Ranma 1/2

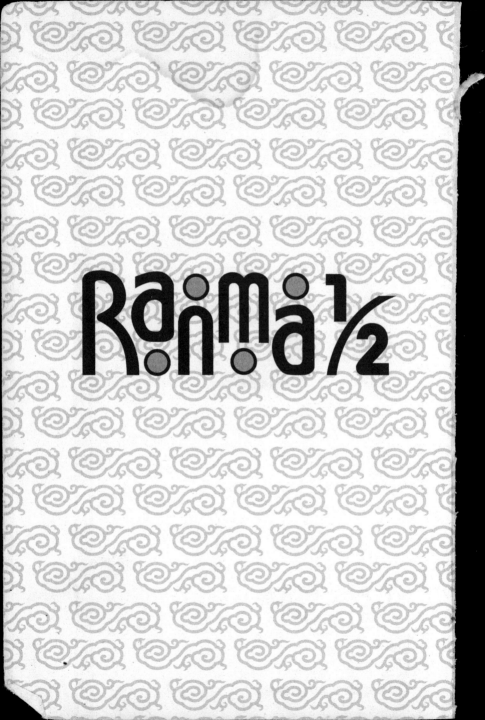

Ranma 1/2
2-in-1 Edition
Vol. 2

STORY AND ART BY
RUMIKO TAKAHASHI

RANMA 1/2 Vol. 3, 4
by Rumiko TAKAHASHI
© 1988 Rumiko TAKAHASHI
All rights reserved.
Original Japanese edition published by SHOGAKUKAN.
English translation rights in the United States of America,
Canada, the United Kingdom and Ireland arranged with
SHOGAKUKAN.

English Adaptation/Gerard Jones, Matt Thorn
Touch-up Art & Lettering/Deron Bennett
Design/Yukiko Whitley
Editors/(First Edition) Satoru Fujii, Trish Ledoux; (Second Edition)
Julie Davis; (2-in-1 Edition) Hope Donovan

The stories, characters and incidents mentioned in
this publication are entirely fictional.

No portion of this book may be reproduced or transmitted in
any form or by any means without written permission from the
copyright holders.

Printed in the U.S.A.

Published by VIZ Media, LLC
P.O. Box 77010
San Francisco, CA 94107

10 9 8 7 6 5 4 3 2 1
First printing, May 2014

www.viz.com   WWW.SHONENSUNDAY.COM

PARENTAL ADVISORY
RANMA 1/2 is rated T+ for Older Teens and is
recommended for ages 16 and up. This volume
contains sexual situations and humor.
FOR OLDER TEEN
ratings.viz.com

Ranma 1/2

3•4

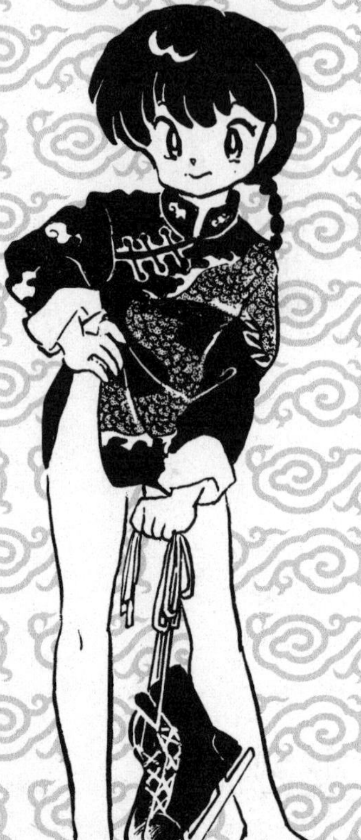

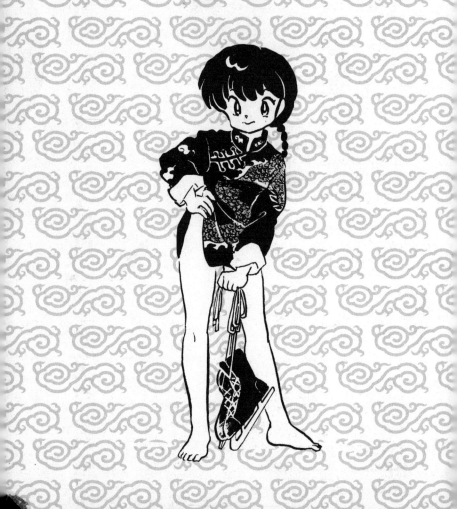

CAST OF CHARACTERS

THE SAOTOMES

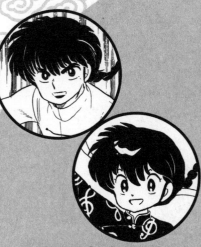

Ranma Saotome
Martial artist with an ego that won't let him quit. Changes into a girl when splashed with cold water.

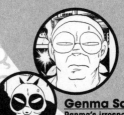

Genma Saotome
Ranma's irresponsible father, recently returned from training his son in China. Changes into a panda.

STORY SO FAR

The Tendos are an average, run-of-the-mill Japanese family—at least on the surface. Soun Tendo is the owner and proprietor of the Tendo Dojo, where "Anything-Goes Martial Arts" is practiced. Like the name says, anything goes and usually does.

When Soun's old friend Genma Saotome comes to visit, Soun's three lovely young daughters—Akane, Nabiki and Kasumi—are told that it's time for one of them to become the fiancée of Genma's teenage son, as per an agreement made between the two fathers years ago. Youngest daughter Akane—who says she hates boys—is quickly nominated for bridal duty by her sisters.

Unfortunately, Ranma and his father have suffered a strange accident. While training in China, both plunged into one of many cursed springs at the legendary martial arts training ground of Jusenkyo. These springs transform the unlucky dunkee into whoever—or whatever—drowned there hundreds of years ago.

From then on, a splash of cold water turns Ranma's father into a giant panda, and Ranma becomes a beautiful, busty young woman. Hot water reverses the effect…but only until next time.

Although their parents are still determined to see Ranma and Akane marry and carry on the dojo, both seem to have a talent for accumulating suitors. Will the two ever work out their differences and get rid of all these extra people, or will they just call the whole thing off? And will Ranma ever get rid of his curse?

THE TENDOS

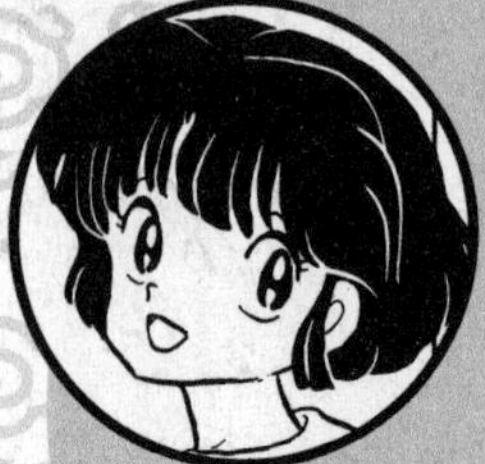

Akane Tendo
A martial artist, tomboy and Ranma's reluctant fiancée. Has no clue who "P-chan" really is.

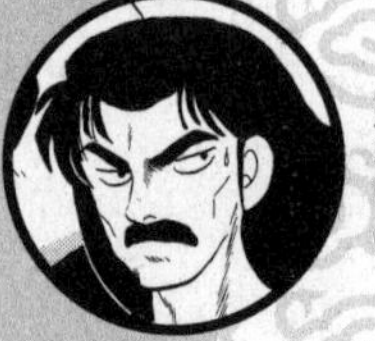

Soun Tendo
Head of the Tendo household and owner of the Tendo Dojo.

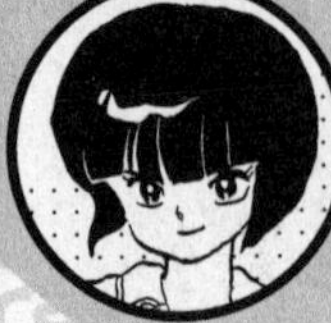

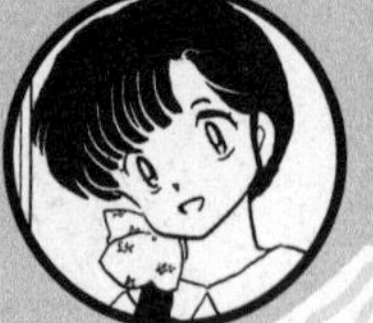

Kasumi Tendo
Sweet-natured eldest daughter and substitute mother figure for the Tendo family.

Nabiki Tendo
Always ready to make a buck off others' suffering, coldhearted capitalist Nabiki is the middle Tendo daughter.

THE SUITORS

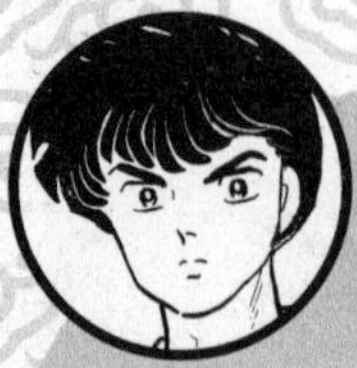

Tatewaki Kuno
Blustering upperclassman who is the kendo team captain. In love with both Akane and girl-type Ranma.

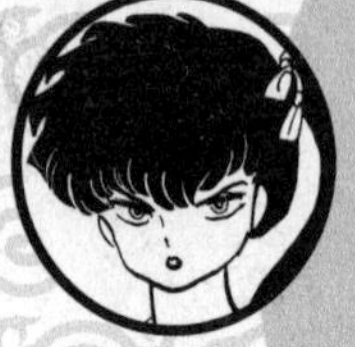

Kodachi Kuno
Twisted sister of Tatewaki. An expert in Martial Rhythmic Gymnastics, she's determined to use her ribbon-whipping skills to tame Ranma.

Shampoo
Chinese Amazon warrior with a serious grudge against Ranma.

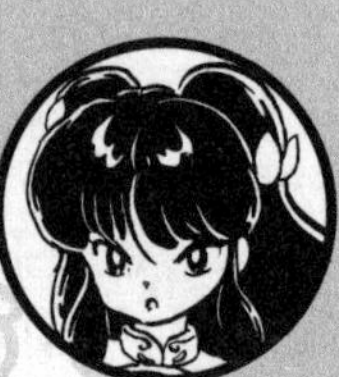

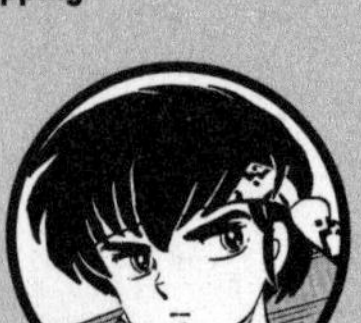

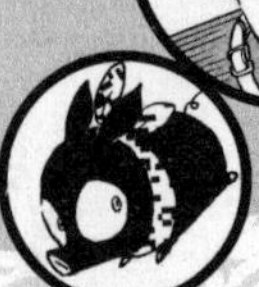

Ryoga Hibiki
A martial artist with a grudge against Ranma, a crush on Akane and no sense of direction. Changes into a piglet Akane calls "P-chan."

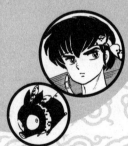

AND IN THIS CORNER...

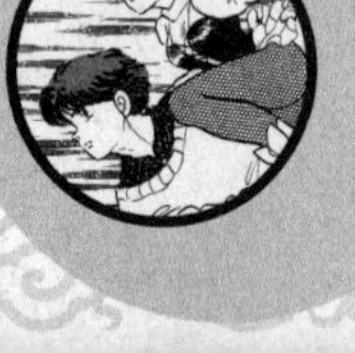

Azusa Shiratori and Mikado Sanzenin
The "Golden Pair" of high school figure skating, this competitive couple has sworn to defeat Ranma and Akane in a skating match with P-chan as the prize.

Contents

PART 1
THE LOVE OF
THE BLACK ROSE

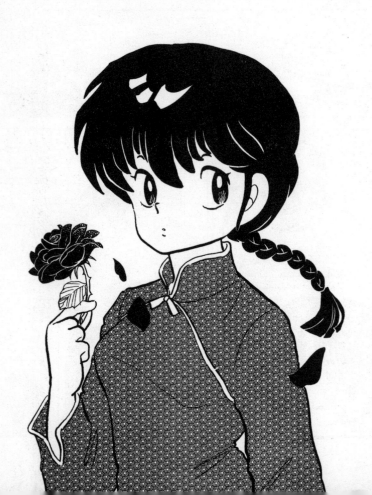

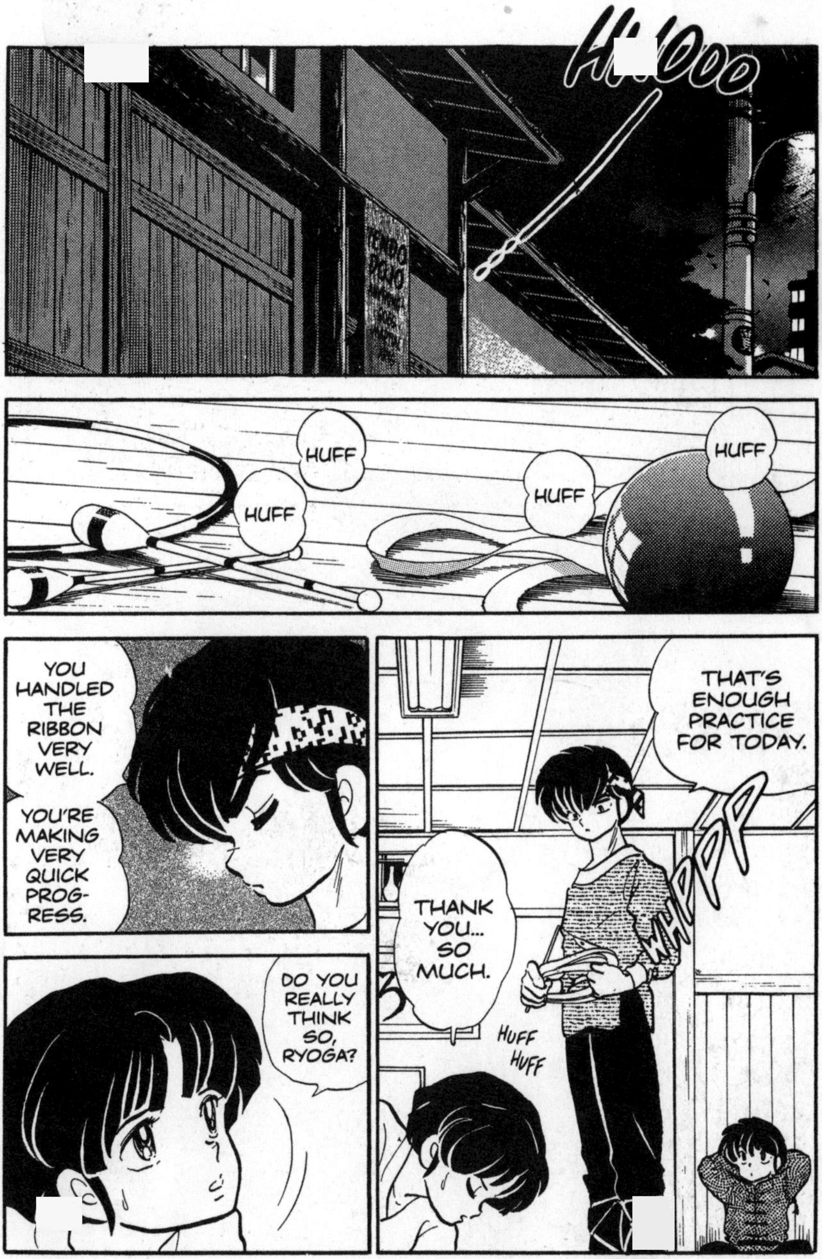
HUFF
HUFF
HUFF
HUFF
THAT'S ENOUGH PRACTICE FOR TODAY.
WHPPP
THANK YOU... SO MUCH.
HUFF HUFF
YOU HANDLED THE RIBBON VERY WELL.
YOU'RE MAKING VERY QUICK PROGRESS.
DO YOU REALLY THINK SO, RYOGA?

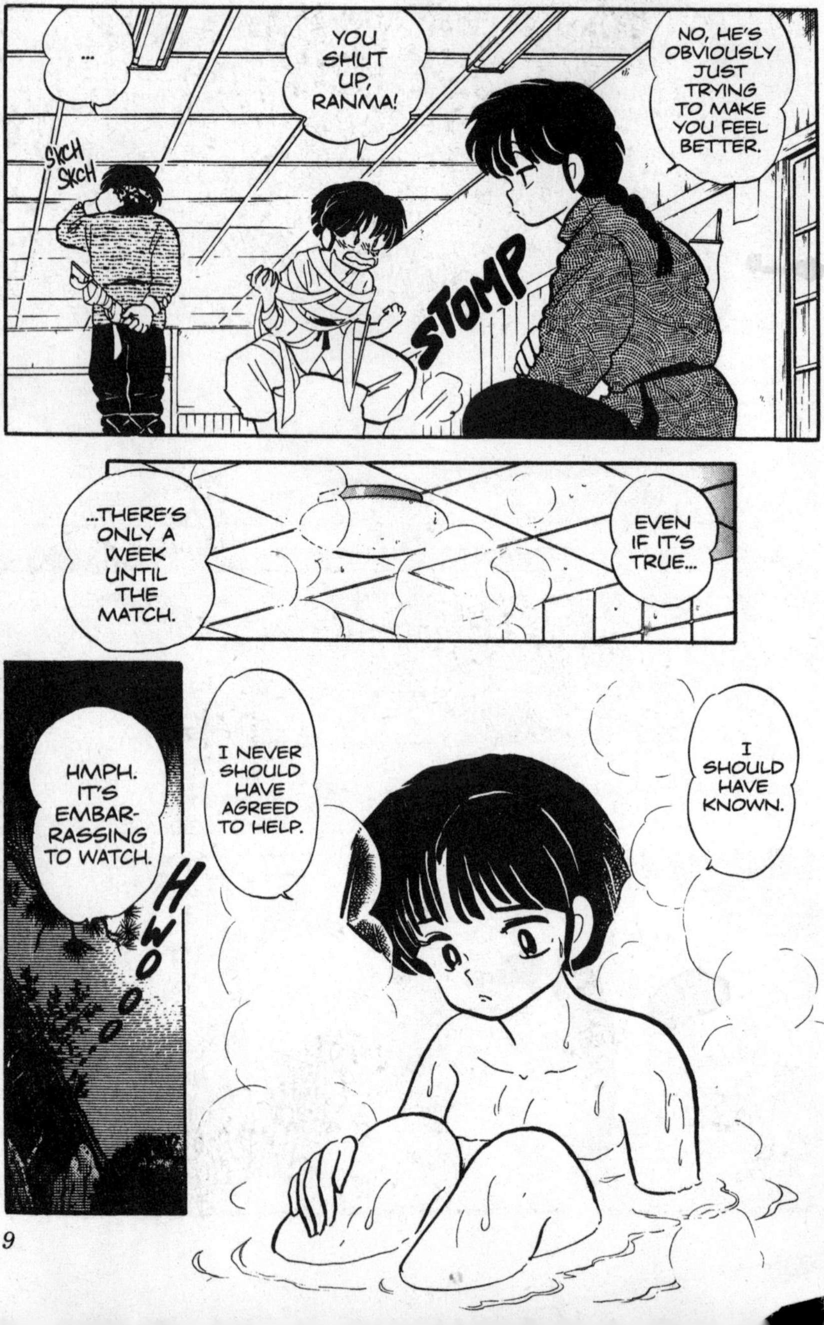
NO, HE'S OBVIOUSLY JUST TRYING TO MAKE YOU FEEL BETTER.
STOMP
YOU SHUT UP, RANMA!
...
SKCH SKCH
EVEN IF IT'S TRUE...
...THERE'S ONLY A WEEK UNTIL THE MATCH.
I SHOULD HAVE KNOWN.
I NEVER SHOULD HAVE AGREED TO HELP.
HMPH. IT'S EMBAR-RASSING TO WATCH.
HWOOOO

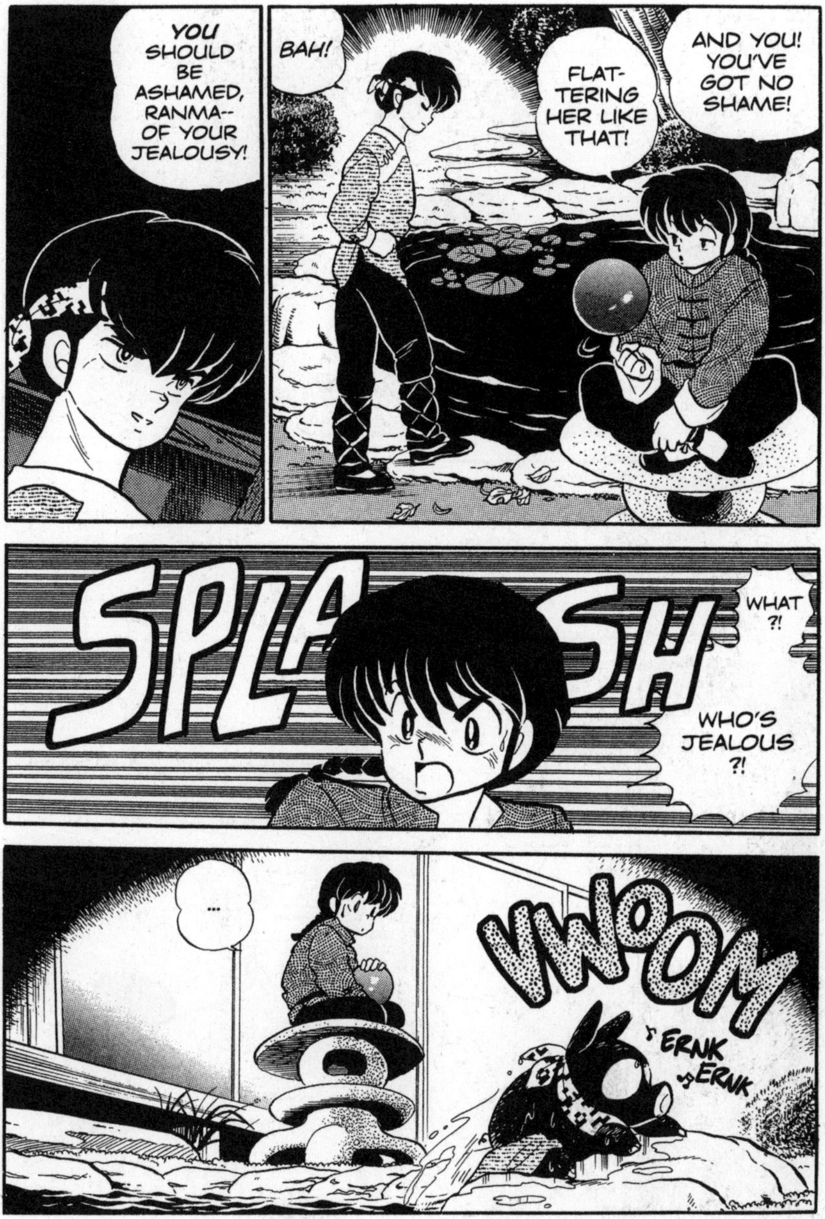
AND YOU! YOU'VE GOT NO SHAME!
FLAT-TERING HER LIKE THAT!
BAH!
YOU SHOULD BE ASHAMED, RANMA-- OF YOUR JEALOUSY!
WHAT ?!
SPLASH
WHO'S JEALOUS ?!
VWOOM
ERNK ERNK
...

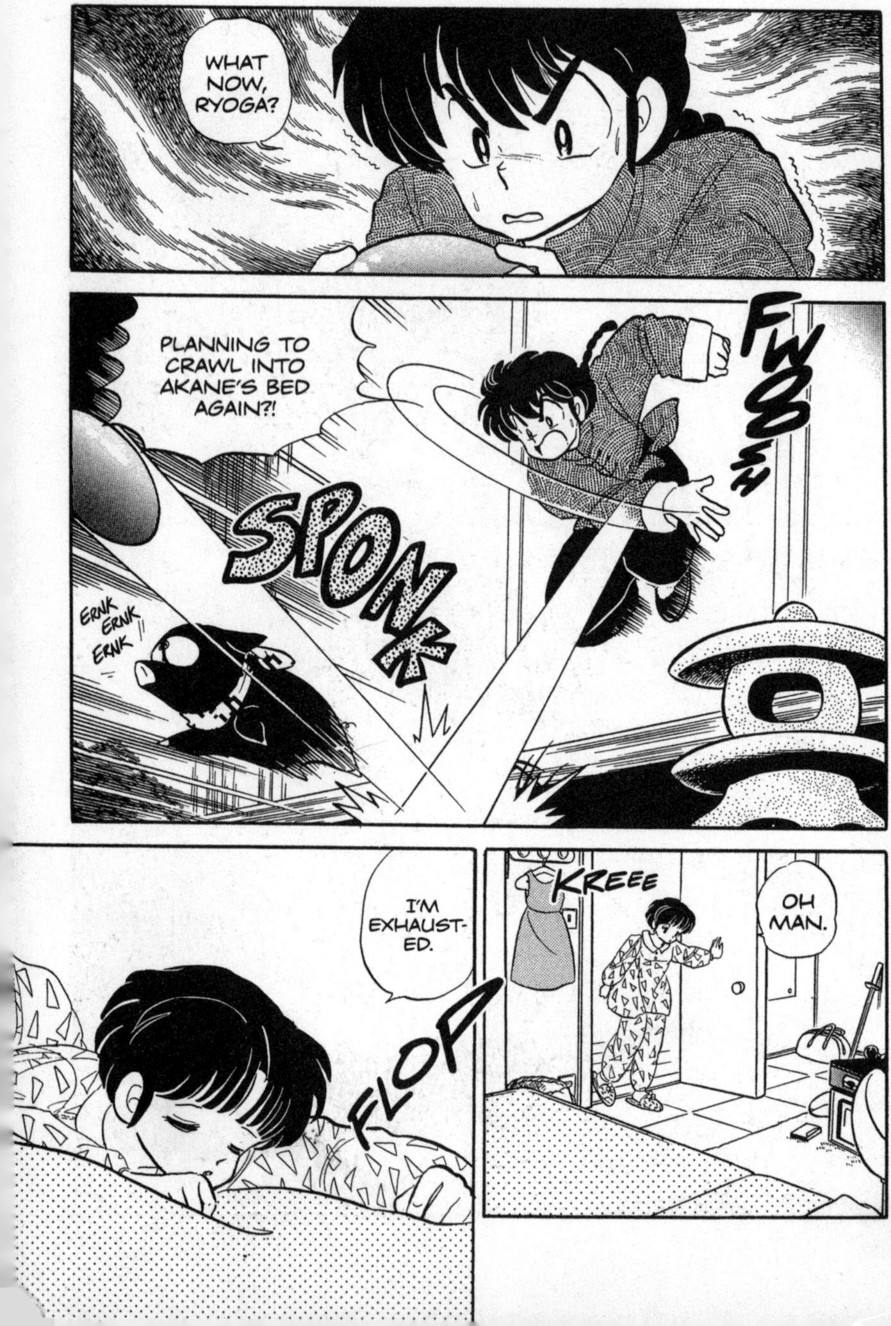
WHAT NOW, RYOGA?
FWOOSH
PLANNING TO CRAWL INTO AKANE'S BED AGAIN?!
SPONK
ERNK ERNK ERNK
OH MAN.
KREEE
I'M EXHAUST-ED.
FLOP

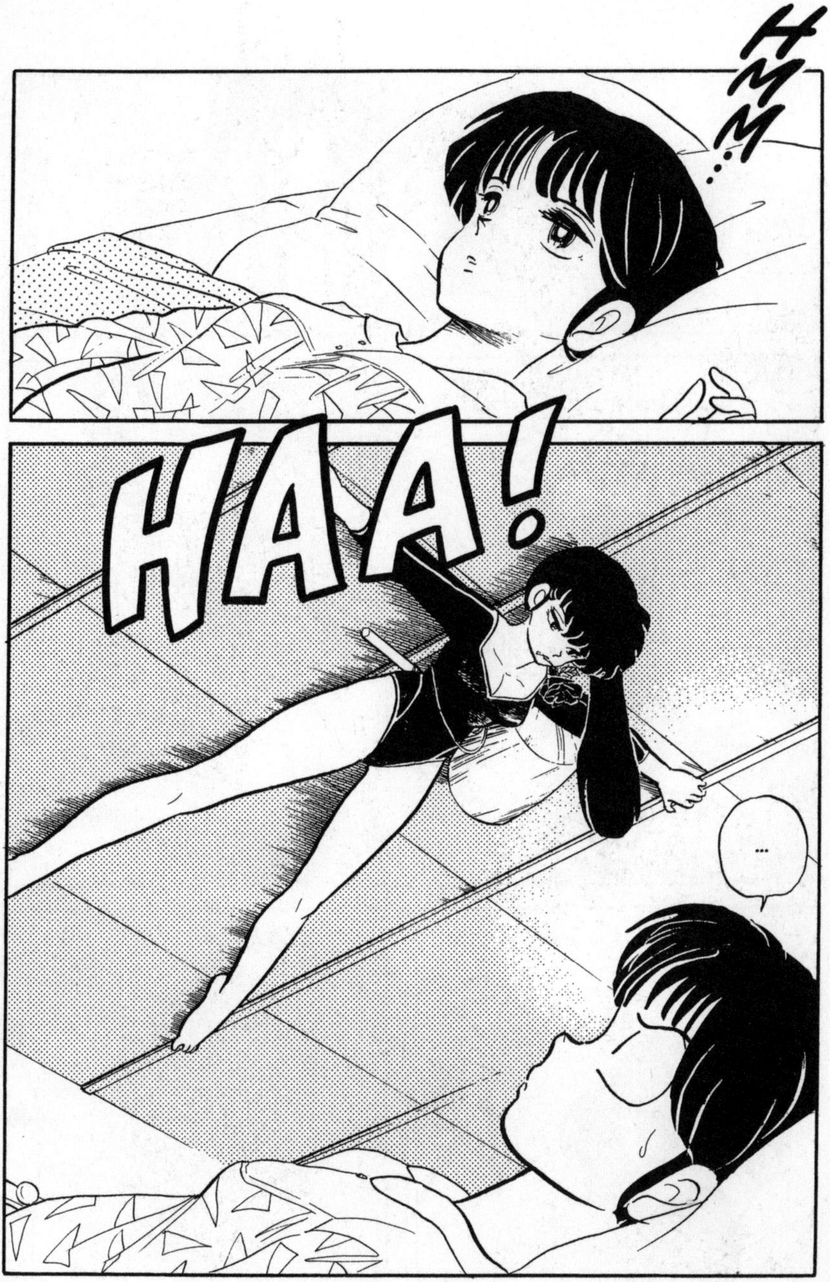
HMMM...
HAA!
...

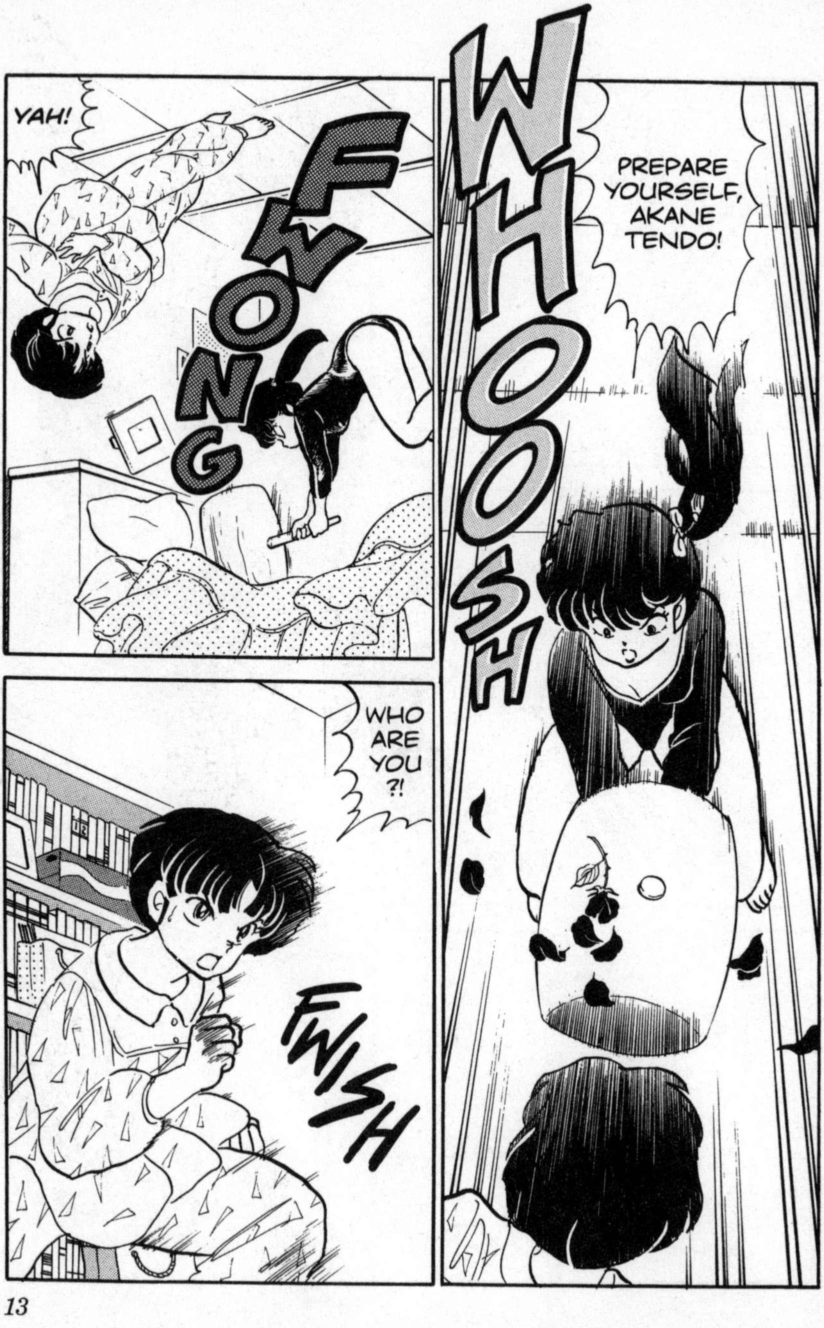
WHOOOSH
PREPARE YOURSELF, AKANE TENDO!
YAH!
FWONG
WHO ARE YOU?!
FWISH

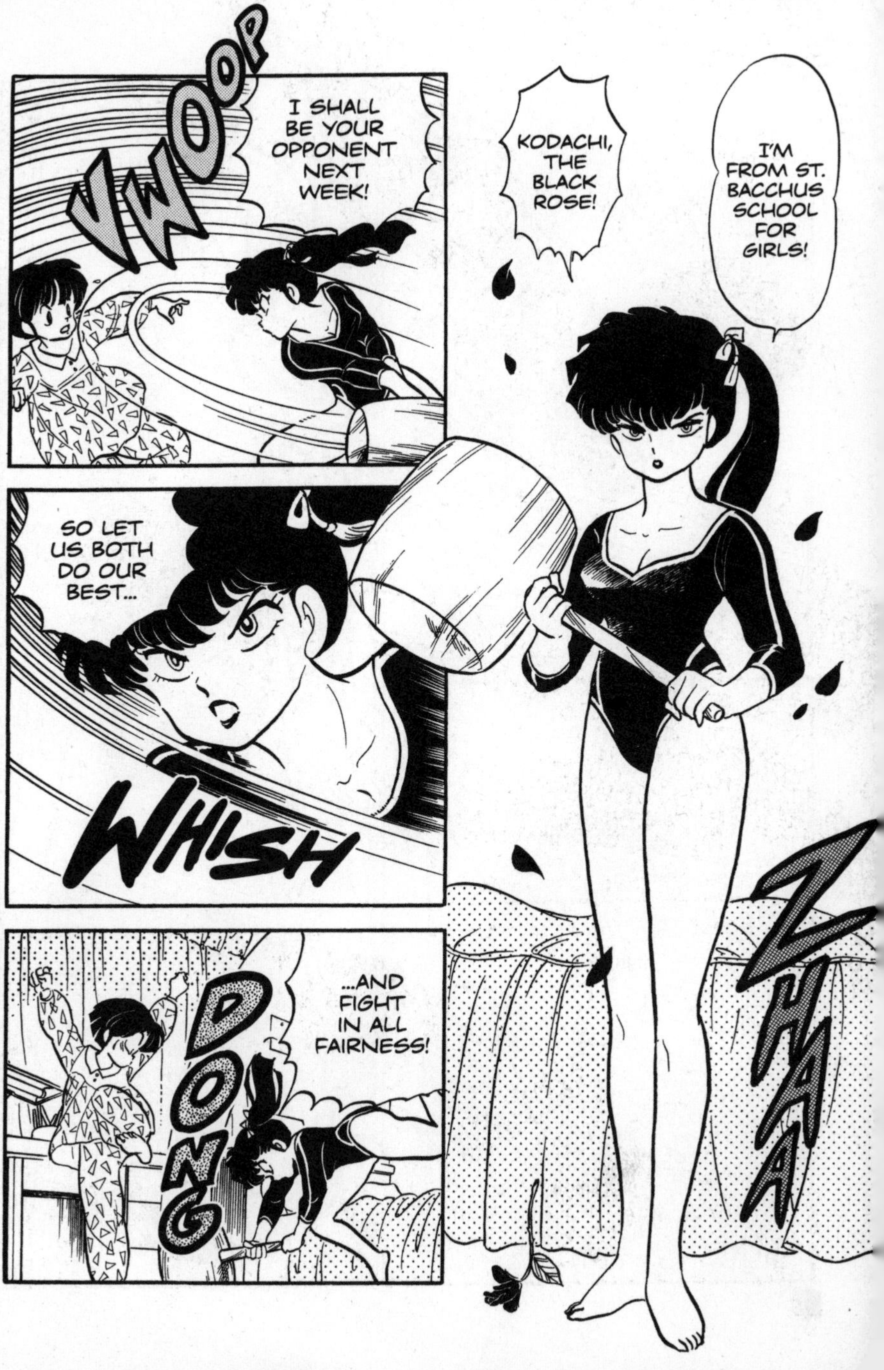
I'M FROM ST. BACCHUS SCHOOL FOR GIRLS!
KODACHI, THE BLACK ROSE!
ZHAA
VWOOP
I SHALL BE YOUR OPPONENT NEXT WEEK!
SO LET US BOTH DO OUR BEST...
WHISH
...AND FIGHT IN ALL FAIRNESS!
DONG

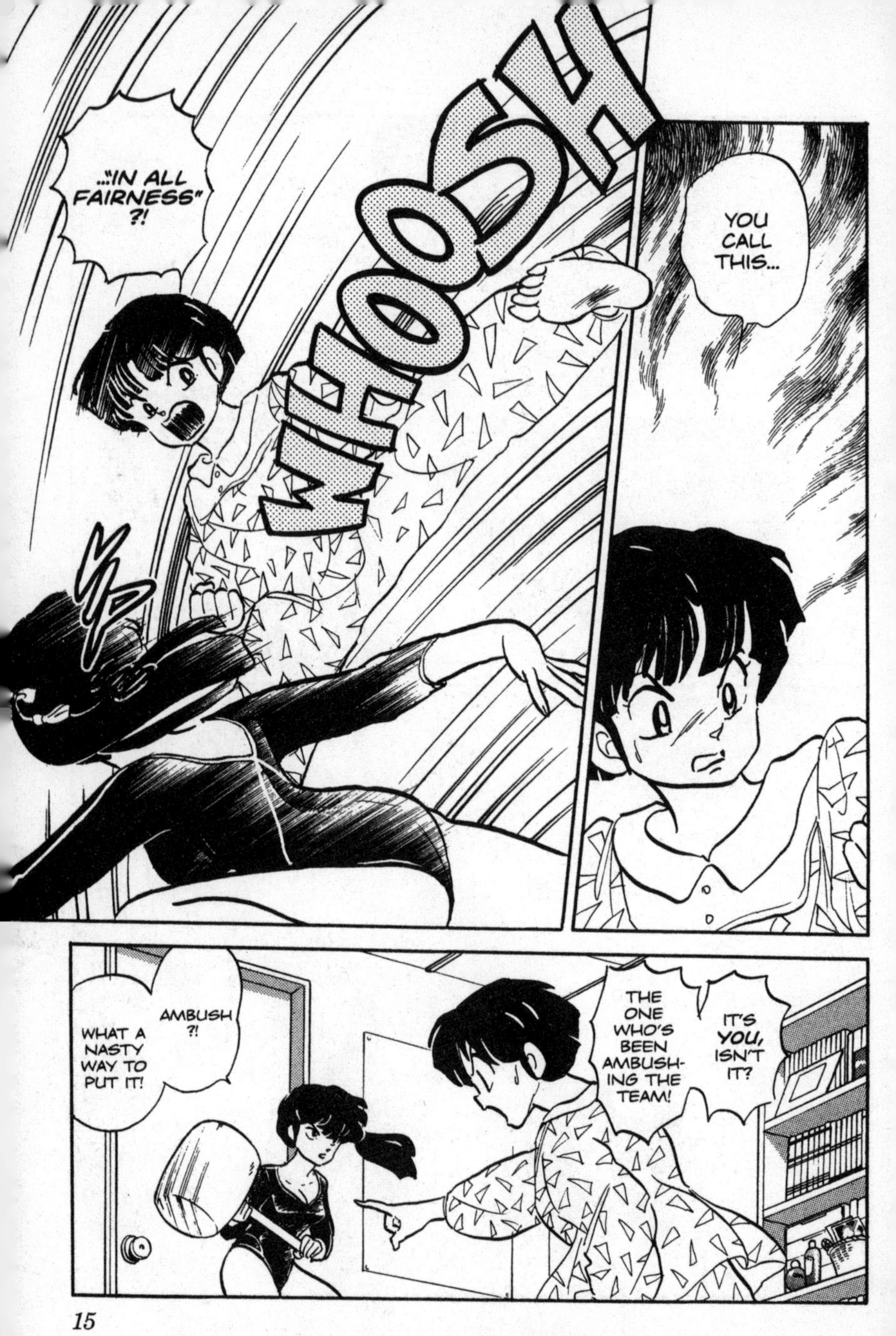
YOU CALL THIS...
WHOOSH!
..."IN ALL FAIRNESS"?!
IT'S YOU, ISN'T IT?
THE ONE WHO'S BEEN AMBUSHING THE TEAM!
AMBUSH?!
WHAT A NASTY WAY TO PUT IT!

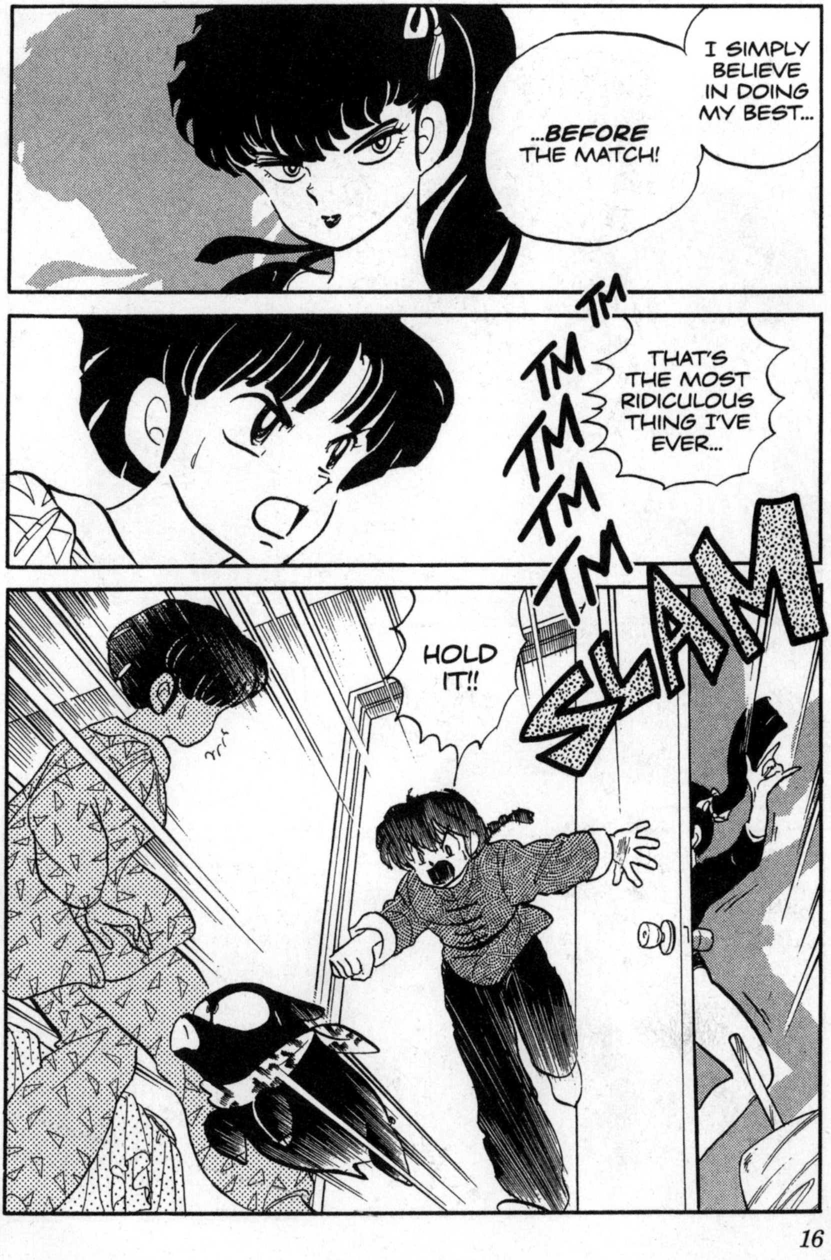
I SIMPLY BELIEVE IN DOING MY BEST...
...BEFORE THE MATCH!
TM TM TM TM TM TM
THAT'S THE MOST RIDICULOUS THING I'VE EVER...
SLAM
HOLD IT!!

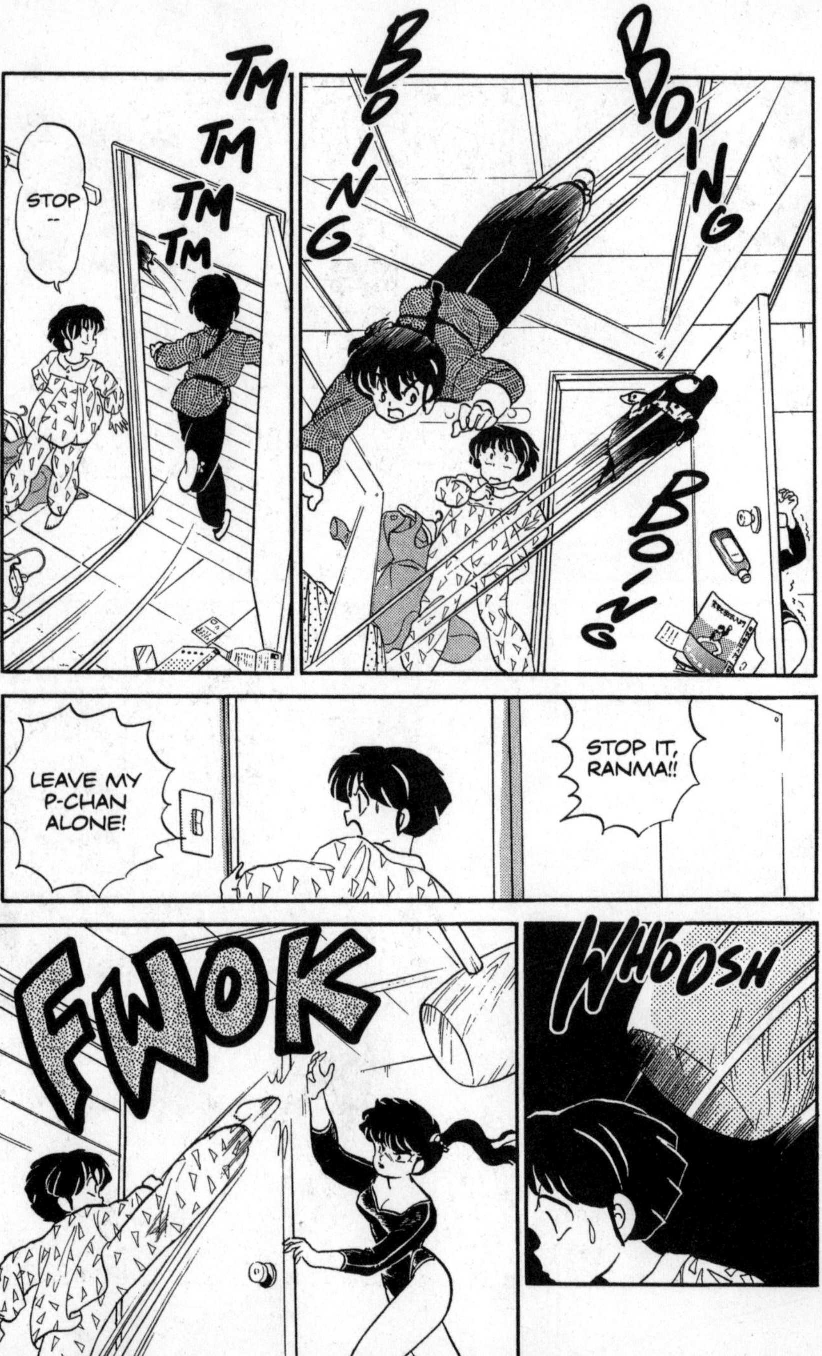
BOING
BOING
BOING
TM
TM
TM
TM
STOP --
STOP IT, RANMA!!
LEAVE MY P-CHAN ALONE!
WHOOSH
FWOK

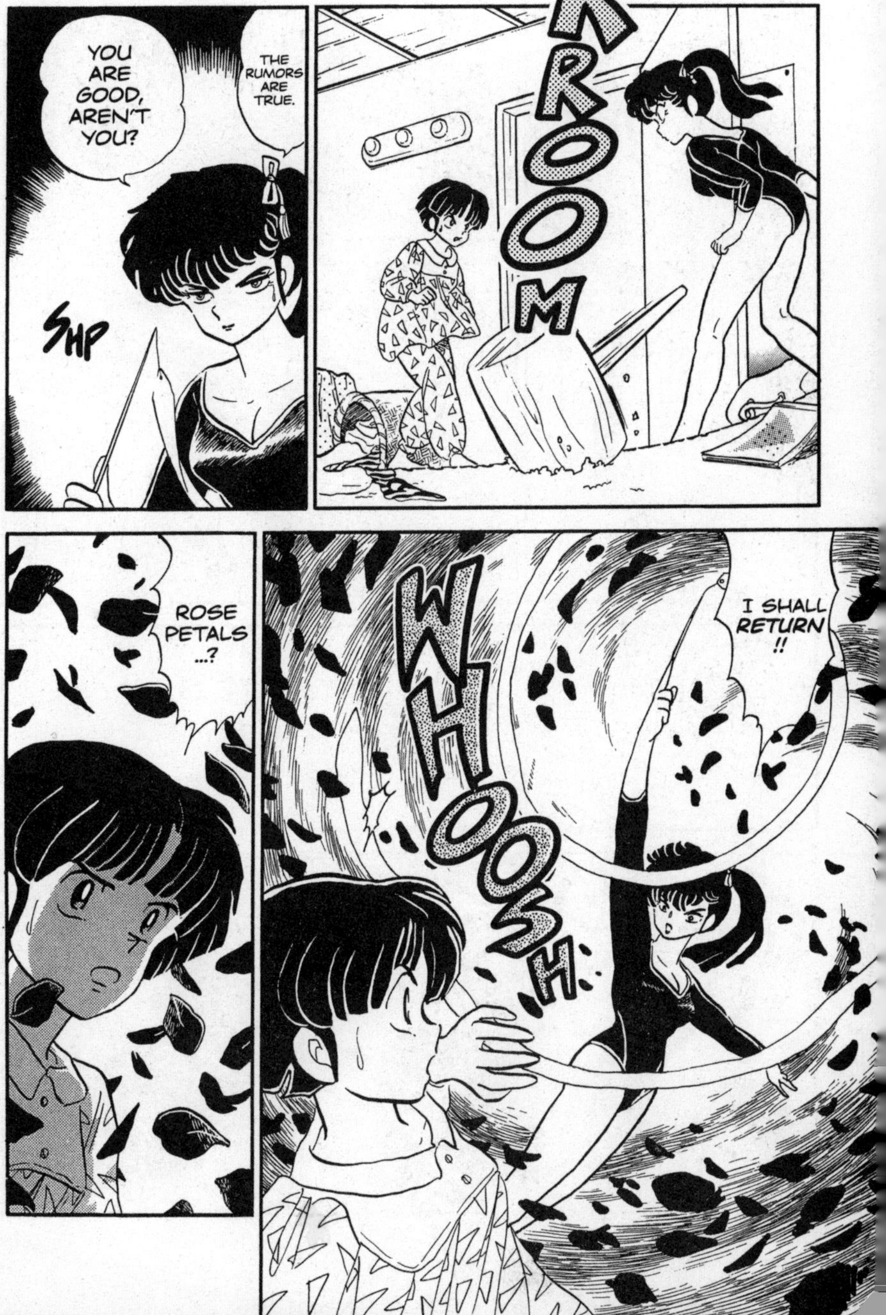
KROOOM
THE RUMORS ARE TRUE.
YOU ARE GOOD, AREN'T YOU?
SHP
I SHALL RETURN !!
WHOOOSH
ROSE PETALS ...?

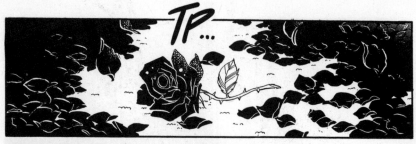

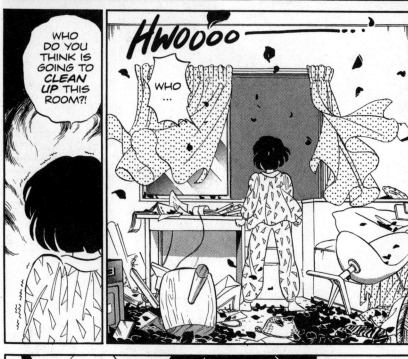

WHO DO YOU THINK IS GOING TO **CLEAN UP** THIS ROOM?!

HWOOOO...

WHO...

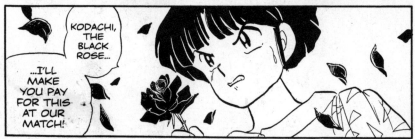

KODACHI, THE BLACK ROSE...

...I'LL MAKE YOU PAY FOR THIS AT OUR MATCH!

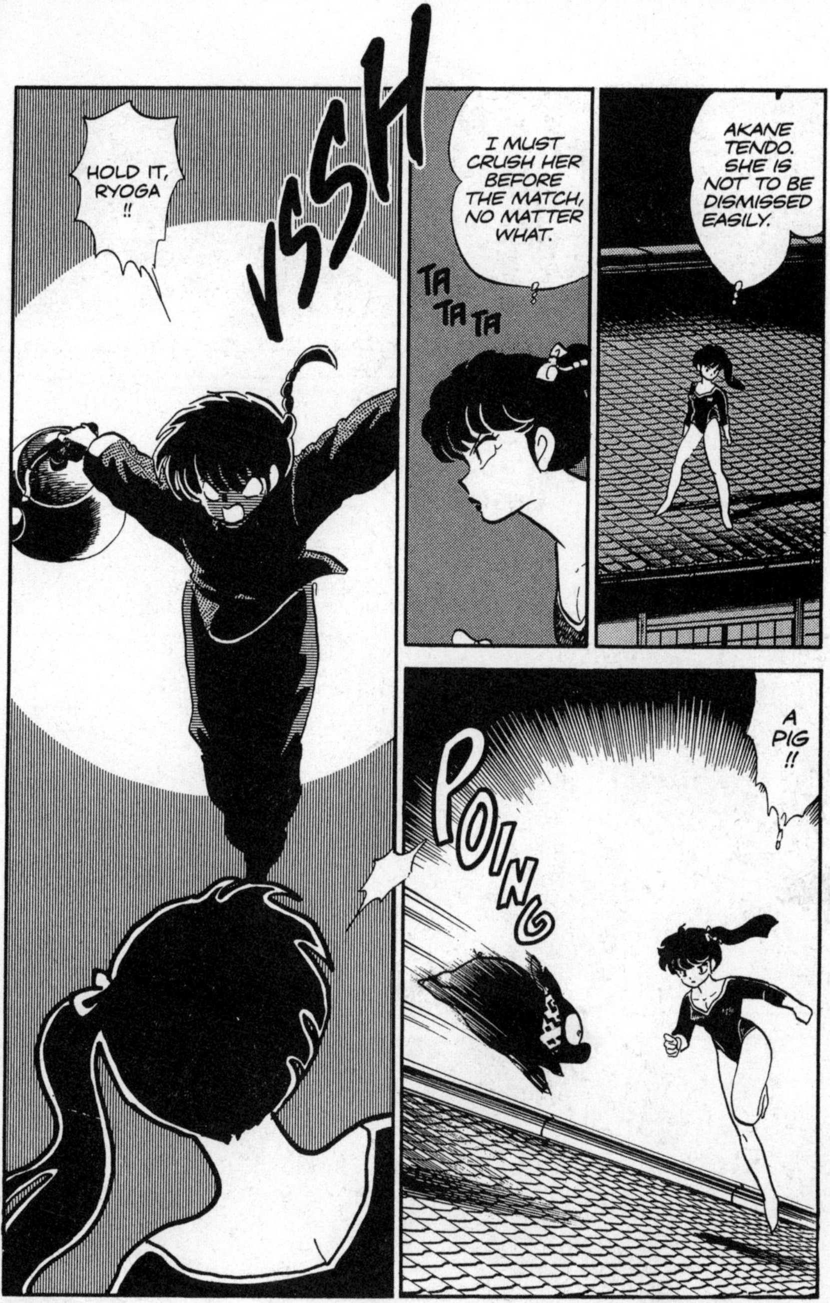
AKANE TENDO. SHE IS NOT TO BE DISMISSED EASILY.
I MUST CRUSH HER BEFORE THE MATCH, NO MATTER WHAT.
TA TA TA
A PIG !!
POING
VSSH
HOLD IT, RYOGA !!

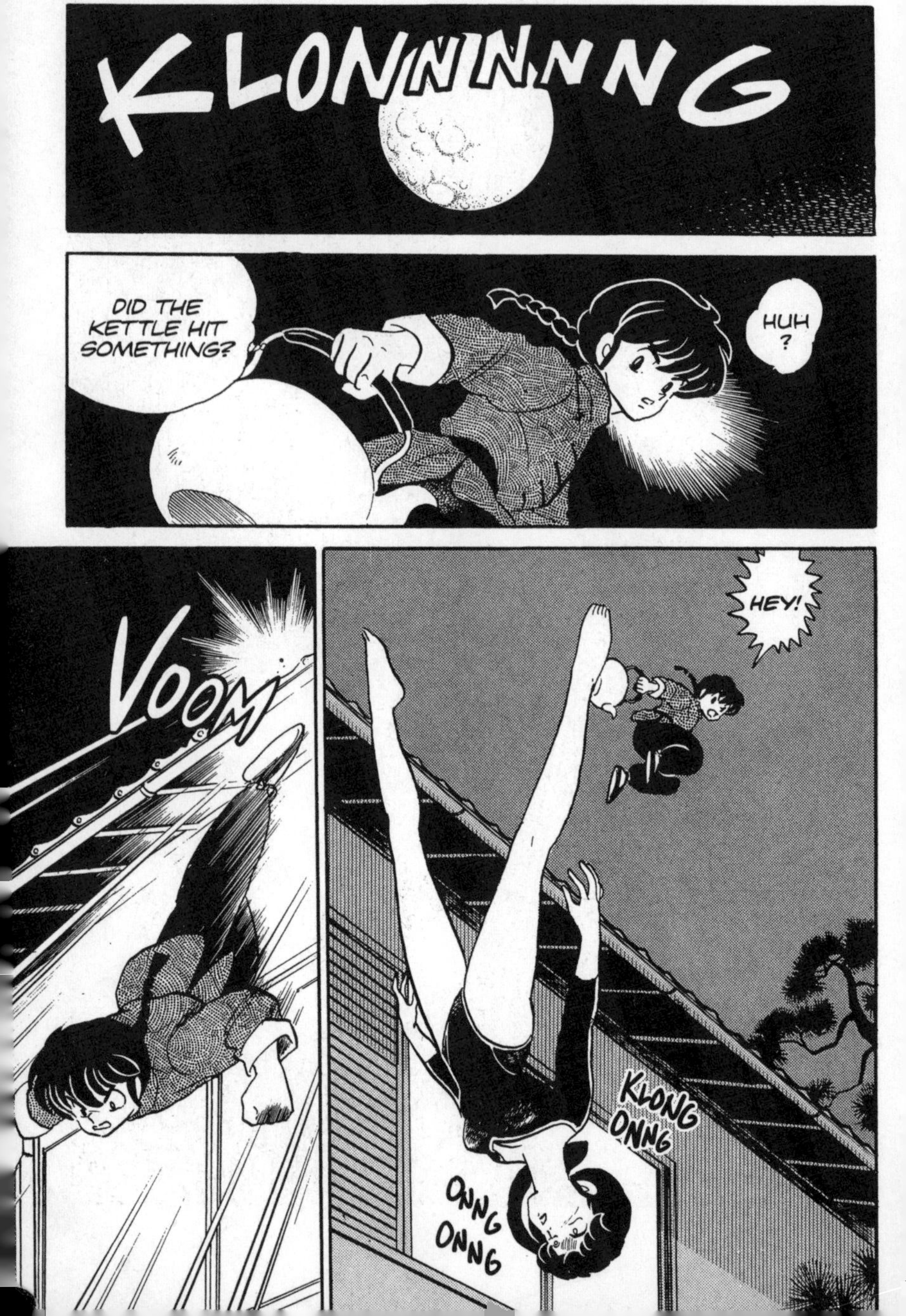
KLONNNNNG
HUH?
DID THE KETTLE HIT SOMETHING?
HEY!
KLONG ONNG
ONNG ONNG
VOOM

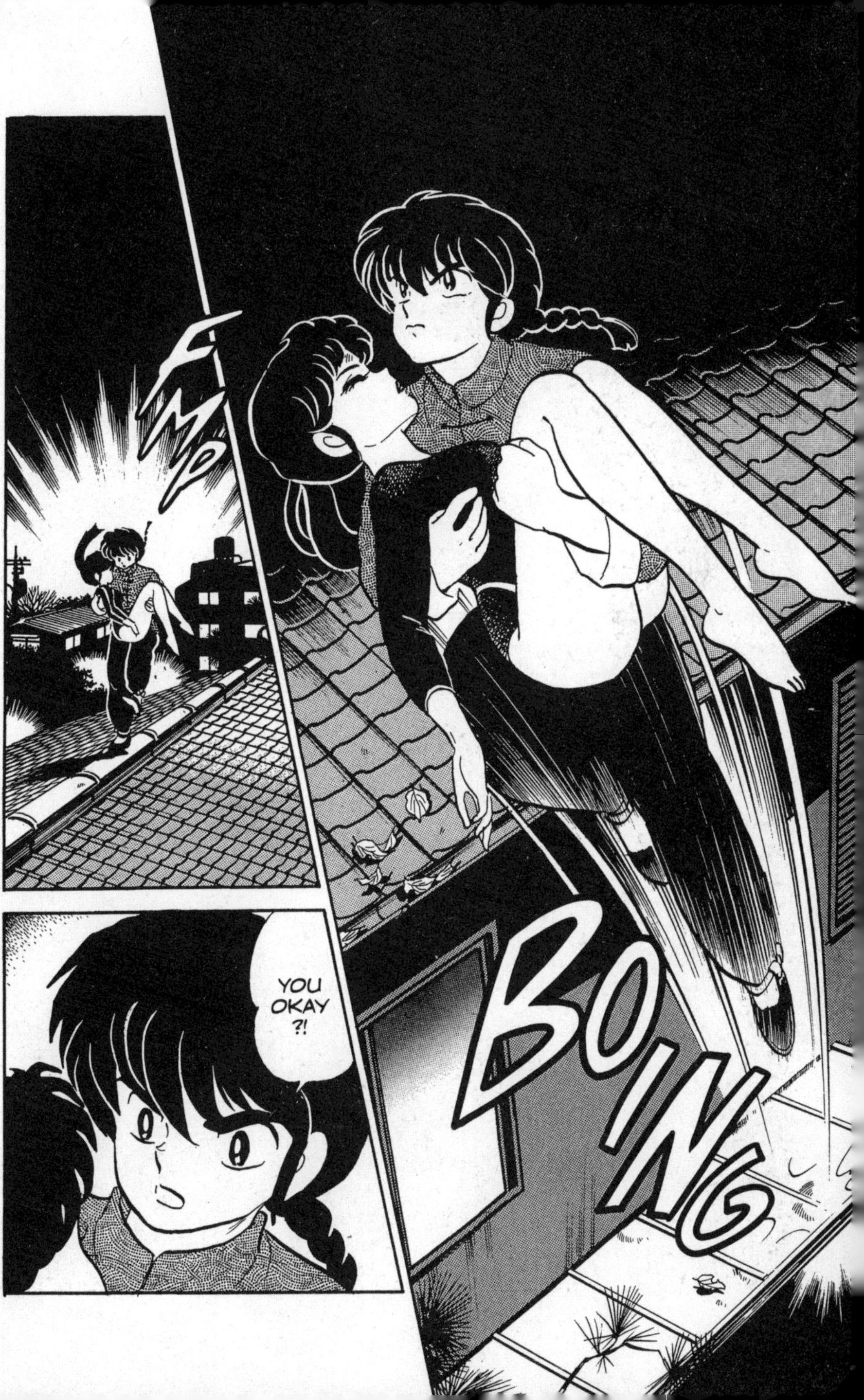
BOING
YOU OKAY ?!

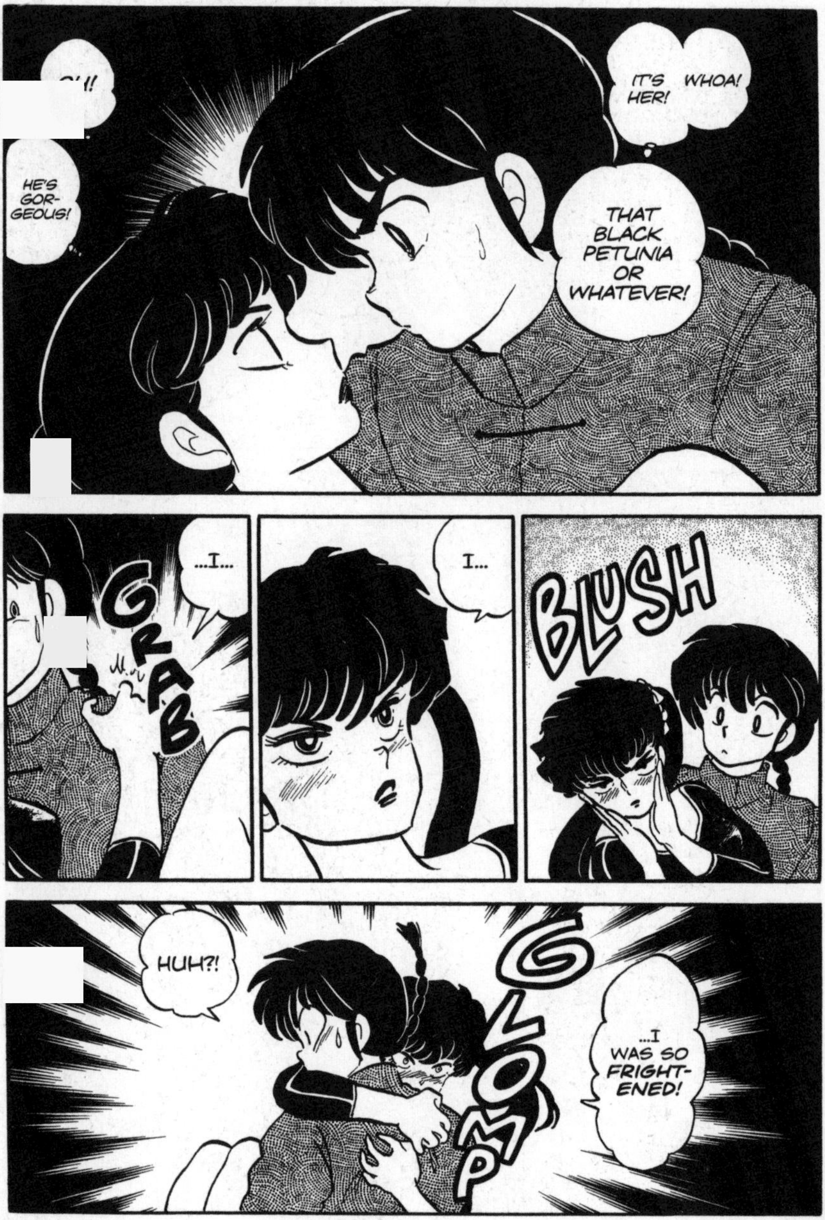
WHOA!
IT'S HER!
THAT BLACK PETUNIA OR WHATEVER!
HE'S GOR-GEOUS!
BLUSH
I...
...I...
GRAB
...I WAS SO FRIGHT-ENED!
GLOMP
HUH?!

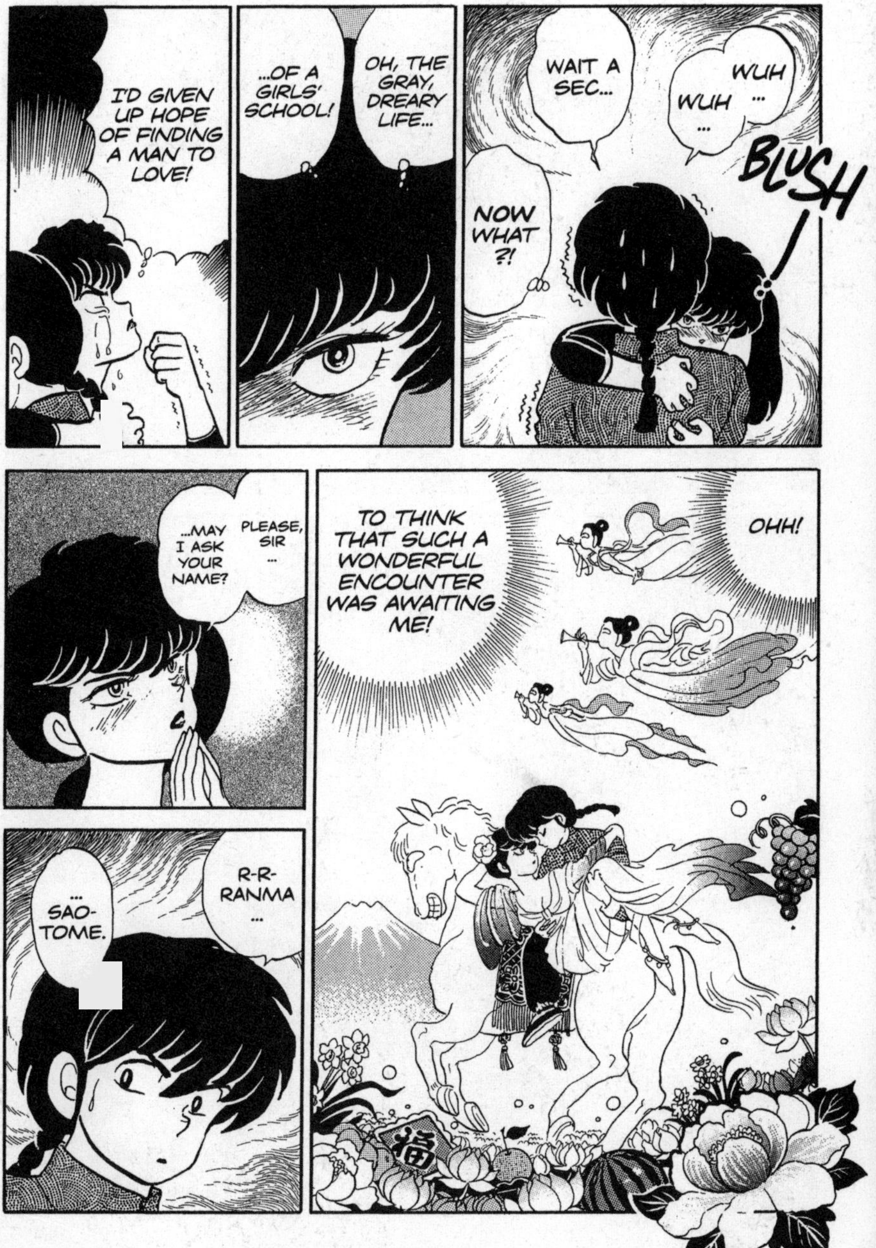
WUH WUH...
BLUSH
WAIT A SEC...
NOW WHAT?!
OH, THE GRAY, DREARY LIFE...
...OF A GIRLS' SCHOOL!
I'D GIVEN UP HOPE OF FINDING A MAN TO LOVE!
OHH!
TO THINK THAT SUCH A WONDERFUL ENCOUNTER WAS AWAITING ME!
PLEASE, SIR...
...MAY I ASK YOUR NAME?
R-R-RANMA...
...SAO-TOME.

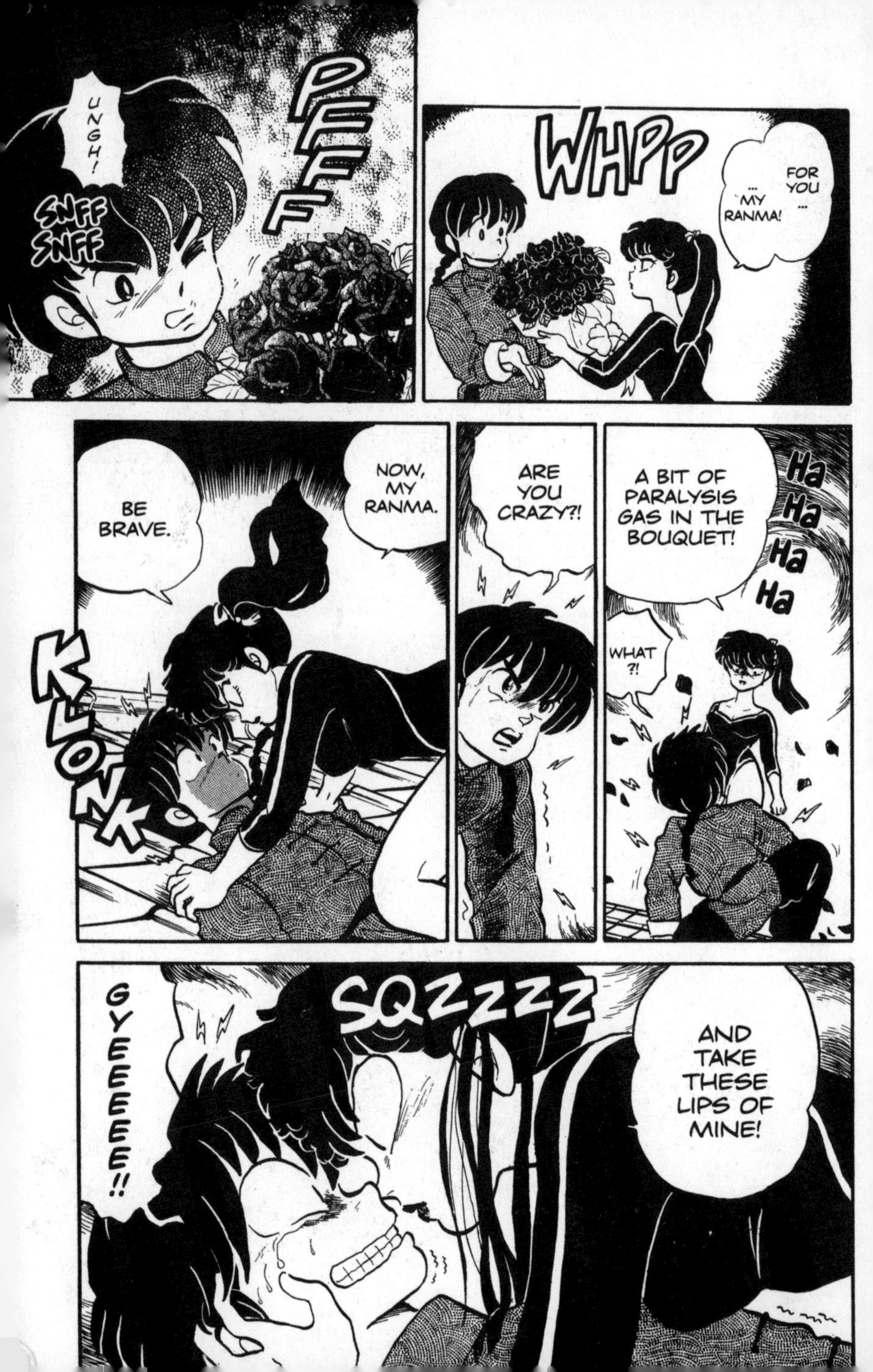
WHPP
FOR YOU ... ... MY RANMA!
PFFFF
UNGH!
SNFF SNFF
A BIT OF PARALYSIS GAS IN THE BOUQUET!
Ha Ha Ha Ha
WHAT ?!
ARE YOU CRAZY?!
NOW, MY RANMA.
BE BRAVE.
KLONK
AND TAKE THESE LIPS OF MINE!
SQZZZZ
GYEEEEEE!!

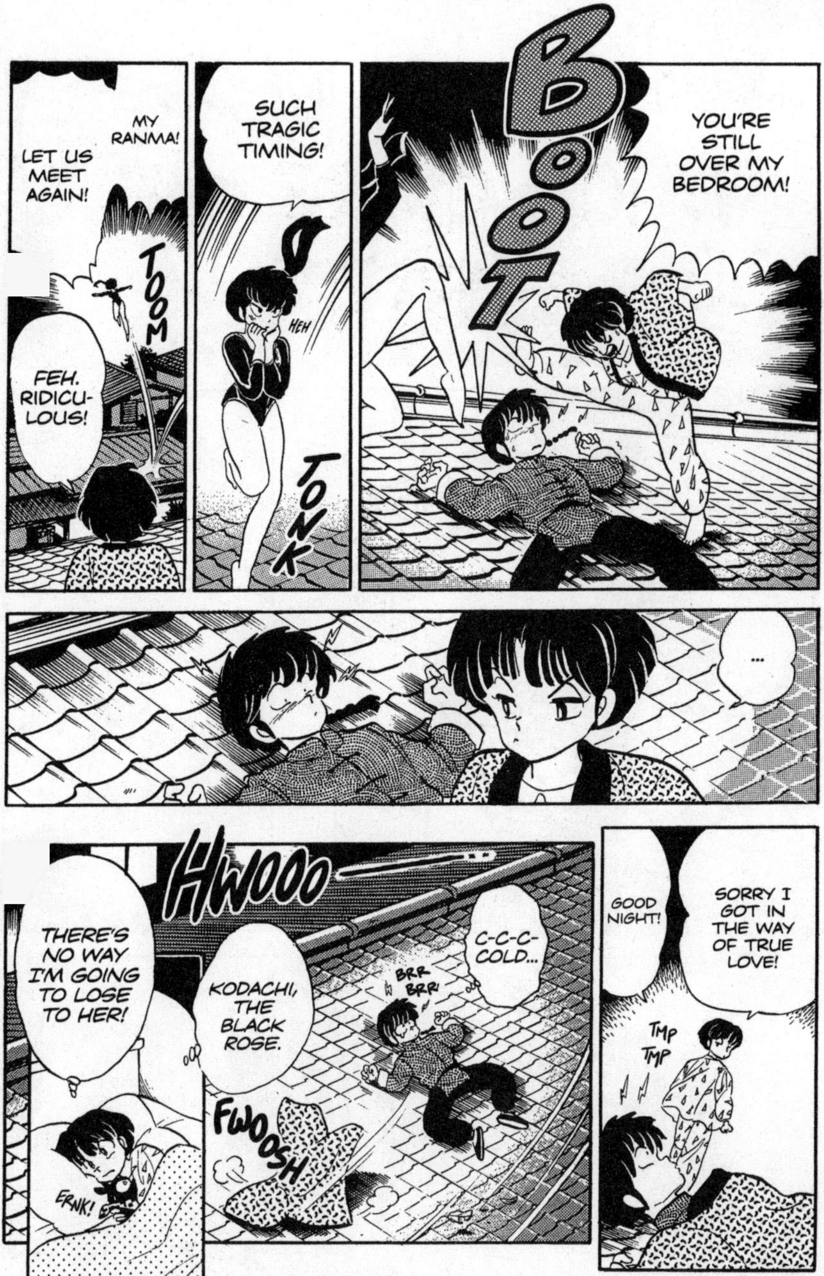

YOU'RE STILL OVER MY BEDROOM!
BOOT
SUCH TRAGIC TIMING!
HEH
TONK
MY RANMA!
LET US MEET AGAIN!
TOOM
FEH. RIDICULOUS!
...
SORRY I GOT IN THE WAY OF TRUE LOVE!
GOOD NIGHT!
TMP TMP
HWOOO
C-C-C-COLD...
BRR BRR
KODACHI, THE BLACK ROSE.
FWOOSH
THERE'S NO WAY I'M GOING TO LOSE TO HER!
ERNK!

PART 2
TAKE CARE OF
MY SISTER

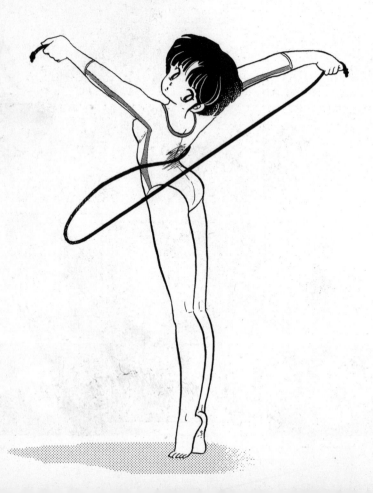

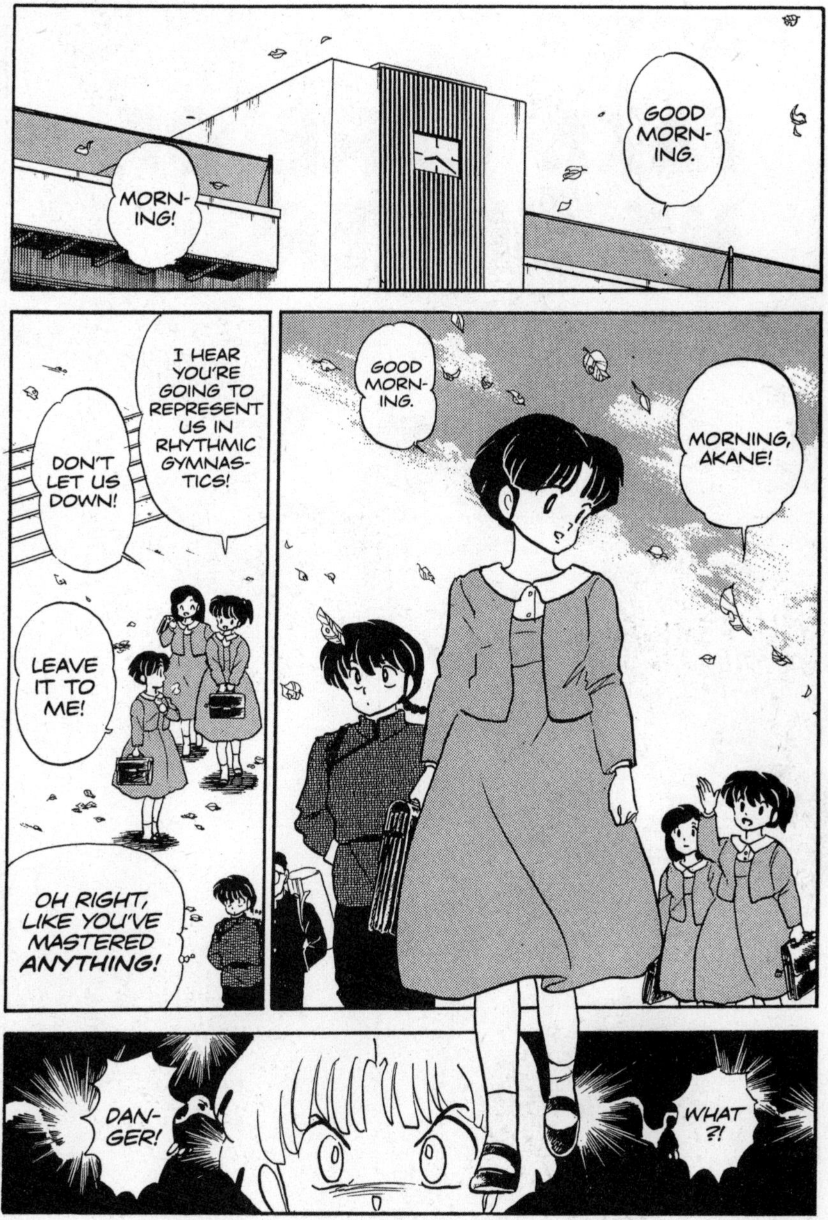
GOOD MORN-ING.
MORN-ING!
MORNING, AKANE!
GOOD MORN-ING.
I HEAR YOU'RE GOING TO REPRESENT US IN RHYTHMIC GYMNAS-TICS!
DON'T LET US DOWN!
LEAVE IT TO ME!
OH RIGHT, LIKE YOU'VE MASTERED ANYTHING!
WHAT ?!
DAN-GER!

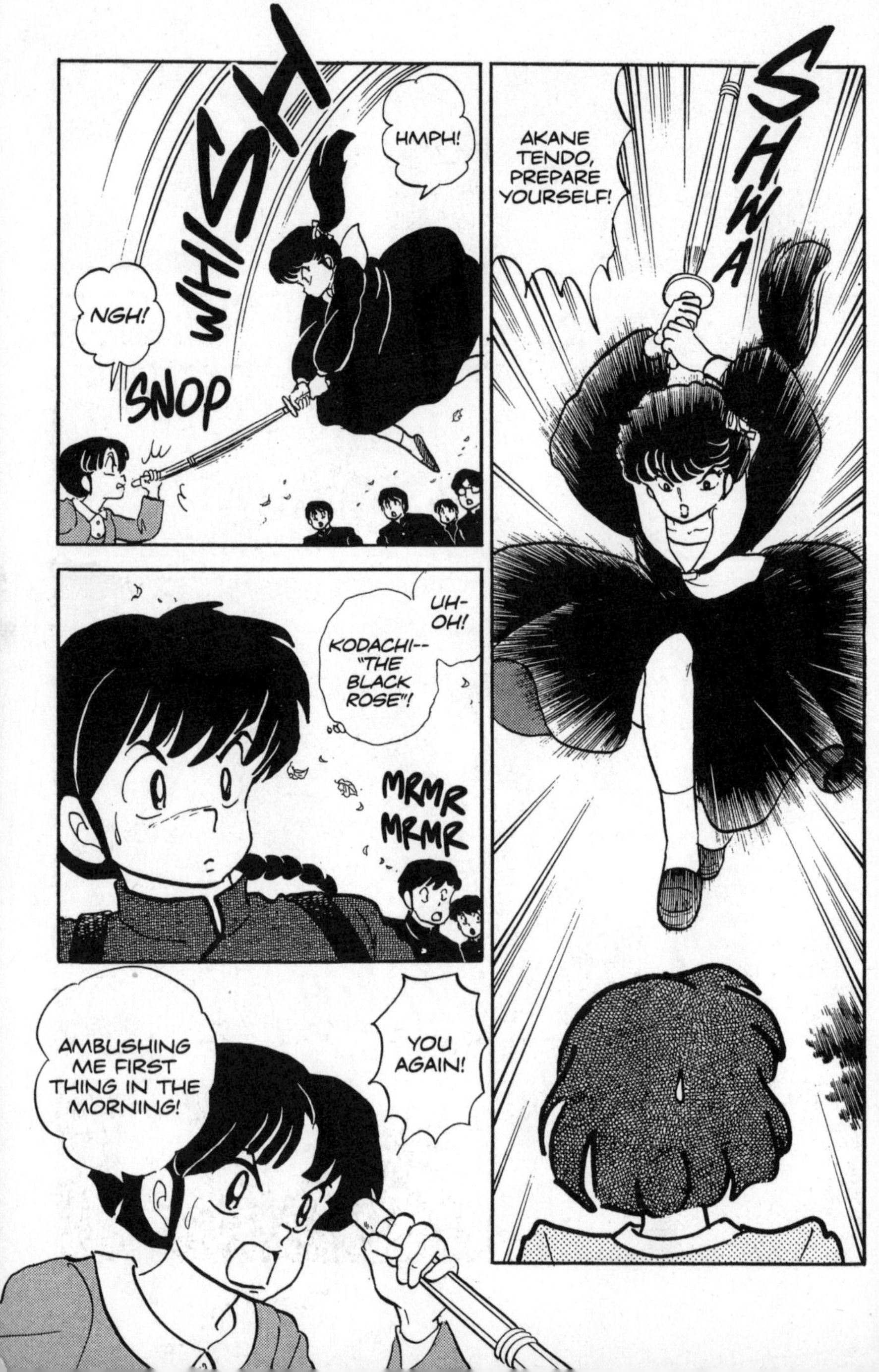
SHWA
AKANE TENDO, PREPARE YOURSELF!
HMPH!
WHISH
NGH!
SNOP
UH-OH! KODACHI-- "THE BLACK ROSE"!
MRMR MRMR
YOU AGAIN!
AMBUSHING ME FIRST THING IN THE MORNING!

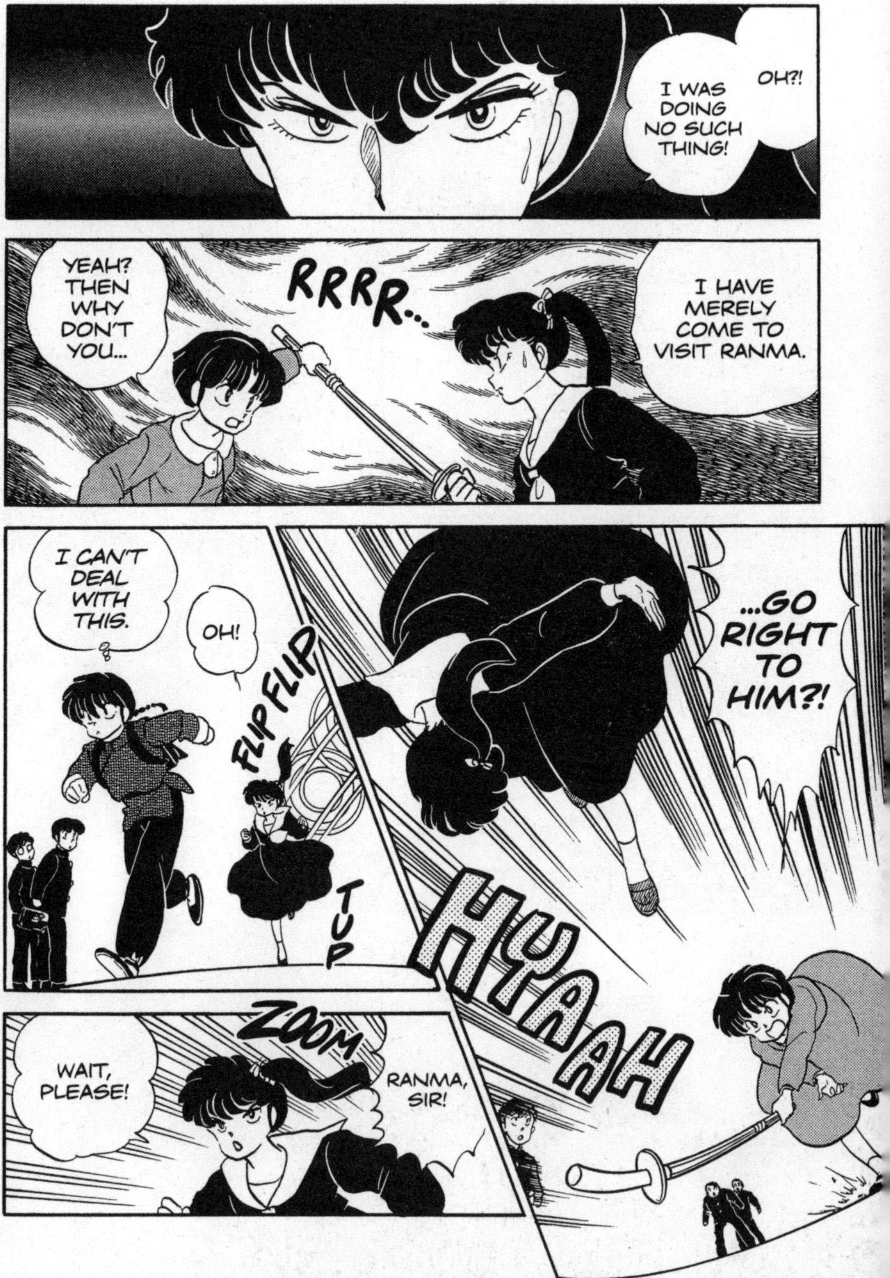
OH?!
I WAS DOING NO SUCH THING!
I HAVE MERELY COME TO VISIT RANMA.
RRRR...
YEAH? THEN WHY DON'T YOU...
...GO RIGHT TO HIM?!
HYAAH
I CAN'T DEAL WITH THIS.
OH!
FLIP FLIP
TUP TUP
ZOOM
RANMA, SIR!
WAIT, PLEASE!

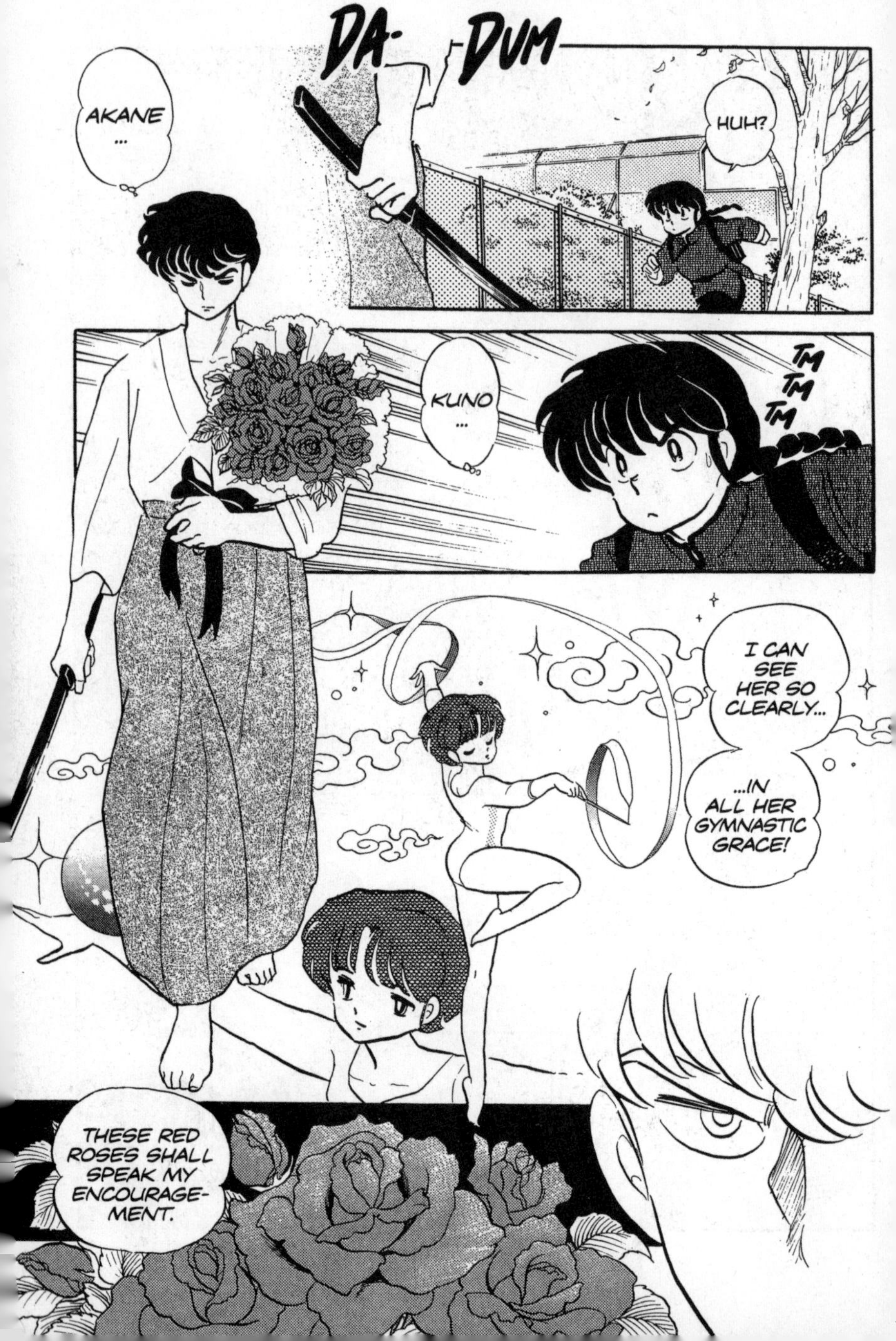
DA-DUM
HUH?
KUNO ...
TM TM TM
AKANE ...
I CAN SEE HER SO CLEARLY...
...IN ALL HER GYMNASTIC GRACE!
THESE RED ROSES SHALL SPEAK MY ENCOURAGEMENT.

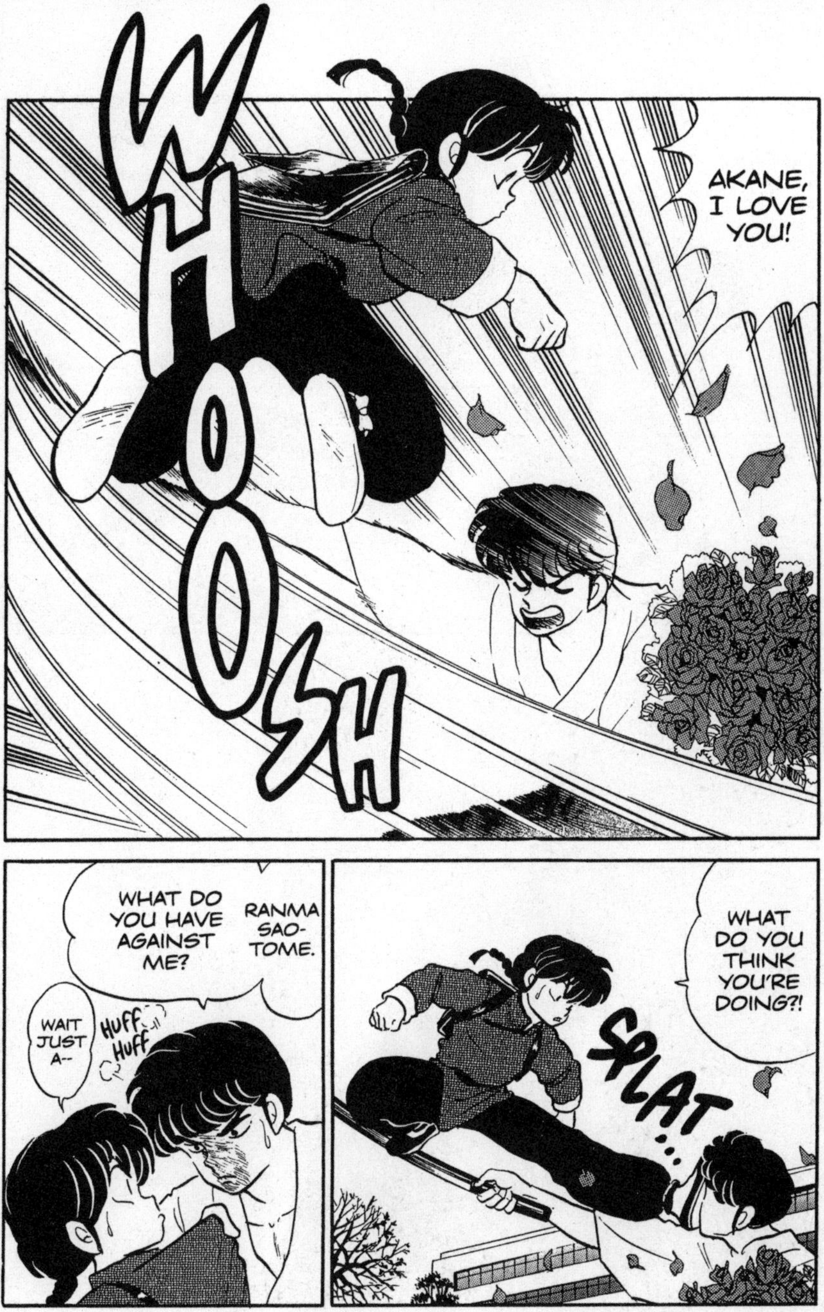
AKANE, I LOVE YOU!
WHOOSH
WHAT DO YOU THINK YOU'RE DOING?!
SPLAT...
RANMA SAOTOME.
WHAT DO YOU HAVE AGAINST ME?
HUFF HUFF
WAIT JUST A--

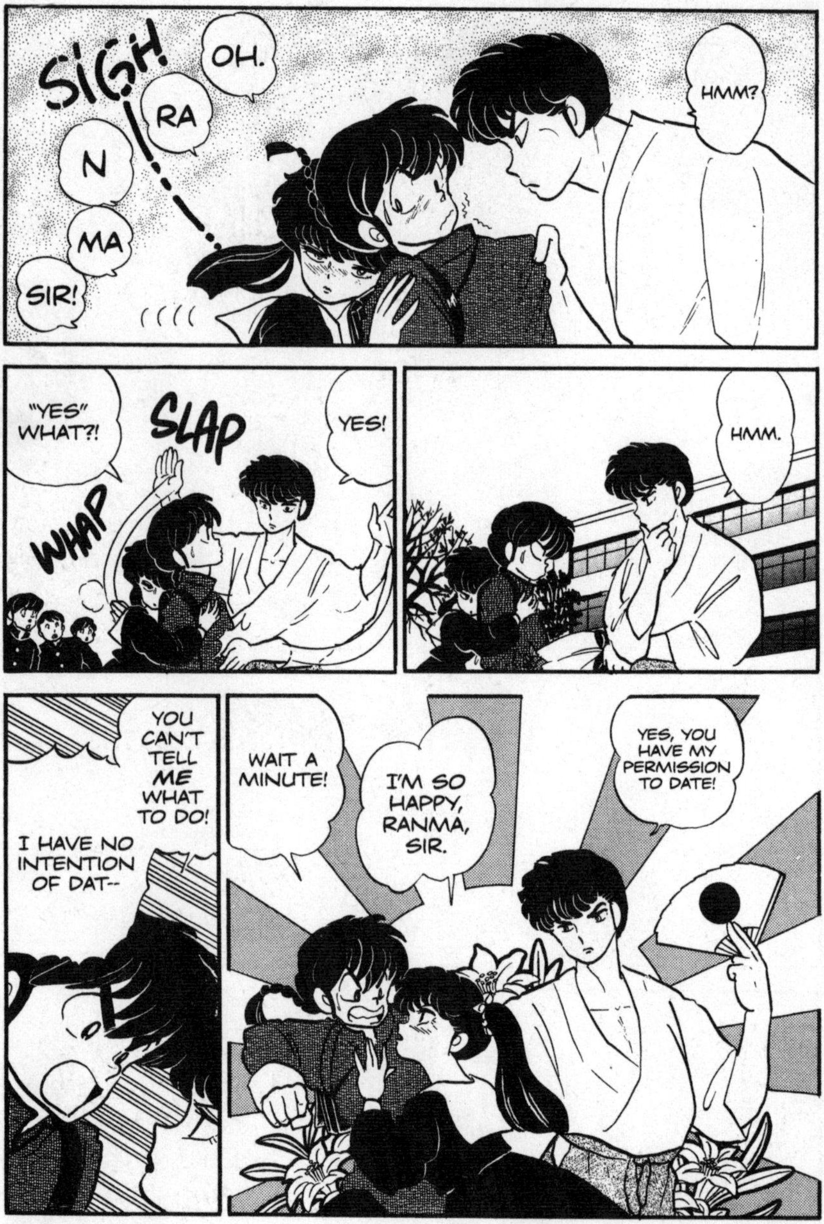
HMM?
OH.
SIGH!
RA
N
MA
SIR!
HMM.
YES!
SLAP
"YES" WHAT?!
WHAP
YES, YOU HAVE MY PERMISSION TO DATE!
I'M SO HAPPY, RANMA, SIR.
WAIT A MINUTE!
YOU CAN'T TELL *ME* WHAT TO DO!
I HAVE NO INTENTION OF DAT--

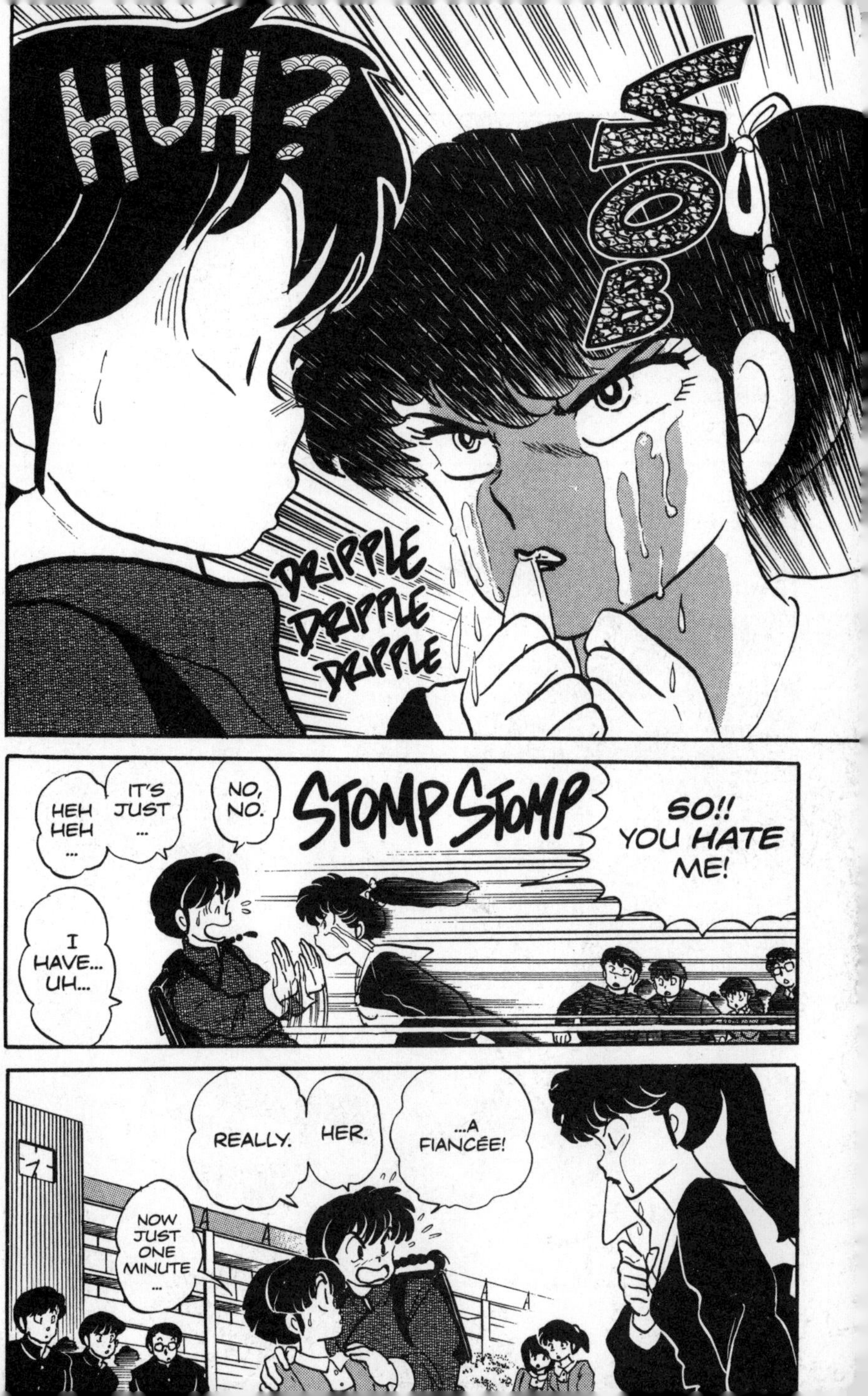
SOB
HUH?
DRIPPLE DRIPPLE DRIPPLE
SO!! YOU HATE ME!
STOMP STOMP
NO, NO.
IT'S JUST ...
HEH HEH ...
I HAVE... UH...
...A FIANCÉE!
HER.
REALLY.
NOW JUST ONE MINUTE ...

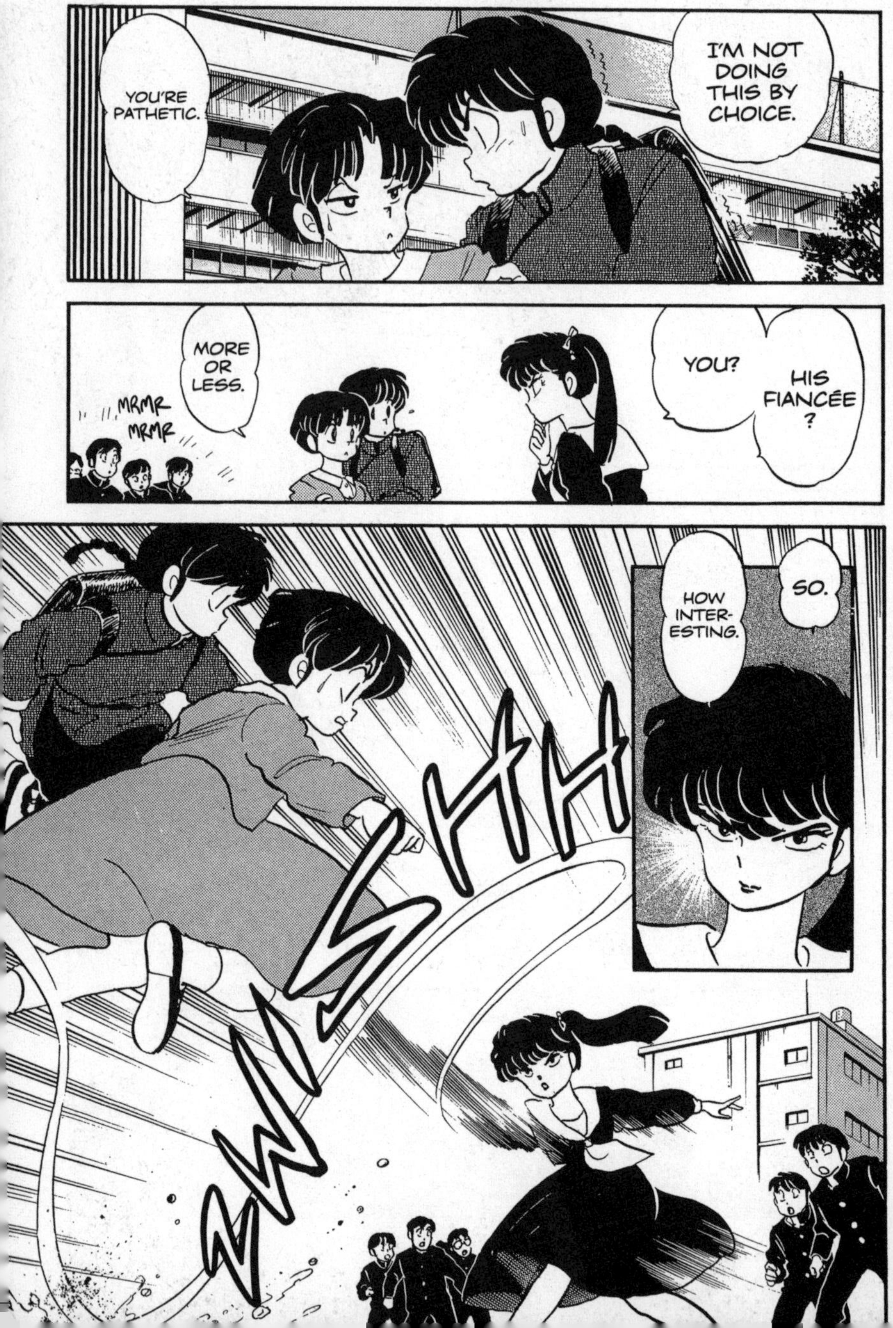
I'M NOT DOING THIS BY CHOICE.
YOU'RE PATHETIC.
HIS FIANCÉE?
YOU?
MORE OR LESS.
MRMR MRMR
SO.
HOW INTER-ESTING.

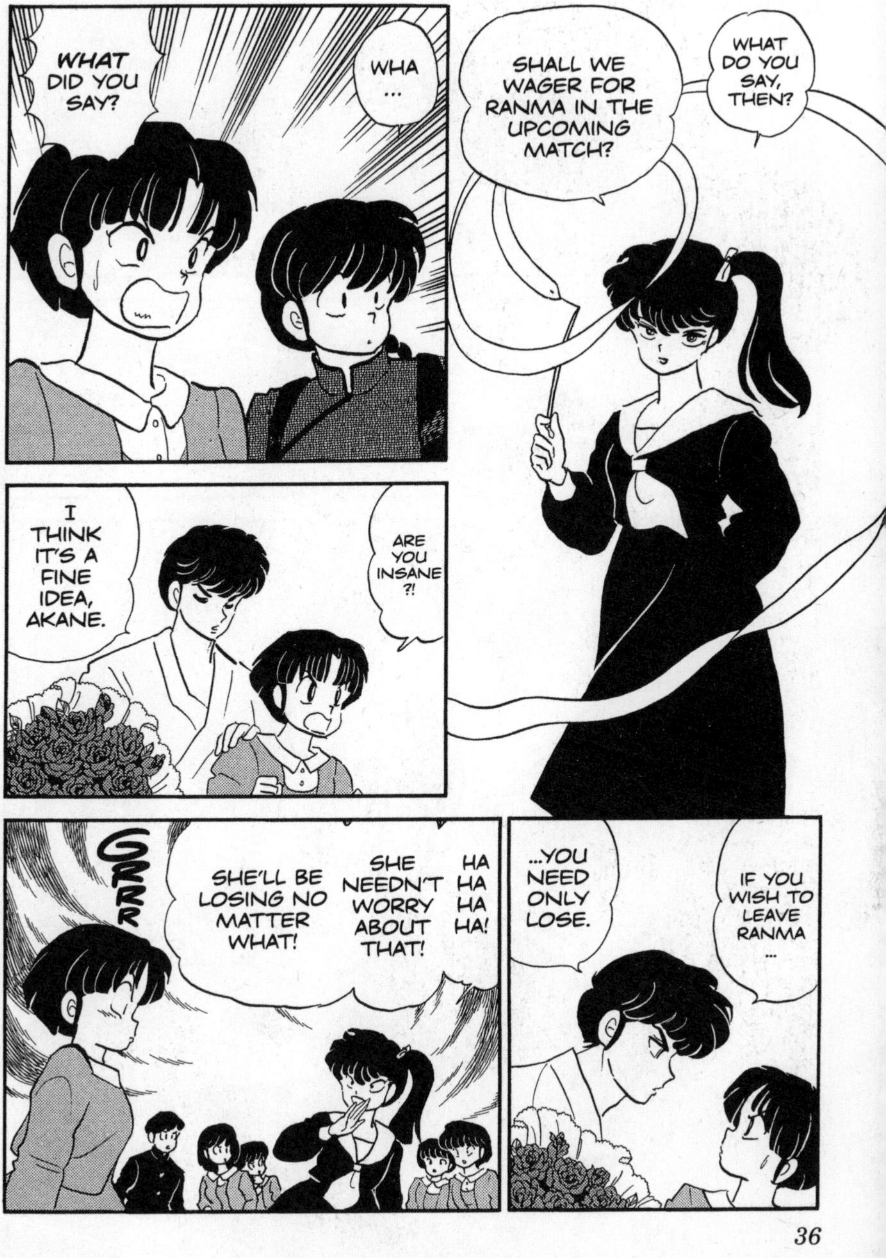
WHAT DO YOU SAY, THEN?
SHALL WE WAGER FOR RANMA IN THE UPCOMING MATCH?
WHA ...
WHAT DID YOU SAY?
ARE YOU INSANE ?!
I THINK IT'S A FINE IDEA, AKANE.
IF YOU WISH TO LEAVE RANMA ...
...YOU NEED ONLY LOSE.
HA HA HA HA!
SHE NEEDN'T WORRY ABOUT THAT!
SHE'LL BE LOSING NO MATTER WHAT!
GRRR

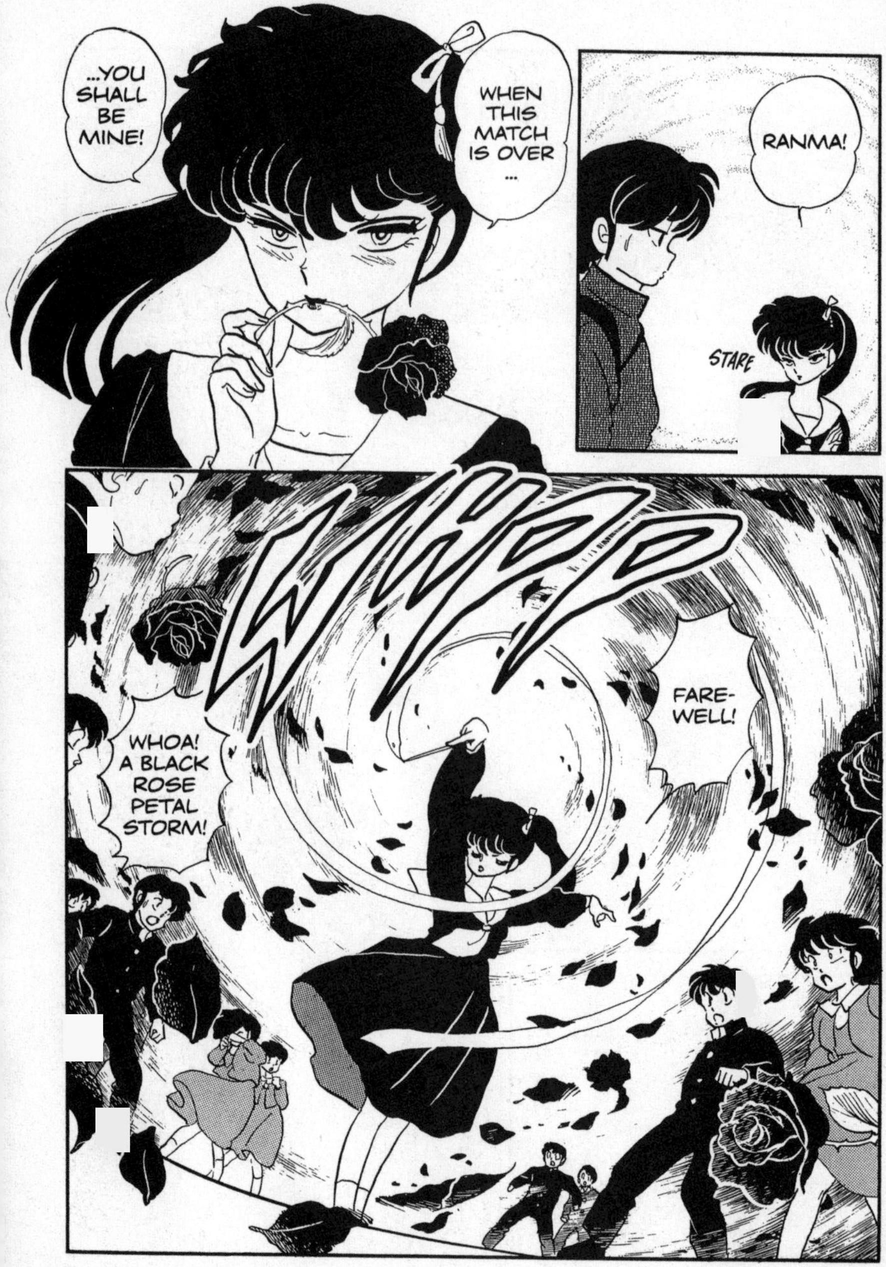
RANMA!
STARE
WHEN THIS MATCH IS OVER ...
...YOU SHALL BE MINE!
WHIPP
FARE-WELL!
WHOA! A BLACK ROSE PETAL STORM!

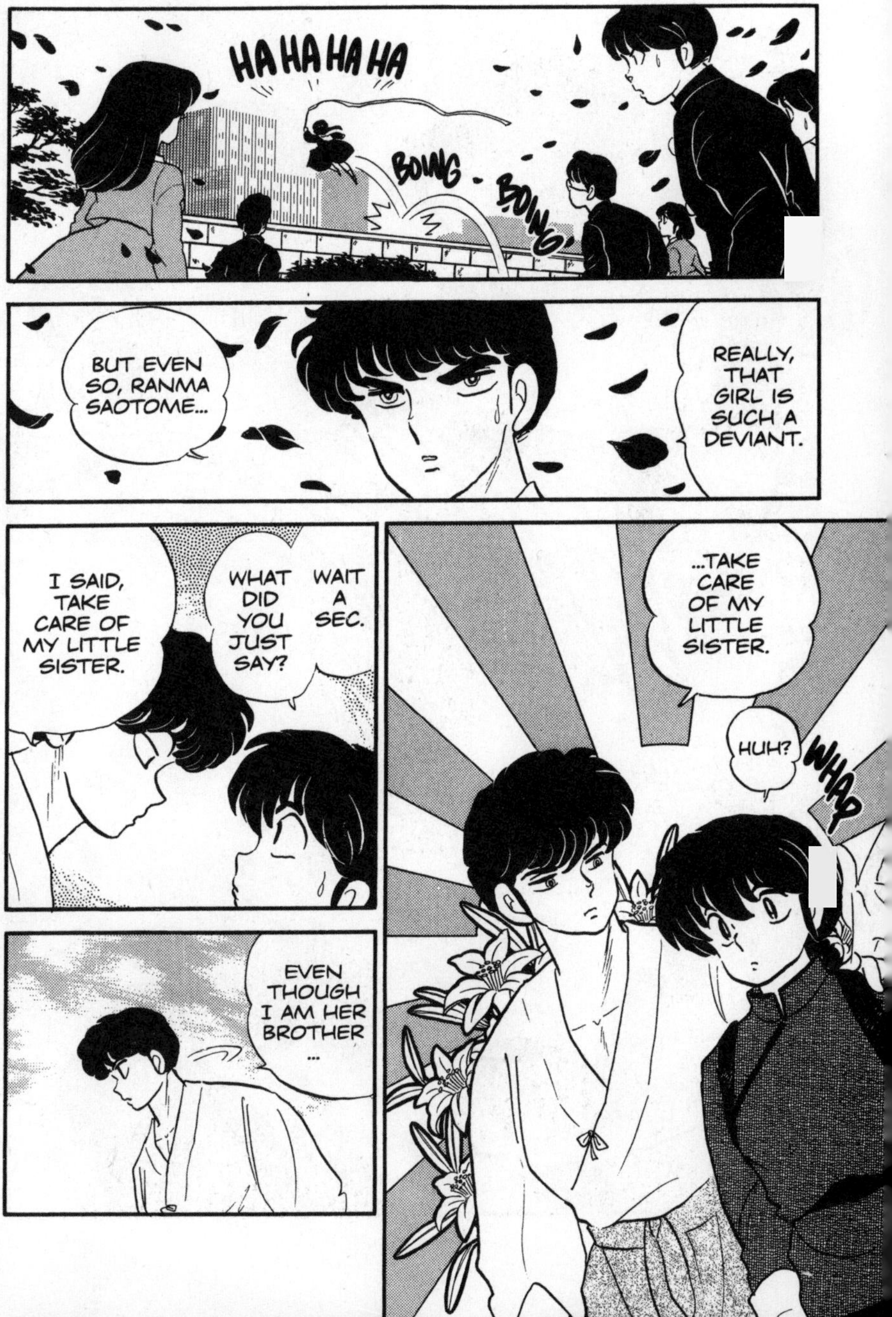
HA HA HA HA
BOING
BOING
REALLY, THAT GIRL IS SUCH A DEVIANT.
BUT EVEN SO, RANMA SAOTOME...
...TAKE CARE OF MY LITTLE SISTER.
HUH?
WHA?
WAIT A SEC.
WHAT DID YOU JUST SAY?
I SAID, TAKE CARE OF MY LITTLE SISTER.
EVEN THOUGH I AM HER BROTHER ...

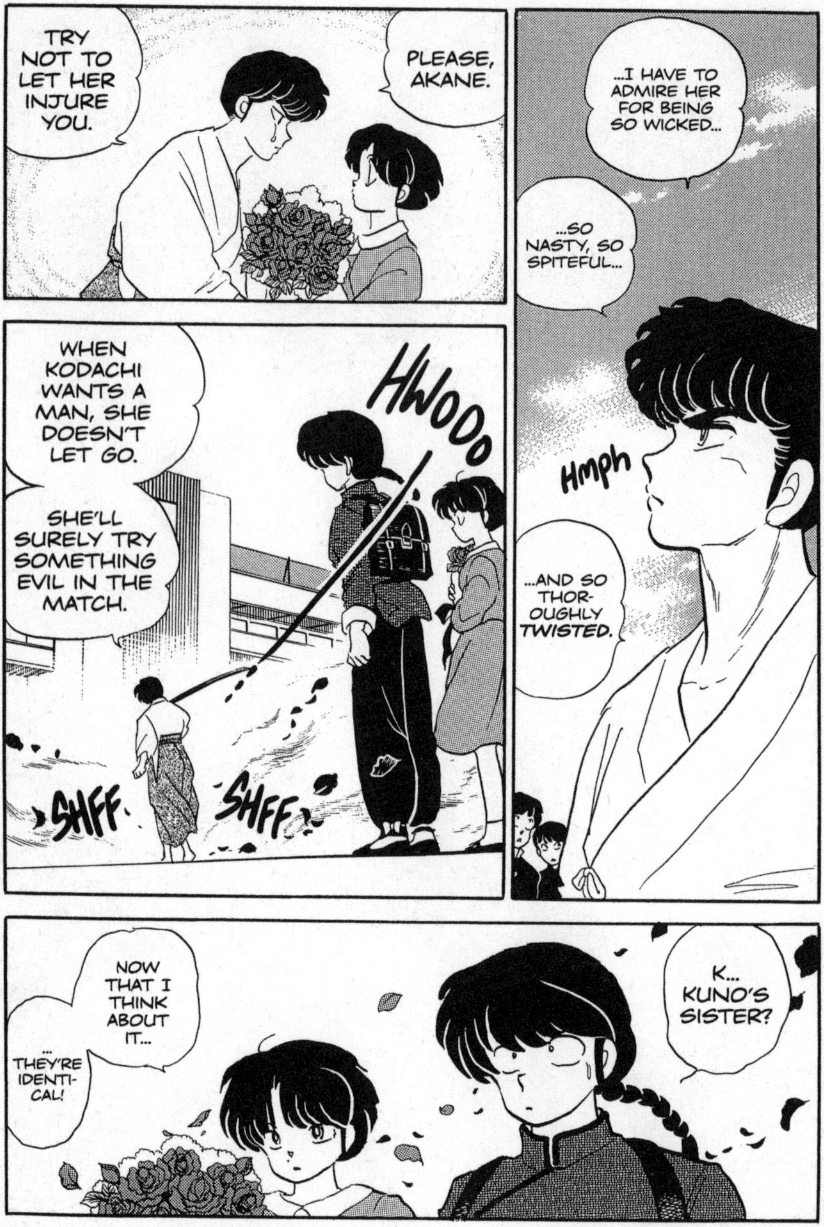
...I HAVE TO ADMIRE HER FOR BEING SO WICKED...
...SO NASTY, SO SPITEFUL...
Hmph
...AND SO THOROUGHLY TWISTED.
PLEASE, AKANE.
TRY NOT TO LET HER INJURE YOU.
HWoDo
WHEN KODACHI WANTS A MAN, SHE DOESN'T LET GO.
SHE'LL SURELY TRY SOMETHING EVIL IN THE MATCH.
SHFF
SHFF
K... KUNO'S SISTER?
NOW THAT I THINK ABOUT IT...
...THEY'RE IDENTICAL!

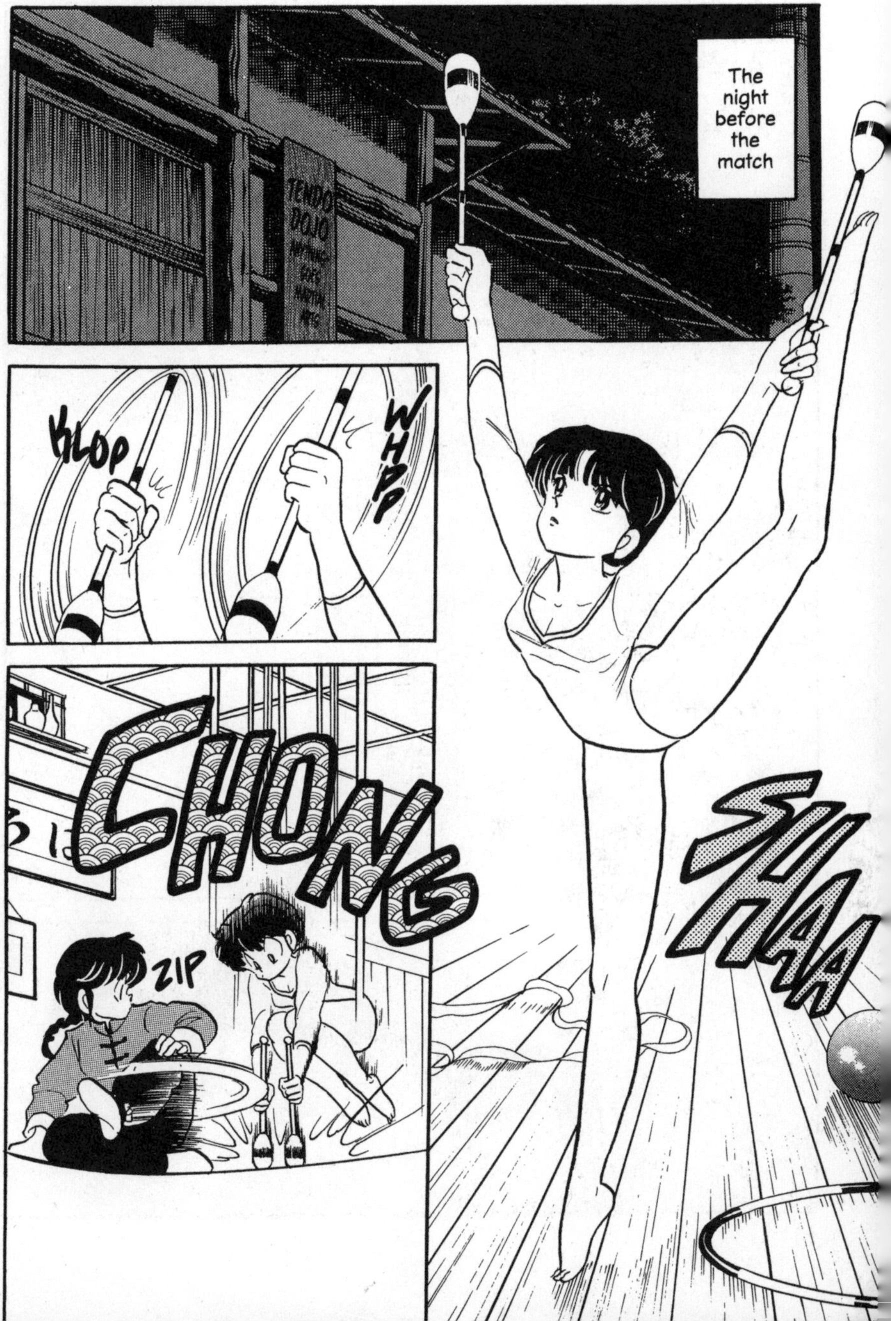
The night before the match
TENDO DOJO
SHAA
WHPP
KLOP
CHONG
ZIP

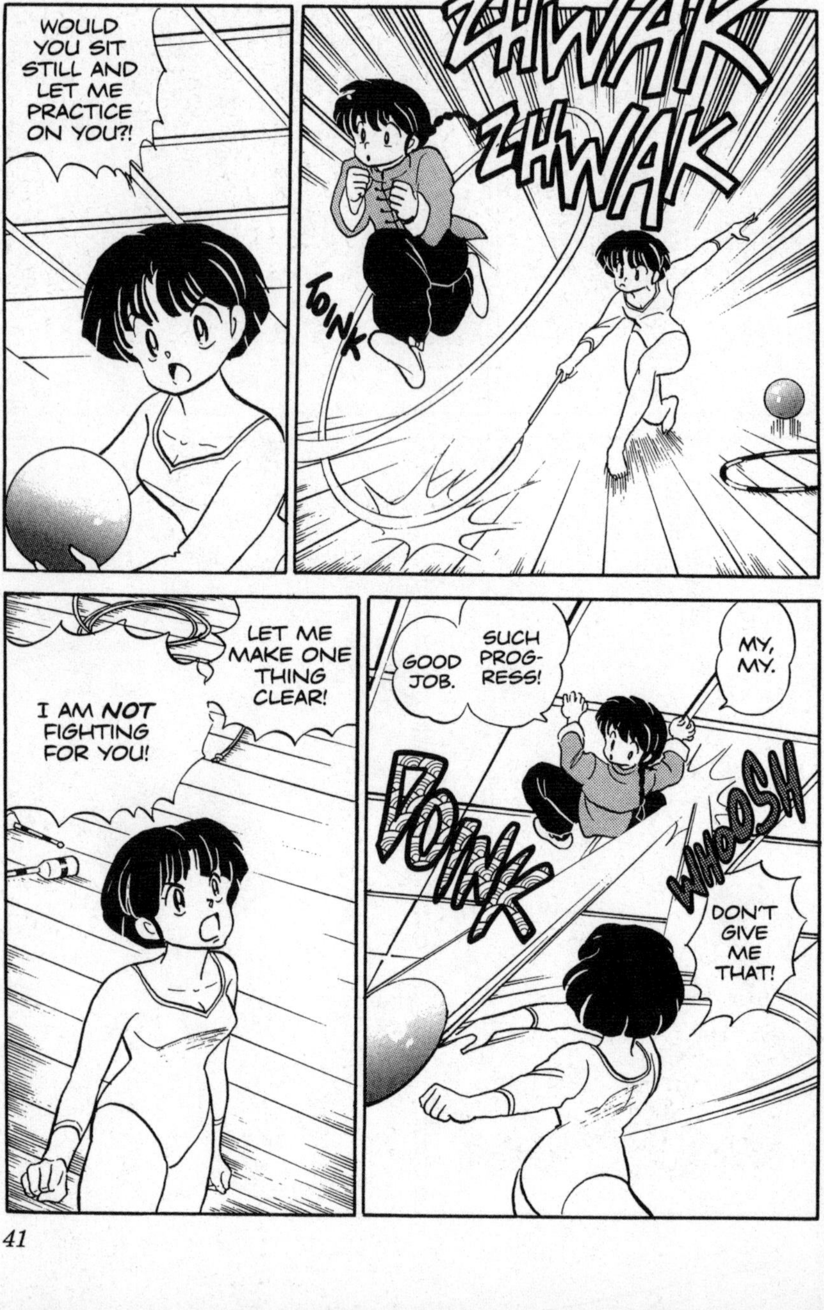
ZHWAK
ZHWAK
TOINK
WOULD YOU SIT STILL AND LET ME PRACTICE ON YOU?!
MY, MY.
SUCH PROG-RESS!
GOOD JOB.
BOINK
WHOOSH
DON'T GIVE ME THAT!
LET ME MAKE ONE THING CLEAR!
I AM **NOT** FIGHTING FOR YOU!

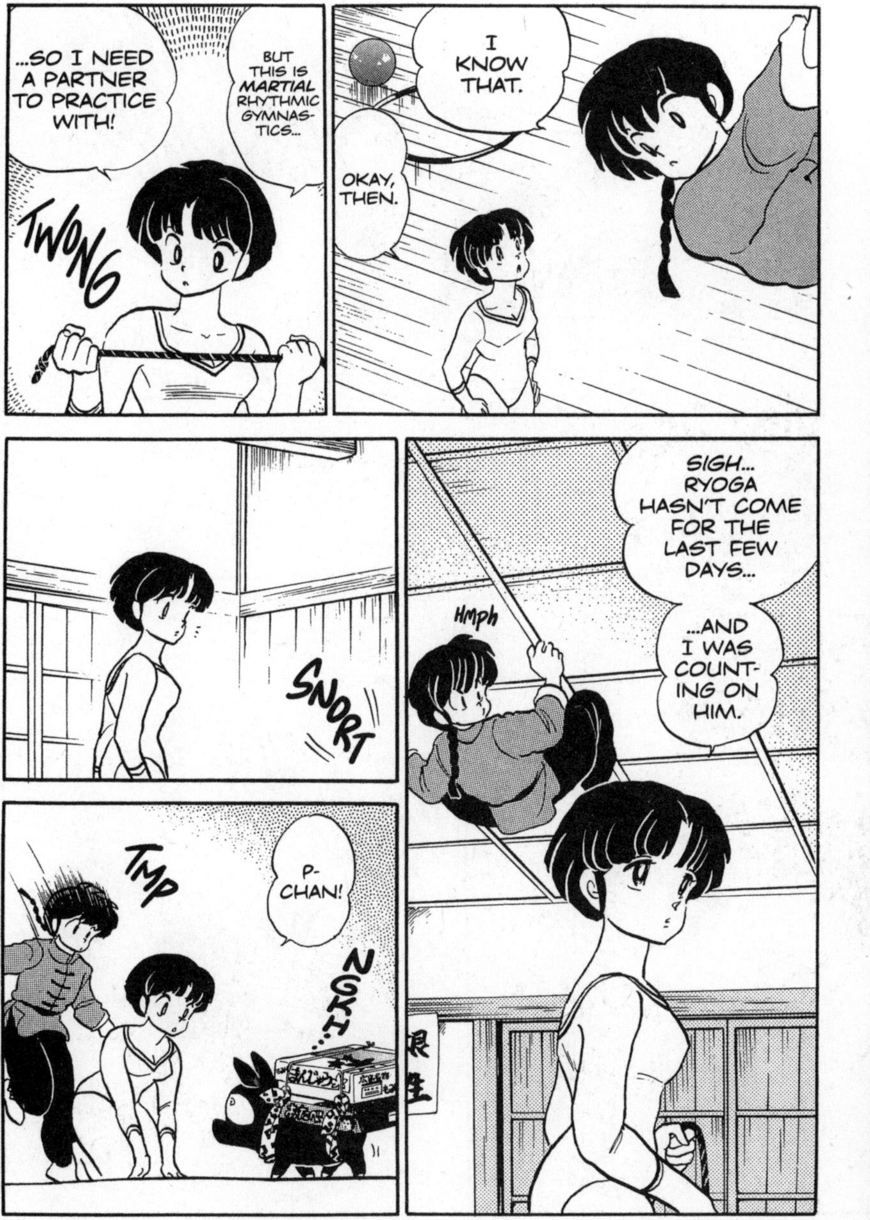
I KNOW THAT.
OKAY, THEN.
BUT THIS IS MARTIAL RHYTHMIC GYMNASTICS...
...SO I NEED A PARTNER TO PRACTICE WITH!
TWONG
SIGH... RYOGA HASN'T COME FOR THE LAST FEW DAYS...
...AND I WAS COUNTING ON HIM.
Hmph
SNORT
P-CHAN!
NGKH...
TMP

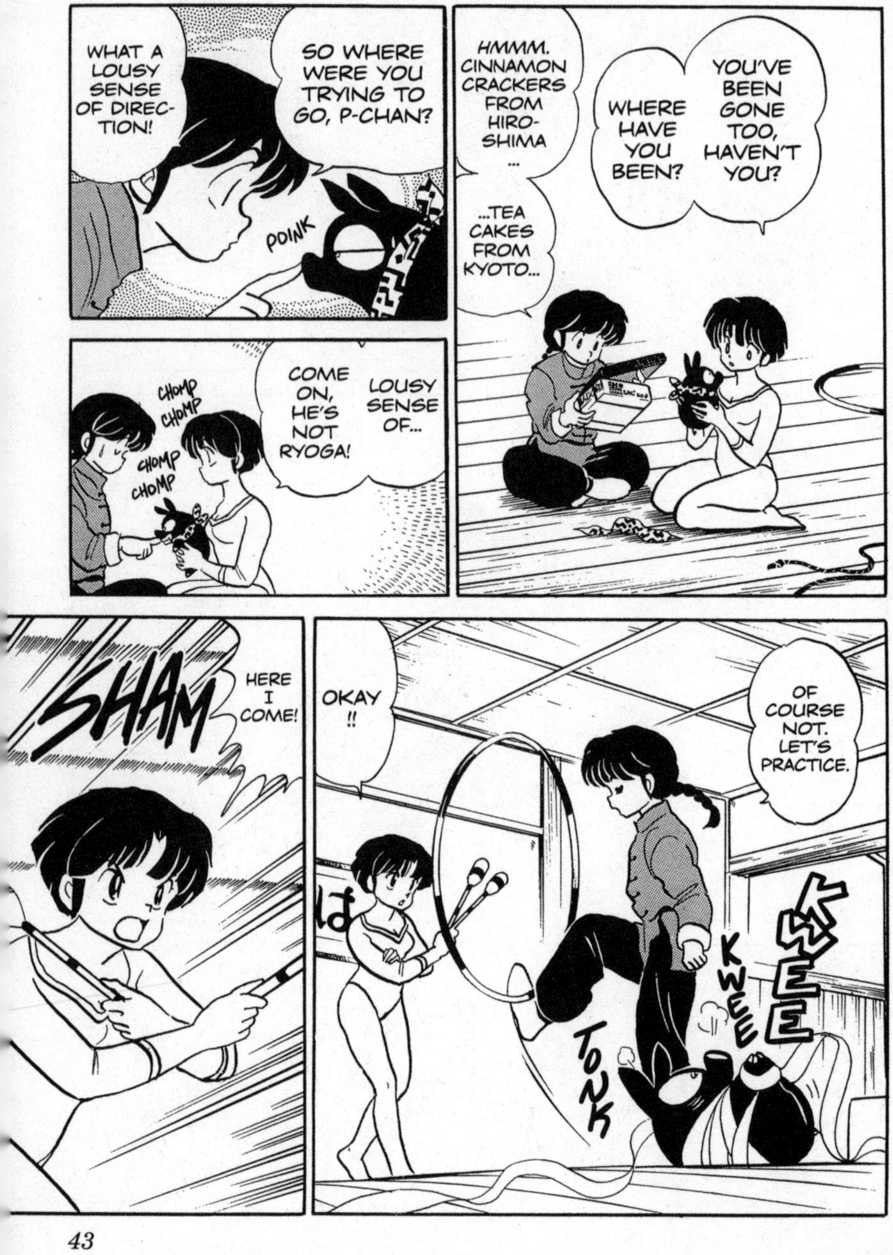
YOU'VE BEEN GONE TOO, HAVEN'T YOU?
WHERE HAVE YOU BEEN?
HMMM. CINNAMON CRACKERS FROM HIRO-SHIMA ...
...TEA CAKES FROM KYOTO...
SO WHERE WERE YOU TRYING TO GO, P-CHAN?
WHAT A LOUSY SENSE OF DIREC-TION!
POINK
LOUSY SENSE OF...
COME ON, HE'S NOT RYOGA!
CHOMP CHOMP
CHOMP CHOMP
OF COURSE NOT. LET'S PRACTICE.
KWEE
KWEE
TONK
OKAY !!
HERE I COME!
SHAM

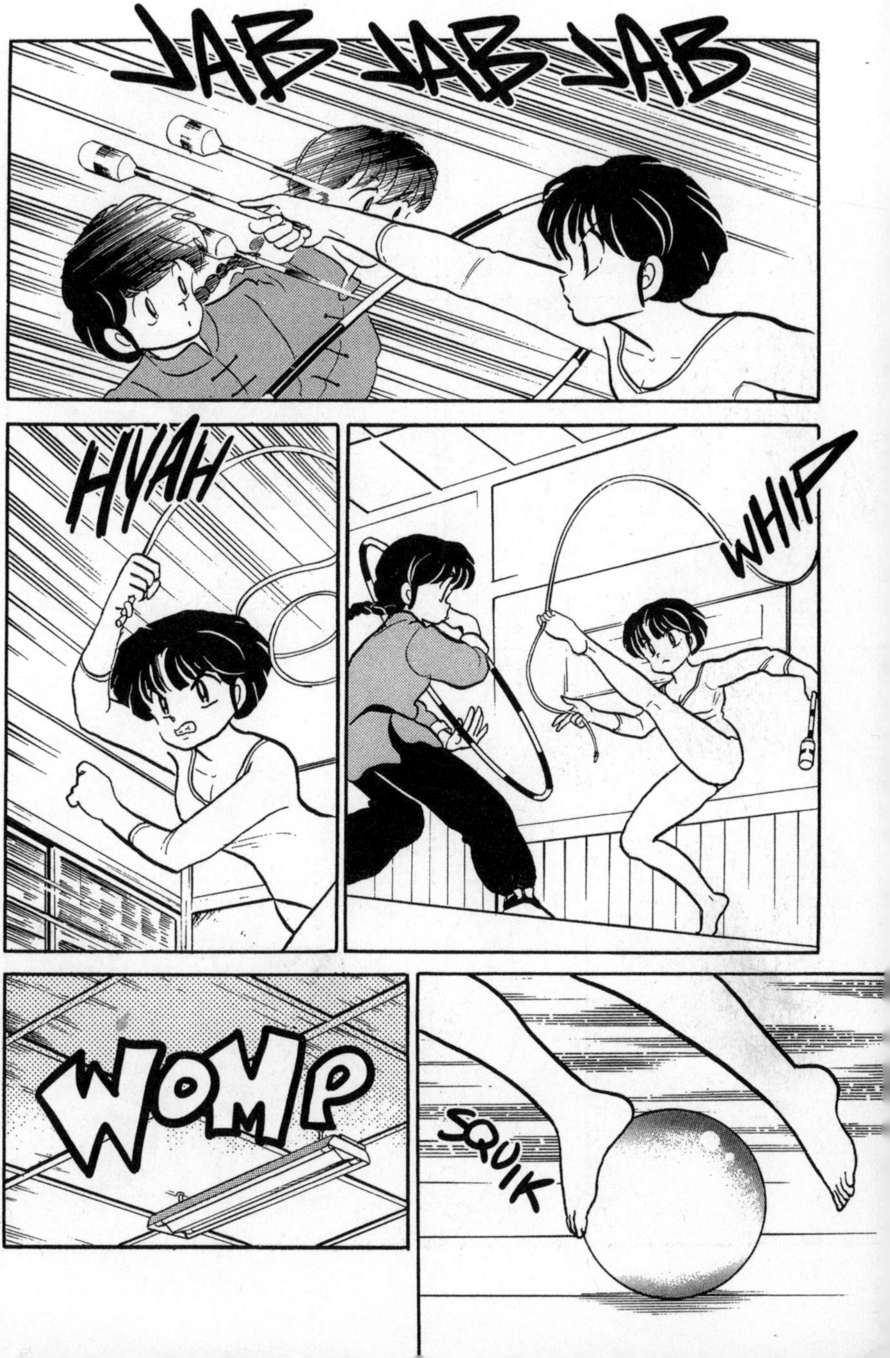
JAB JAB JAB
WHIP
HYAH
SQUIK
WOMP

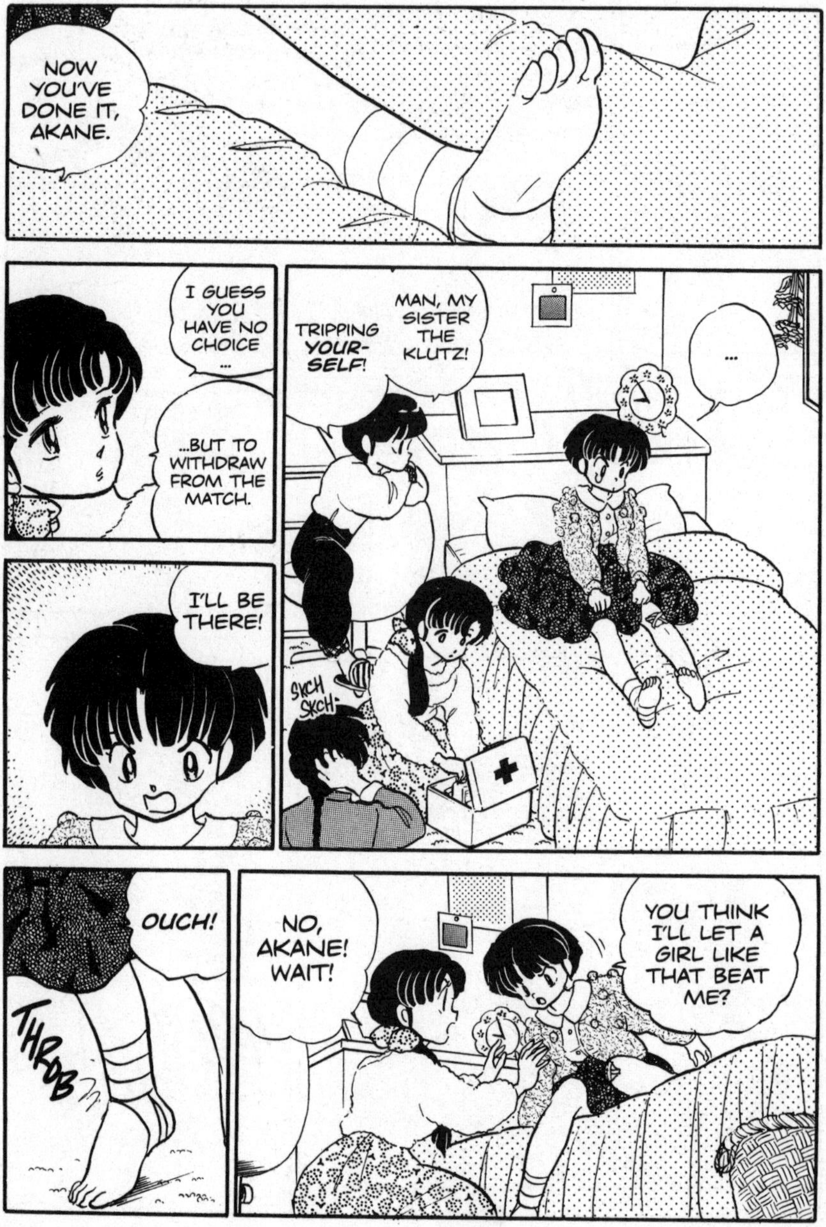
NOW YOU'VE DONE IT, AKANE.
...
MAN, MY SISTER THE KLUTZ!
TRIPPING *YOURSELF*!
SKCH SKCH
I GUESS YOU HAVE NO CHOICE ...
...BUT TO WITHDRAW FROM THE MATCH.
I'LL BE THERE!
YOU THINK I'LL LET A GIRL LIKE THAT BEAT ME?
NO, AKANE! WAIT!
OUCH!
THROB

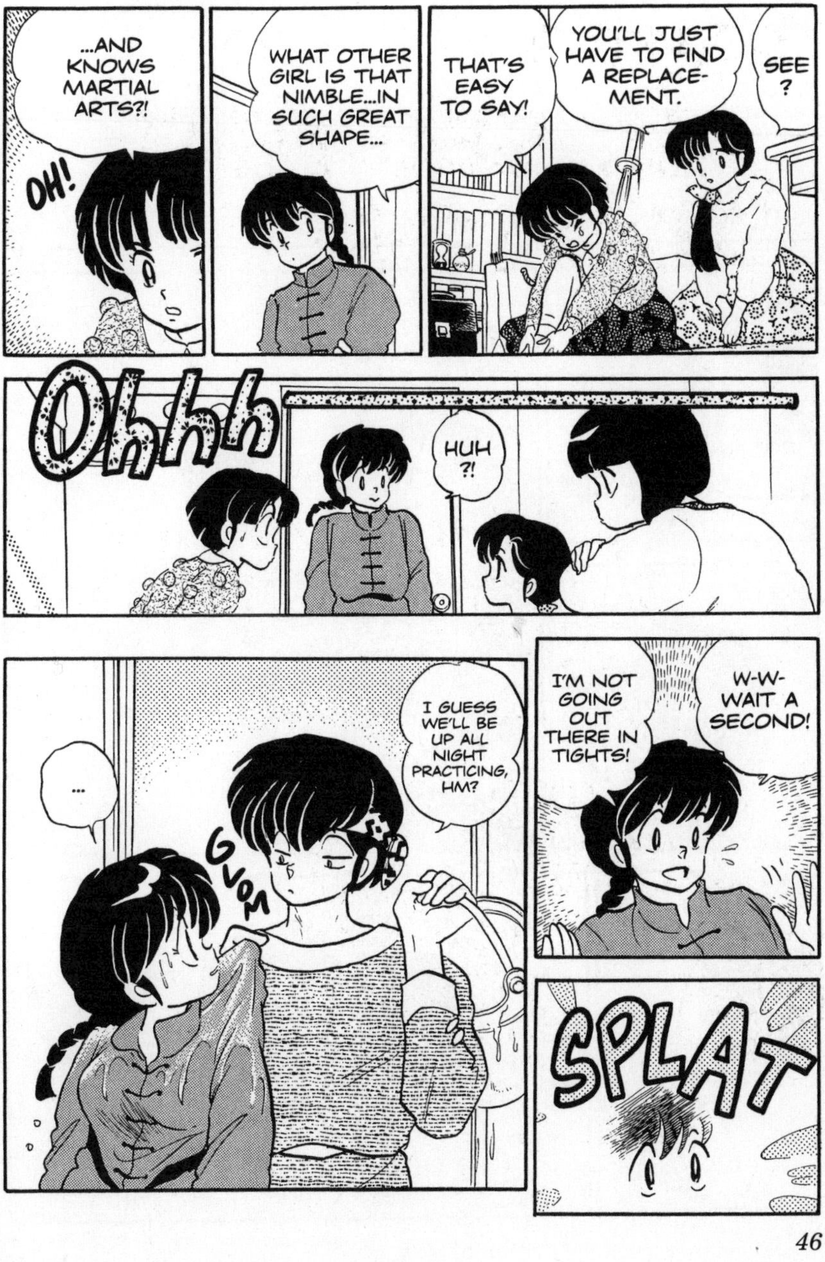
SEE ?
YOU'LL JUST HAVE TO FIND A REPLACE-MENT.
THAT'S EASY TO SAY!
WHAT OTHER GIRL IS THAT NIMBLE...IN SUCH GREAT SHAPE...
...AND KNOWS MARTIAL ARTS?!
OH!
HUH ?!
Ohhh
W-W-WAIT A SECOND!
I'M NOT GOING OUT THERE IN TIGHTS!
SPLAT
I GUESS WE'LL BE UP ALL NIGHT PRACTICING, HM?
GLOM
...

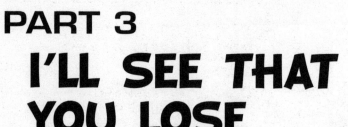

PART 3
I'LL SEE THAT
YOU LOSE

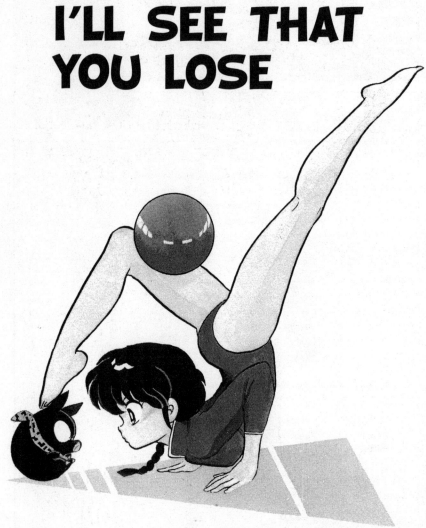

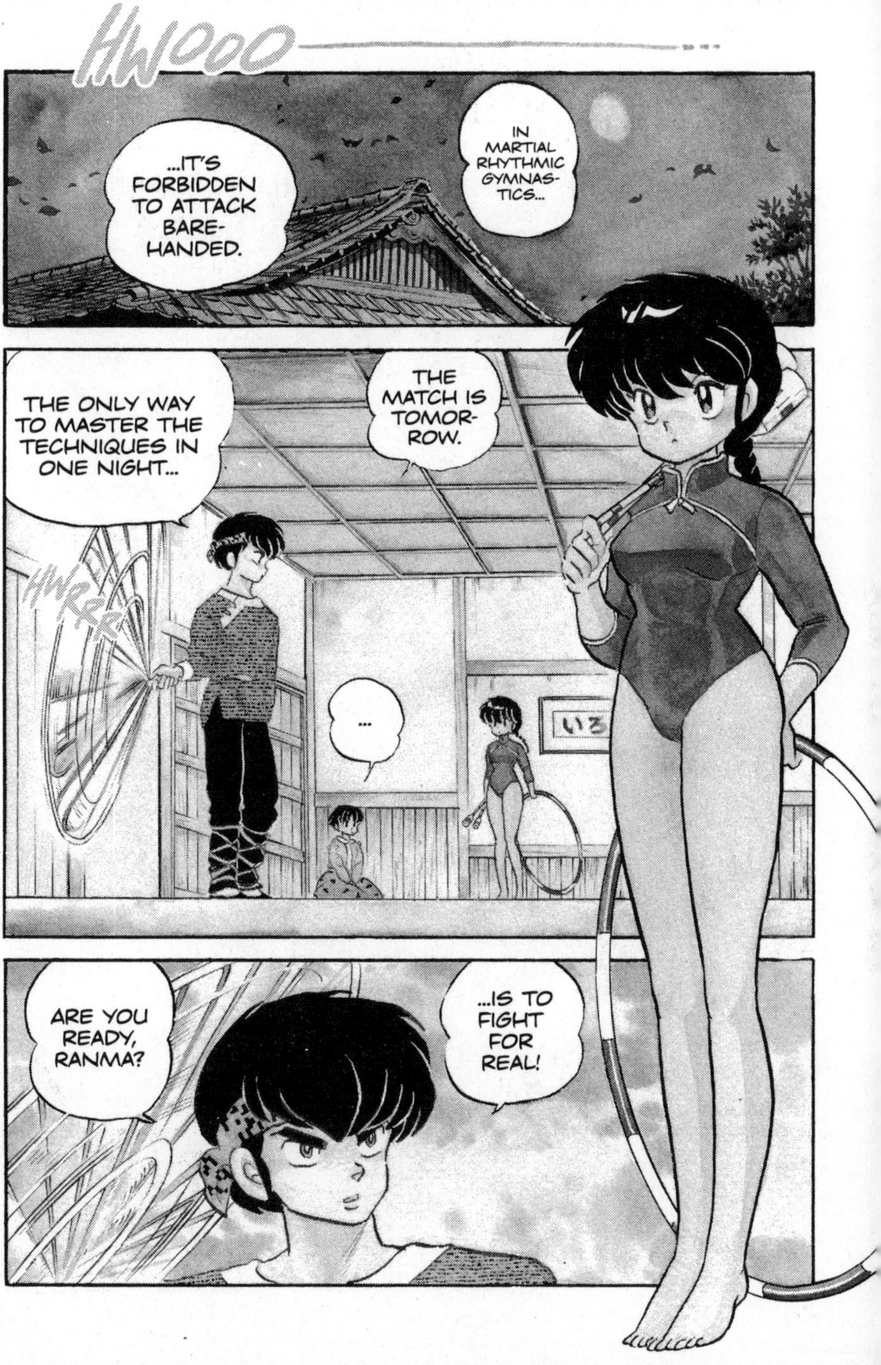
HWOOO
IN MARTIAL RHYTHMIC GYMNAS-TICS...
...IT'S FORBIDDEN TO ATTACK BARE-HANDED.
THE MATCH IS TOMOR-ROW.
THE ONLY WAY TO MASTER THE TECHNIQUES IN ONE NIGHT...
HWRRRR
...
いろ
...IS TO FIGHT FOR REAL!
ARE YOU READY, RANMA?

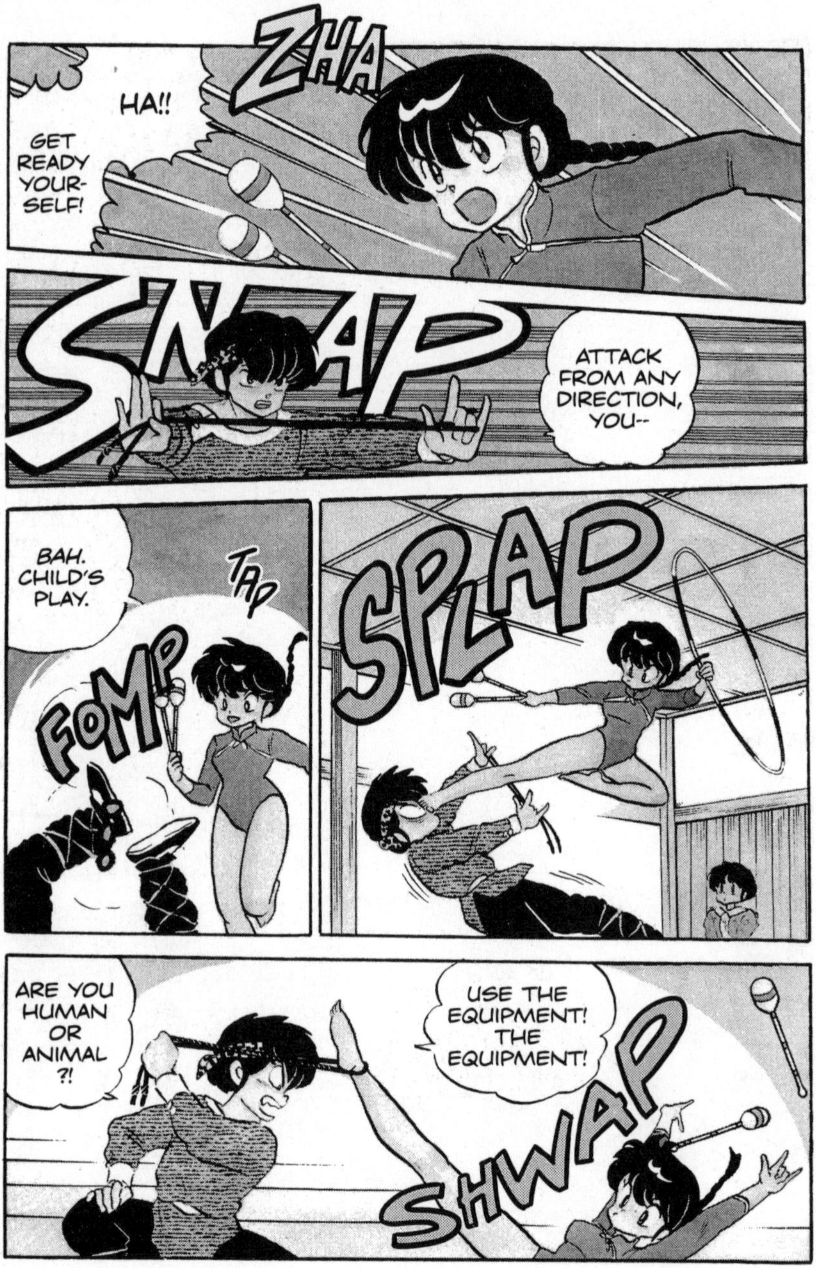
ZHA
HA!!
GET READY YOUR-SELF!
SNAP
ATTACK FROM ANY DIRECTION, YOU--
SPLAP
BAH. CHILD'S PLAY.
TAP
FOMP
USE THE EQUIPMENT! THE EQUIPMENT!
ARE YOU HUMAN OR ANIMAL ?!
SHWAP

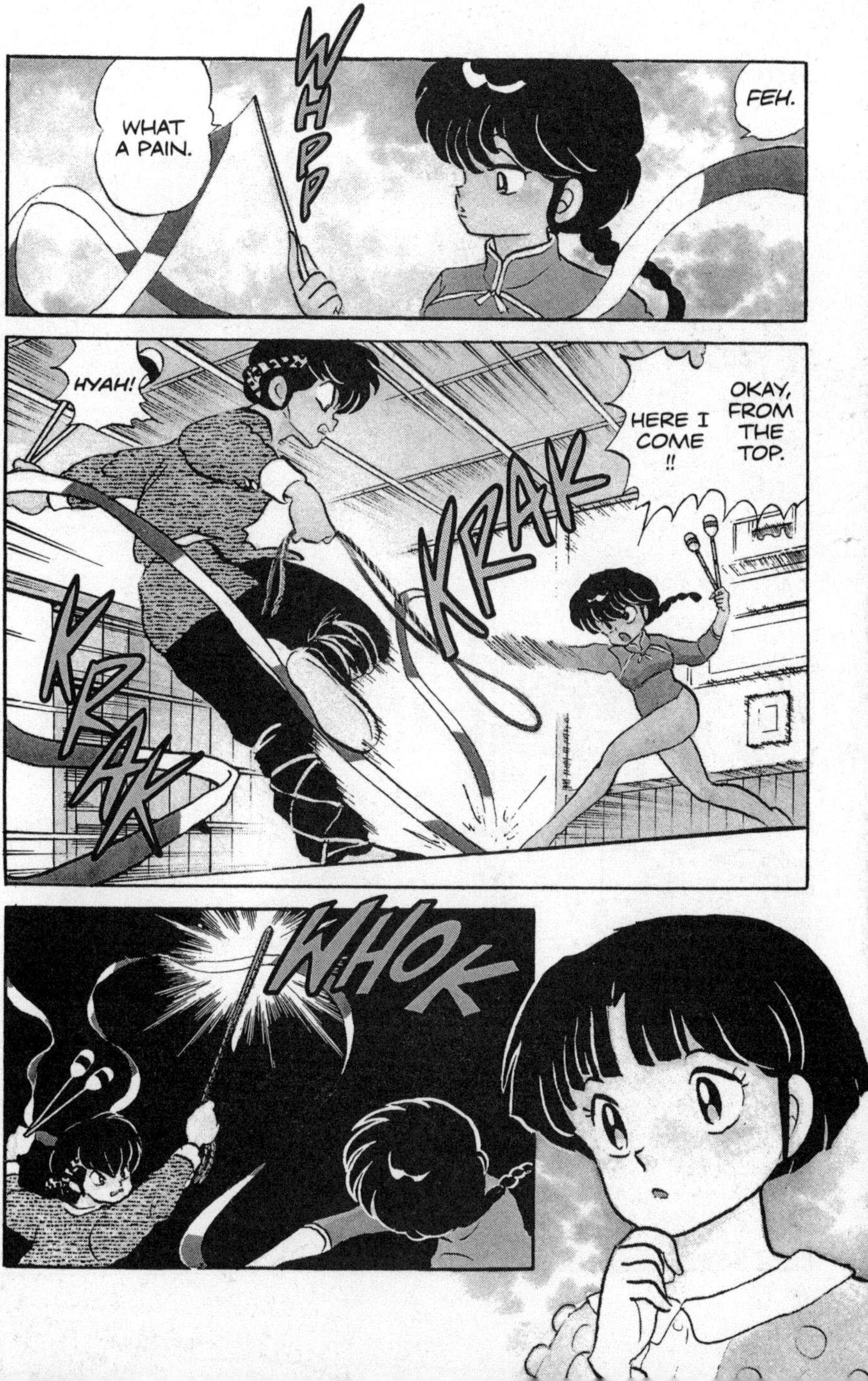
FEH.
WHPP
WHAT A PAIN.
OKAY, FROM THE TOP.
HERE I COME !!
KRAK
HYAH!
KRAK
WHOK

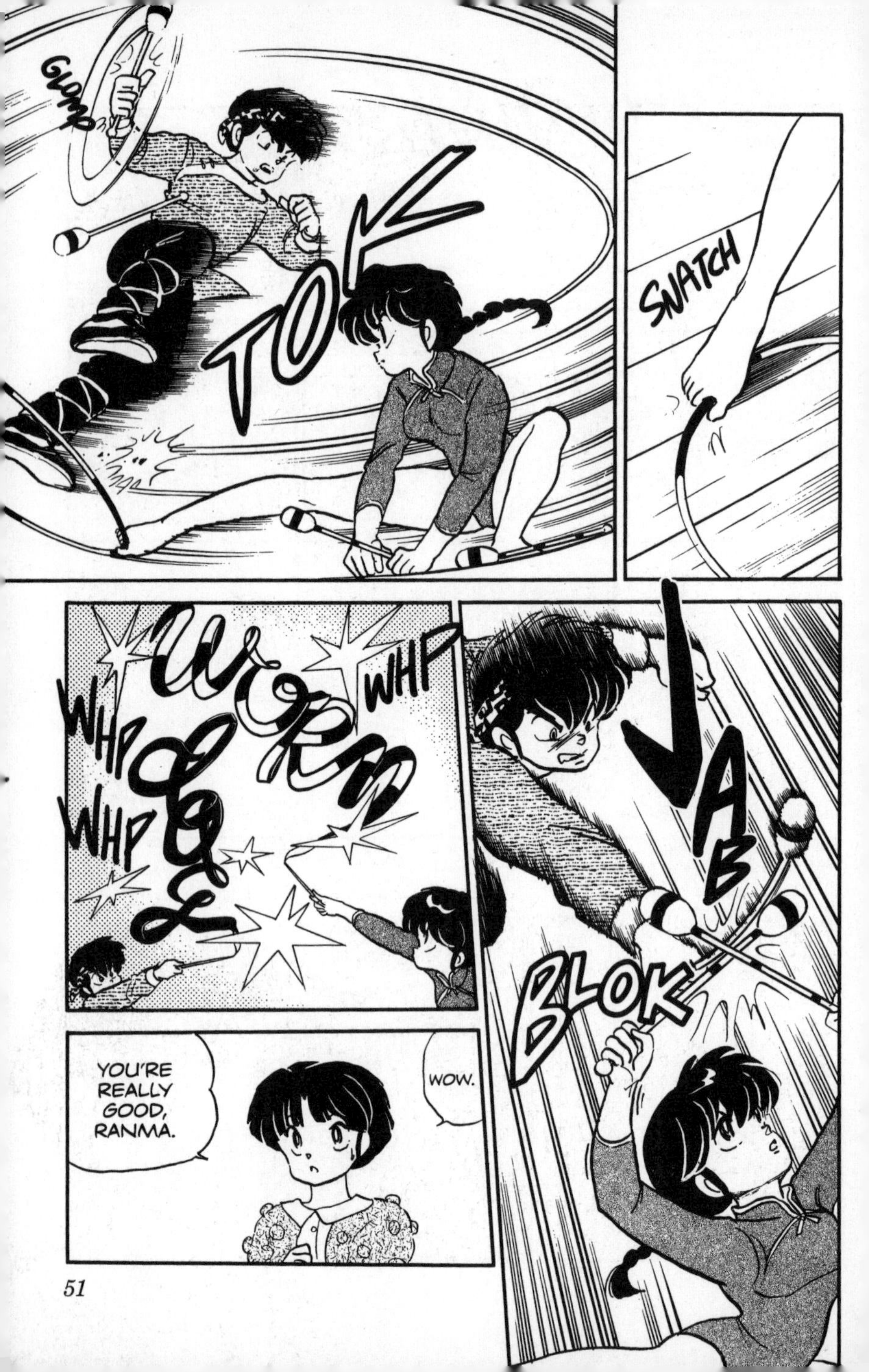
SNATCH
GLOMP
TOK
JAB
BLOK
WHP
WHP
WHP
WOW.
YOU'RE REALLY GOOD, RANMA.

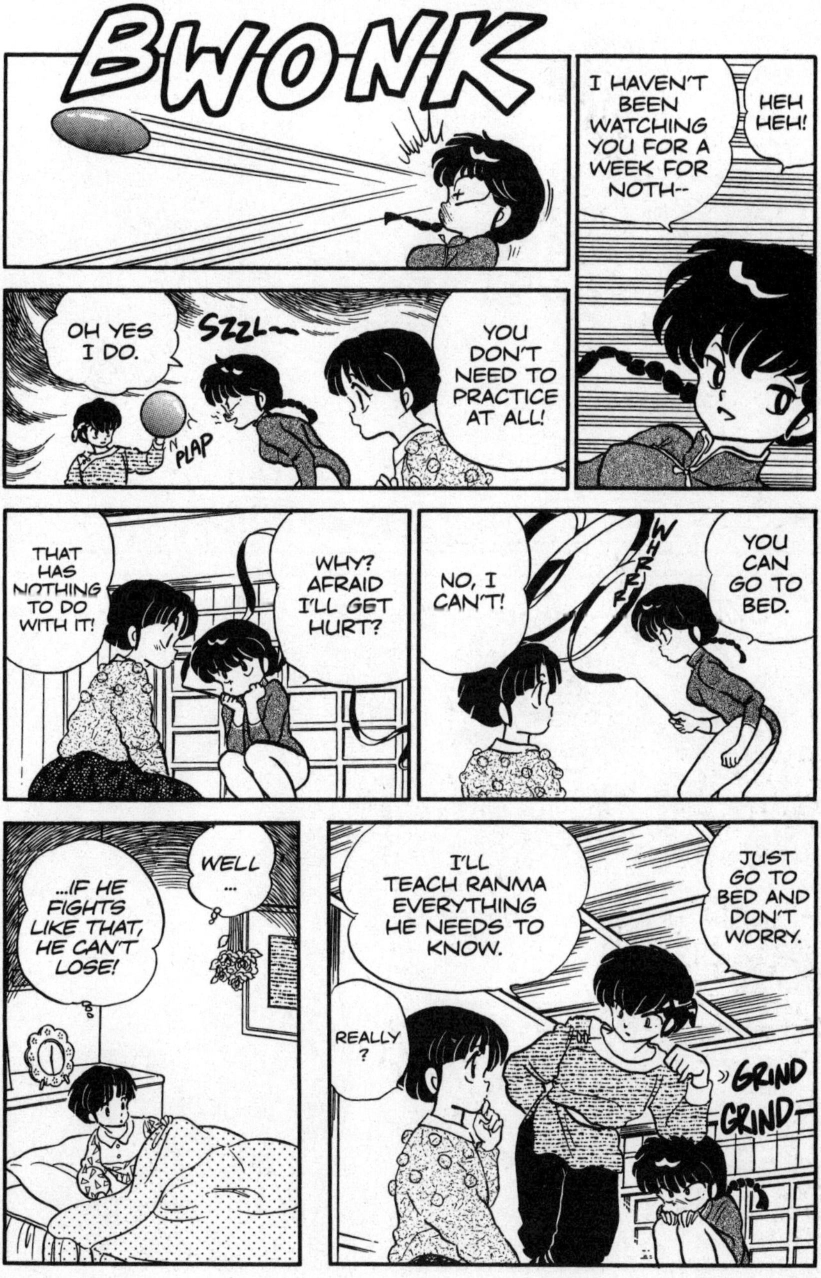
HEH HEH!
I HAVEN'T BEEN WATCHING YOU FOR A WEEK FOR NOTH--
BWONK
YOU DON'T NEED TO PRACTICE AT ALL!
SZZL--
OH YES I DO.
PLAP
YOU CAN GO TO BED.
WHRRR
NO, I CAN'T!
WHY? AFRAID I'LL GET HURT?
THAT HAS NOTHING TO DO WITH IT!
JUST GO TO BED AND DON'T WORRY.
I'LL TEACH RANMA EVERYTHING HE NEEDS TO KNOW.
REALLY?
GRIND GRIND
WELL ...
...IF HE FIGHTS LIKE THAT, HE CAN'T LOSE!

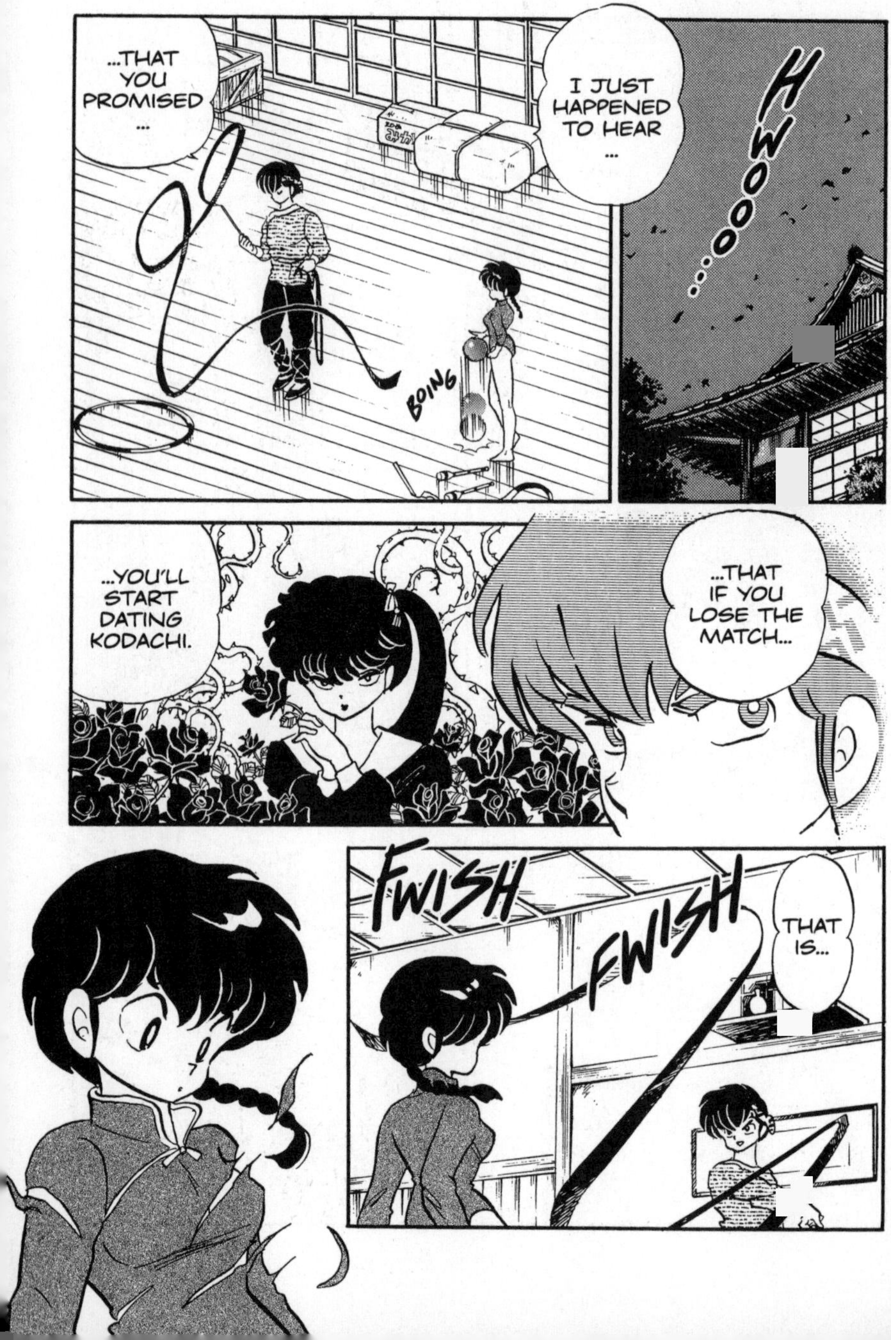
HWOOOO...
I JUST HAPPENED TO HEAR ...
...THAT YOU PROMISED ...
BOING
...THAT IF YOU LOSE THE MATCH...
...YOU'LL START DATING KODACHI.
FWISH
FWISH
THAT IS...

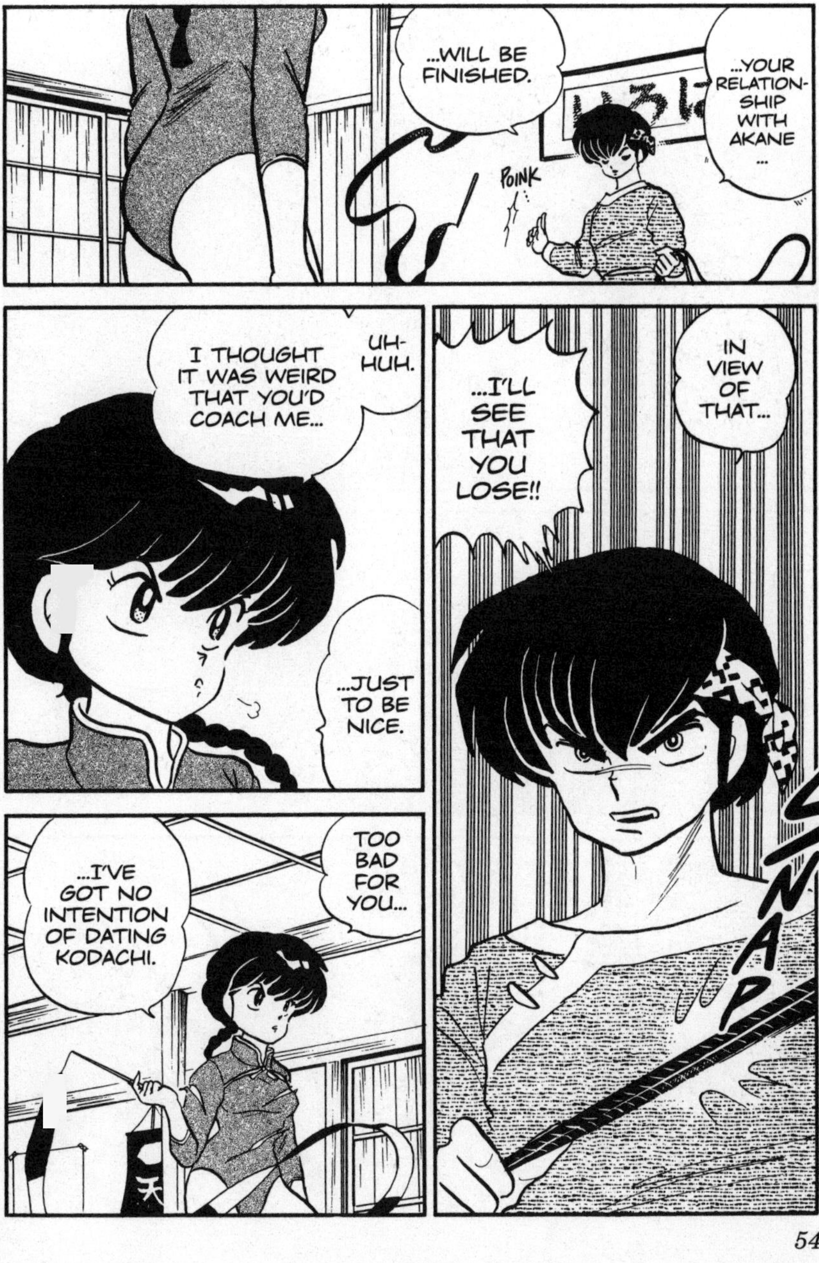
...YOUR RELATIONSHIP WITH AKANE ...
...WILL BE FINISHED.
POINK
IN VIEW OF THAT...
...I'LL SEE THAT YOU LOSE!!
SNAP
UH-HUH.
I THOUGHT IT WAS WEIRD THAT YOU'D COACH ME...
...JUST TO BE NICE.
TOO BAD FOR YOU...
...I'VE GOT NO INTENTION OF DATING KODACHI.

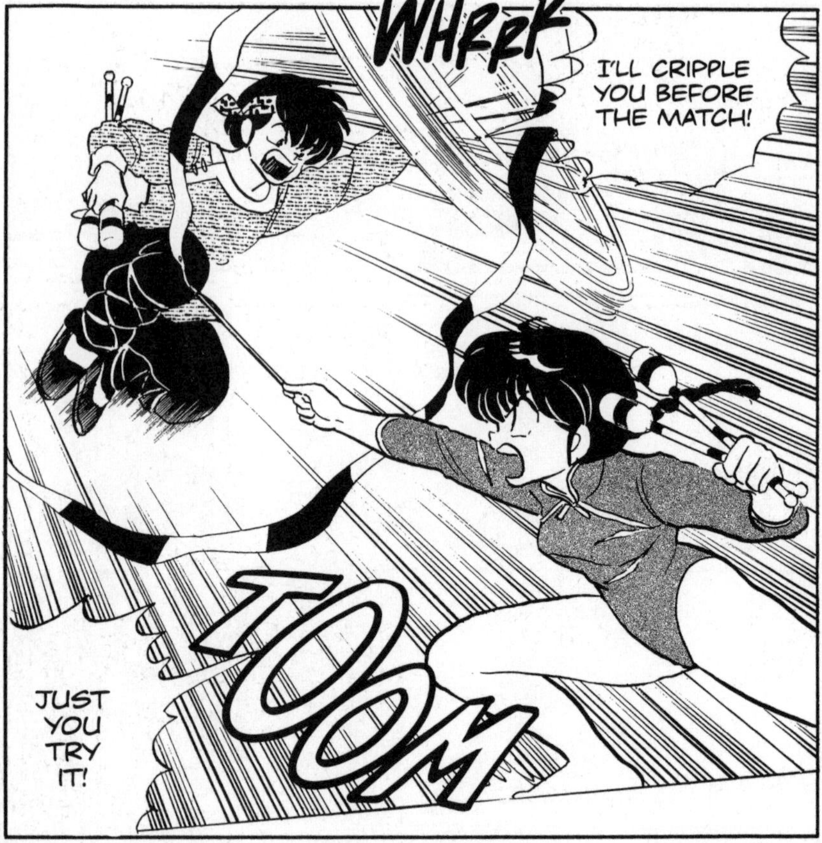
WHRRR
I'LL CRIPPLE YOU BEFORE THE MATCH!
TOOM
JUST YOU TRY IT!

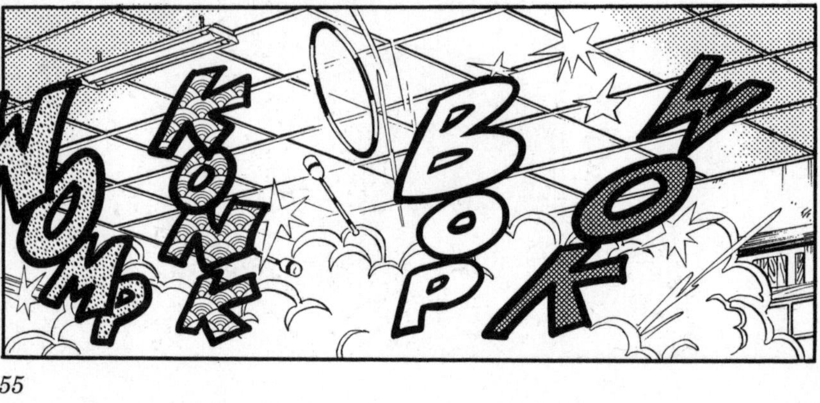
WOK
BOOP
KONK
WOMP

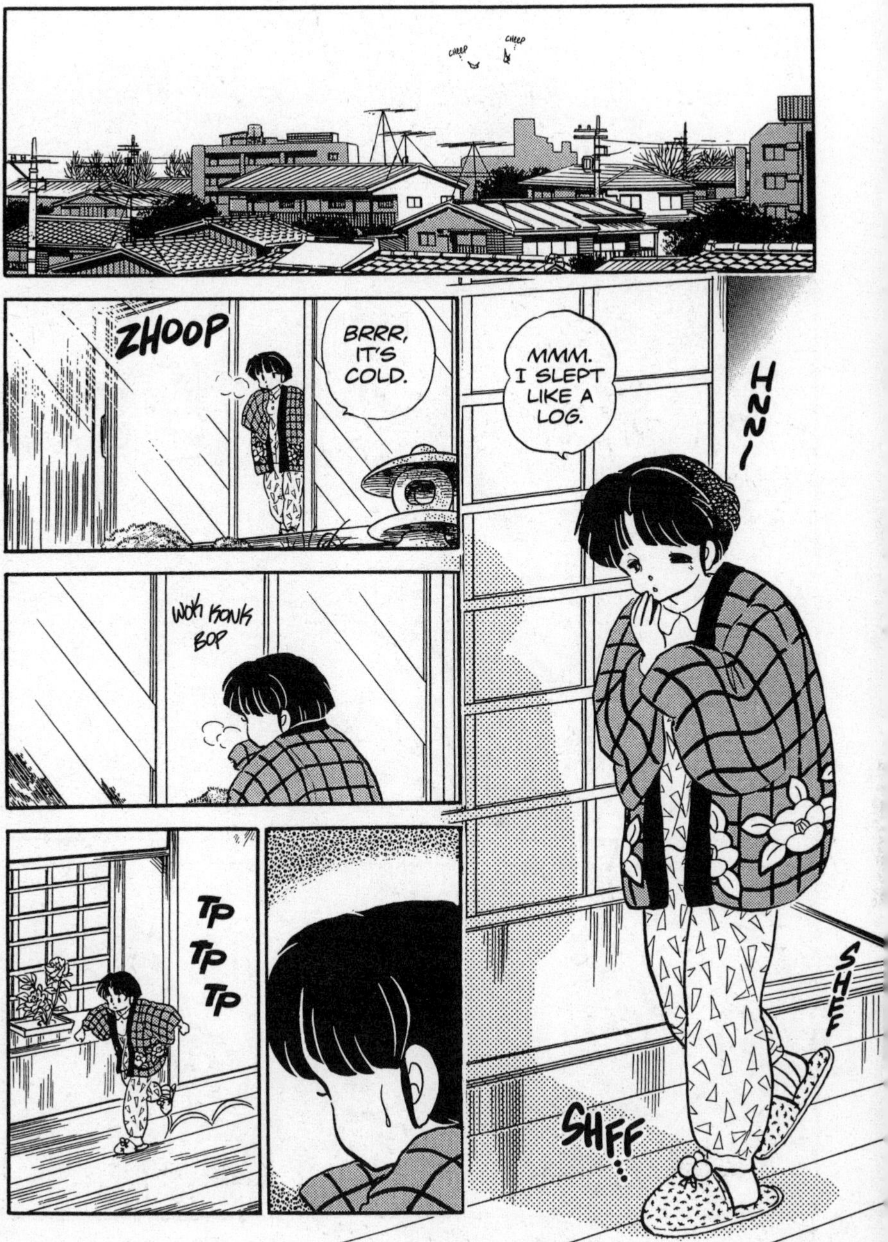
CHEEP
CHEEP
HNN
MMM. I SLEPT LIKE A LOG.
SHEF
SHFF
ZHOOP
BRRR, IT'S COLD.
WOK KONK BOP
TP TP TP

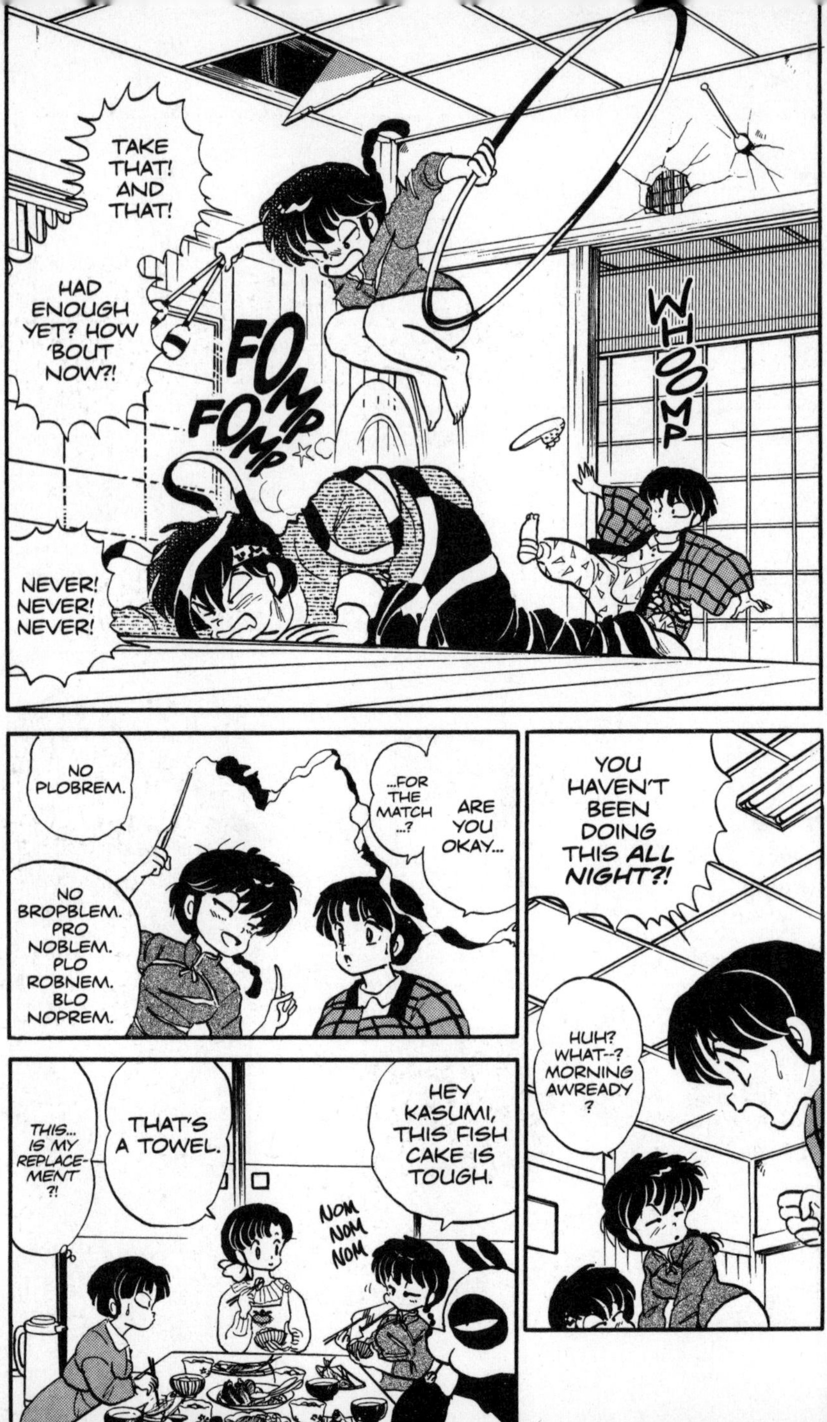

WHOOMP
TAKE THAT! AND THAT!
HAD ENOUGH YET? HOW 'BOUT NOW?!
FOMP FOMP
NEVER! NEVER! NEVER!
YOU HAVEN'T BEEN DOING THIS ALL NIGHT?!
HUH? WHAT--? MORNING AWREADY?
ARE YOU OKAY...
...FOR THE MATCH...?
NO PLOBREM.
NO BROPBLEM. PRO NOBLEM. PLO ROBNEM. BLO NOPREM.
HEY KASUMI, THIS FISH CAKE IS TOUGH.
NOM NOM NOM
THAT'S A TOWEL.
THIS... IS MY REPLACEMENT?!

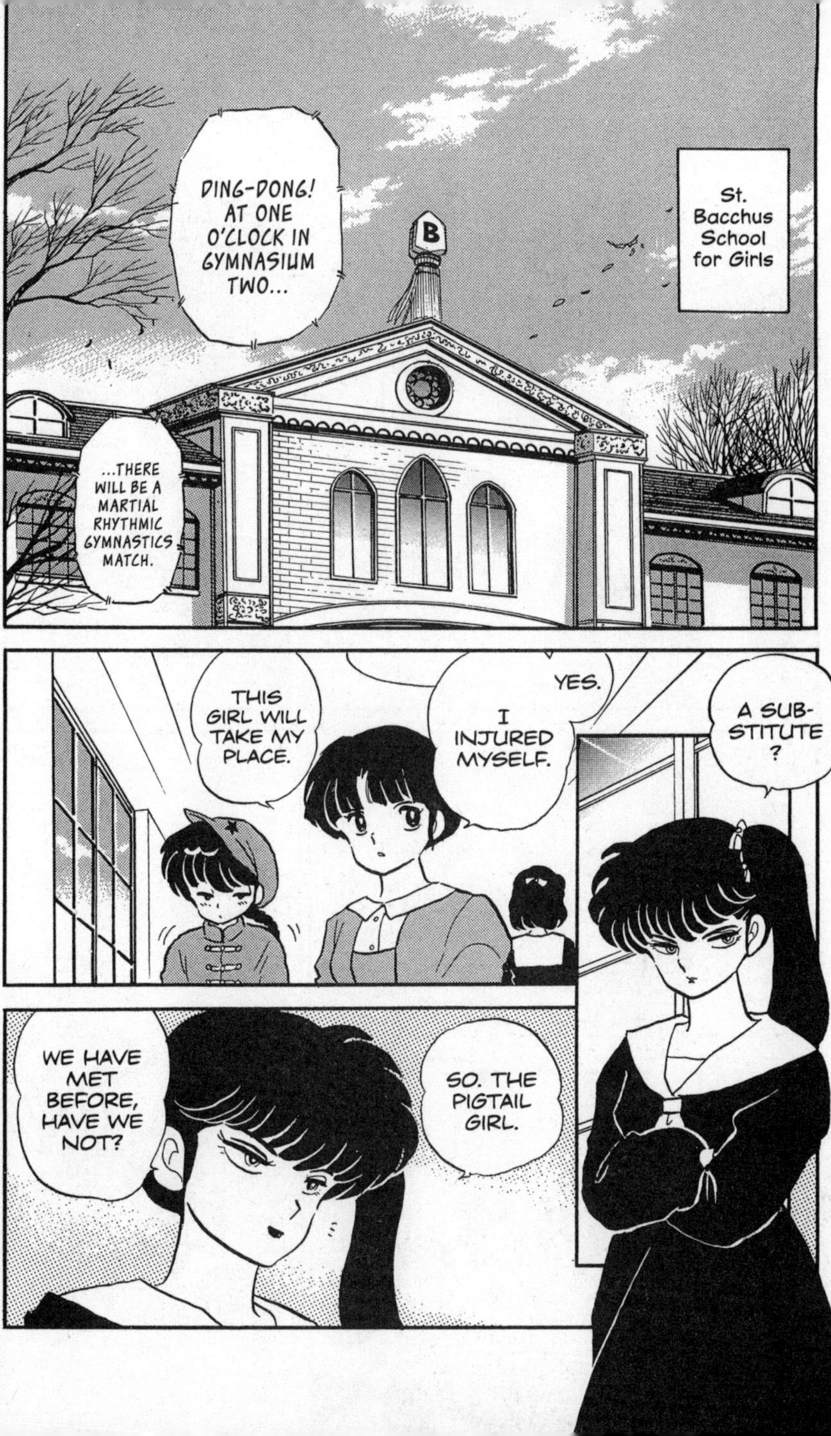
St. Bacchus School for Girls
DING-DONG! AT ONE O'CLOCK IN GYMNASIUM TWO...
...THERE WILL BE A MARTIAL RHYTHMIC GYMNASTICS MATCH.
A SUB-STITUTE?
YES.
I INJURED MYSELF.
THIS GIRL WILL TAKE MY PLACE.
SO. THE PIGTAIL GIRL.
WE HAVE MET BEFORE, HAVE WE NOT?

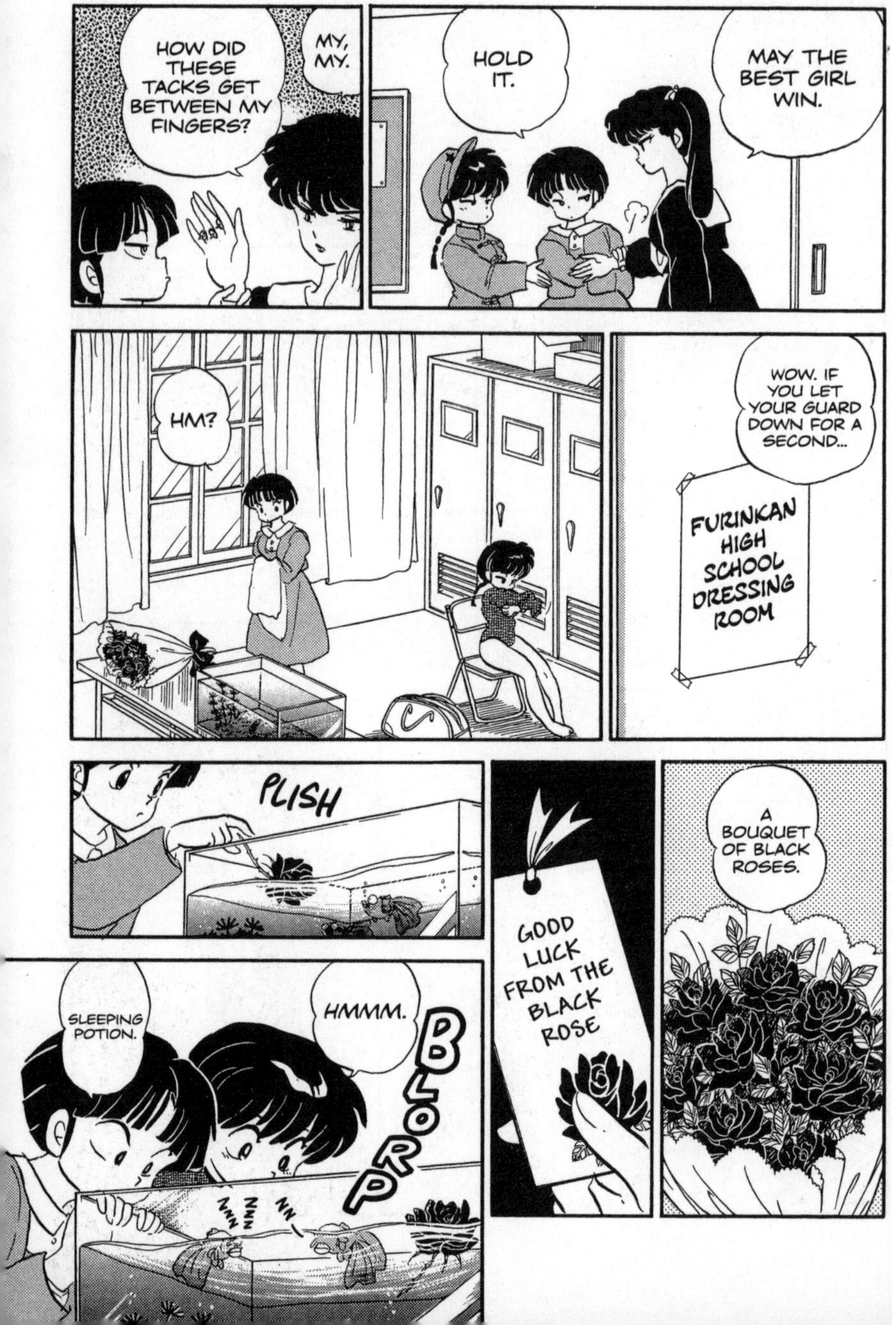
MAY THE BEST GIRL WIN.
HOLD IT.
MY, MY.
HOW DID THESE TACKS GET BETWEEN MY FINGERS?
WOW. IF YOU LET YOUR GUARD DOWN FOR A SECOND...
FURINKAN HIGH SCHOOL DRESSING ROOM
HM?
A BOUQUET OF BLACK ROSES.
GOOD LUCK FROM THE BLACK ROSE
PLISH
HMMM.
SLEEPING POTION.
BLORP
ZZZ
ZZZ
ZZ

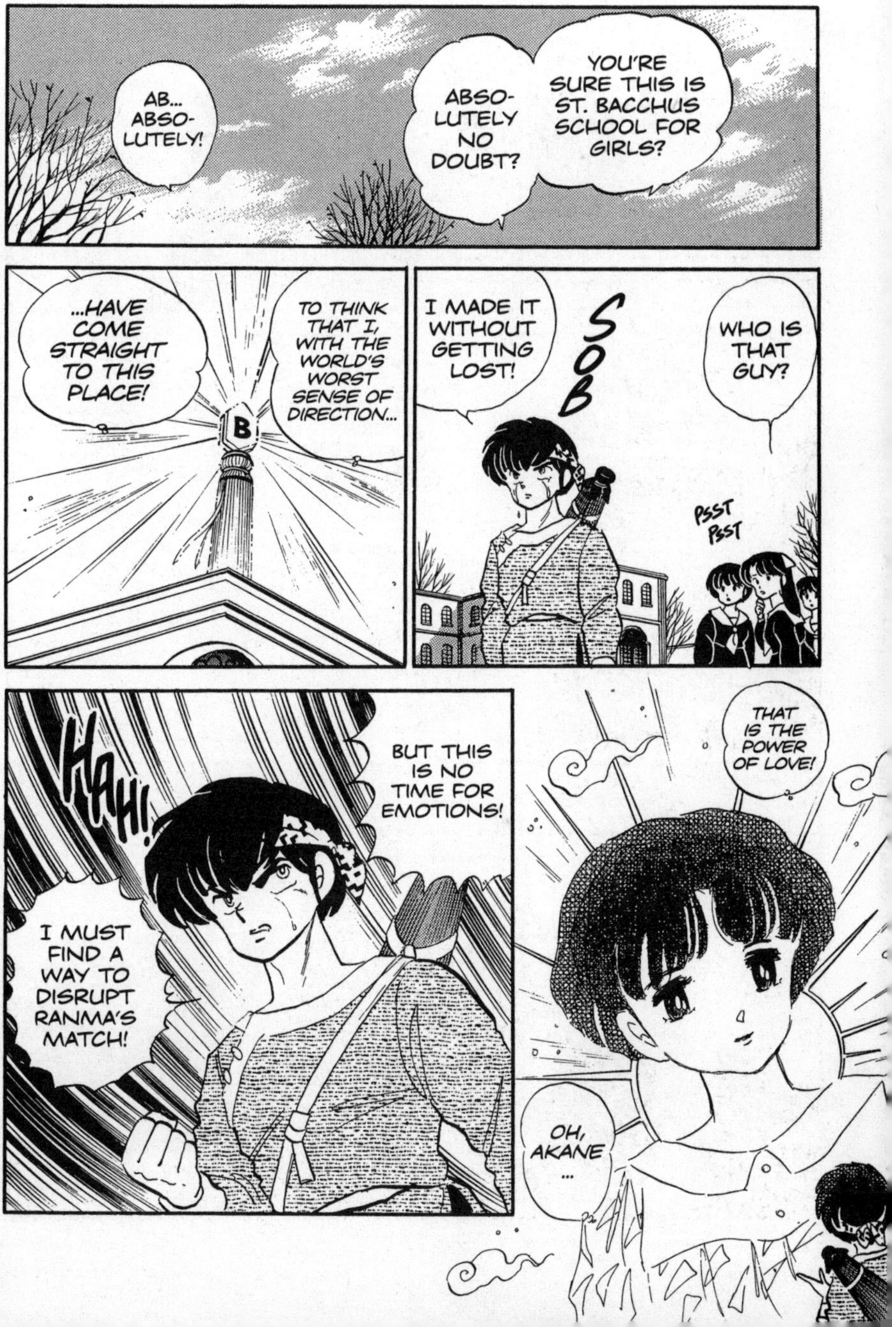
YOU'RE SURE THIS IS ST. BACCHUS SCHOOL FOR GIRLS?
ABSO-LUTELY NO DOUBT?
AB... ABSO-LUTELY!
WHO IS THAT GUY?
PSST PSST
SOB
I MADE IT WITHOUT GETTING LOST!
TO THINK THAT I, WITH THE WORLD'S WORST SENSE OF DIRECTION...
...HAVE COME STRAIGHT TO THIS PLACE!
B
THAT IS THE POWER OF LOVE!
OH, AKANE ...
BUT THIS IS NO TIME FOR EMOTIONS!
HAH!
I MUST FIND A WAY TO DISRUPT RANMA'S MATCH!

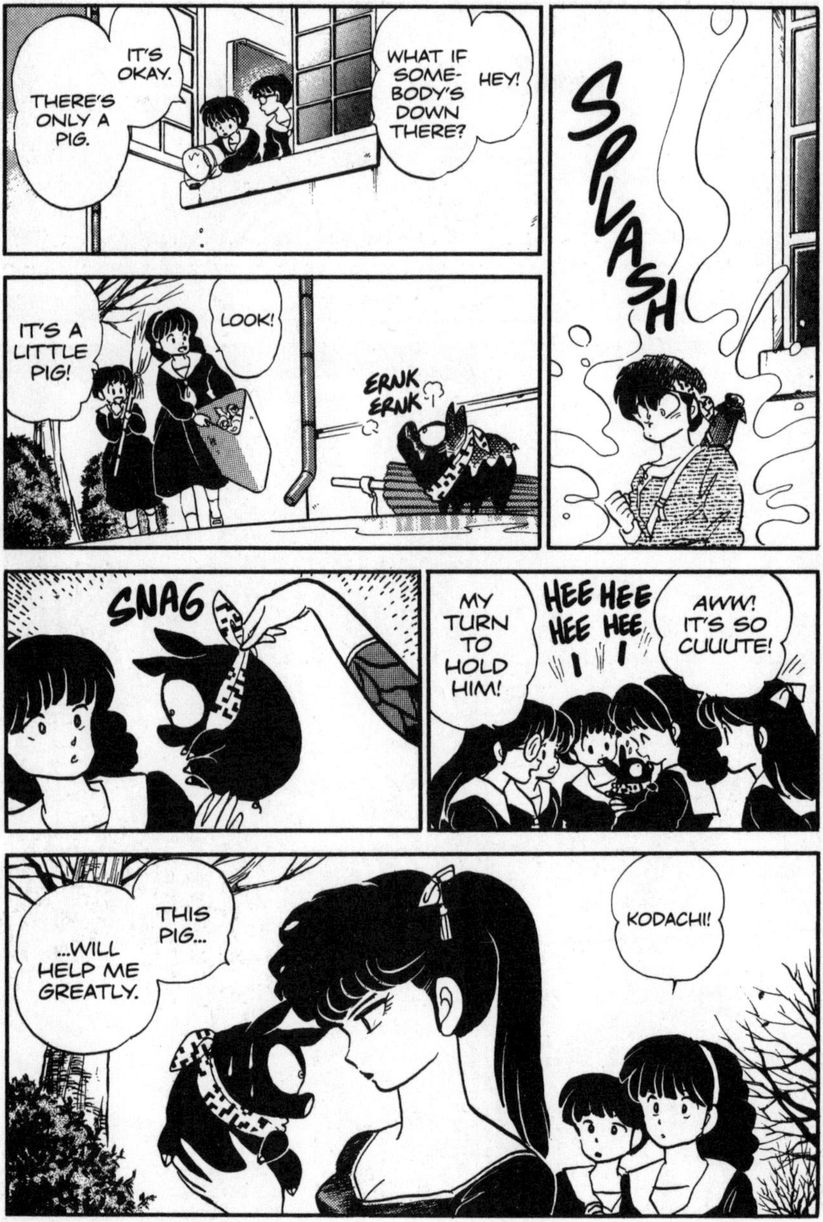
SPLASH
HEY!
WHAT IF SOME-BODY'S DOWN THERE?
IT'S OKAY.
THERE'S ONLY A PIG.
ERNK ERNK
LOOK!
IT'S A LITTLE PIG!
AWW! IT'S SO CUUUTE!
HEE HEE HEE HEE
MY TURN TO HOLD HIM!
SNAG
KODACHI!
THIS PIG...
...WILL HELP ME GREATLY.

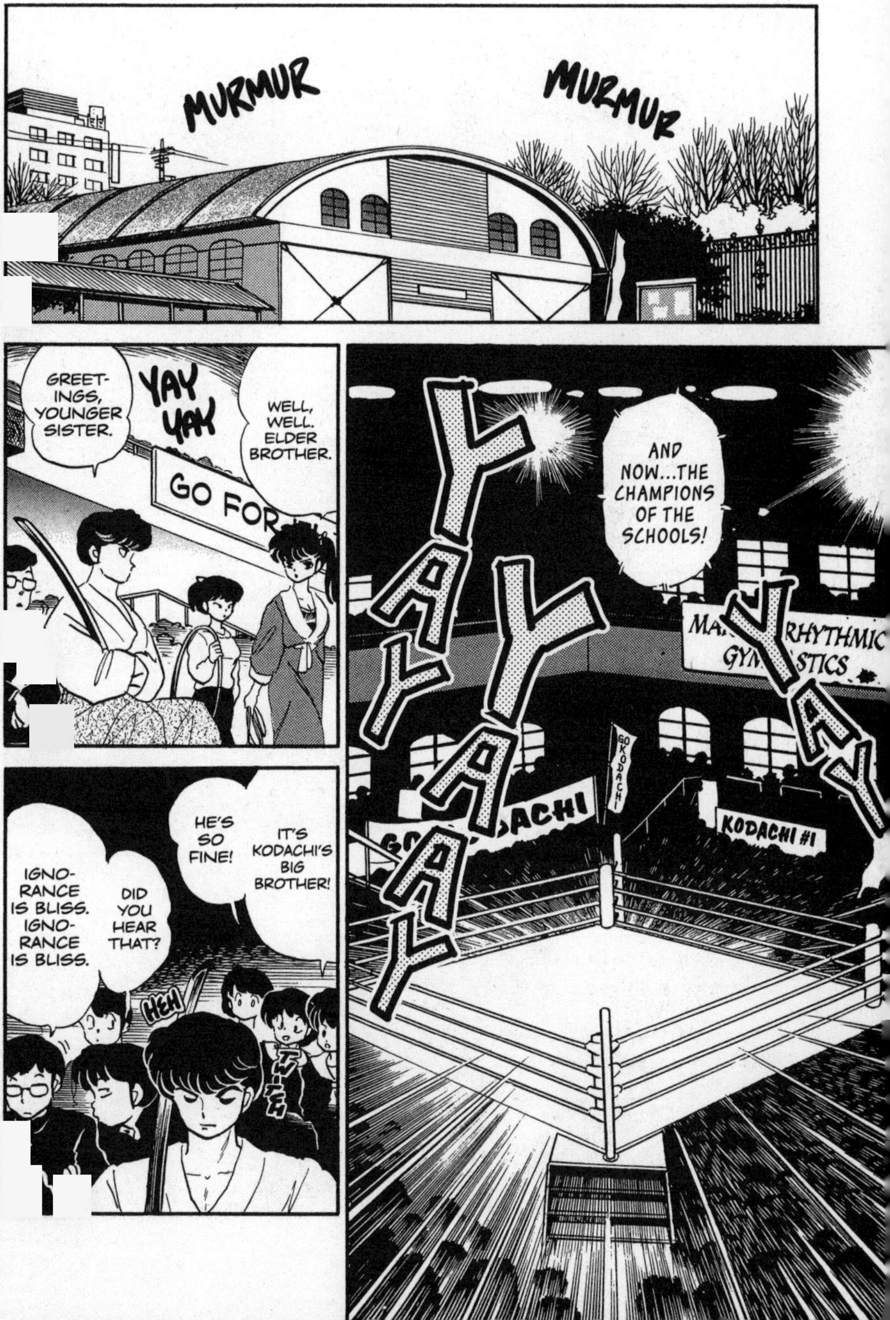
MURMUR
MURMUR
YAY YAY YAY YAY
AND NOW...THE CHAMPIONS OF THE SCHOOLS!
GO KODACHI
KODACHI #1
WELL, WELL. ELDER BROTHER.
YAY YAY
GREET-INGS, YOUNGER SISTER.
IT'S KODACHI'S BIG BROTHER!
HE'S SO FINE!
DID YOU HEAR THAT?
IGNO-RANCE IS BLISS. IGNO-RANCE IS BLISS.
HEH
TWITCH

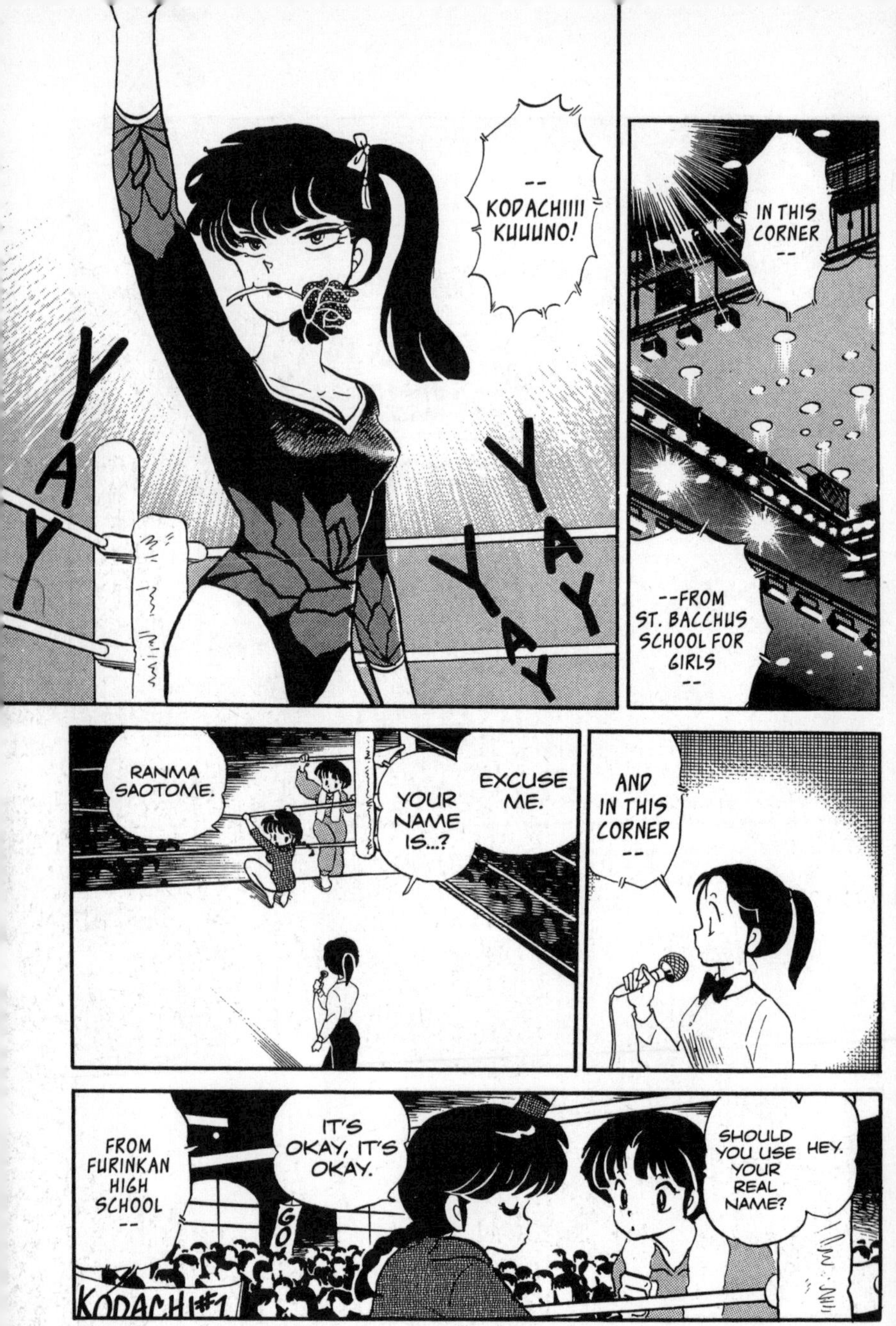
IN THIS CORNER --
--FROM ST. BACCHUS SCHOOL FOR GIRLS --
-- KODACHIIIII KUUUNO!
YAY
YAY
YAY
AND IN THIS CORNER --
EXCUSE ME.
YOUR NAME IS...?
RANMA SAOTOME.
HEY.
SHOULD YOU USE YOUR REAL NAME?
IT'S OKAY, IT'S OKAY.
FROM FURINKAN HIGH SCHOOL --
GO
KODACHI#1

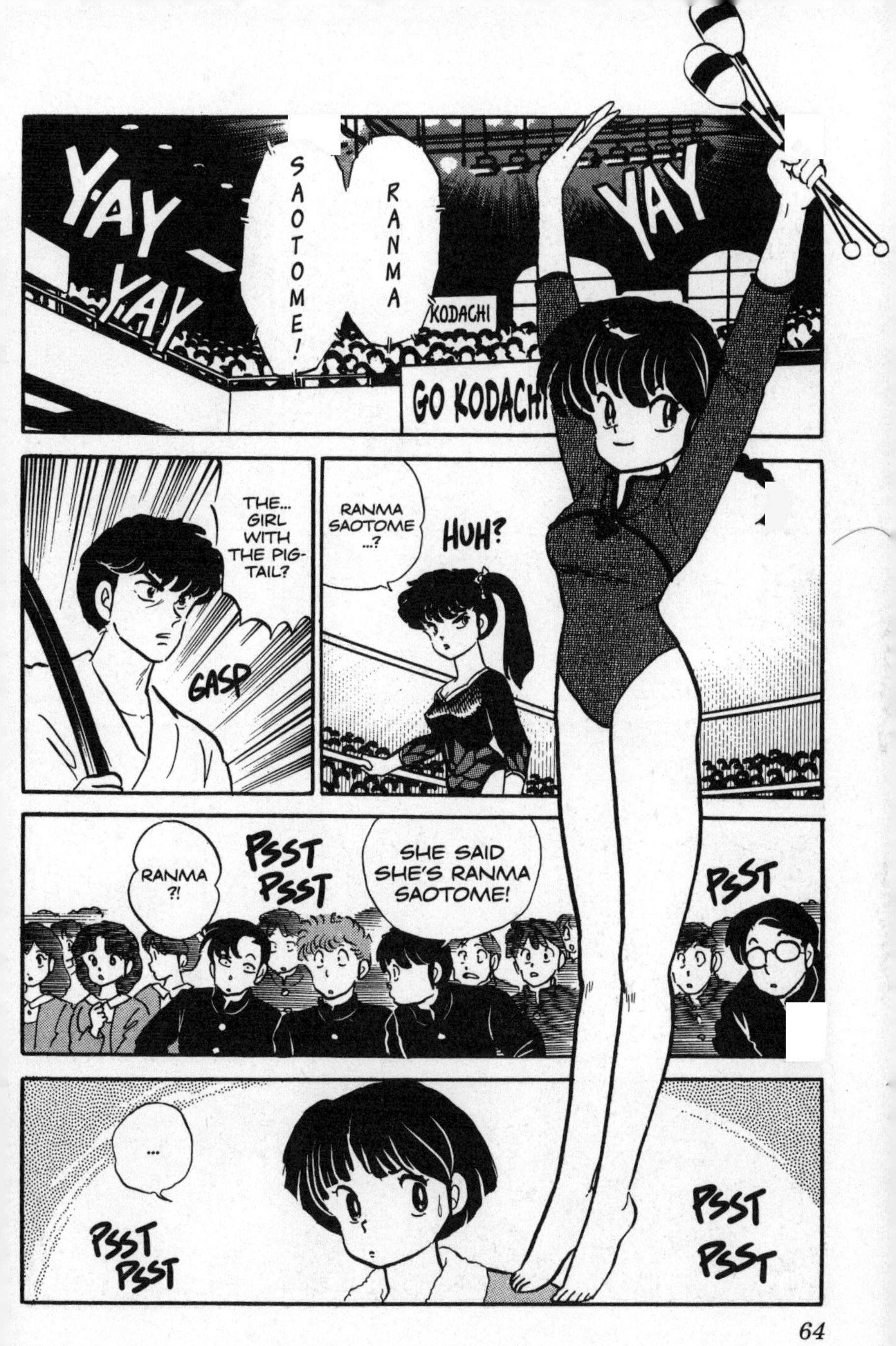
YAY
RANMA SAOTOME!
YAY
YAY
KODACHI
GO KODACHI
HUH?
RANMA SAOTOME ...?
THE... GIRL WITH THE PIG-TAIL?
GASP
PSST
SHE SAID SHE'S RANMA SAOTOME!
PSST PSST
RANMA ?!
PSST PSST
...
PSST PSST

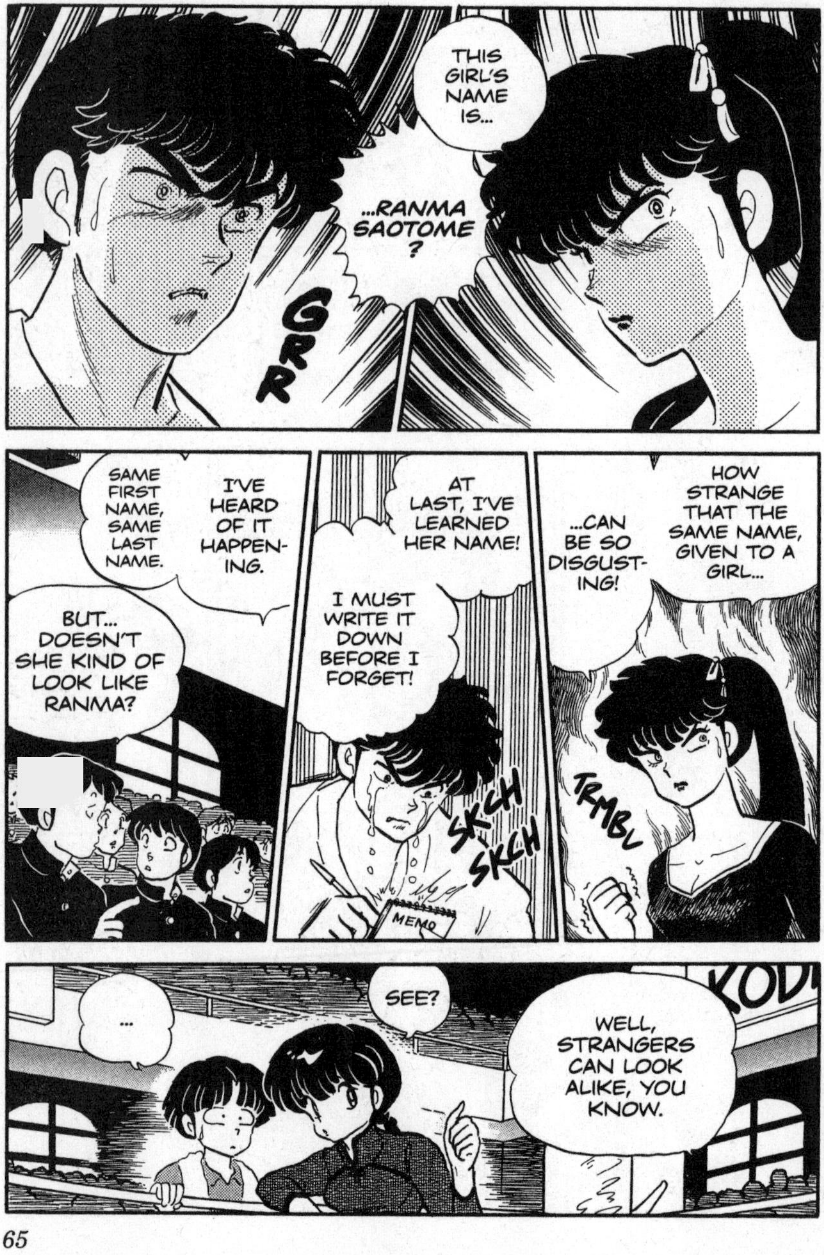
THIS GIRL'S NAME IS...
...RANMA SAOTOME ?
GRR
HOW STRANGE THAT THE SAME NAME, GIVEN TO A GIRL...
...CAN BE SO DISGUST-ING!
TRMBL
AT LAST, I'VE LEARNED HER NAME!
I MUST WRITE IT DOWN BEFORE I FORGET!
SKCH SKCH
MEMO
I'VE HEARD OF IT HAPPEN-ING.
SAME FIRST NAME, SAME LAST NAME.
BUT... DOESN'T SHE KIND OF LOOK LIKE RANMA?
WELL, STRANGERS CAN LOOK ALIKE, YOU KNOW.
SEE?
...

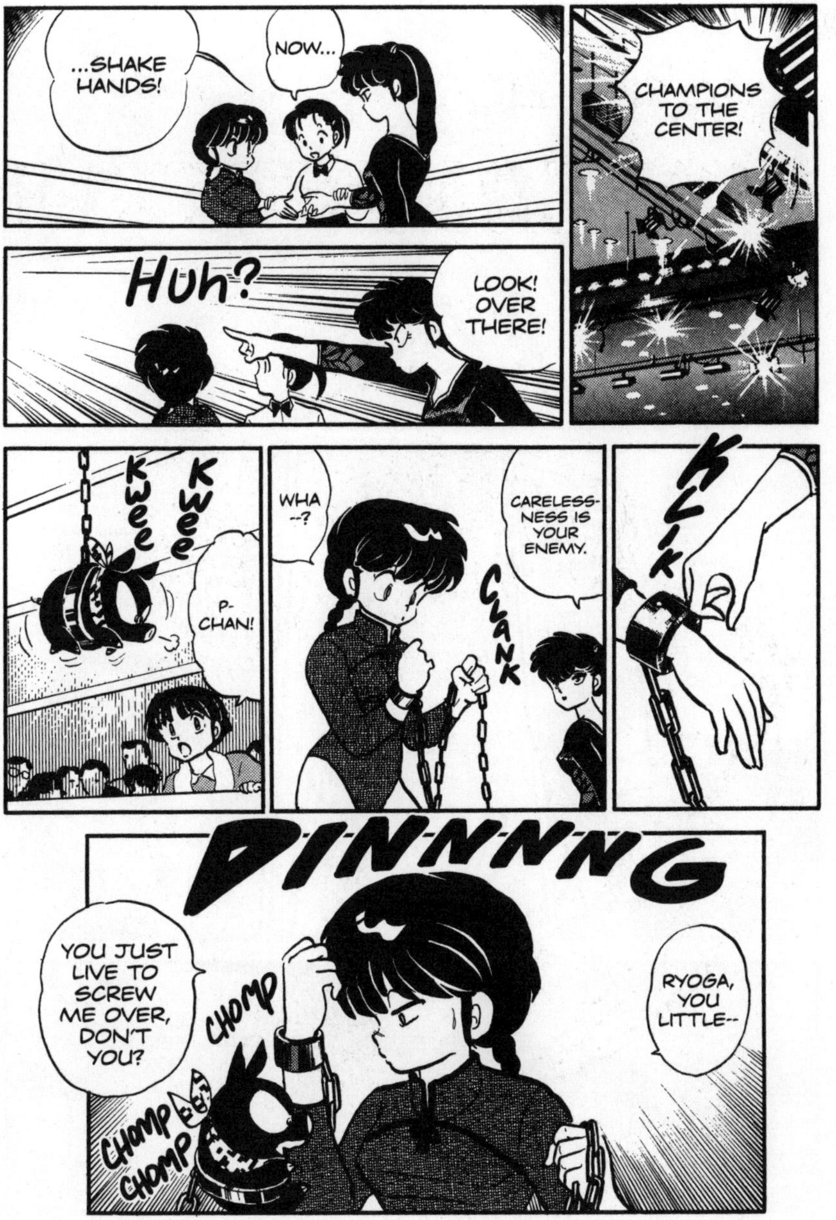
CHAMPIONS TO THE CENTER!
NOW...
...SHAKE HANDS!
LOOK! OVER THERE!
Huh?
KLIK
CARELESS-NESS IS YOUR ENEMY.
CLANK
WHA --?
KWEE KWEE
P-CHAN!
DINNNNG
RYOGA, YOU LITTLE--
YOU JUST LIVE TO SCREW ME OVER, DON'T YOU?
CHOMP
CHOMP CHOMP

PART 4
HOT COMPETITION

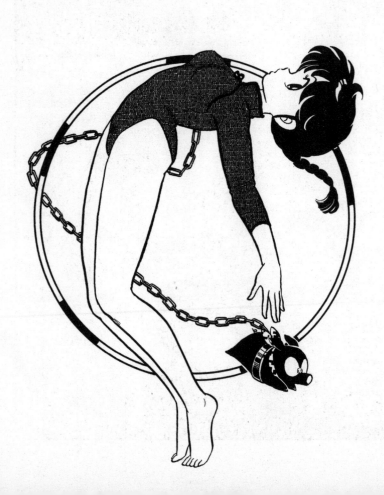

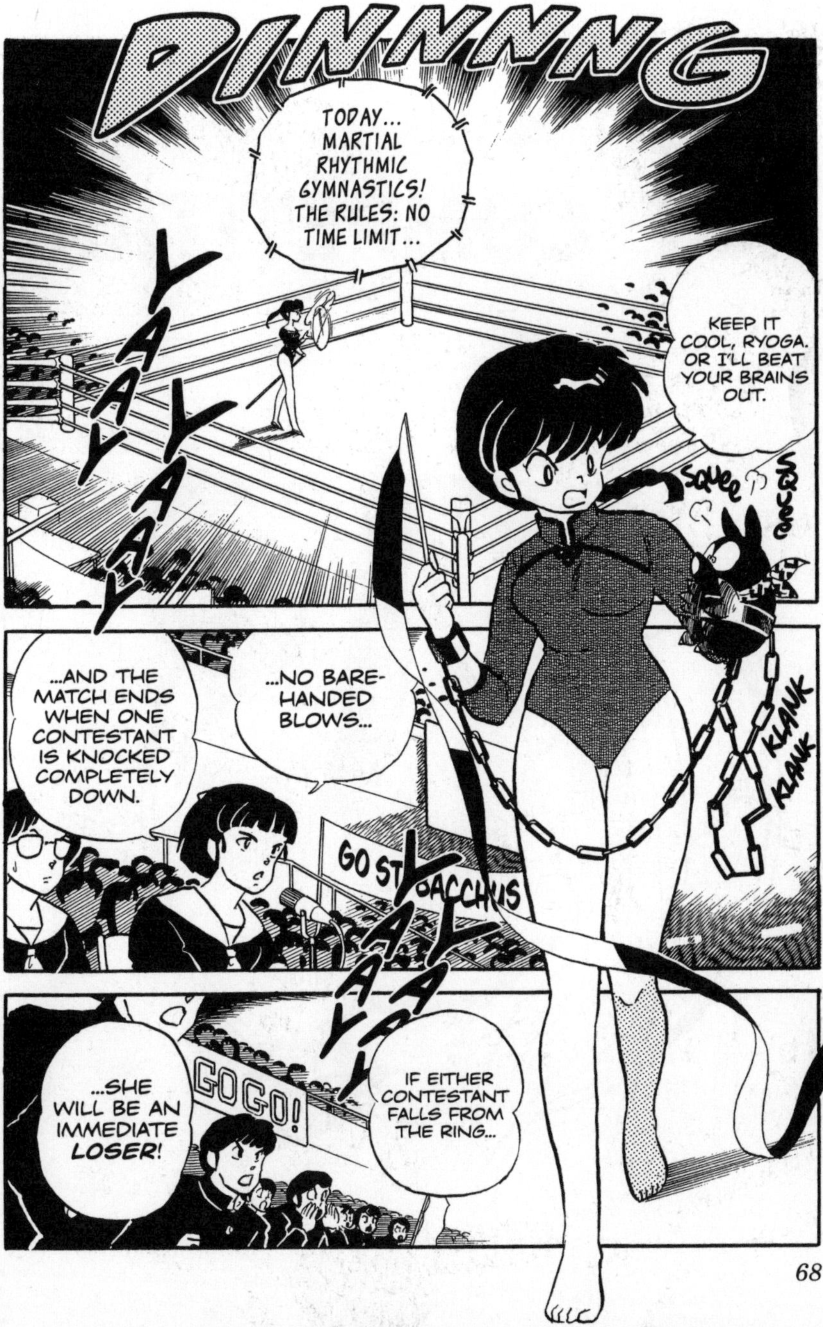
DINNNNG
TODAY... MARTIAL RHYTHMIC GYMNASTICS! THE RULES: NO TIME LIMIT...
YAAAY
KEEP IT COOL, RYOGA. OR I'LL BEAT YOUR BRAINS OUT.
SQUEE
SQUEE
YAAAY
...NO BARE-HANDED BLOWS...
...AND THE MATCH ENDS WHEN ONE CONTESTANT IS KNOCKED COMPLETELY DOWN.
KLANK
KLANK
YAAAY
IF EITHER CONTESTANT FALLS FROM THE RING...
...SHE WILL BE AN IMMEDIATE *LOSER*!
GOGO!

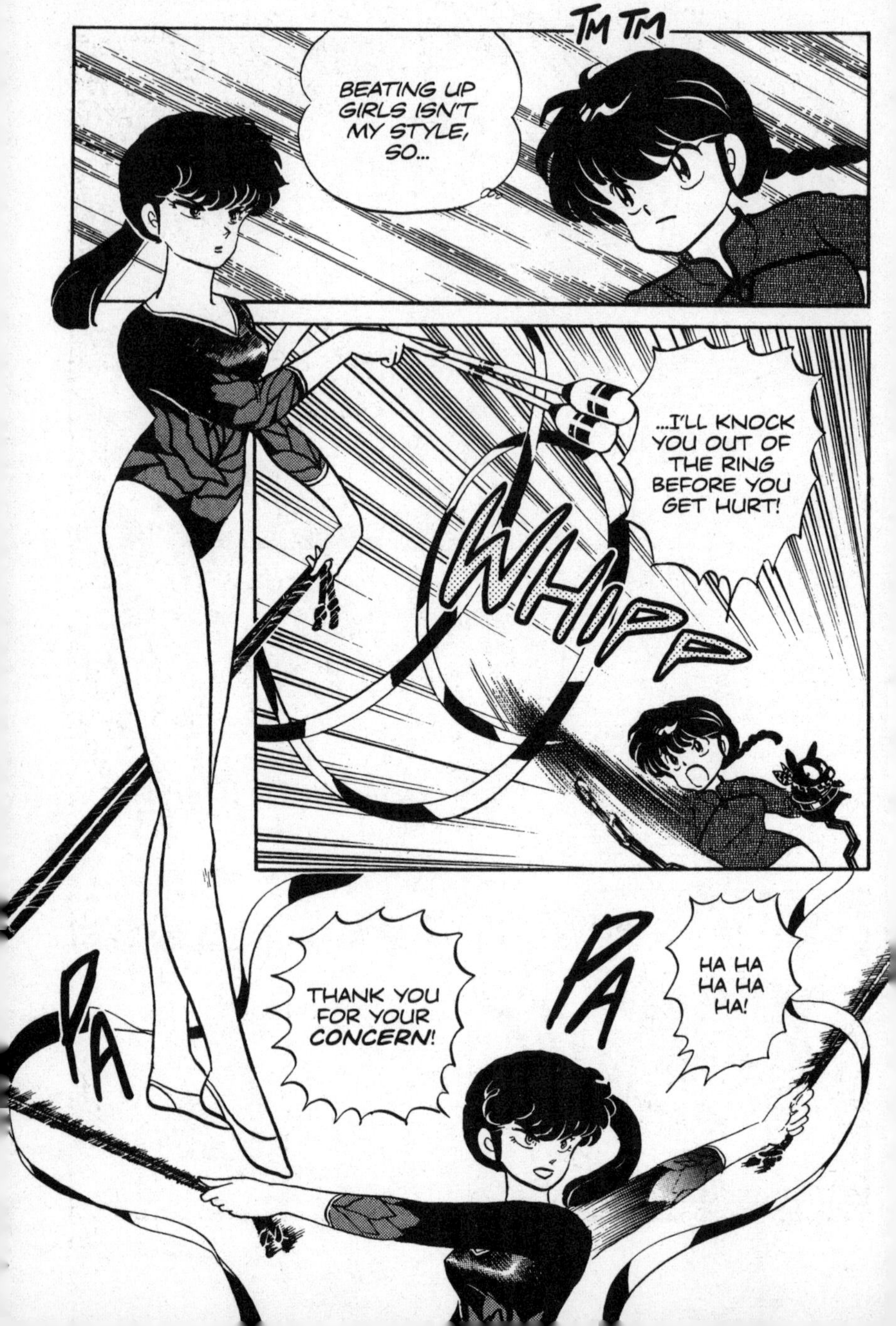
TM TM
BEATING UP GIRLS ISN'T MY STYLE, SO...
...I'LL KNOCK YOU OUT OF THE RING BEFORE YOU GET HURT!
WHIPP
PA
HA HA HA HA HA!
PA
THANK YOU FOR YOUR CONCERN!

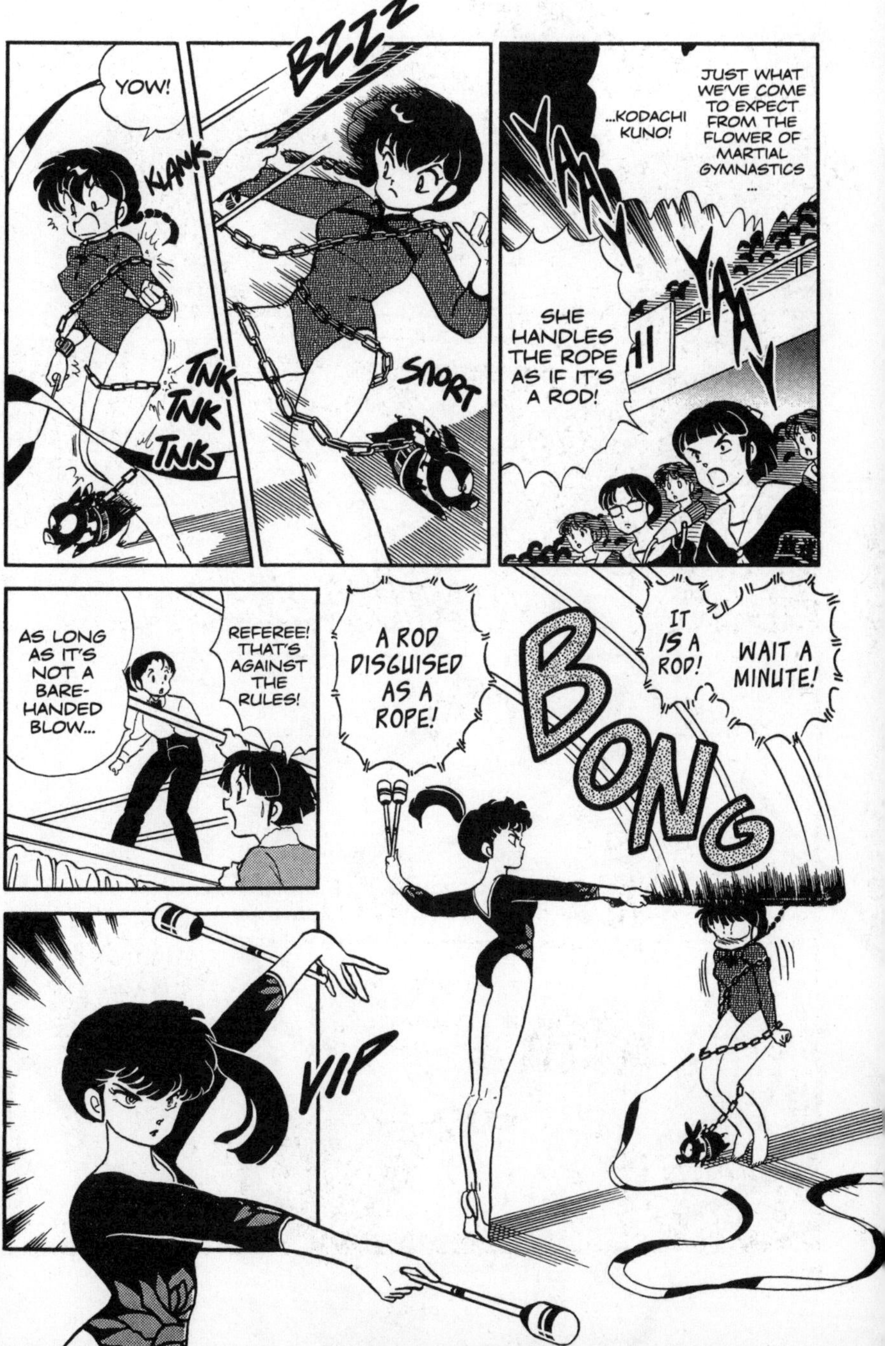
JUST WHAT WE'VE COME TO EXPECT FROM THE FLOWER OF MARTIAL GYMNASTICS ...
...KODACHI KUNO!
YAAAY
YAAAY
SHE HANDLES THE ROPE AS IF IT'S A ROD!
BZZZ
SNORT
YOW!
KLANK
TNK
TNK
TNK
WAIT A MINUTE!
IT IS A ROD!
A ROD DISGUISED AS A ROPE!
BONG
REFEREE! THAT'S AGAINST THE RULES!
AS LONG AS IT'S NOT A BARE-HANDED BLOW...
VIP

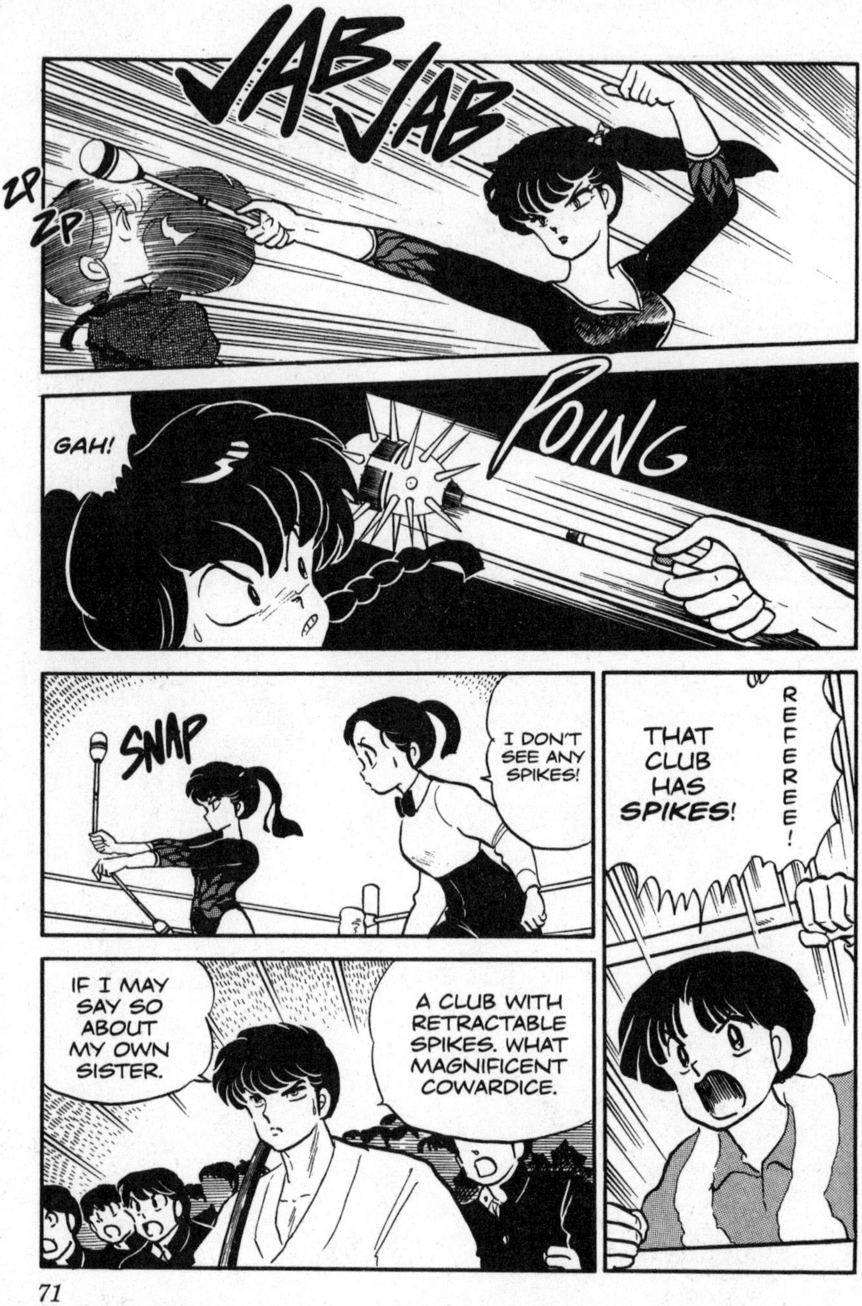
JAB JAB
ZP
ZP
POING
GAH!
REFEREE!
THAT CLUB HAS SPIKES!
I DON'T SEE ANY SPIKES!
SNAP
A CLUB WITH RETRACTABLE SPIKES. WHAT MAGNIFICENT COWARDICE.
IF I MAY SAY SO ABOUT MY OWN SISTER.

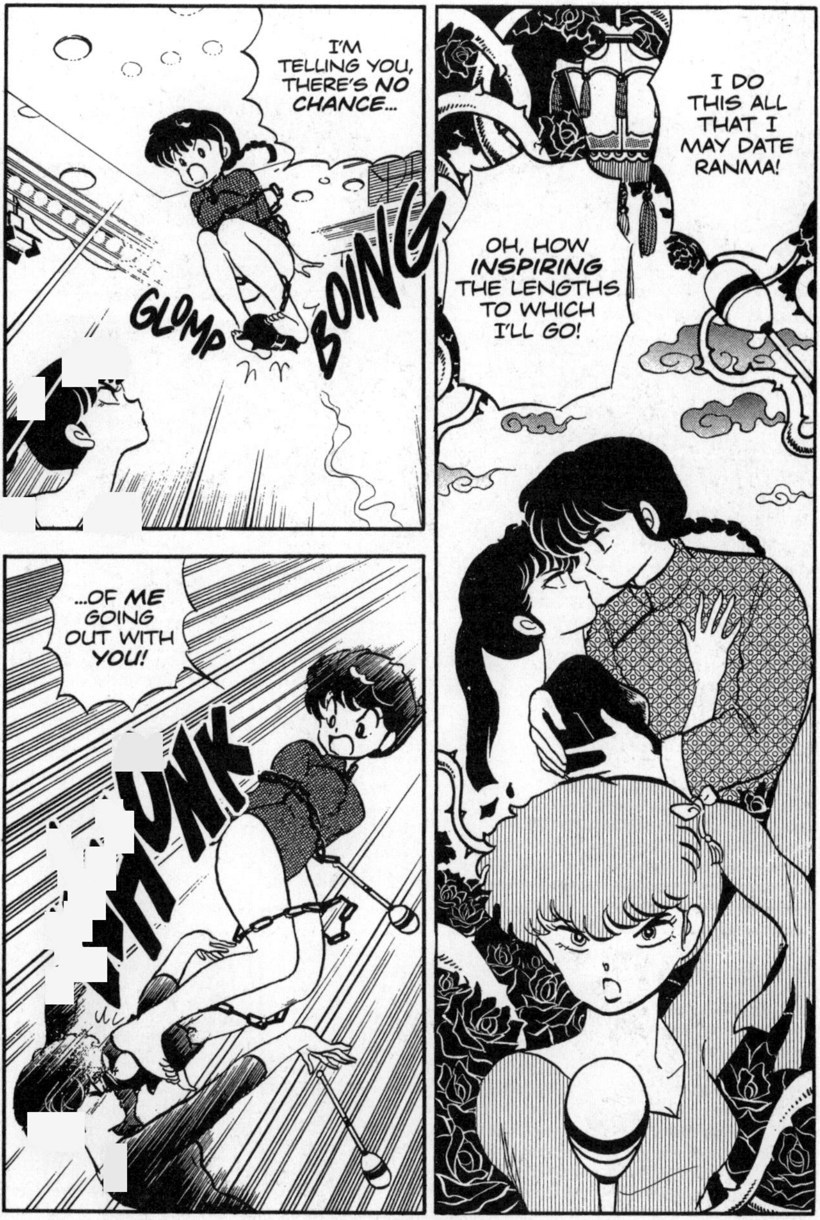
I DO THIS ALL THAT I MAY DATE RANMA!
OH, HOW INSPIRING THE LENGTHS TO WHICH I'LL GO!
I'M TELLING YOU, THERE'S NO CHANCE...
BOING
GLOMP
...OF ME GOING OUT WITH YOU!
THUNK

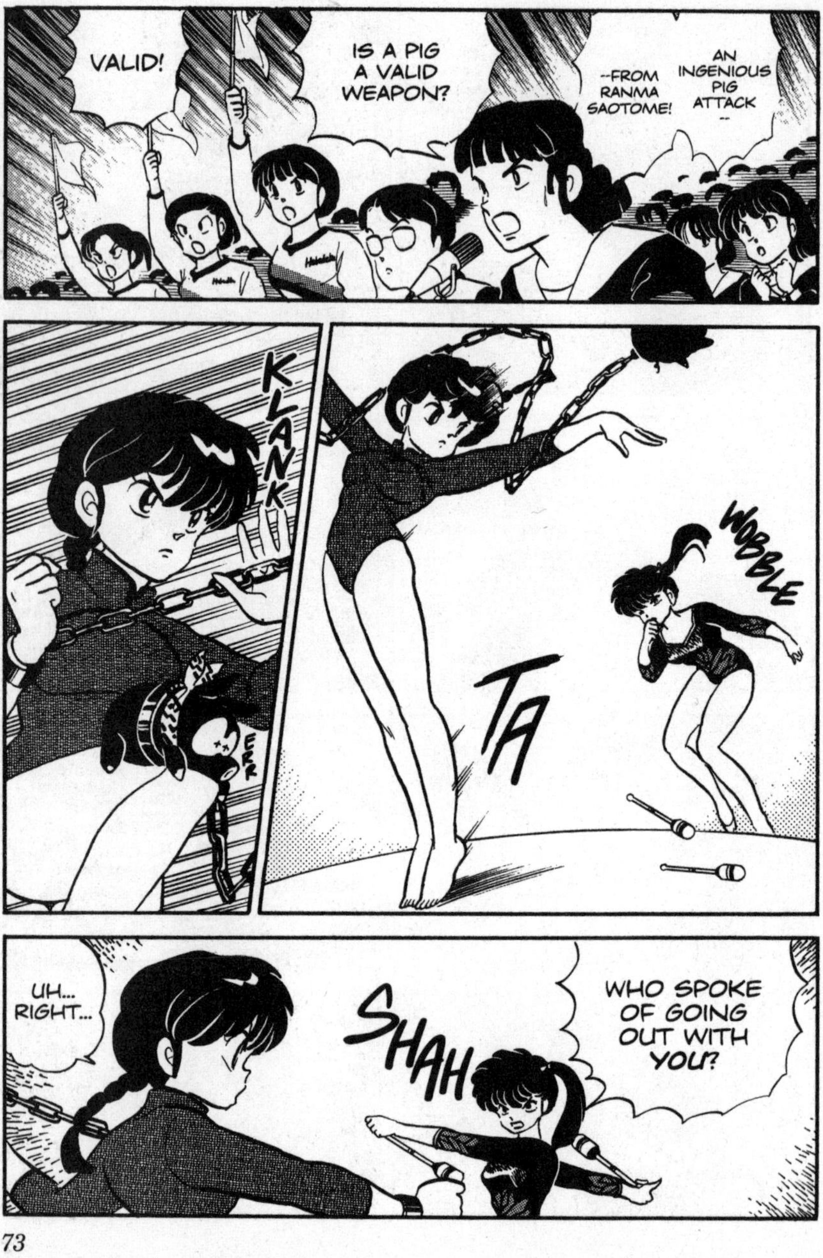
AN INGENIOUS PIG ATTACK --
--FROM RANMA SAOTOME!
IS A PIG A VALID WEAPON?
VALID!
WOBBLE
TA
KLANK
ERR
WHO SPOKE OF GOING OUT WITH YOU?
SHAH
UH... RIGHT...

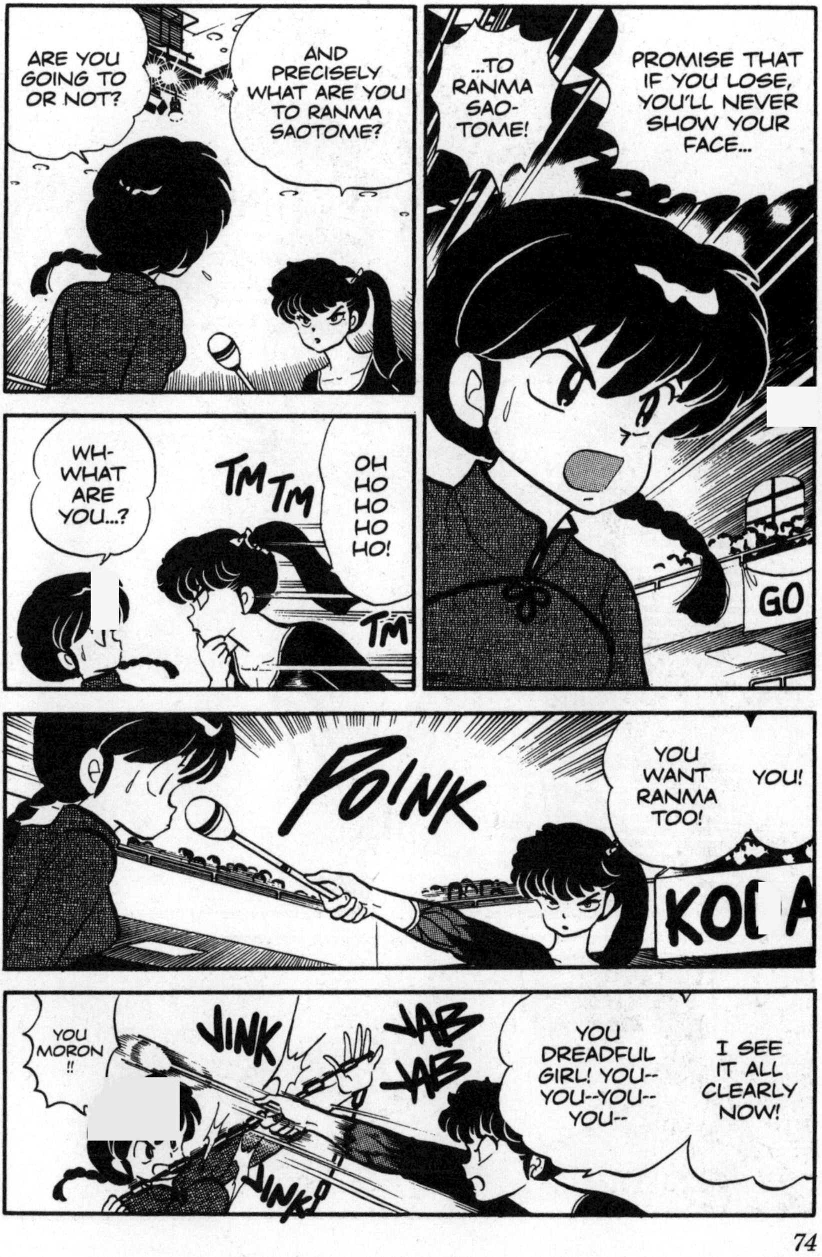
PROMISE THAT IF YOU LOSE, YOU'LL NEVER SHOW YOUR FACE...
...TO RANMA SAO-TOME!
GO
AND PRECISELY WHAT ARE YOU TO RANMA SAOTOME?
ARE YOU GOING TO OR NOT?
OH HO HO HO HO!
TM TM
WH-WHAT ARE YOU...?
TM
YOU!
YOU WANT RANMA TOO!
POINK
I SEE IT ALL CLEARLY NOW!
YOU DREADFUL GIRL! YOU--YOU--YOU--YOU--
JAB
JAB
JINK
JINK
YOU MORON !!

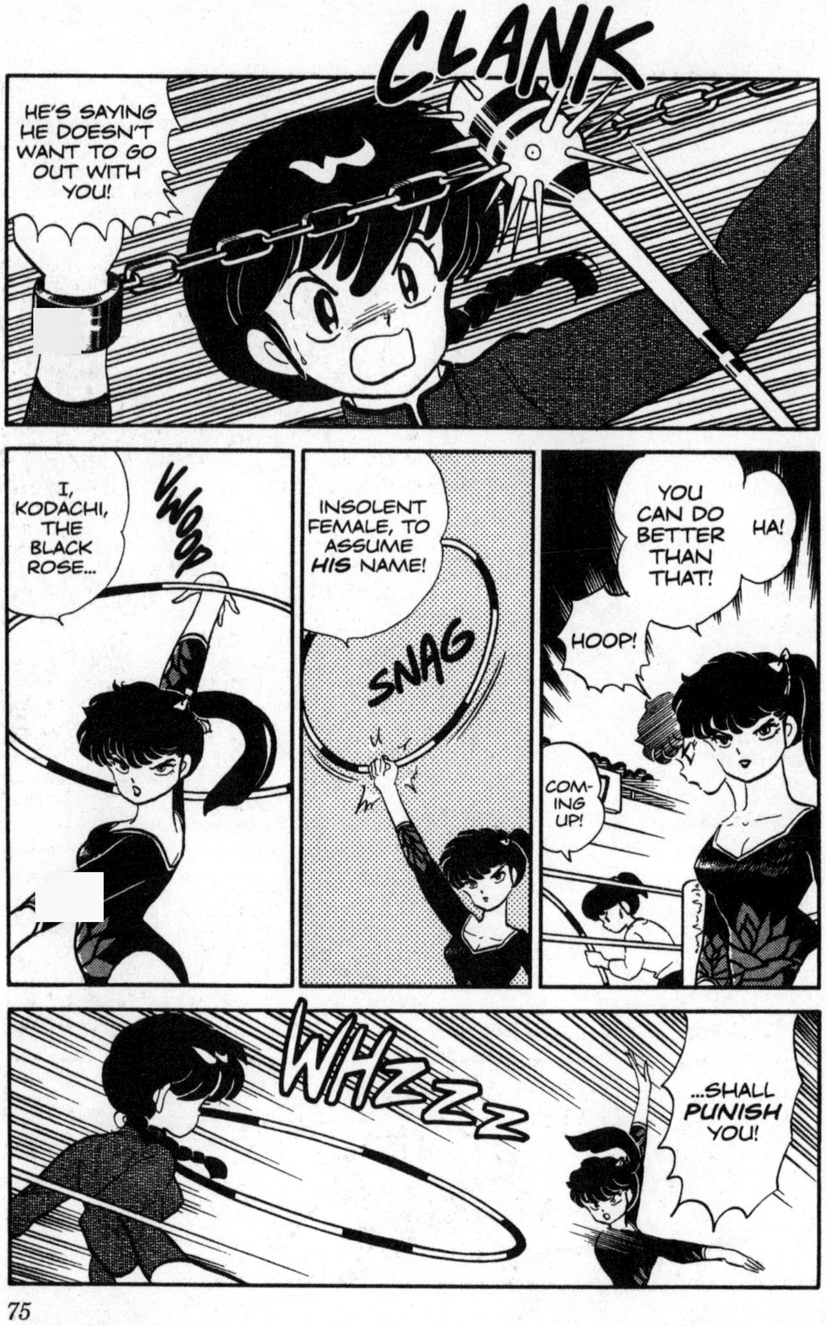
CLANK
HE'S SAYING HE DOESN'T WANT TO GO OUT WITH YOU!
HA!
YOU CAN DO BETTER THAN THAT!
HOOP!
COM-ING UP!
INSOLENT FEMALE, TO ASSUME HIS NAME!
SNAG
I, KODACHI, THE BLACK ROSE...
VWOOP
...SHALL PUNISH YOU!
WHZZZ

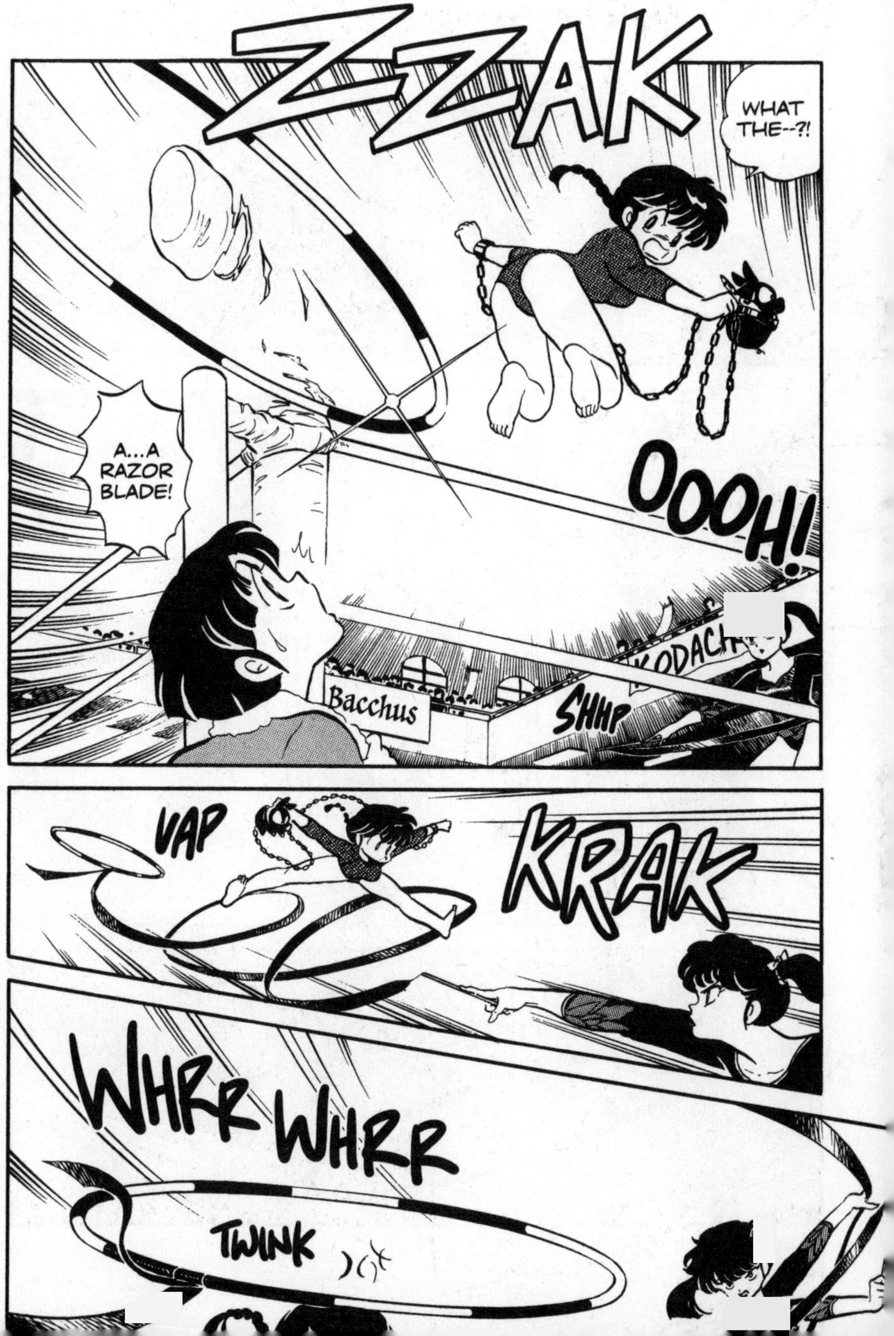
ZZAK
WHAT THE--?!
A...A RAZOR BLADE!
OOOH!
SHHP
Bacchus
KRAK
VAP
WHRR WHRR
TWINK

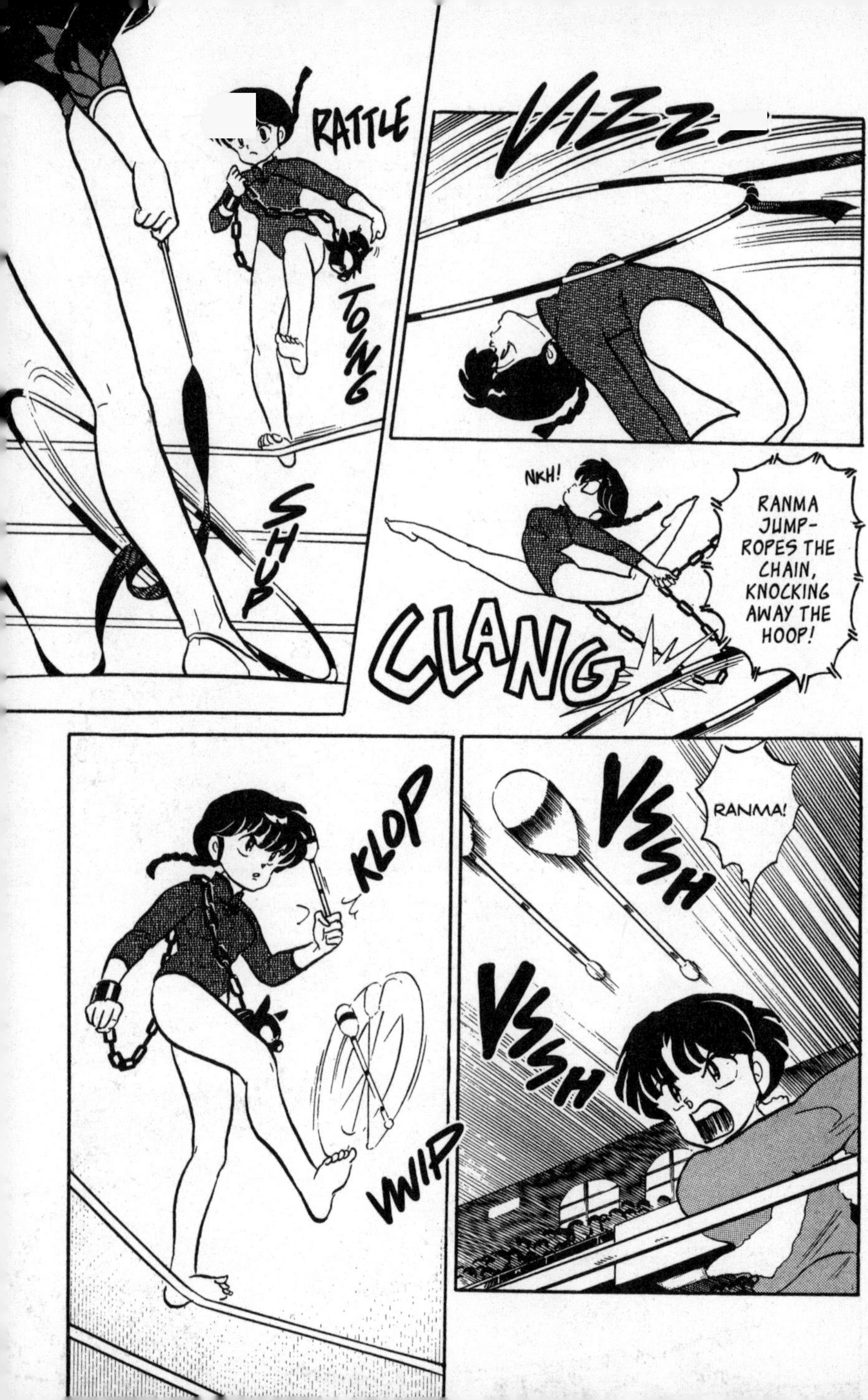
VIZZZ
NKH!
RANMA JUMP-ROPES THE CHAIN, KNOCKING AWAY THE HOOP!
CLANG
RATTLE
TOING
SHUP
VSSH
RANMA!
VSSH
KLOP
VWIP

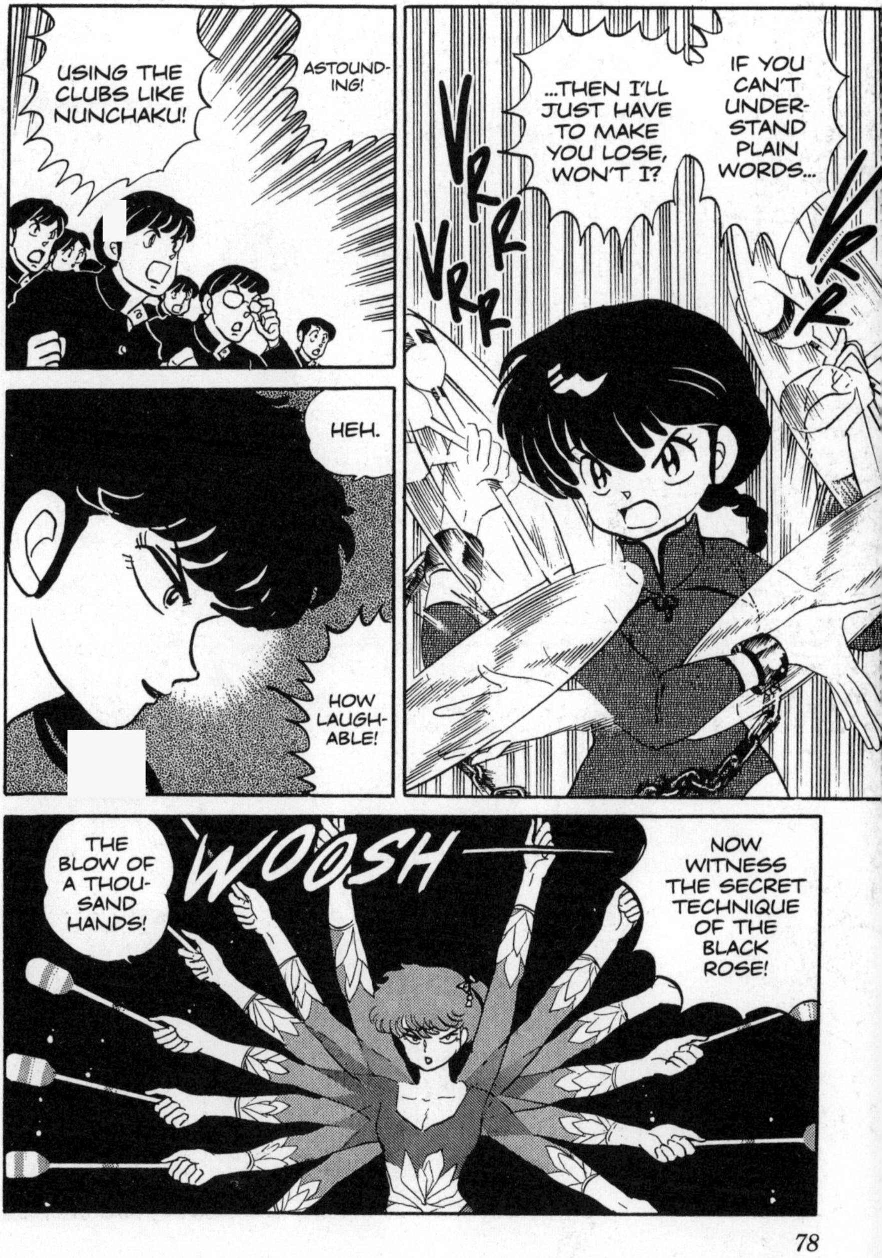
IF YOU CAN'T UNDERSTAND PLAIN WORDS...
...THEN I'LL JUST HAVE TO MAKE YOU LOSE, WON'T I?
VRR
VRRR
VRRR
ASTOUNDING!
USING THE CLUBS LIKE NUNCHAKU!
HEH.
HOW LAUGHABLE!
NOW WITNESS THE SECRET TECHNIQUE OF THE BLACK ROSE!
WOOSH
THE BLOW OF A THOUSAND HANDS!

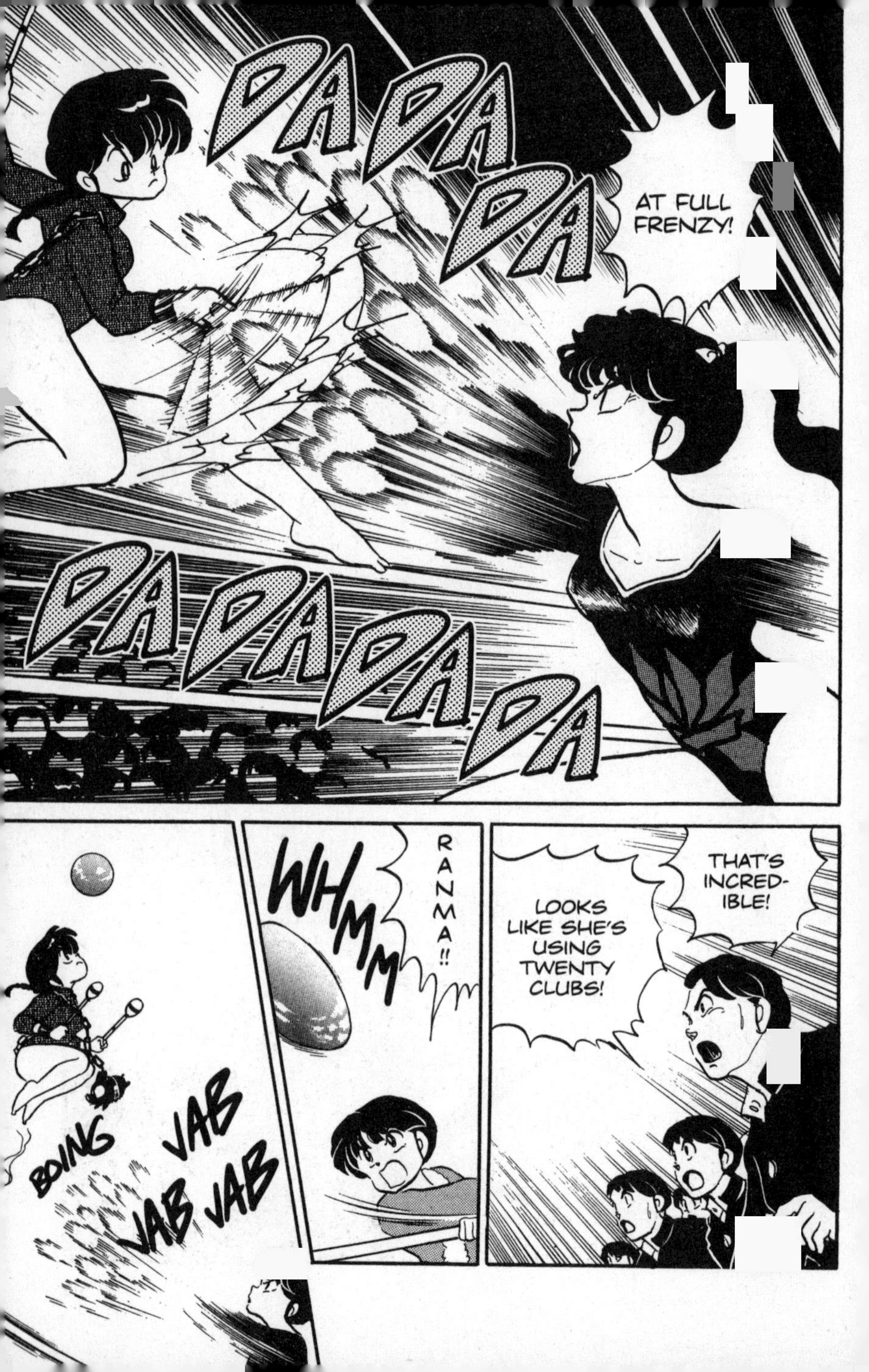
AT FULL FRENZY!
DADADADA
DADADADADADA
THAT'S INCRED-IBLE!
LOOKS LIKE SHE'S USING TWENTY CLUBS!
RANMA!!
WHMMM
BOING
JAB JAB JAB

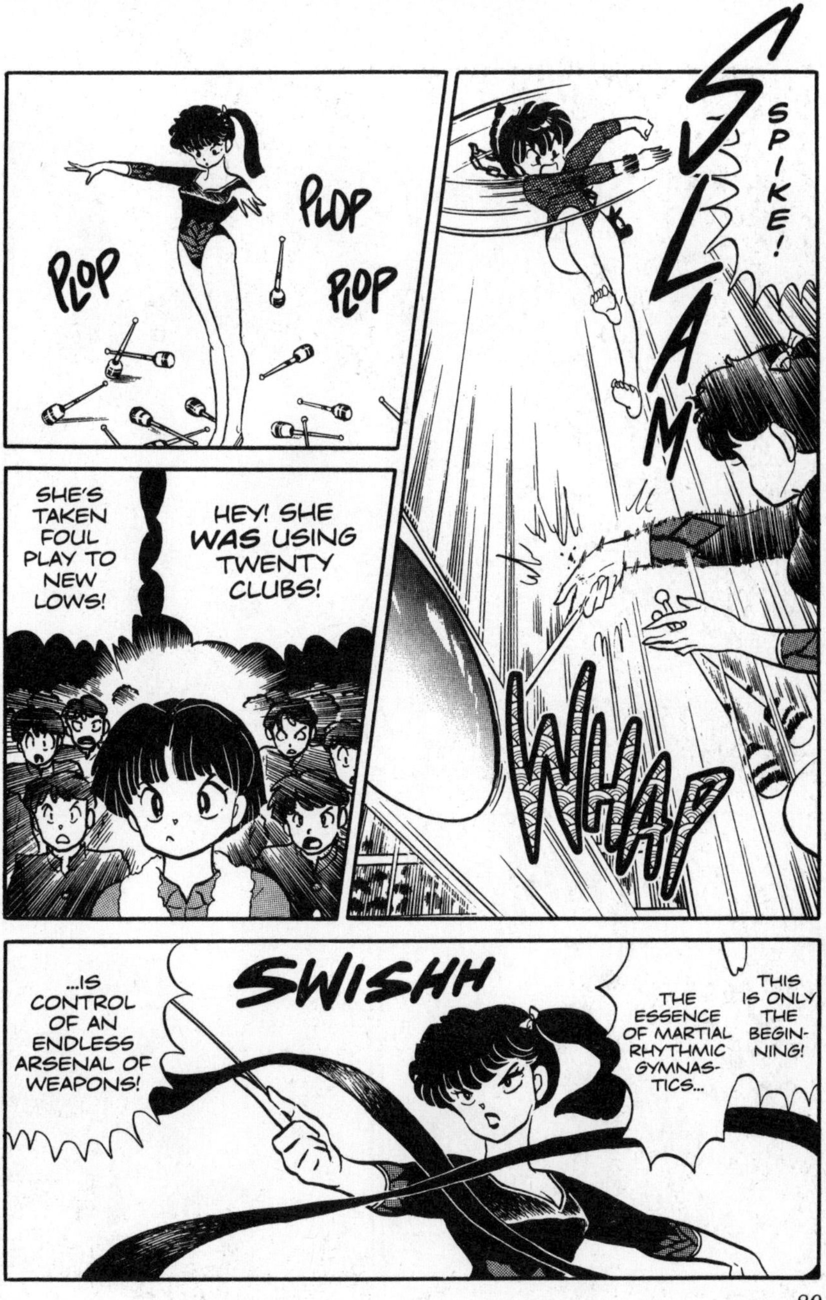
SPIKE!
SLAM
WHAP
PLOP
PLOP
PLOP
HEY! SHE WAS USING TWENTY CLUBS!
SHE'S TAKEN FOUL PLAY TO NEW LOWS!
THIS IS ONLY THE BEGIN-NING!
THE ESSENCE OF MARTIAL RHYTHMIC GYMNAS-TICS...
SWISHH
...IS CONTROL OF AN ENDLESS ARSENAL OF WEAPONS!

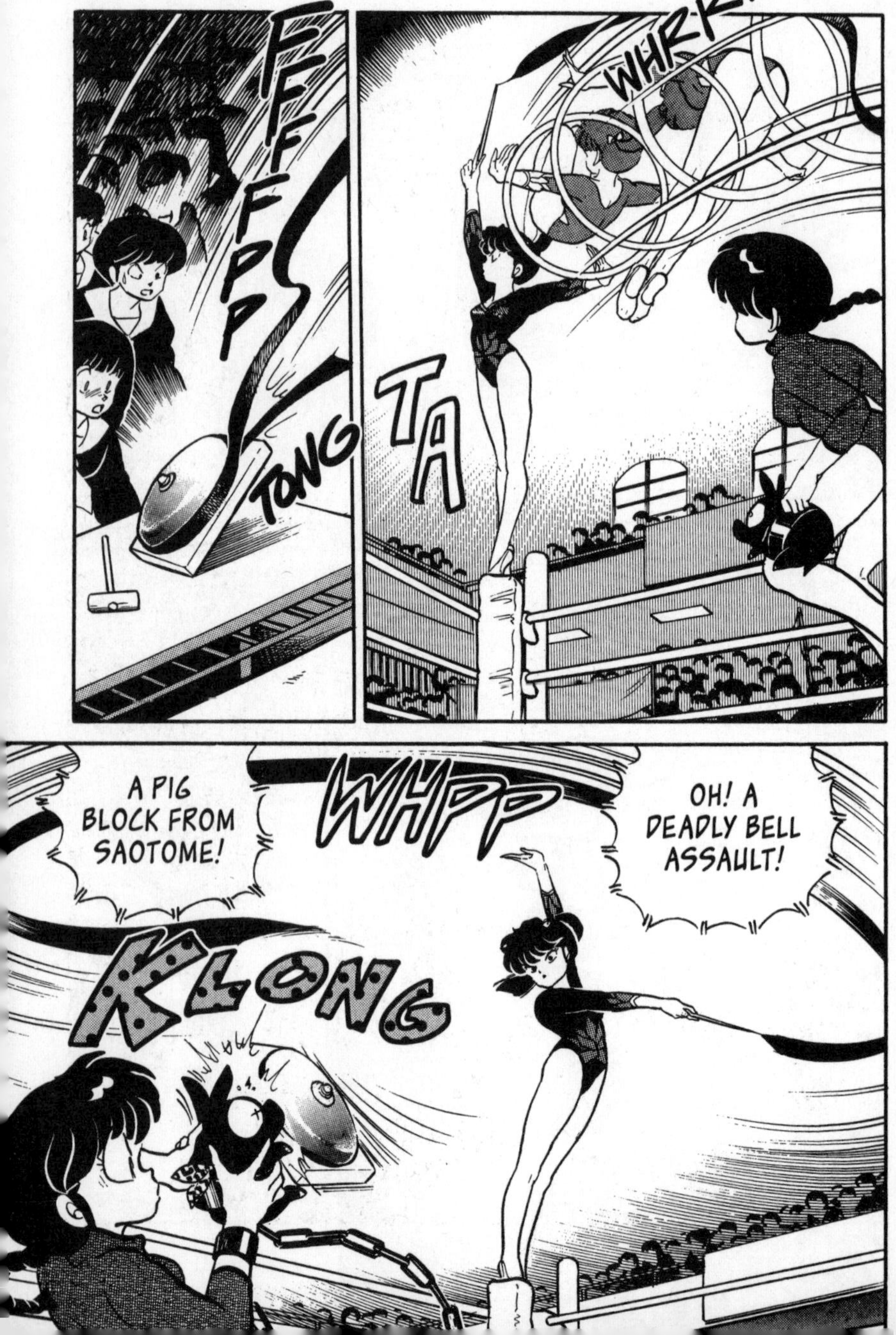
WHRRR
TA
FFFFPP
TONG
OH! A DEADLY BELL ASSAULT!
WHPP
A PIG BLOCK FROM SAOTOME!
KLONG

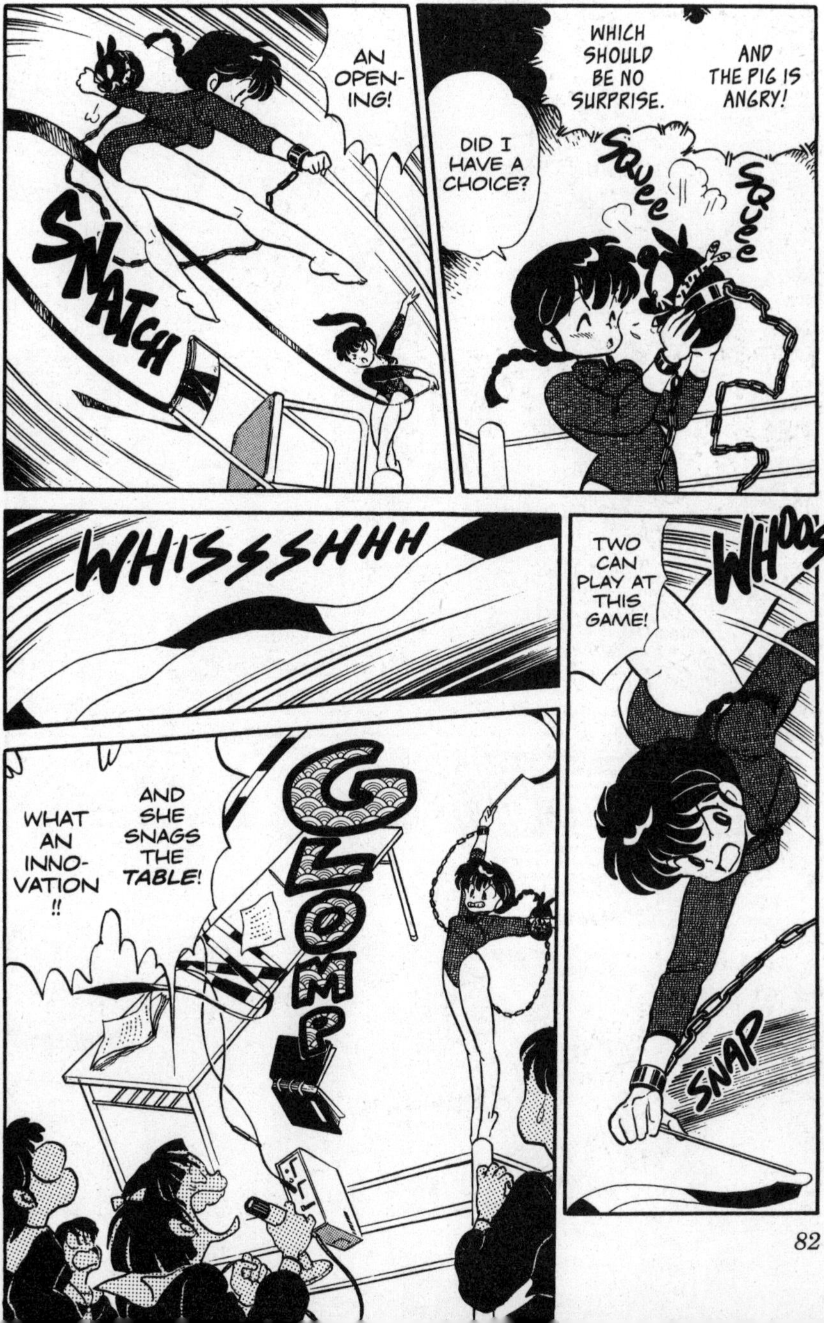
AND THE PIG IS ANGRY!
WHICH SHOULD BE NO SURPRISE.
DID I HAVE A CHOICE?
SQUEE
SQUEE
AN OPEN-ING!
SNATCH
WHOOSH
TWO CAN PLAY AT THIS GAME!
SNAP
WHISSSHHH
AND SHE SNAGS THE TABLE!
WHAT AN INNO-VATION!!
GLOMP

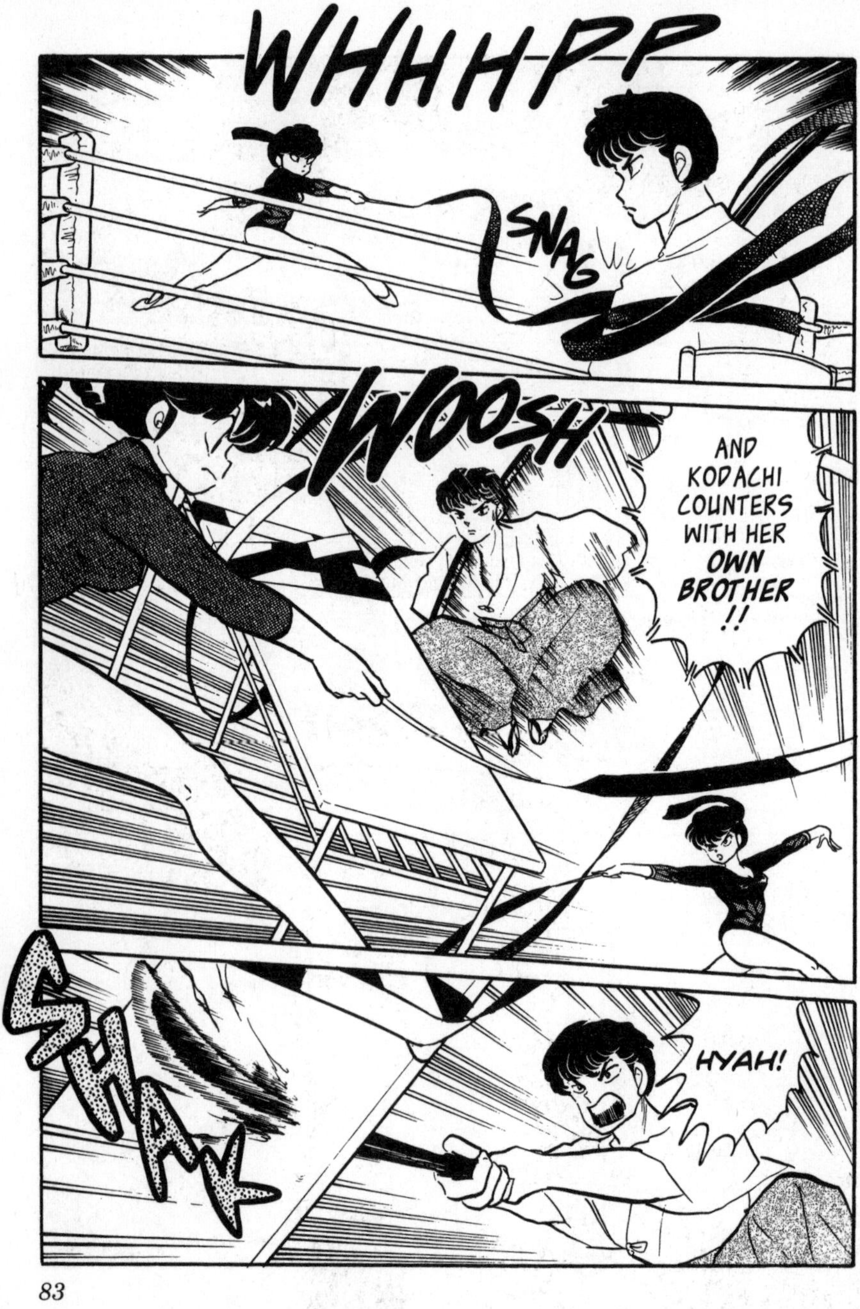
WHHHPP
SNAG
WOOSH
AND KODACHI COUNTERS WITH HER OWN BROTHER!!
HYAH!
SHAK

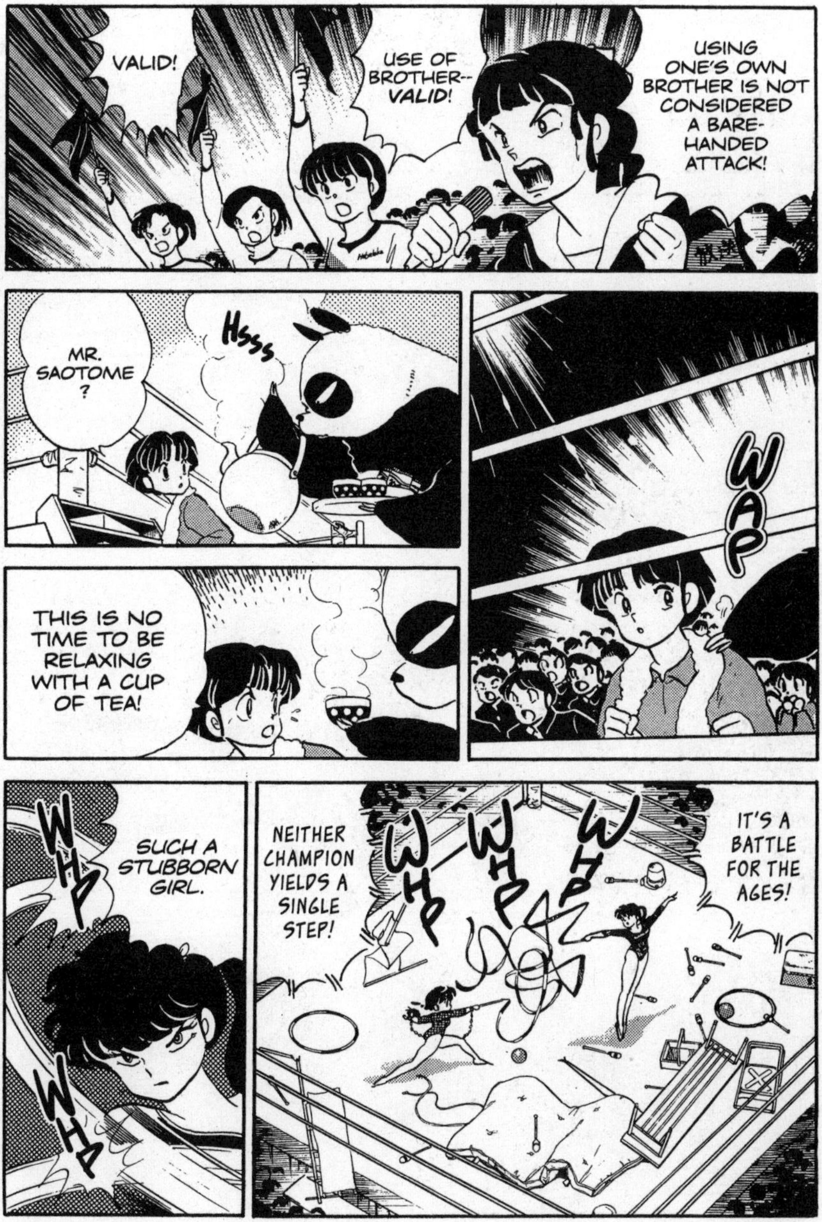
USING ONE'S OWN BROTHER IS NOT CONSIDERED A BARE-HANDED ATTACK!
USE OF BROTHER-- VALID!
VALID!
WAP
Hsss
MR. SAOTOME ?
THIS IS NO TIME TO BE RELAXING WITH A CUP OF TEA!
IT'S A BATTLE FOR THE AGES!
WHP
WHP
WHP
NEITHER CHAMPION YIELDS A SINGLE STEP!
SUCH A STUBBORN GIRL.
WHAP
WHAP

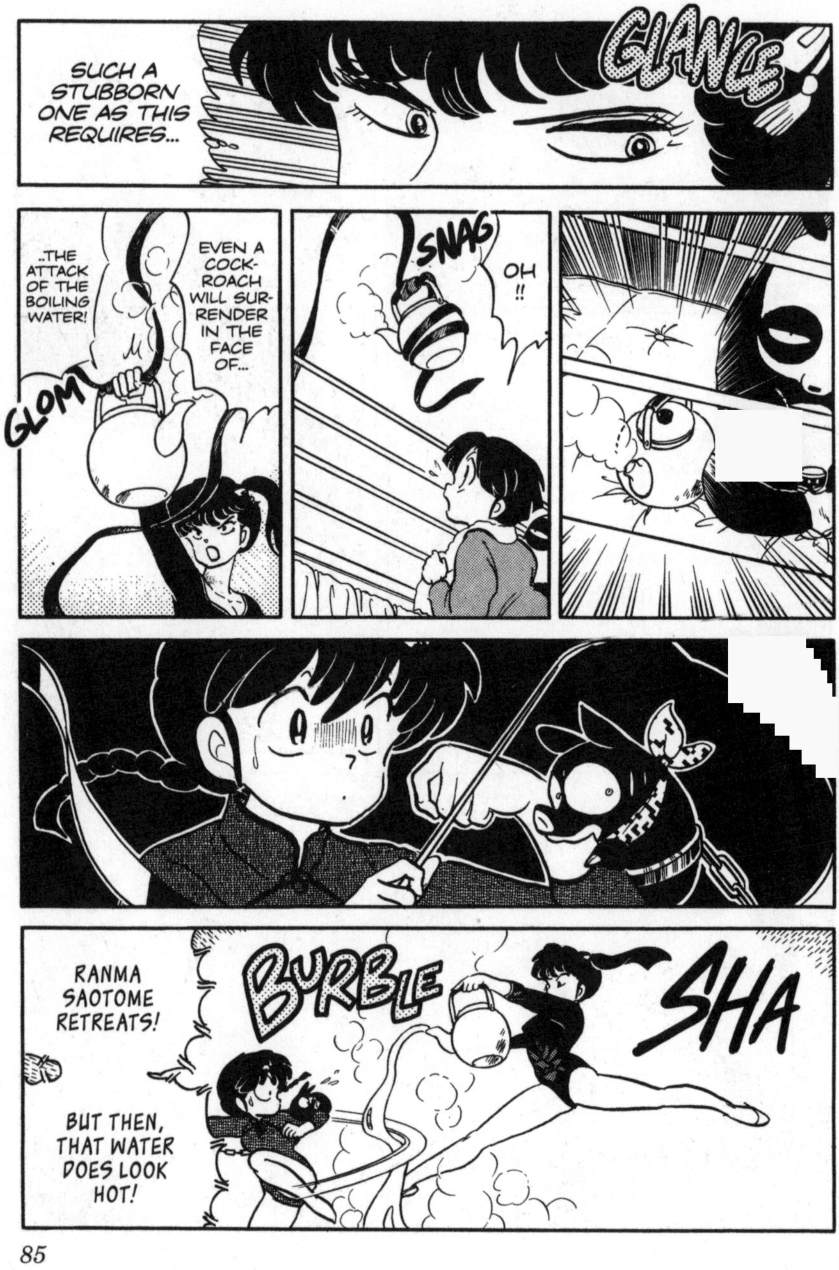
GLANCE
SUCH A STUBBORN ONE AS THIS REQUIRES...
SNAG
OH !!
EVEN A COCK-ROACH WILL SUR-RENDER IN THE FACE OF...
..THE ATTACK OF THE BOILING WATER!
GLOM
SHA
BURBLE
RANMA SAOTOME RETREATS!
BUT THEN, THAT WATER DOES LOOK HOT!

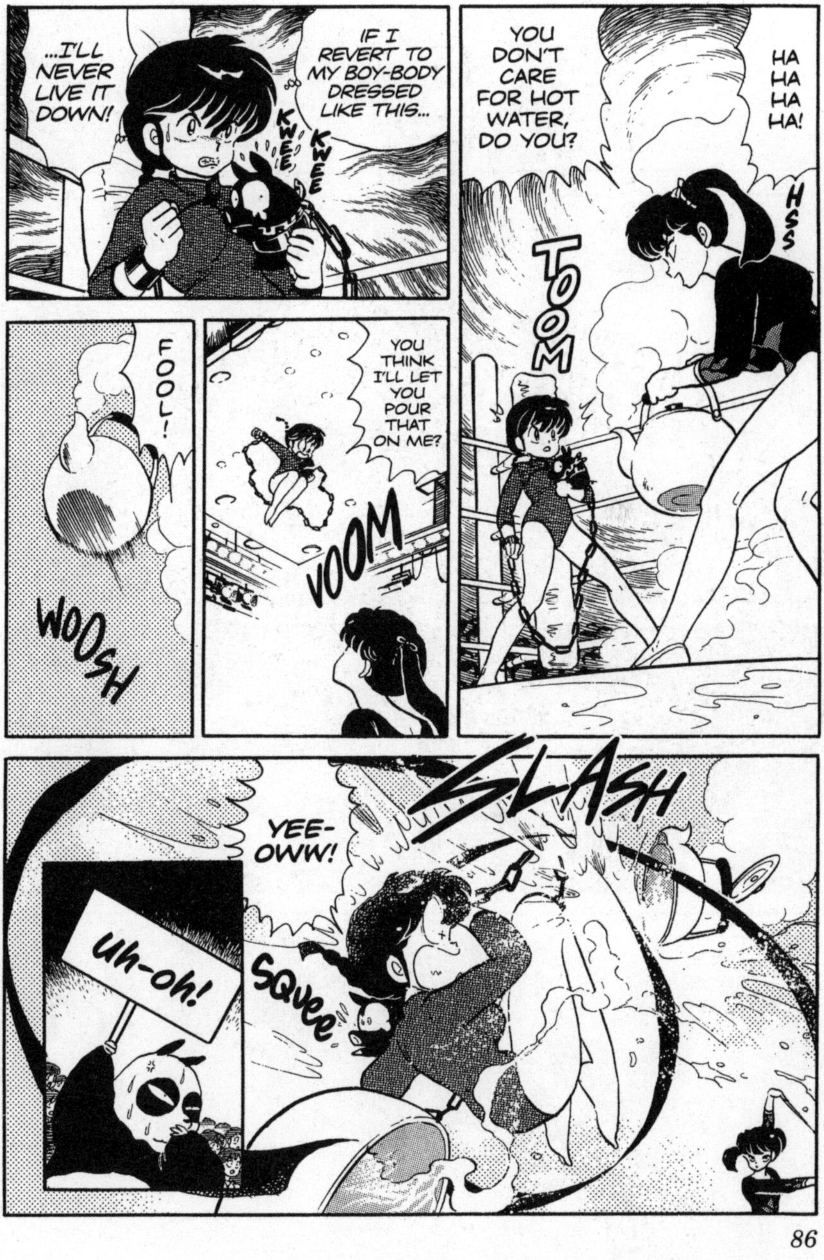
HA HA HA HA!
YOU DON'T CARE FOR HOT WATER, DO YOU?
HSS
TOOM
IF I REVERT TO MY BOY-BODY DRESSED LIKE THIS...
...I'LL NEVER LIVE IT DOWN!
KWEE KWEE
KWEE
YOU THINK I'LL LET YOU POUR THAT ON ME?
VOOM
FOOL!
WOOSH
SLASH
YEE-OWW!
SQUEE
uh-oh!

PART 5
I GIVE UP

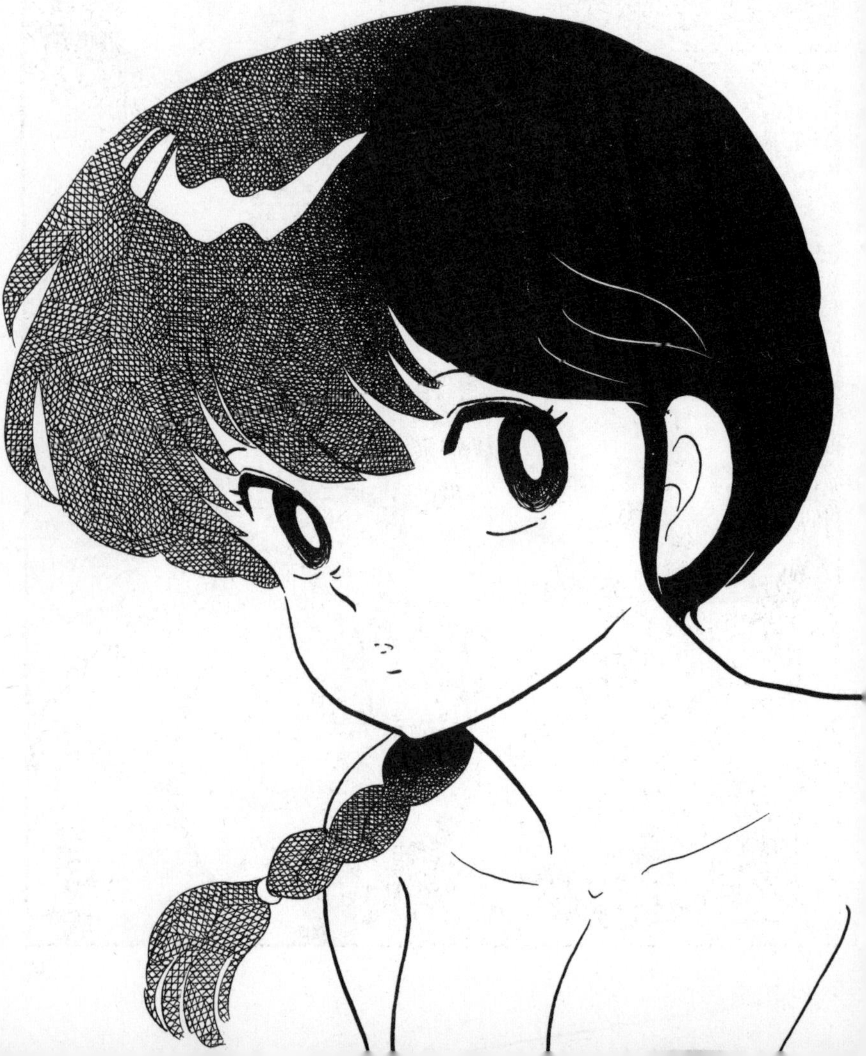

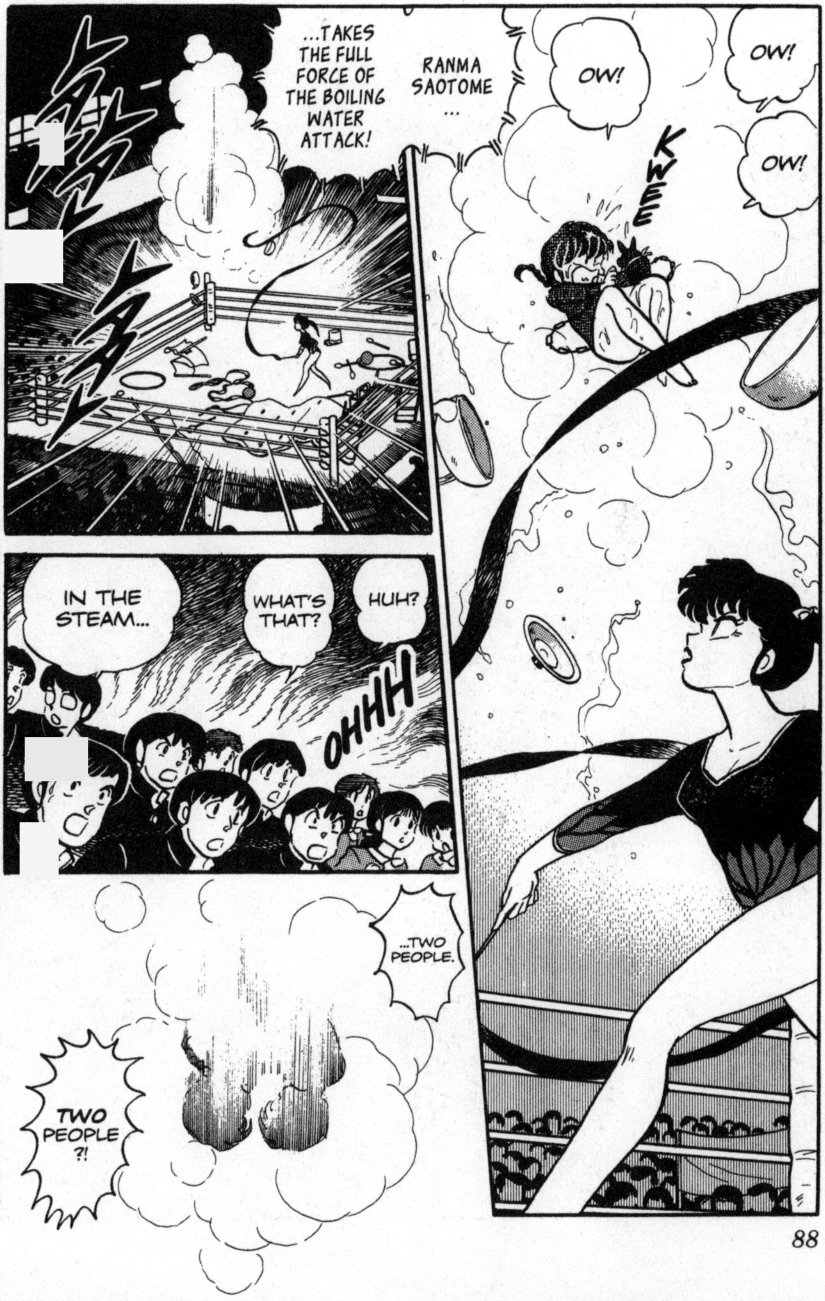
OW!
OW!
OW!
KWEE
RANMA SAOTOME ...
...TAKES THE FULL FORCE OF THE BOILING WATER ATTACK!
HUH?
WHAT'S THAT?
IN THE STEAM...
OHHH
...TWO PEOPLE.
TWO PEOPLE ?!

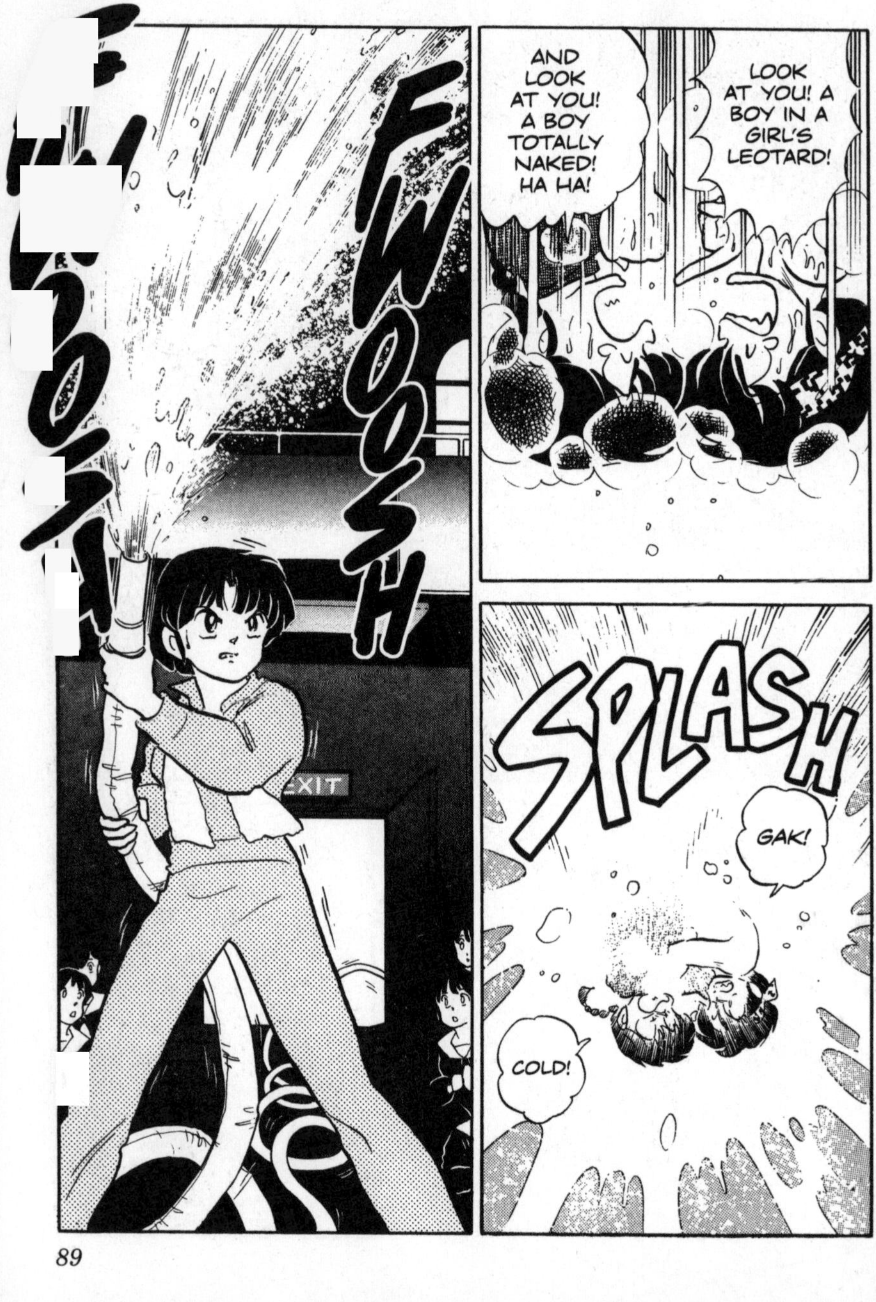
LOOK AT YOU! A BOY IN A GIRL'S LEOTARD!
AND LOOK AT YOU! A BOY TOTALLY NAKED! HA HA!
SPLASH
GAK!
COLD!
FWOOSH

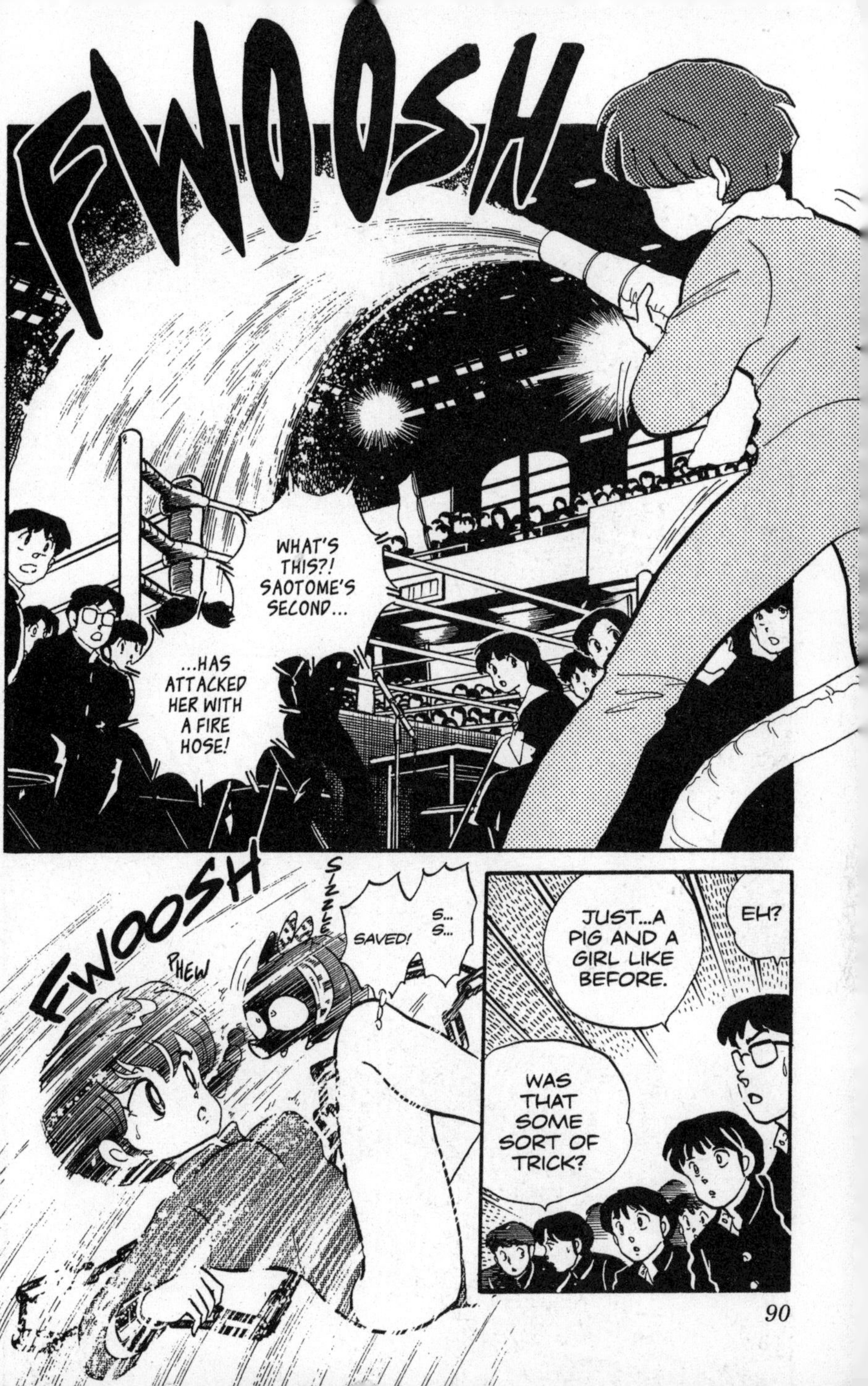
F-W-O-O-S-H
WHAT'S THIS?! SAOTOME'S SECOND...
...HAS ATTACKED HER WITH A FIRE HOSE!
EH?
JUST...A PIG AND A GIRL LIKE BEFORE.
WAS THAT SOME SORT OF TRICK?
SIZZLE
S... S...
SAVED!
FWOOSH
PHEW

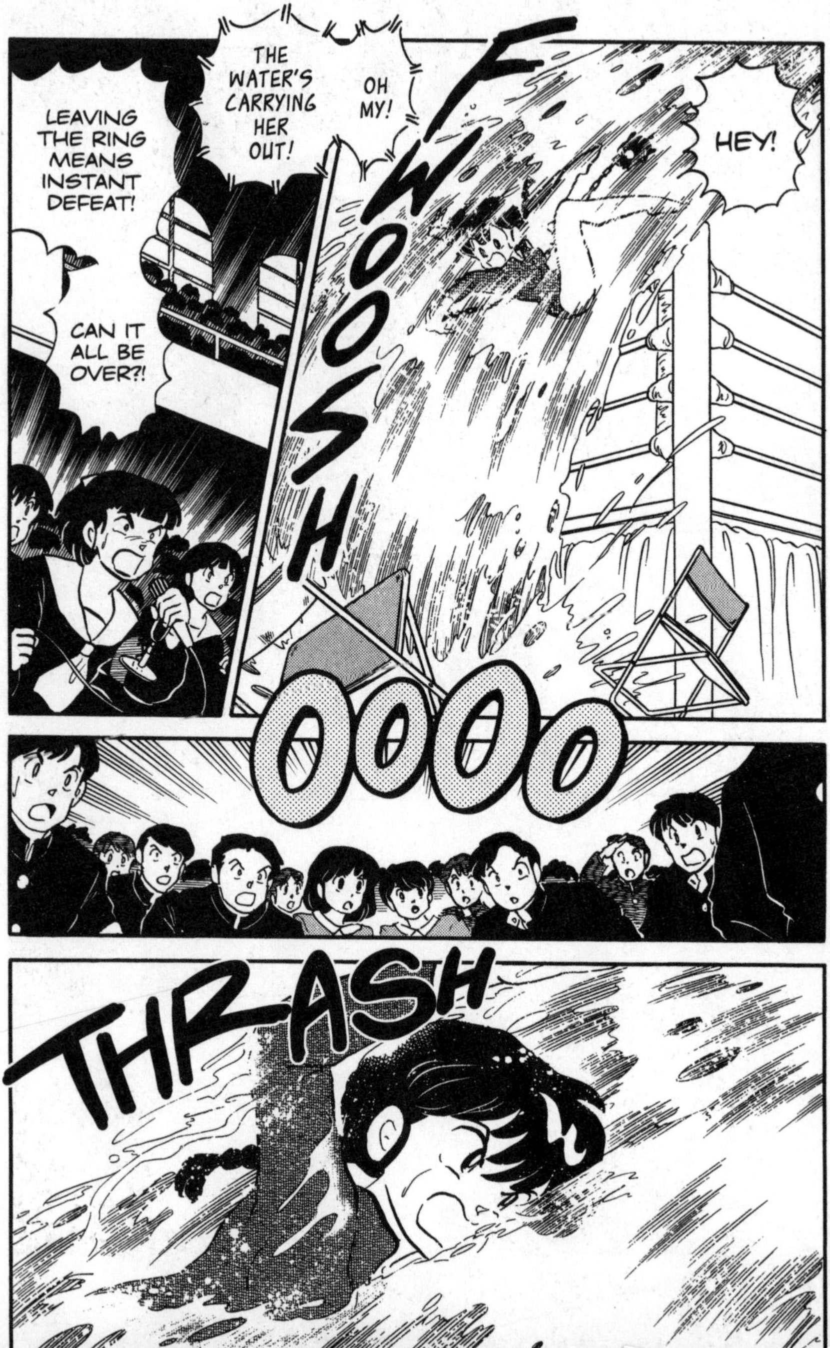
HEY!
FWOOSH
OH MY!
THE WATER'S CARRYING HER OUT!
LEAVING THE RING MEANS INSTANT DEFEAT!
CAN IT ALL BE OVER?!
OOOO
THRASH

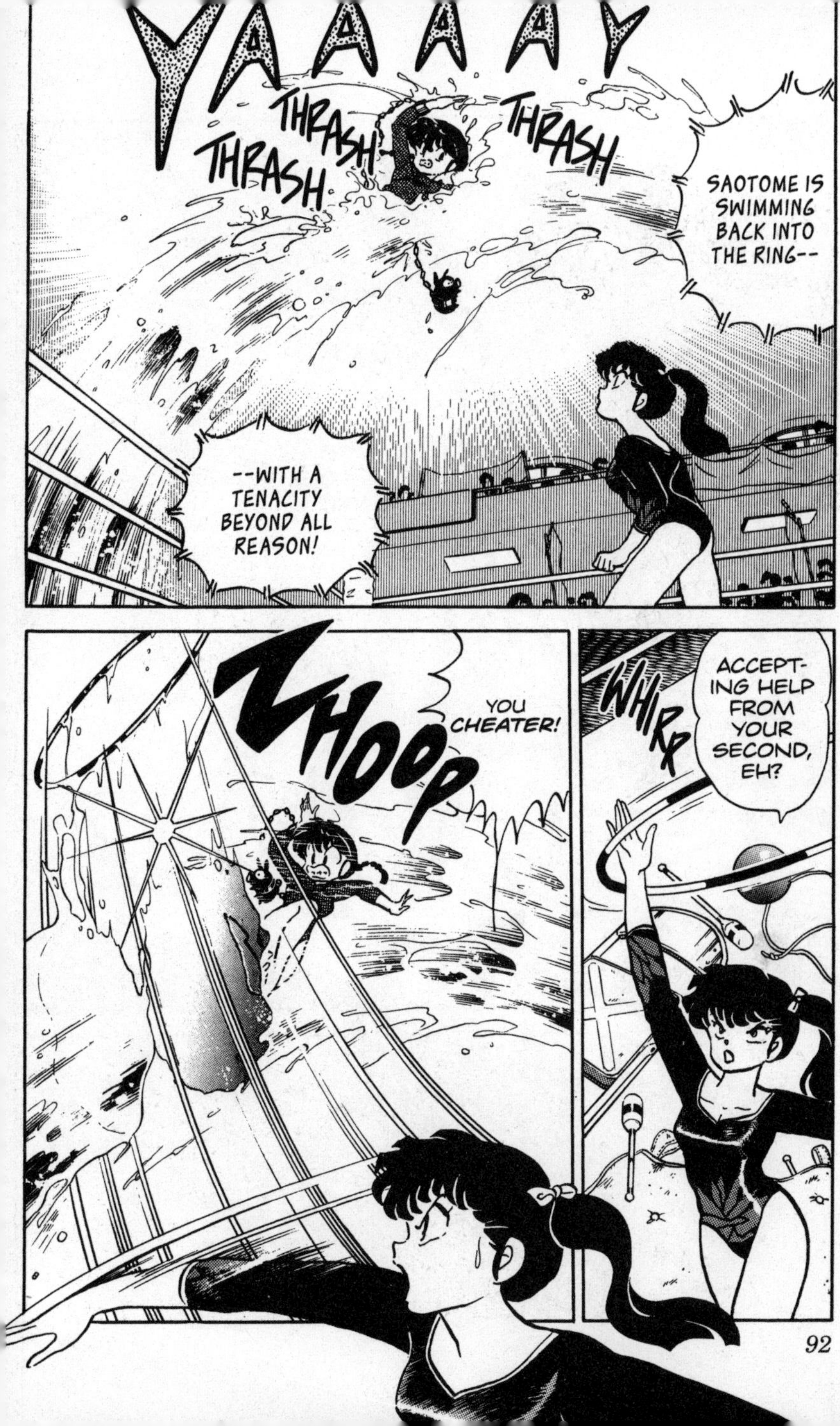
YAAAAY
THRASH THRASH
THRASH
THRASH
SAOTOME IS SWIMMING BACK INTO THE RING--
--WITH A TENACITY BEYOND ALL REASON!
WHIRR
ACCEPT-ING HELP FROM YOUR SECOND, EH?
YOU CHEATER!
WHOOP

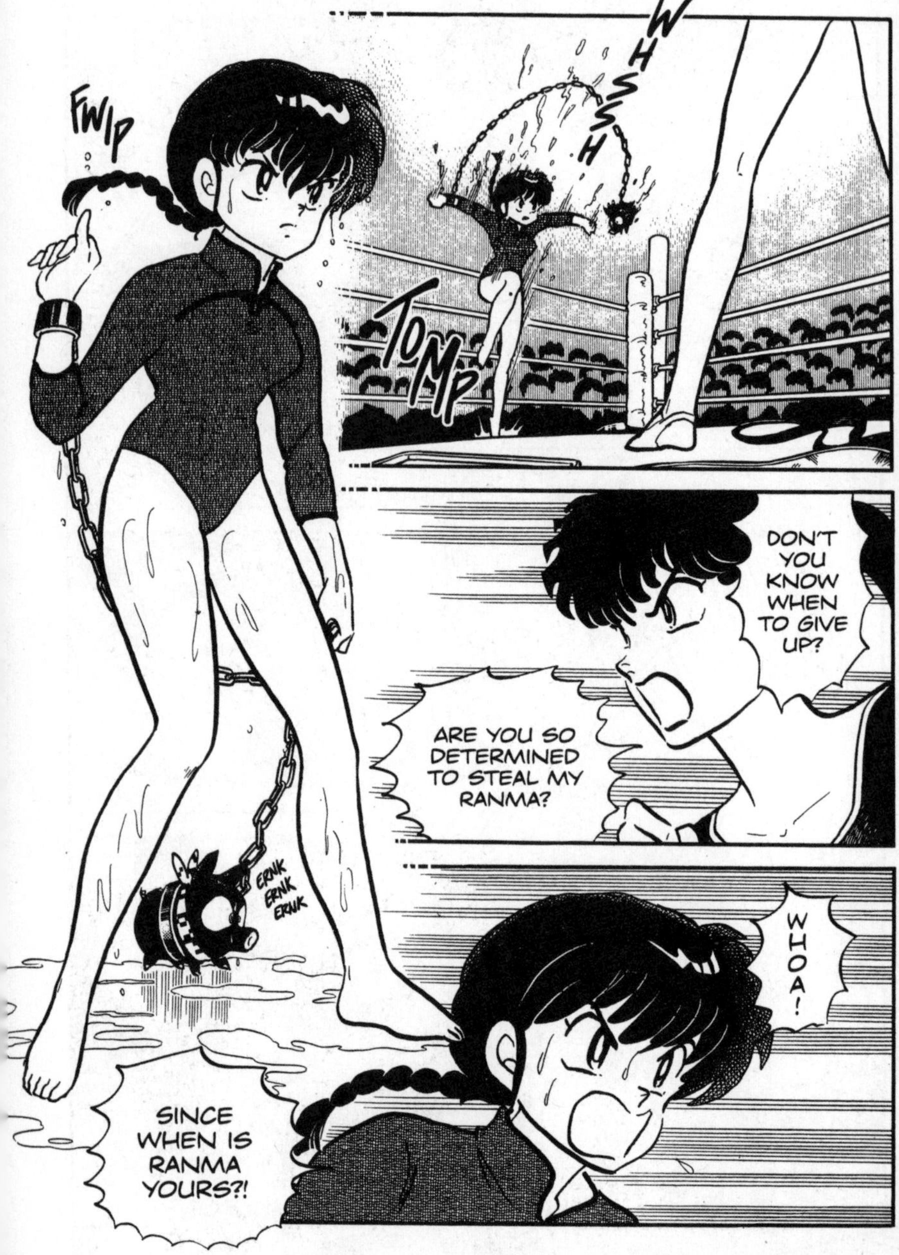
WHHSSH
TOMP
DON'T YOU KNOW WHEN TO GIVE UP?
ARE YOU SO DETERMINED TO STEAL MY RANMA?
WHOA!
FWIP
ERNK ERNK ERNK
SINCE WHEN IS RANMA YOURS?!

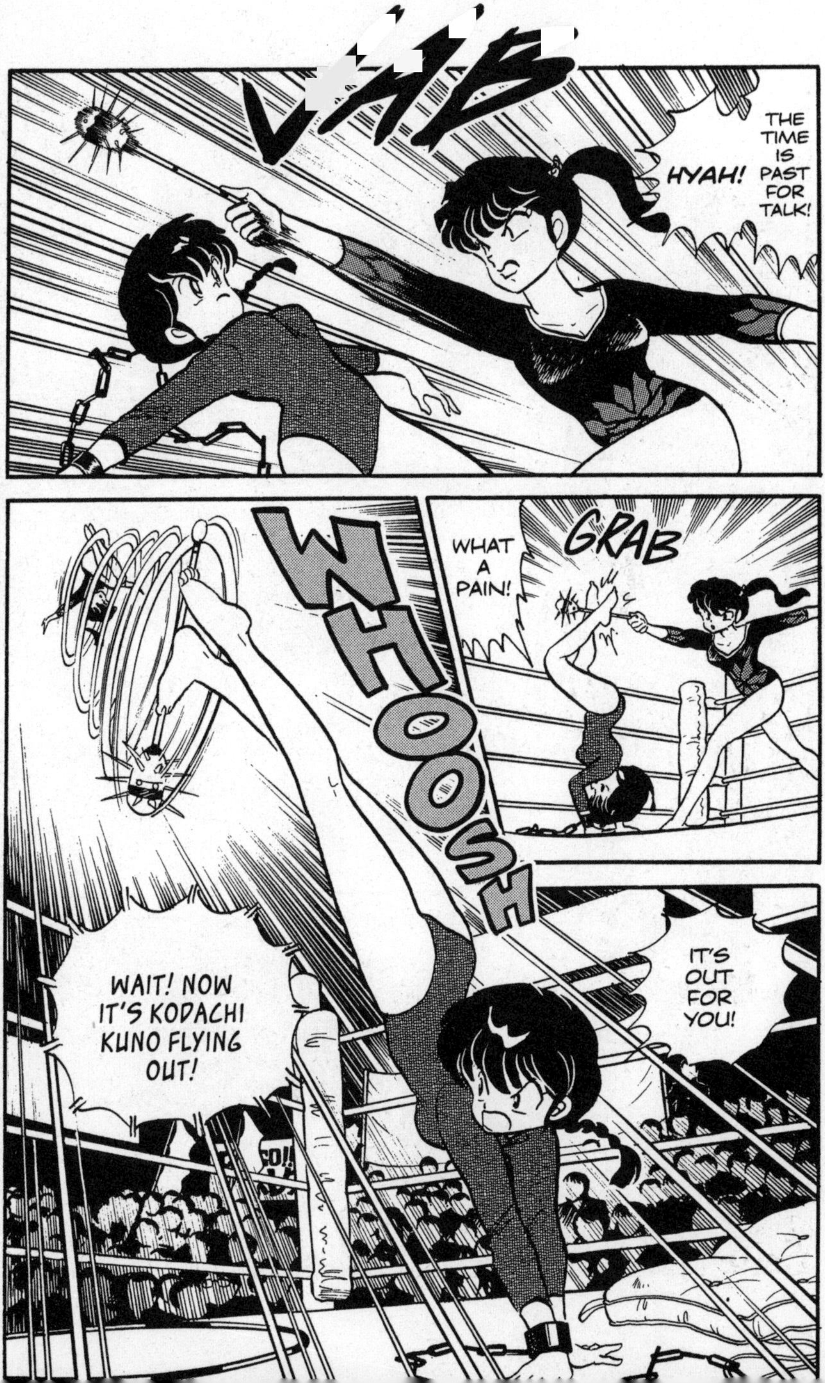
JAB
THE TIME IS PAST FOR TALK!
HYAH!
GRAB
WHAT A PAIN!
WHOOSH
IT'S OUT FOR YOU!
WAIT! NOW IT'S KODACHI KUNO FLYING OUT!

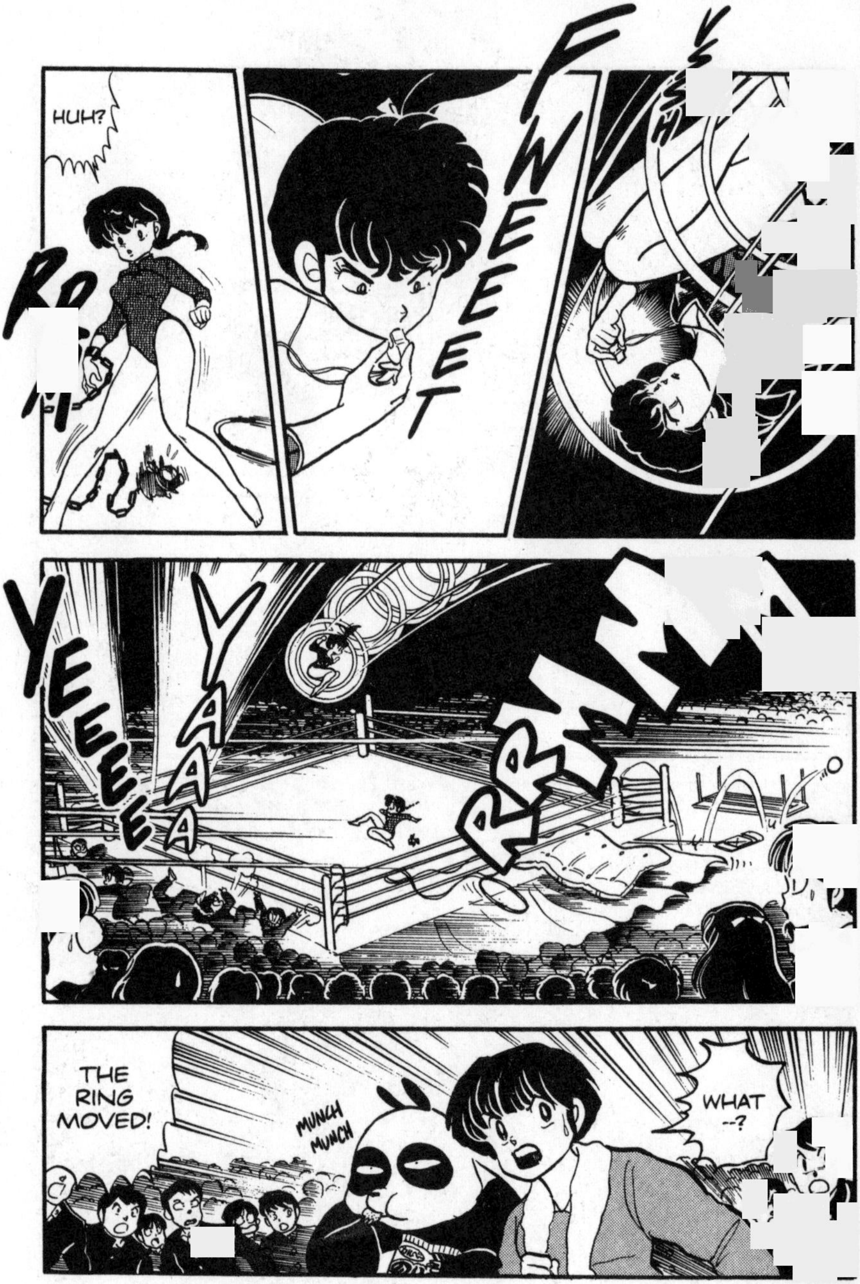
FWEEEEET
HUH?
WHAT --?
MUNCH MUNCH
THE RING MOVED!

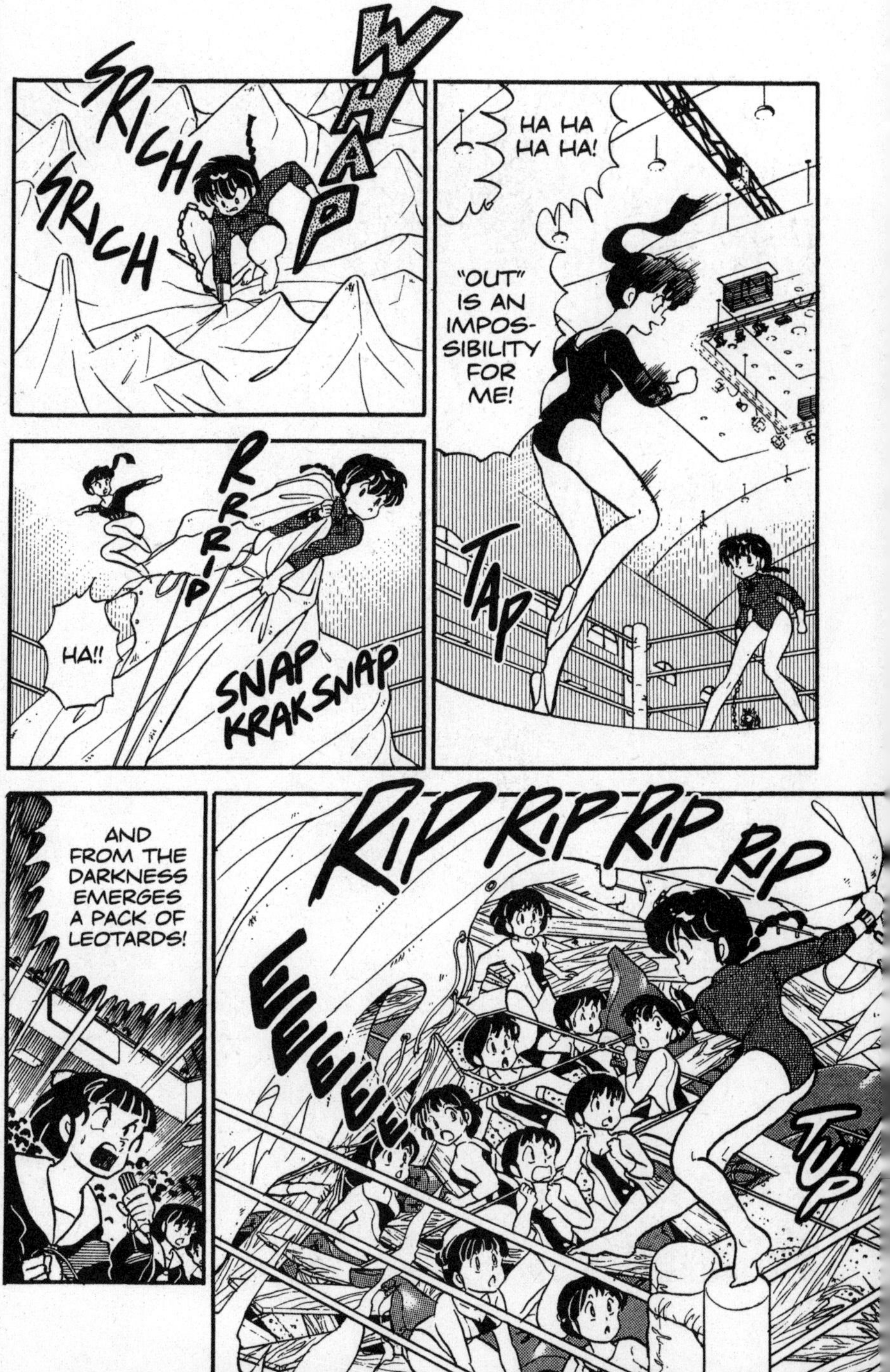
HA HA HA HA!
"OUT" IS AN IMPOSSIBILITY FOR ME!
TAP
WHAP
SRICH SRICH SRICH
RRRRIP
HA!!
SNAP KRAKSNAP
RIP RIP RIP RIP RIP
EEEEEE
TUP
AND FROM THE DARKNESS EMERGES A PACK OF LEOTARDS!

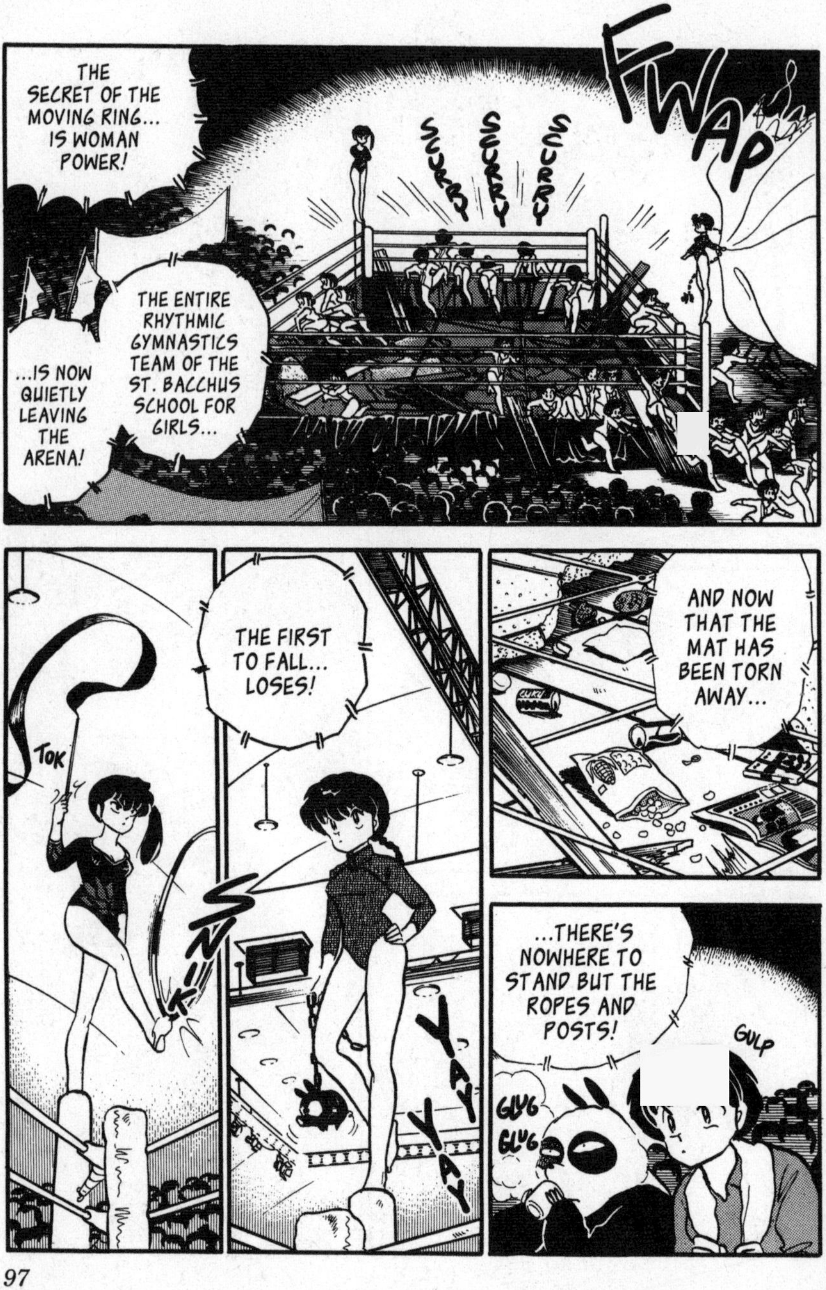
FWAP
SCURRY
SCURRY
SCURRY
THE SECRET OF THE MOVING RING... IS WOMAN POWER!
THE ENTIRE RHYTHMIC GYMNASTICS TEAM OF THE ST. BACCHUS SCHOOL FOR GIRLS...
...IS NOW QUIETLY LEAVING THE ARENA!
AND NOW THAT THE MAT HAS BEEN TORN AWAY...
...THERE'S NOWHERE TO STAND BUT THE ROPES AND POSTS!
GULP
GLUG
GLUG
THE FIRST TO FALL... LOSES!
YAY
YAY
TOK
SNIK

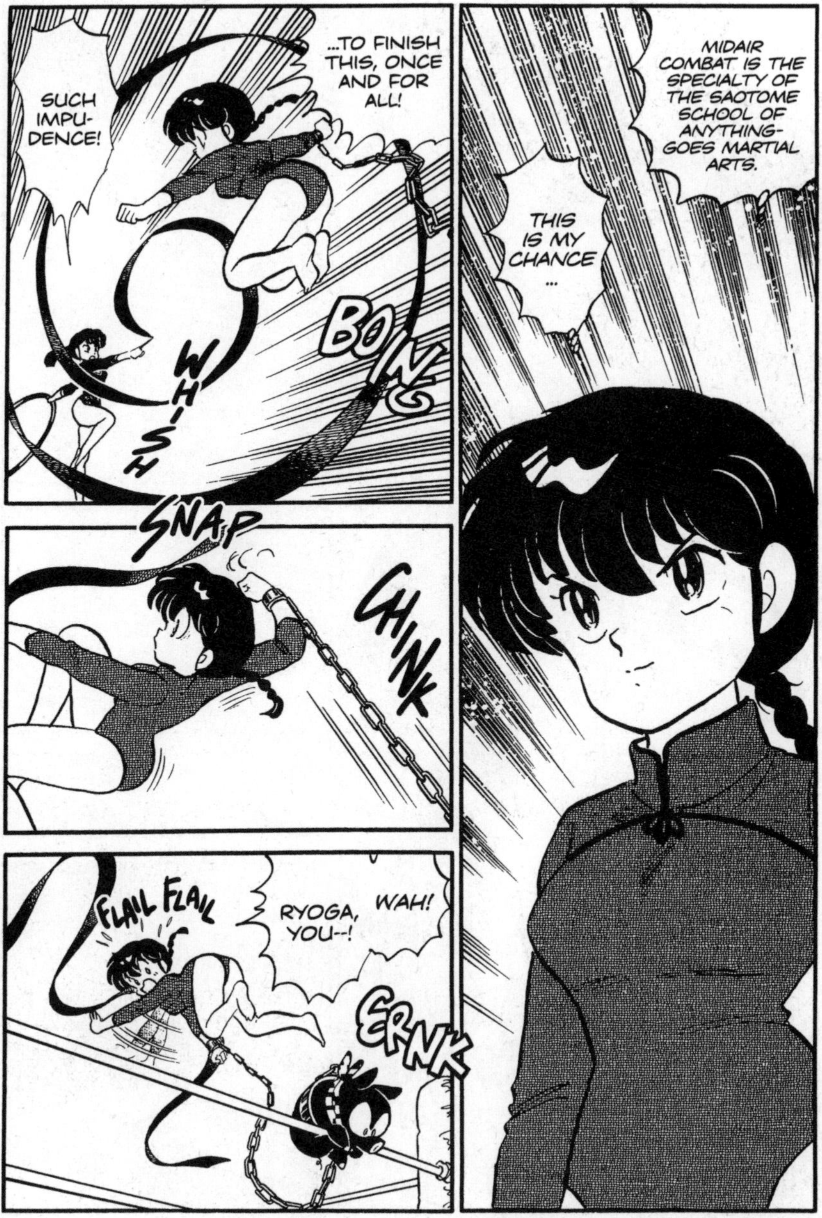
MIDAIR COMBAT IS THE SPECIALTY OF THE SAOTOME SCHOOL OF ANYTHING-GOES MARTIAL ARTS.
THIS IS MY CHANCE ...
...TO FINISH THIS, ONCE AND FOR ALL!
BOING
SUCH IMPU-DENCE!
WHISH
SNAP
CHINK
WAH!
RYOGA, YOU--!
FLAIL FLAIL
ERNK

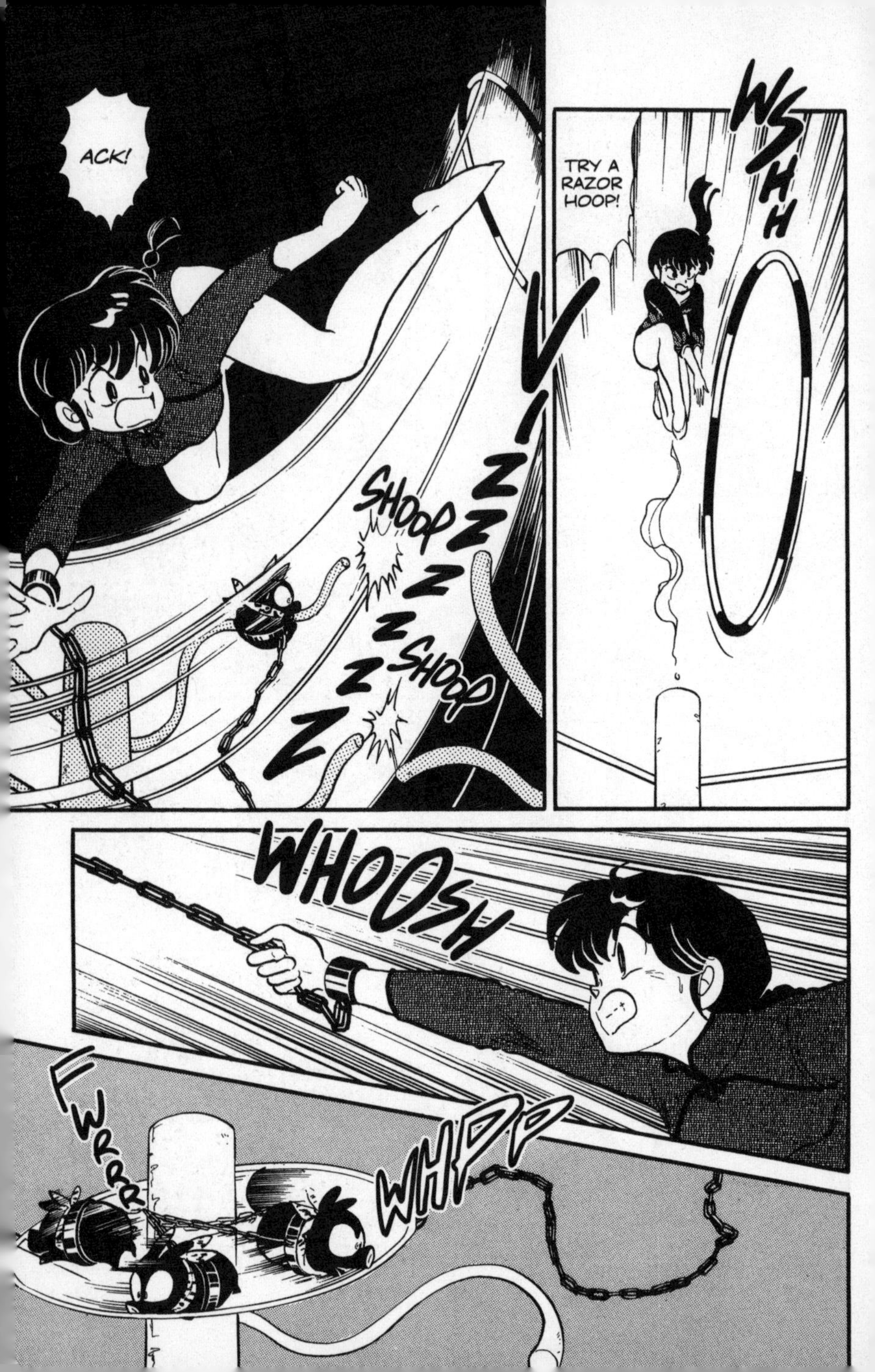
WSHHH
TRY A RAZOR HOOP!
ACK!
SHOOP
SHOOP
WHOOSH
WHPP
FWRRRR

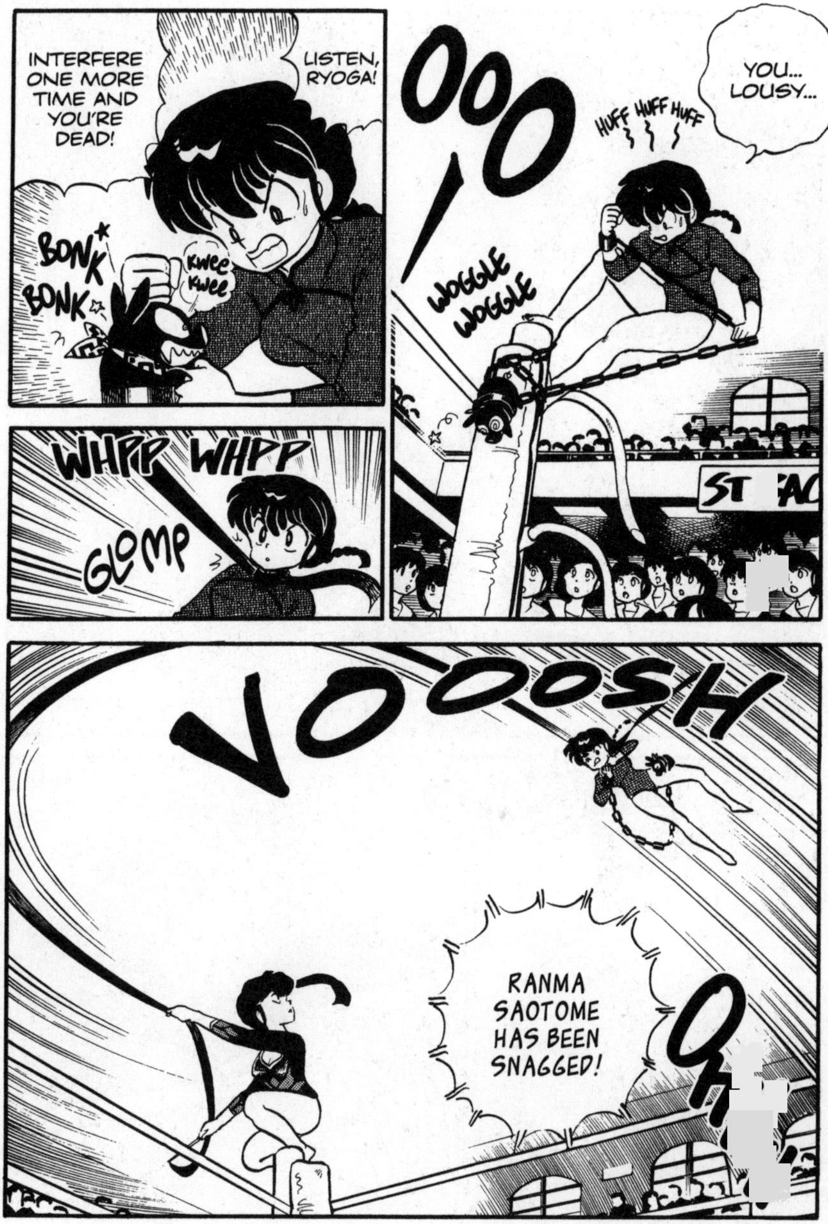
YOU... LOUSY...
HUFF HUFF HUFF
OOOO
WOGGLE WOGGLE
LISTEN, RYOGA!
INTERFERE ONE MORE TIME AND YOU'RE DEAD!
KWEE KWEE
BONK BONK
WHPP WHPP
GLOMP
VOOOSH
RANMA SAOTOME HAS BEEN SNAGGED!

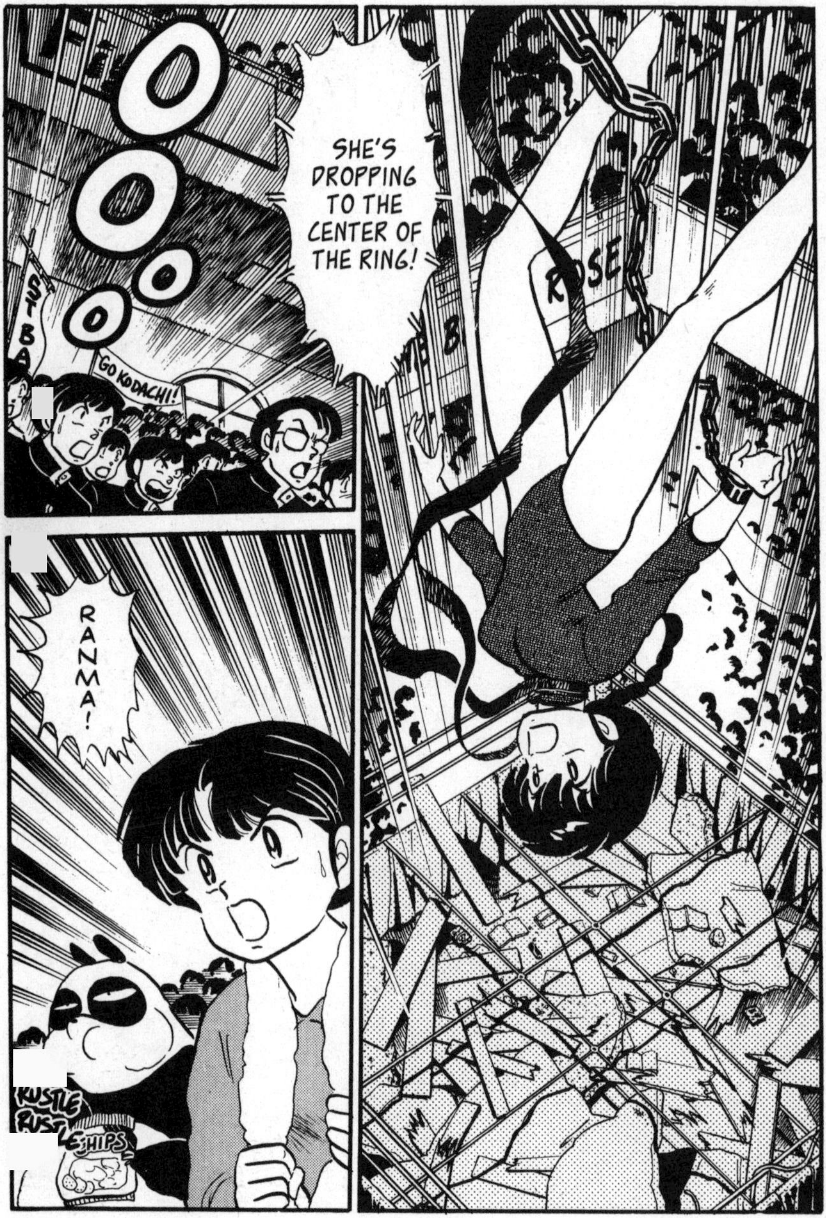
ROSE
SHE'S DROPPING TO THE CENTER OF THE RING!
OOOO
GO KODACHI!
RANMA!

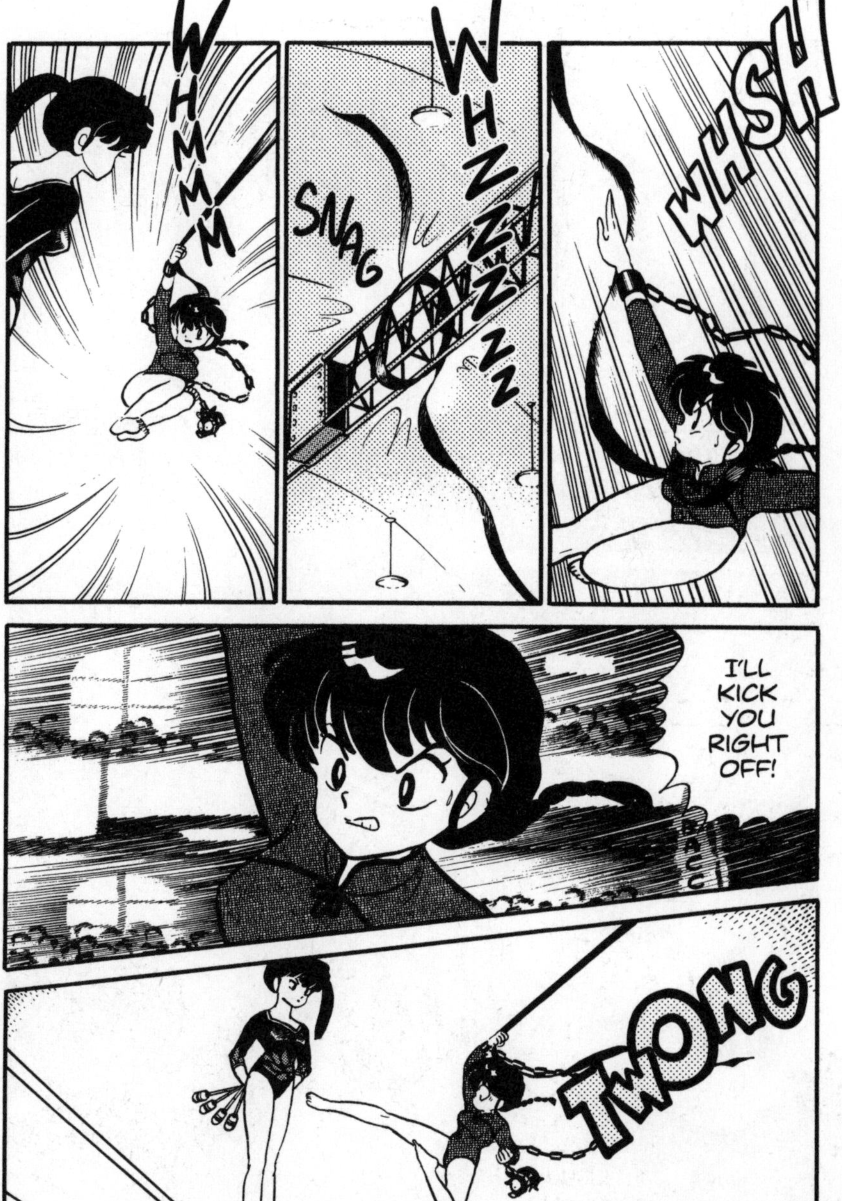
WHSH
WHZZZZZ
SNAG
WHMMMM
I'LL KICK YOU RIGHT OFF!
TWONG

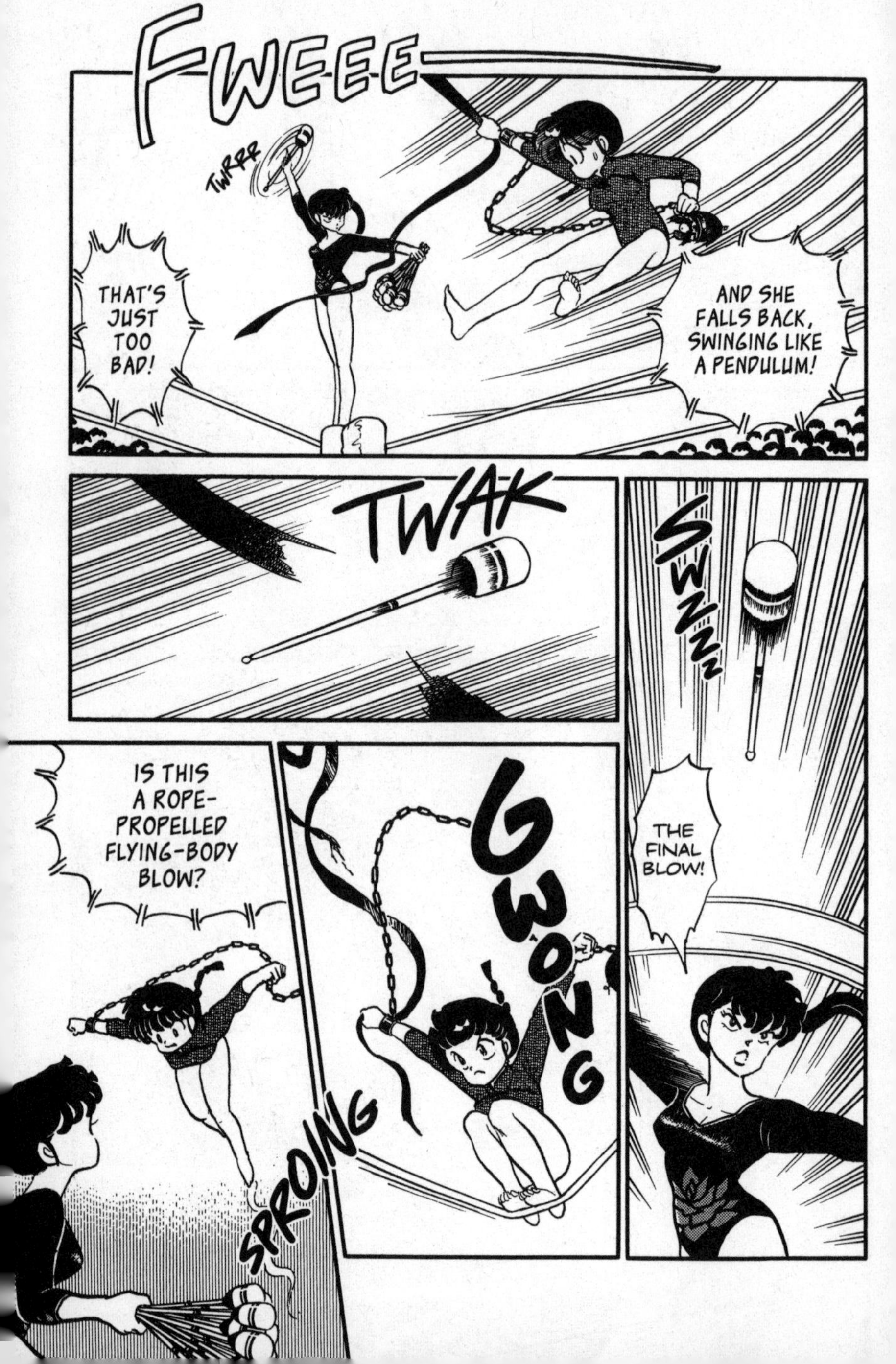
FWEEE
AND SHE FALLS BACK, SWINGING LIKE A PENDULUM!
TWRRR
THAT'S JUST TOO BAD!
SWZZZ
THE FINAL BLOW!
TWAK
GWONG
IS THIS A ROPE-PROPELLED FLYING-BODY BLOW?
SPROING

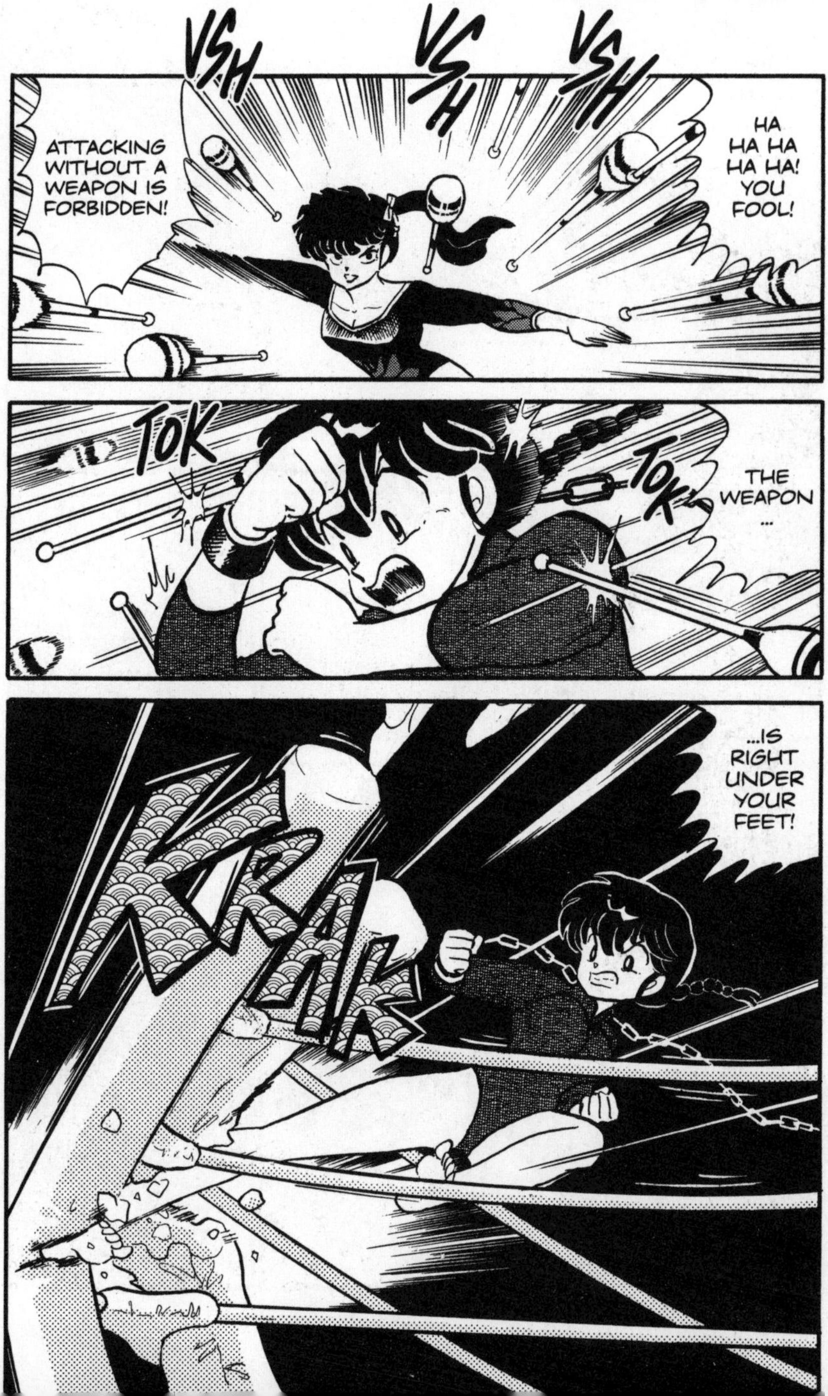
VSH
VSH
VSH
HA HA HA HA HA! YOU FOOL!
ATTACKING WITHOUT A WEAPON IS FORBIDDEN!
TOK
TOK
THE WEAPON ...
...IS RIGHT UNDER YOUR FEET!
KRAK

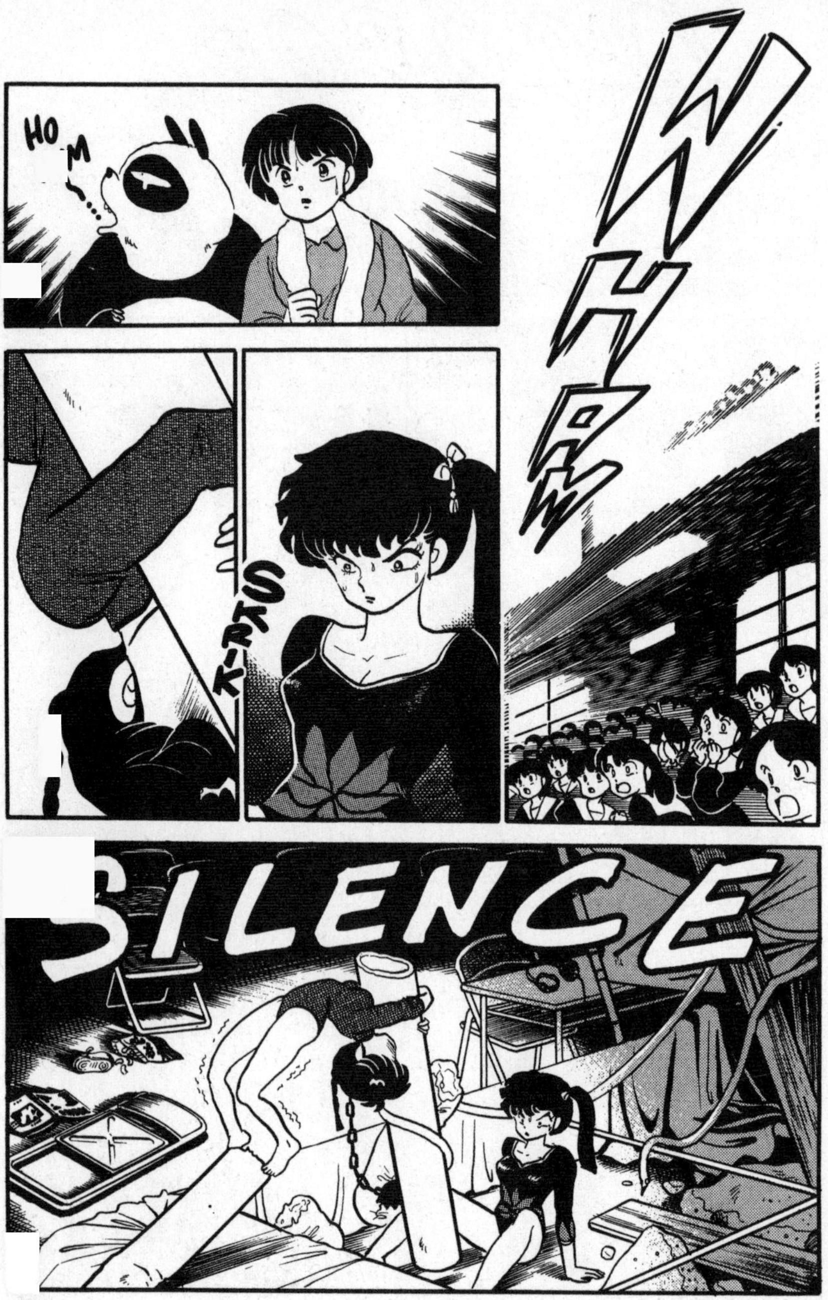
WHAM
HO M
SKRIK
SILENCE

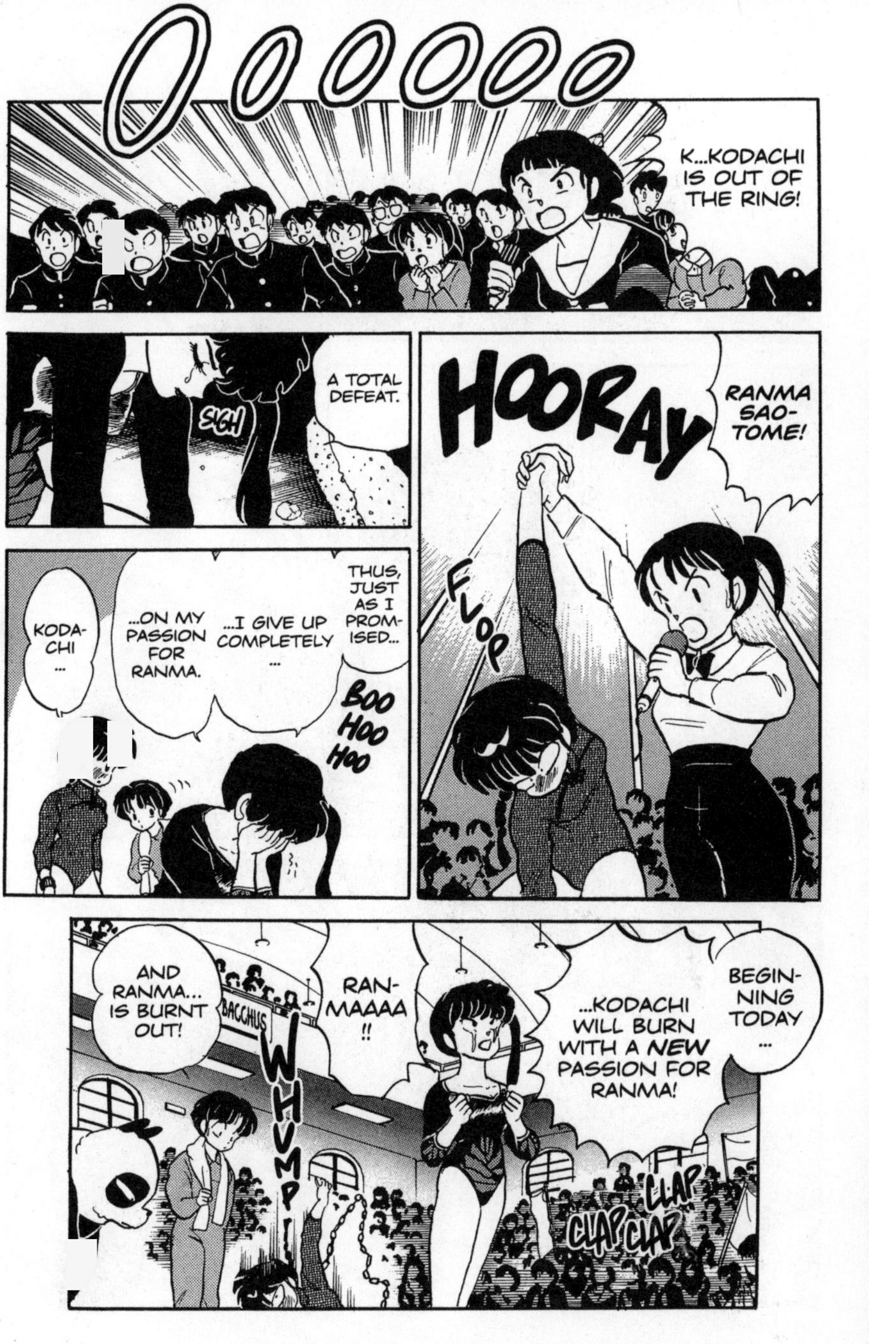
OOOOOO
K...KODACHI IS OUT OF THE RING!
HOORAY
RANMA SAO-TOME!
FLOP
A TOTAL DEFEAT.
SIGH
THUS, JUST AS I PROM-ISED...
...I GIVE UP COMPLETELY ...
...ON MY PASSION FOR RANMA.
KODA-CHI ...
BOO HOO HOO
BEGIN-NING TODAY ...
...KODACHI WILL BURN WITH A *NEW* PASSION FOR RANMA!
RAN-MAAAA !!
AND RANMA... IS BURNT OUT!
BACCHUS
WHUMP!
CLAP
CLAP CLAP

PART 6
DARLING CHARLOTTE

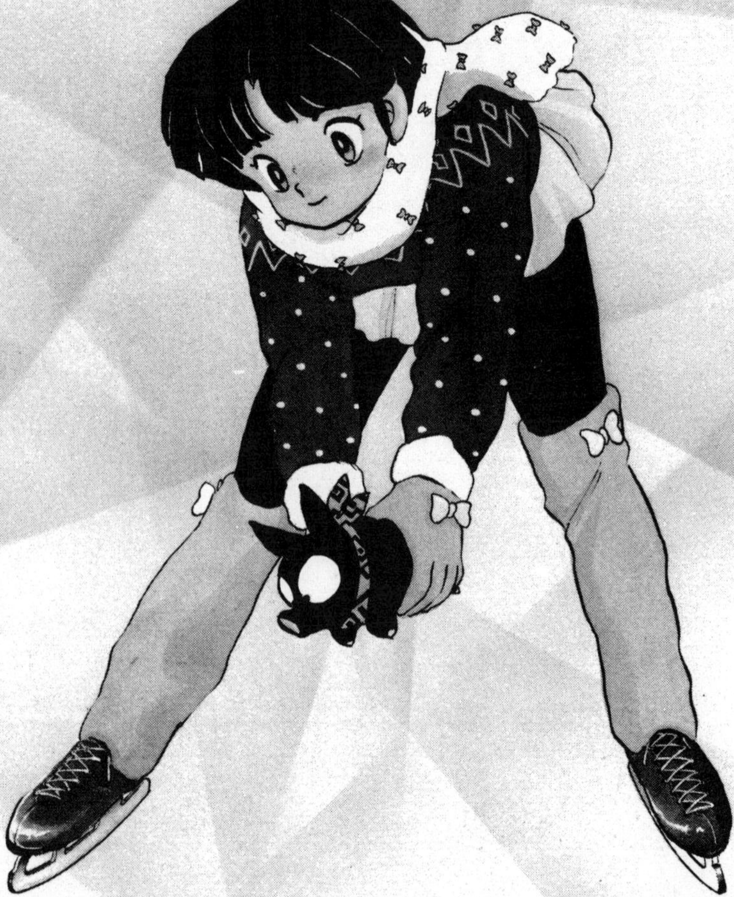

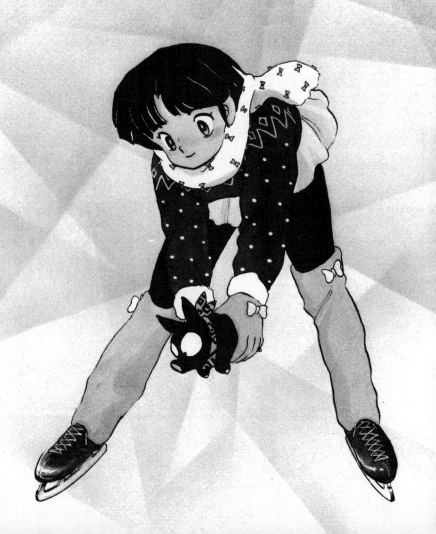

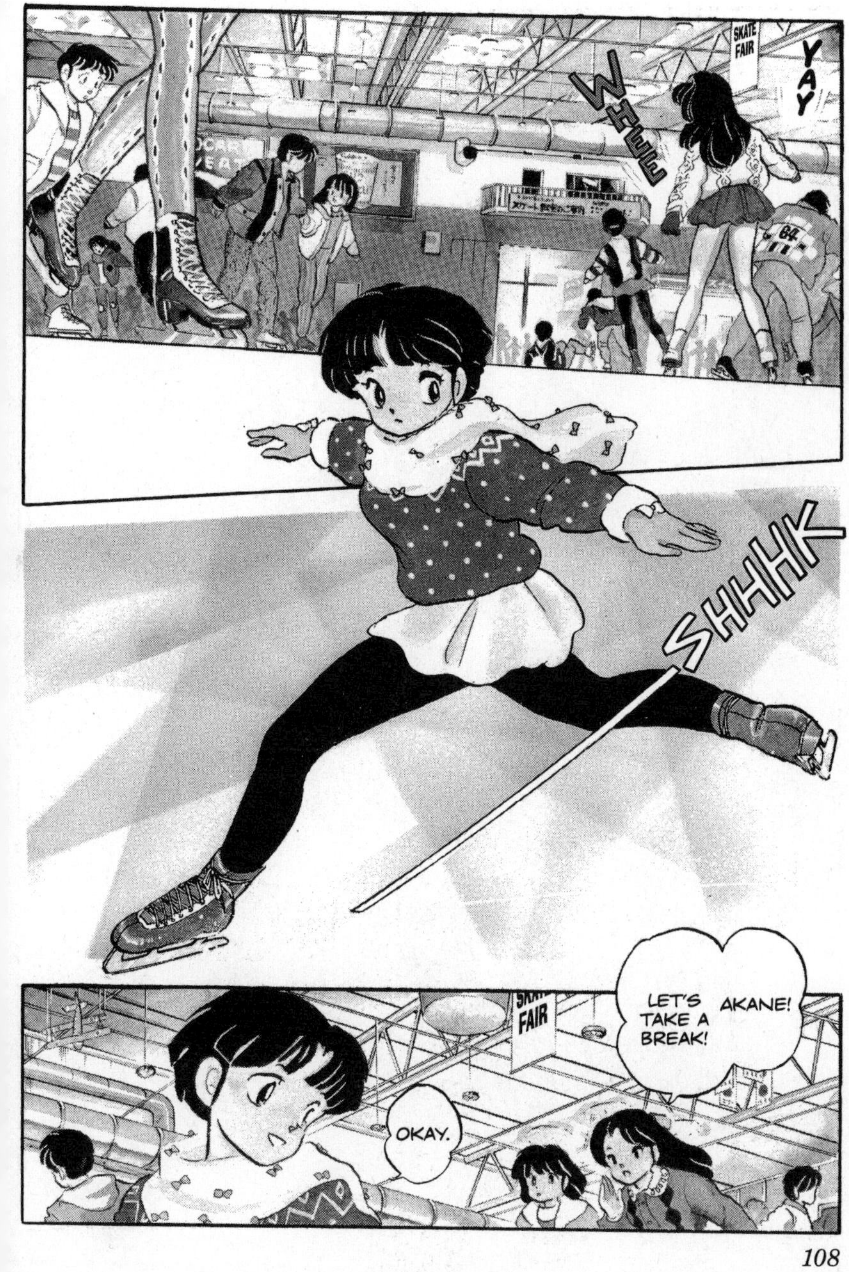
YAY
SKATE FAIR
WHEEE
SHHHK
AKANE!
LET'S TAKE A BREAK!
SKATE FAIR
OKAY.

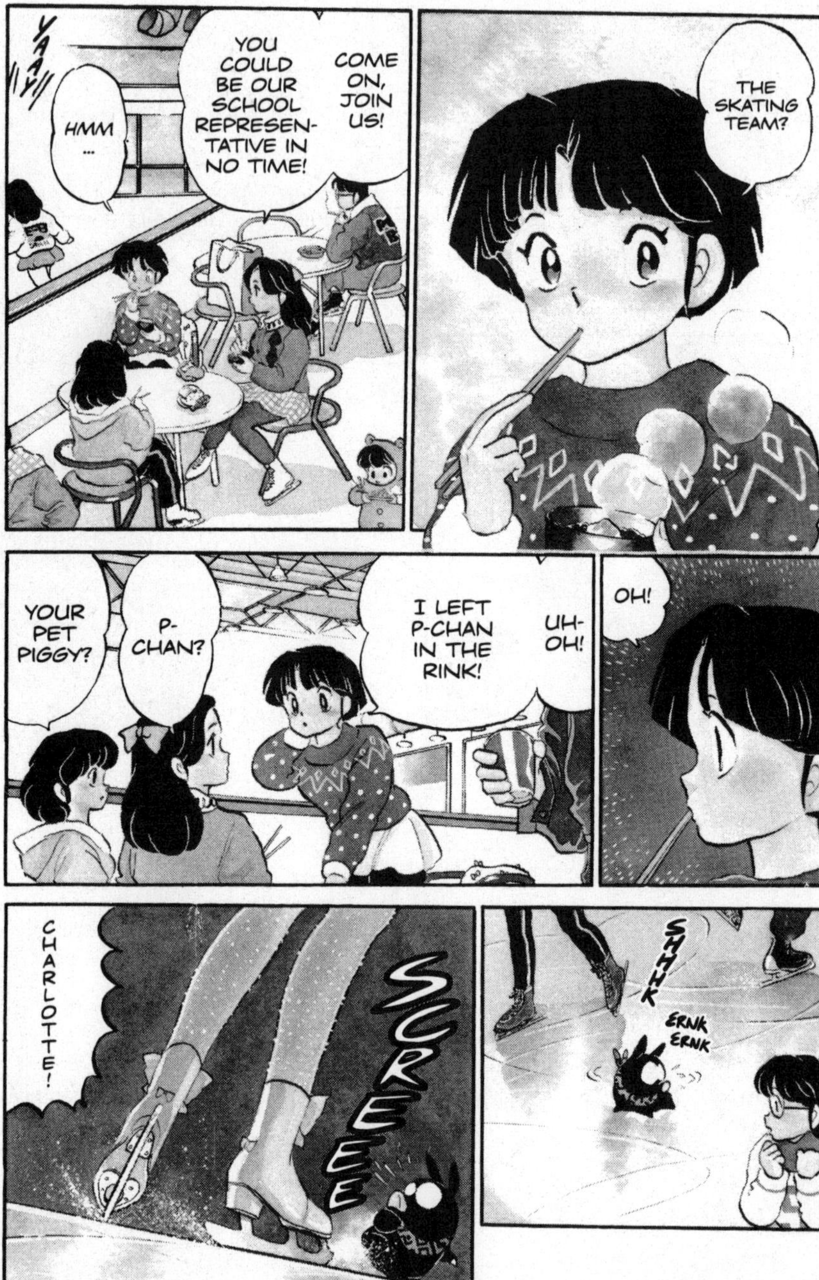
THE SKATING TEAM?
COME ON, JOIN US!
YOU COULD BE OUR SCHOOL REPRESEN-TATIVE IN NO TIME!
YAAAY
HMM ...
OH!
UH-OH!
I LEFT P-CHAN IN THE RINK!
P-CHAN?
YOUR PET PIGGY?
SHHHK
ERNK ERNK
SCREEEE
CHARLOTTE!

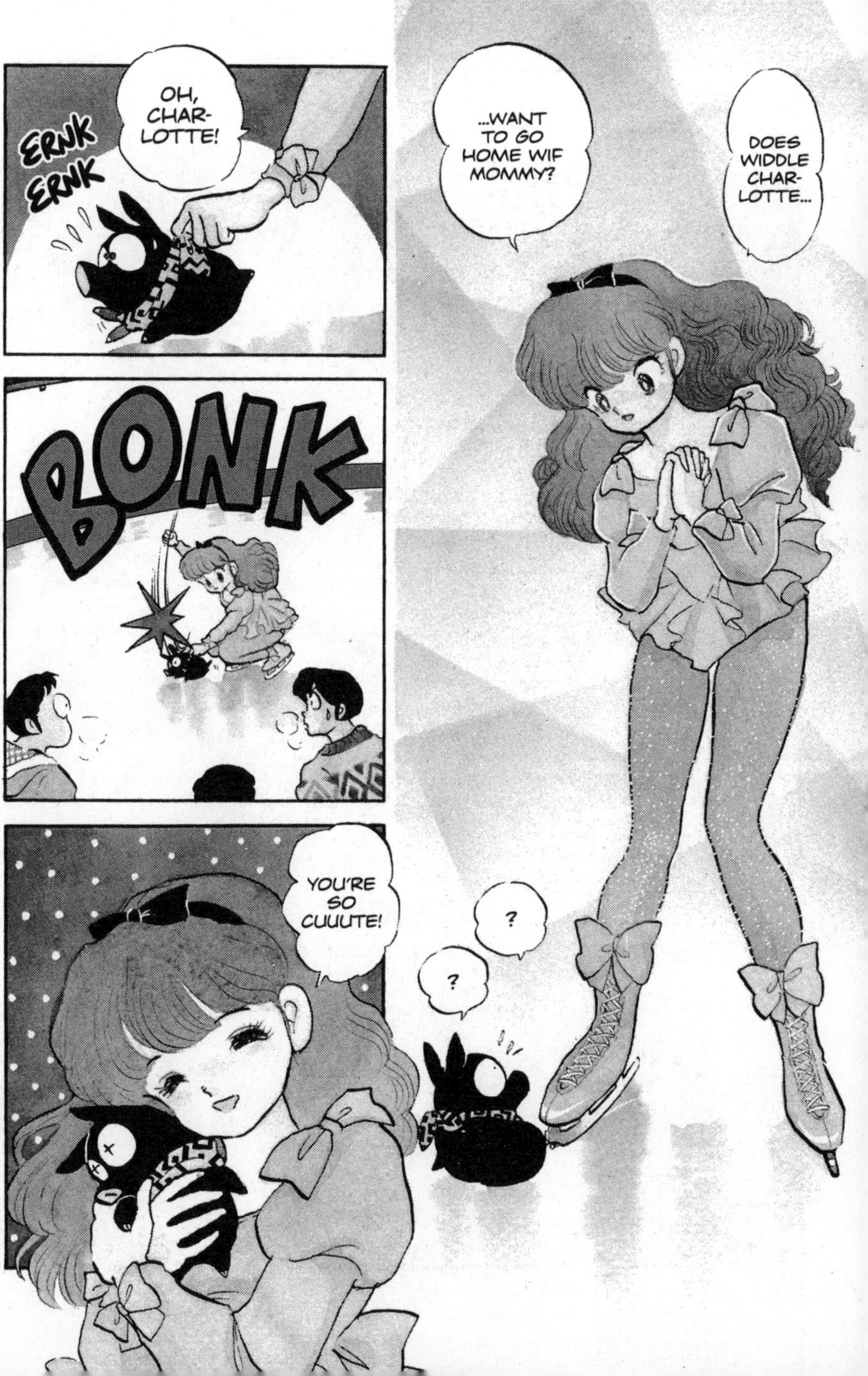
DOES WIDDLE CHAR-LOTTE...
...WANT TO GO HOME WIF MOMMY?
?
?
OH, CHAR-LOTTE!
ERNK ERNK
BONK
YOU'RE SO CUUUTE!

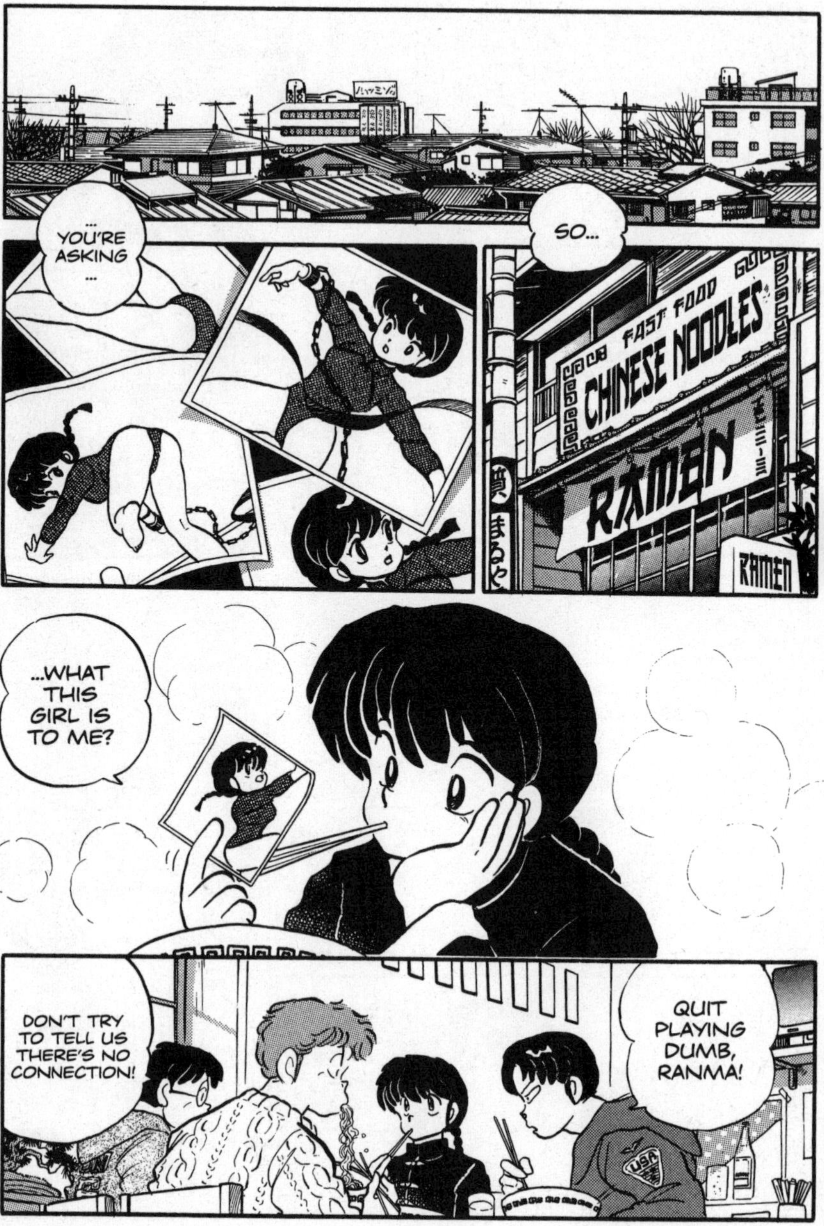
SO...
FAST FOOD
CHINESE NOODLES
RAMEN
RAMEN
... YOU'RE ASKING ...
...WHAT THIS GIRL IS TO ME?
QUIT PLAYING DUMB, RANMA!
DON'T TRY TO TELL US THERE'S NO CONNECTION!

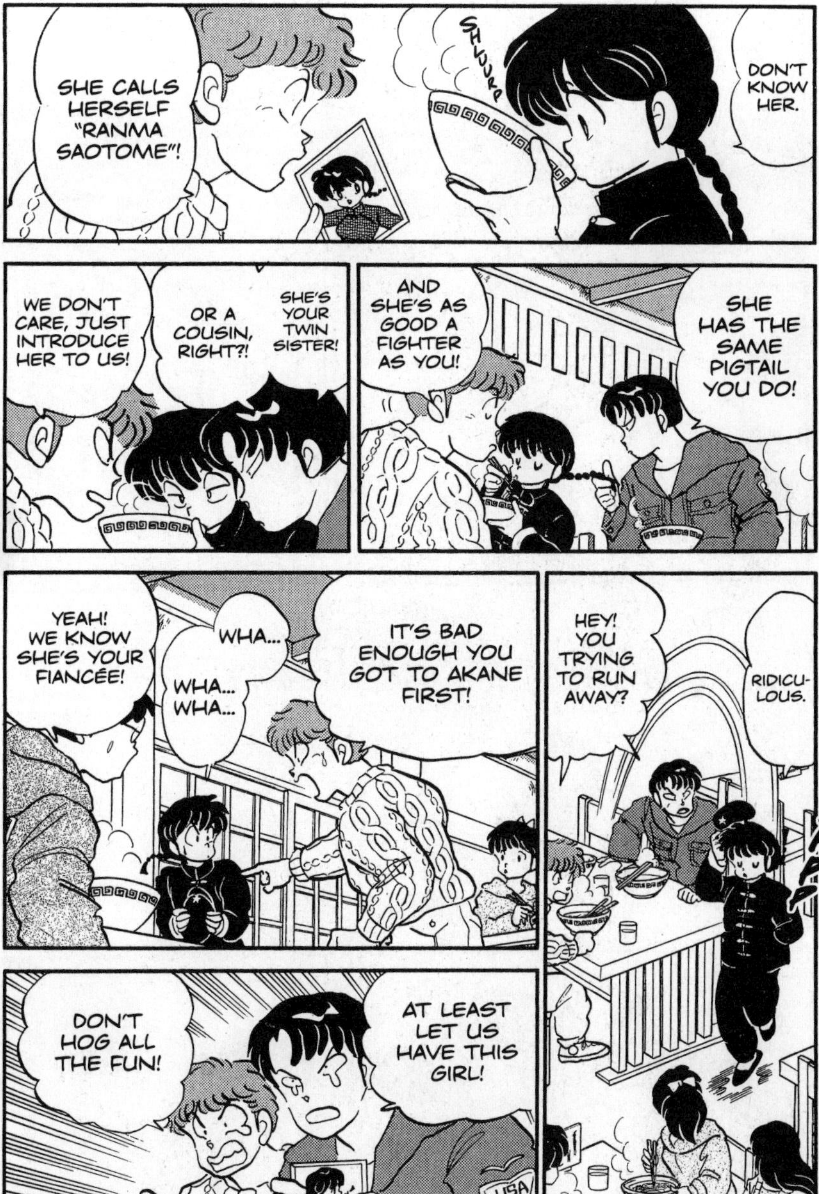
DON'T KNOW HER.
SHVUURP
SHE CALLS HERSELF "RANMA SAOTOME"!
SHE HAS THE SAME PIGTAIL YOU DO!
AND SHE'S AS GOOD A FIGHTER AS YOU!
SHE'S YOUR TWIN SISTER!
OR A COUSIN, RIGHT?!
WE DON'T CARE, JUST INTRODUCE HER TO US!
RIDICU-LOUS.
HEY! YOU TRYING TO RUN AWAY?
SHPP
IT'S BAD ENOUGH YOU GOT TO AKANE FIRST!
WHA...
WHA... WHA...
YEAH! WE KNOW SHE'S YOUR FIANCÉE!
AT LEAST LET US HAVE THIS GIRL!
DON'T HOG ALL THE FUN!
USA

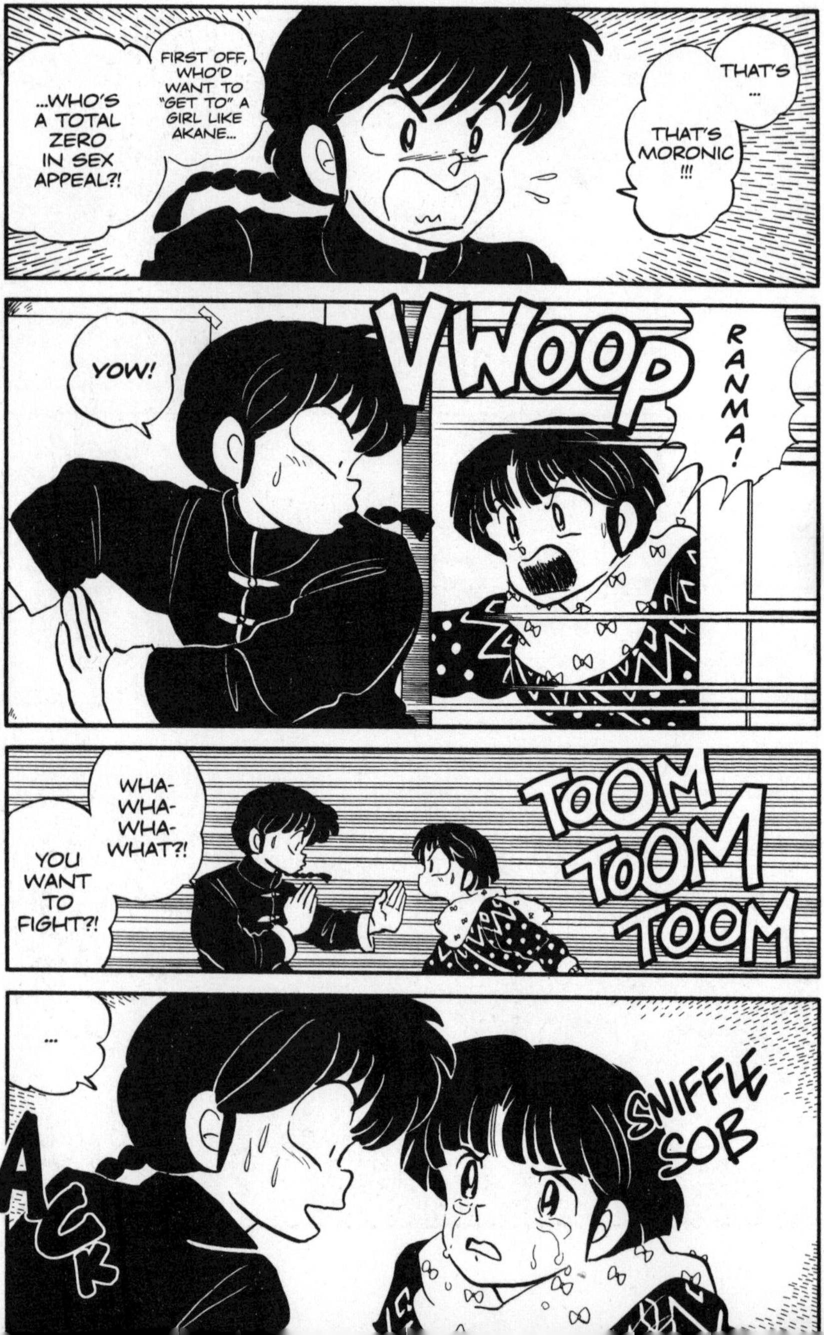
THAT'S... THAT'S MORONIC!!!
FIRST OFF, WHO'D WANT TO "GET TO" A GIRL LIKE AKANE...
...WHO'S A TOTAL ZERO IN SEX APPEAL?!
RANMA!
VWOOP
YOW!
TOOM TOOM TOOM
WHA-WHA-WHA-WHAT?!
YOU WANT TO FIGHT?!
SNIFFLE SOB
...
AUCK

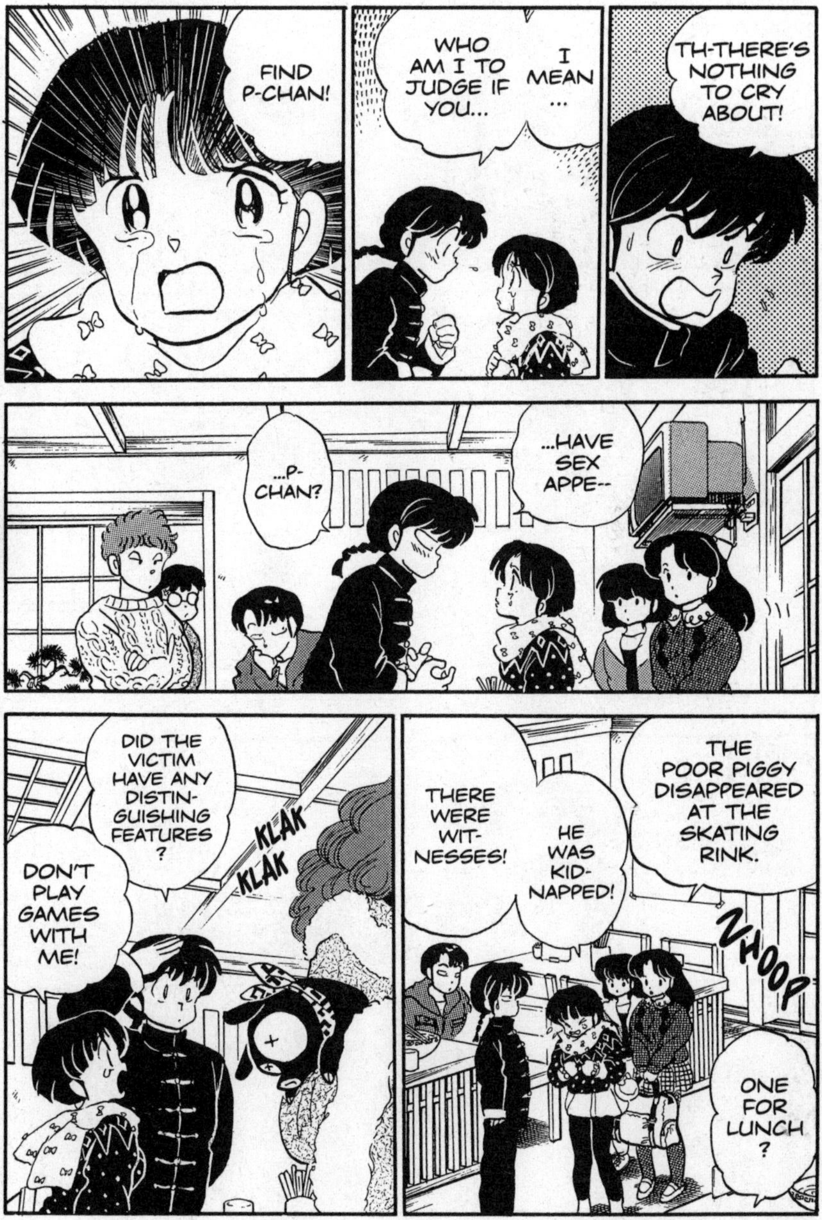
TH-THERE'S NOTHING TO CRY ABOUT!
I MEAN ...
WHO AM I TO JUDGE IF YOU...
FIND P-CHAN!
...HAVE SEX APPE--
...P-CHAN?
THE POOR PIGGY DISAPPEARED AT THE SKATING RINK.
ZHOOP
HE WAS KID-NAPPED!
THERE WERE WIT-NESSES!
ONE FOR LUNCH?
DID THE VICTIM HAVE ANY DISTIN-GUISHING FEATURES?
KLAK KLAK
DON'T PLAY GAMES WITH ME!

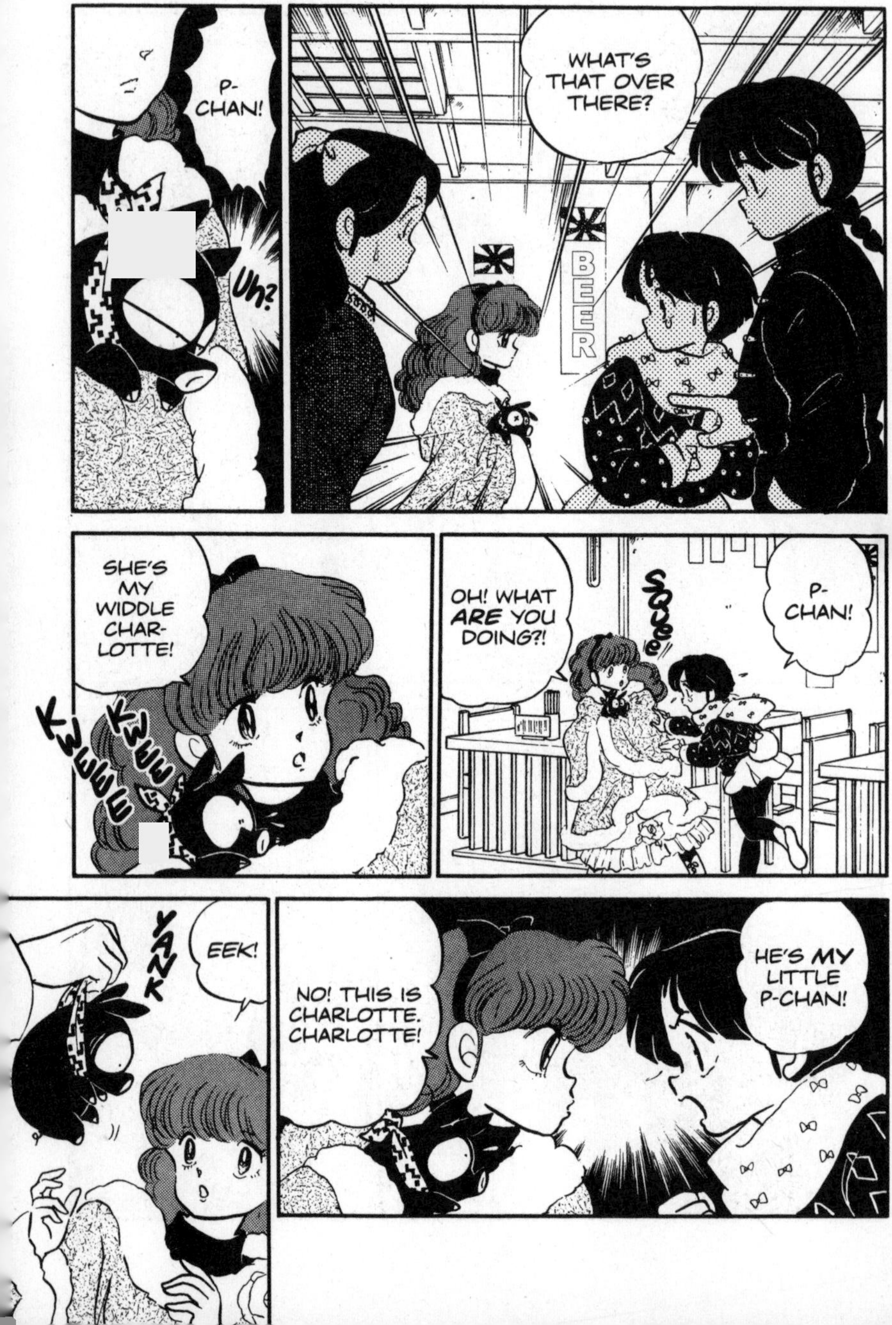
WHAT'S THAT OVER THERE?
Uh?
P-CHAN!
P-CHAN!
SQUEEE
OH! WHAT ARE YOU DOING?!
SHE'S MY WIDDLE CHAR-LOTTE!
KWEE
KWEEEE
HE'S MY LITTLE P-CHAN!
NO! THIS IS CHARLOTTE. CHARLOTTE!
EEK!
YANK

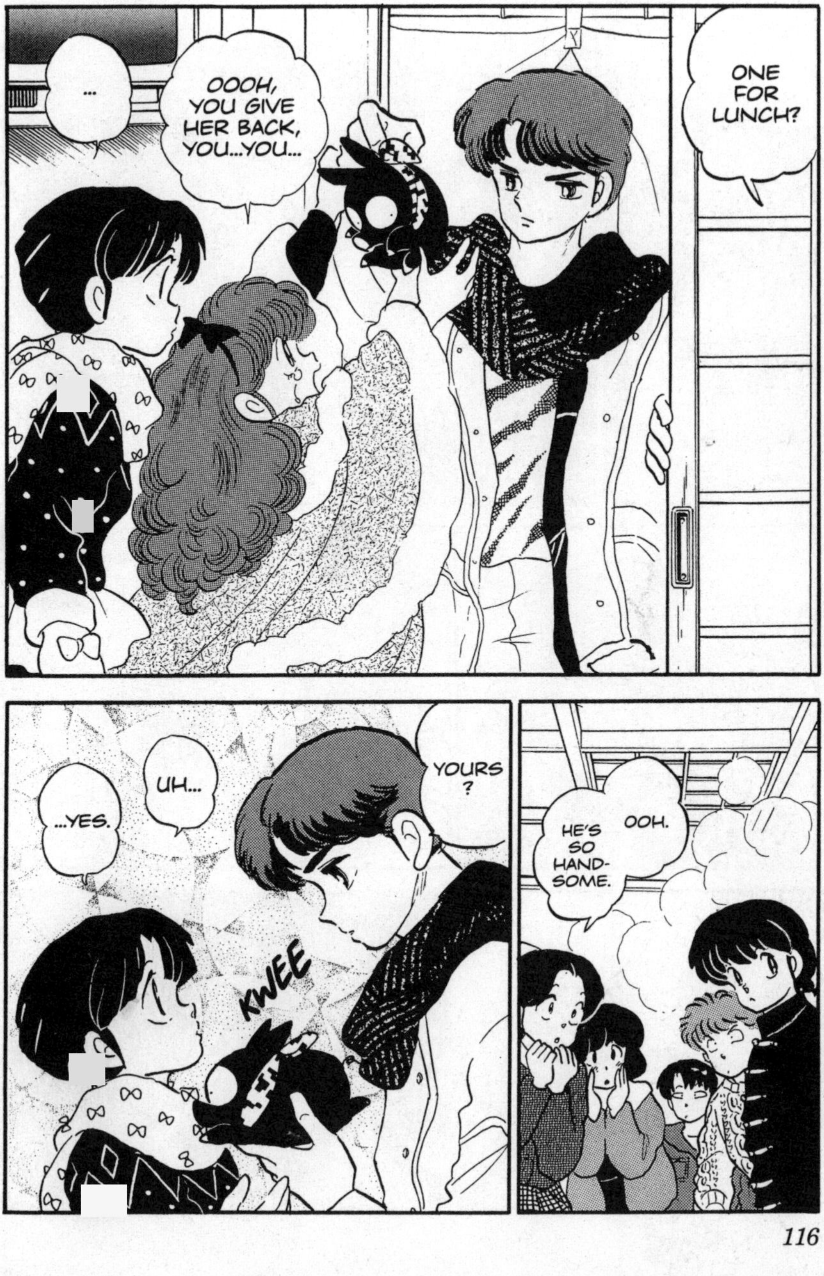
ONE FOR LUNCH?
OOOH, YOU GIVE HER BACK, YOU...YOU...
...
OOH.
HE'S SO HANDSOME.
YOURS?
UH...
...YES.
KWEE

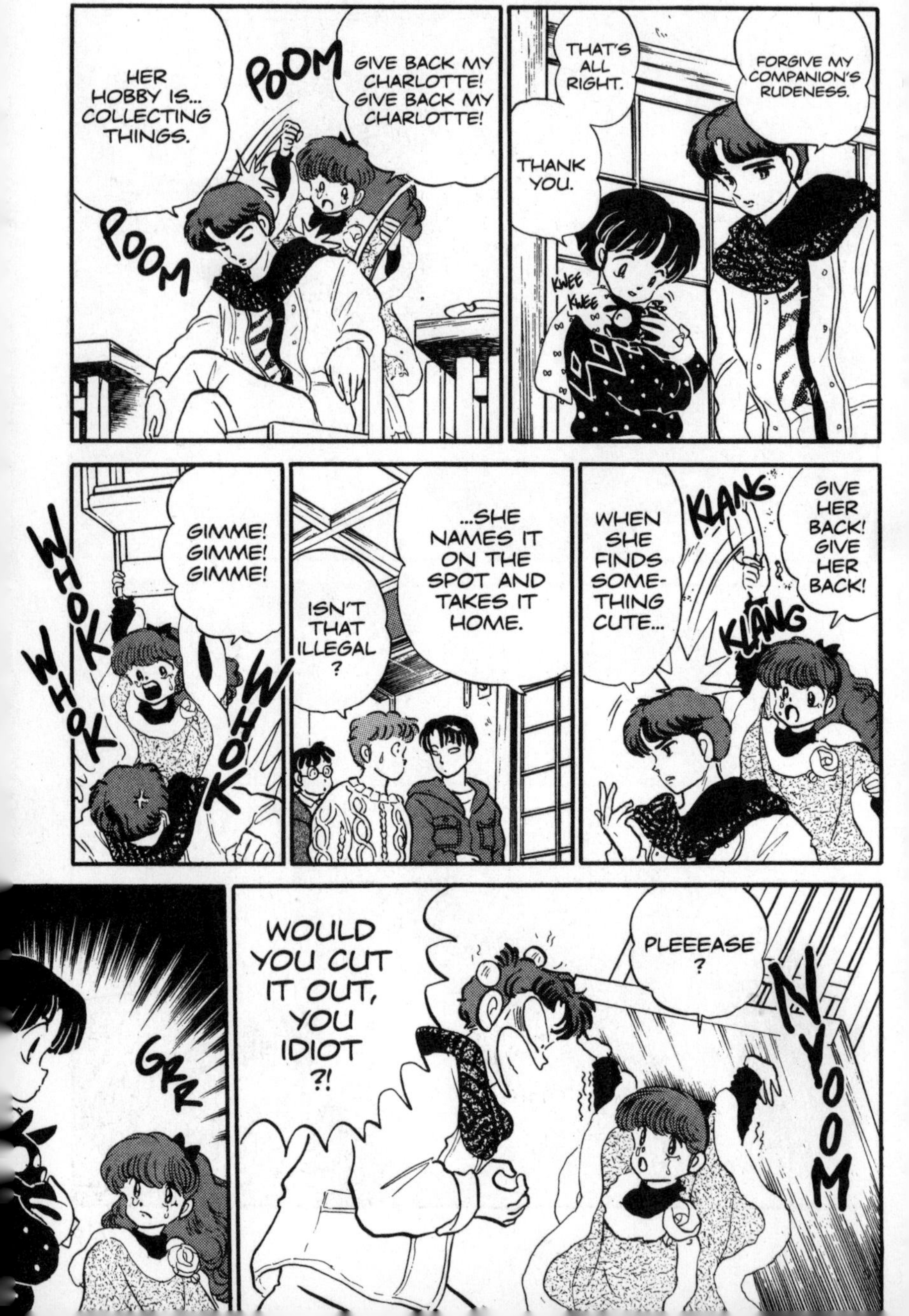
FORGIVE MY COMPANION'S RUDENESS.
THAT'S ALL RIGHT.
THANK YOU.
KWEE KWEE
GIVE BACK MY CHARLOTTE! GIVE BACK MY CHARLOTTE!
POOM
HER HOBBY IS... COLLECTING THINGS.
POOM
GIVE HER BACK! GIVE HER BACK!
KLANG
WHEN SHE FINDS SOME-THING CUTE...
KLANG
...SHE NAMES IT ON THE SPOT AND TAKES IT HOME.
ISN'T THAT ILLEGAL?
GIMME! GIMME! GIMME!
WHOK WHOK
WHOK WHOK
PLEEEASE?
NYOOM
WOULD YOU CUT IT OUT, YOU IDIOT?!
GRR

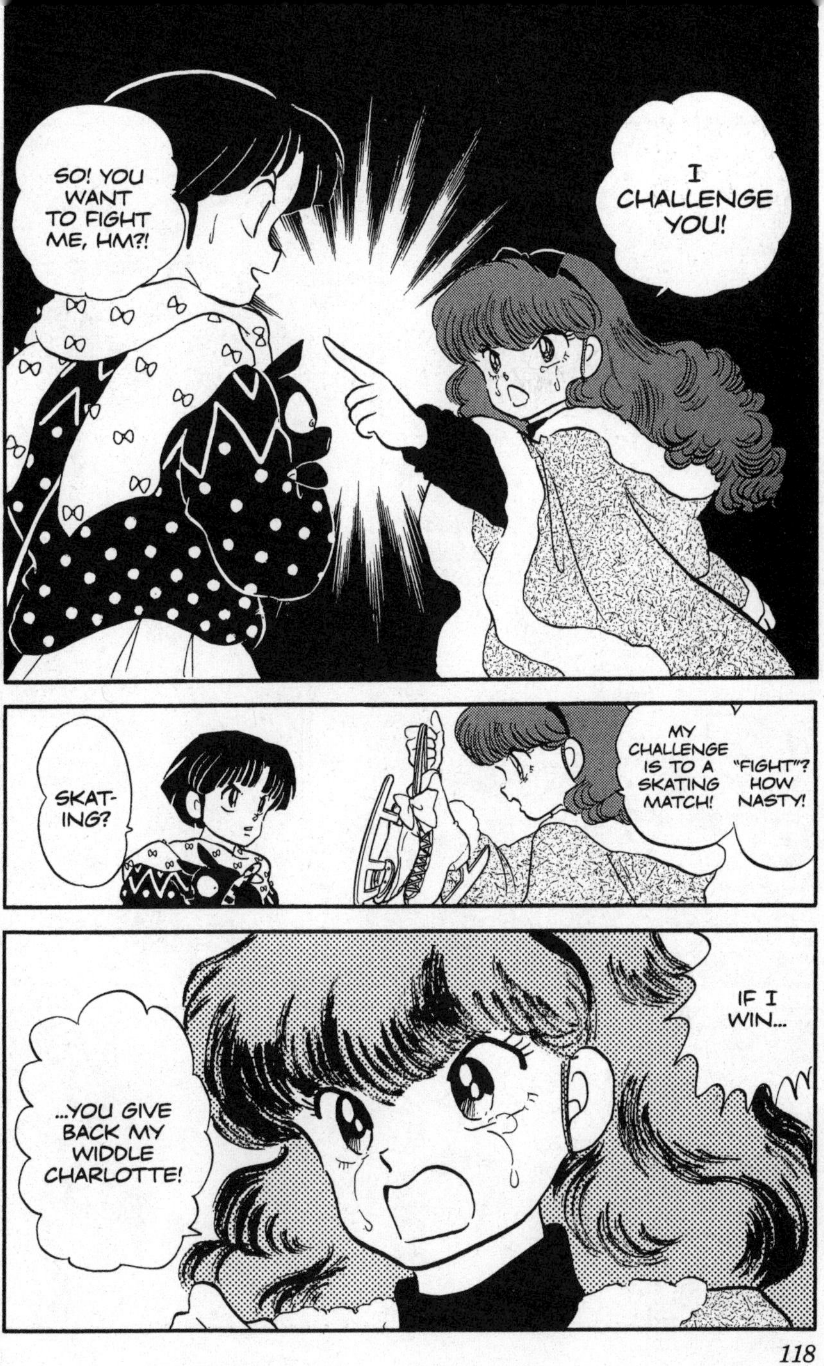
I CHALLENGE YOU!
SO! YOU WANT TO FIGHT ME, HM?!
"FIGHT"? HOW NASTY!
MY CHALLENGE IS TO A SKATING MATCH!
SKAT-ING?
IF I WIN...
...YOU GIVE BACK MY WIDDLE CHARLOTTE!

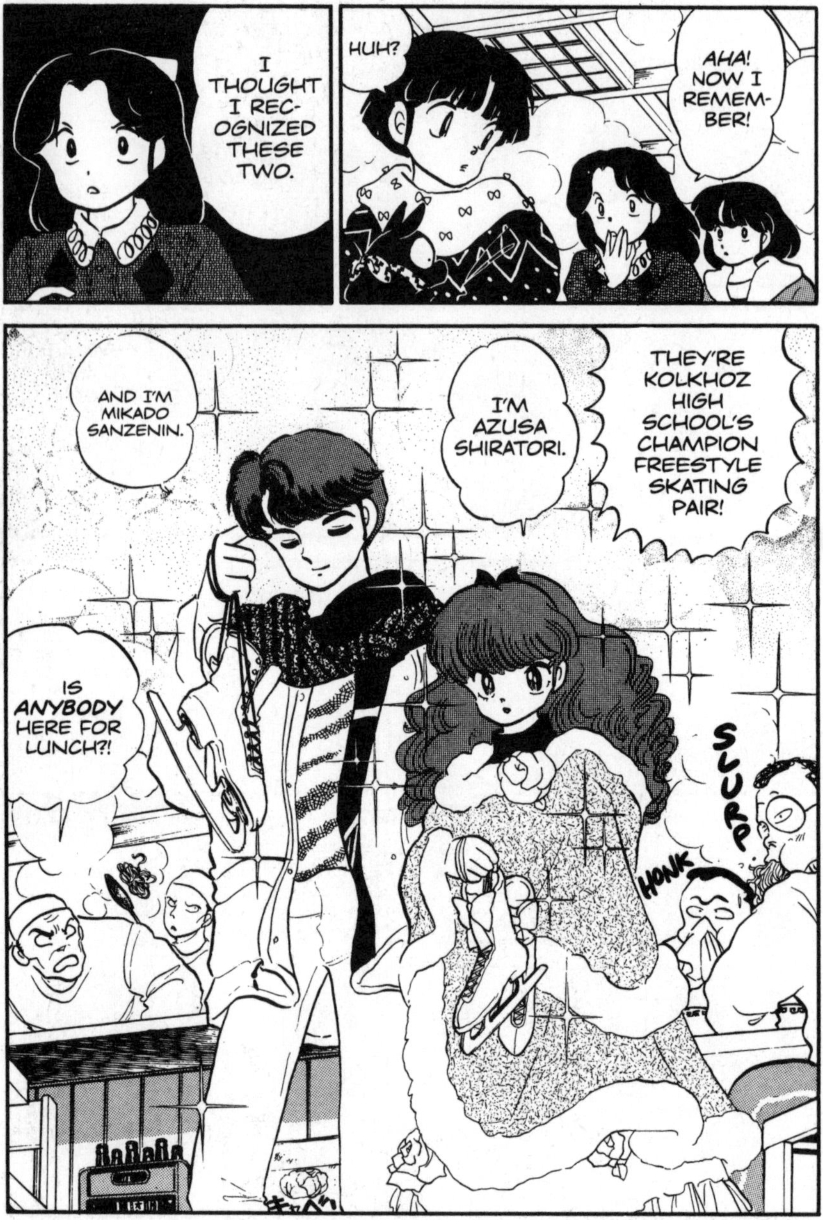
AHA! NOW I REMEMBER!
HUH?
I THOUGHT I RECOGNIZED THESE TWO.
THEY'RE KOLKHOZ HIGH SCHOOL'S CHAMPION FREESTYLE SKATING PAIR!
I'M AZUSA SHIRATORI.
AND I'M MIKADO SANZENIN.
SLURP
HONK
IS ANYBODY HERE FOR LUNCH?!

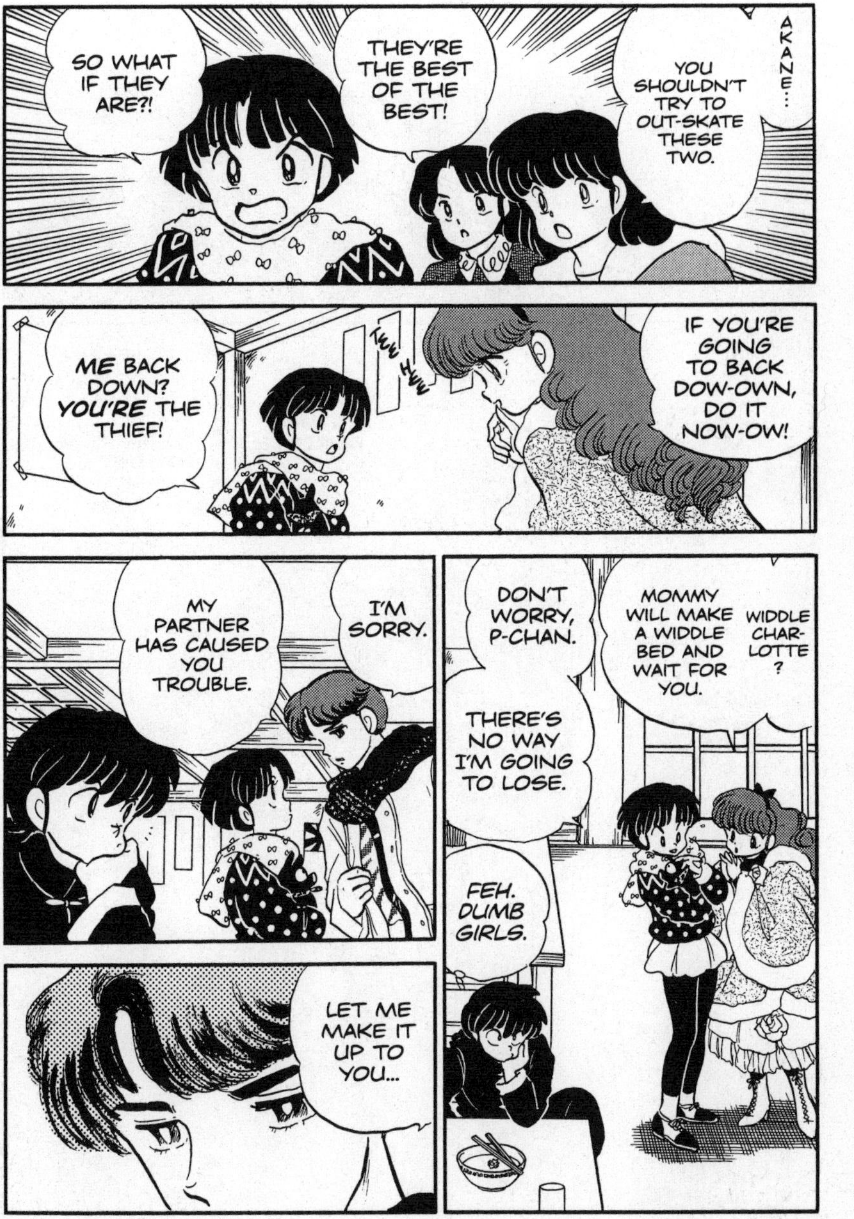
AKANE...
YOU SHOULDN'T TRY TO OUT-SKATE THESE TWO.
THEY'RE THE BEST OF THE BEST!
SO WHAT IF THEY ARE?!
IF YOU'RE GOING TO BACK DOW-OWN, DO IT NOW-OW!
HEE HEE
ME BACK DOWN? *YOU'RE* THE THIEF!
WIDDLE CHAR-LOTTE ?
MOMMY WILL MAKE A WIDDLE BED AND WAIT FOR YOU.
DON'T WORRY, P-CHAN.
THERE'S NO WAY I'M GOING TO LOSE.
FEH. DUMB GIRLS.
I'M SORRY.
MY PARTNER HAS CAUSED YOU TROUBLE.
LET ME MAKE IT UP TO YOU...

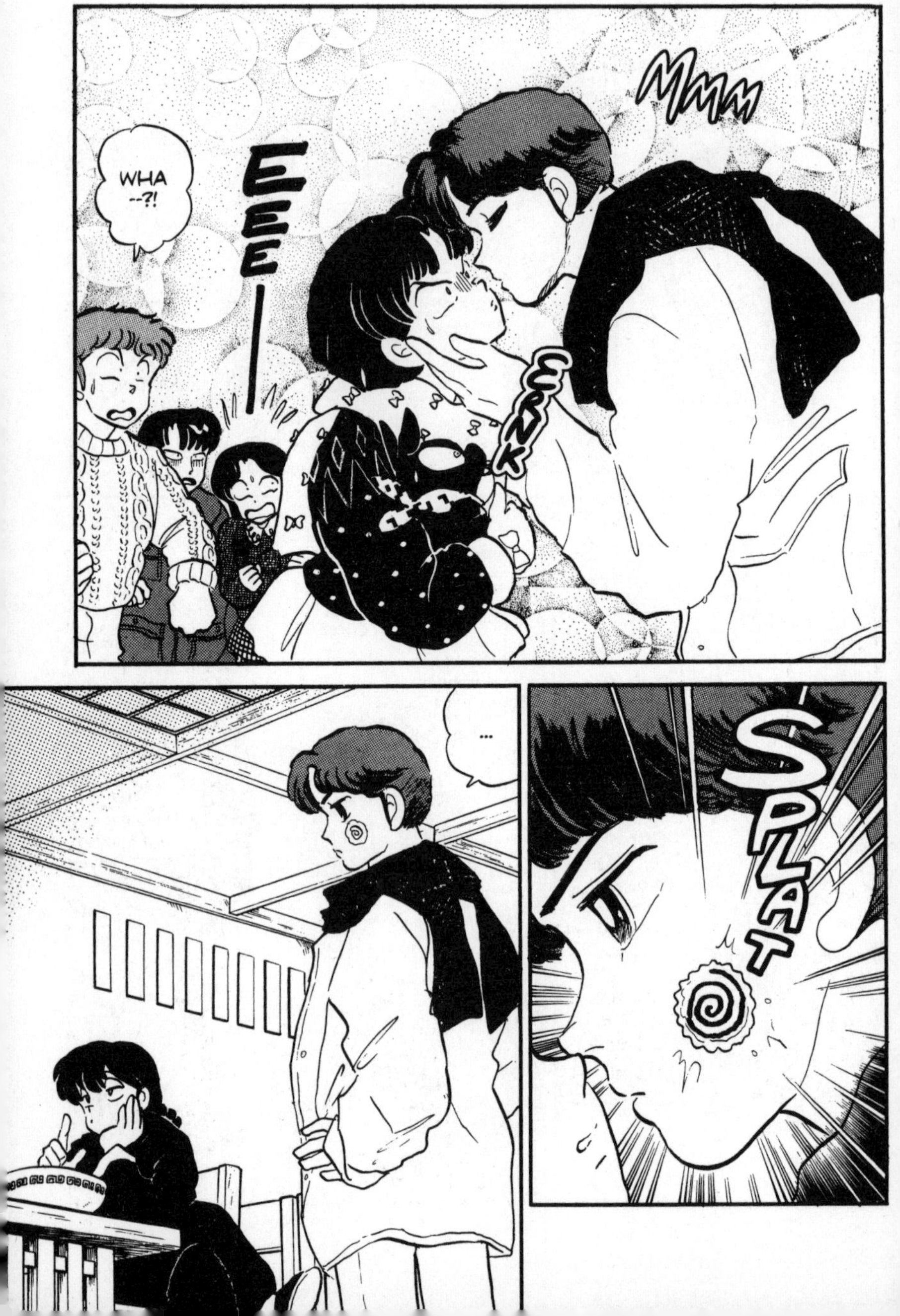
MMM
EENK
EEE—
WHA --?!
SPLAT
...

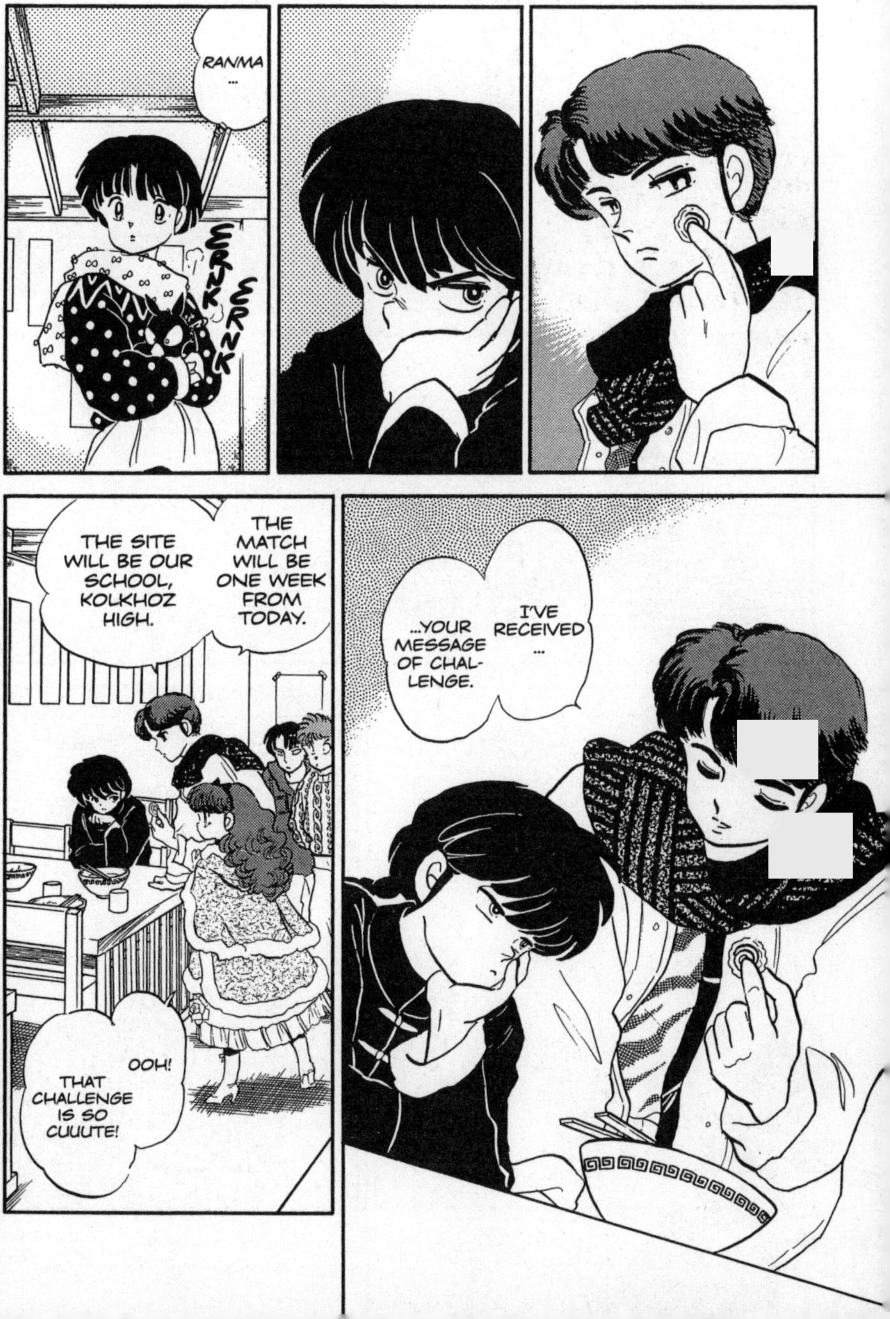
RANMA ...
ERNK ERNK
I'VE RECEIVED ...
...YOUR MESSAGE OF CHAL-LENGE.
THE MATCH WILL BE ONE WEEK FROM TODAY.
THE SITE WILL BE OUR SCHOOL, KOLKHOZ HIGH.
OOH!
THAT CHALLENGE IS SO CUUUTE!

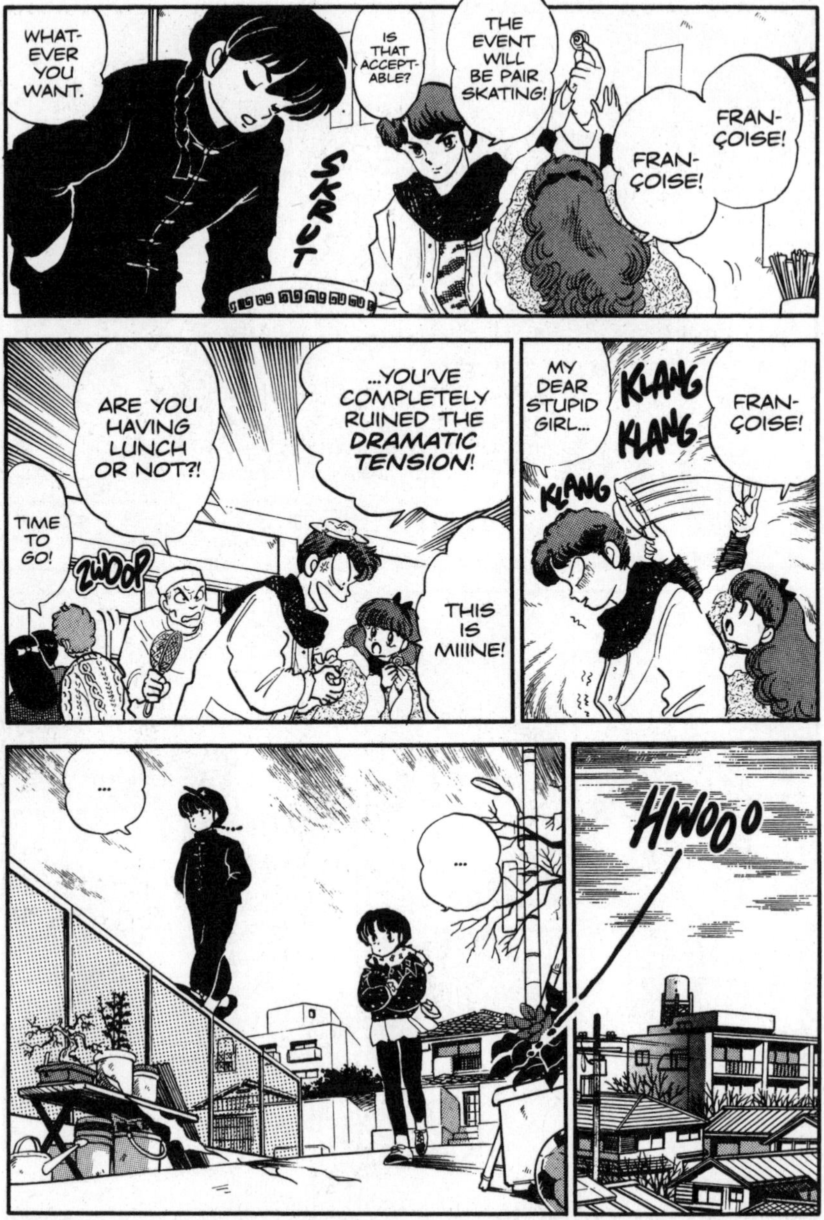
FRANÇOISE!
FRANÇOISE!
THE EVENT WILL BE PAIR SKATING!
IS THAT ACCEPTABLE?
WHATEVER YOU WANT.
SKRUT
FRANÇOISE!
KLANG
KLANG
MY DEAR STUPID GIRL...
KLANG
...YOU'VE COMPLETELY RUINED THE DRAMATIC TENSION!
ARE YOU HAVING LUNCH OR NOT?!
TIME TO GO!
ZWOOP
THIS IS MIIINE!
HWOOO
...
...

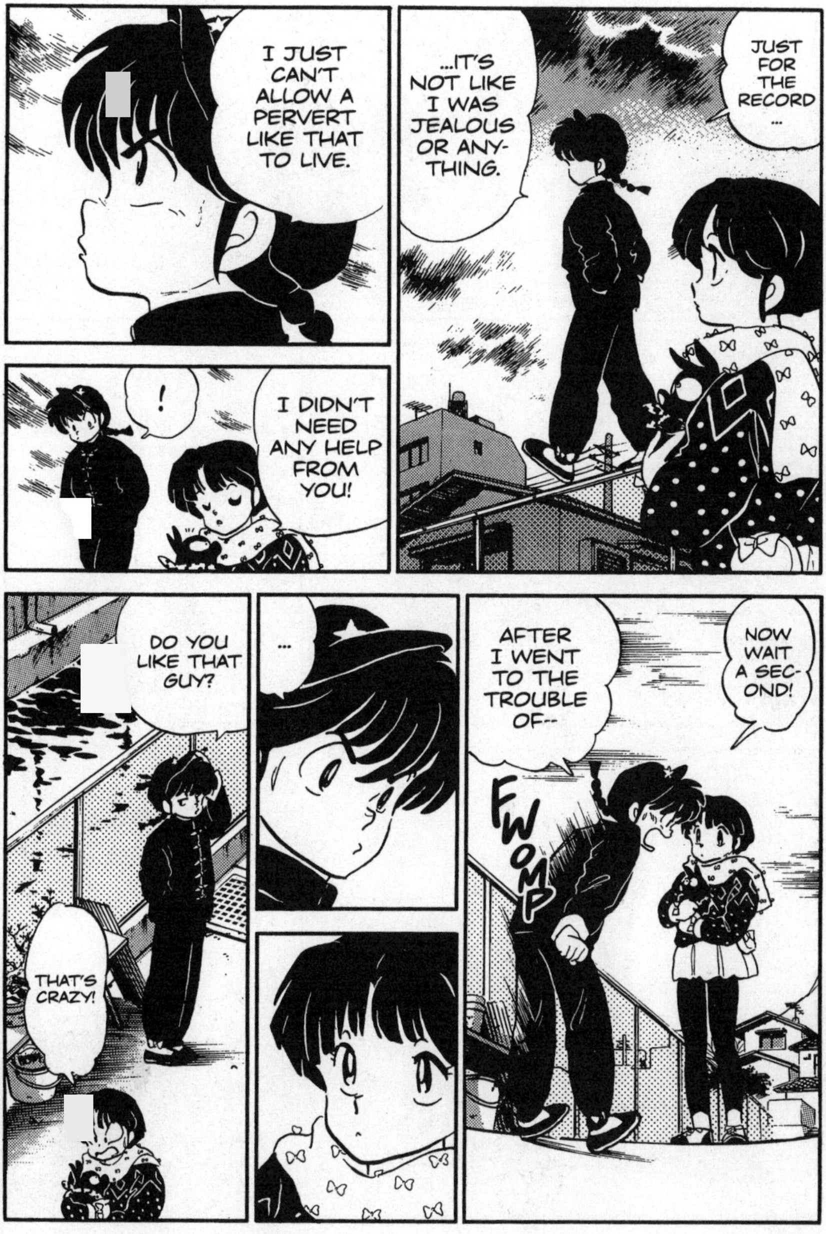

JUST FOR THE RECORD...
...IT'S NOT LIKE I WAS JEALOUS OR ANYTHING.
I JUST CAN'T ALLOW A PERVERT LIKE THAT TO LIVE.
I DIDN'T NEED ANY HELP FROM YOU!
!
NOW WAIT A SECOND!
AFTER I WENT TO THE TROUBLE OF--
FWOMP
...
DO YOU LIKE THAT GUY?
THAT'S CRAZY!

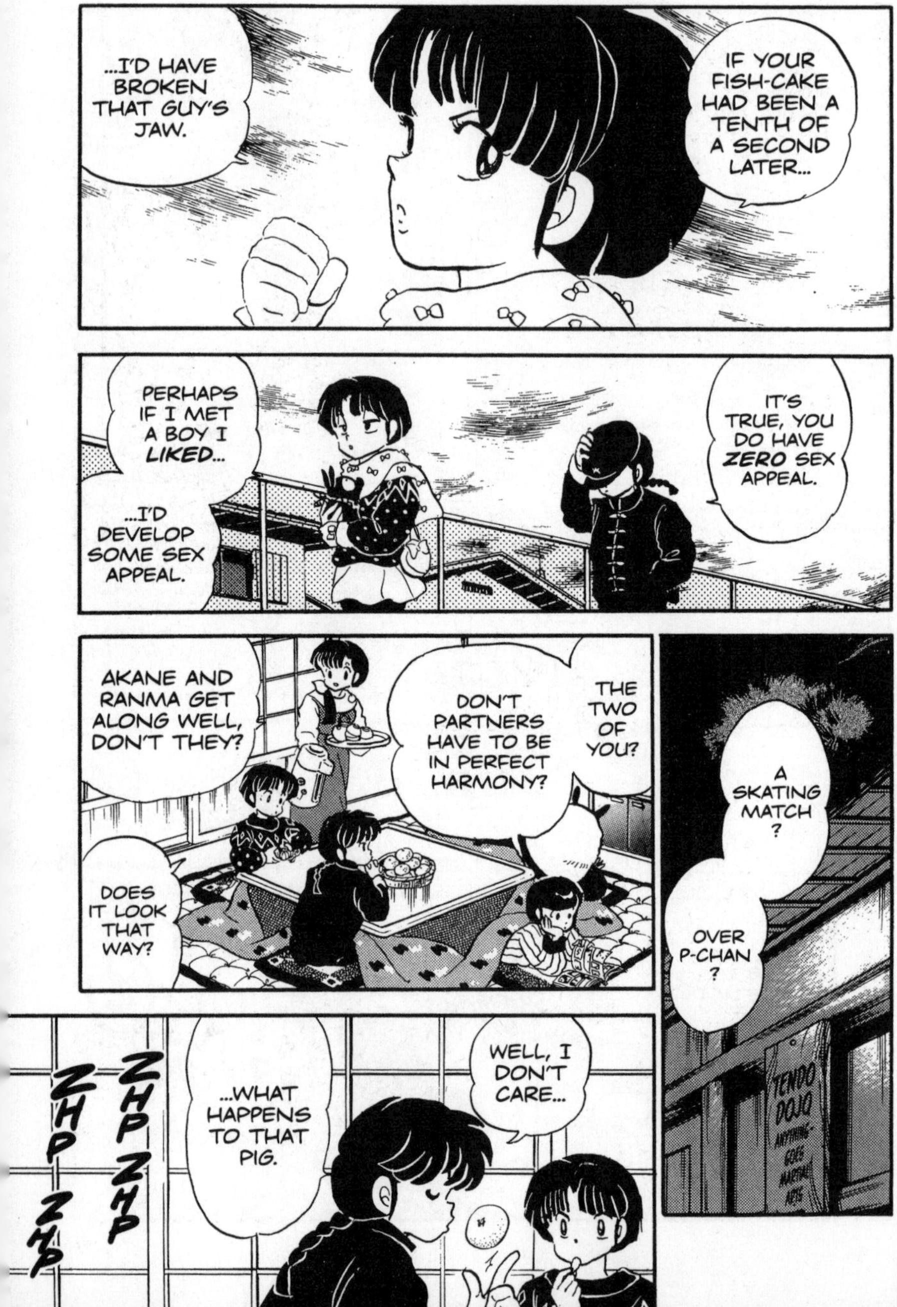
IF YOUR FISH-CAKE HAD BEEN A TENTH OF A SECOND LATER...
...I'D HAVE BROKEN THAT GUY'S JAW.
IT'S TRUE, YOU DO HAVE **ZERO** SEX APPEAL.
PERHAPS IF I MET A BOY I **LIKED**...
...I'D DEVELOP SOME SEX APPEAL.
TENDO DOJO ANYTHING-GOES MARTIAL ARTS
A SKATING MATCH?
OVER P-CHAN?
THE TWO OF YOU?
DON'T PARTNERS HAVE TO BE IN PERFECT HARMONY?
AKANE AND RANMA GET ALONG WELL, DON'T THEY?
DOES IT LOOK THAT WAY?
WELL, I DON'T CARE...
...WHAT HAPPENS TO THAT PIG.
ZHP ZHP ZHP
ZHP ZHP

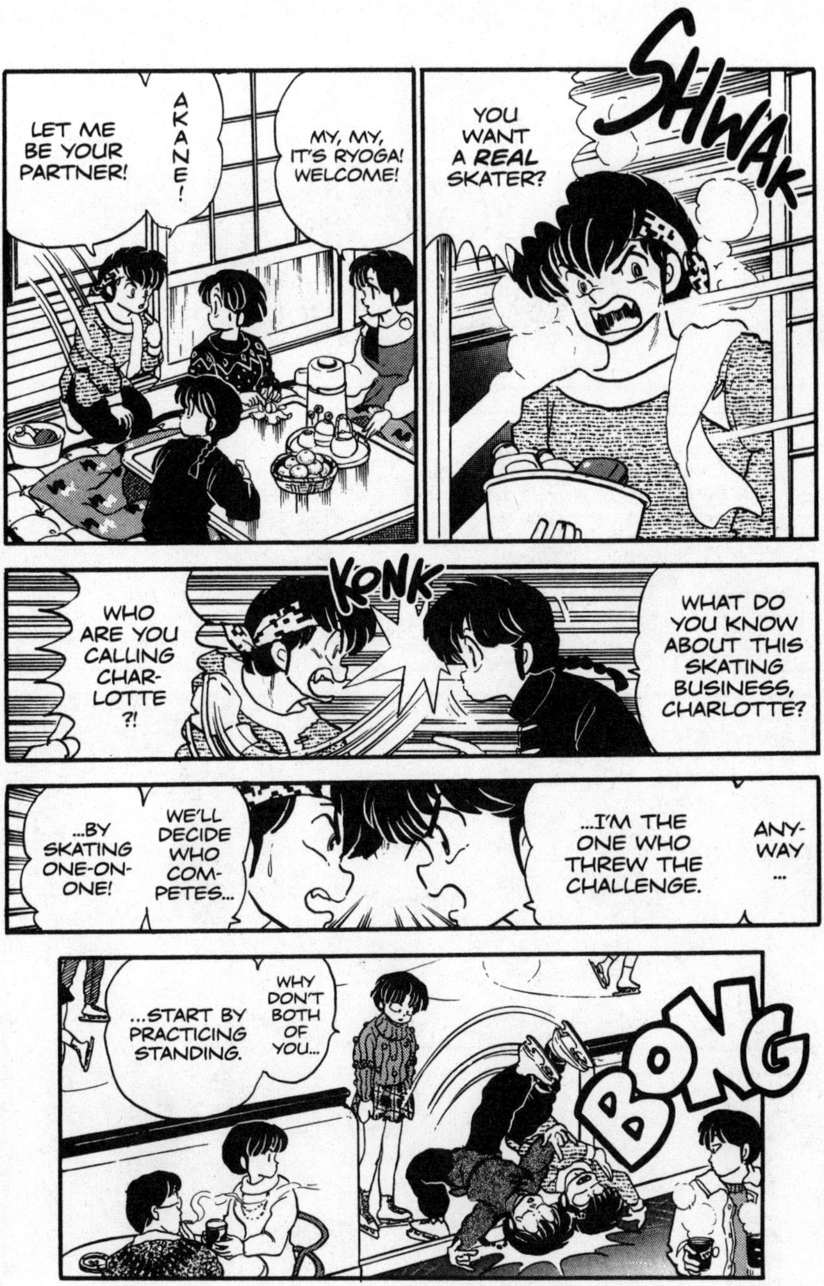
SHWAK
YOU WANT A REAL SKATER?
MY, MY, IT'S RYOGA! WELCOME!
AKANE!
LET ME BE YOUR PARTNER!
WHAT DO YOU KNOW ABOUT THIS SKATING BUSINESS, CHARLOTTE?
KONK
WHO ARE YOU CALLING CHAR-LOTTE ?!
ANY-WAY ...
...I'M THE ONE WHO THREW THE CHALLENGE.
WE'LL DECIDE WHO COM-PETES...
...BY SKATING ONE-ON-ONE!
BONG
WHY DON'T BOTH OF YOU...
...START BY PRACTICING STANDING.

PART 7
A KISS IN THE RINK

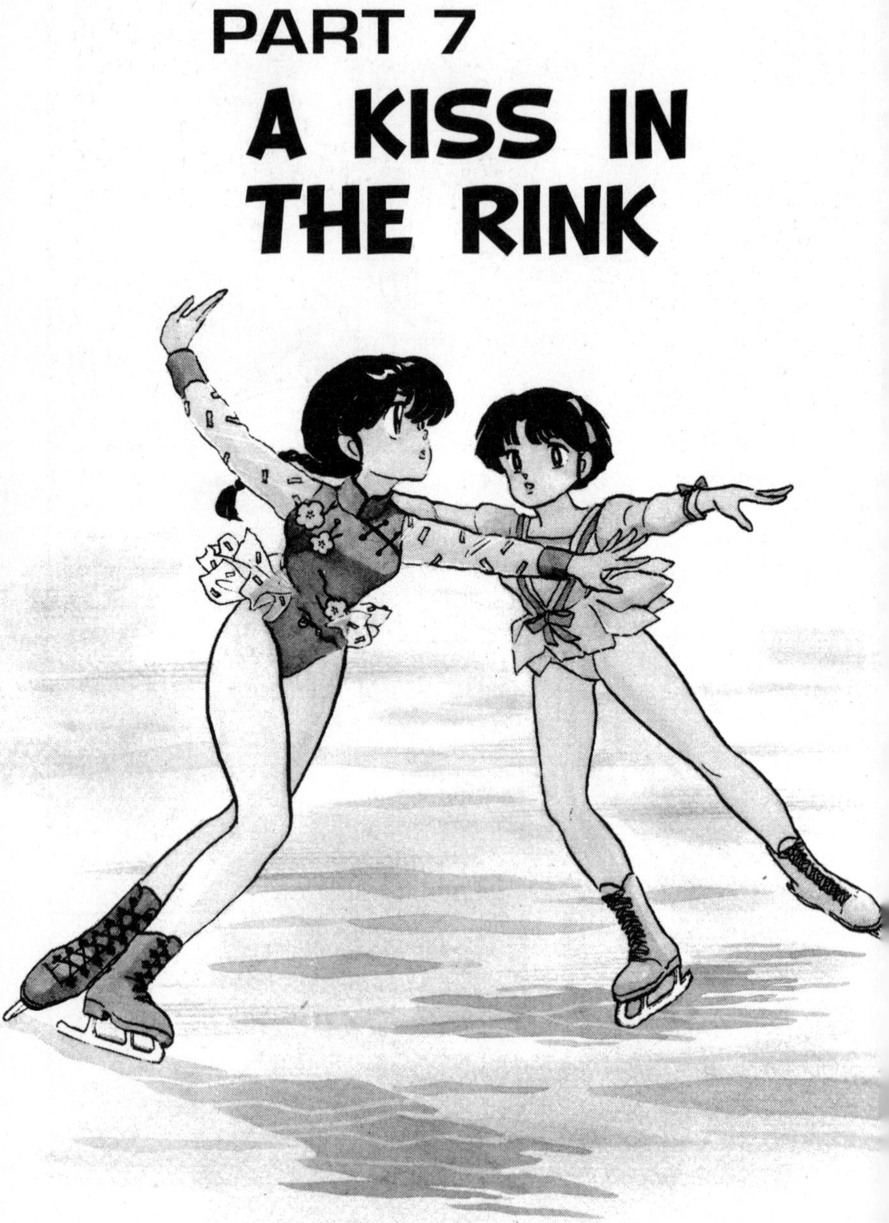

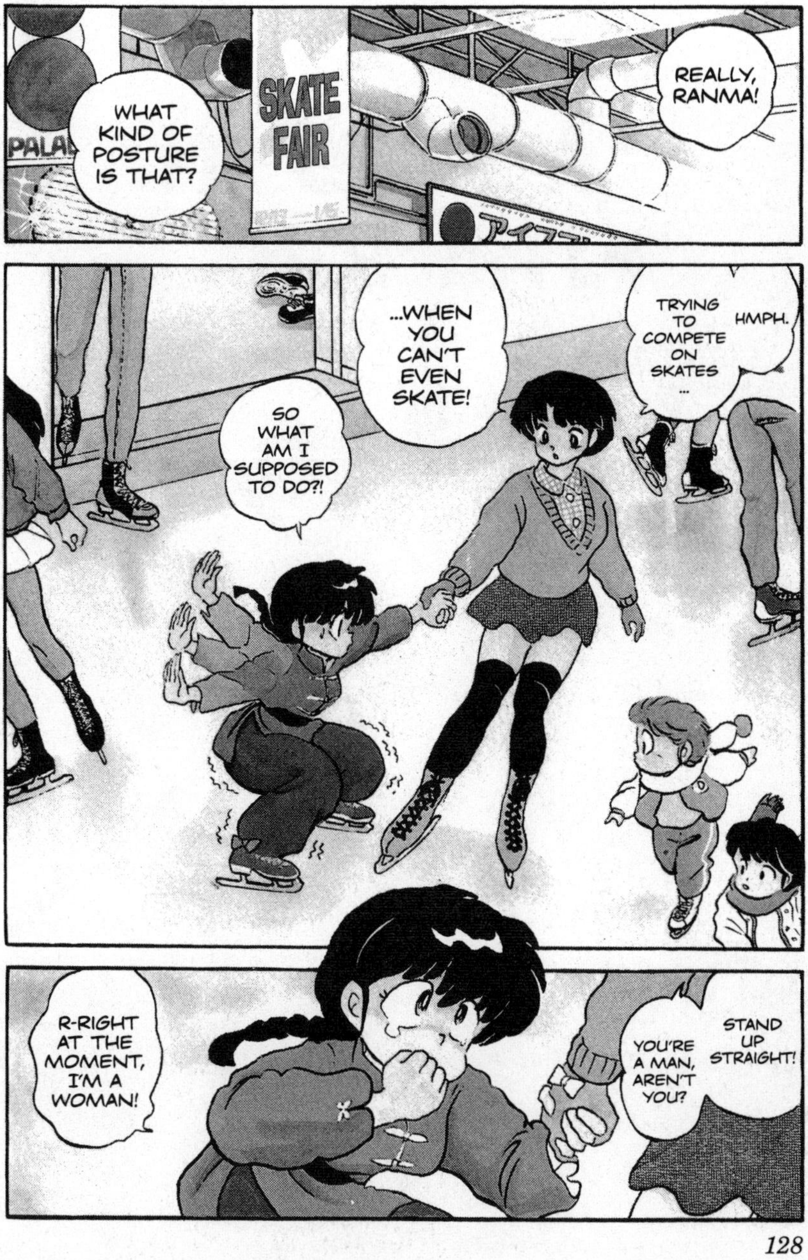
REALLY, RANMA!
SKATE FAIR
WHAT KIND OF POSTURE IS THAT?
HMPH.
TRYING TO COMPETE ON SKATES ...
...WHEN YOU CAN'T EVEN SKATE!
SO WHAT AM I SUPPOSED TO DO?!
STAND UP STRAIGHT!
YOU'RE A MAN, AREN'T YOU?
R-RIGHT AT THE MOMENT, I'M A WOMAN!

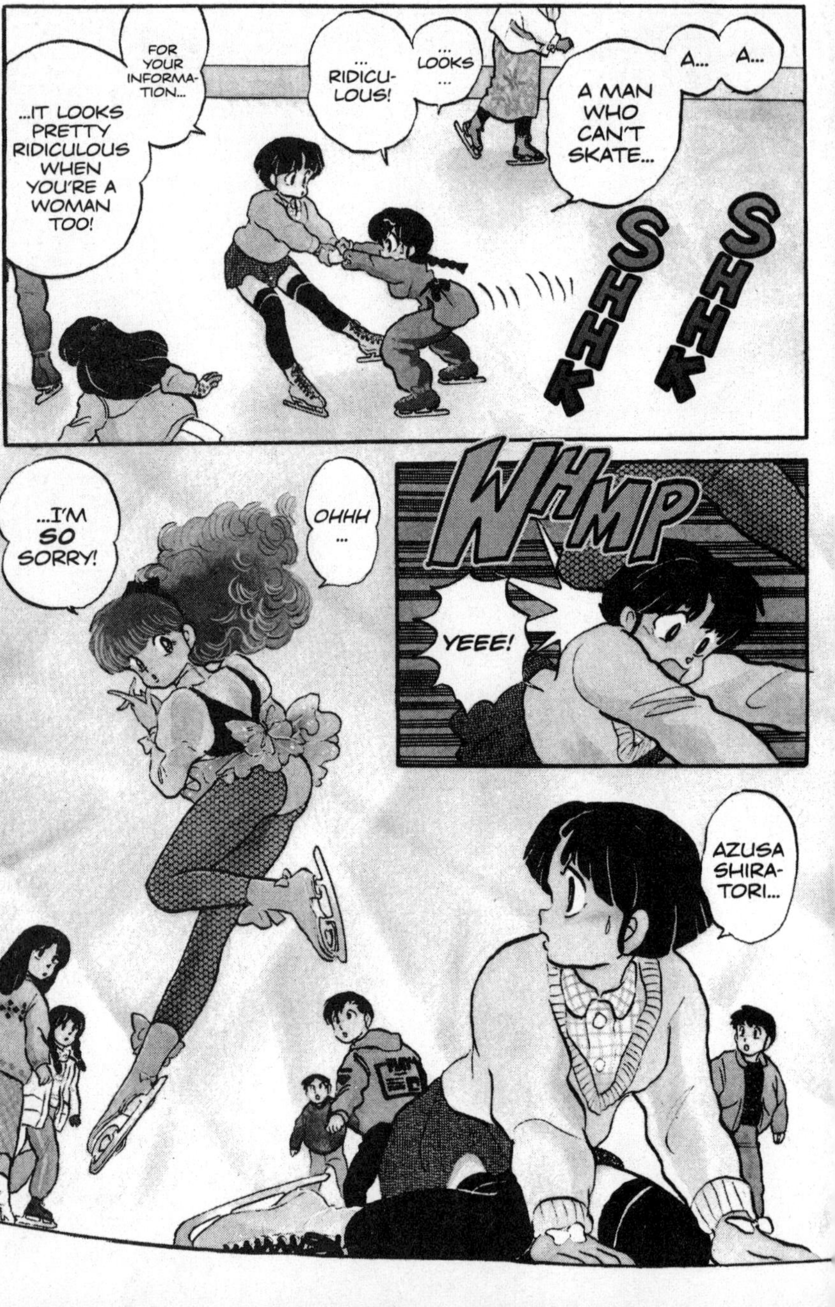
A... A...
A MAN WHO CAN'T SKATE...
...LOOKS...
...RIDICULOUS!
FOR YOUR INFORMATION...
...IT LOOKS PRETTY RIDICULOUS WHEN YOU'RE A WOMAN TOO!
SHHHK
SHHHK
WHMP
YEEE!
OHHH...
...I'M SO SORRY!
AZUSA SHIRATORI...

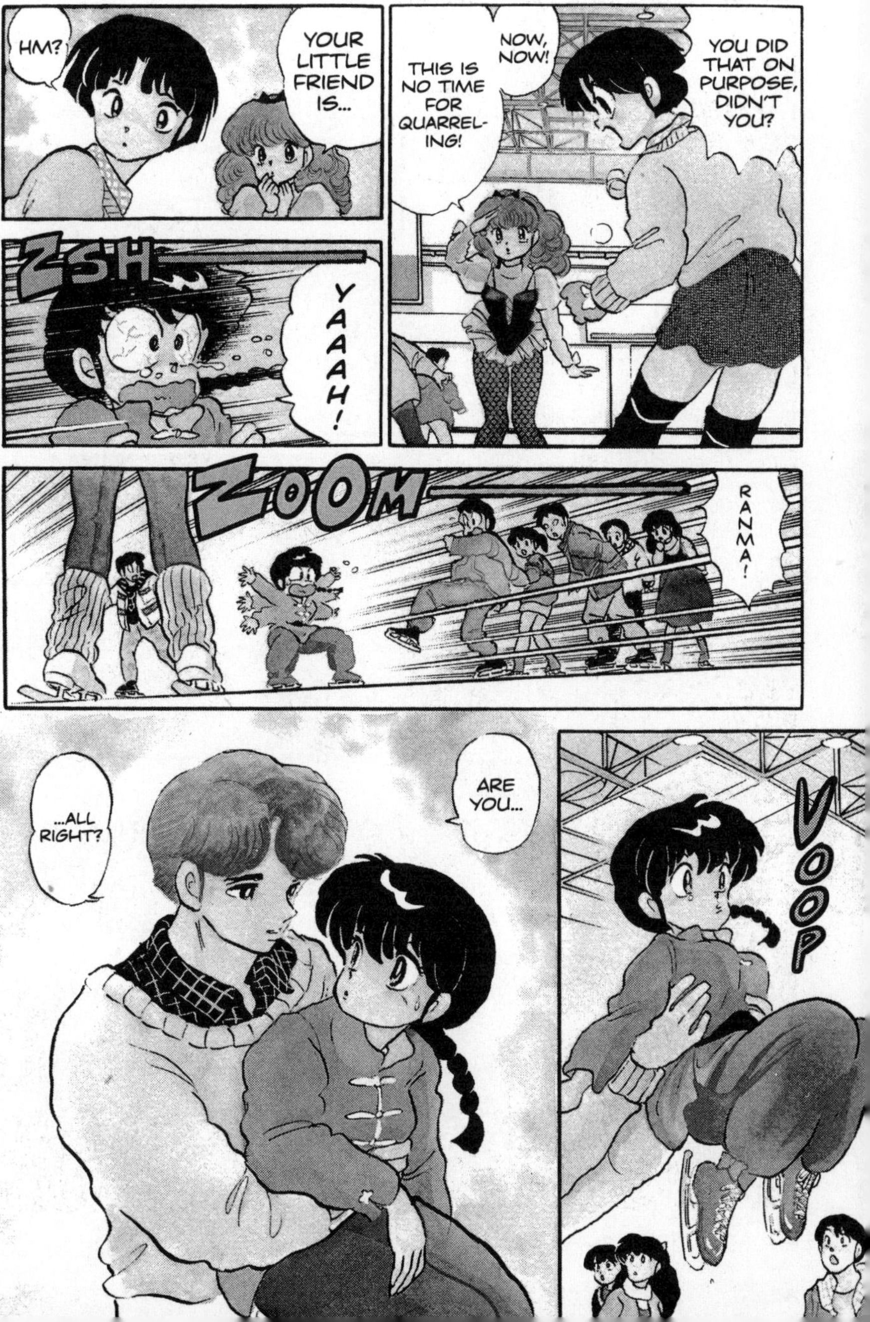
YOU DID THAT ON PURPOSE, DIDN'T YOU?
NOW, NOW!
THIS IS NO TIME FOR QUARREL-ING!
YOUR LITTLE FRIEND IS...
HM?
YAAAAH!
ZSH
RANMA!
ZOOM
VOOP
ARE YOU...
...ALL RIGHT?

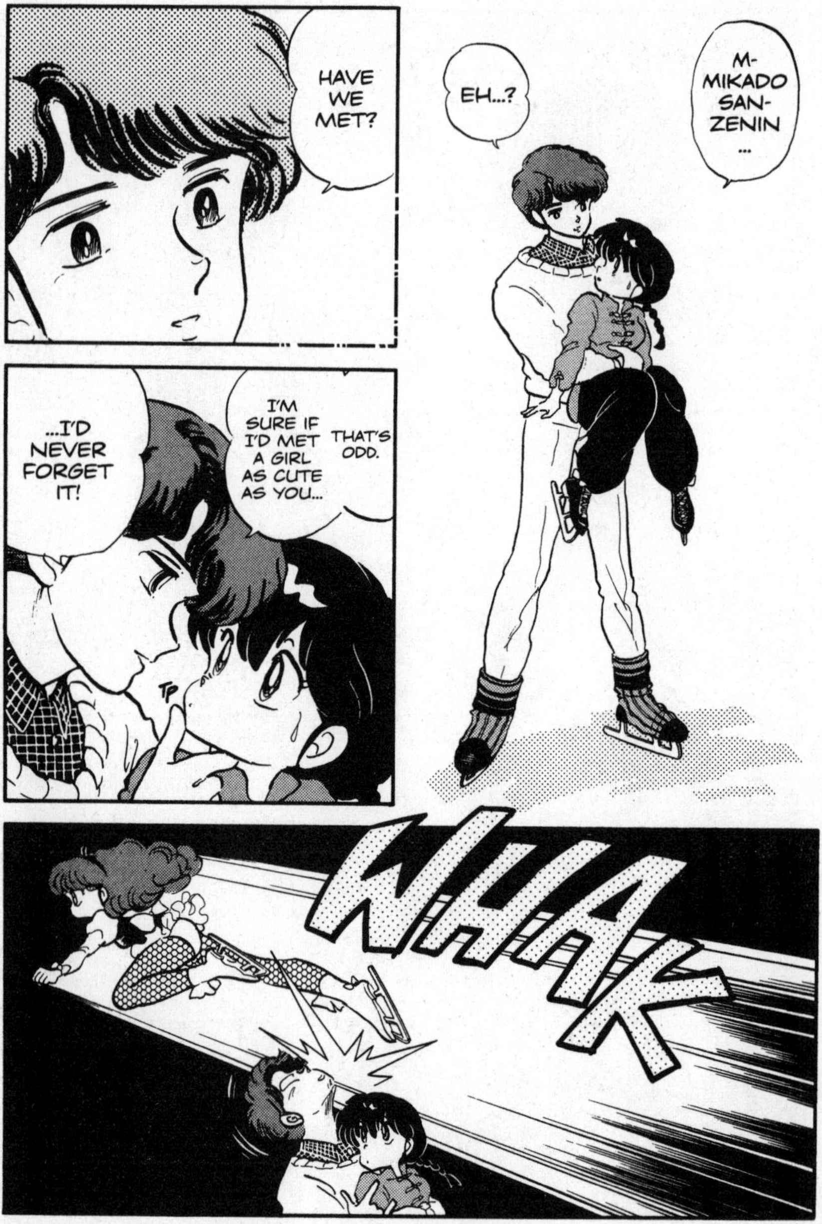
M-MIKADO SAN-ZENIN ...
EH...?
HAVE WE MET?
THAT'S ODD.
I'M SURE IF I'D MET A GIRL AS CUTE AS YOU...
...I'D NEVER FORGET IT!
TP
WHAK

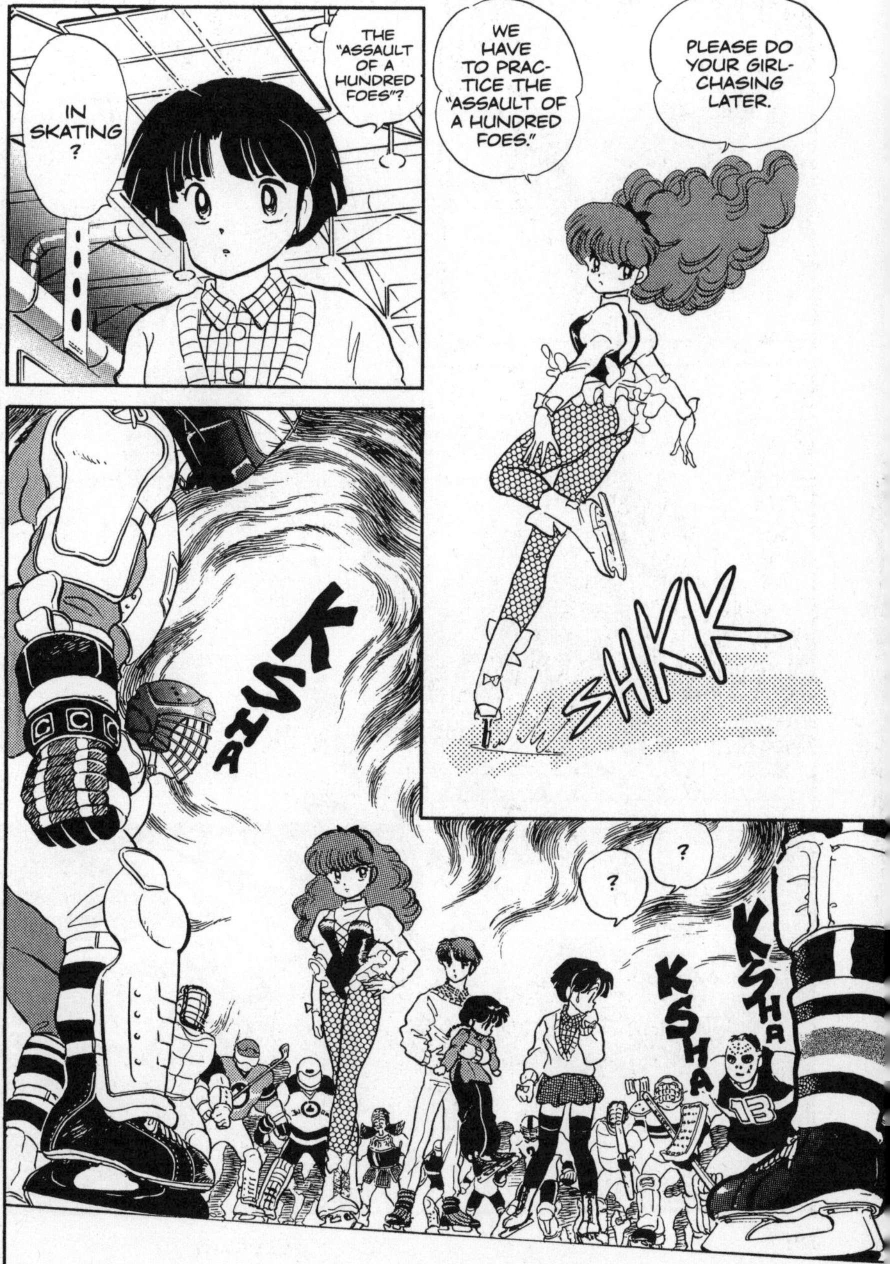
PLEASE DO YOUR GIRL-CHASING LATER.
WE HAVE TO PRACTICE THE "ASSAULT OF A HUNDRED FOES."
SHKK
THE "ASSAULT OF A HUNDRED FOES"?
IN SKATING?
....
KSHA
?
?
KSHA
KSHA

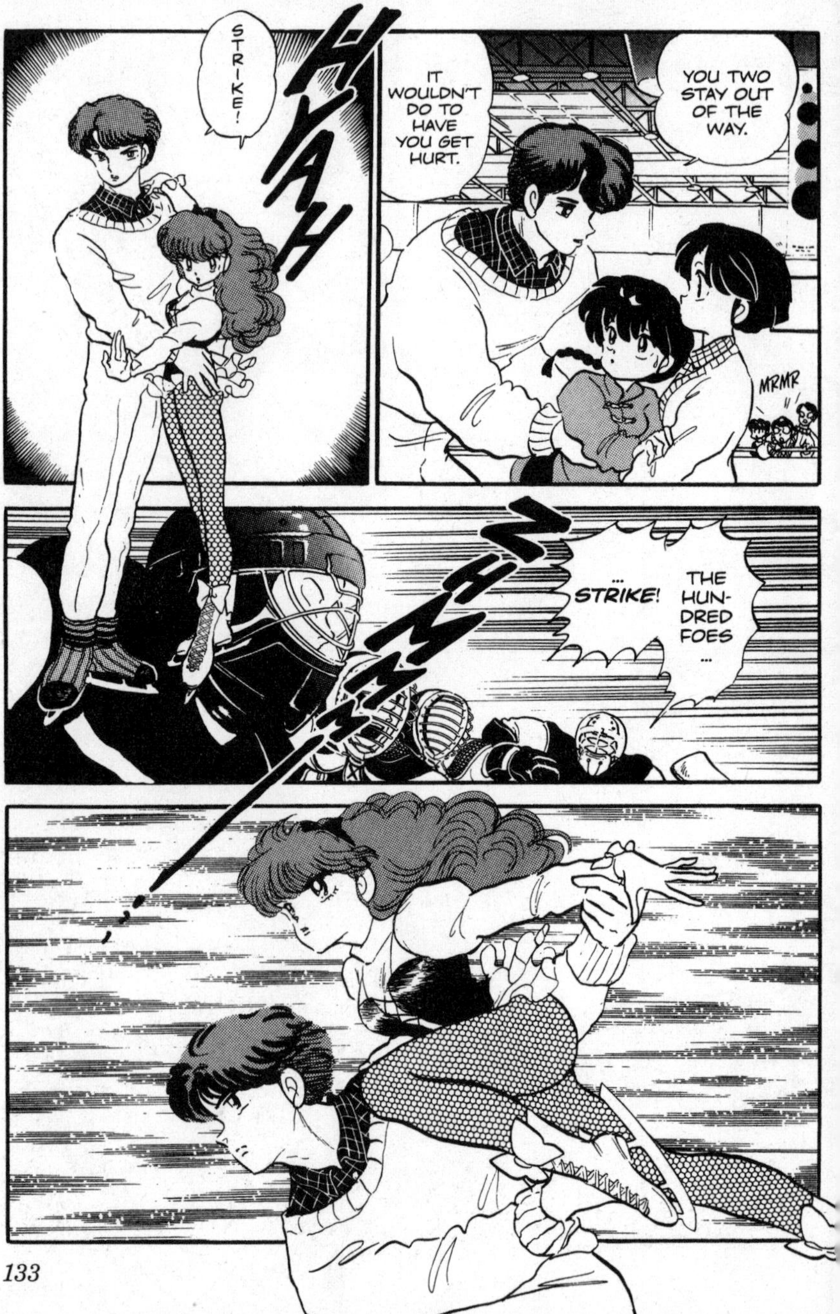
YOU TWO STAY OUT OF THE WAY.
IT WOULDN'T DO TO HAVE YOU GET HURT.
MRMR
STRIKE!
HYAH
THE HUNDRED FOES...
...STRIKE!
ZHMMMM

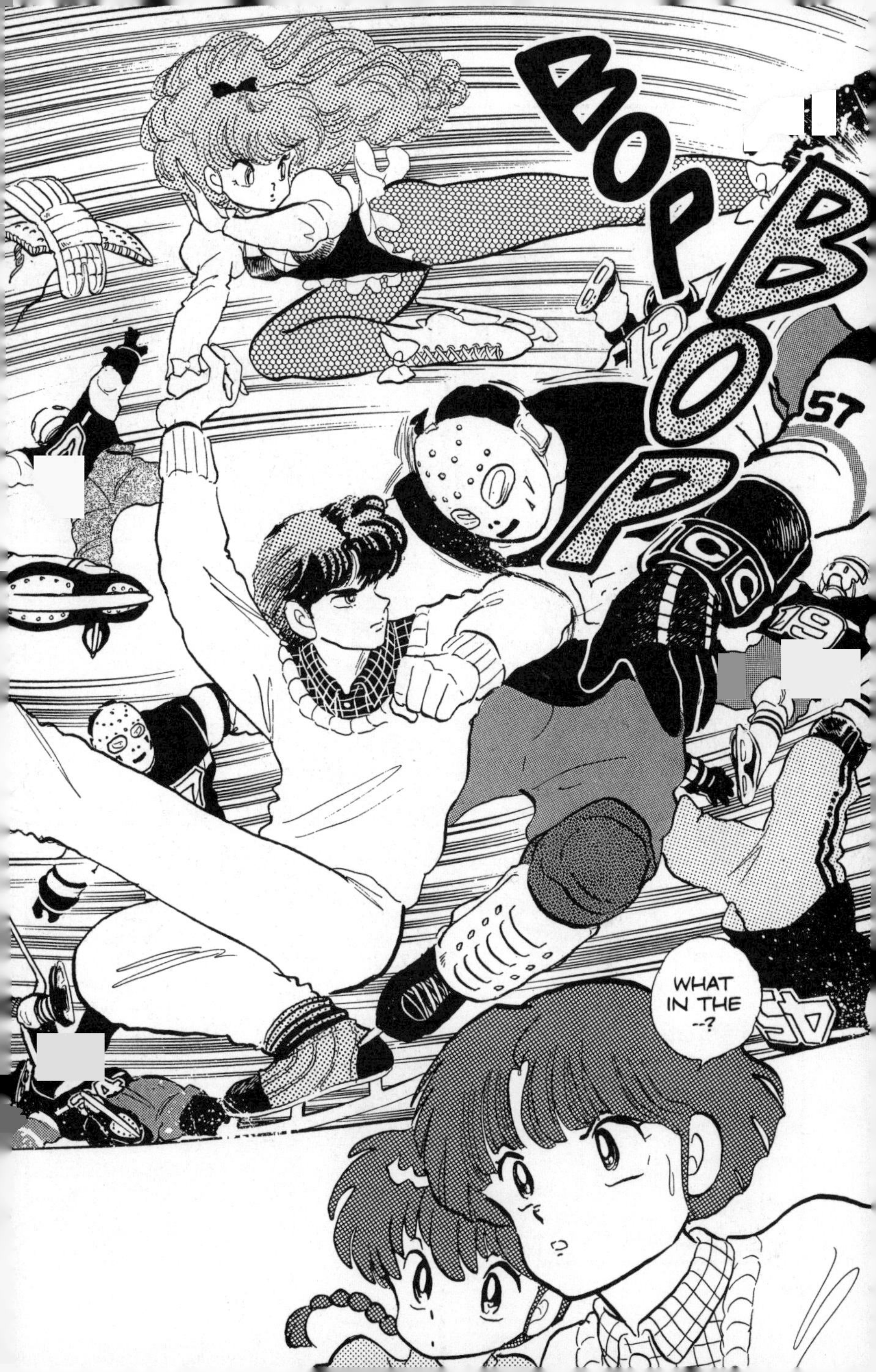
BOP
BOP
WHAT IN THE --?

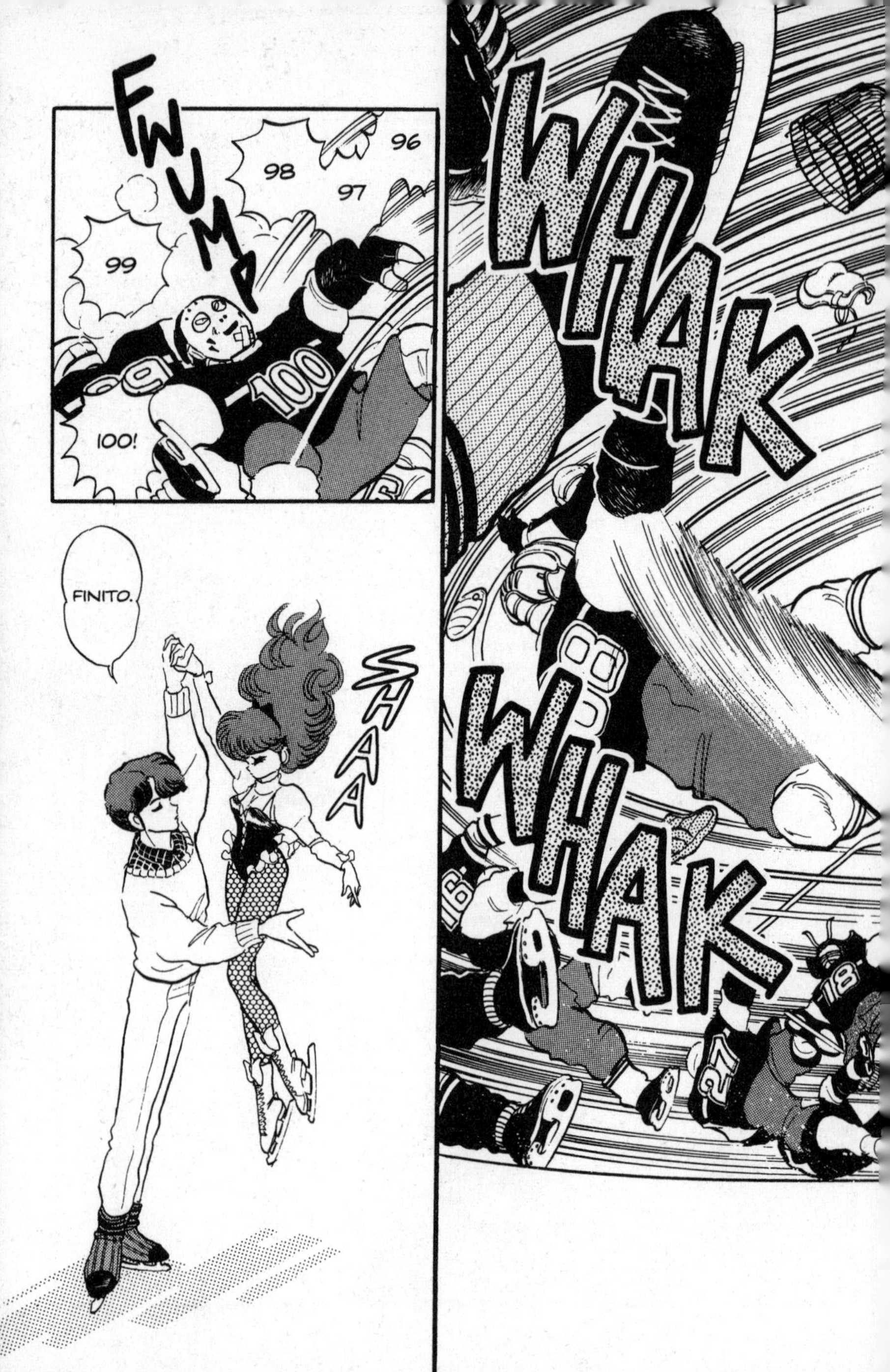
WHAK
WHAK
96
98
97
FWUMP
99
100!
FINITO.
SHAAA

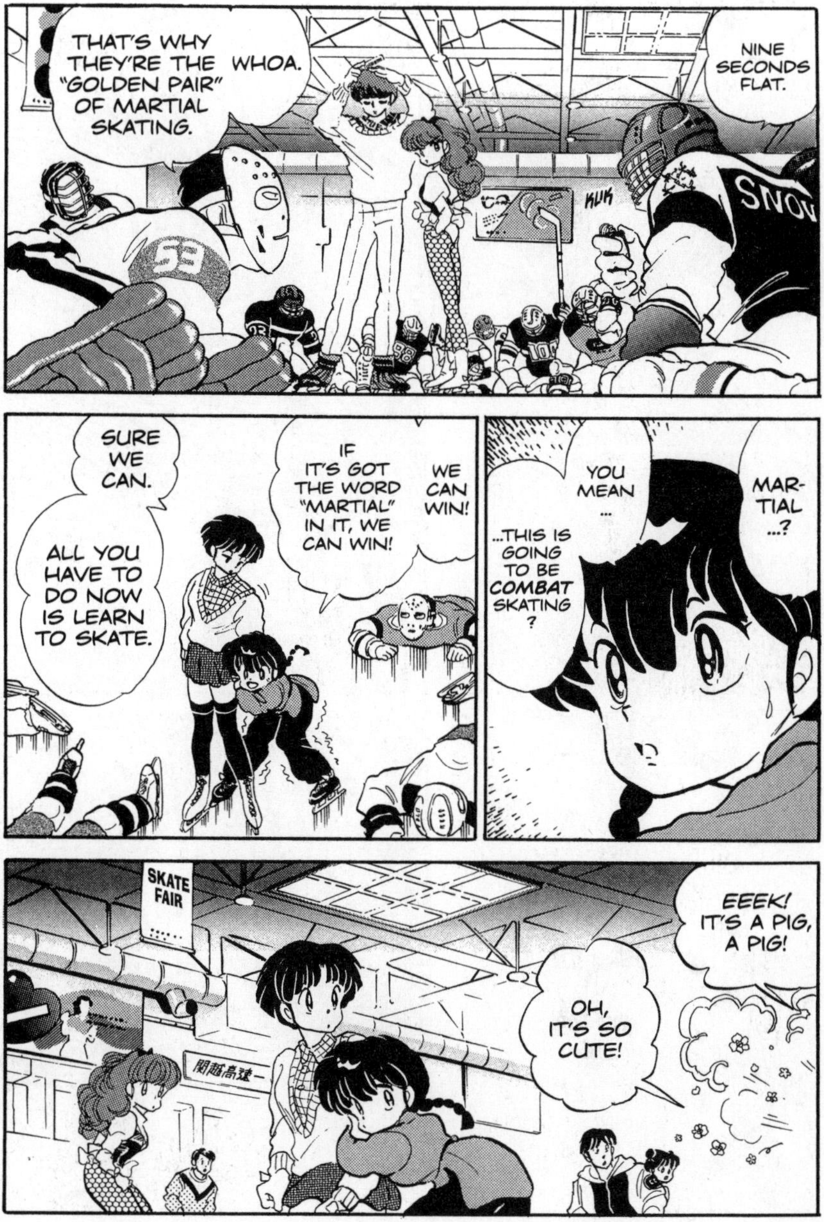
NINE SECONDS FLAT.
KUK
WHOA.
THAT'S WHY THEY'RE THE "GOLDEN PAIR" OF MARTIAL SKATING.
MAR-TIAL ...?
YOU MEAN ...
...THIS IS GOING TO BE COMBAT SKATING ?
WE CAN WIN!
IF IT'S GOT THE WORD "MARTIAL" IN IT, WE CAN WIN!
SURE WE CAN.
ALL YOU HAVE TO DO NOW IS LEARN TO SKATE.
EEEK! IT'S A PIG, A PIG!
OH, IT'S SO CUTE!
SKATE FAIR

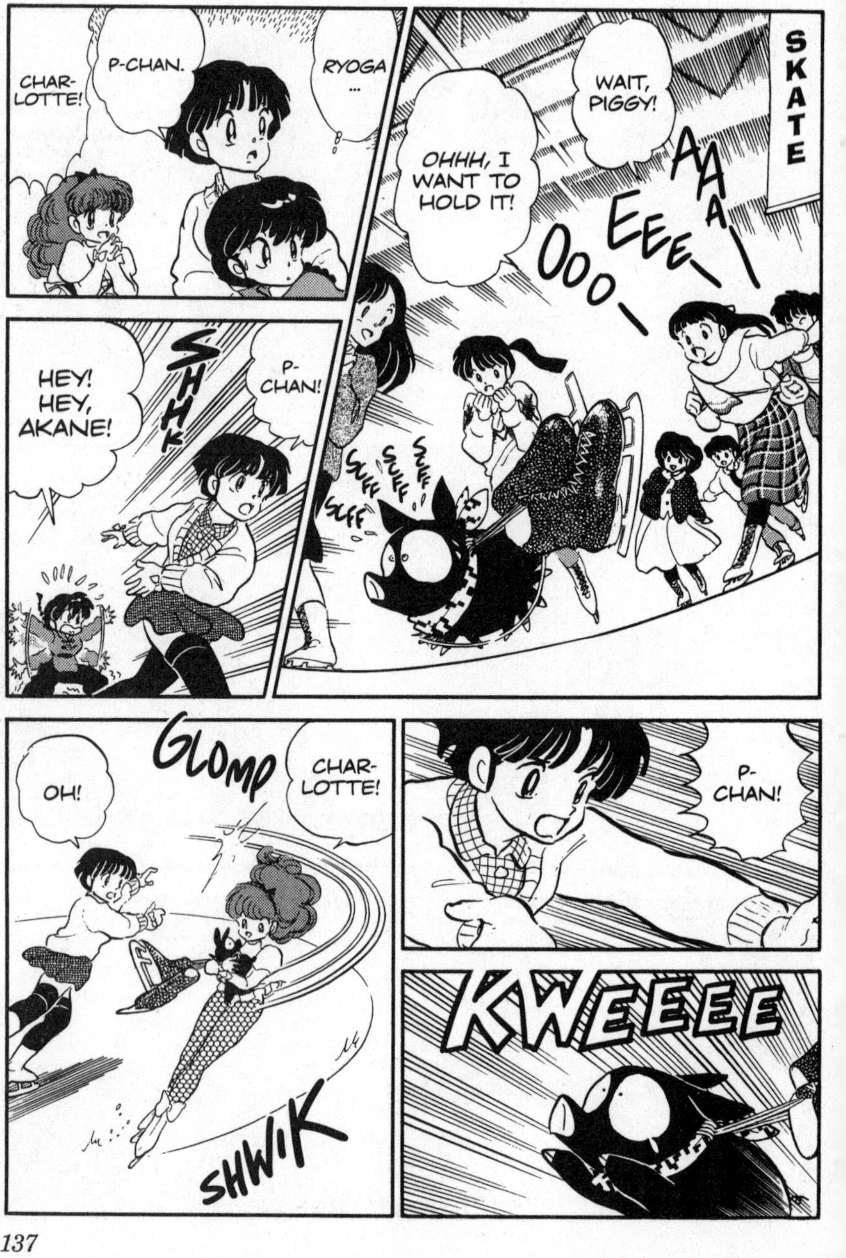
SKATE
WAIT, PIGGY!
OHHH, I WANT TO HOLD IT!
AAA
EEE
OOO
RYOGA ...
P-CHAN.
CHAR-LOTTE!
P-CHAN!
HEY! HEY, AKANE!
SHHK
SCUFF SCUFF SCUFF SCUFF
P-CHAN!
KWEEEE
CHAR-LOTTE!
GLOMP
OH!
SHWIK

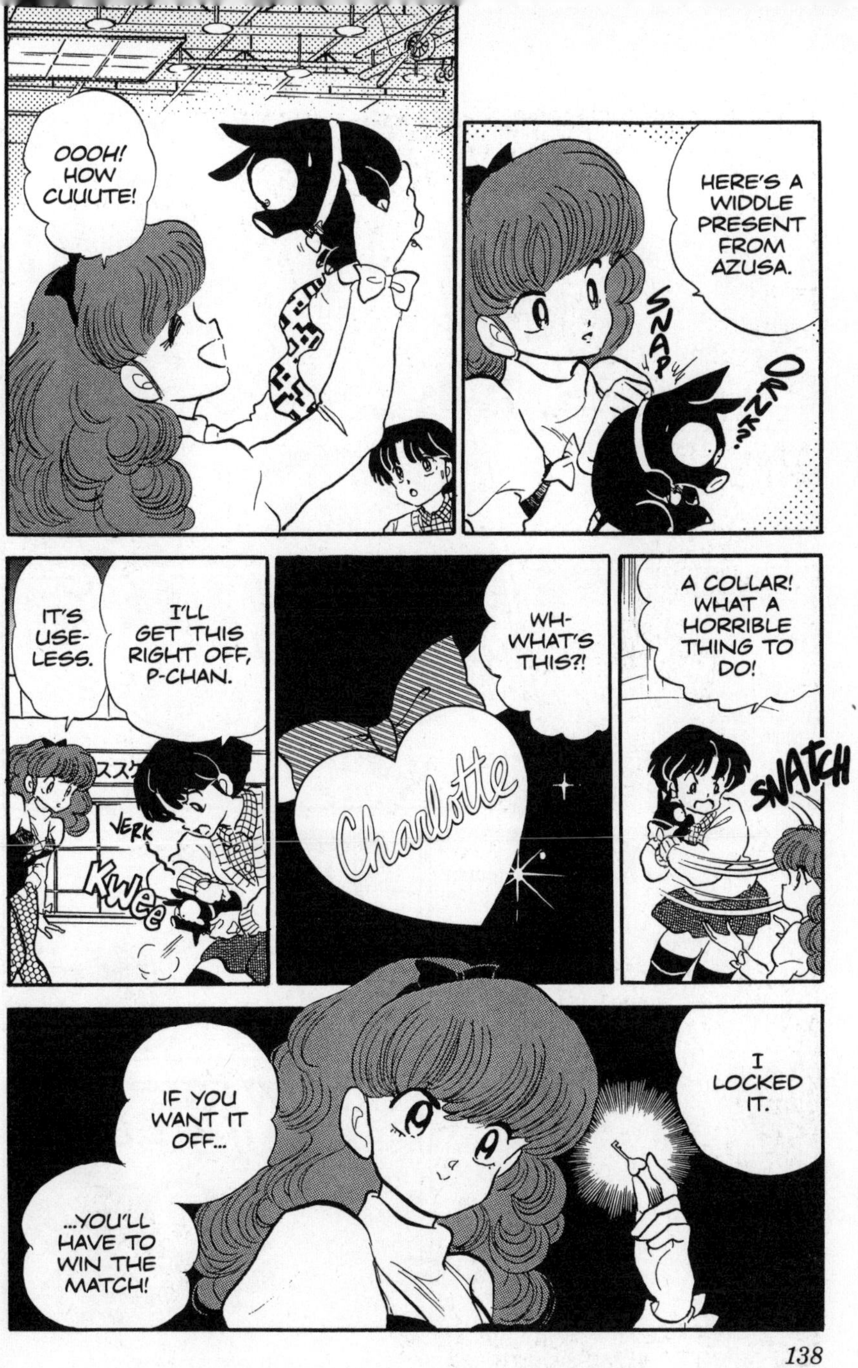
HERE'S A WIDDLE PRESENT FROM AZUSA.
SNAP
ORNK?!
OOOH! HOW CUUUTE!
A COLLAR! WHAT A HORRIBLE THING TO DO!
SNATCH
WH- WHAT'S THIS?!
Charlotte
I'LL GET THIS RIGHT OFF, P-CHAN.
IT'S USE- LESS.
VERK
Kwee
I LOCKED IT.
IF YOU WANT IT OFF...
...YOU'LL HAVE TO WIN THE MATCH!

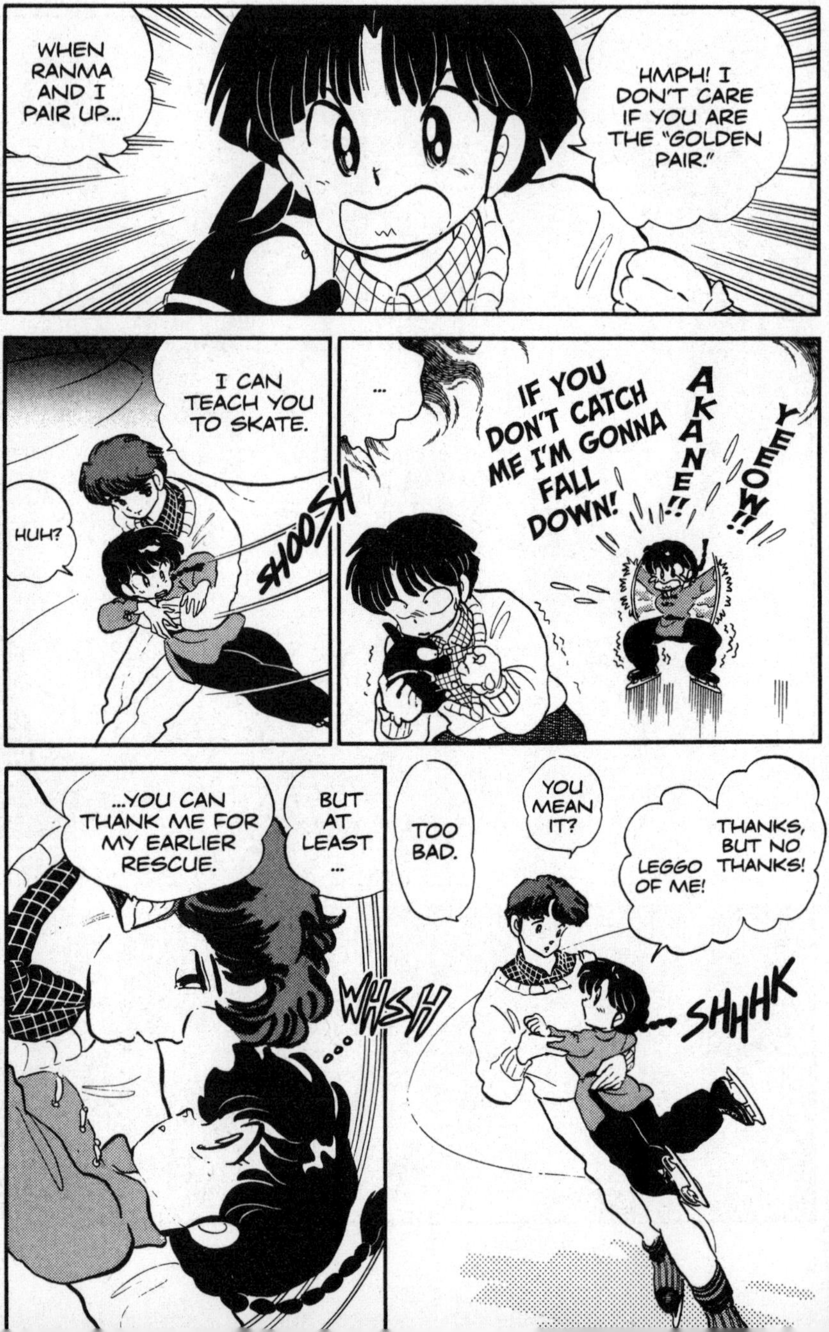
HMPH! I DON'T CARE IF YOU ARE THE "GOLDEN PAIR."
WHEN RANMA AND I PAIR UP...
YEEOW!!
AKANE!!
IF YOU DON'T CATCH ME I'M GONNA FALL DOWN!
...
I CAN TEACH YOU TO SKATE.
SHOOSH
HUH?
THANKS, BUT NO THANKS!
LEGGO OF ME!
YOU MEAN IT?
SHHHK
TOO BAD.
BUT AT LEAST ...
...YOU CAN THANK ME FOR MY EARLIER RESCUE.
WHSH

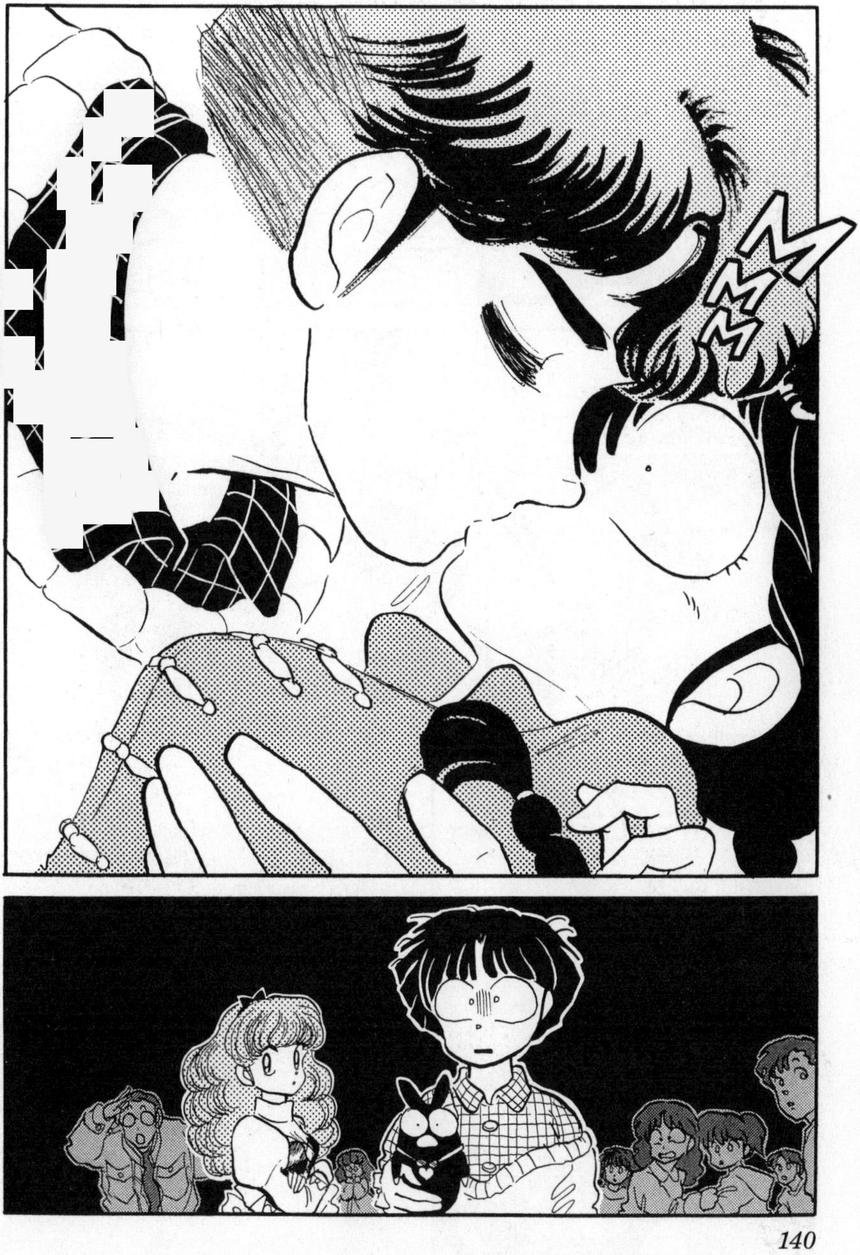
MMMM

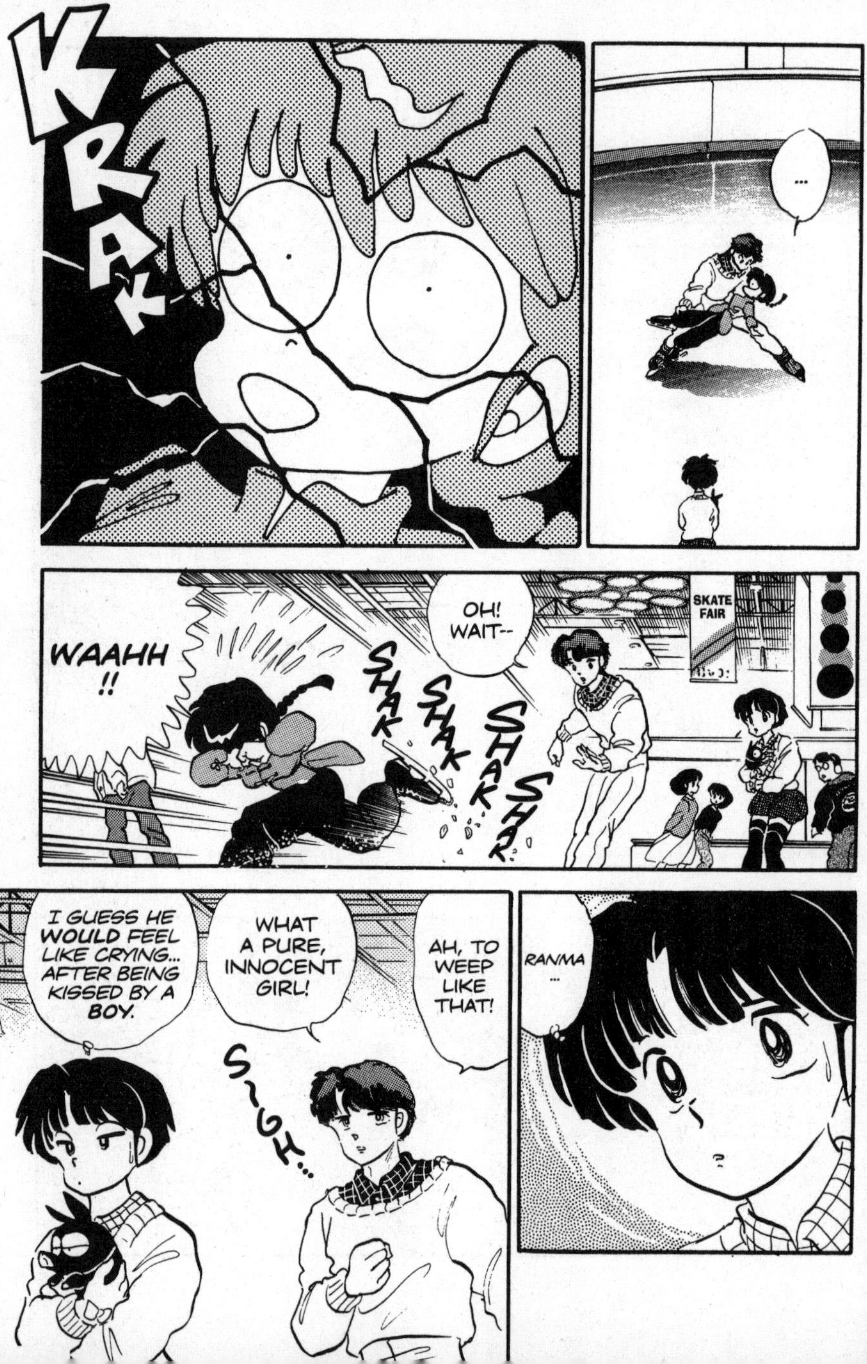
...
KRAK
OH! WAIT--
SKATE FAIR
SHAK SHAK SHAK SHAK
WAAHH !!
RANMA ...
AH, TO WEEP LIKE THAT!
WHAT A PURE, INNOCENT GIRL!
I GUESS HE WOULD FEEL LIKE CRYING... AFTER BEING KISSED BY A BOY.
S~IGH...

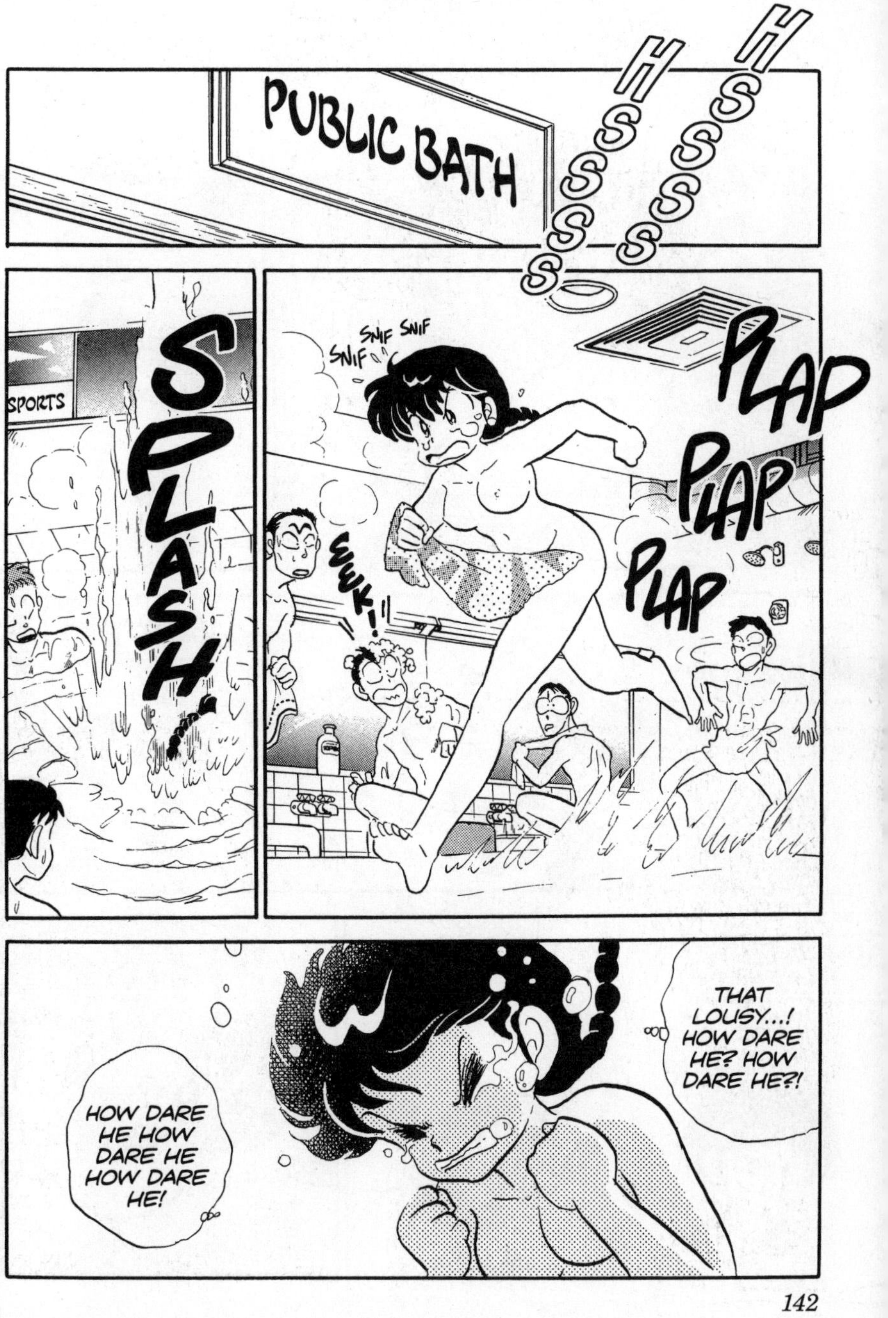
PUBLIC BATH
HSSSSS
HSSSSS
SNIF SNIF SNIF
PLAP PLAP PLAP
EEEK!!
SPORTS
SPLASH
THAT LOUSY...! HOW DARE HE? HOW DARE HE?!
HOW DARE HE HOW DARE HE HOW DARE HE!

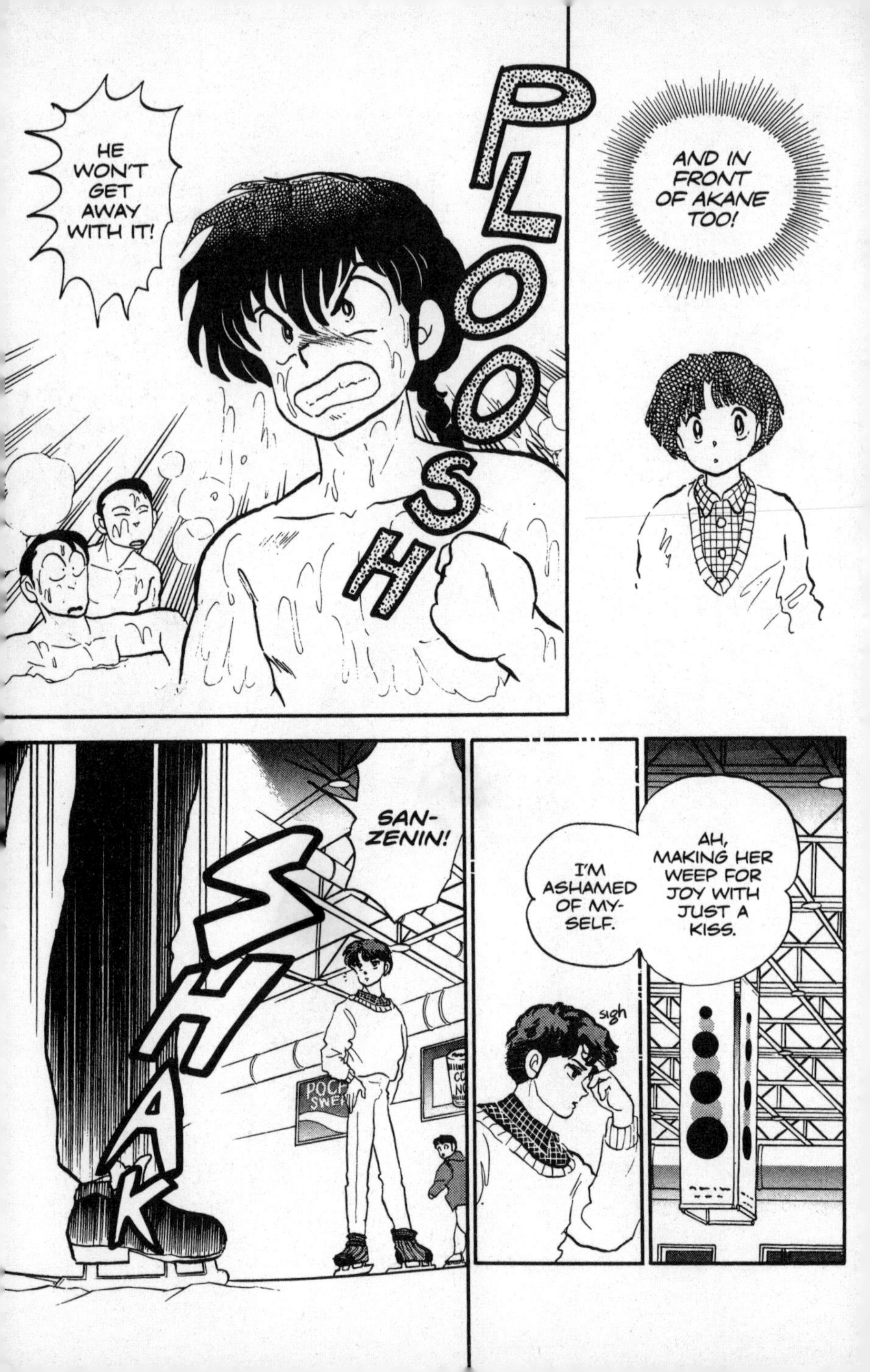
AND IN FRONT OF AKANE TOO!
PLOOOSH
HE WON'T GET AWAY WITH IT!
AH, MAKING HER WEEP FOR JOY WITH JUST A KISS.
I'M ASHAMED OF MY-SELF.
sigh
SAN-ZENIN!
SHHAK

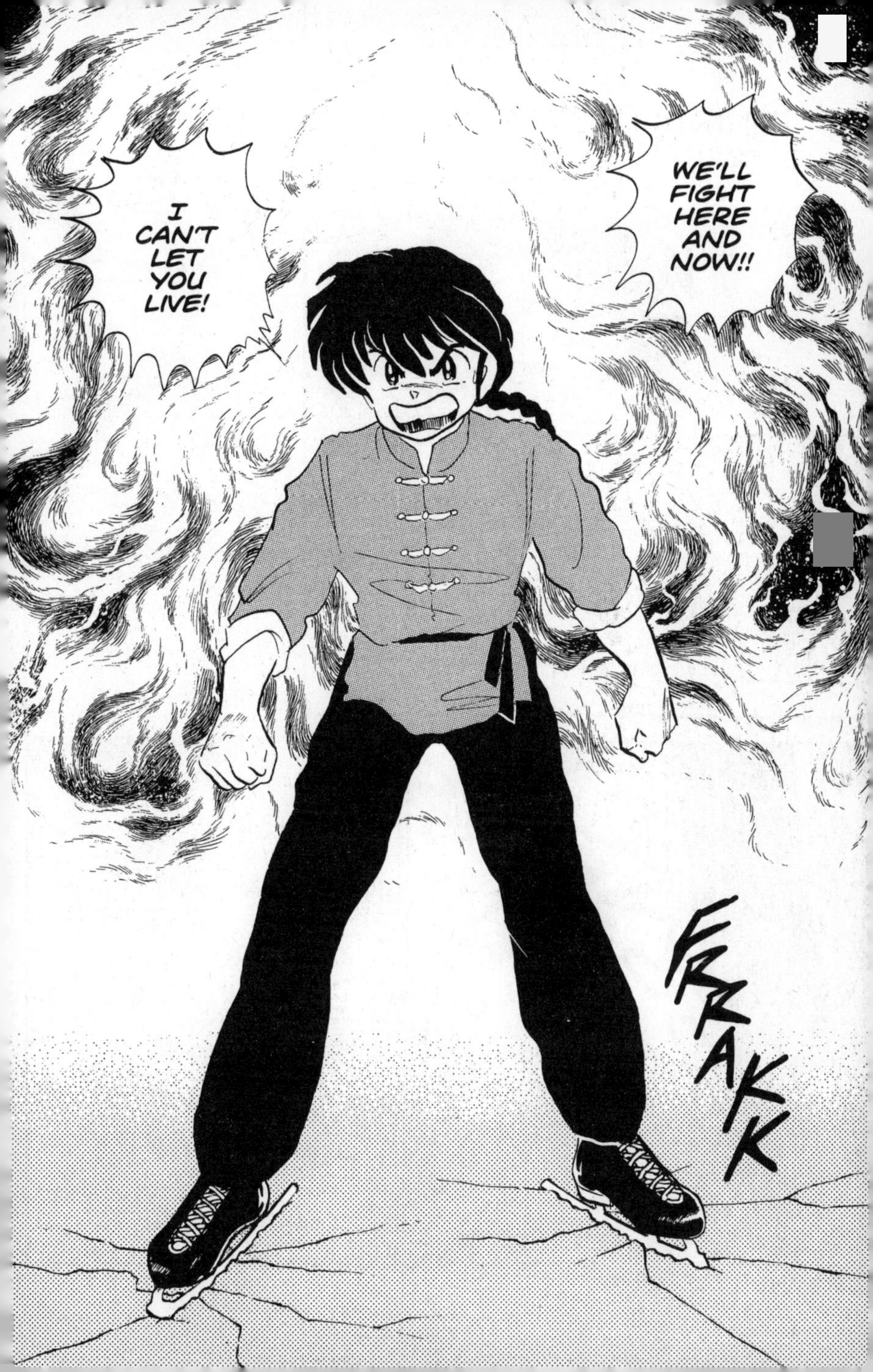
WE'LL FIGHT HERE AND NOW!!
I CAN'T LET YOU LIVE!
FRRAKK

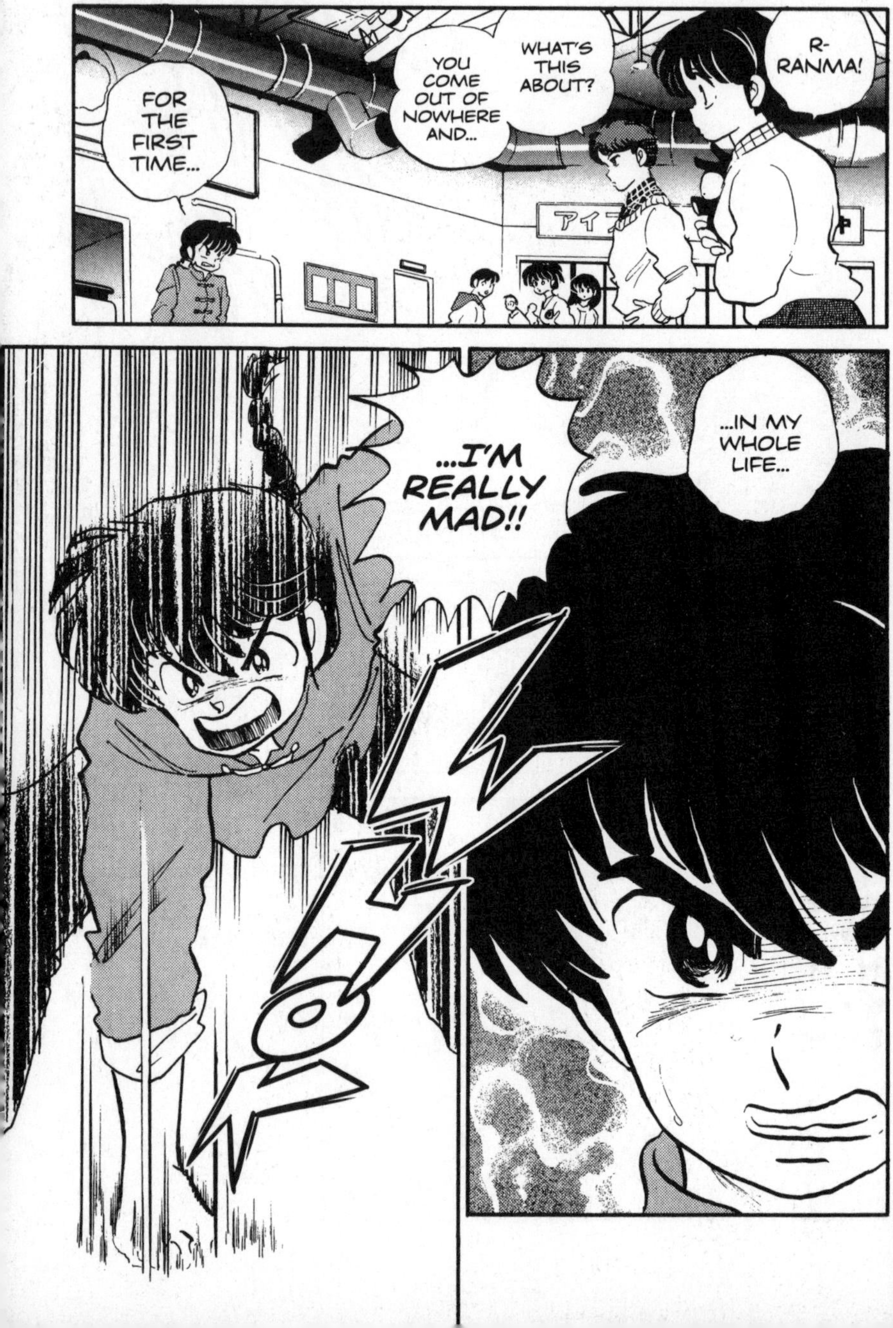
R-RANMA!
WHAT'S THIS ABOUT?
YOU COME OUT OF NOWHERE AND...
FOR THE FIRST TIME...
...IN MY WHOLE LIFE...
...I'M REALLY MAD!!

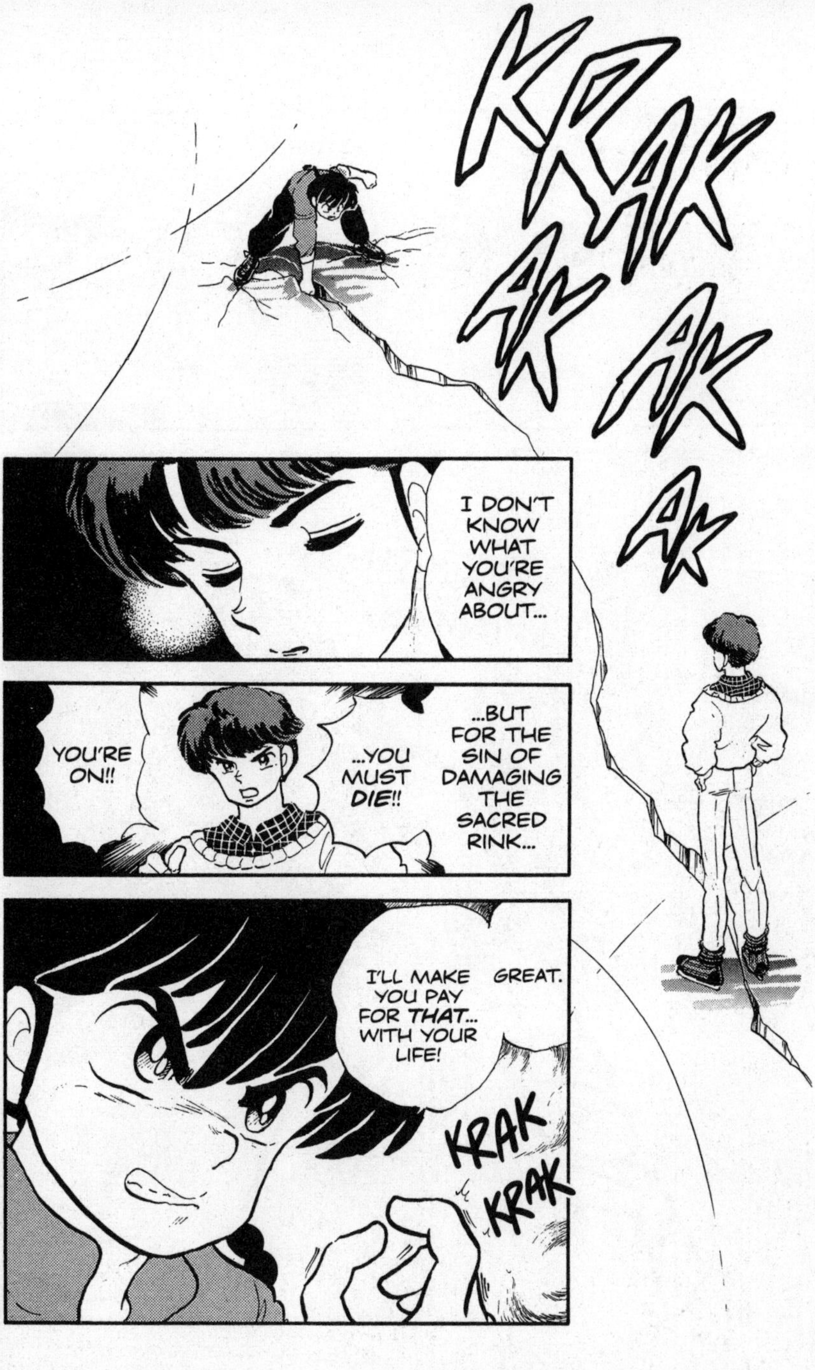
KRAK AK AK AK
I DON'T KNOW WHAT YOU'RE ANGRY ABOUT...
...BUT FOR THE SIN OF DAMAGING THE SACRED RINK...
...YOU MUST DIE!!
YOU'RE ON!!
GREAT.
I'LL MAKE YOU PAY FOR THAT... WITH YOUR LIFE!
KRAK
KRAK

PART 8
LIPS AT A LOSS

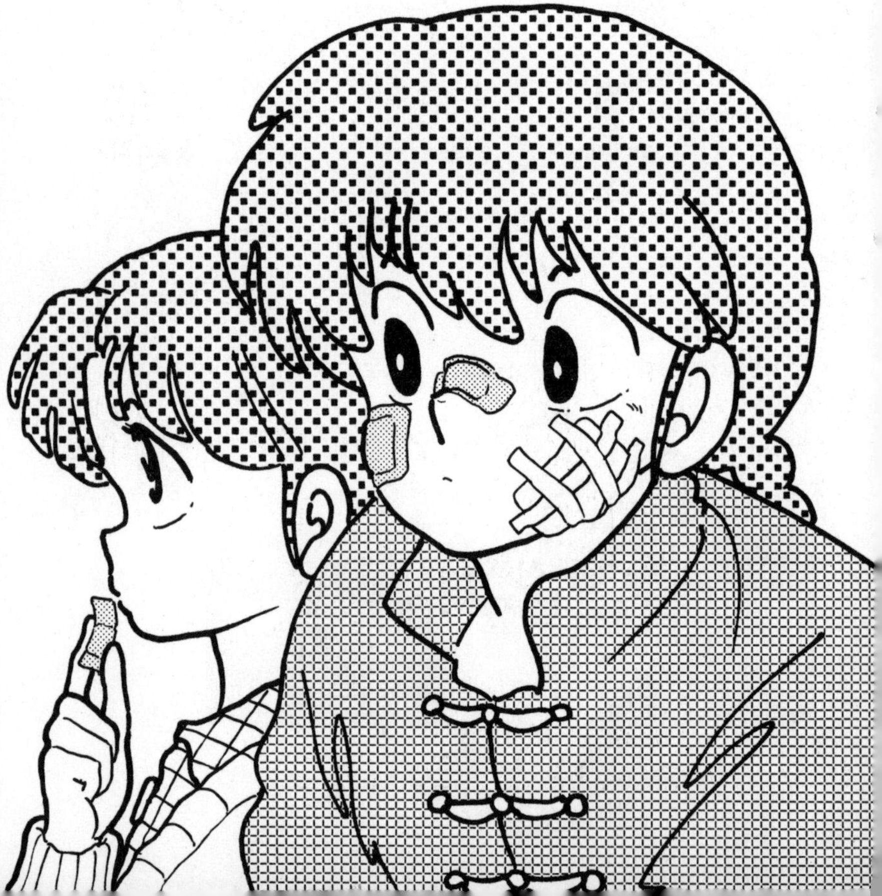

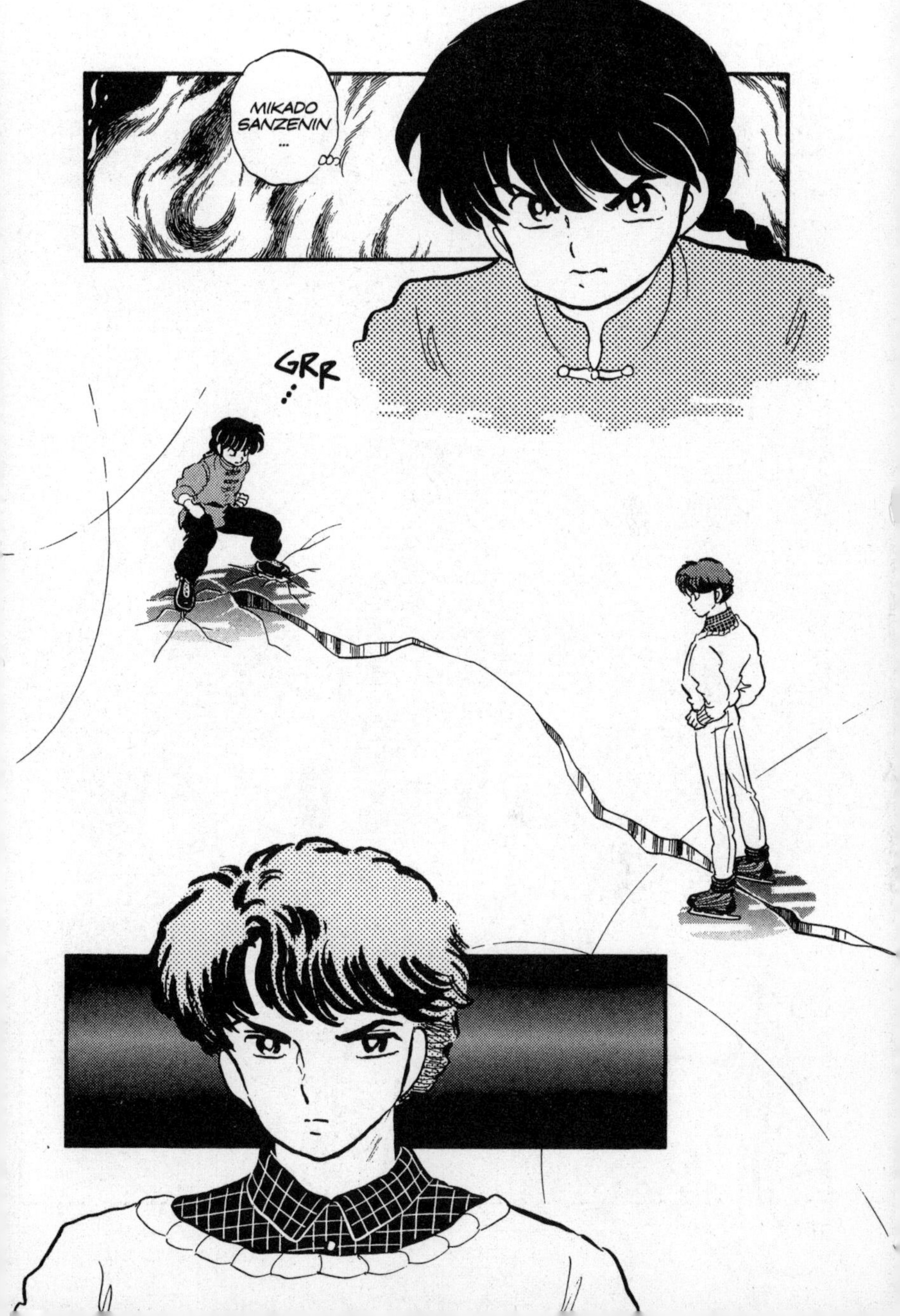

MIKADO SANZENIN ...
GRR ...

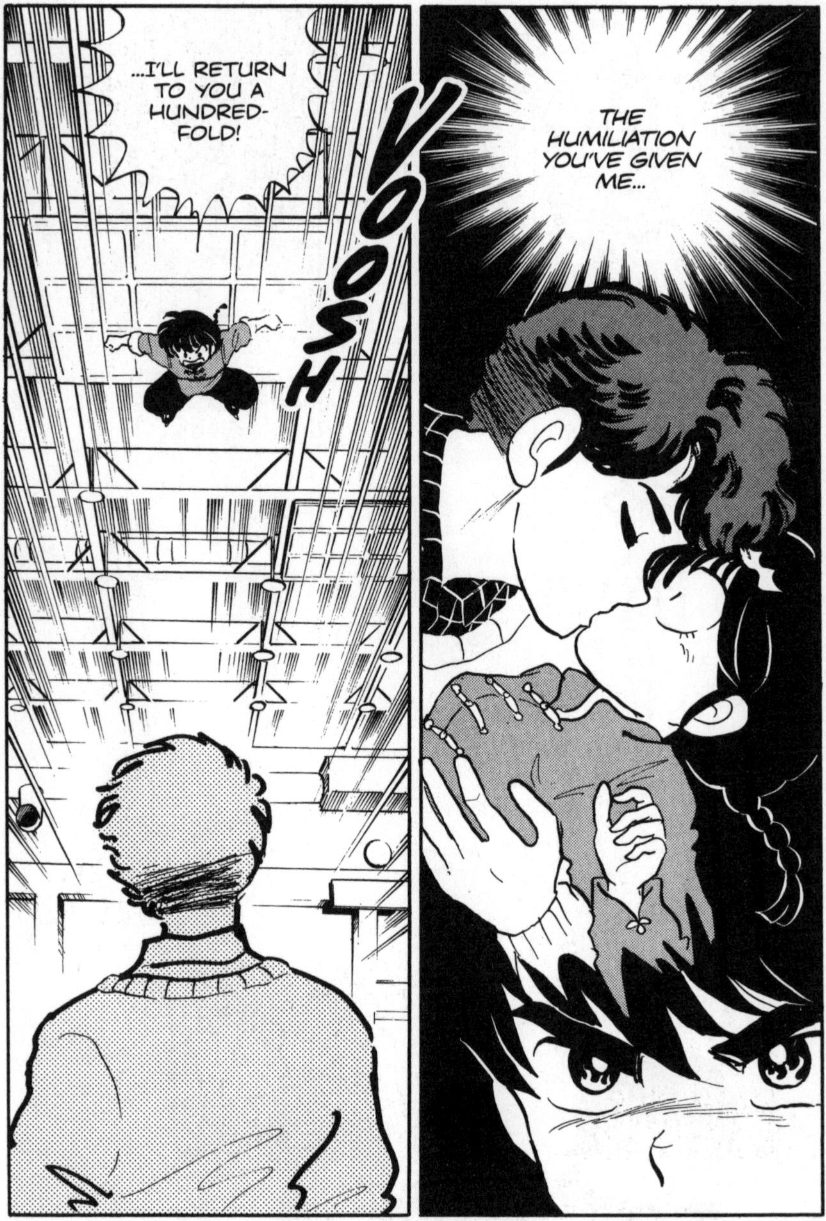
THE HUMILIATION YOU'VE GIVEN ME...
...I'LL RETURN TO YOU A HUNDRED-FOLD!
VOOSH

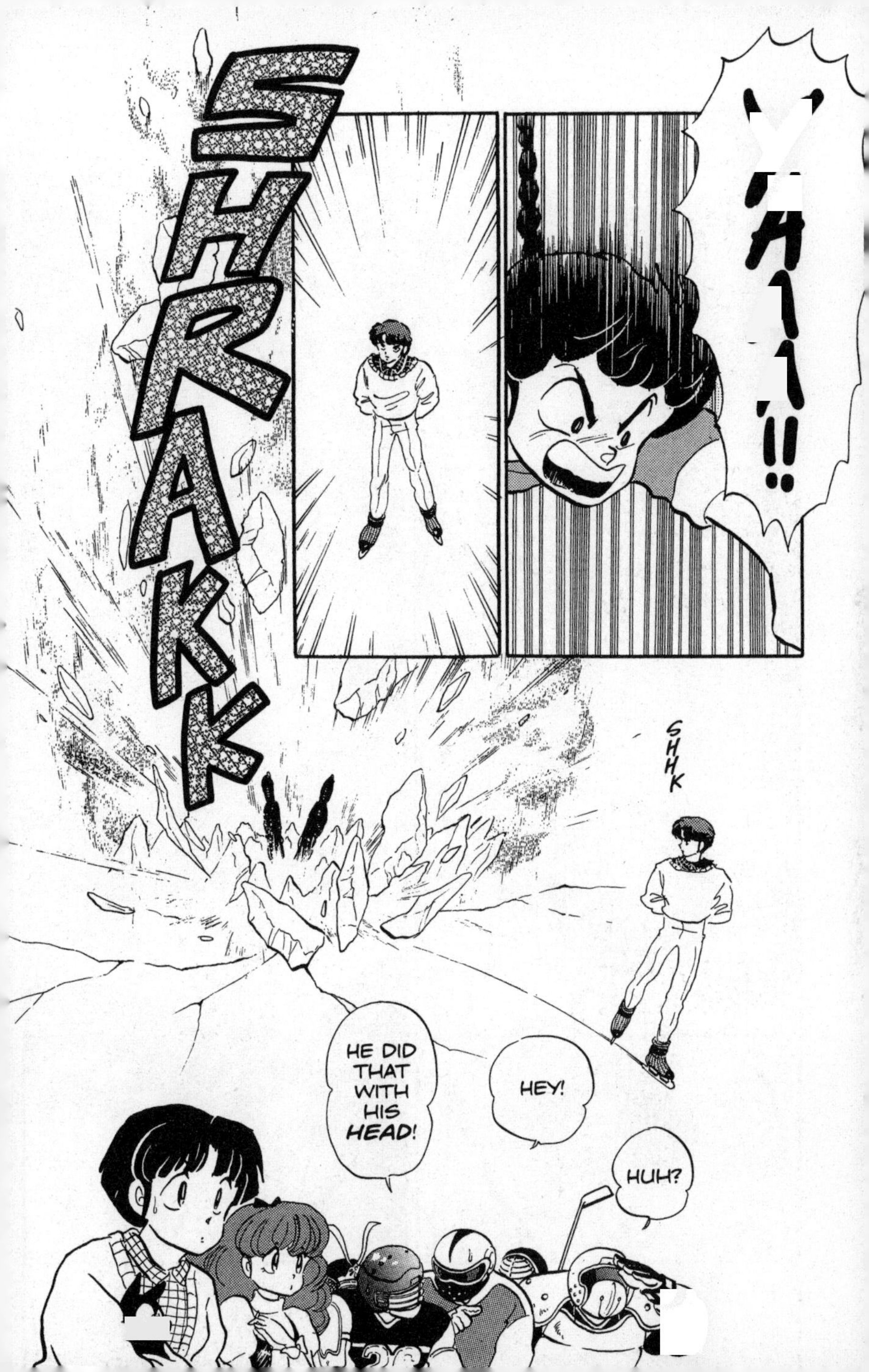
SHRAKK
SHHK
HEY!
HE DID THAT WITH HIS HEAD!
HUH?

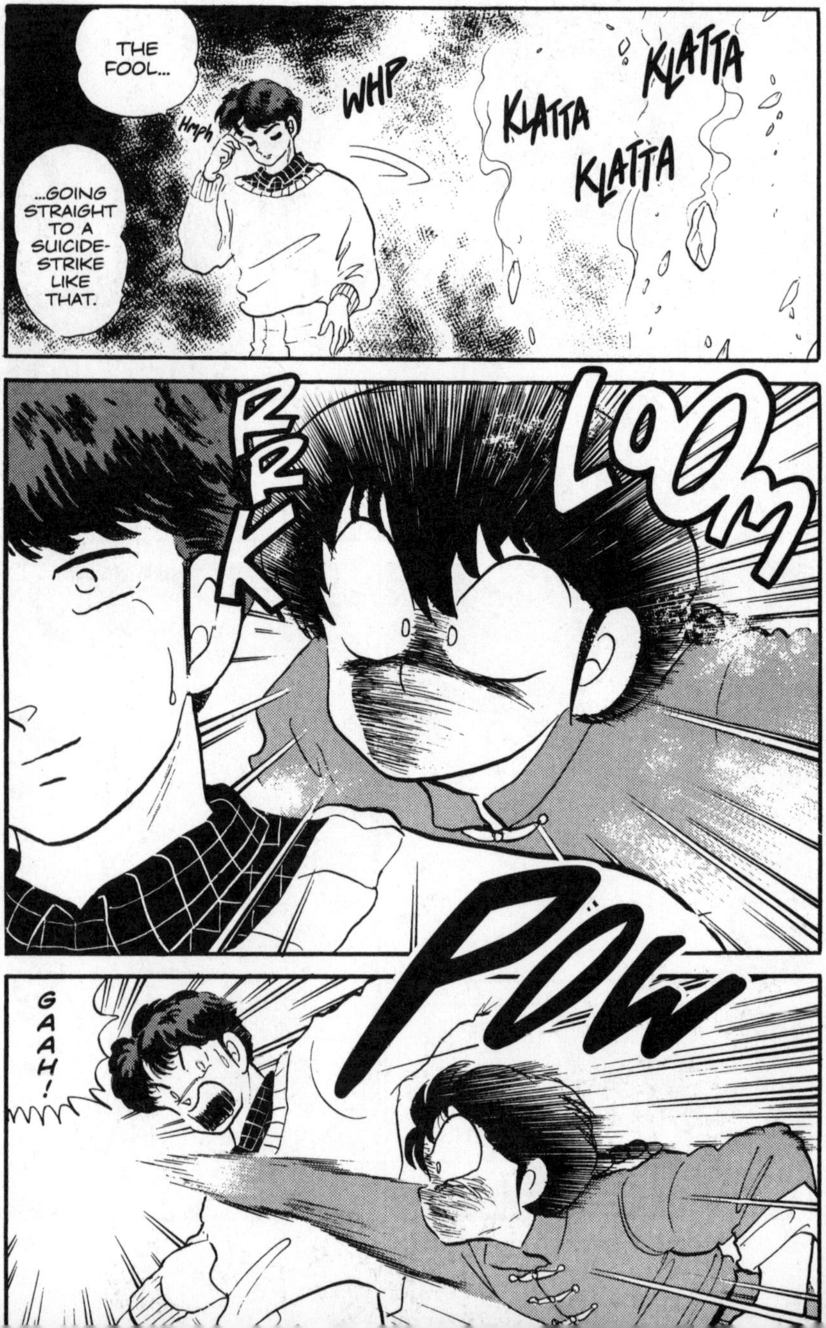
KLATTA
KLATTA
KLATTA
WHP
THE FOOL...
Hmph
...GOING STRAIGHT TO A SUICIDE-STRIKE LIKE THAT.
LOOM
RRK
POW
GAAH!

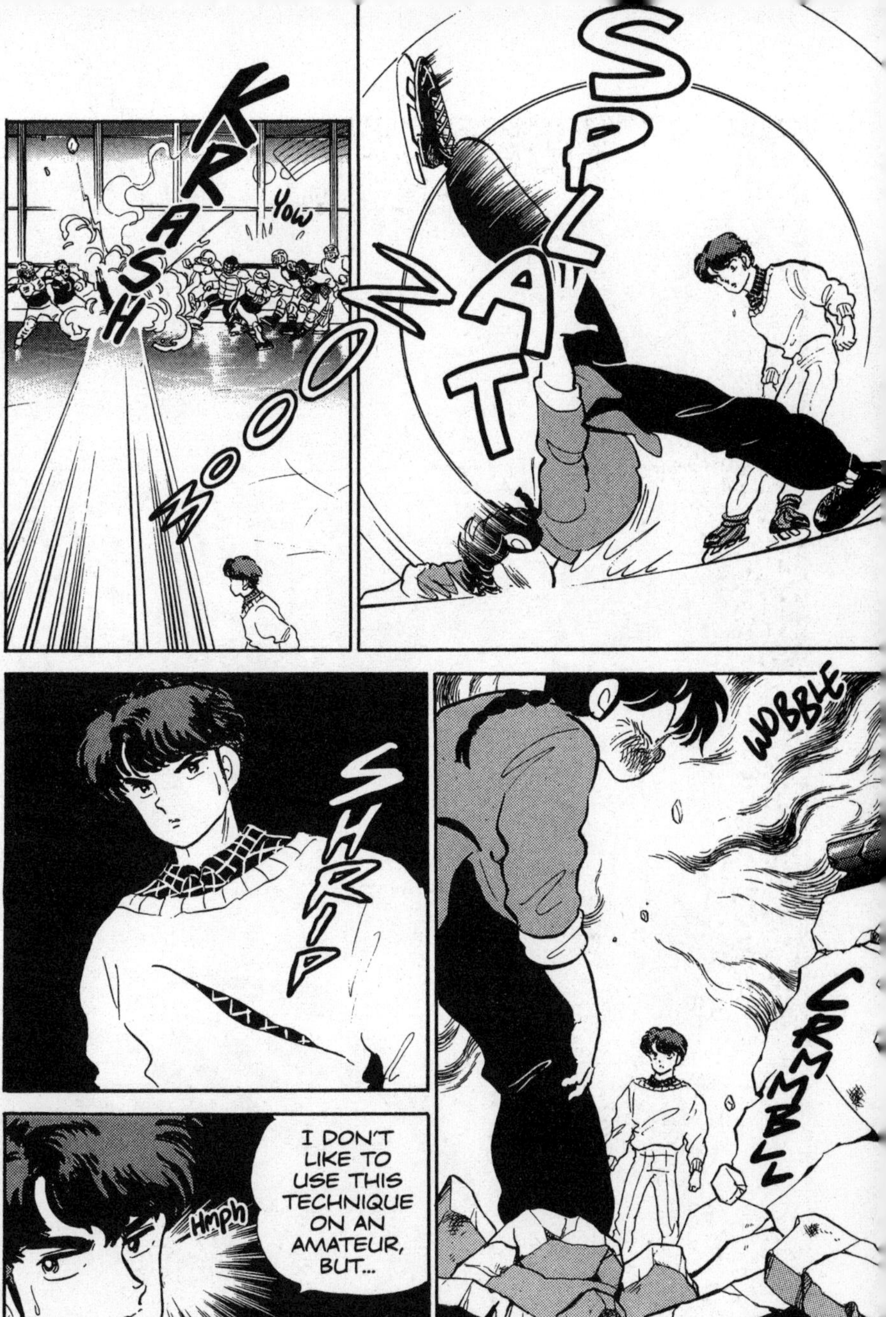
SPLAT
ZOOOOM
KRASH
YOW
WOBBLE
CRMMBLL
SHRIP
Hmph
I DON'T LIKE TO USE THIS TECHNIQUE ON AN AMATEUR, BUT...

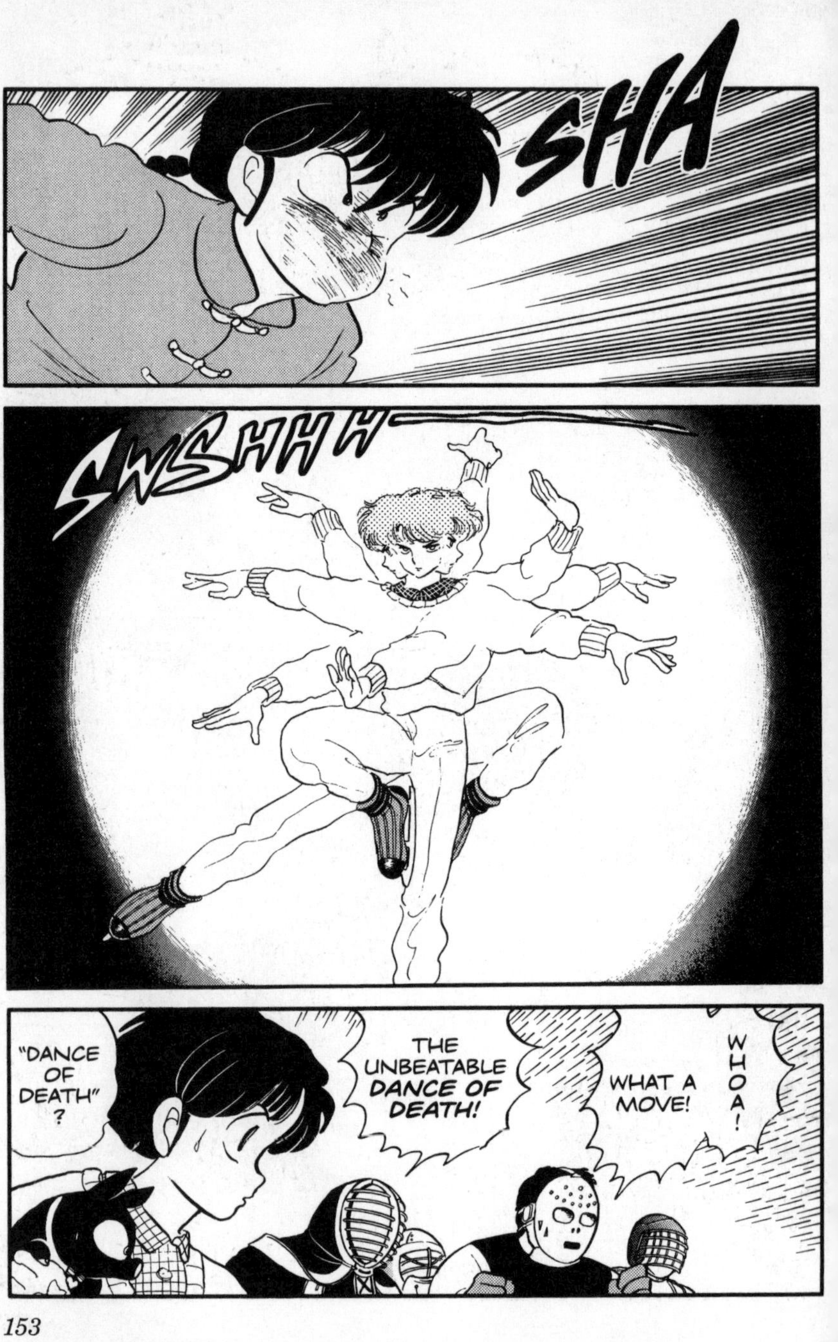
SHA
SWSHHH
WHOA!
WHAT A MOVE!
THE UNBEATABLE DANCE OF DEATH!
"DANCE OF DEATH"?

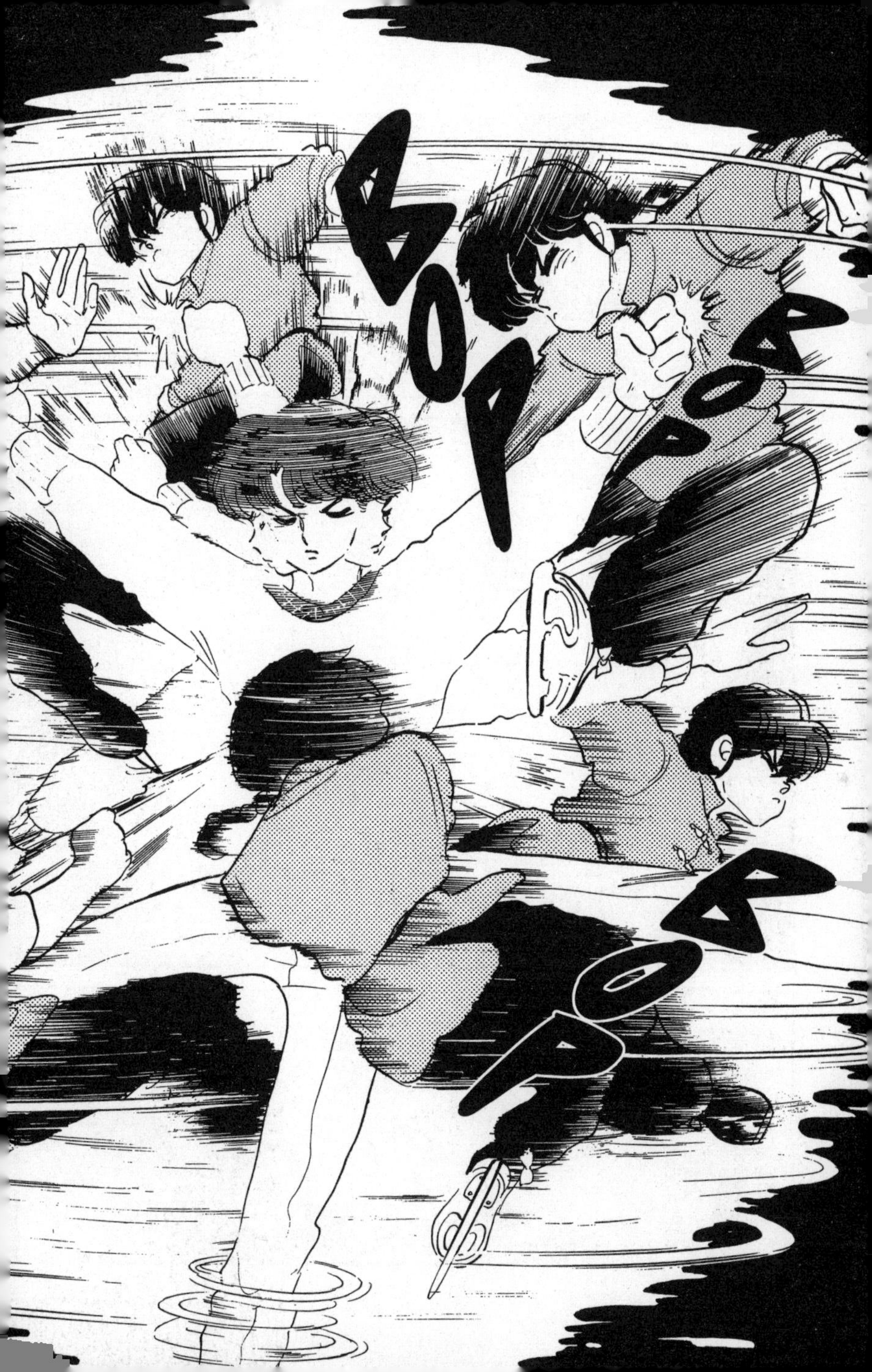
BOP
BOP
BOP

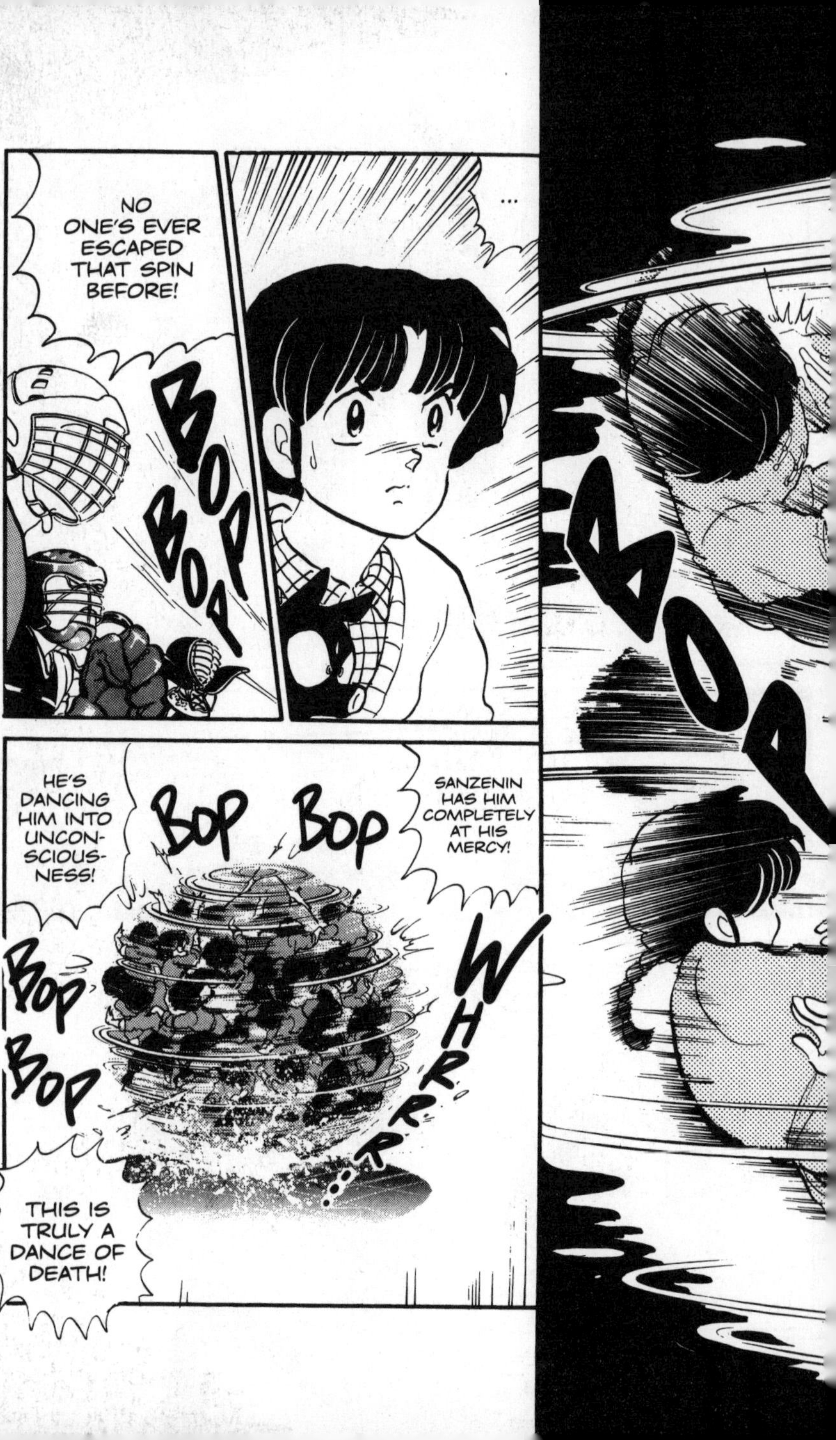
BOOP
...
BOP BOP
NO ONE'S EVER ESCAPED THAT SPIN BEFORE!
SANZENIN HAS HIM COMPLETELY AT HIS MERCY!
WHRRRR...
BOP BOP
HE'S DANCING HIM INTO UNCON-SCIOUS-NESS!
BOP BOP
THIS IS TRULY A DANCE OF DEATH!

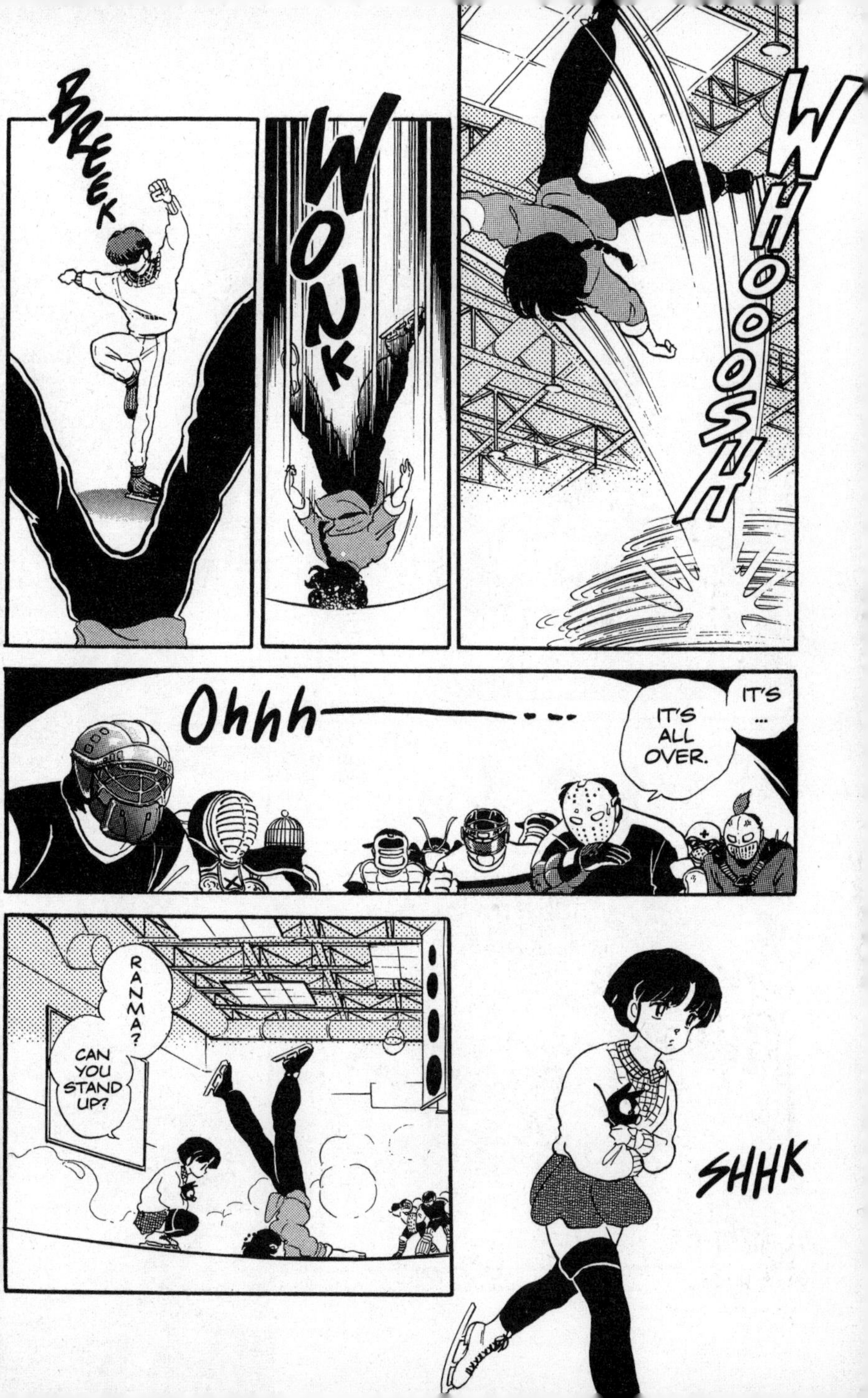
WHOOOOSH
WONK
BREEK
IT'S ...
IT'S ALL OVER.
Ohhh———...
SHHK
RANMA?
CAN YOU STAND UP?

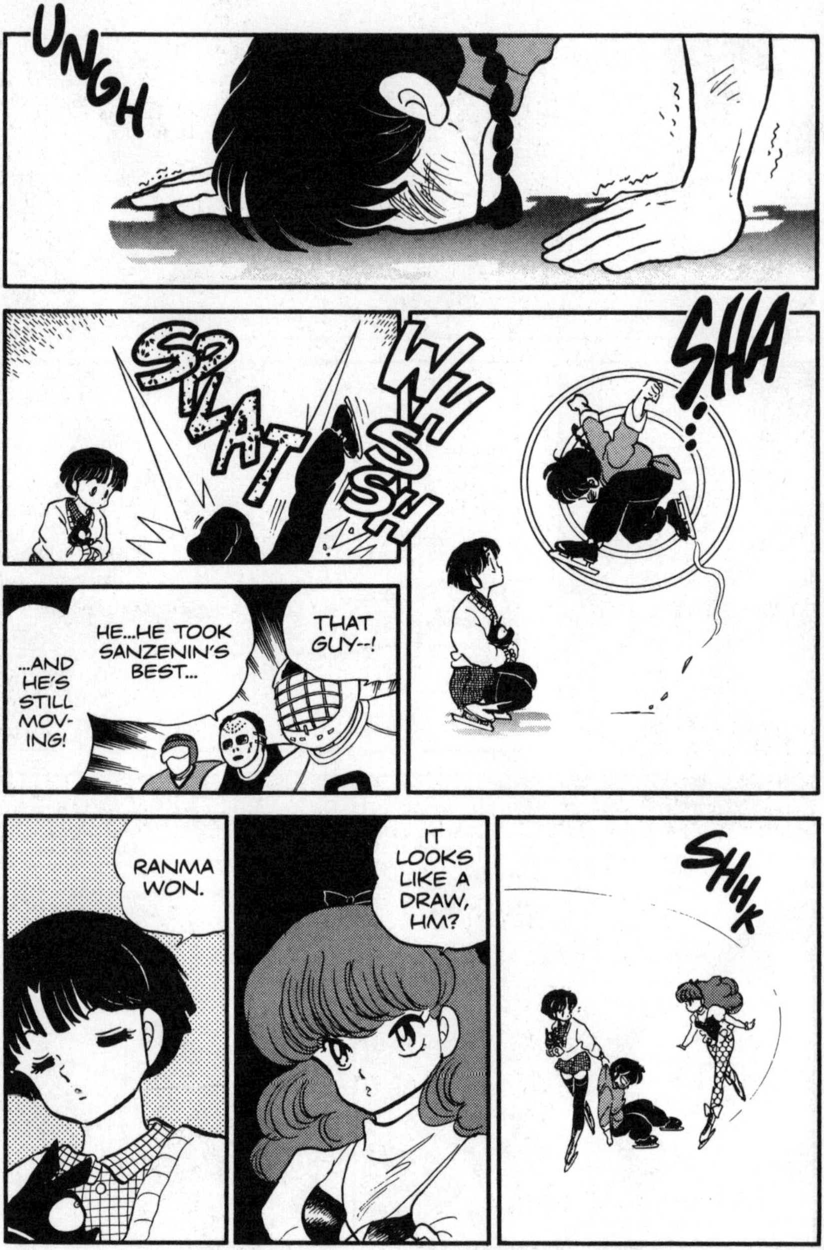
UNGH
SHA
SPLAT
WHSSH
THAT GUY--!
HE...HE TOOK SANZENIN'S BEST...
...AND HE'S STILL MOVING!
SHHK
IT LOOKS LIKE A DRAW, HM?
RANMA WON.

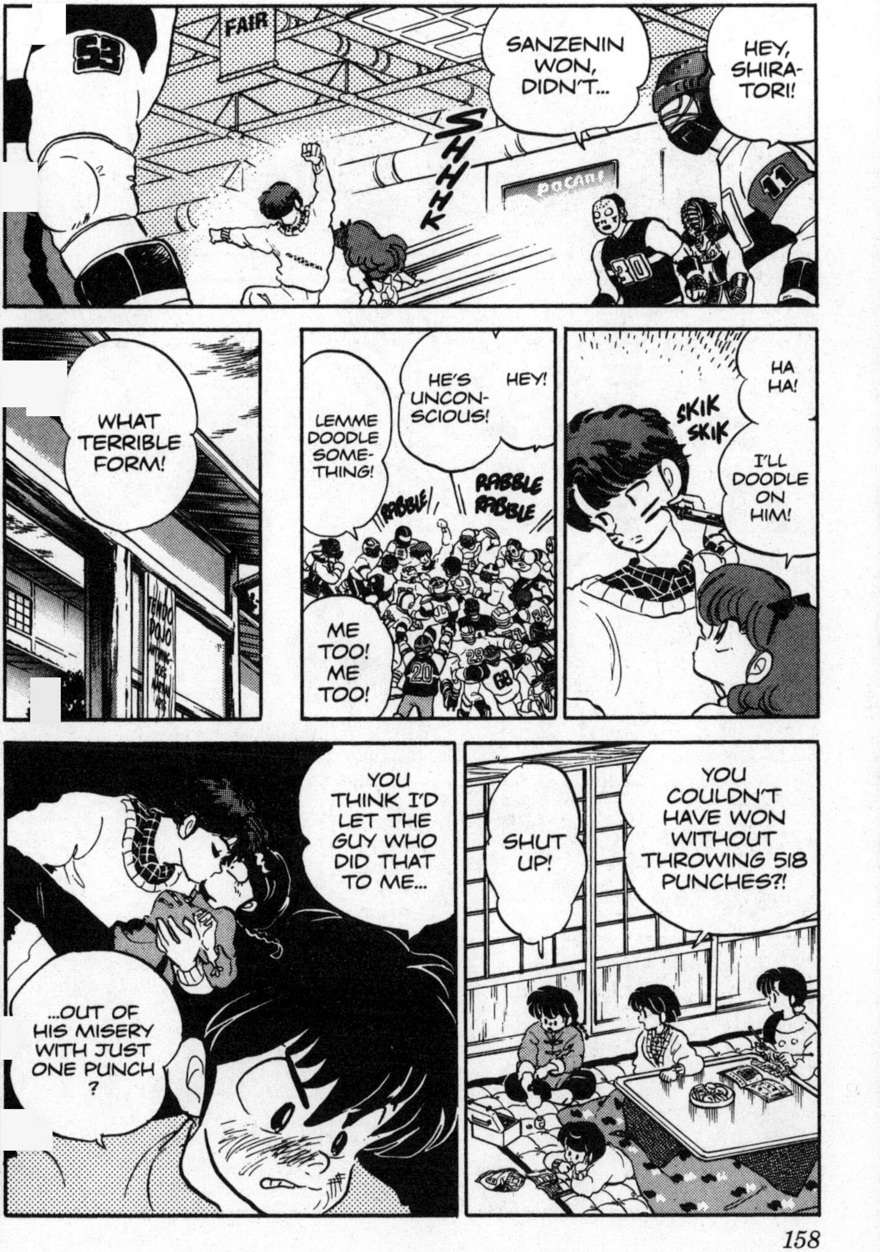
HEY, SHIRATORI!
SANZENIN WON, DIDN'T...
SHHHHK
HA HA!
I'LL DOODLE ON HIM!
SKIK SKIK
HEY!
HE'S UNCONSCIOUS!
LEMME DOODLE SOMETHING!
RABBLE RABBLE
RABBLE
ME TOO! ME TOO!
WHAT TERRIBLE FORM!
YOU COULDN'T HAVE WON WITHOUT THROWING 518 PUNCHES?!
SHUT UP!
YOU THINK I'D LET THE GUY WHO DID THAT TO ME...
...OUT OF HIS MISERY WITH JUST ONE PUNCH?

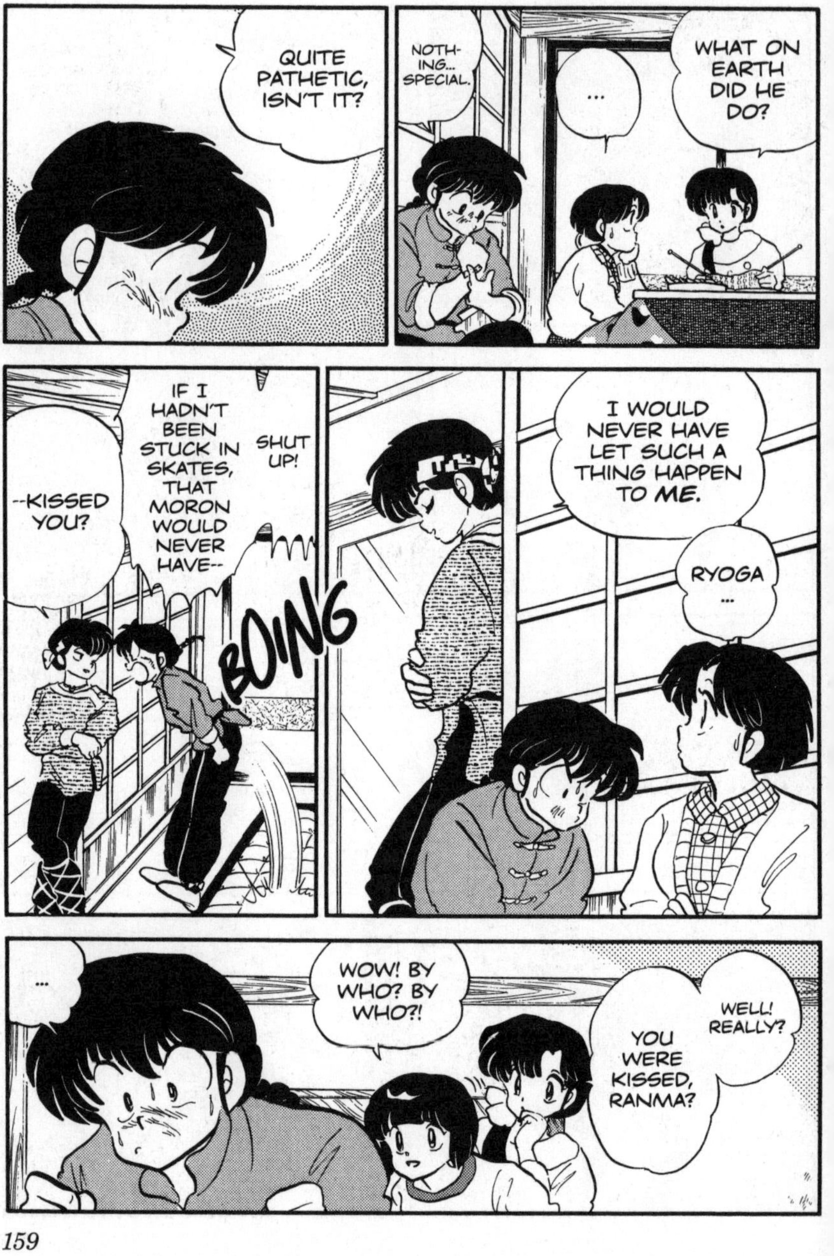
WHAT ON EARTH DID HE DO?
...
NOTH-ING... SPECIAL.
QUITE PATHETIC, ISN'T IT?
I WOULD NEVER HAVE LET SUCH A THING HAPPEN TO ME.
RYOGA ...
SHUT UP!
IF I HADN'T BEEN STUCK IN SKATES, THAT MORON WOULD NEVER HAVE--
--KISSED YOU?
BOING
WELL! REALLY?
YOU WERE KISSED, RANMA?
WOW! BY WHO? BY WHO?!
...

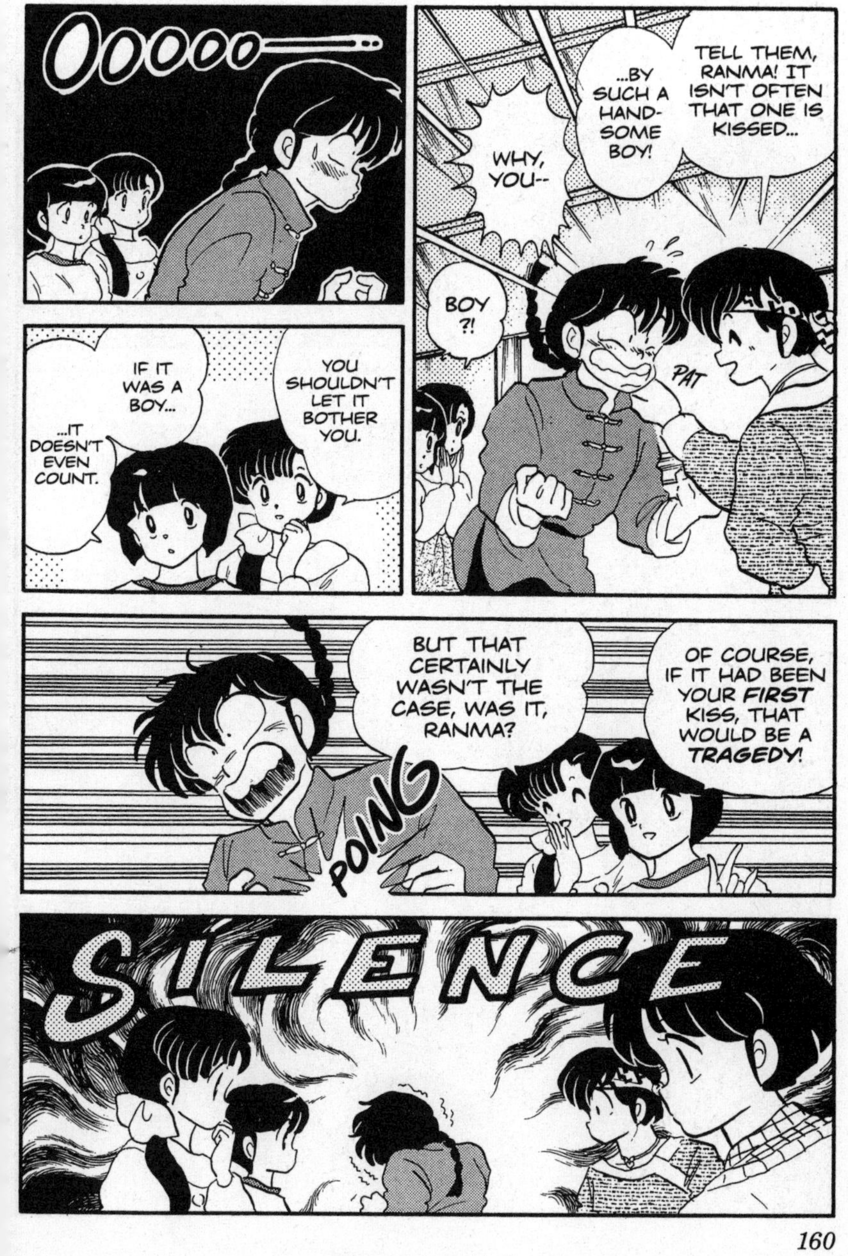
TELL THEM, RANMA! IT ISN'T OFTEN THAT ONE IS KISSED...
...BY SUCH A HAND-SOME BOY!
WHY, YOU--
BOY ?!
PAT
OOOOO—
YOU SHOULDN'T LET IT BOTHER YOU.
IF IT WAS A BOY...
...IT DOESN'T EVEN COUNT.
OF COURSE, IF IT HAD BEEN YOUR FIRST KISS, THAT WOULD BE A TRAGEDY!
BUT THAT CERTAINLY WASN'T THE CASE, WAS IT, RANMA?
POING
SILENCE

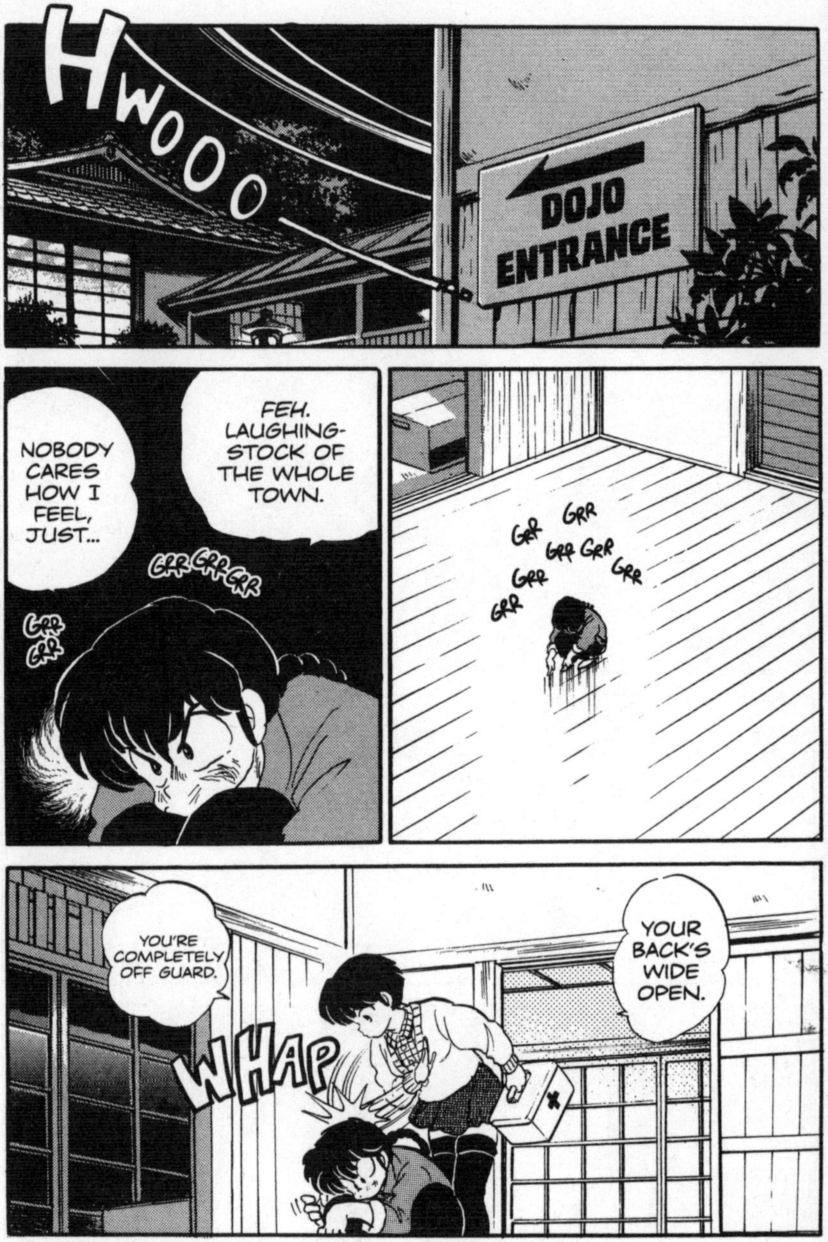
HWOOOO
DOJO ENTRANCE
GRR GRR GRR GRR GRR GRR GRR
FEH. LAUGHING-STOCK OF THE WHOLE TOWN.
NOBODY CARES HOW I FEEL, JUST...
GRR GRR GRR
GRR GRR
YOUR BACK'S WIDE OPEN.
YOU'RE COMPLETELY OFF GUARD.
WHAP

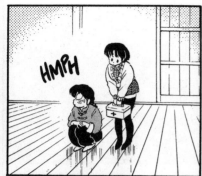

HMPH

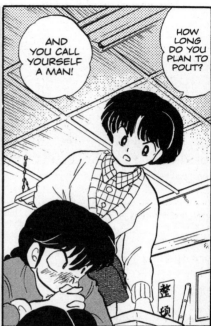

HOW LONG DO YOU PLAN TO POUT?

AND YOU CALL YOURSELF A MAN!

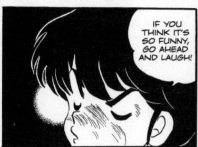

IF YOU THINK IT'S SO FUNNY, GO AHEAD AND LAUGH!

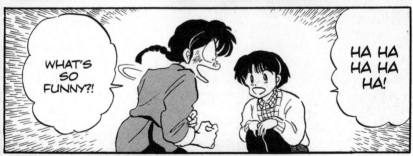

WHAT'S SO FUNNY?!

HA HA HA HA HA!

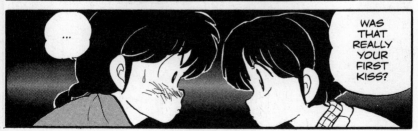

...

WAS THAT REALLY YOUR FIRST KISS?

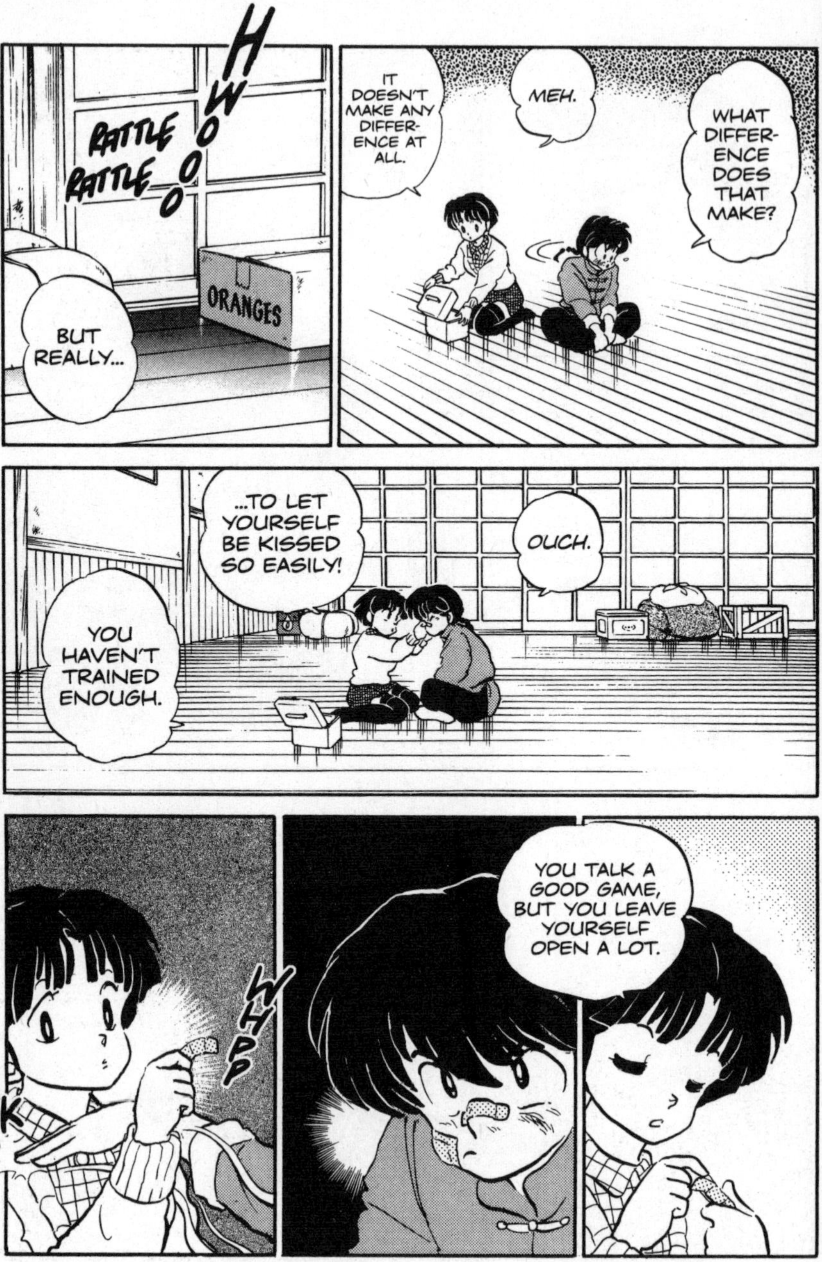
WHAT DIFFERENCE DOES THAT MAKE?
MEH.
IT DOESN'T MAKE ANY DIFFER-ENCE AT ALL.
HWOOOO
RATTLE RATTLE
ORANGES
BUT REALLY...
OUCH.
...TO LET YOURSELF BE KISSED SO EASILY!
YOU HAVEN'T TRAINED ENOUGH.
YOU TALK A GOOD GAME, BUT YOU LEAVE YOURSELF OPEN A LOT.
WHPP
POIK

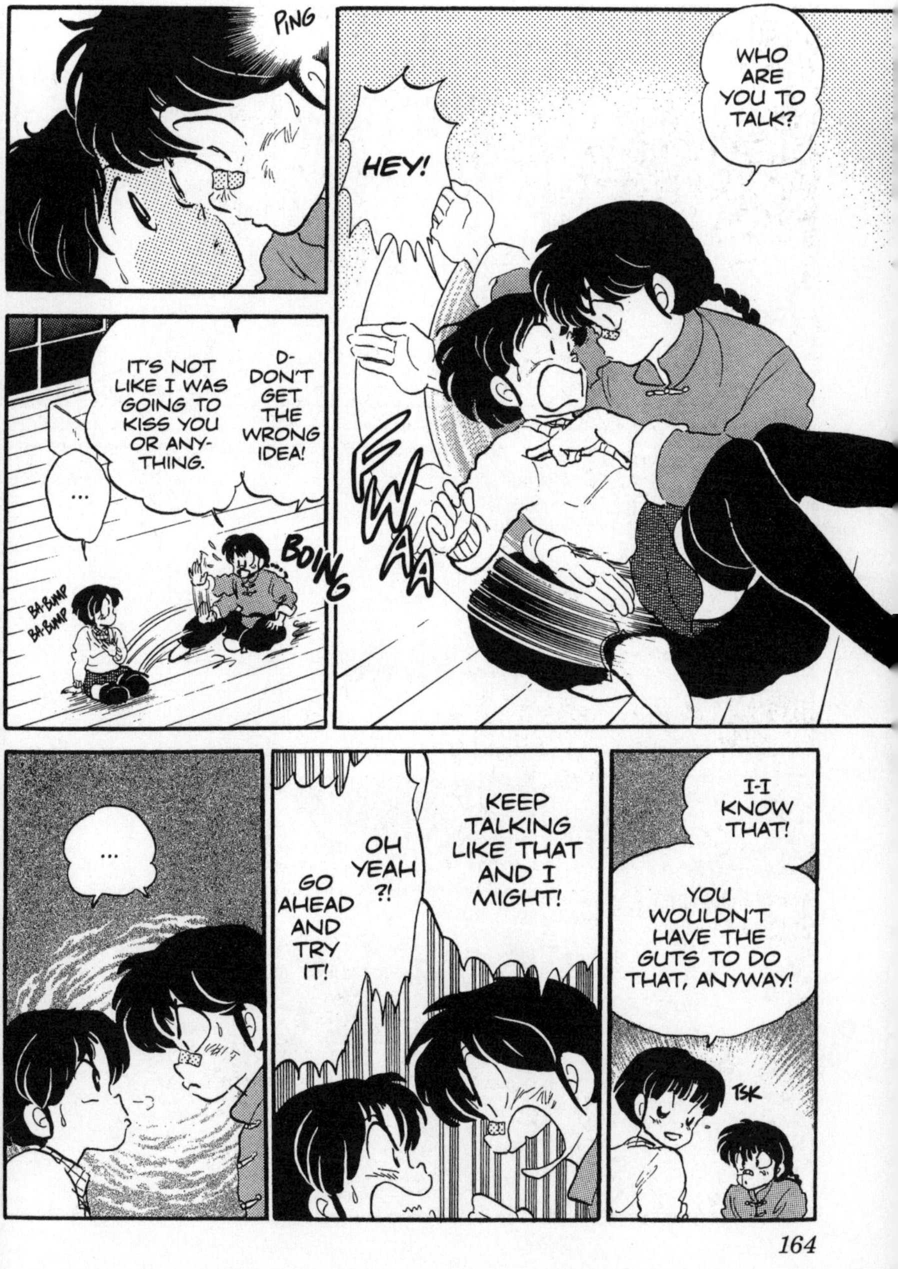
WHO ARE YOU TO TALK?
HEY!
FWAAA
PING
D-DON'T GET THE WRONG IDEA!
IT'S NOT LIKE I WAS GOING TO KISS YOU OR ANYTHING.
...
BOING
BA-BUMP BA-BUMP
I-I KNOW THAT!
YOU WOULDN'T HAVE THE GUTS TO DO THAT, ANYWAY!
TSK
KEEP TALKING LIKE THAT AND I MIGHT!
OH YEAH?!
GO AHEAD AND TRY IT!
...

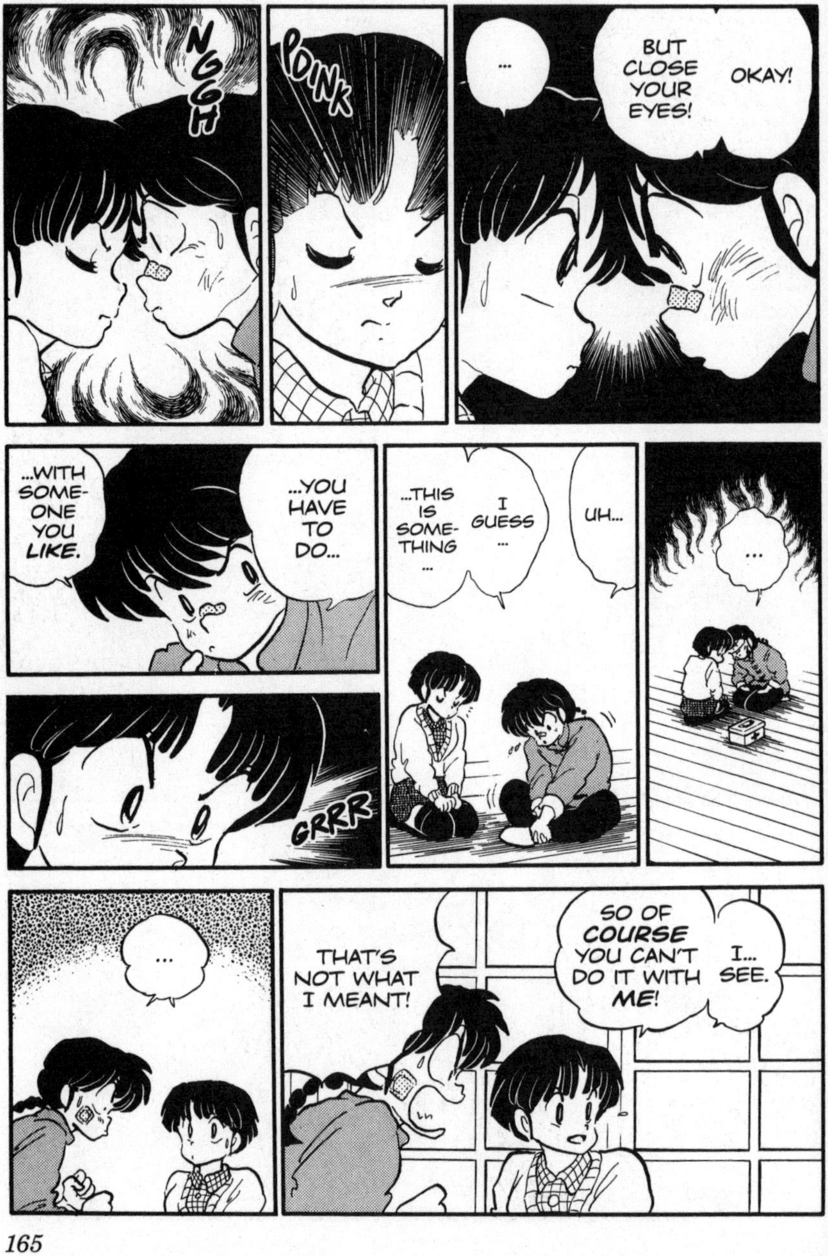
OKAY!
BUT CLOSE YOUR EYES!
...
POINK
NGGH
...
UH...
I GUESS ...
...THIS IS SOMETHING ...
...YOU HAVE TO DO...
...WITH SOMEONE YOU **LIKE.**
GRRR
I... SEE.
SO OF **COURSE** YOU CAN'T DO IT WITH **ME**!
THAT'S NOT WHAT I MEANT!
...

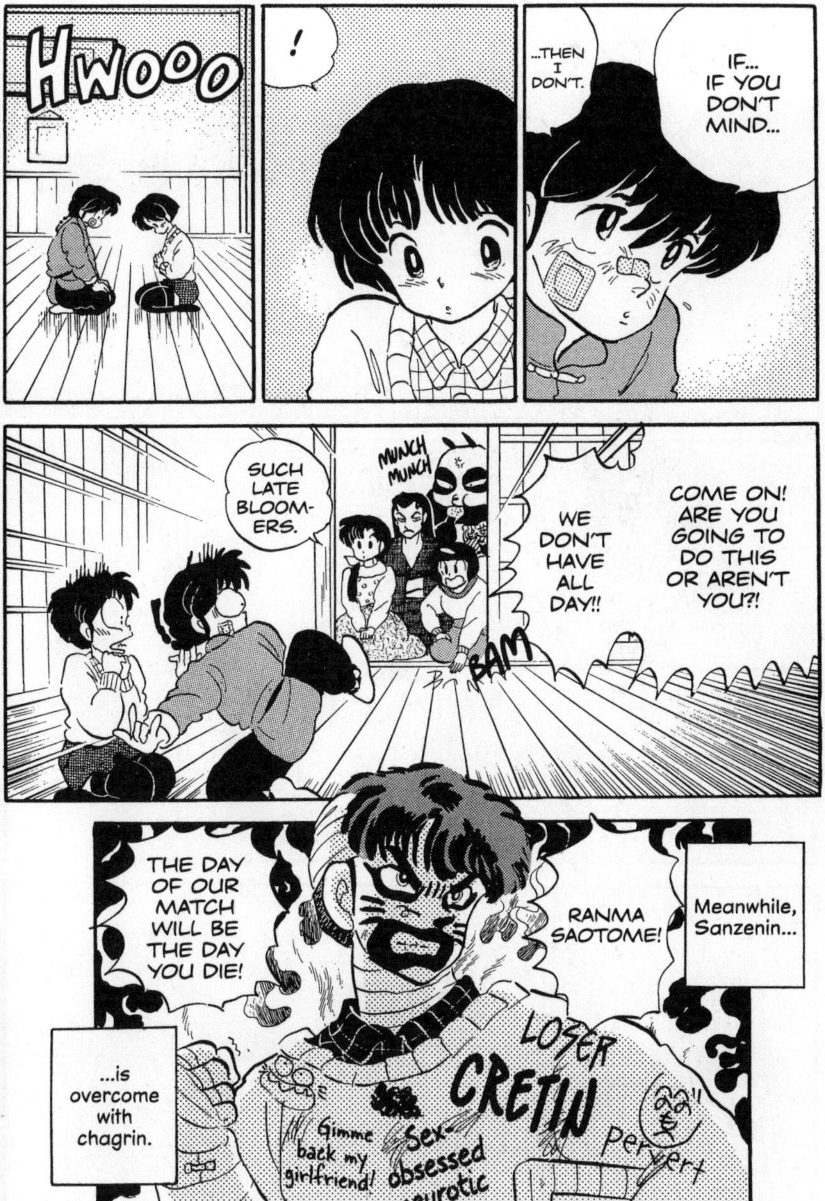
IF... IF YOU DON'T MIND...
...THEN I DON'T.
!
HWOOO
COME ON! ARE YOU GOING TO DO THIS OR AREN'T YOU?!
WE DON'T HAVE ALL DAY!!
MUNCH MUNCH
SUCH LATE BLOOMERS.
BAM
Meanwhile, Sanzenin...
RANMA SAOTOME!
THE DAY OF OUR MATCH WILL BE THE DAY YOU DIE!
LOSER
CRETIN
Pervert
Sex-obsessed neurotic
Gimme back my girlfriend!
...is overcome with chagrin.

PART 9
LIPS AT WAR

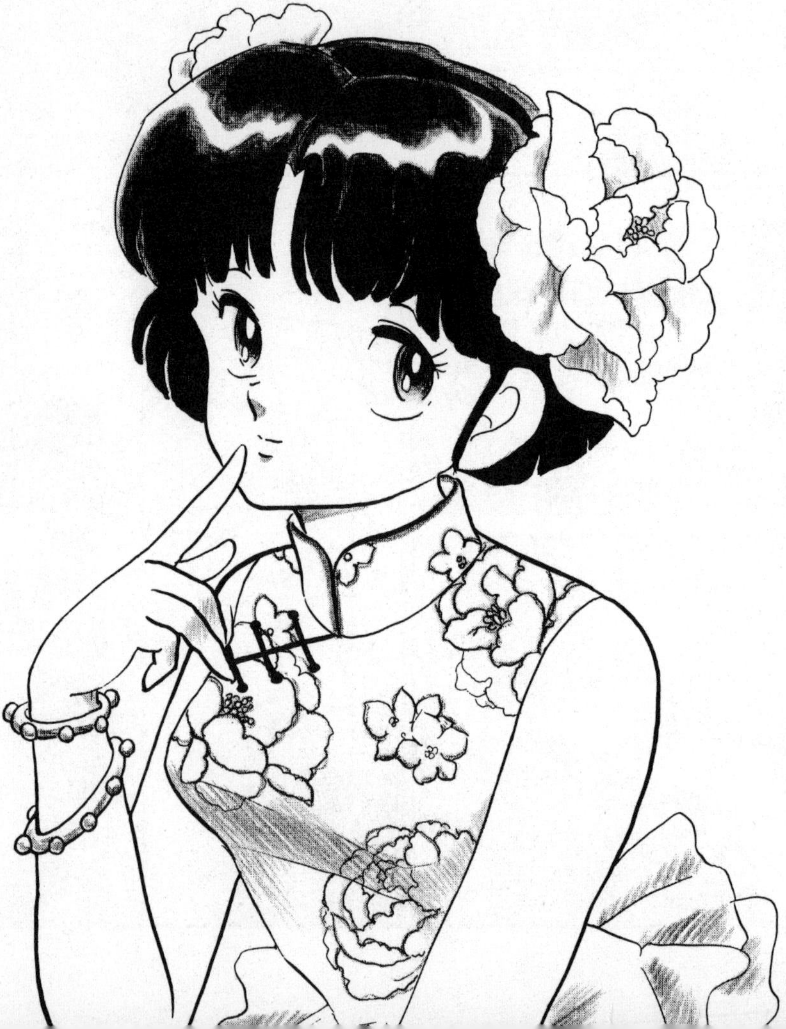

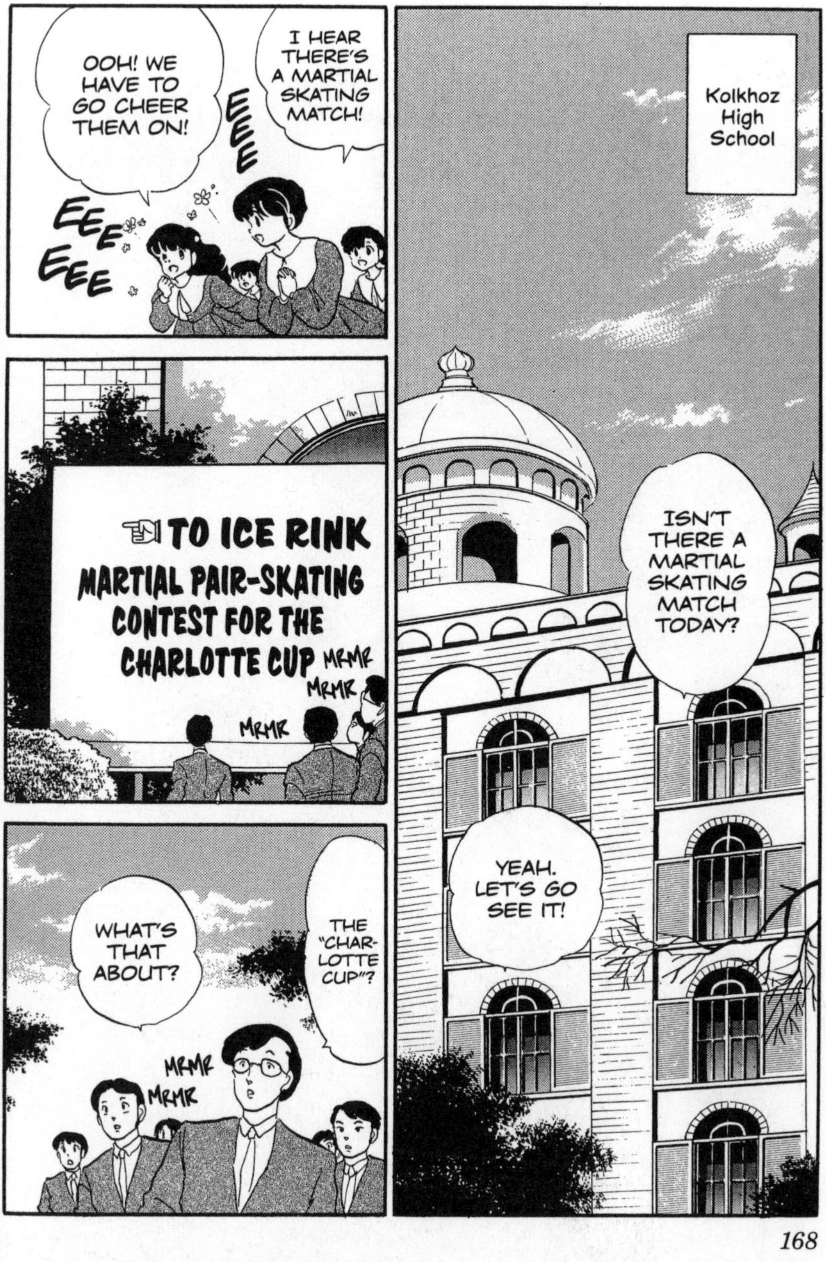
Kolkhoz High School
ISN'T THERE A MARTIAL SKATING MATCH TODAY?
YEAH. LET'S GO SEE IT!
I HEAR THERE'S A MARTIAL SKATING MATCH!
EEE
OOH! WE HAVE TO GO CHEER THEM ON!
EEE EEE
TO ICE RINK
MARTIAL PAIR-SKATING CONTEST FOR THE CHARLOTTE CUP
MRMR MRMR
MRMR
THE "CHARLOTTE CUP"?
WHAT'S THAT ABOUT?
MRMR MRMR

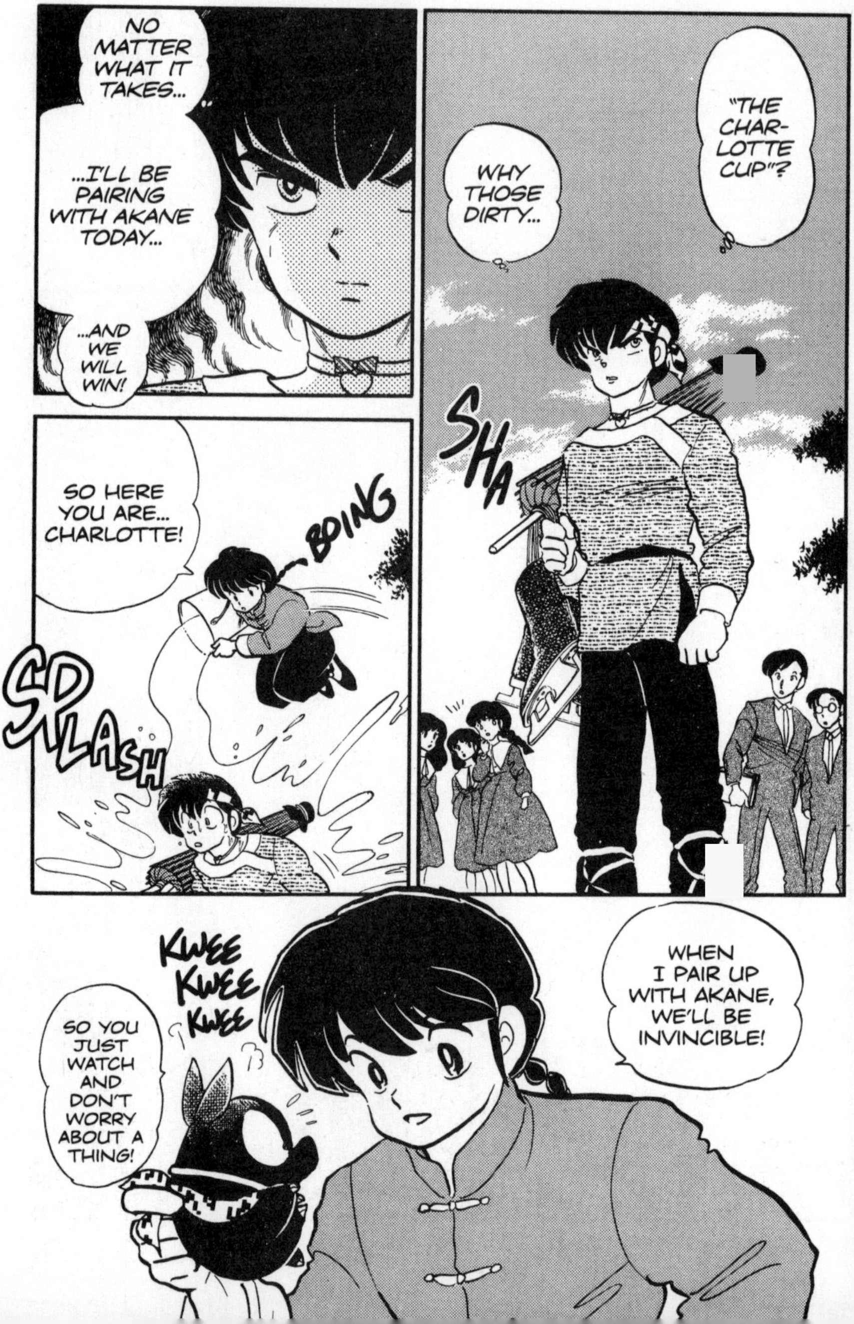
"THE CHARLOTTE CUP"?
WHY THOSE DIRTY...
SHA
NO MATTER WHAT IT TAKES...
...I'LL BE PAIRING WITH AKANE TODAY...
...AND WE WILL WIN!
BOING
SO HERE YOU ARE... CHARLOTTE!
SPLASH
WHEN I PAIR UP WITH AKANE, WE'LL BE INVINCIBLE!
KWEE KWEE KWEE
SO YOU JUST WATCH AND DON'T WORRY ABOUT A THING!

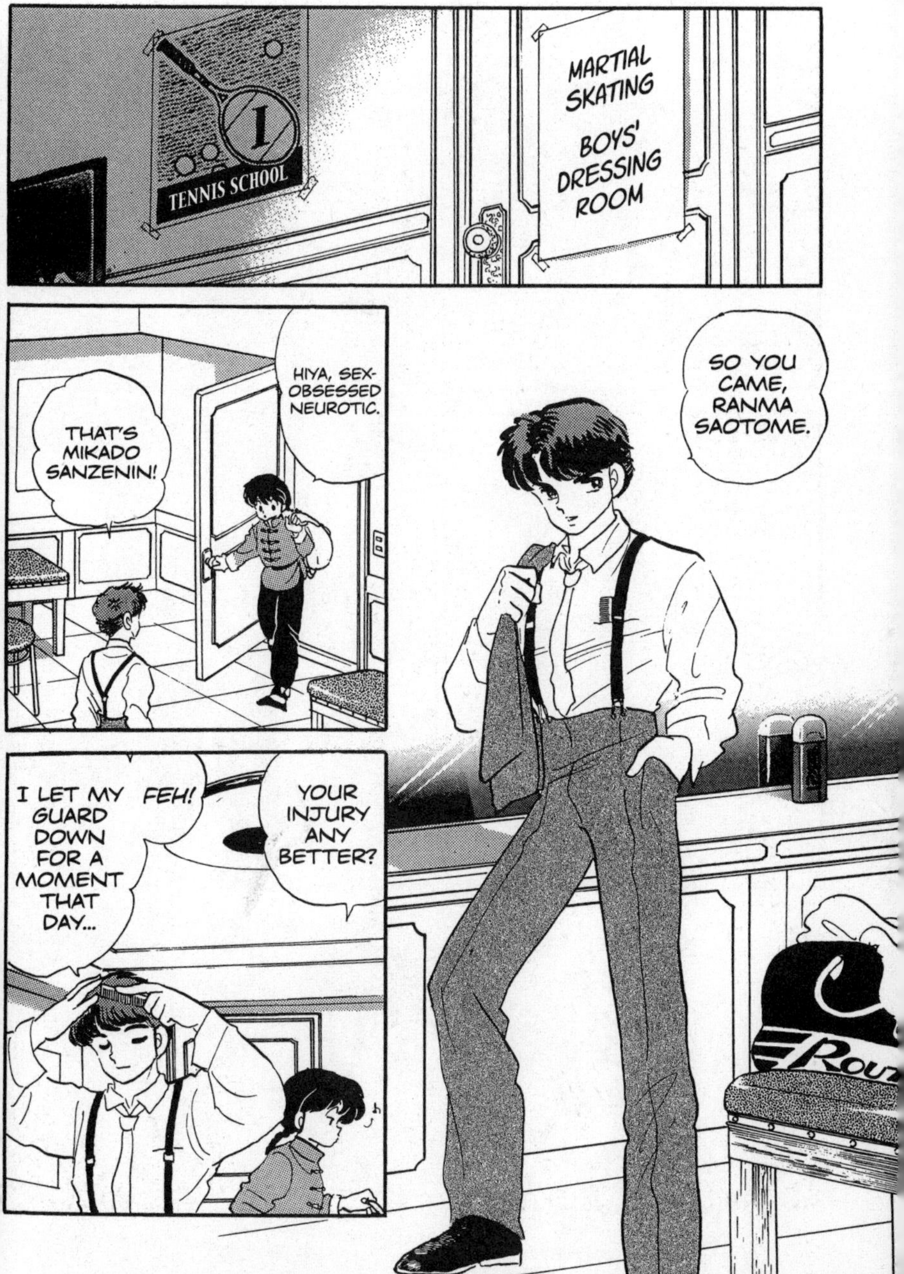
MARTIAL SKATING
BOYS' DRESSING ROOM
1
TENNIS SCHOOL
SO YOU CAME, RANMA SAOTOME.
HIYA, SEX-OBSESSED NEUROTIC.
THAT'S MIKADO SANZENIN!
YOUR INJURY ANY BETTER?
FEH!
I LET MY GUARD DOWN FOR A MOMENT THAT DAY...

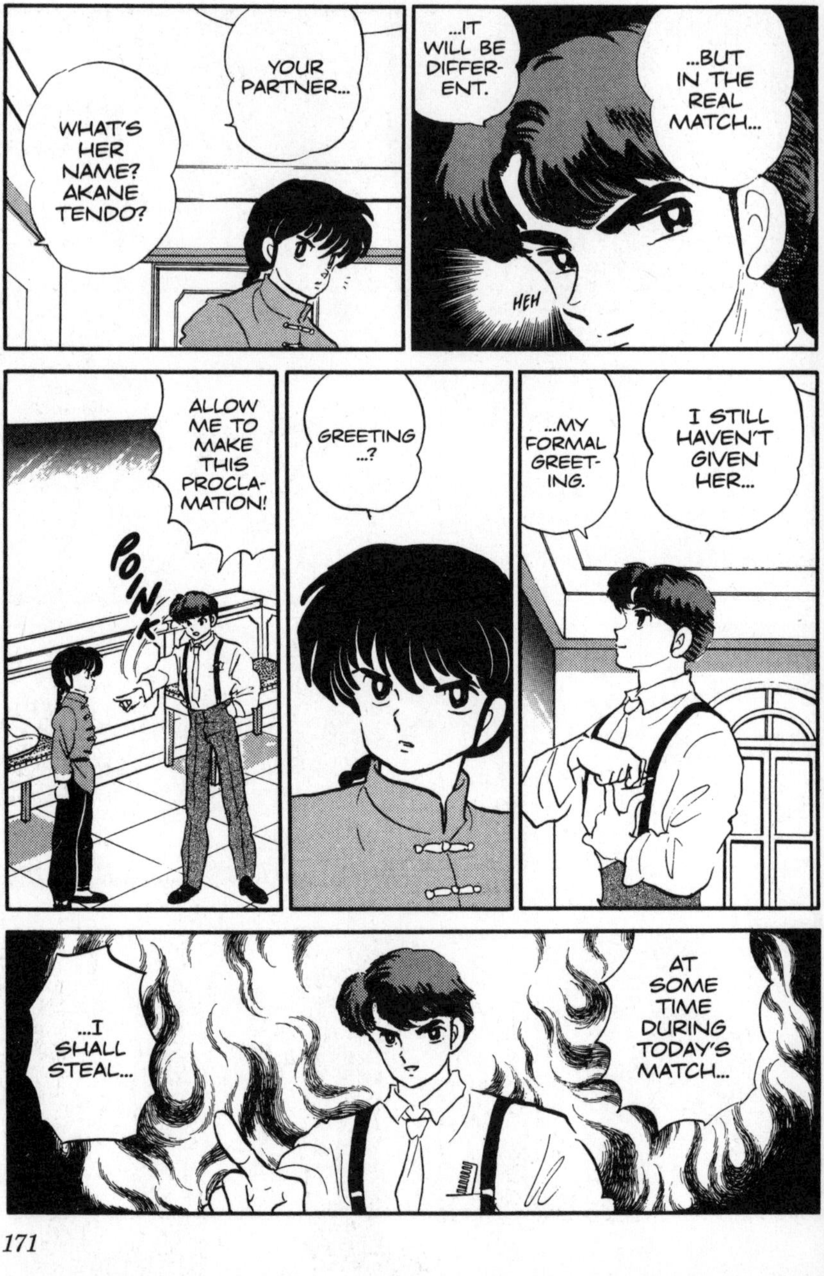
...BUT IN THE REAL MATCH...
...IT WILL BE DIFFER-ENT.
HEH
YOUR PARTNER...
WHAT'S HER NAME? AKANE TENDO?
I STILL HAVEN'T GIVEN HER...
...MY FORMAL GREET-ING.
GREETING ...?
ALLOW ME TO MAKE THIS PROCLA-MATION!
POINK
AT SOME TIME DURING TODAY'S MATCH...
...I SHALL STEAL...

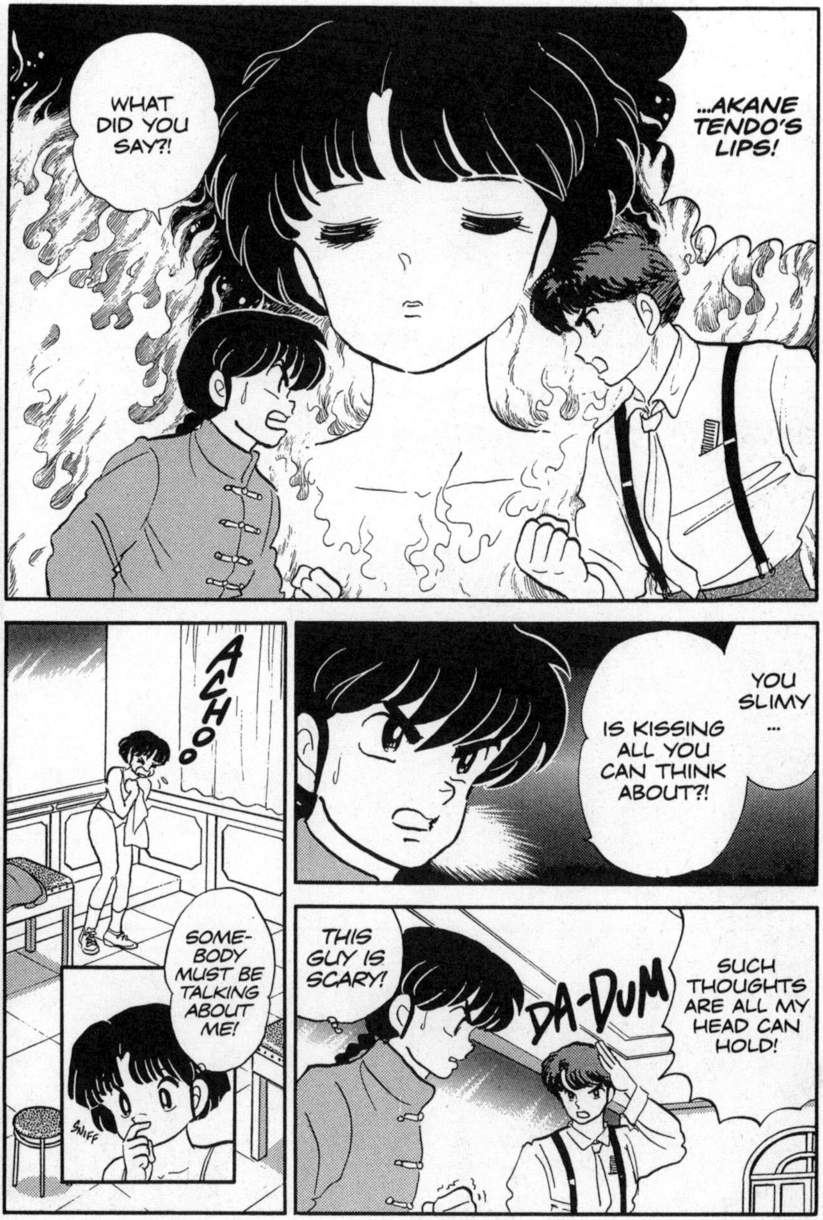
...AKANE TENDO'S LIPS!
WHAT DID YOU SAY?!
YOU SLIMY ...
IS KISSING ALL YOU CAN THINK ABOUT?!
SUCH THOUGHTS ARE ALL MY HEAD CAN HOLD!
DA-DUM
THIS GUY IS SCARY!
ACHOO
SOME-BODY MUST BE TALKING ABOUT ME!
SNIFF

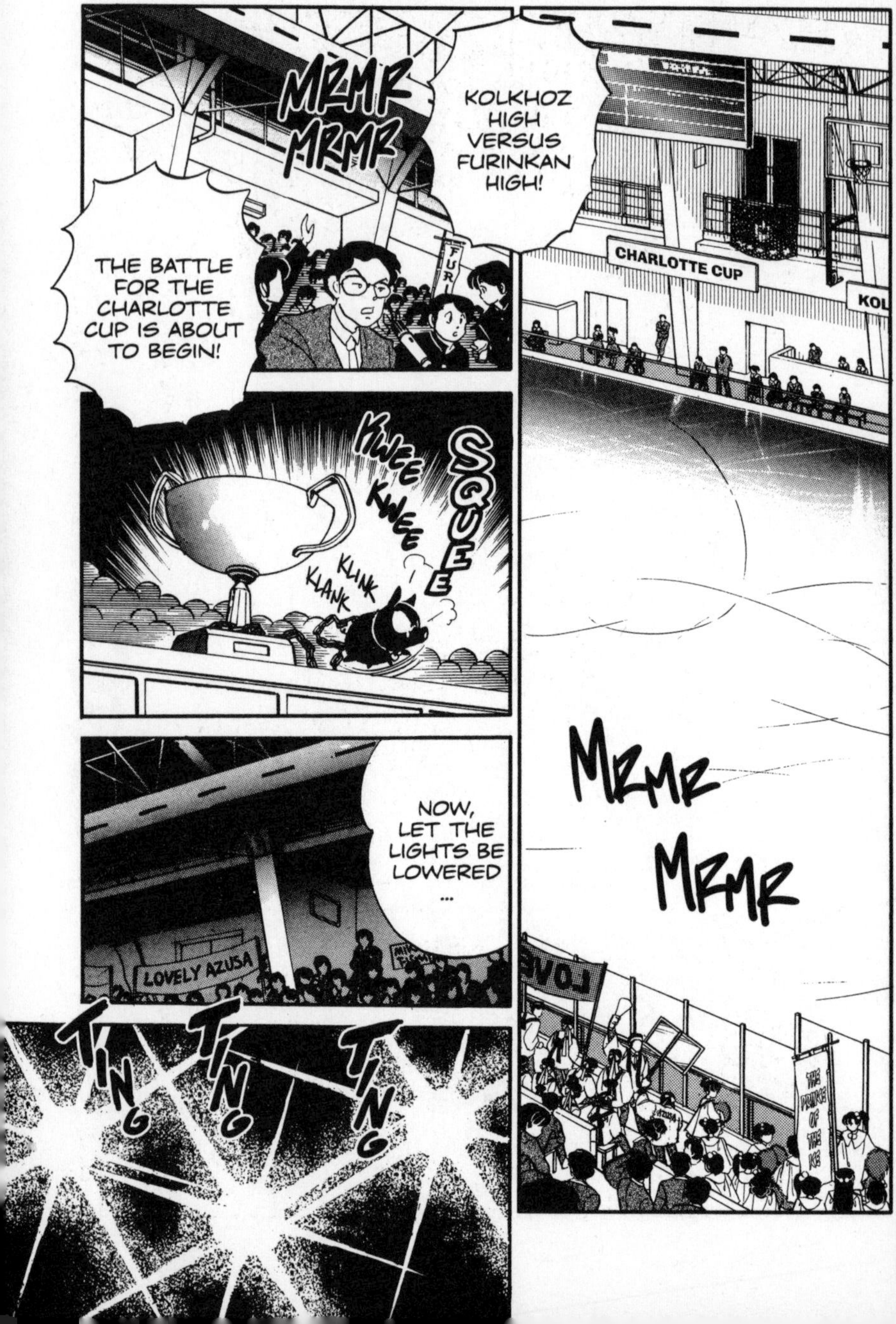
CHARLOTTE CUP
KOL
MRMR
MRMR
THE PRINCE OF THE ICE
MRMR
MRMR
KOLKHOZ HIGH VERSUS FURINKAN HIGH!
THE BATTLE FOR THE CHARLOTTE CUP IS ABOUT TO BEGIN!
FURI
SQUEE
KWEE KWEE
KLINK KLANK
NOW, LET THE LIGHTS BE LOWERED ...
LOVELY AZUSA
TING TING TING

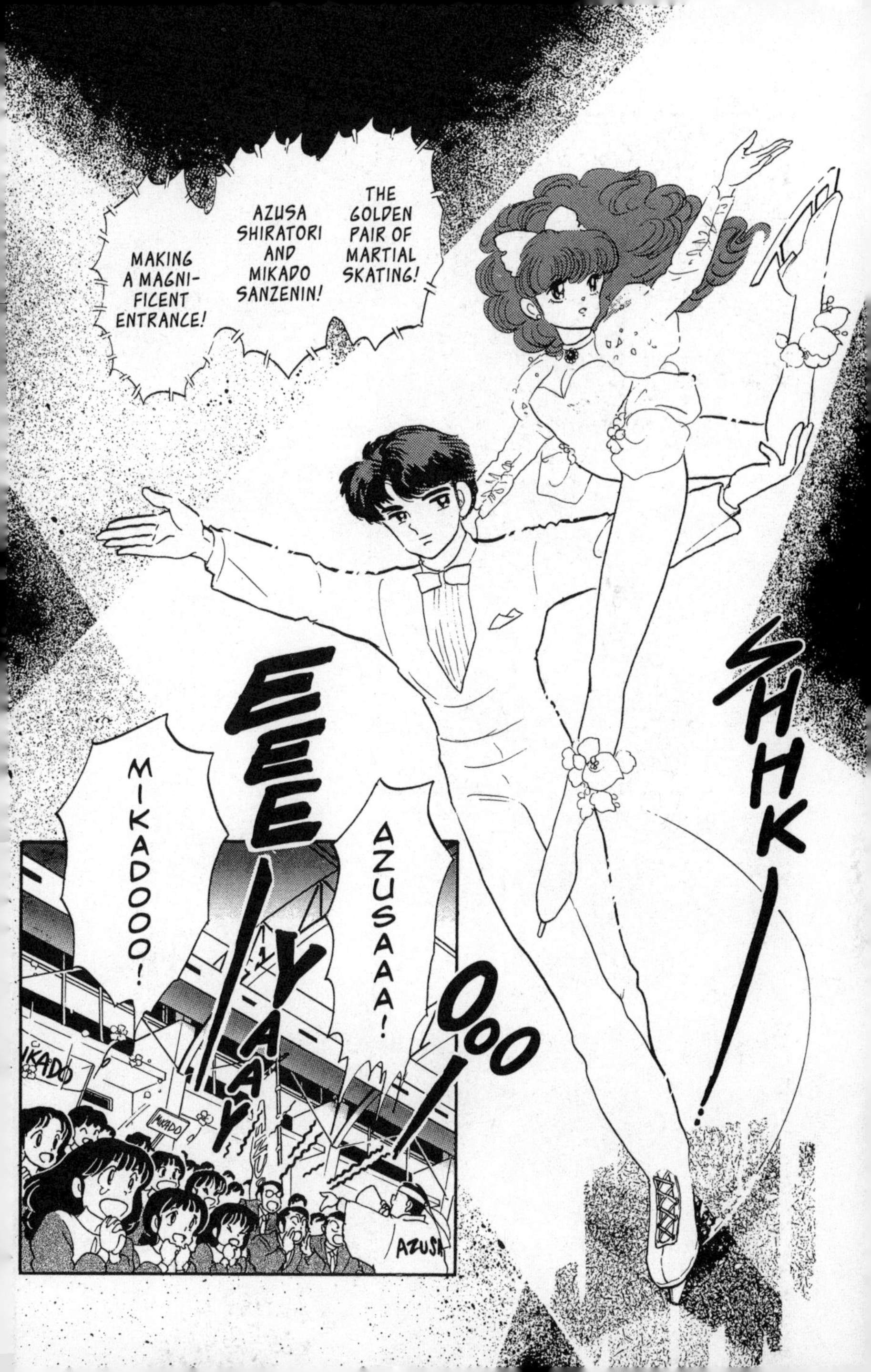
THE GOLDEN PAIR OF MARTIAL SKATING!
AZUSA SHIRATORI AND MIKADO SANZENIN!
MAKING A MAGNIFICENT ENTRANCE!
SHHK!
OOO!
AZUSAAAA!
EEE-YAAAY
MIKADOOOO!
MIKADO
MIKADO
AZUSA

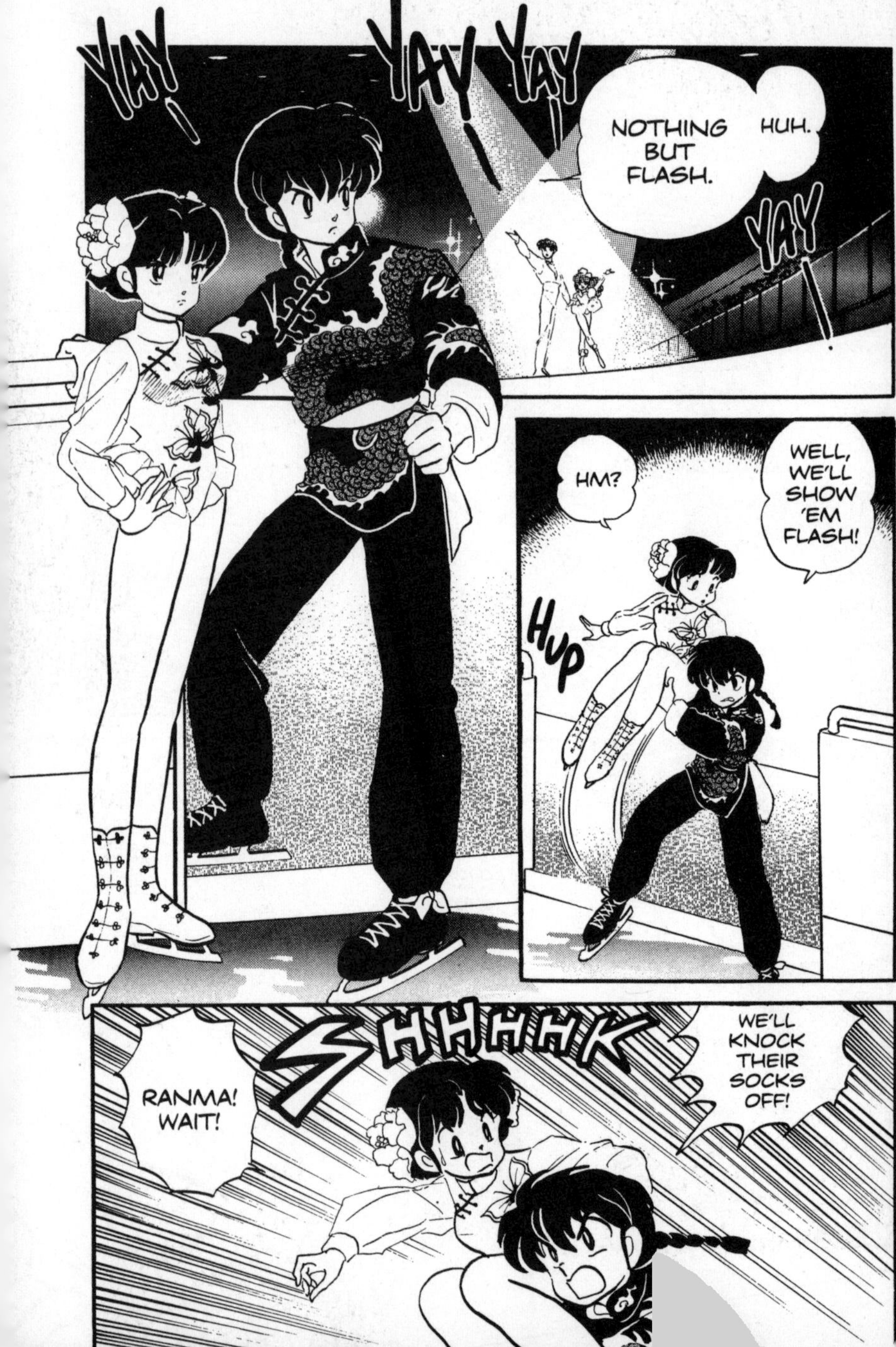
YAY
HUH.
NOTHING BUT FLASH.
YAY YAY
YAY
WELL, WE'LL SHOW 'EM FLASH!
HM?
HUP
WE'LL KNOCK THEIR SOCKS OFF!
SHHHHK
RANMA! WAIT!

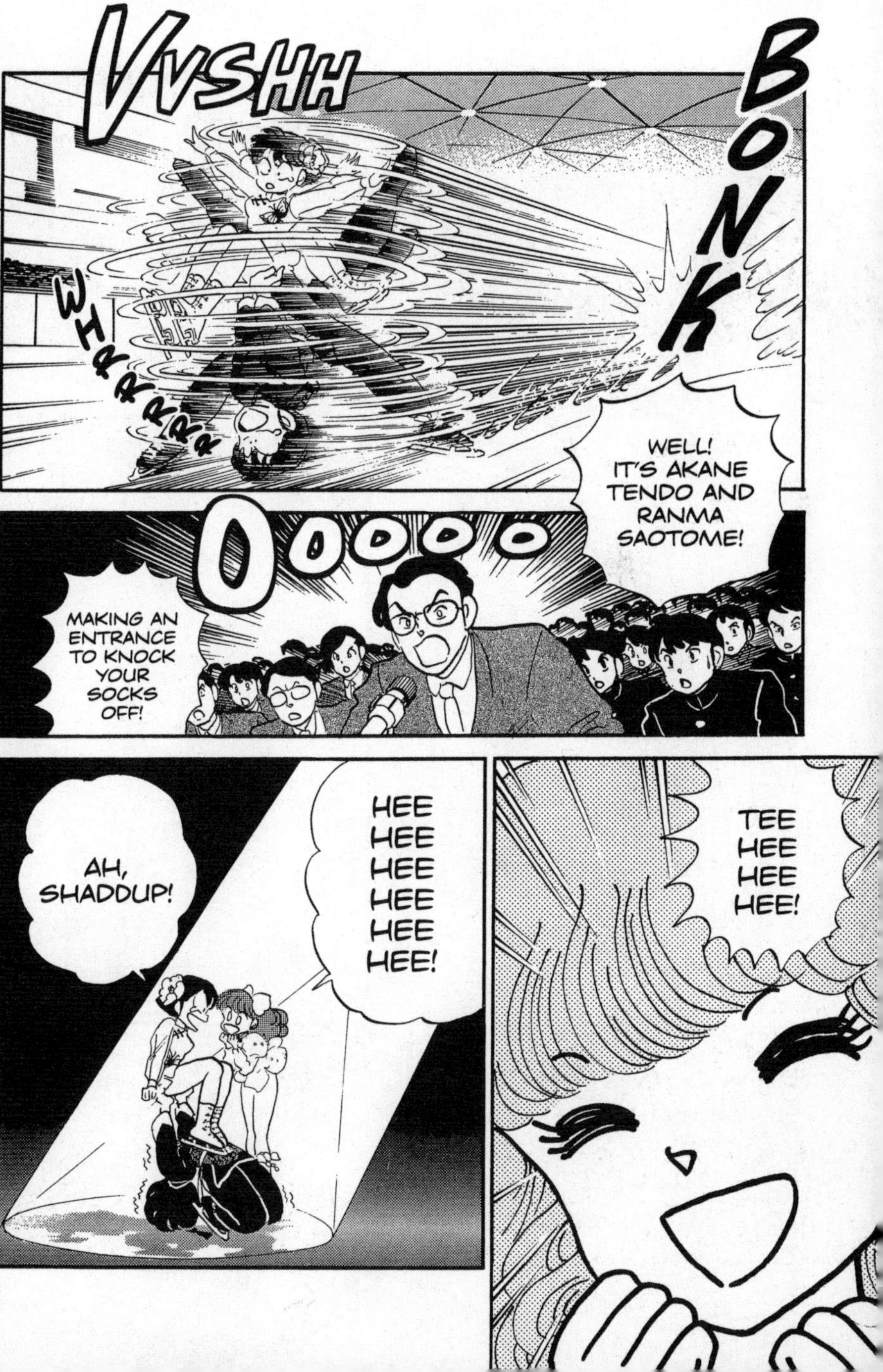
BONK
VVSHH
WHRRRRRR
WELL! IT'S AKANE TENDO AND RANMA SAOTOME!
OOOOO
MAKING AN ENTRANCE TO KNOCK YOUR SOCKS OFF!
TEE HEE HEE HEE!
HEE HEE HEE HEE HEE HEE!
AH, SHADDUP!

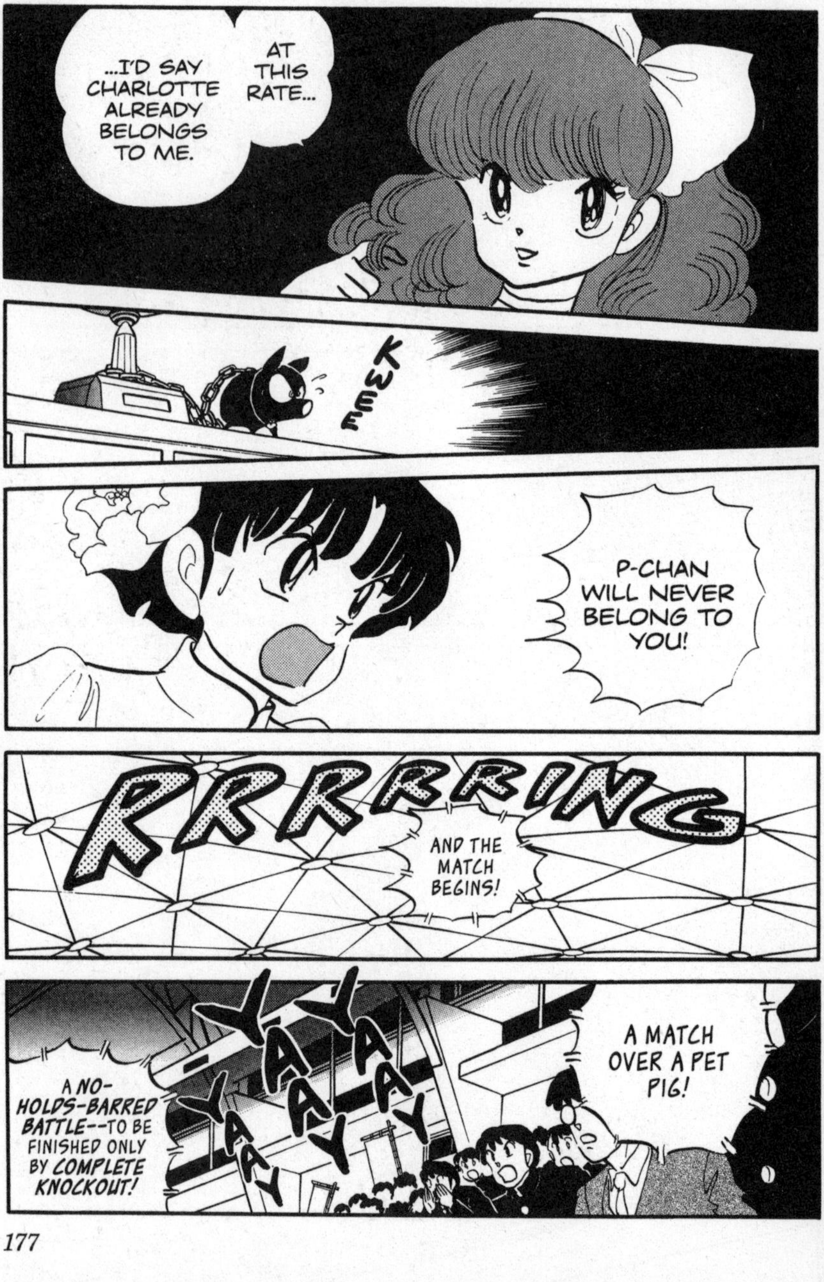
AT THIS RATE...
...I'D SAY CHARLOTTE ALREADY BELONGS TO ME.
KWEEE
P-CHAN WILL NEVER BELONG TO YOU!
RRRRRING
AND THE MATCH BEGINS!
A MATCH OVER A PET PIG!
A NO-HOLDS-BARRED BATTLE--TO BE FINISHED ONLY BY COMPLETE KNOCKOUT!

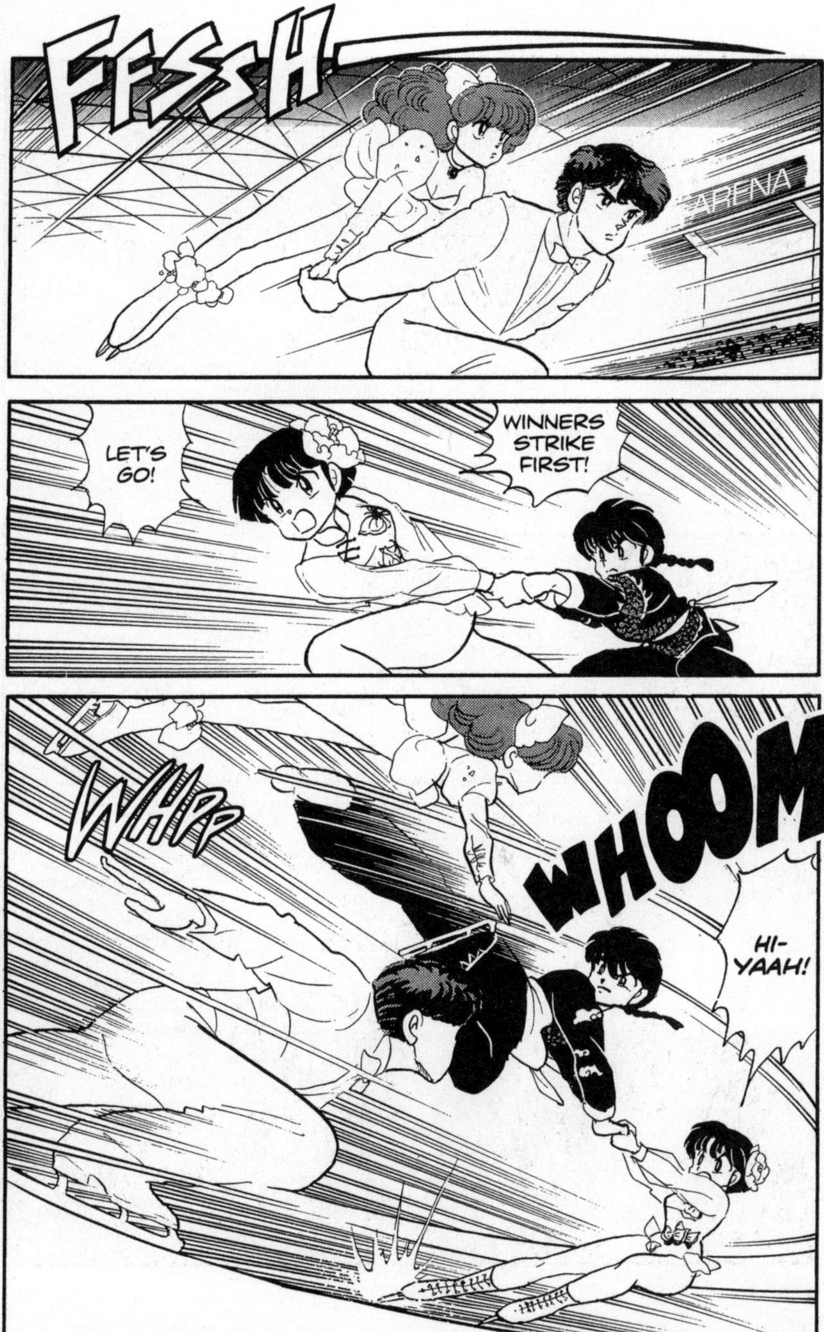
FFSSH
WINNERS STRIKE FIRST!
LET'S GO!
WHOOM
HI-YAAH!
WHPP

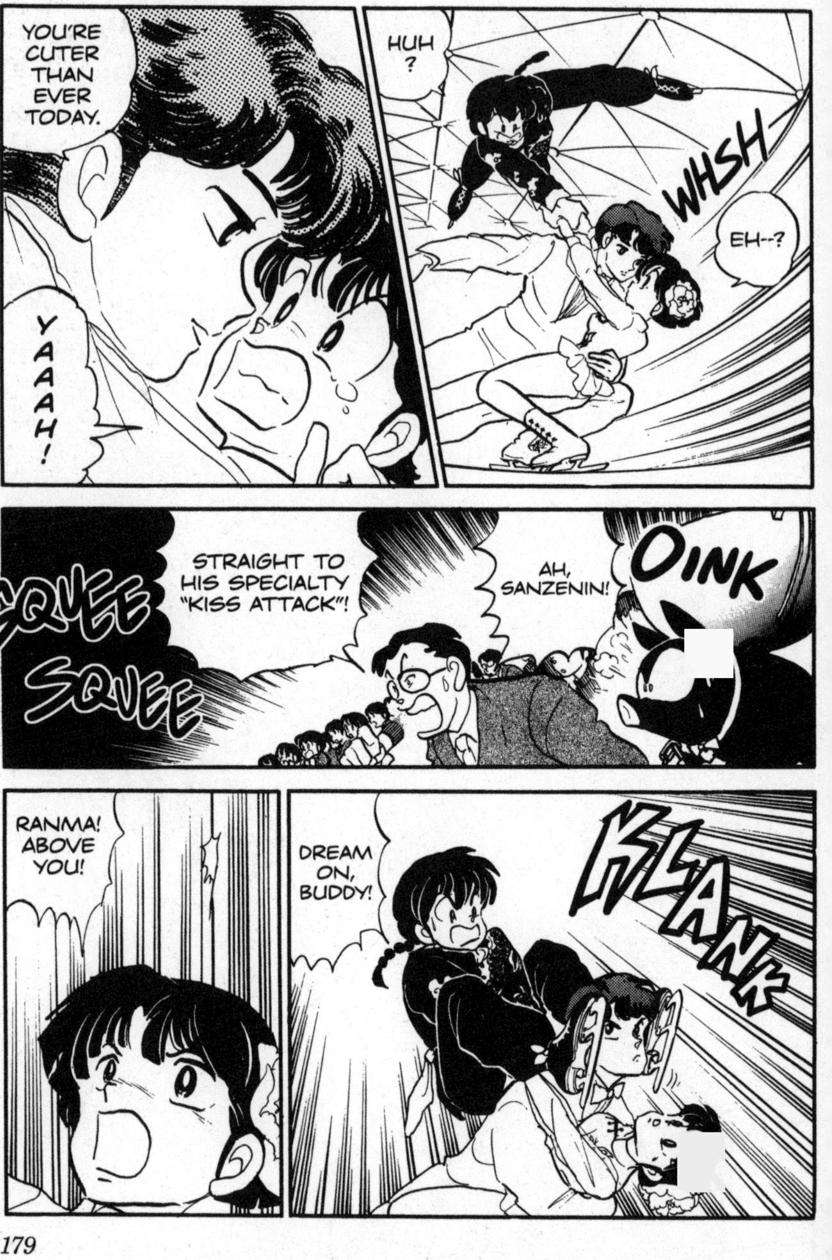
HUH?
WHSH
EH--?
YOU'RE CUTER THAN EVER TODAY.
YAAAAH!
OINK
AH, SANZENIN!
STRAIGHT TO HIS SPECIALTY "KISS ATTACK"!
SQUEE SQUEE
KLANK
DREAM ON, BUDDY!
RANMA! ABOVE YOU!

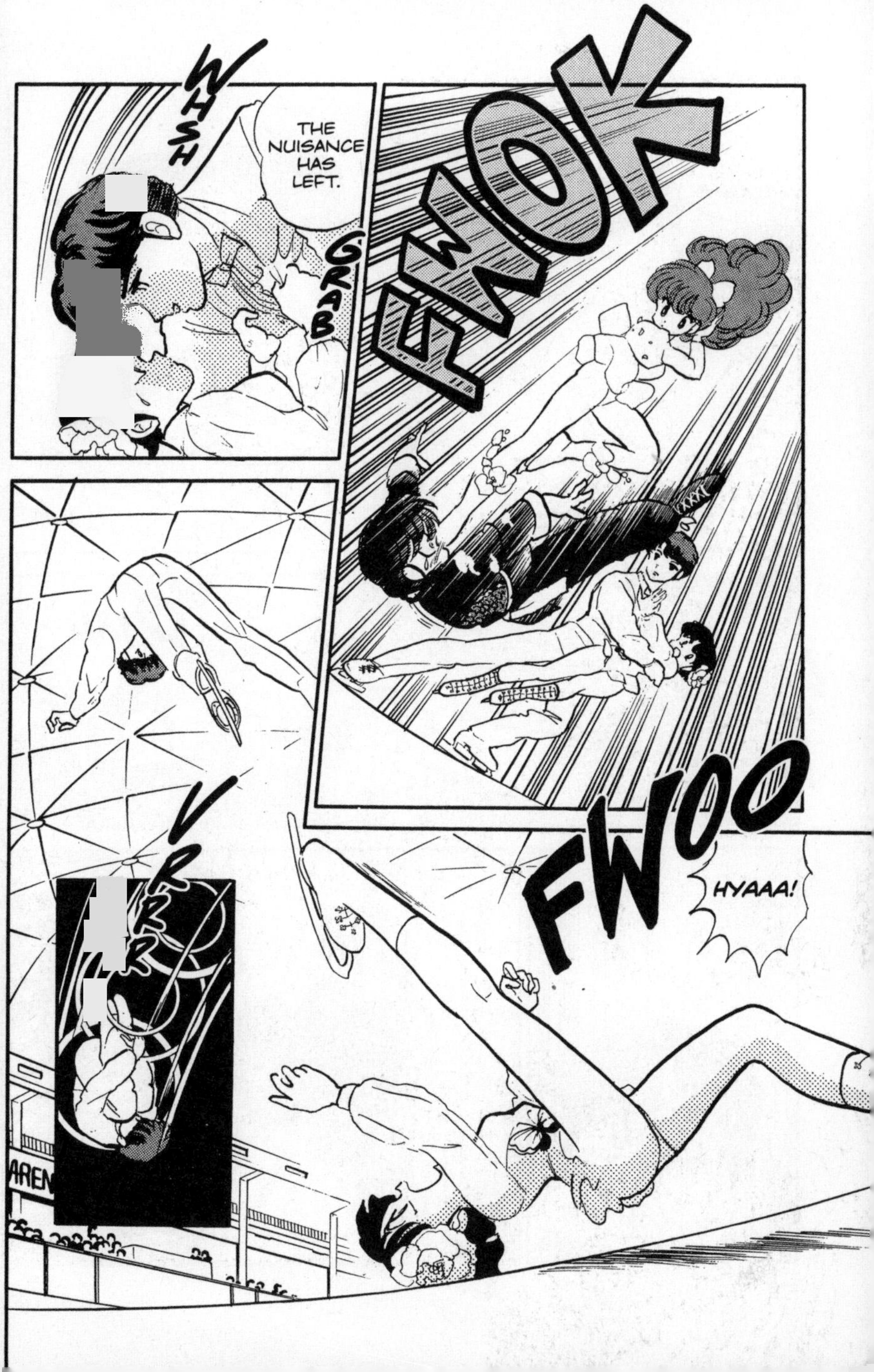

FWOK
WHSH
THE NUISANCE HAS LEFT.
GRAB
FWOO
HYAAA!
VRRR
AREN

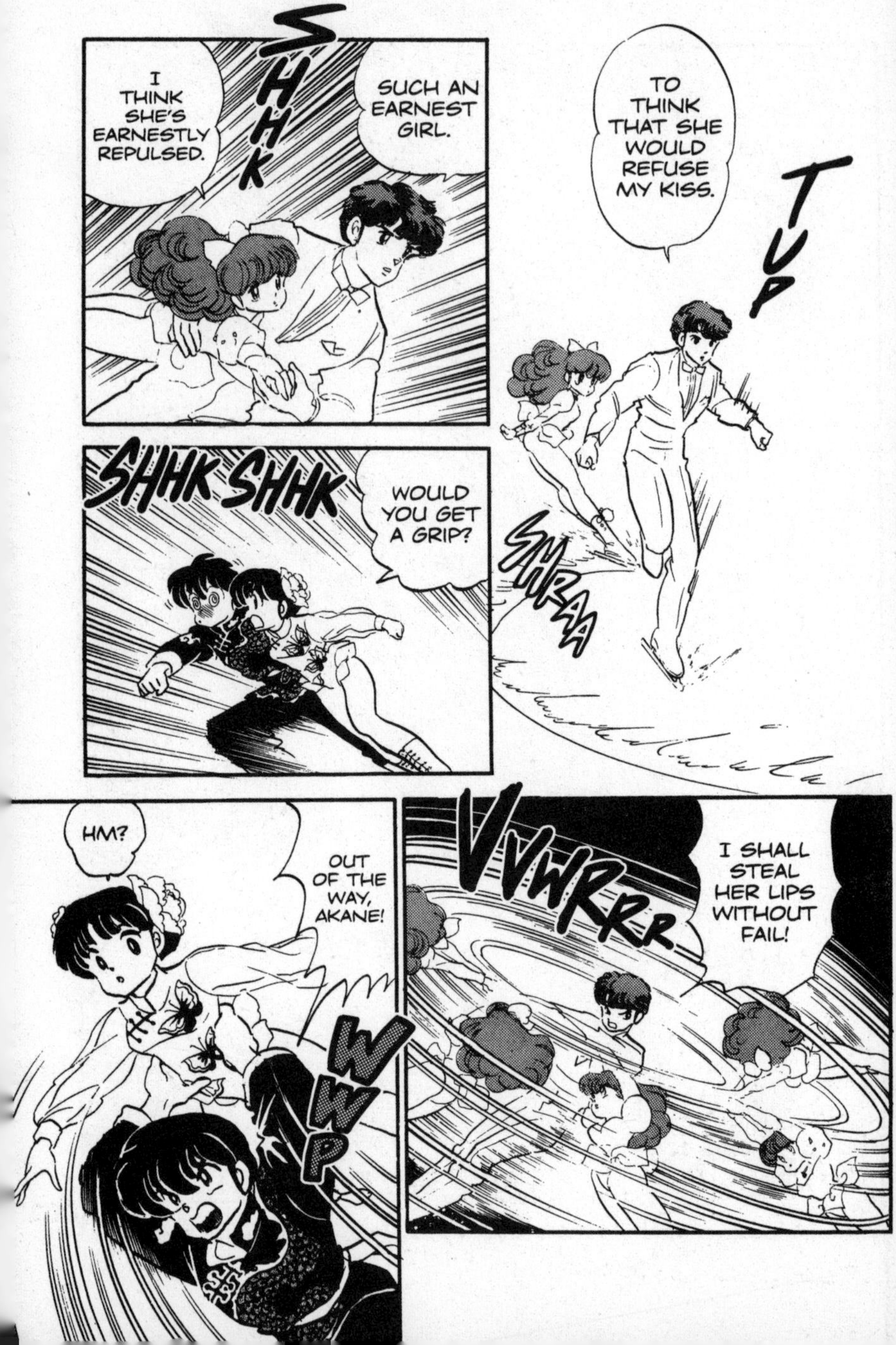
TO THINK THAT SHE WOULD REFUSE MY KISS.
TUP
SHRAA
SHHHK
SUCH AN EARNEST GIRL.
I THINK SHE'S EARNESTLY REPULSED.
SHHK SHHK
WOULD YOU GET A GRIP?
VVWRRR
I SHALL STEAL HER LIPS WITHOUT FAIL!
HM?
OUT OF THE WAY, AKANE!
WWP

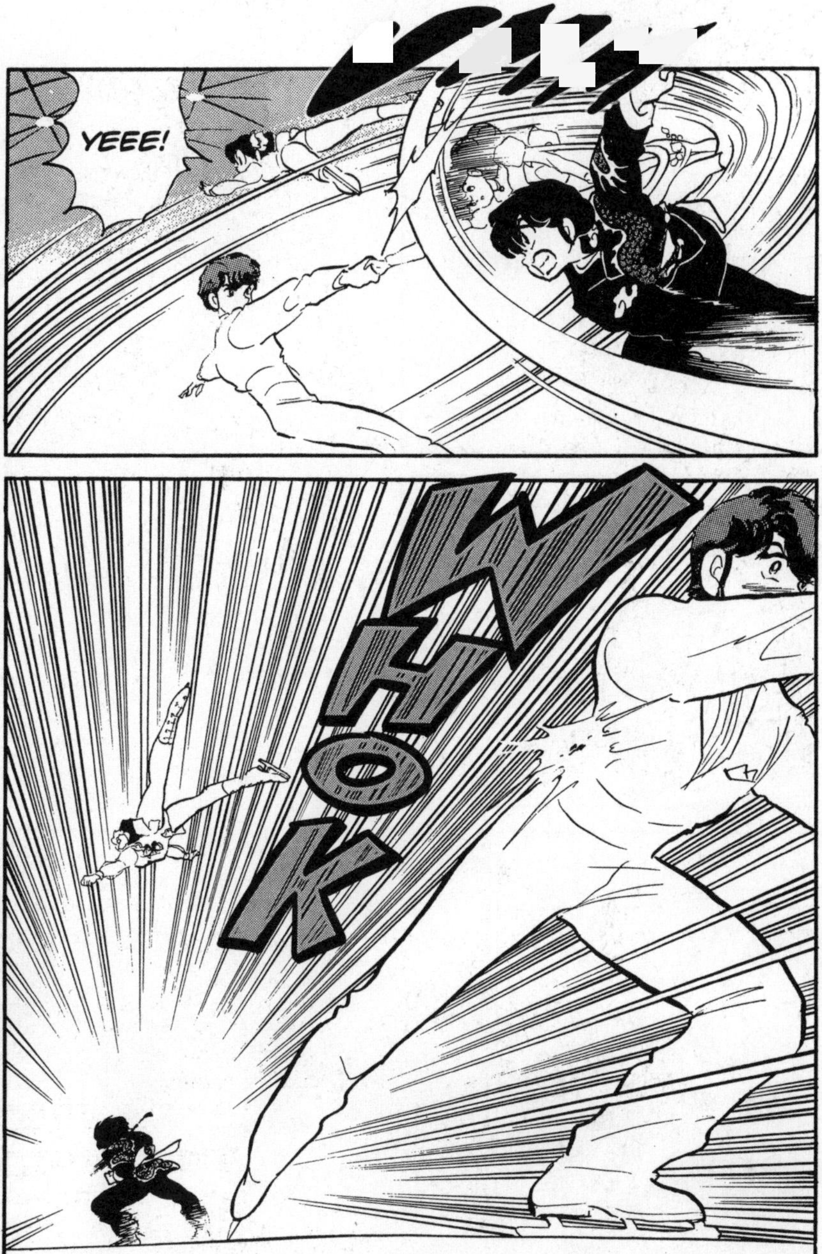
YEEE!
WHOK

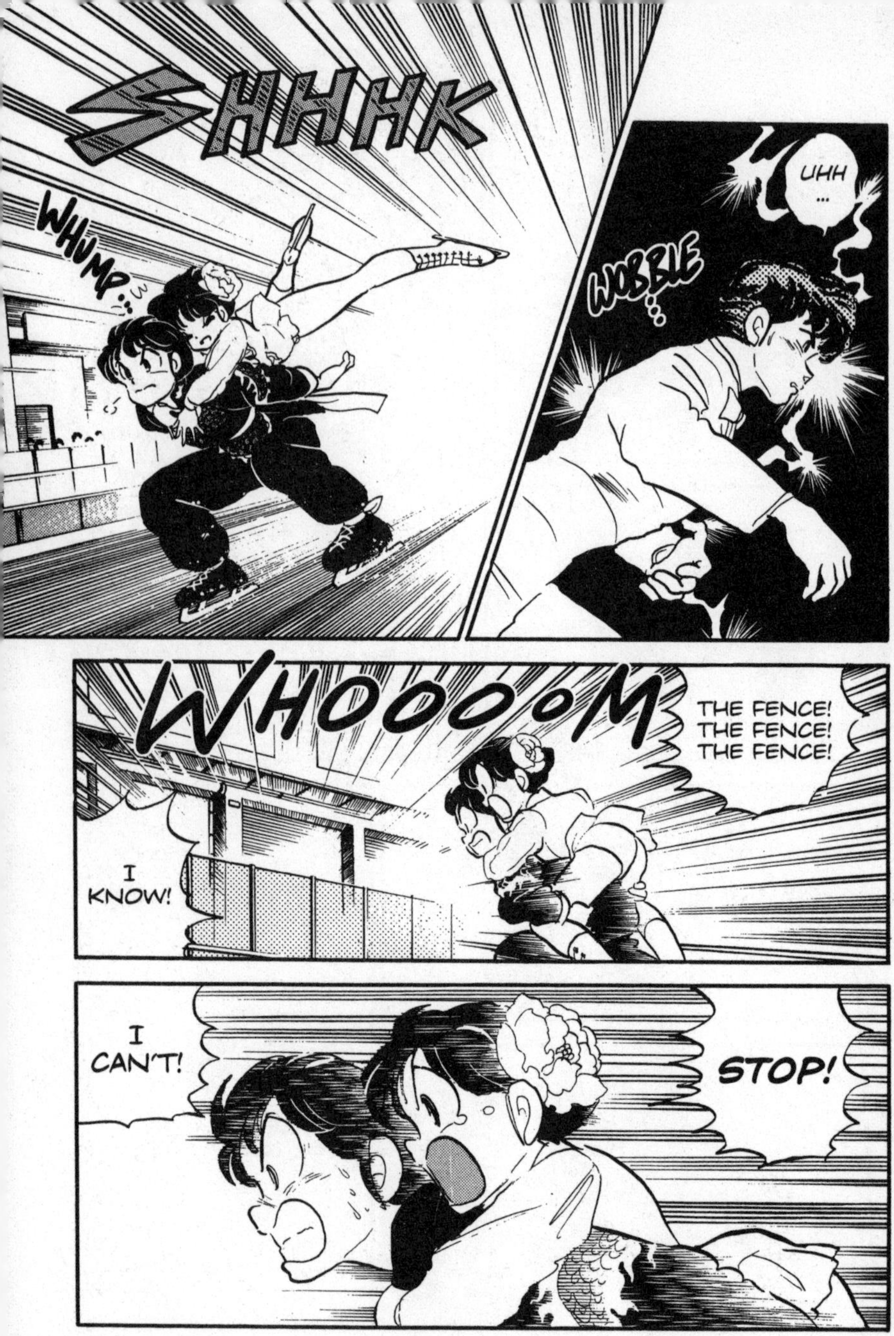
UHH ...
WOBBLE
SHHHK
WHUMP
WHOOOOM
THE FENCE! THE FENCE! THE FENCE!
I KNOW!
STOP!
I CAN'T!

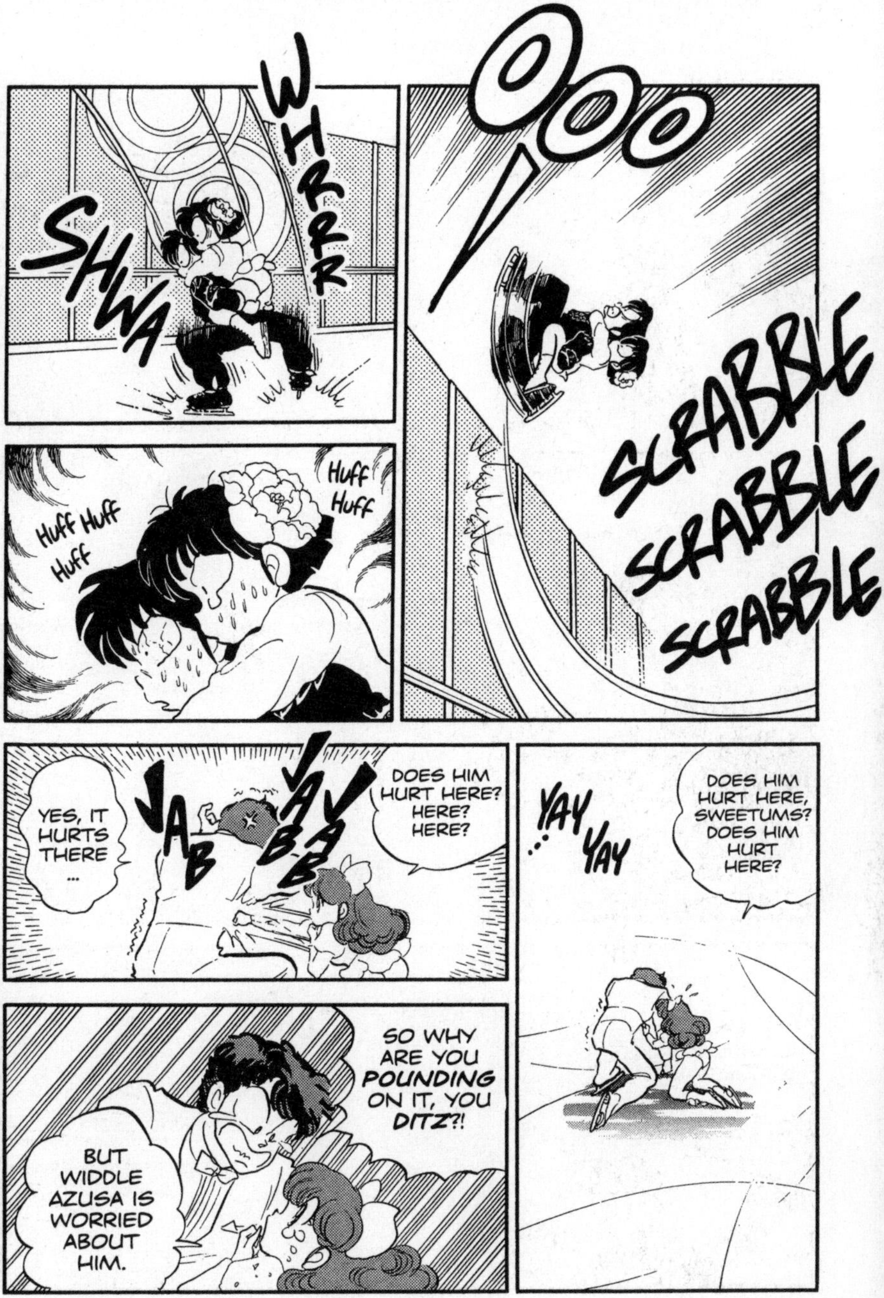
OOOO
SCRABBLE
SCRABBLE
SCRABBLE
WHRRRR
SHWA
Huff Huff
Huff Huff
Huff
DOES HIM HURT HERE, SWEETUMS? DOES HIM HURT HERE?
YAY YAY
DOES HIM HURT HERE? HERE? HERE?
JAB JAB JAB
YES, IT HURTS THERE ...
SO WHY ARE YOU **POUNDING** ON IT, YOU ***DITZ***?!
BUT WIDDLE AZUSA IS WORRIED ABOUT HIM.

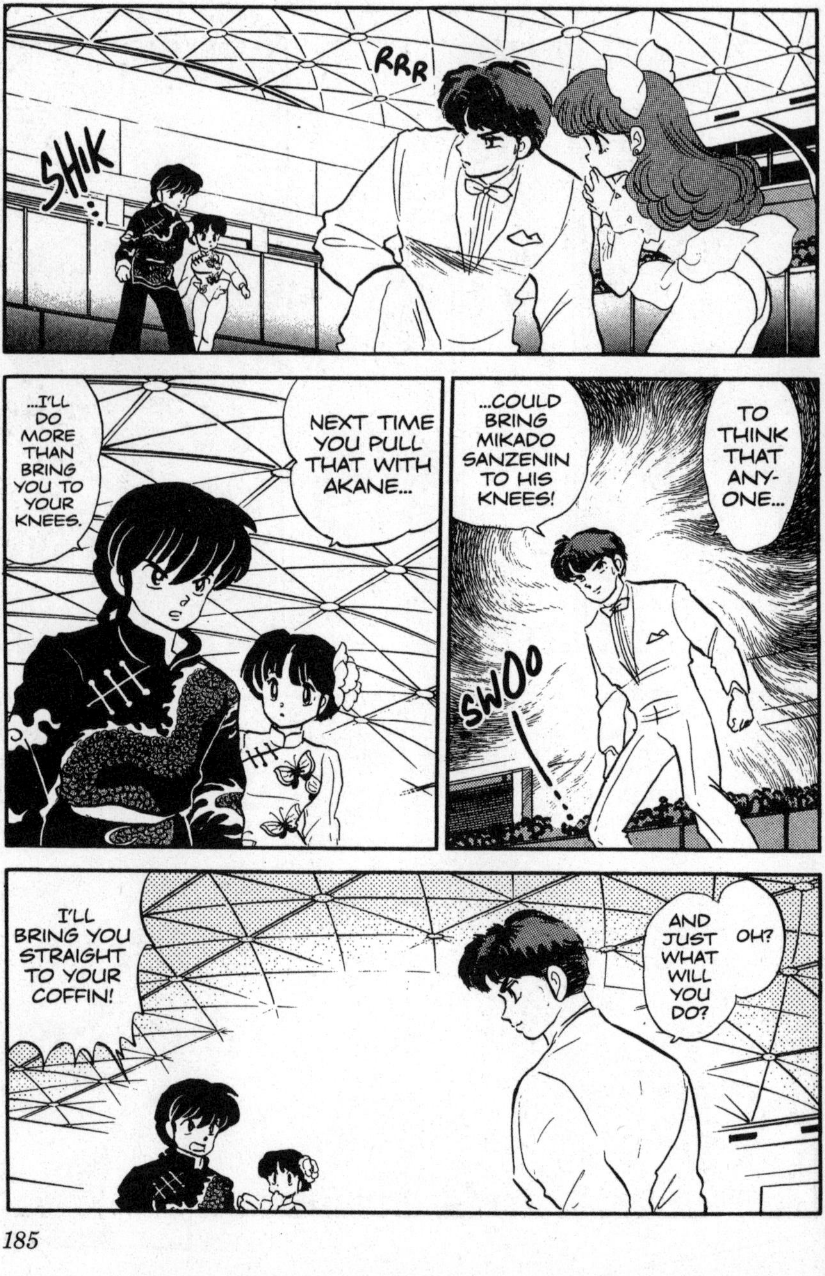
RRR
SHIK
TO THINK THAT ANY-ONE...
...COULD BRING MIKADO SANZENIN TO HIS KNEES!
SWOO
NEXT TIME YOU PULL THAT WITH AKANE...
...I'LL DO MORE THAN BRING YOU TO YOUR KNEES.
OH?
AND JUST WHAT WILL YOU DO?
I'LL BRING YOU STRAIGHT TO YOUR COFFIN!

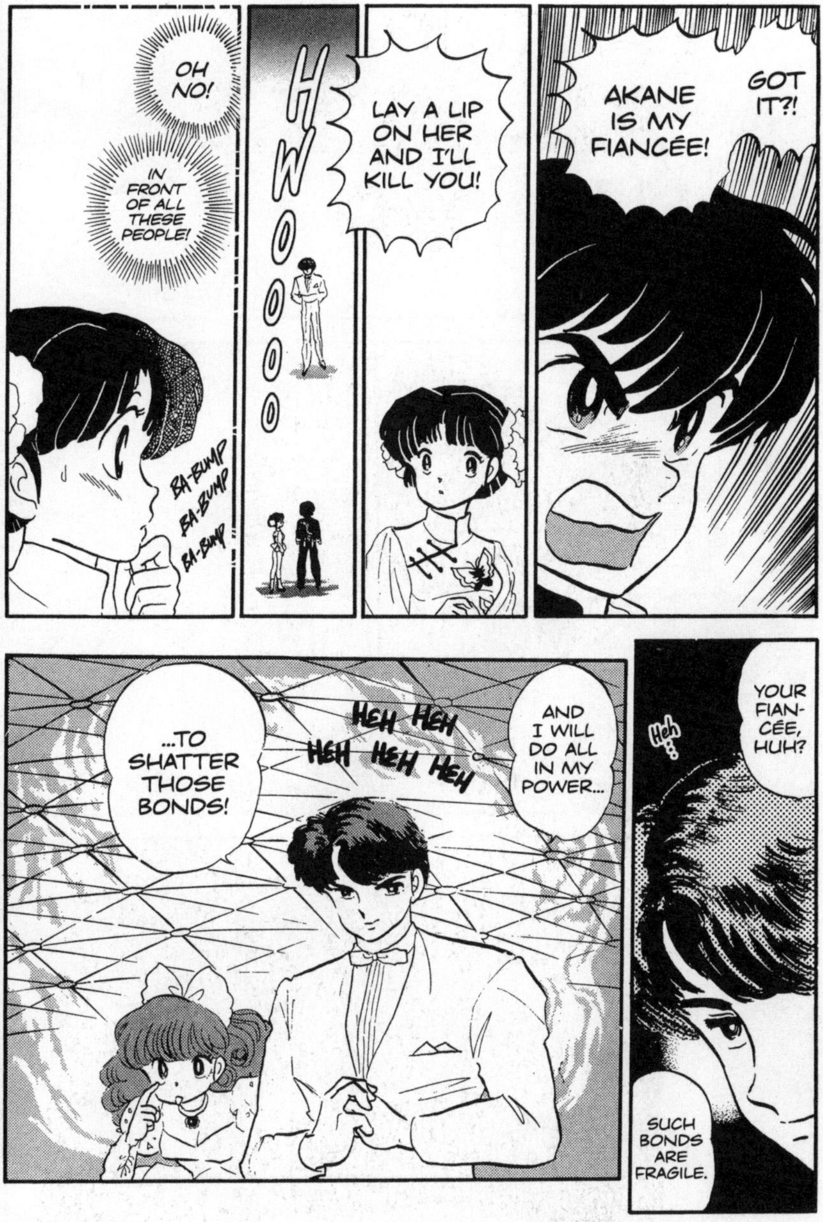
AKANE IS MY FIANCÉE!
GOT IT?!
LAY A LIP ON HER AND I'LL KILL YOU!
HWOOOOOO
OH NO!
IN FRONT OF ALL THESE PEOPLE!
BA-BUMP BA-BUMP BA-BUMP
Heh...
YOUR FIAN-CÉE, HUH?
SUCH BONDS ARE FRAGILE.
AND I WILL DO ALL IN MY POWER...
HEH HEH HEH HEH HEH
...TO SHATTER THOSE BONDS!

PART 10
I'LL NEVER
LET GO

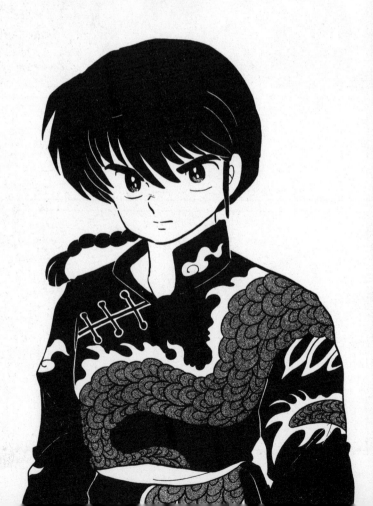

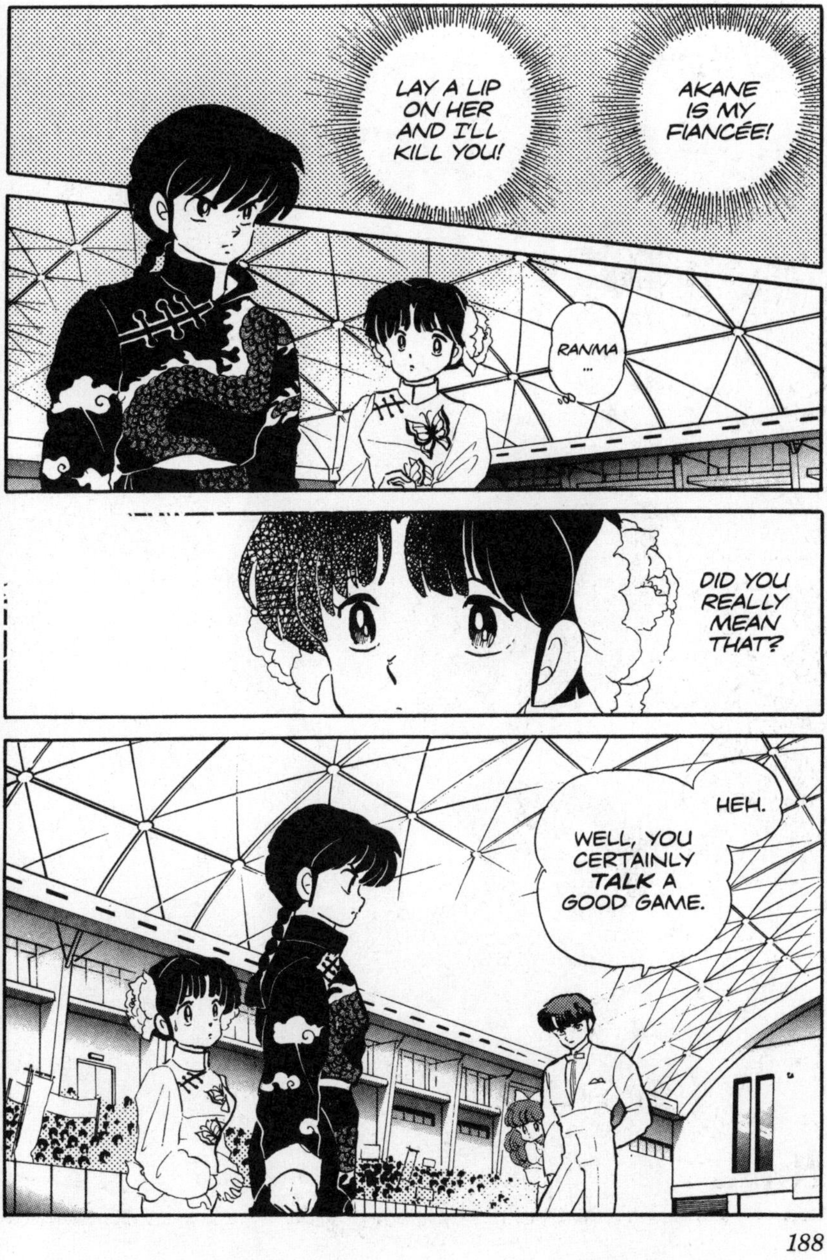
AKANE IS MY FIANCÉE!
LAY A LIP ON HER AND I'LL KILL YOU!
RANMA ...
DID YOU REALLY MEAN THAT?
HEH.
WELL, YOU CERTAINLY TALK A GOOD GAME.

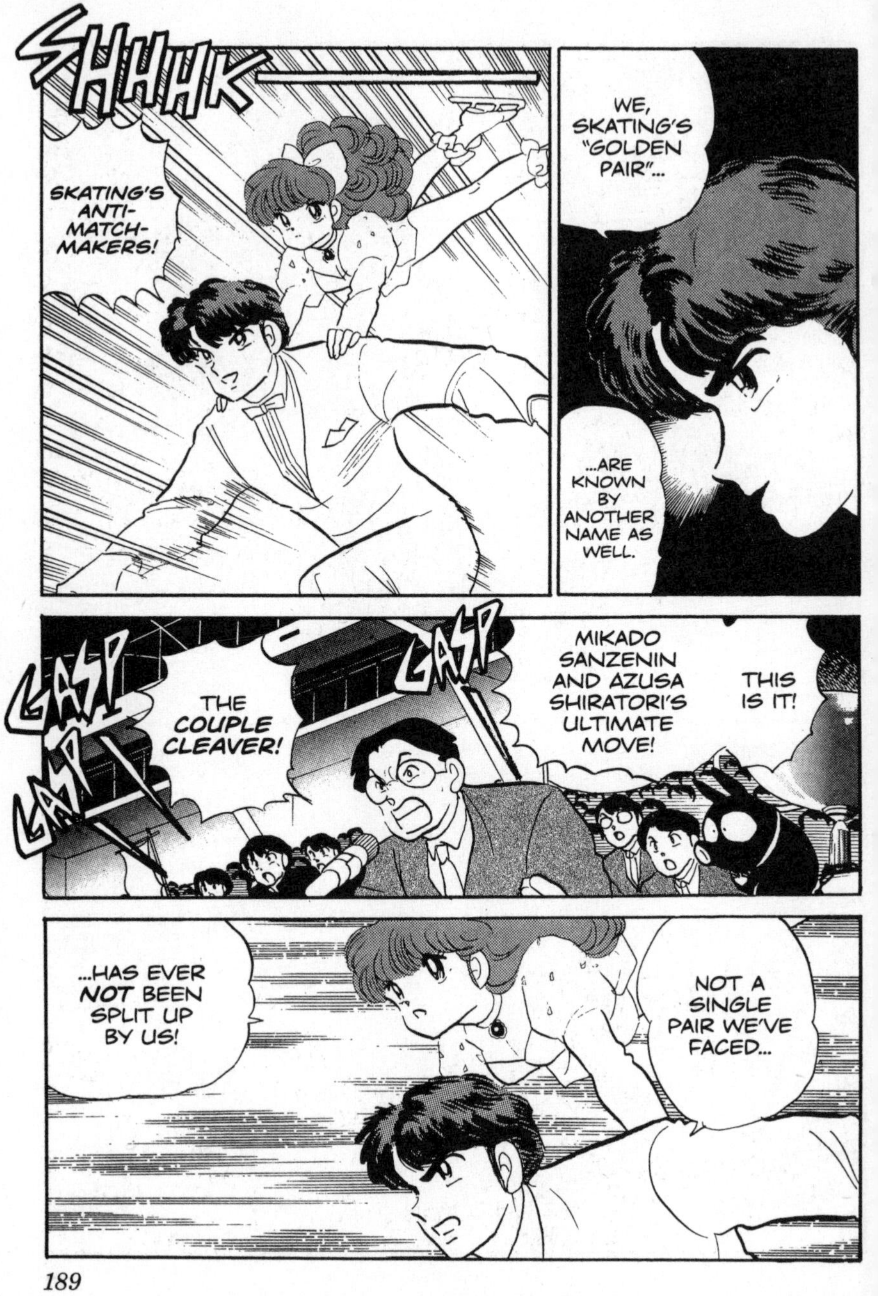
WE, SKATING'S "GOLDEN PAIR"...
...ARE KNOWN BY ANOTHER NAME AS WELL.
SHHHK
SKATING'S ANTI-MATCH-MAKERS!
THIS IS IT!
MIKADO SANZENIN AND AZUSA SHIRATORI'S ULTIMATE MOVE!
GASP
THE *COUPLE CLEAVER!*
GASP
GASP
NOT A SINGLE PAIR WE'VE FACED...
...HAS EVER **NOT** BEEN SPLIT UP BY US!

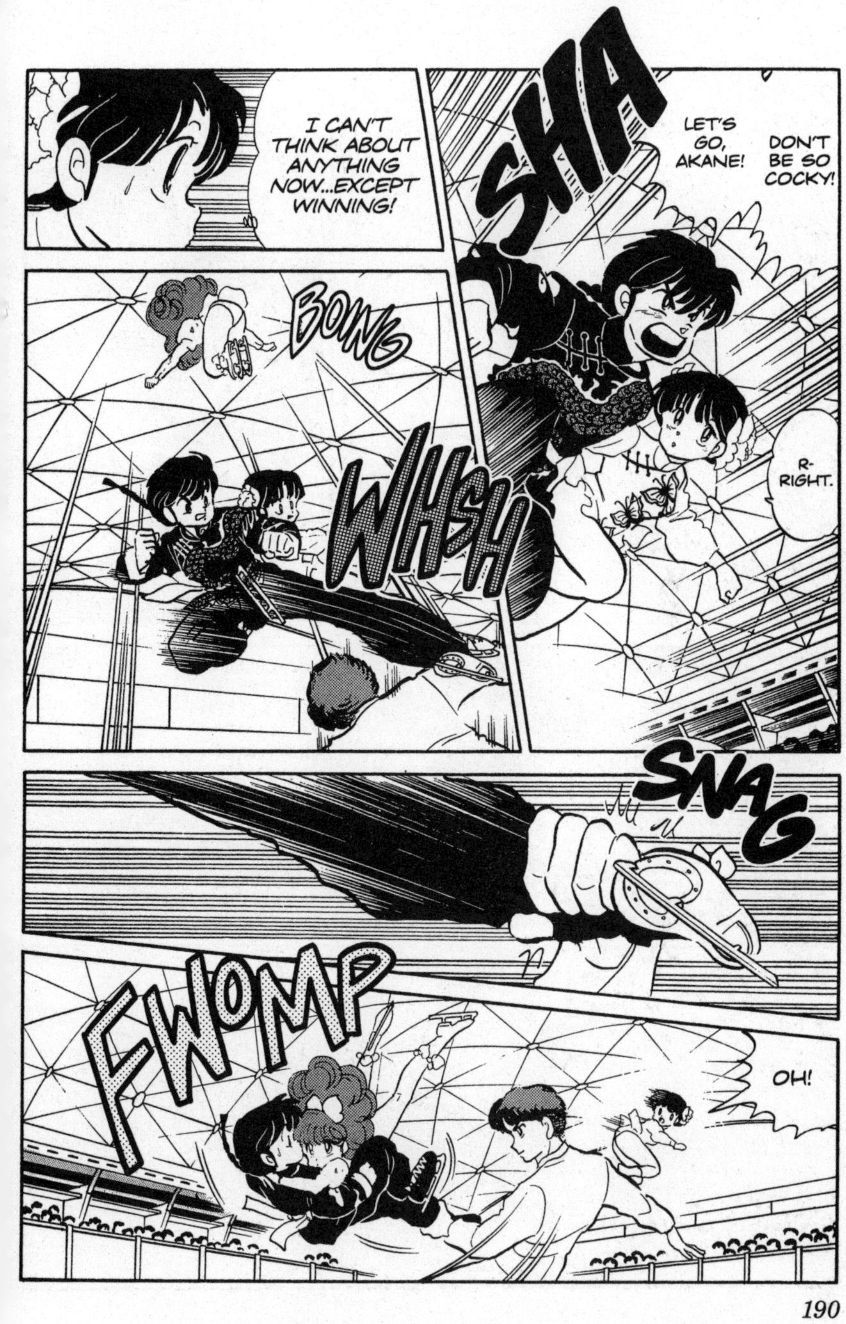
SHA
DON'T BE SO COCKY!
LET'S GO, AKANE!
R-RIGHT.
I CAN'T THINK ABOUT ANYTHING NOW...EXCEPT WINNING!
BOING
WHSH
SNAG
OH!
FWOMP

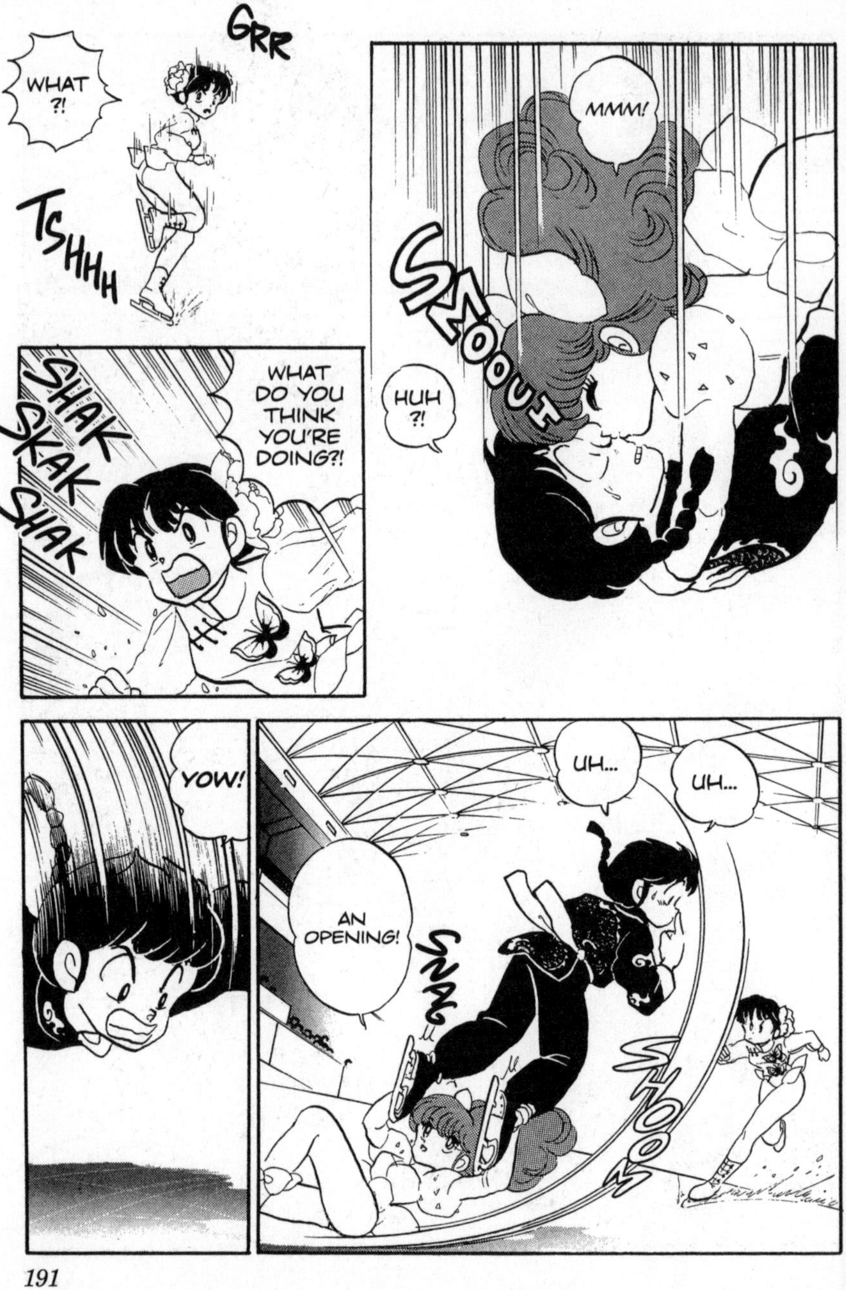
MMM!
SWOOOSH
HUH?!
GRR
WHAT ?!
TSHHHH
WHAT DO YOU THINK YOU'RE DOING?!
SHAK SKAK SHAK
UH...
UH...
AN OPENING!
SNAG
WHOOOM
YOW!

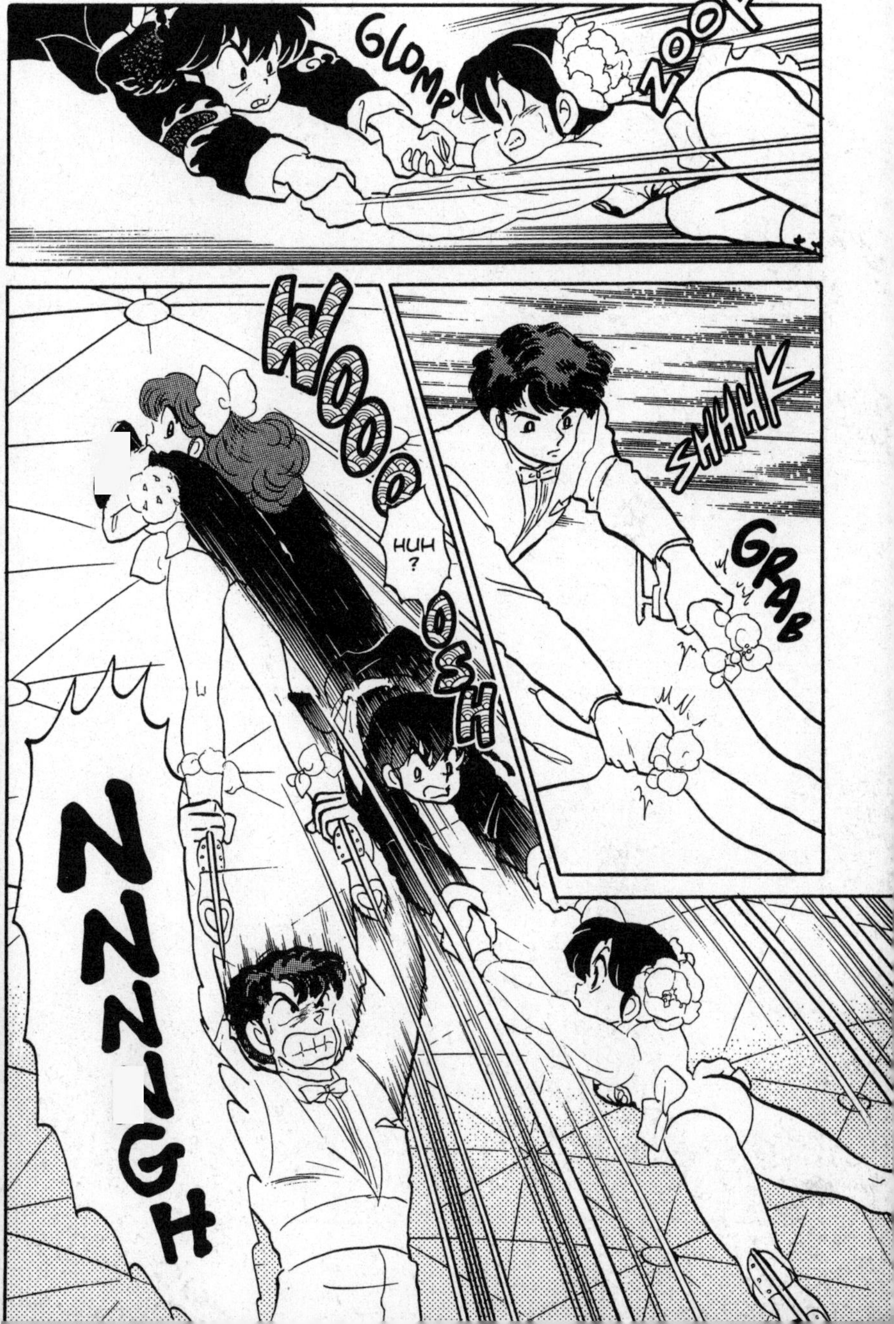
ZOOP
GLOMP
SHHHK
GRAB
WOOOOOSH
HUH?
NNNGH

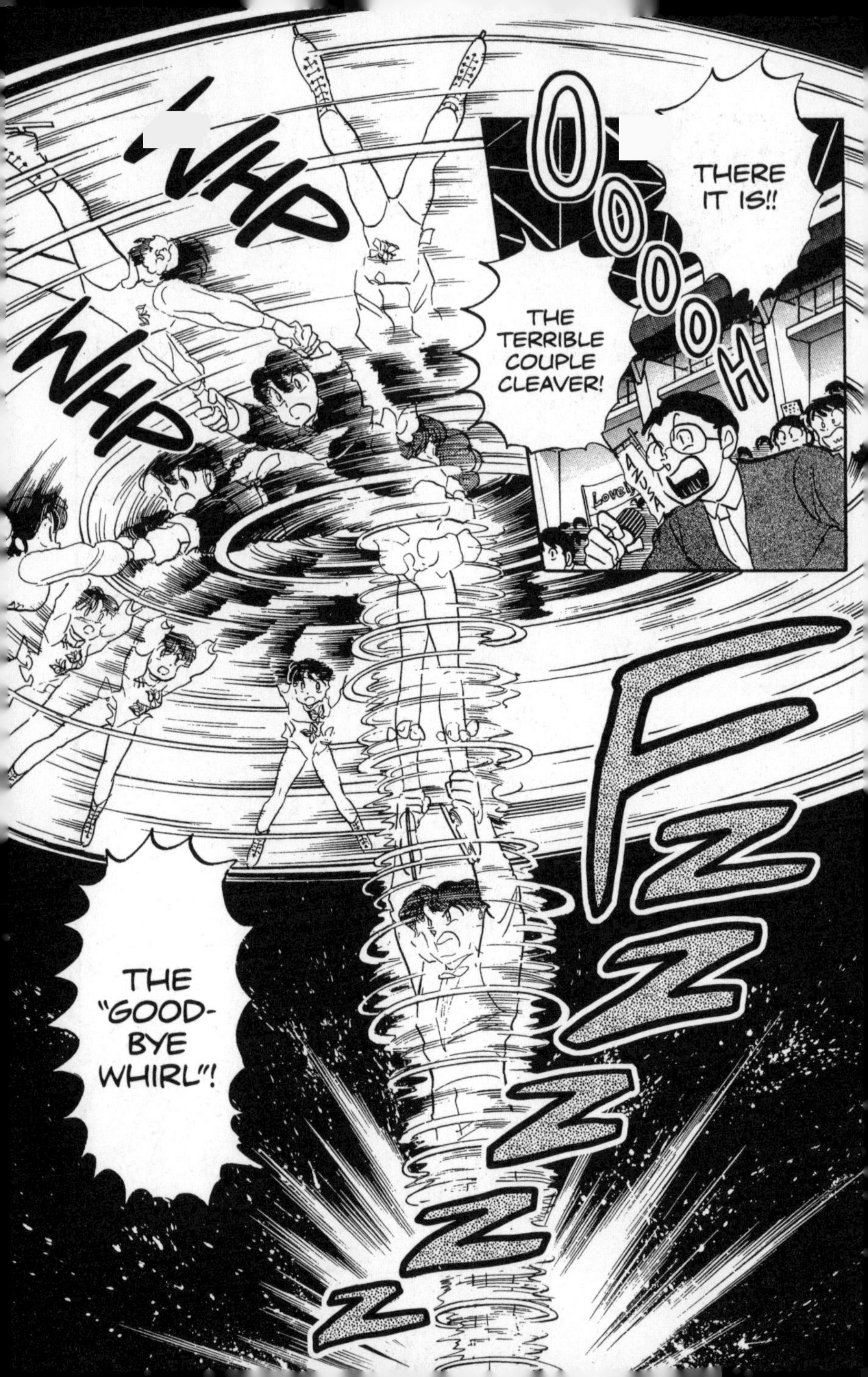
THERE IT IS!!
OOOOOH
THE TERRIBLE COUPLE CLEAVER!
WHP
WHP
WHP
FZZZZZZ
THE "GOOD-BYE WHIRL"!

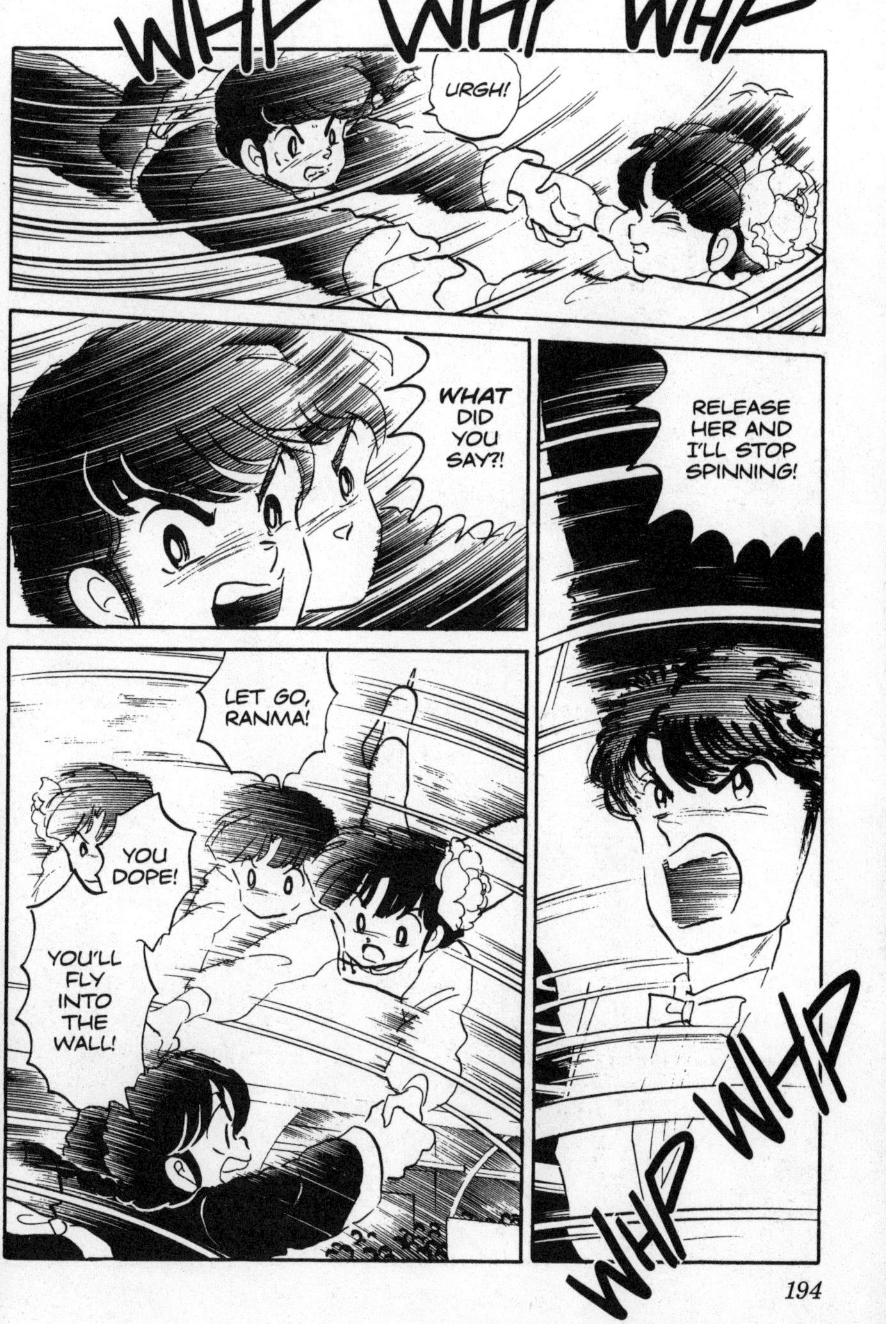
WHP WHP WHP
URGH!
RELEASE HER AND I'LL STOP SPINNING!
WHP WHP
WHAT DID YOU SAY?!
LET GO, RANMA!
YOU DOPE!
YOU'LL FLY INTO THE WALL!

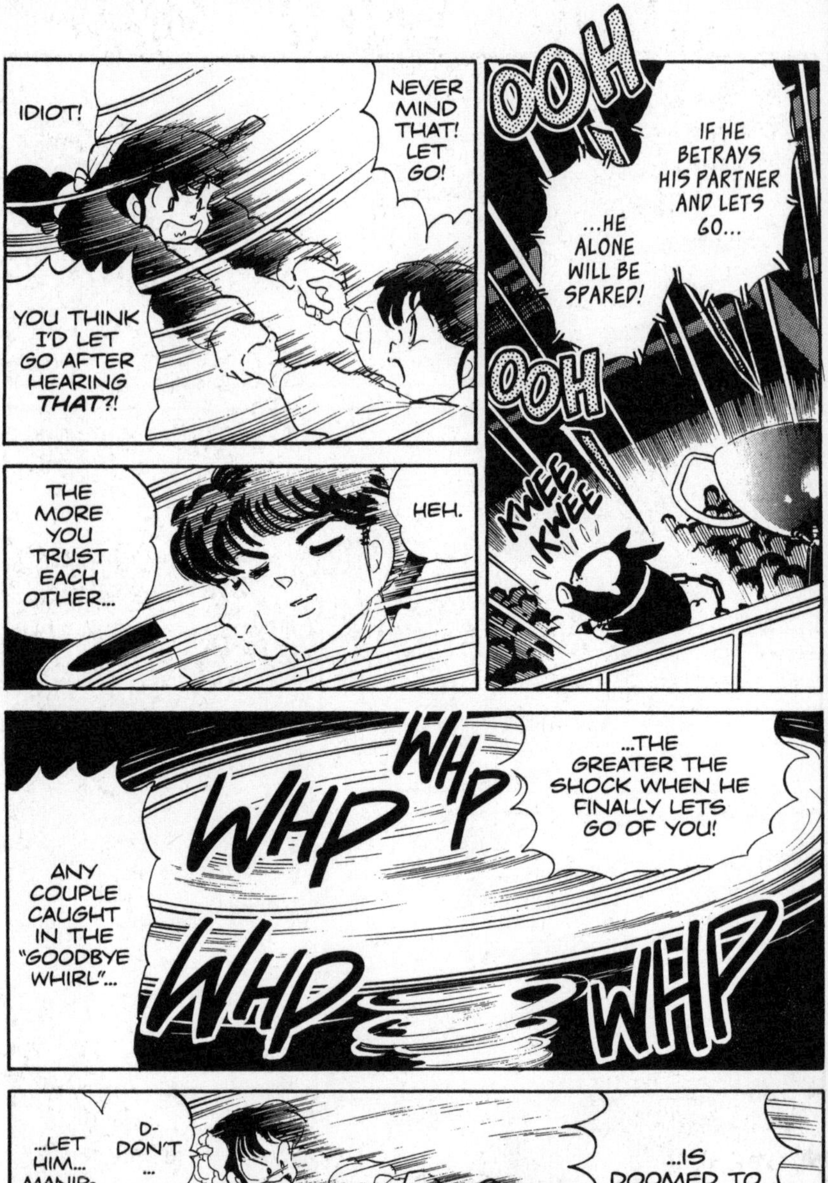
OOH
IF HE BETRAYS HIS PARTNER AND LETS GO...
...HE ALONE WILL BE SPARED!
OOH
KWEE KWEE
NEVER MIND THAT! LET GO!
IDIOT!
YOU THINK I'D LET GO AFTER HEARING *THAT*?!
HEH.
THE MORE YOU TRUST EACH OTHER...
WHP
...THE GREATER THE SHOCK WHEN HE FINALLY LETS GO OF YOU!
WHP
ANY COUPLE CAUGHT IN THE "GOODBYE WHIRL"...
WHP
WHP
...IS DOOMED TO DISASTER!
D-DON'T ...
...LET HIM... MANIP-ULATE YOU!

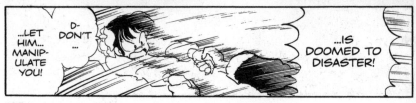

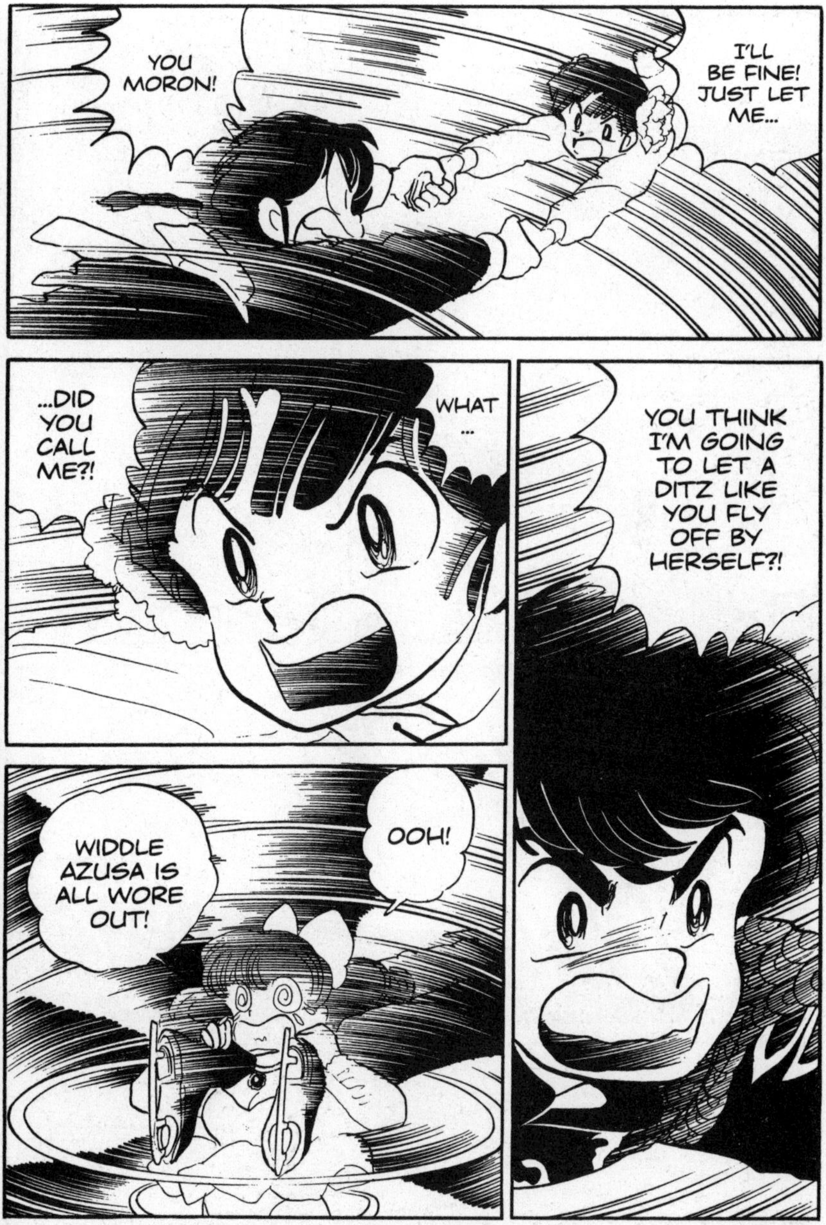
I'LL BE FINE! JUST LET ME...
YOU MORON!
YOU THINK I'M GOING TO LET A DITZ LIKE YOU FLY OFF BY HERSELF?!
WHAT ...
...DID YOU CALL ME?!
OOH!
WIDDLE AZUSA IS ALL WORE OUT!

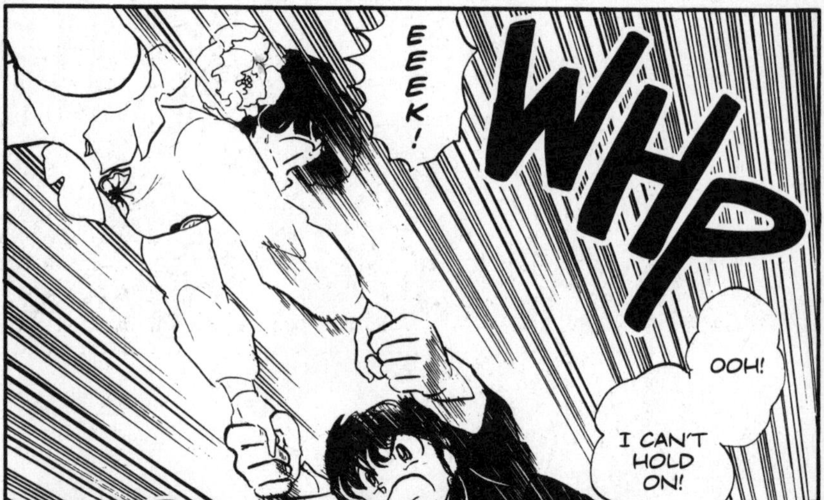
WHIP
EEEEK!
OOH!
I CAN'T HOLD ON!
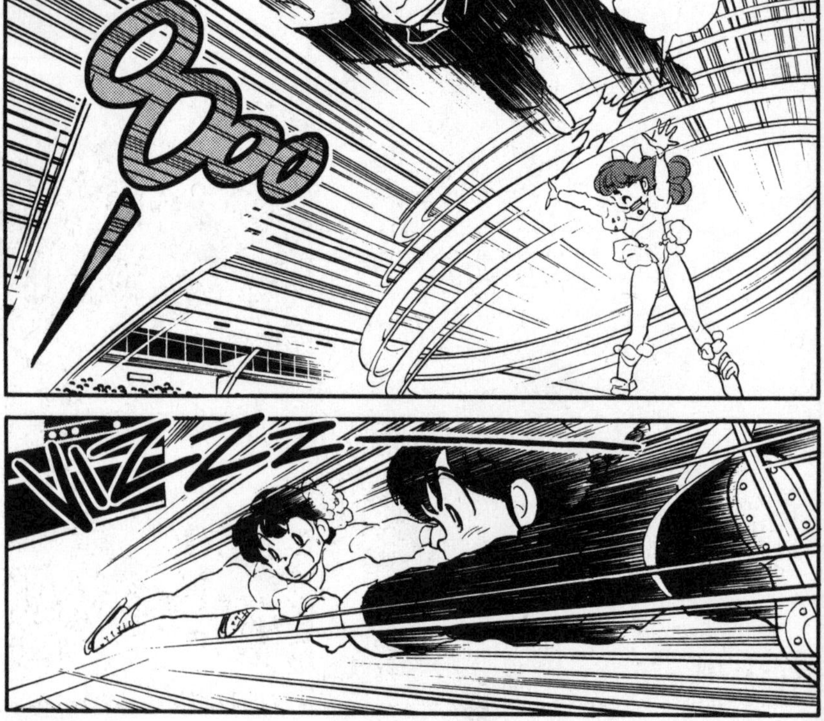
VIZZZZ

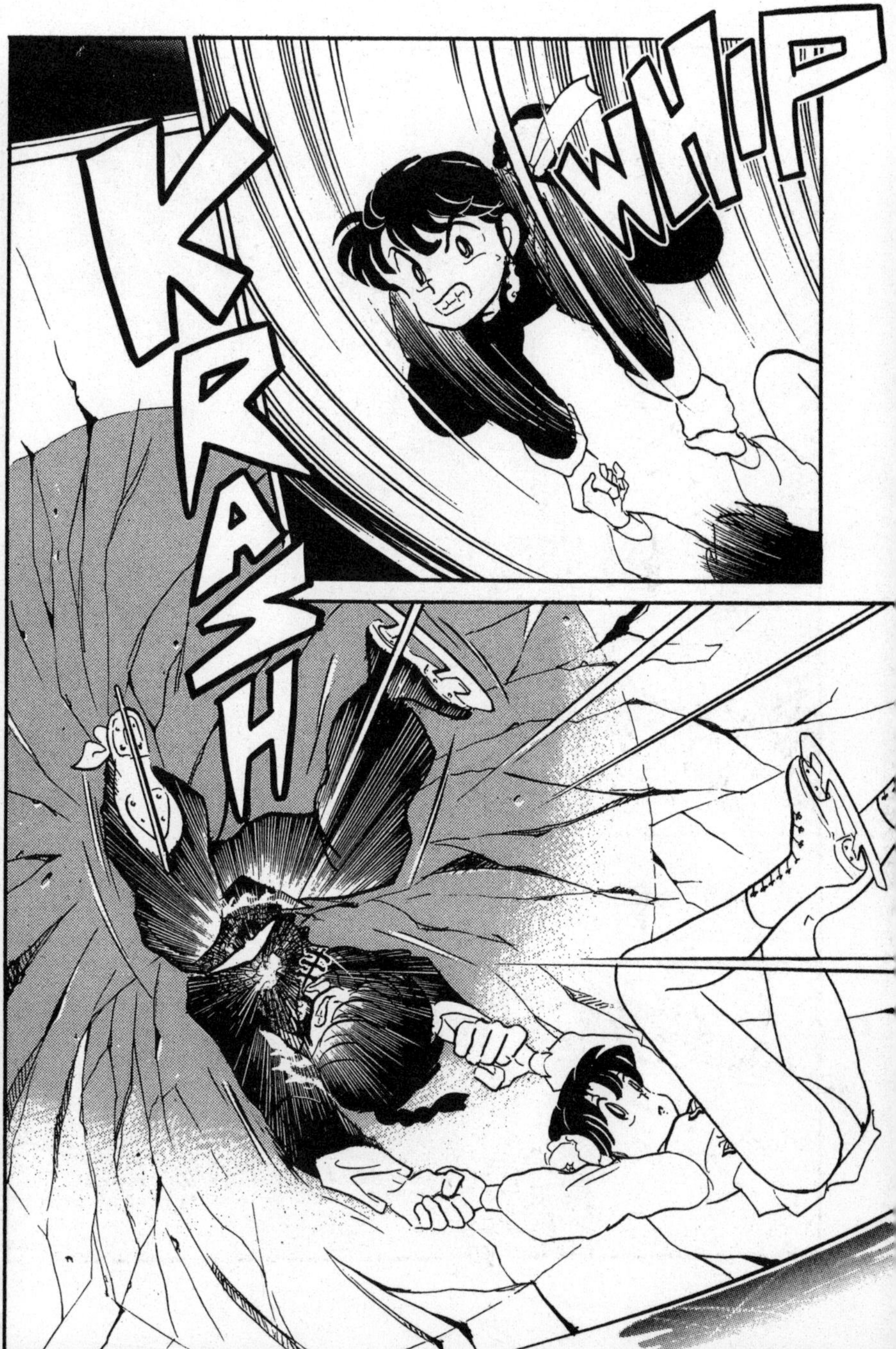
WHIP
KRASH

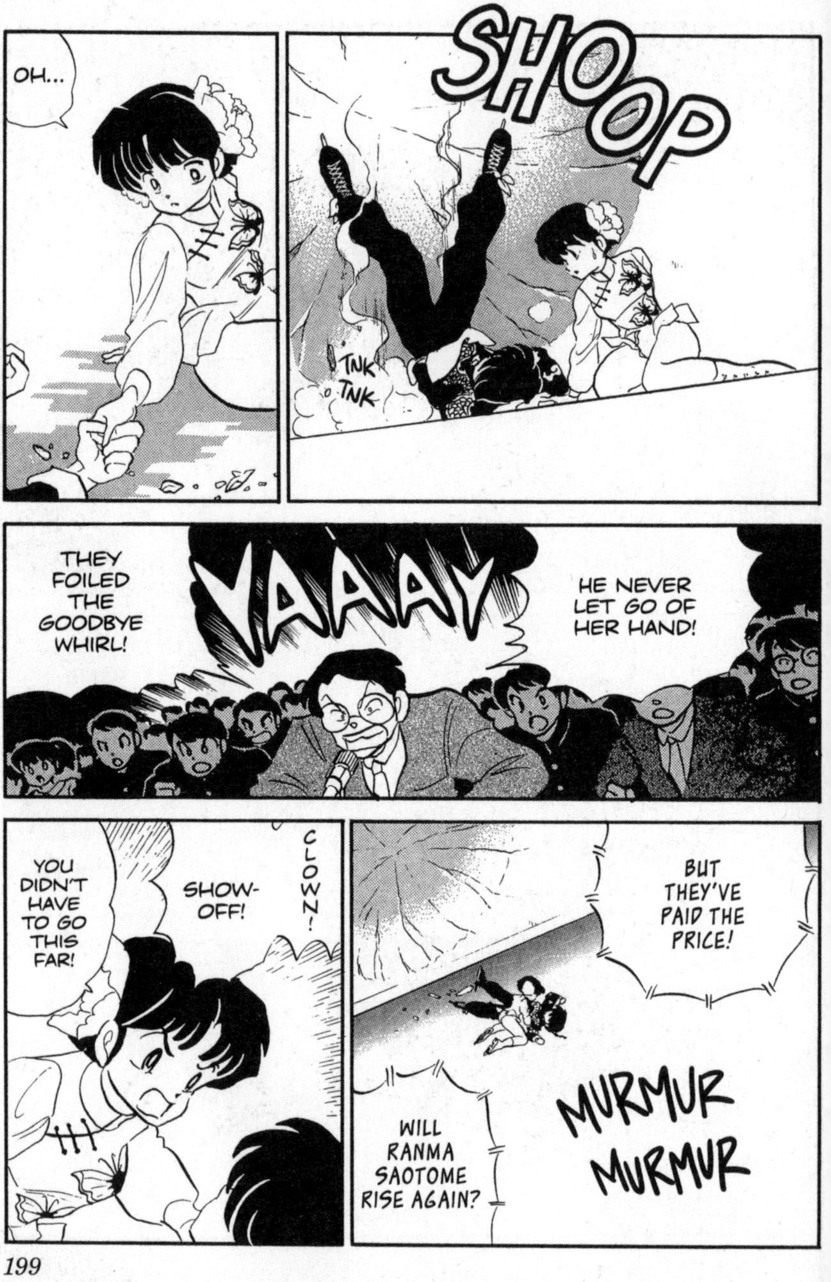
SHOOP
TNK TNK
OH...
HE NEVER LET GO OF HER HAND!
YAAAY
THEY FOILED THE GOODBYE WHIRL!
BUT THEY'VE PAID THE PRICE!
MURMUR MURMUR
WILL RANMA SAOTOME RISE AGAIN?
CLOWN!
SHOW-OFF!
YOU DIDN'T HAVE TO GO THIS FAR!

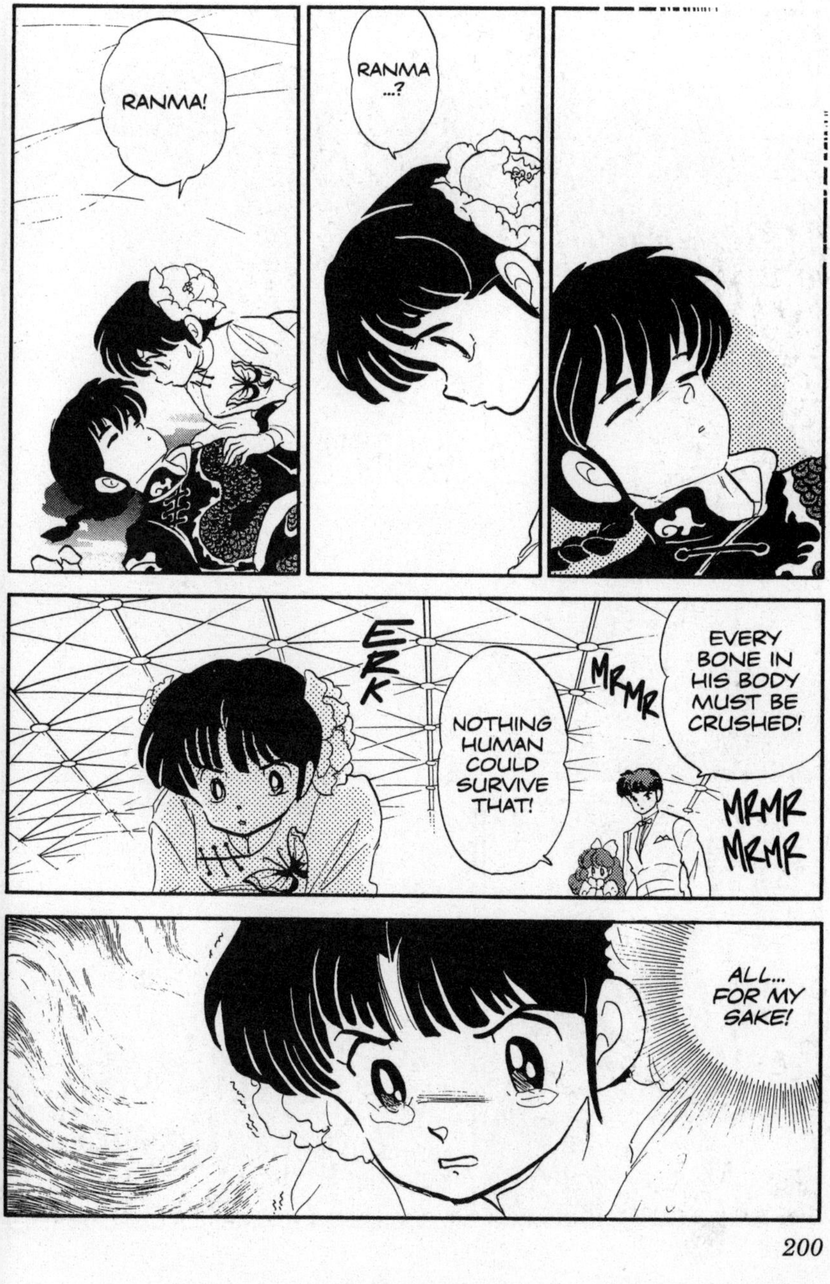
RANMA ...?
RANMA!
MRMR MRMR
EVERY BONE IN HIS BODY MUST BE CRUSHED!
MRMR
NOTHING HUMAN COULD SURVIVE THAT!
ERK
ALL... FOR MY SAKE!

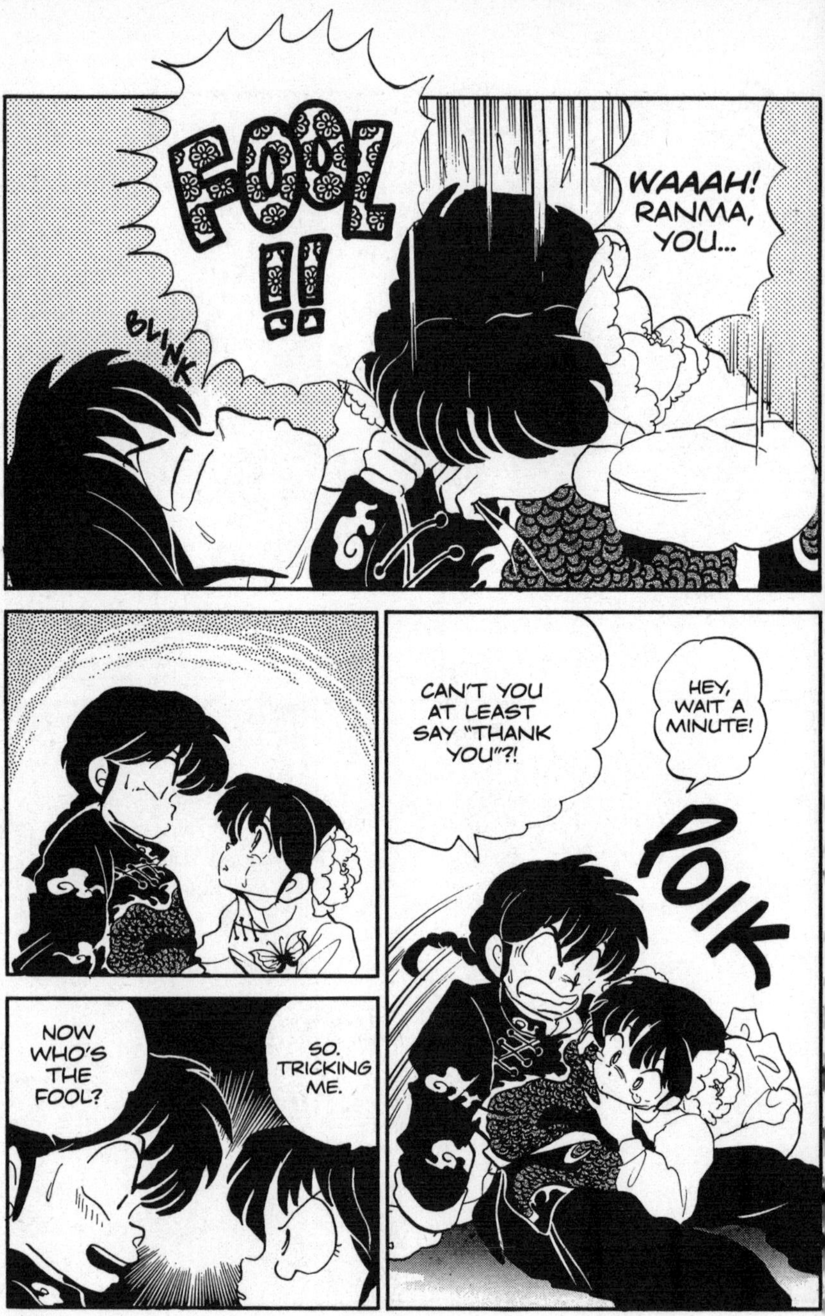
WAAAH! RANMA, YOU...
FOOL!!
BLINK
HEY, WAIT A MINUTE!
CAN'T YOU AT LEAST SAY "THANK YOU"?!
POIK
SO. TRICKING ME.
NOW WHO'S THE FOOL?

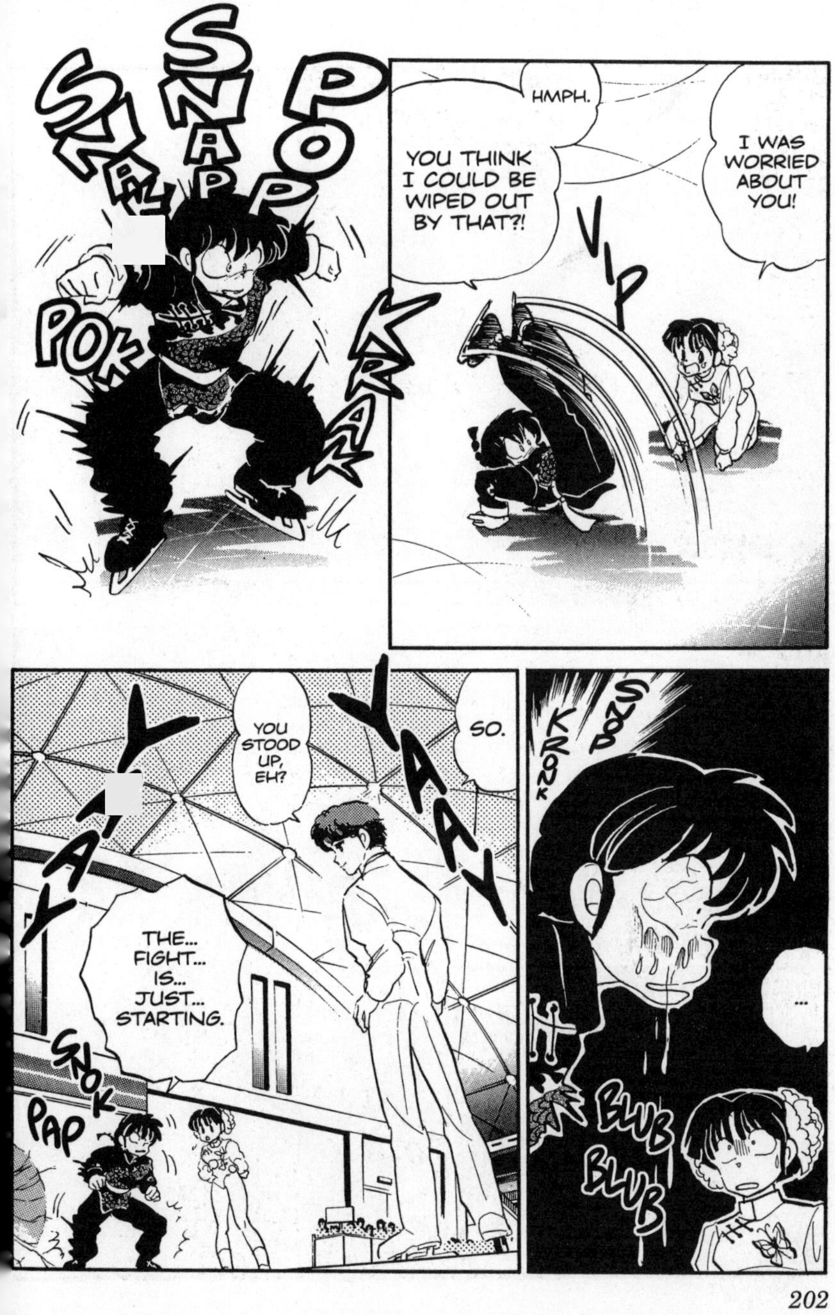
I WAS WORRIED ABOUT YOU!
HMPH.
YOU THINK I COULD BE WIPED OUT BY THAT?!
VIP
POP
SNAP
SNAP
POK
KRAK
SNOP
KRONK
...
BLUB
BLUB
SO.
YOU STOOD UP, EH?
YAAAY
THE... FIGHT... IS... JUST... STARTING.
SNOK
PAP

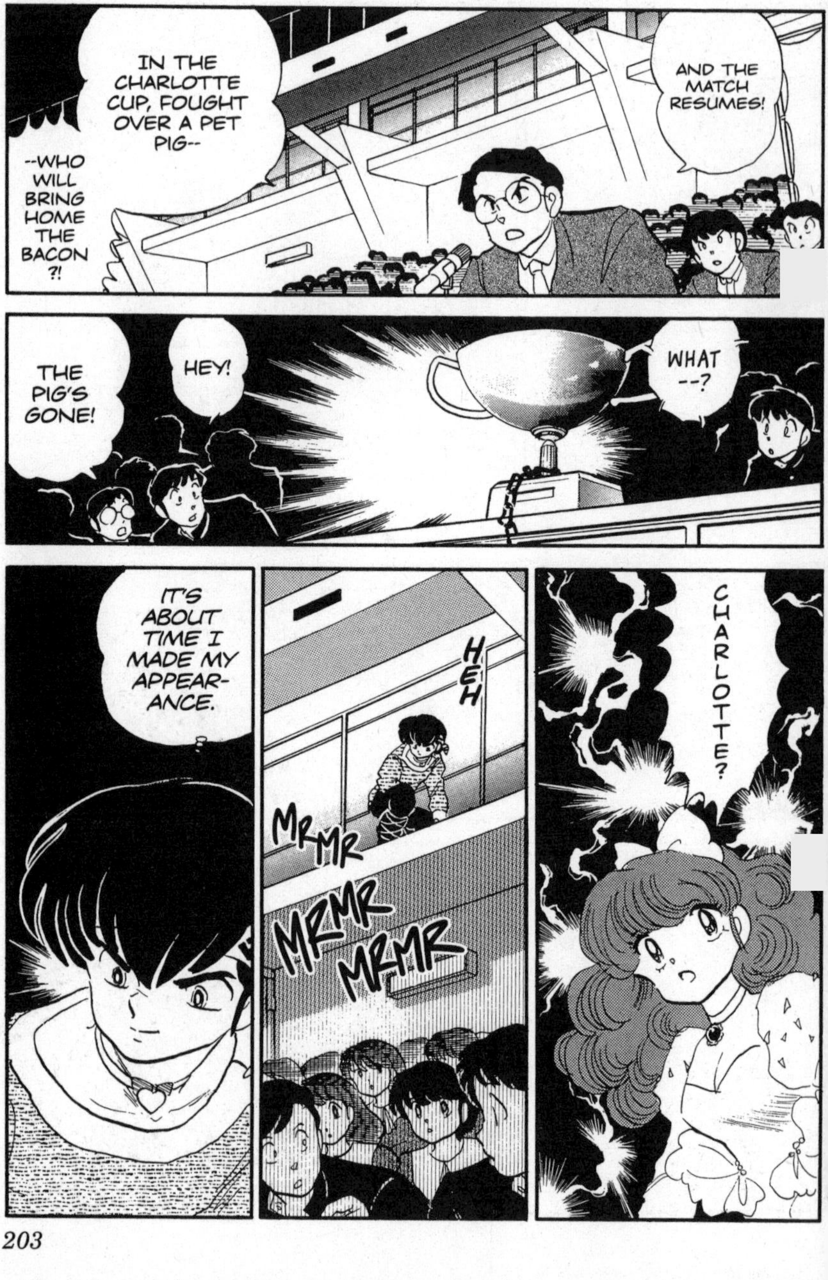
AND THE MATCH RESUMES!
IN THE CHARLOTTE CUP, FOUGHT OVER A PET PIG--
--WHO WILL BRING HOME THE BACON ?!
WHAT --?
HEY!
THE PIG'S GONE!
CHARLOTTE?
HEH
MRMR
MRMR MRMR
IT'S ABOUT TIME I MADE MY APPEARANCE.

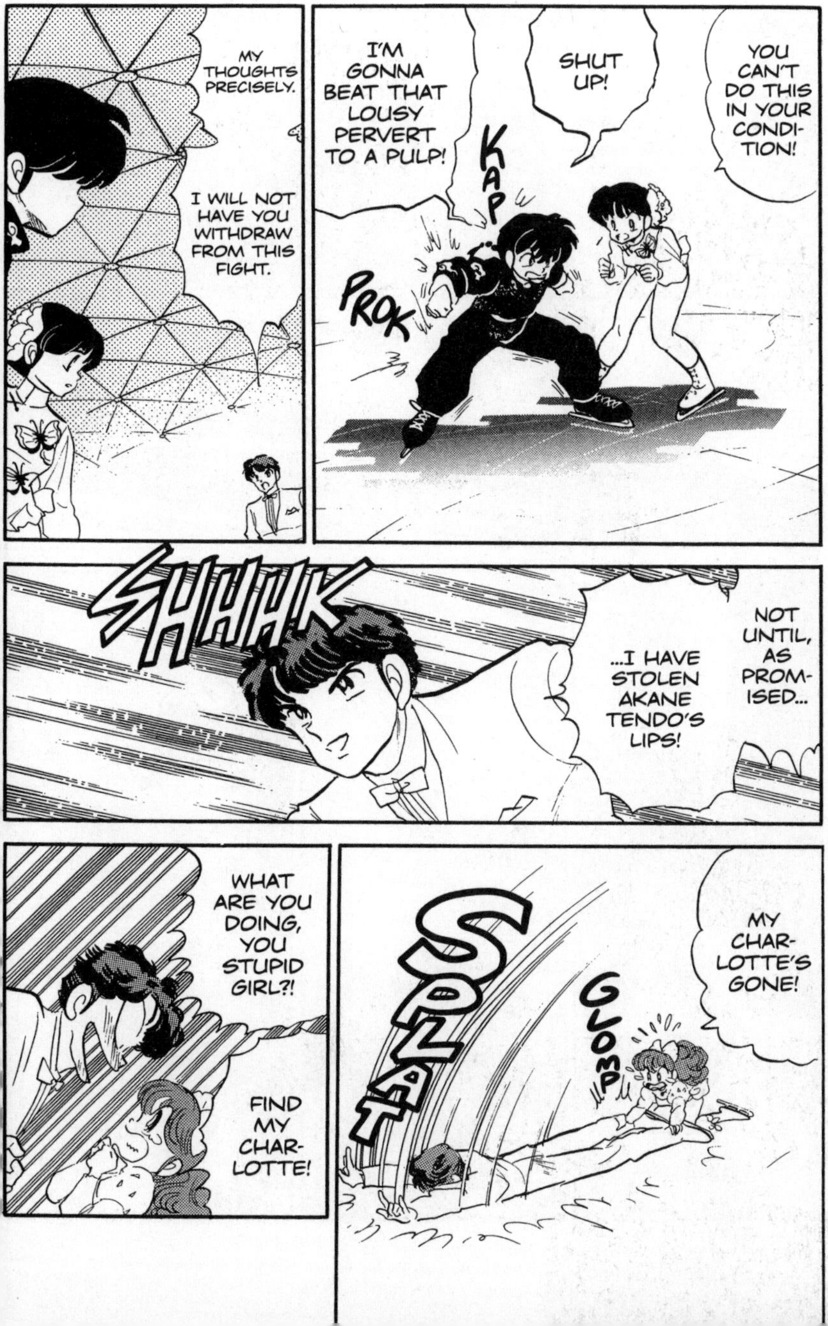
YOU CAN'T DO THIS IN YOUR CONDITION!
SHUT UP!
I'M GONNA BEAT THAT LOUSY PERVERT TO A PULP!
KAP
PROK
MY THOUGHTS PRECISELY.
I WILL NOT HAVE YOU WITHDRAW FROM THIS FIGHT.
SHHHK
NOT UNTIL, AS PROMISED...
...I HAVE STOLEN AKANE TENDO'S LIPS!
MY CHARLOTTE'S GONE!
GLOMP
SPLAT
WHAT ARE YOU DOING, YOU STUPID GIRL?!
FIND MY CHARLOTTE!

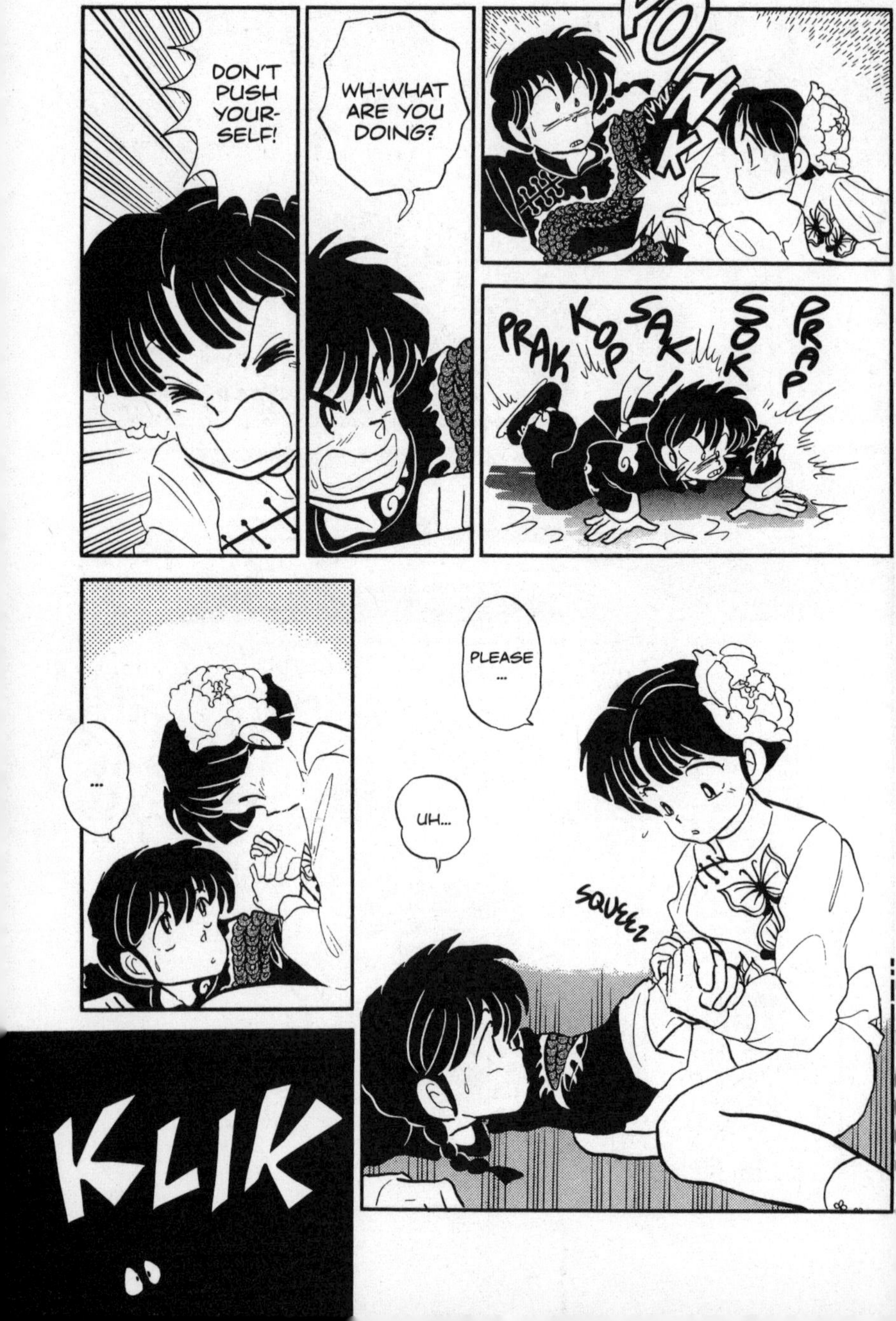
POINK
PRAP
SOK
SAK
KOP
PRAK
WH-WHAT ARE YOU DOING?
DON'T PUSH YOURSELF!
PLEASE ...
UH...
SQUEEZ
...
KLIK

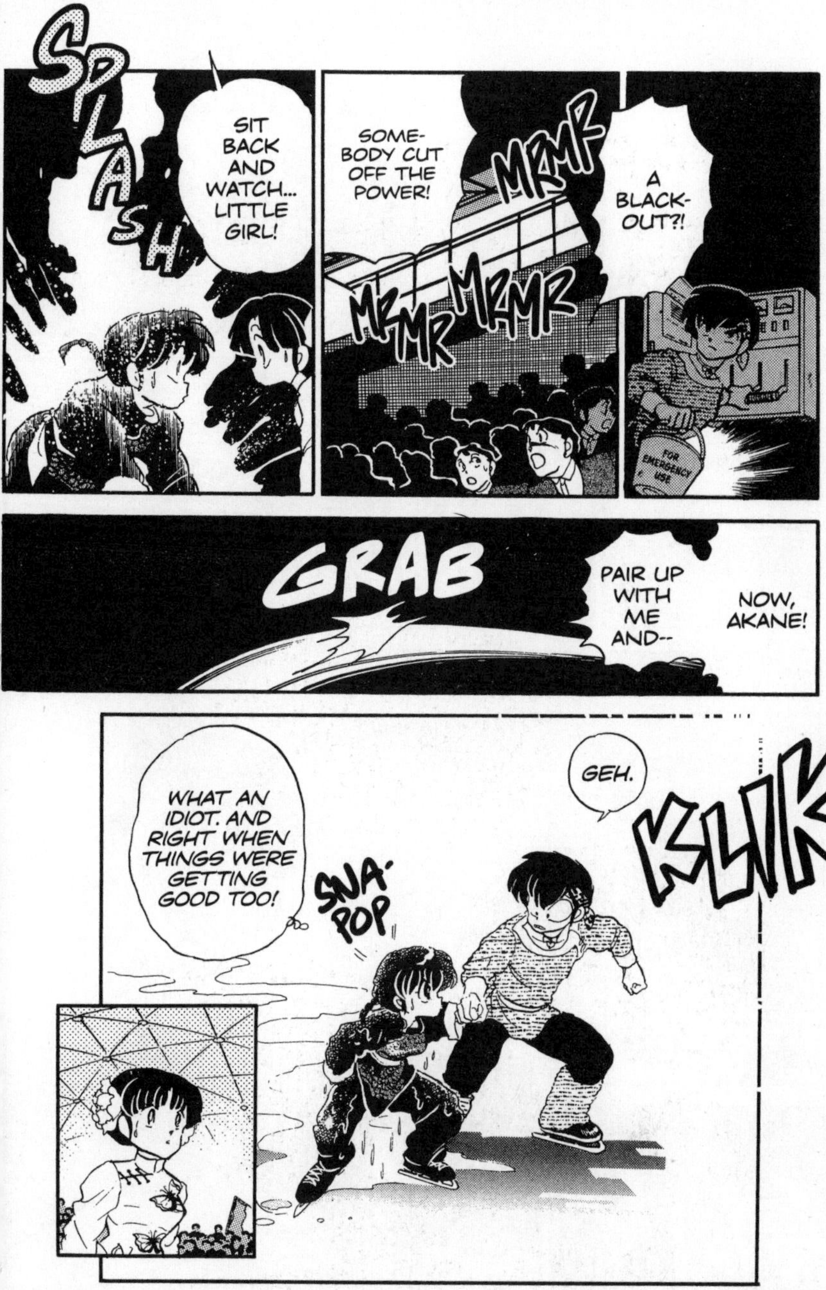
A BLACK-OUT?!
MRMR
SOME-BODY CUT OFF THE POWER!
MRMR MRMR
SPLASH
SIT BACK AND WATCH... LITTLE GIRL!
NOW, AKANE!
PAIR UP WITH ME AND--
GRAB
KLIK
GEH.
SNA-POP
WHAT AN IDIOT. AND RIGHT WHEN THINGS WERE GETTING GOOD TOO!

PART 11
BURNING THE BRIDGES

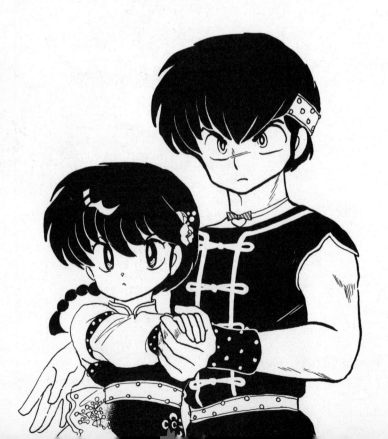

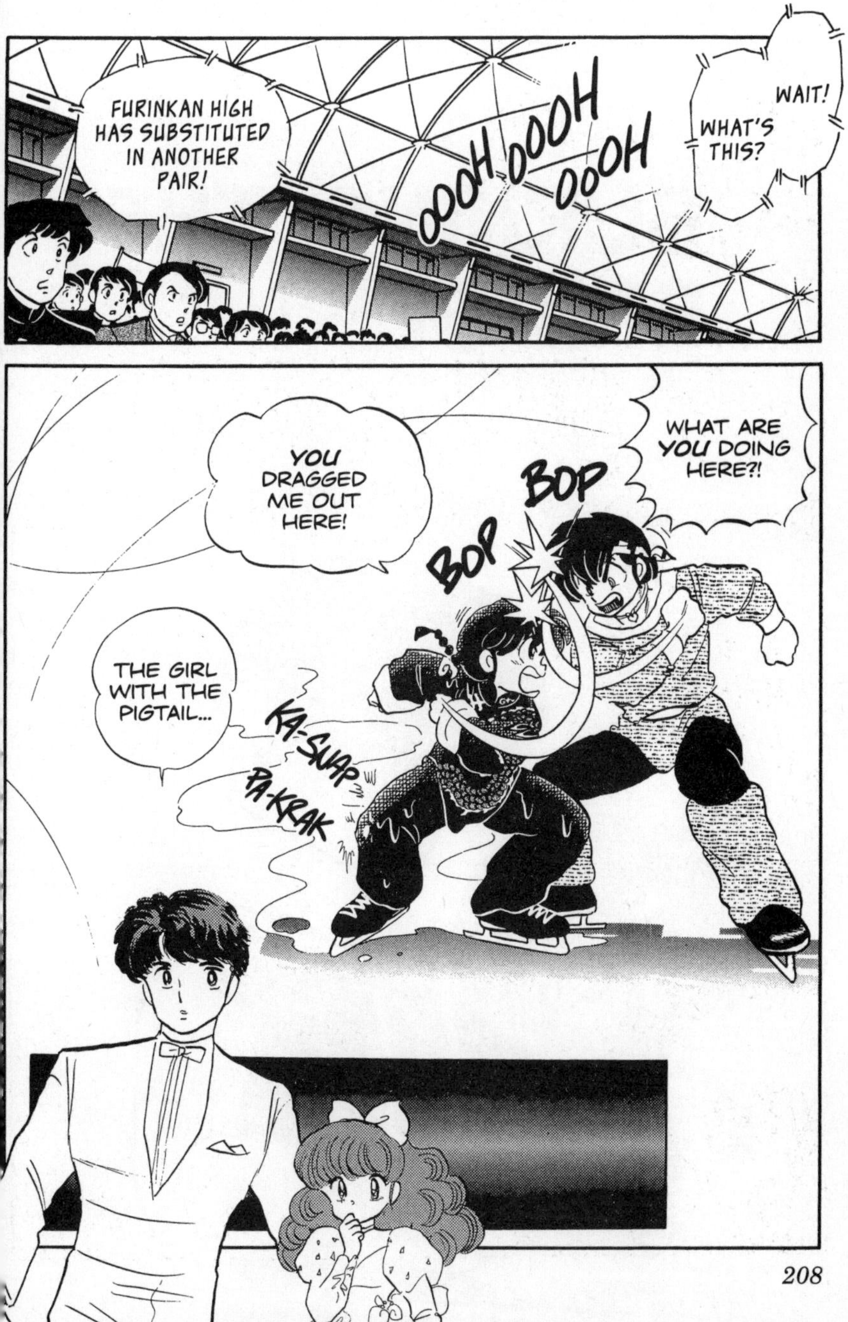
WAIT! WHAT'S THIS?
OOOH OOOH OOOH
FURINKAN HIGH HAS SUBSTITUTED IN ANOTHER PAIR!
WHAT ARE YOU DOING HERE?!
BOP BOP
BOP
YOU DRAGGED ME OUT HERE!
THE GIRL WITH THE PIGTAIL...
KA-SNAP
PA-KRAK

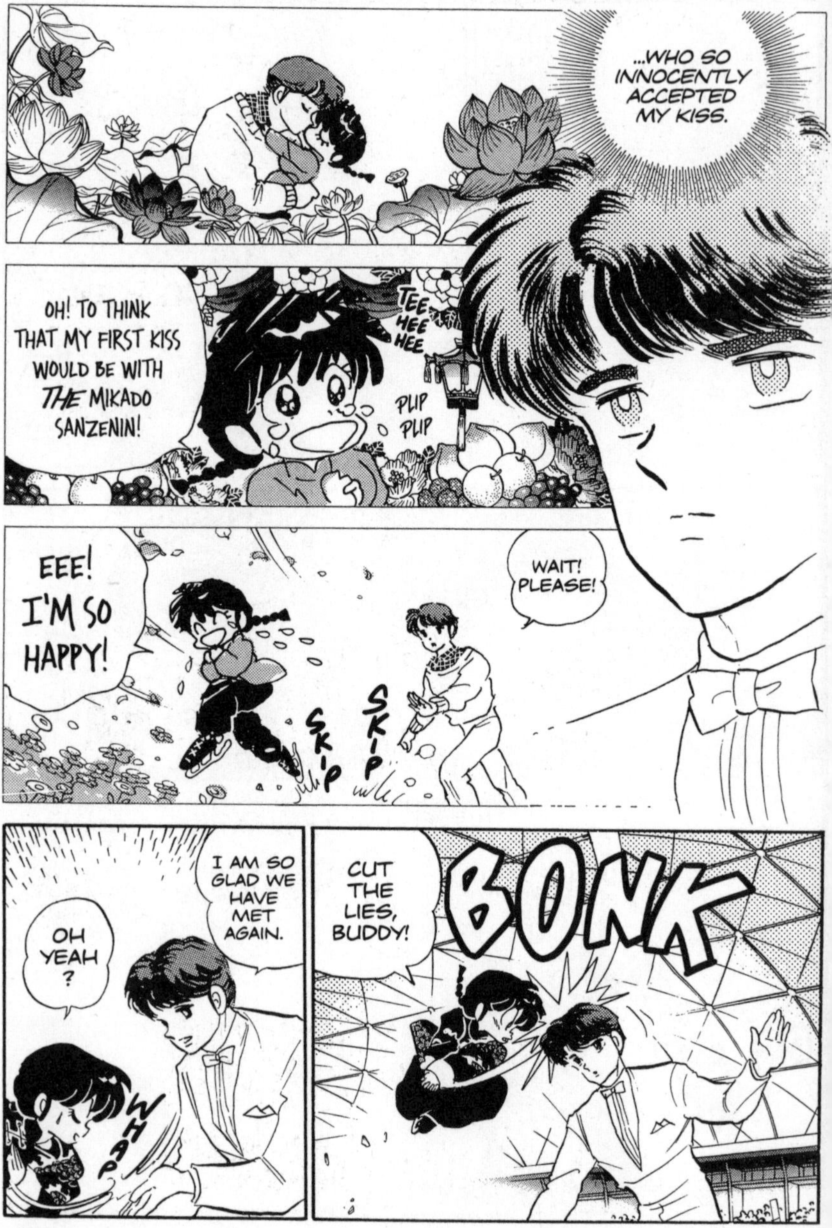
...WHO SO INNOCENTLY ACCEPTED MY KISS.
OH! TO THINK THAT MY FIRST KISS WOULD BE WITH THE MIKADO SANZENIN!
TEE HEE HEE
PLIP PLIP
WAIT! PLEASE!
EEE! I'M SO HAPPY!
SKIP
SKIP
CUT THE LIES, BUDDY!
BONK
I AM SO GLAD WE HAVE MET AGAIN.
OH YEAH?
WHAP

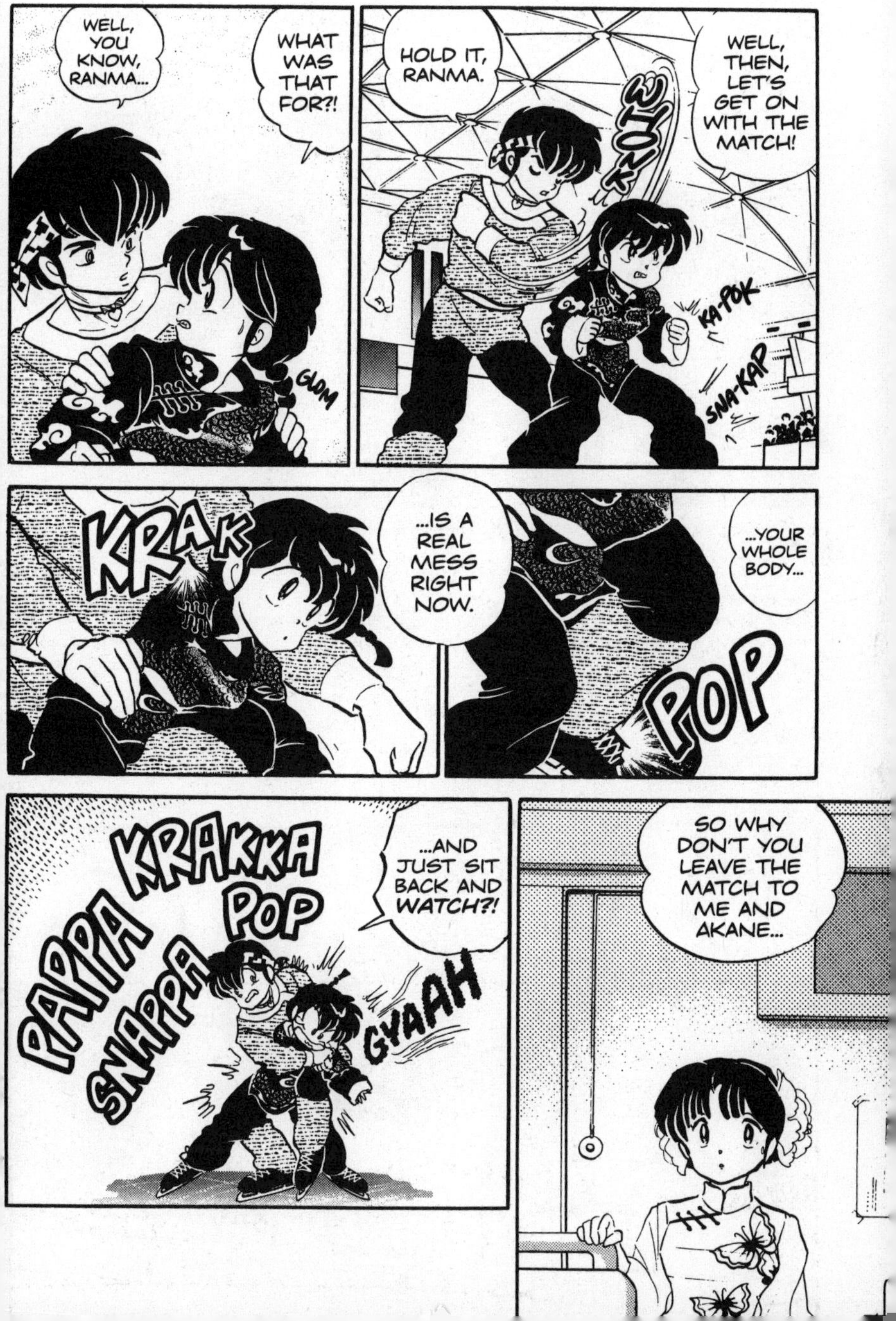
WELL, THEN, LET'S GET ON WITH THE MATCH!
HOLD IT, RANMA.
WHONK
KA-POK
SNA-KAP
WHAT WAS THAT FOR?!
WELL, YOU KNOW, RANMA...
GLOM
...YOUR WHOLE BODY...
POP
...IS A REAL MESS RIGHT NOW.
KRAK
SO WHY DON'T YOU LEAVE THE MATCH TO ME AND AKANE...
...AND JUST SIT BACK AND WATCH?!
KRAKKA POP
PAPPA SNAPPA
GYAAH

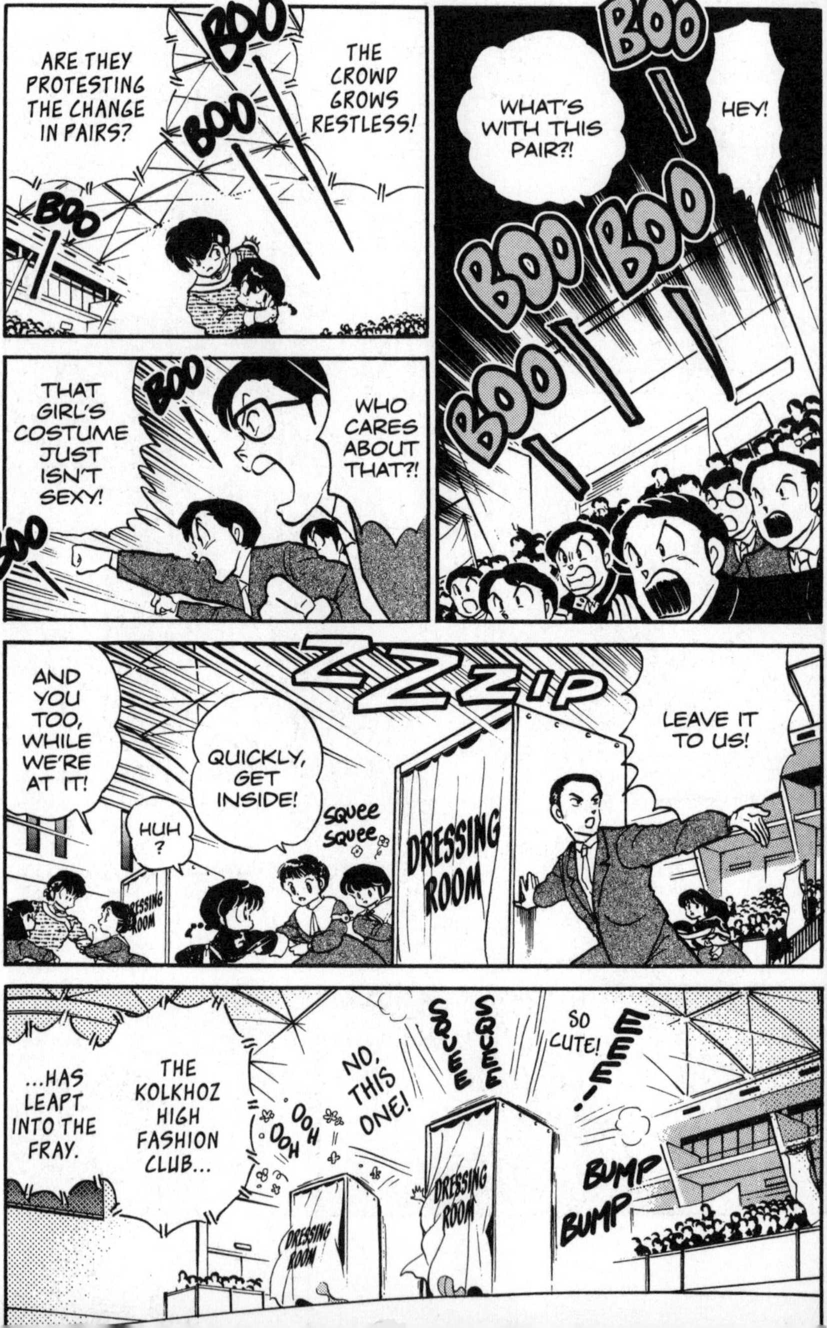
BOO
HEY!
WHAT'S WITH THIS PAIR?!
BOO BOO
BOO
THE CROWD GROWS RESTLESS!
BOO
BOO
ARE THEY PROTESTING THE CHANGE IN PAIRS?
BOO
WHO CARES ABOUT THAT?!
BOO
THAT GIRL'S COSTUME JUST ISN'T SEXY!
BOO
ZZZIP
LEAVE IT TO US!
DRESSING ROOM
QUICKLY, GET INSIDE!
AND YOU TOO, WHILE WE'RE AT IT!
SQUEE SQUEE
HUH?
DRESSING ROOM
SO CUTE!
EEEE!
SQUEE SQUEE
BUMP BUMP
DRESSING ROOM
NO, THIS ONE!
OOH OOH
DRESSING ROOM
THE KOLKHOZ HIGH FASHION CLUB...
...HAS LEAPT INTO THE FRAY.

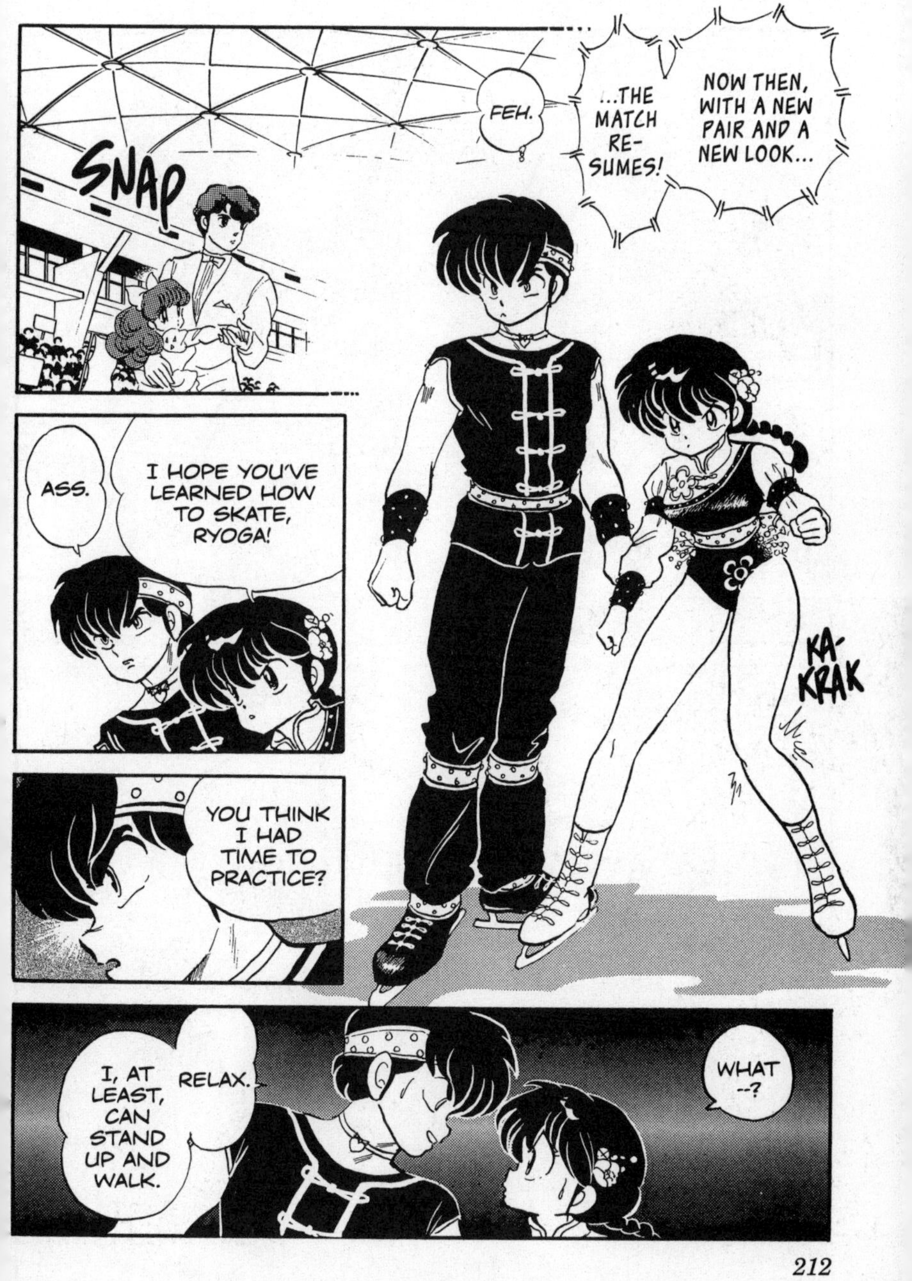
NOW THEN, WITH A NEW PAIR AND A NEW LOOK...
...THE MATCH RE-SUMES!
KA-KRAK
FEH.
SNAP
I HOPE YOU'VE LEARNED HOW TO SKATE, RYOGA!
ASS.
YOU THINK I HAD TIME TO PRACTICE?
WHAT --?
RELAX.
I, AT LEAST, CAN STAND UP AND WALK.

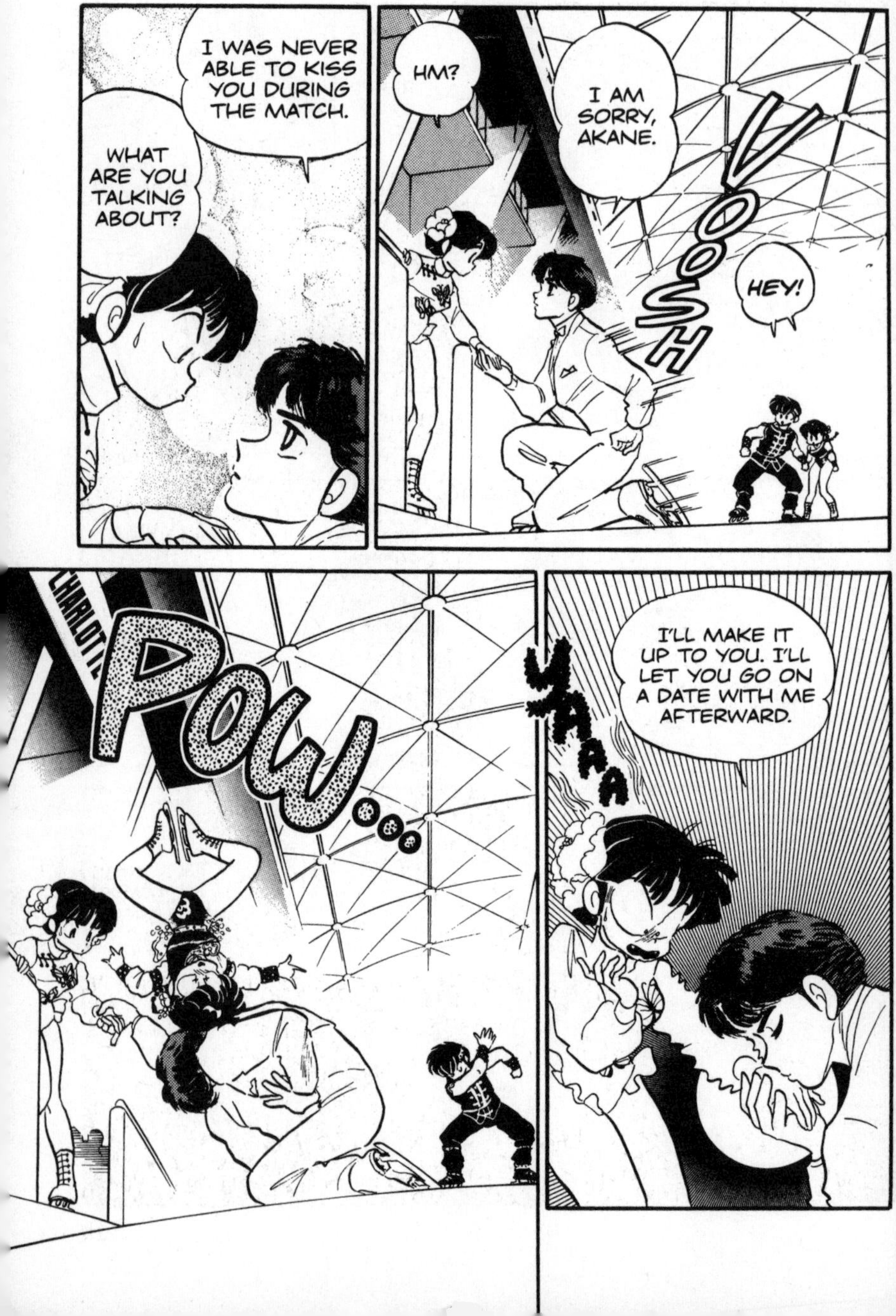
I AM SORRY, AKANE.
HM?
VOOSH
HEY!
I WAS NEVER ABLE TO KISS YOU DURING THE MATCH.
WHAT ARE YOU TALKING ABOUT?
I'LL MAKE IT UP TO YOU. I'LL LET YOU GO ON A DATE WITH ME AFTERWARD.
YAAAA
CHARLOTTE
POW...

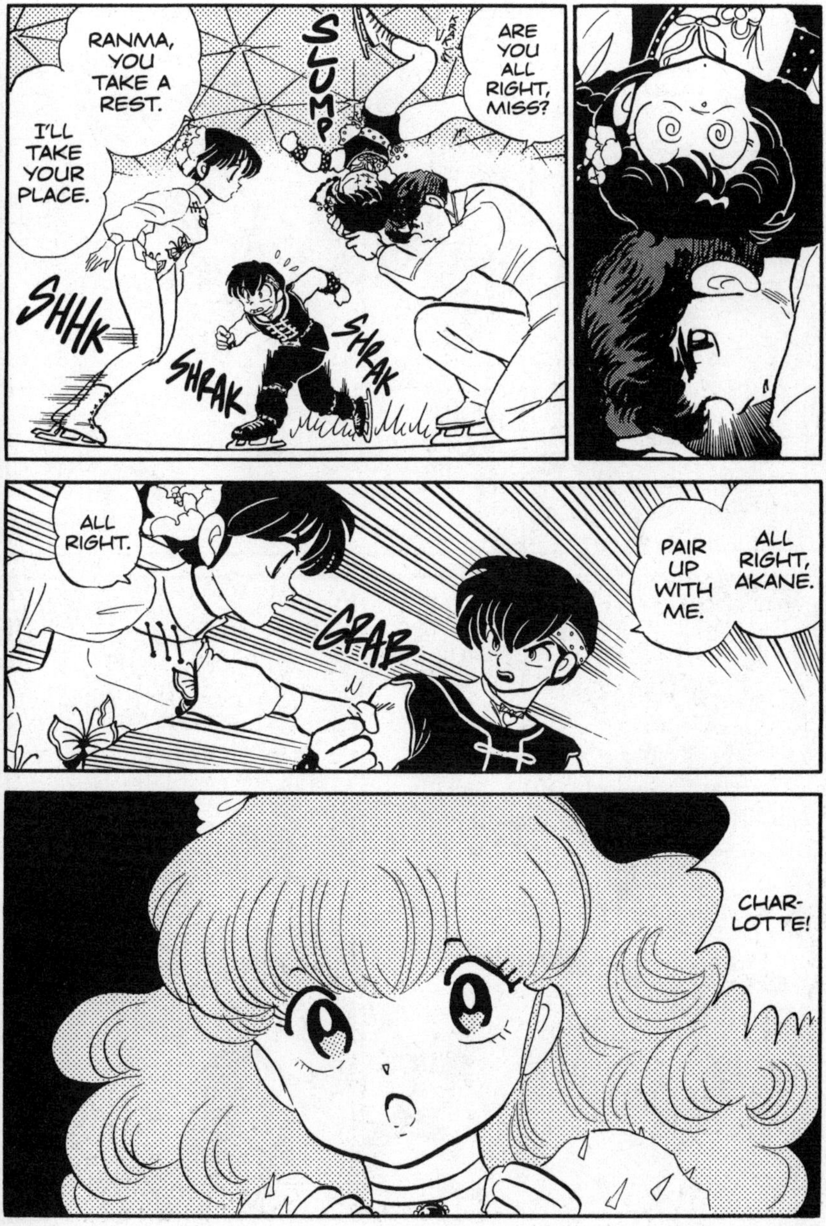
ARE YOU ALL RIGHT, MISS?
SLUMP
RANMA, YOU TAKE A REST.
I'LL TAKE YOUR PLACE.
SHRAK
SHRAK
SHHK
ALL RIGHT, AKANE.
PAIR UP WITH ME.
GRAB
ALL RIGHT.
CHAR-LOTTE!

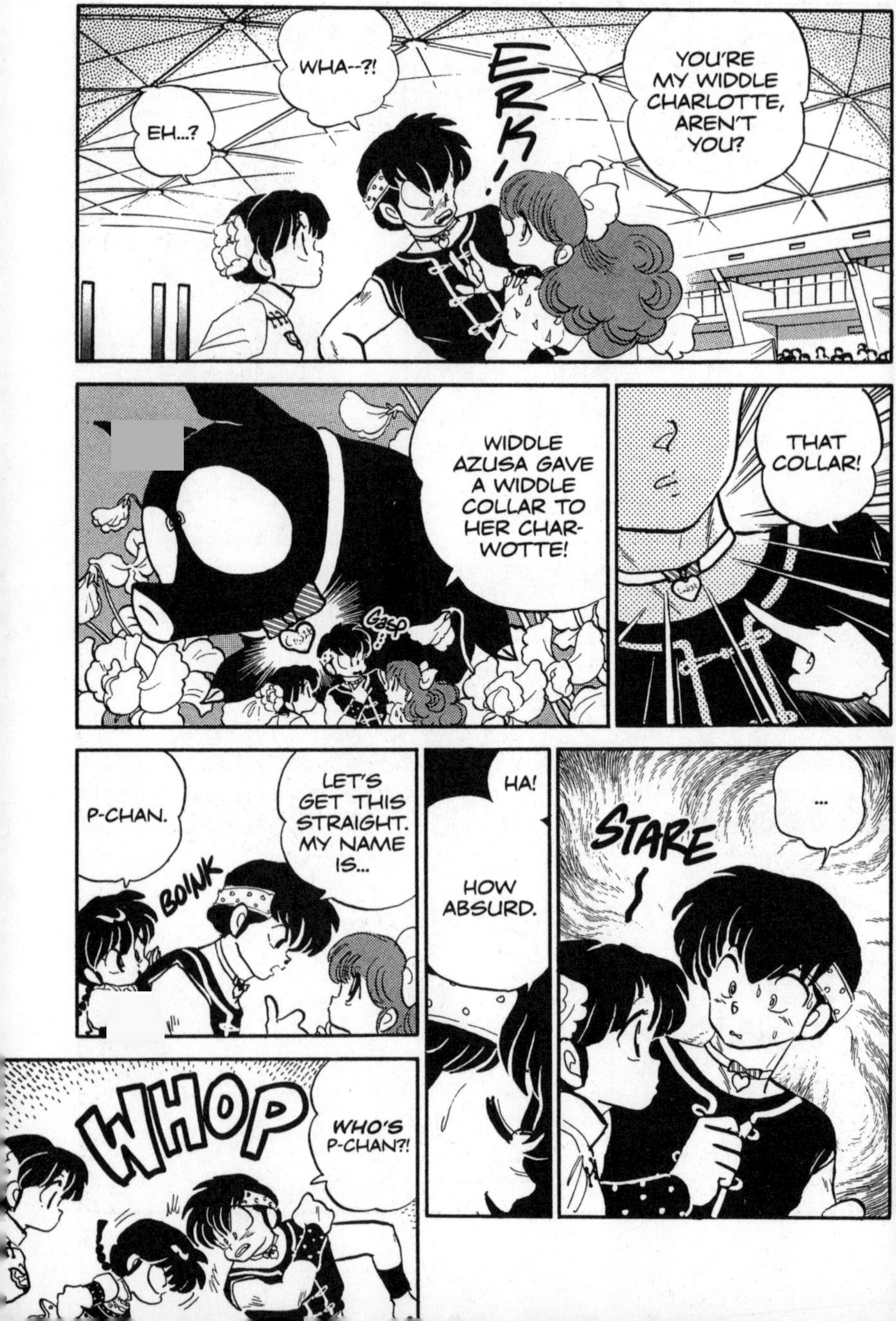
YOU'RE MY WIDDLE CHARLOTTE, AREN'T YOU?
ERK!
WHA--?!
EH...?
THAT COLLAR!
WIDDLE AZUSA GAVE A WIDDLE COLLAR TO HER CHAR-WOTTE!
Gasp
...
STARE
HA!
HOW ABSURD.
LET'S GET THIS STRAIGHT. MY NAME IS...
P-CHAN.
BOINK
WHO'S P-CHAN?!
WHOP

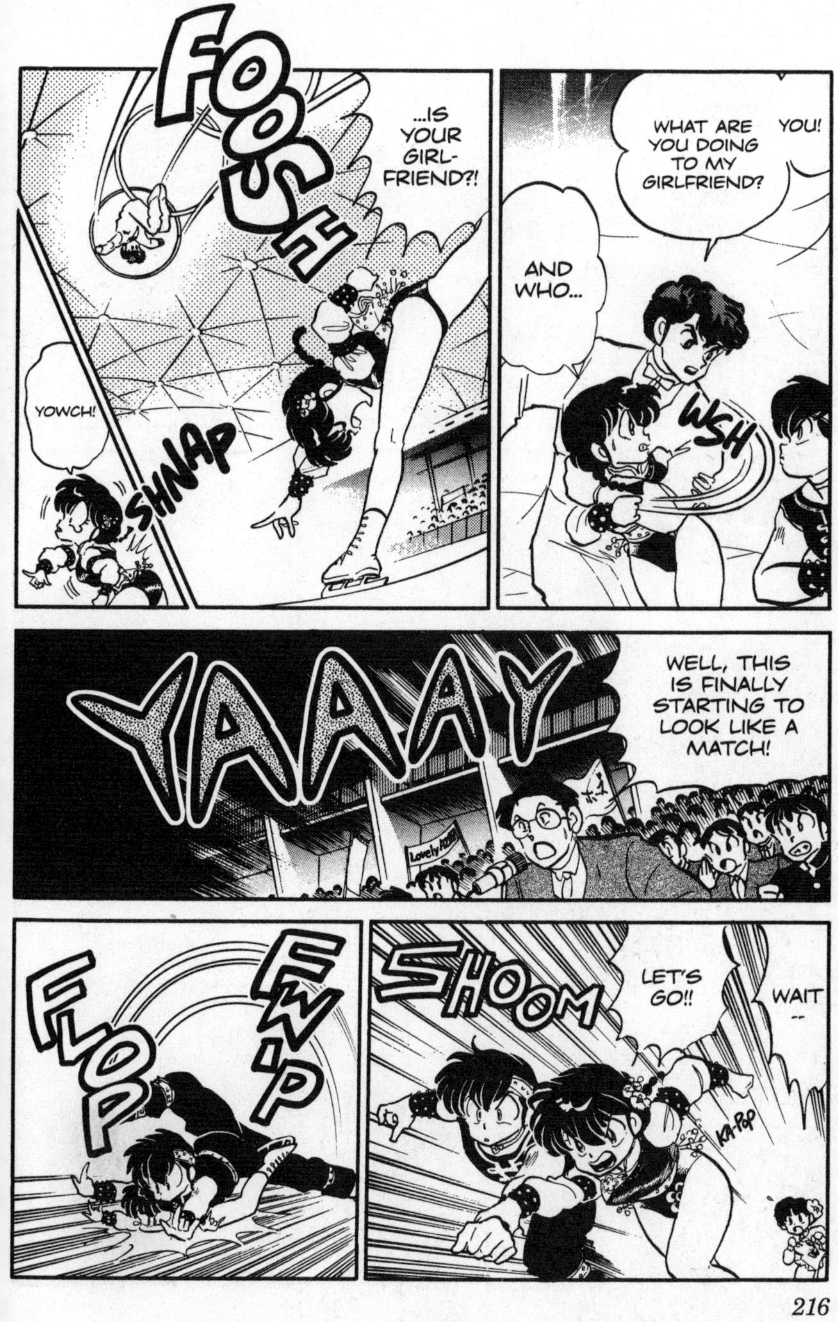
YOU!
WHAT ARE YOU DOING TO MY GIRLFRIEND?
AND WHO...
WSH
...IS YOUR GIRL-FRIEND?!
FOOSH
YOWCH!
SHNAP
WELL, THIS IS FINALLY STARTING TO LOOK LIKE A MATCH!
YAAAY
WAIT --
LET'S GO!!
SHOOM
KA-POP
FWIP
FLOP

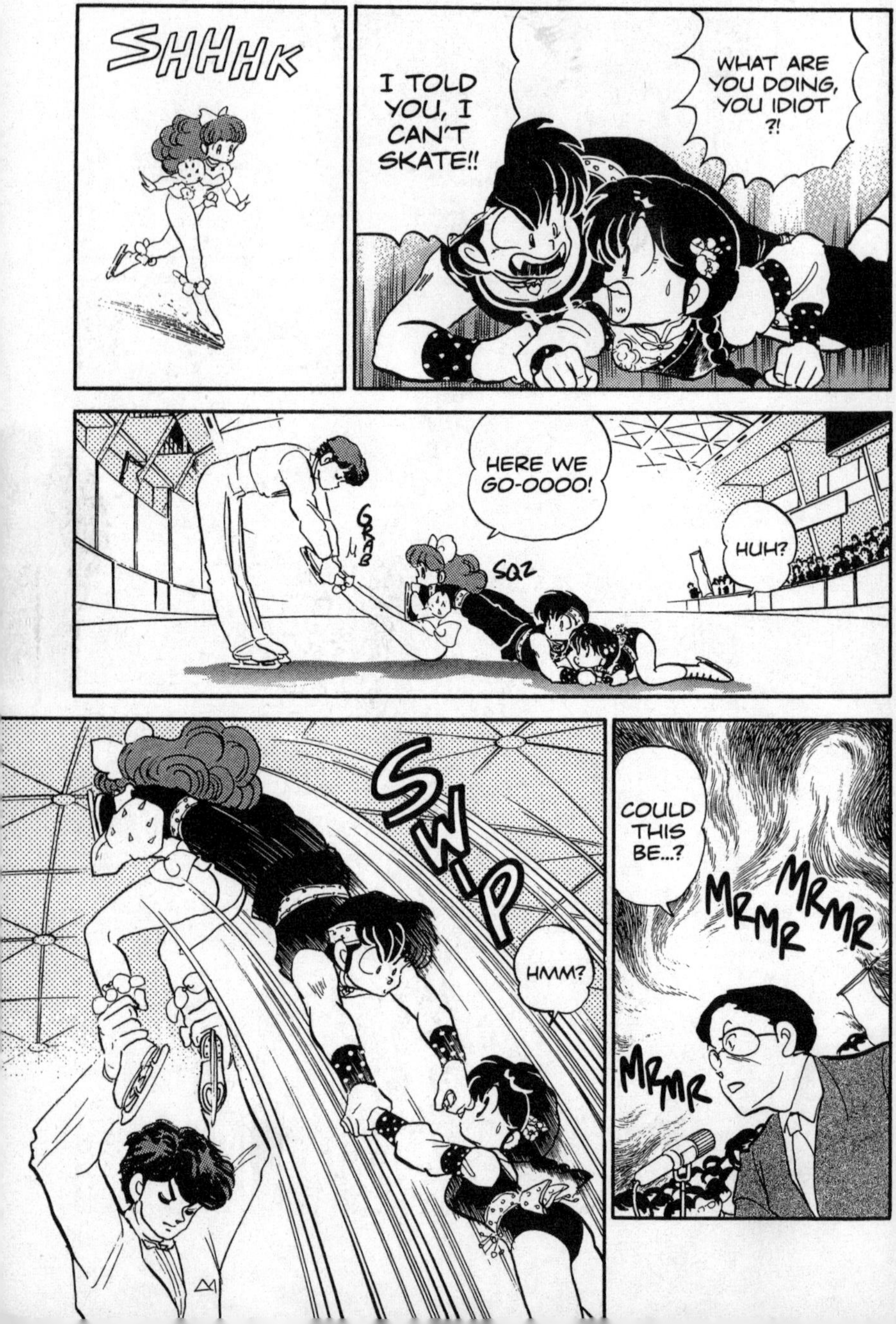
WHAT ARE YOU DOING, YOU IDIOT ?!
I TOLD YOU, I CAN'T SKATE!!
SHHHK
HUH?
HERE WE GO-OOOO!
SQZ
GRAB
COULD THIS BE...?
MRMR
MRMR
MRMR
SWIP
HMM?

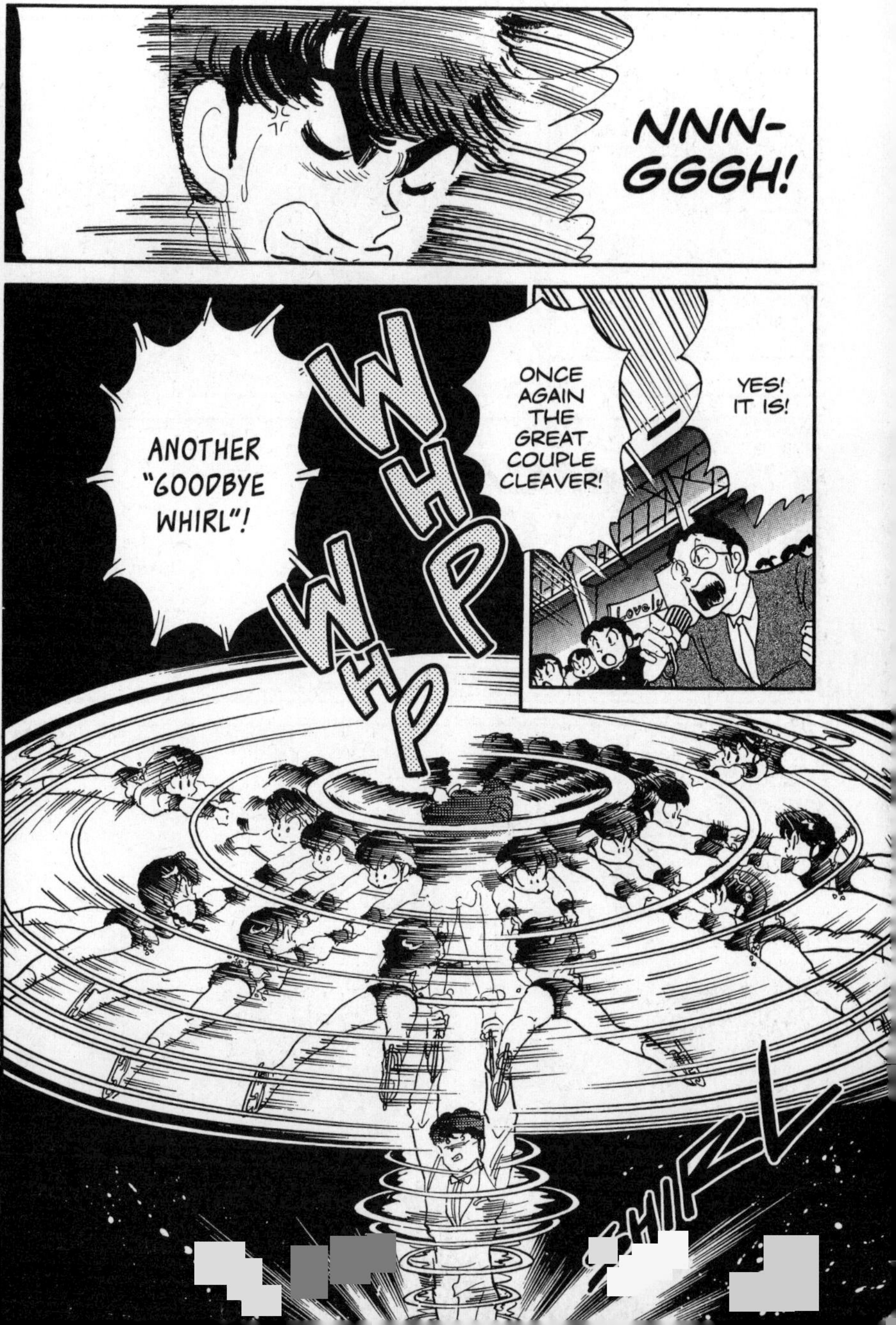
NNN-GGGH!
YES! IT IS!
ONCE AGAIN THE GREAT COUPLE CLEAVER!
Lovely
WHIP WHIP
ANOTHER "GOODBYE WHIRL"!
WHIRL

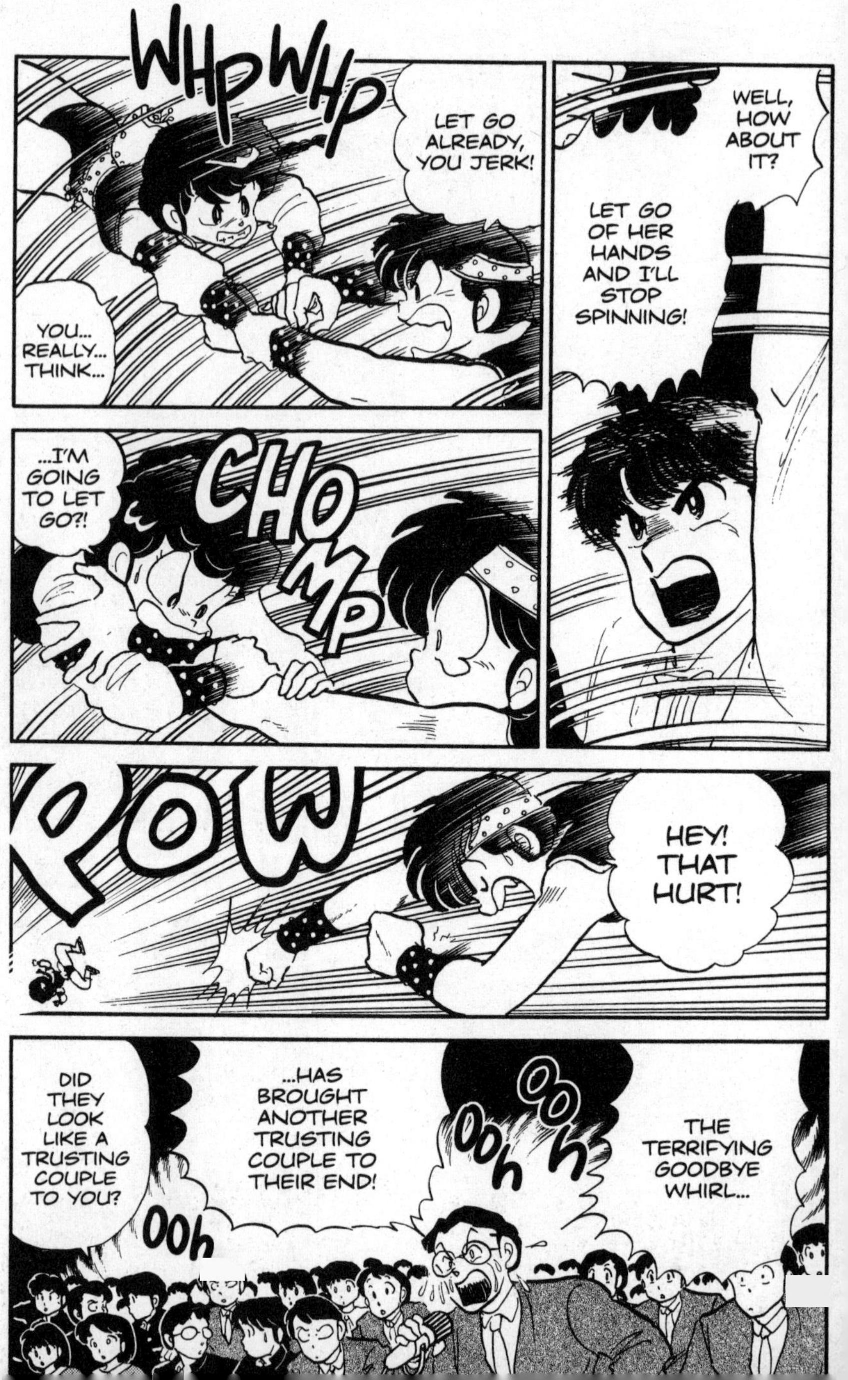
WELL, HOW ABOUT IT?
LET GO OF HER HANDS AND I'LL STOP SPINNING!
WHPWHP
LET GO ALREADY, YOU JERK!
YOU... REALLY... THINK...
CHOMP
...I'M GOING TO LET GO?!
HEY! THAT HURT!
POW
THE TERRIFYING GOODBYE WHIRL...
OOh
OOh
...HAS BROUGHT ANOTHER TRUSTING COUPLE TO THEIR END!
OOh
DID THEY LOOK LIKE A TRUSTING COUPLE TO YOU?

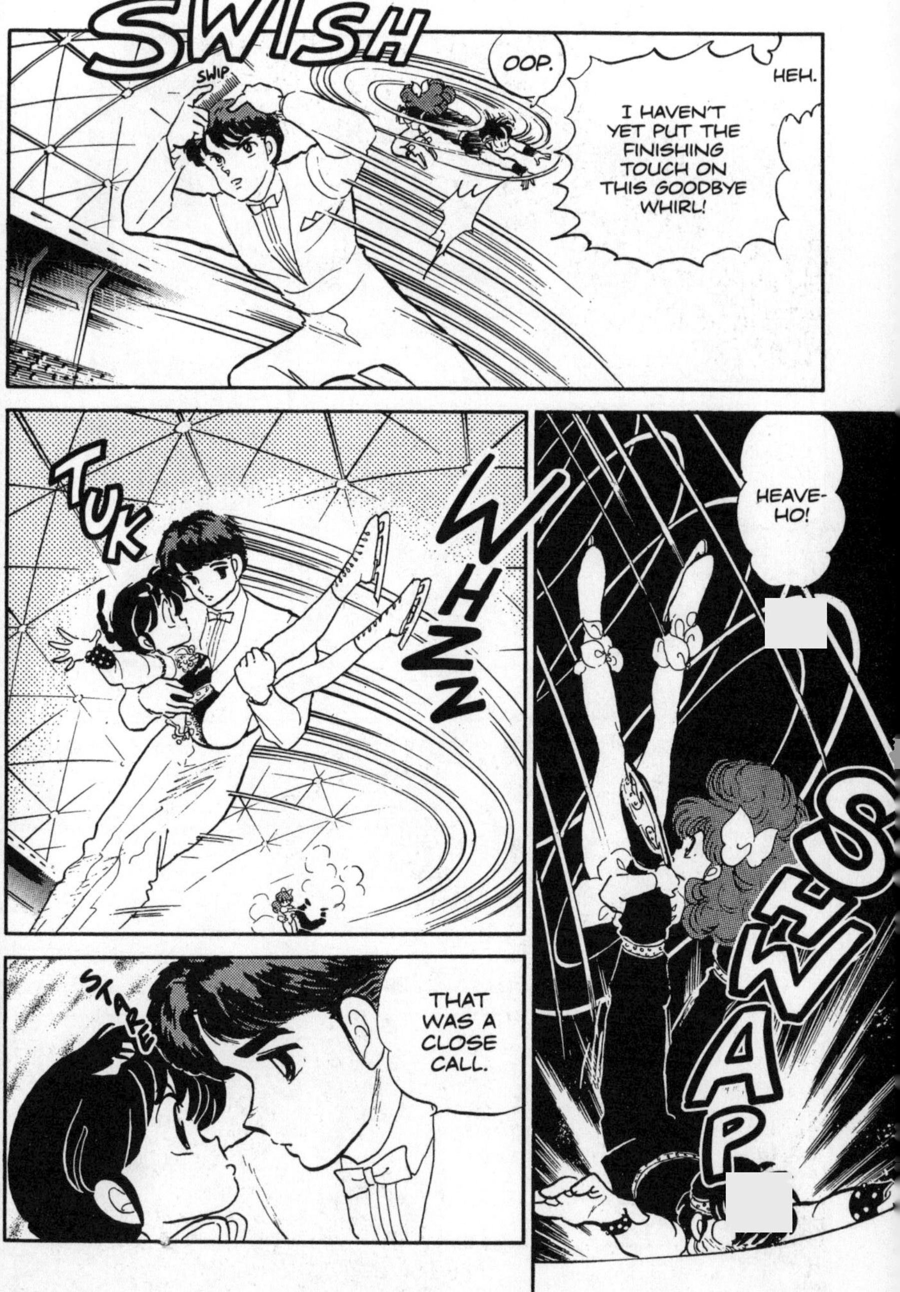
HEH.
I HAVEN'T YET PUT THE FINISHING TOUCH ON THIS GOODBYE WHIRL!
OOP.
SWISH
SWIP
HEAVE-HO!
SWAP
WHZZ
TUK
THAT WAS A CLOSE CALL.
SKATE

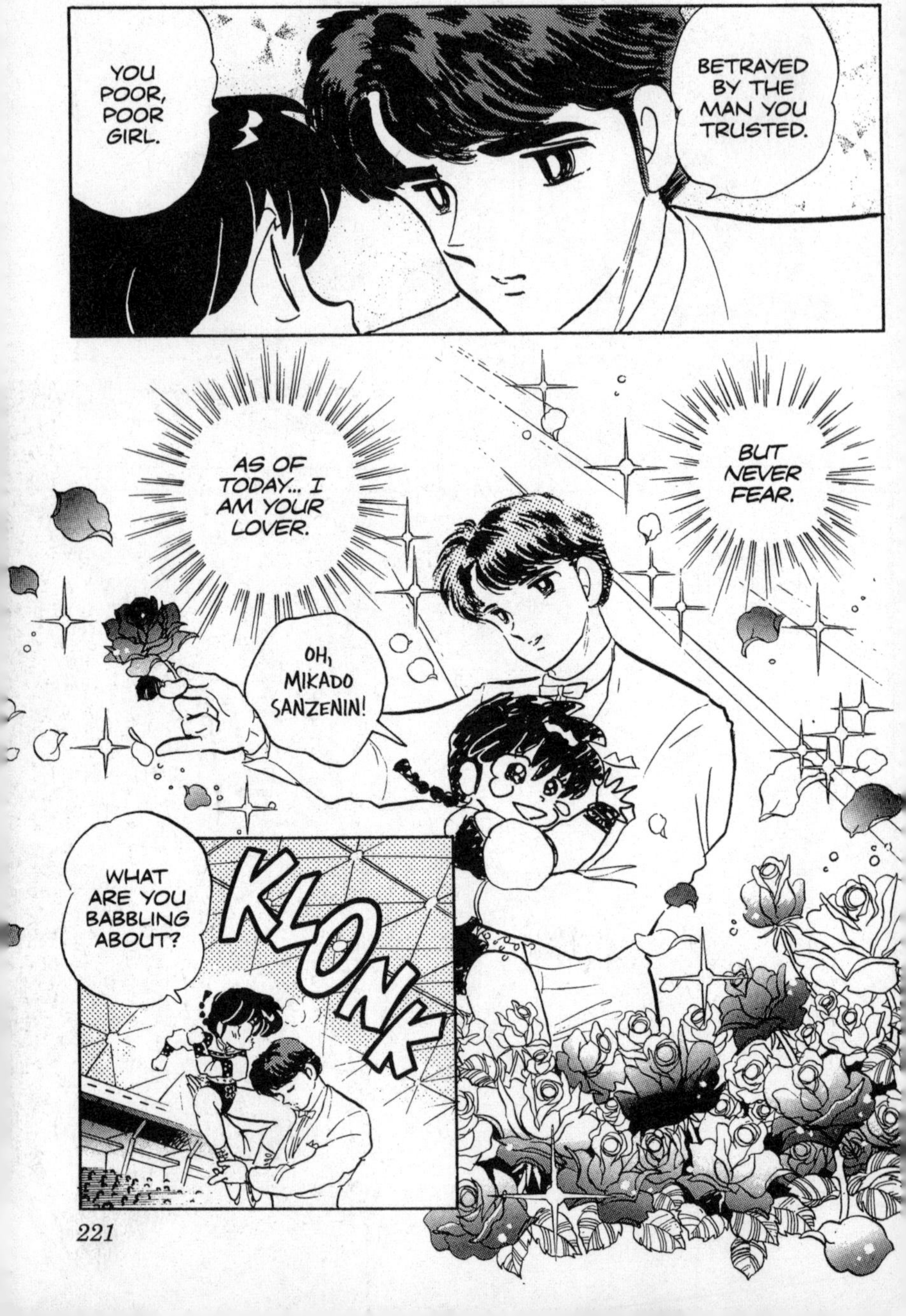
BETRAYED BY THE MAN YOU TRUSTED.
YOU POOR, POOR GIRL.
BUT NEVER FEAR.
AS OF TODAY... I AM YOUR LOVER.
OH, MIKADO SANZENIN!
KLONK
WHAT ARE YOU BABBLING ABOUT?

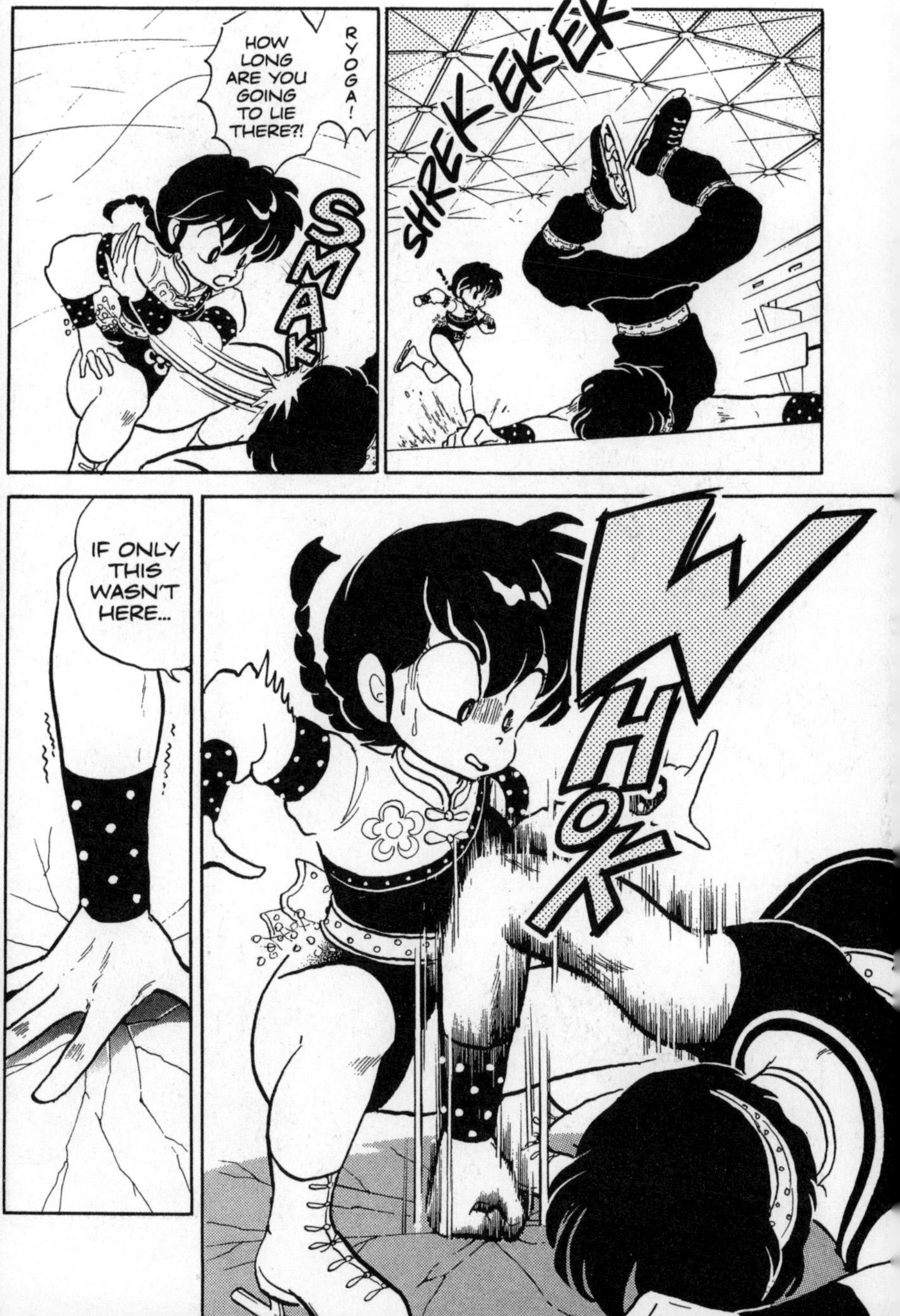
SHREKEKEK
RYOGA!
HOW LONG ARE YOU GOING TO LIE THERE?!
SMAK
WHOK
IF ONLY THIS WASN'T HERE...

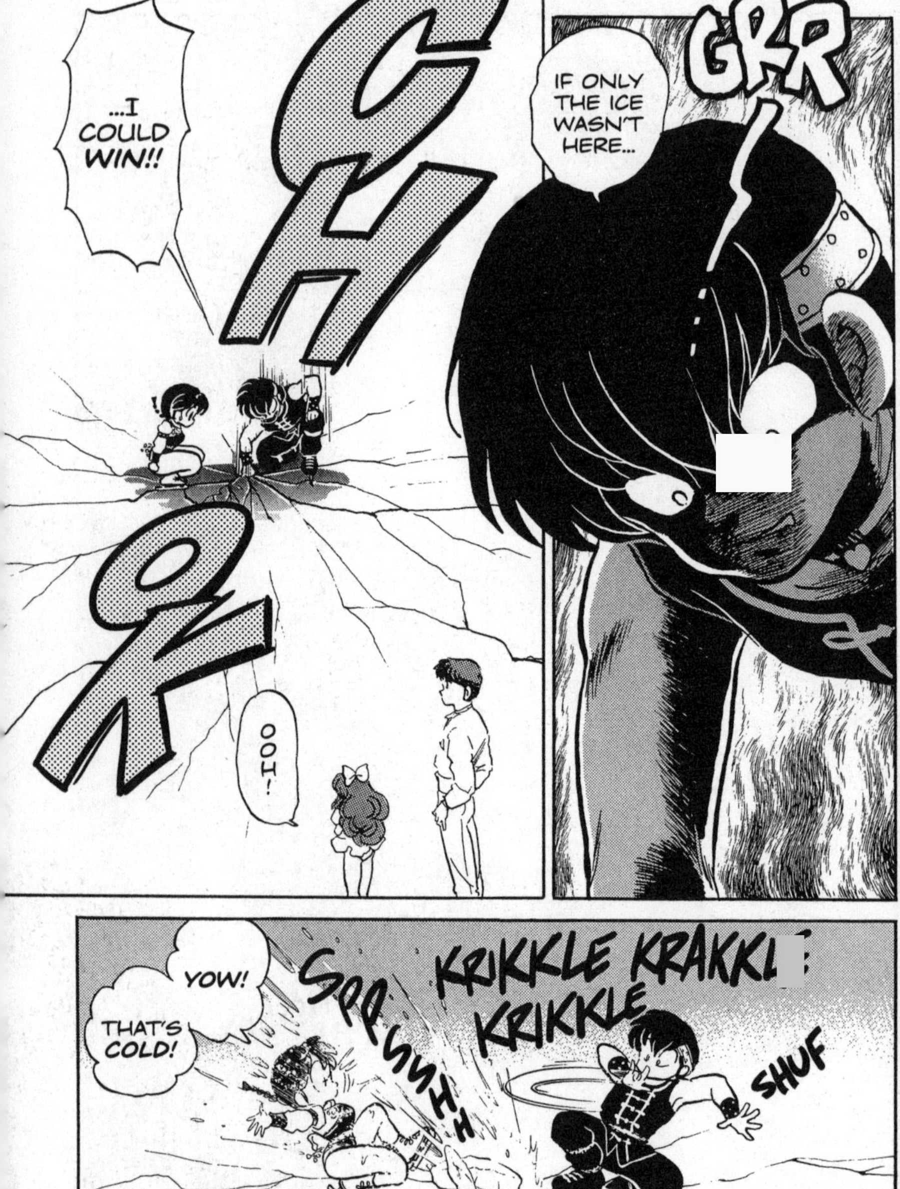
GRR
IF ONLY THE ICE WASN'T HERE...
...I COULD WIN!!
CHONK
OOH!
KRIKKLE KRAKKL
KRIKKLE
SHUF
SPPLSSHH
YOW!
THAT'S COLD!

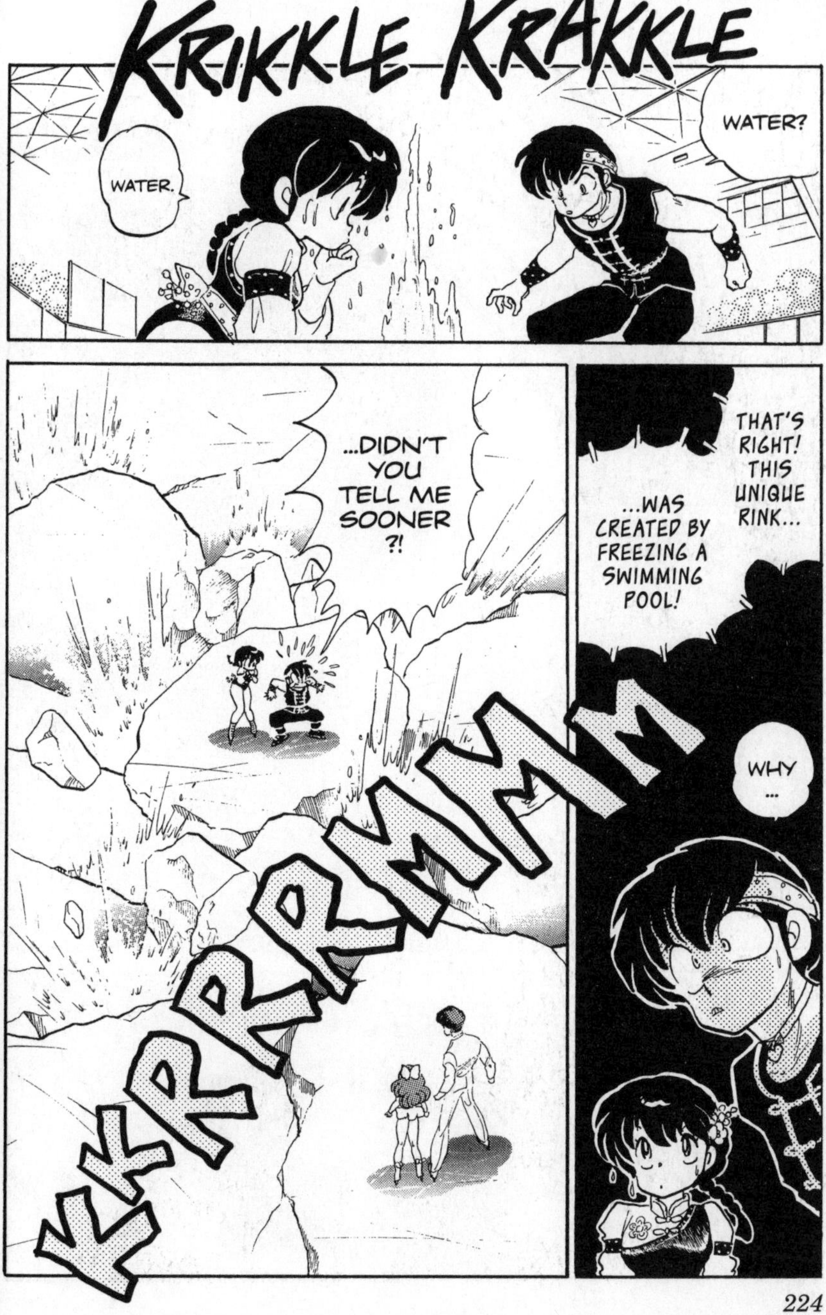
KRIKKLE KRAKKLE
WATER?
WATER.
THAT'S RIGHT! THIS UNIQUE RINK...
...WAS CREATED BY FREEZING A SWIMMING POOL!
WHY ...
...DIDN'T YOU TELL ME SOONER ?!
KKRRRMMMM

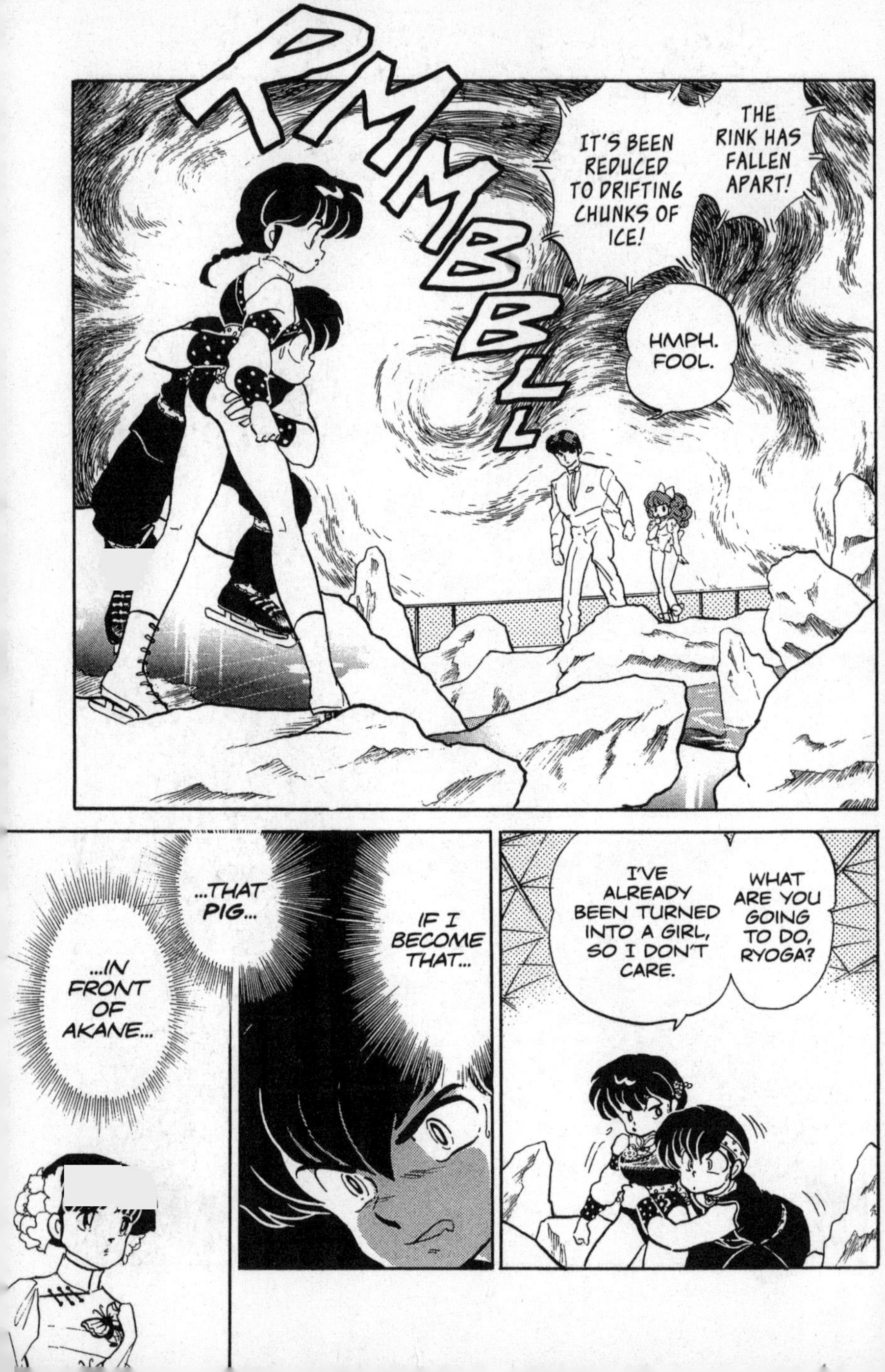
RMMBBLL
THE RINK HAS FALLEN APART!
IT'S BEEN REDUCED TO DRIFTING CHUNKS OF ICE!
HMPH. FOOL.
WHAT ARE YOU GOING TO DO, RYOGA?
I'VE ALREADY BEEN TURNED INTO A GIRL, SO I DON'T CARE.
IF I BECOME THAT...
...THAT PIG...
...IN FRONT OF AKANE...

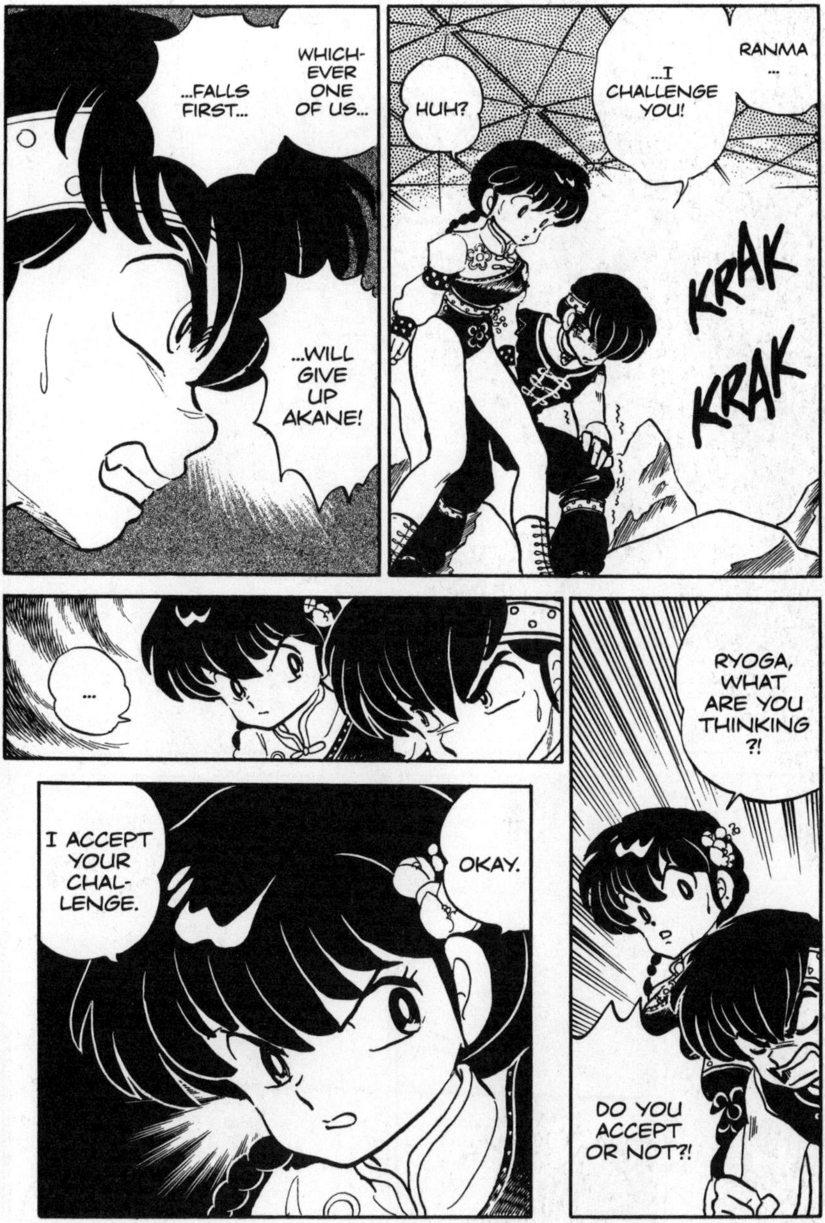
RANMA ...
...I CHALLENGE YOU!
HUH?
KRAK
KRAK
WHICH-EVER ONE OF US...
...FALLS FIRST...
...WILL GIVE UP AKANE!
RYOGA, WHAT ARE YOU THINKING ?!
DO YOU ACCEPT OR NOT?!
...
OKAY.
I ACCEPT YOUR CHAL-LENGE.

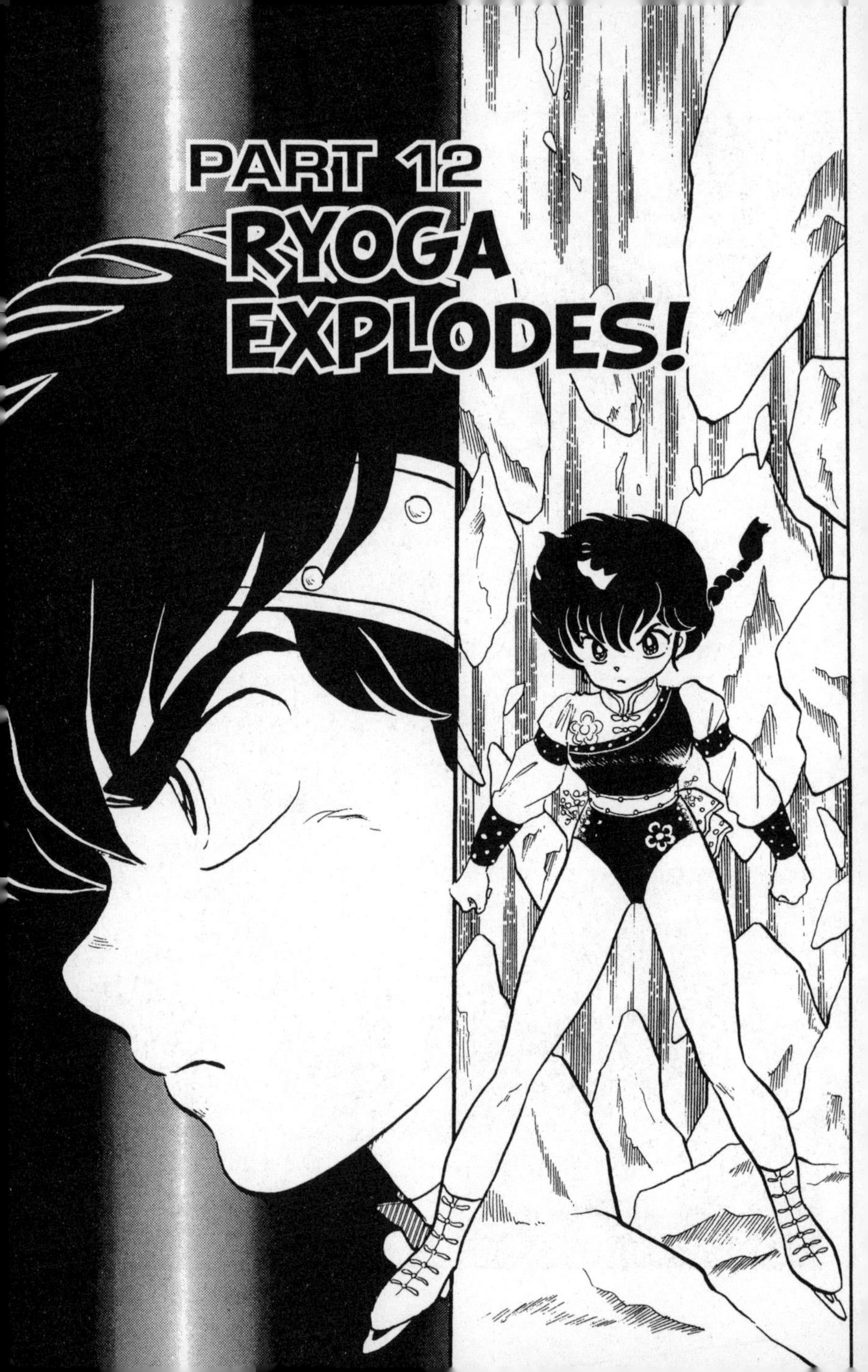
PART 12
RYOGA EXPLODES!

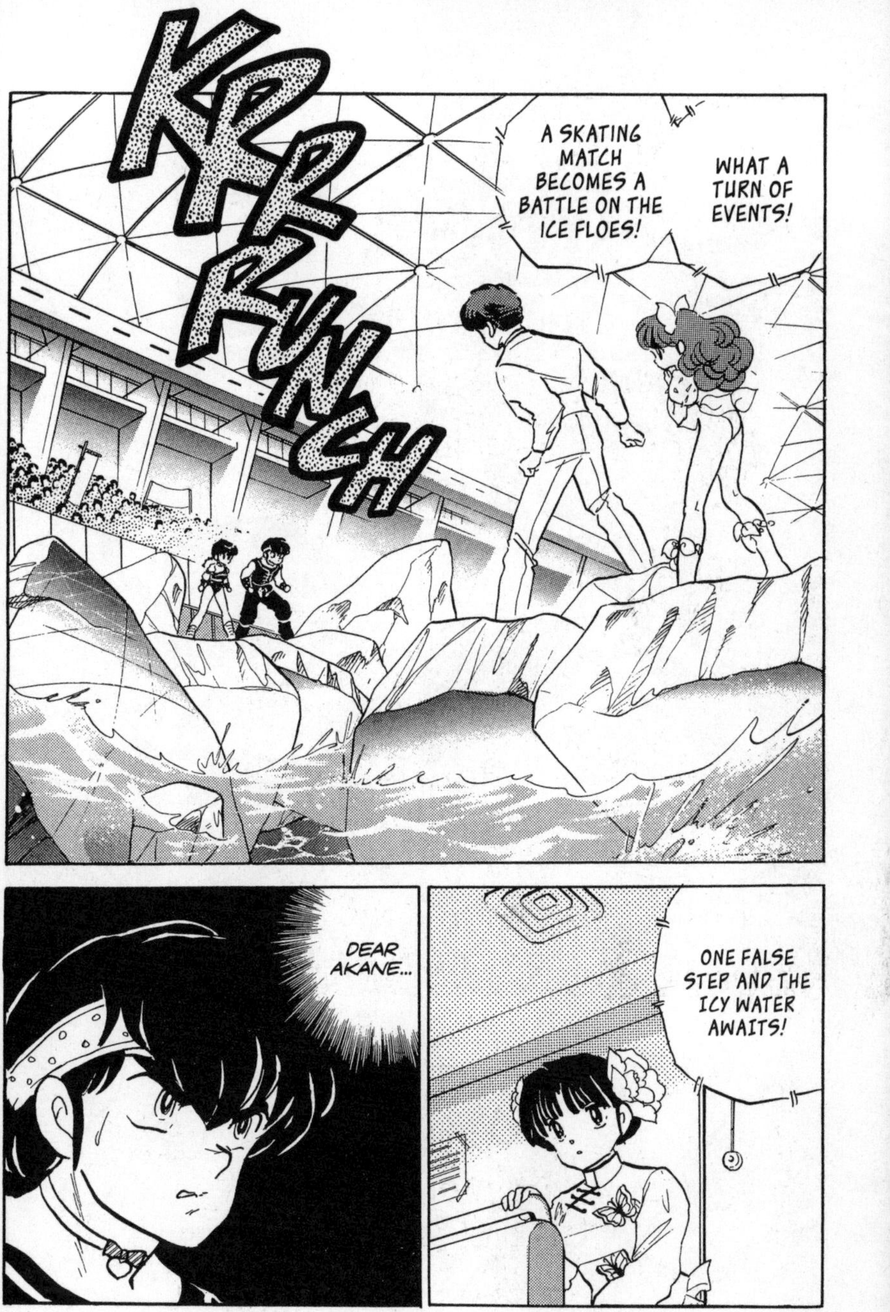
KRRRUNCH
A SKATING MATCH BECOMES A BATTLE ON THE ICE FLOES!
WHAT A TURN OF EVENTS!
ONE FALSE STEP AND THE ICY WATER AWAITS!
DEAR AKANE...

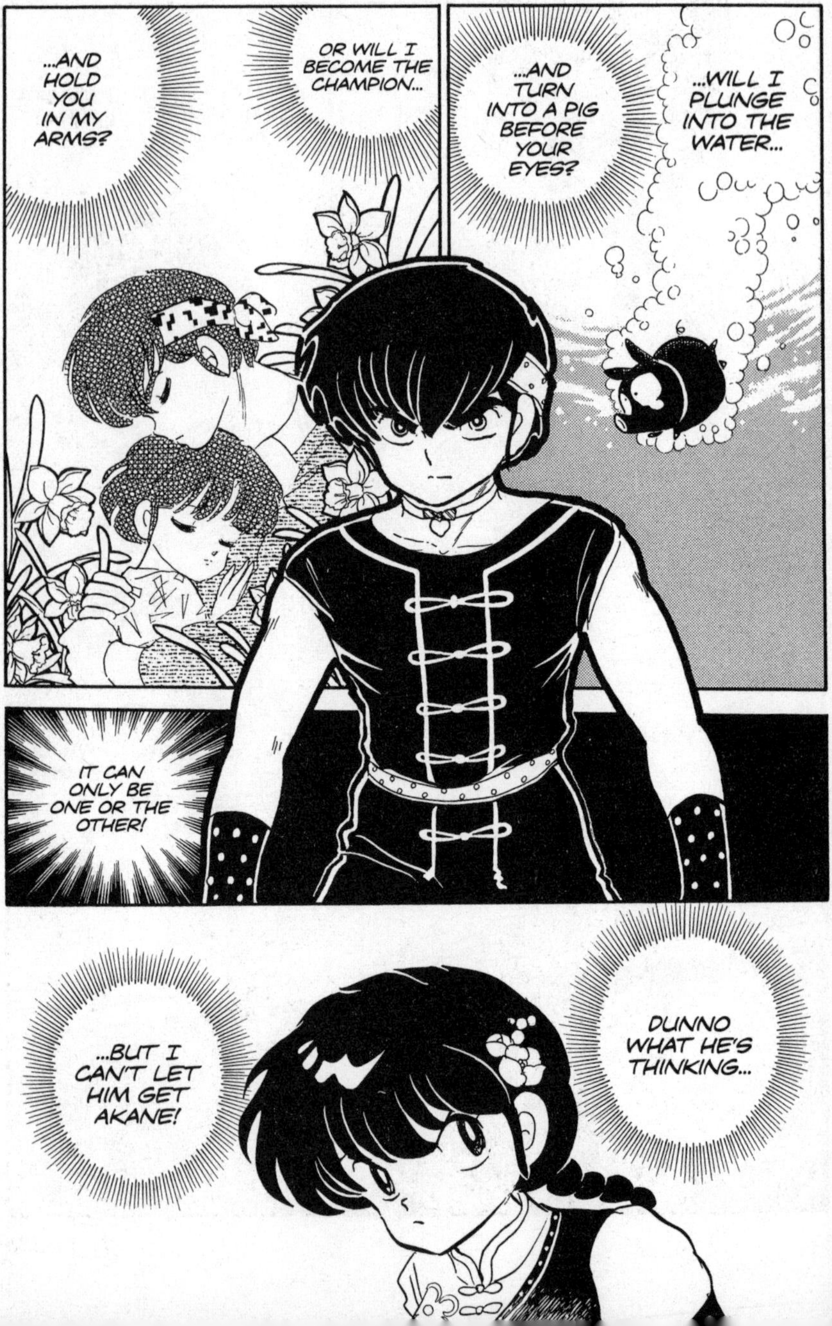
...WILL I PLUNGE INTO THE WATER...
...AND TURN INTO A PIG BEFORE YOUR EYES?
OR WILL I BECOME THE CHAMPION...
...AND HOLD YOU IN MY ARMS?
IT CAN ONLY BE ONE OR THE OTHER!
DUNNO WHAT HE'S THINKING...
...BUT I CAN'T LET HIM GET AKANE!

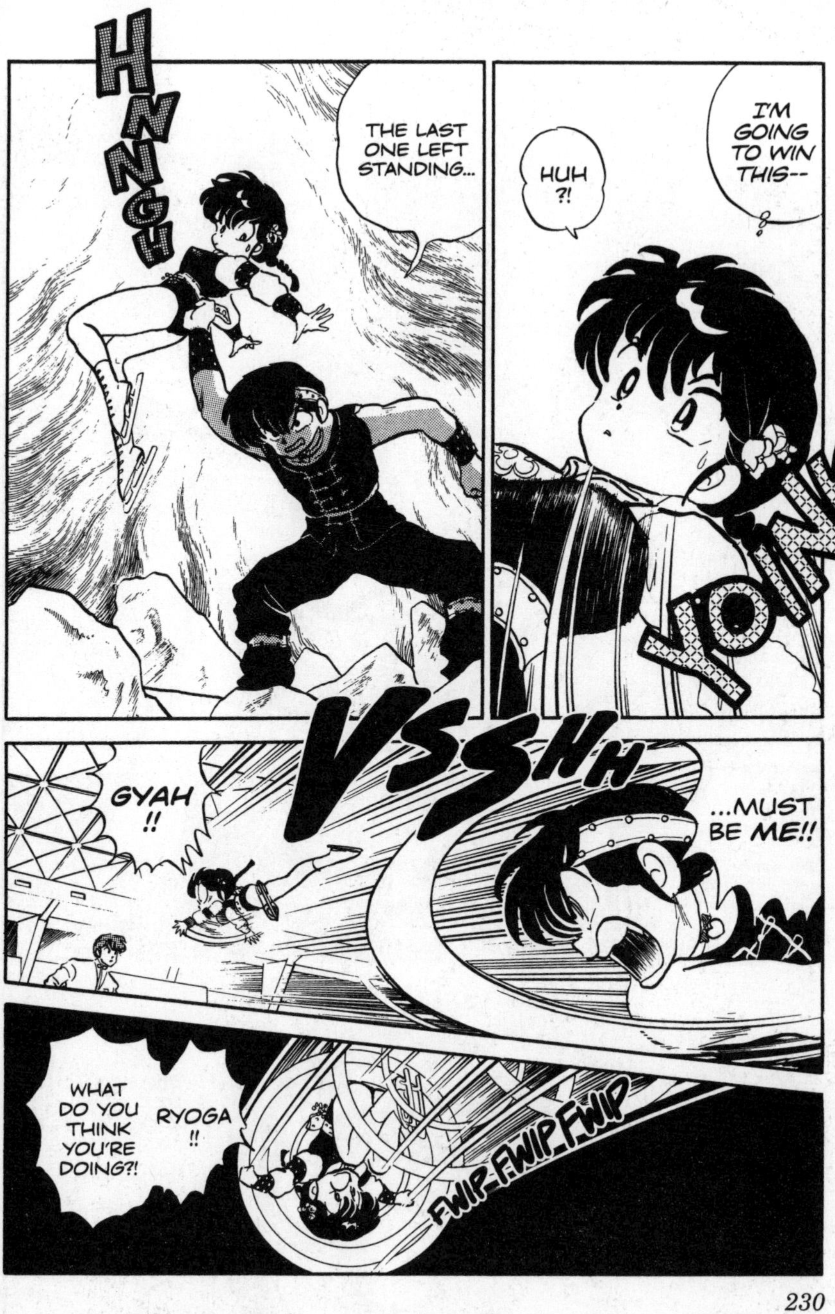
I'M GOING TO WIN THIS--
HUH ?!
YOINK
THE LAST ONE LEFT STANDING...
HNNGH
VSSHH
...MUST BE ME!!
GYAH !!
FWIP FWIP FWIP
RYOGA !!
WHAT DO YOU THINK YOU'RE DOING?!

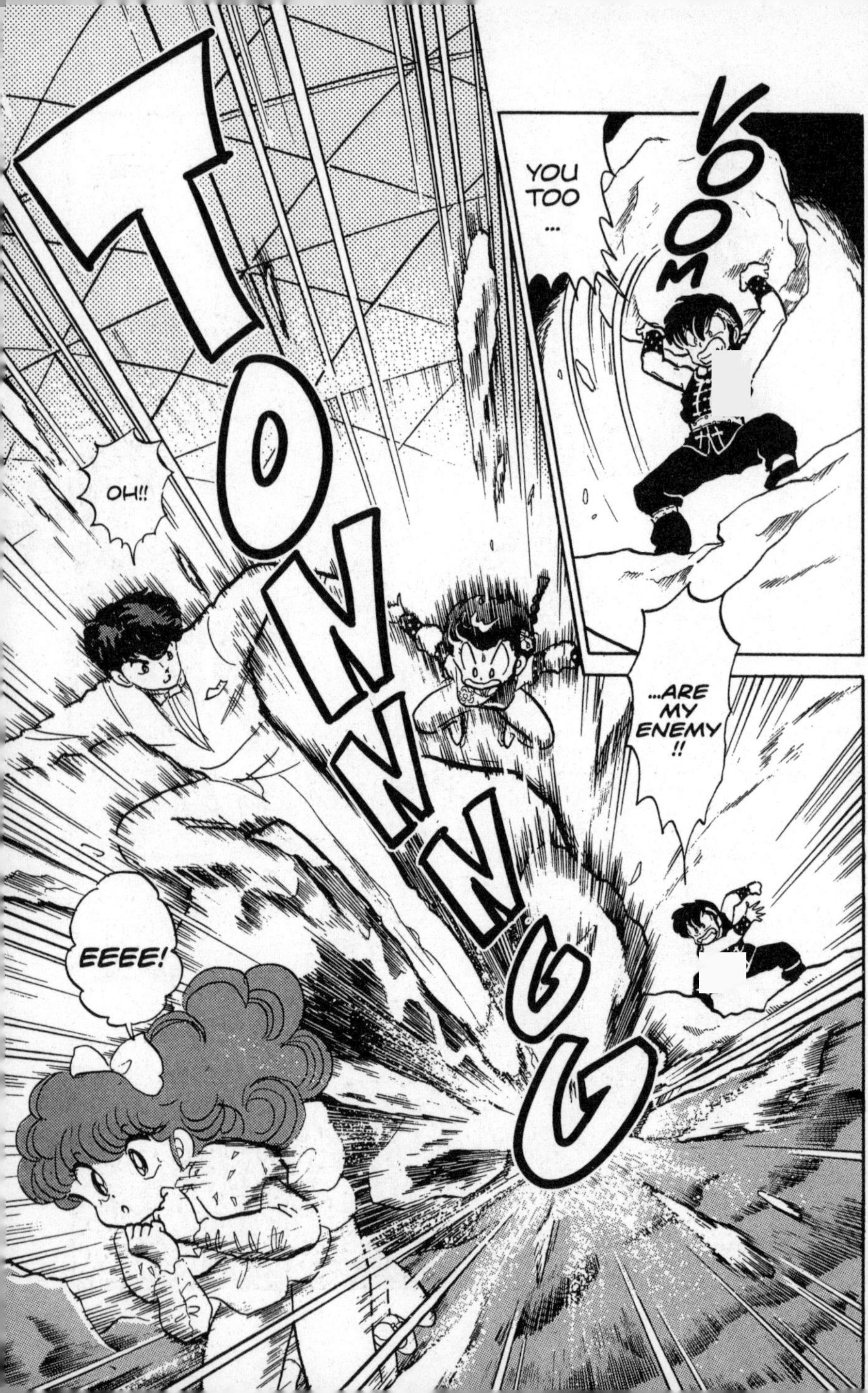
VOOM
YOU TOO ...
...ARE MY ENEMY !!
TONNNGG
OH!!
EEEE!

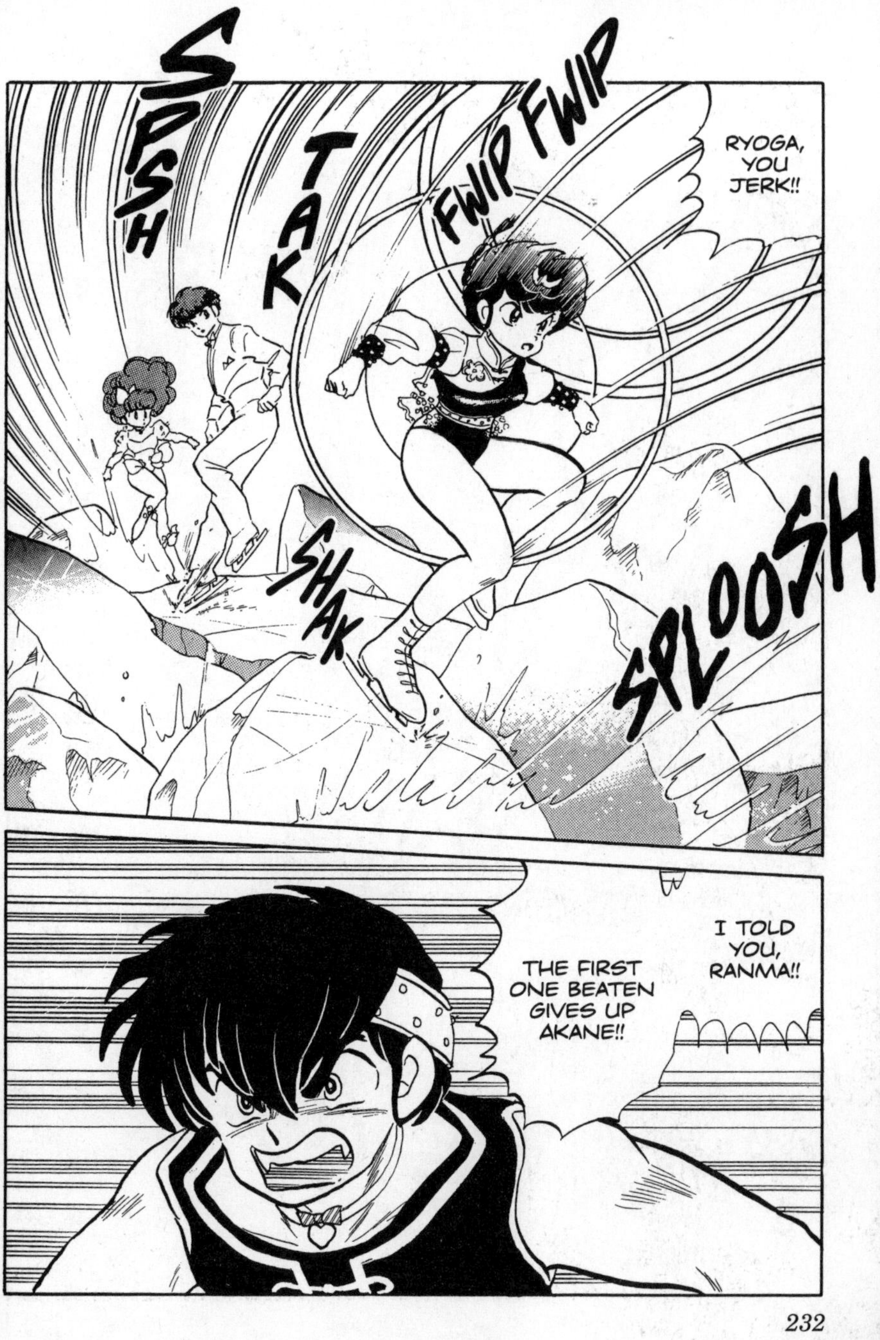
RYOGA, YOU JERK!!
FWIP FWIP
TAK
SPSH
SPLOOSH
SHAK
I TOLD YOU, RANMA!!
THE FIRST ONE BEATEN GIVES UP AKANE!!

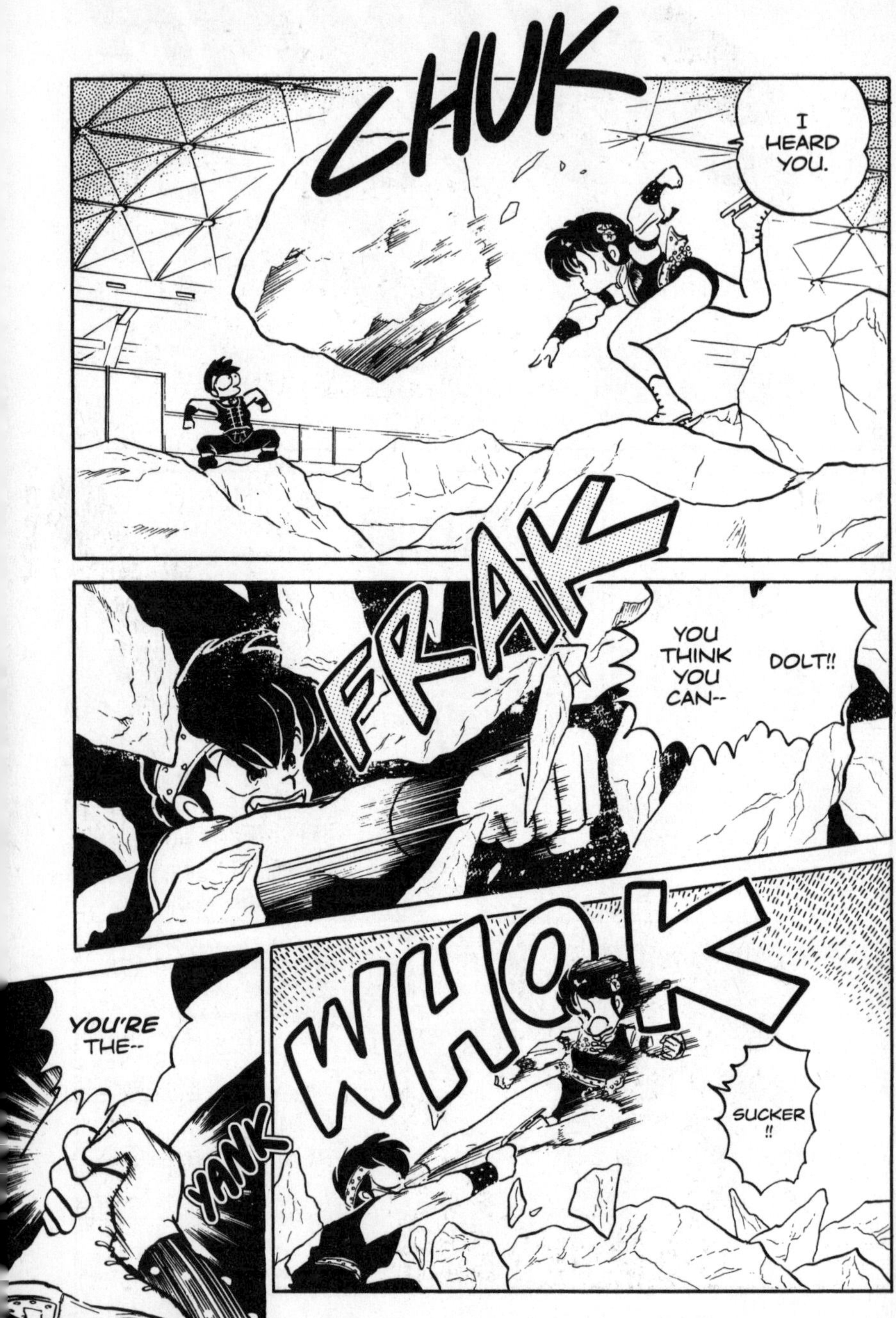
CHUK
I HEARD YOU.
FRAK
DOLT!!
YOU THINK YOU CAN--
WHOK
SUCKER !!
YOU'RE THE--
YANK

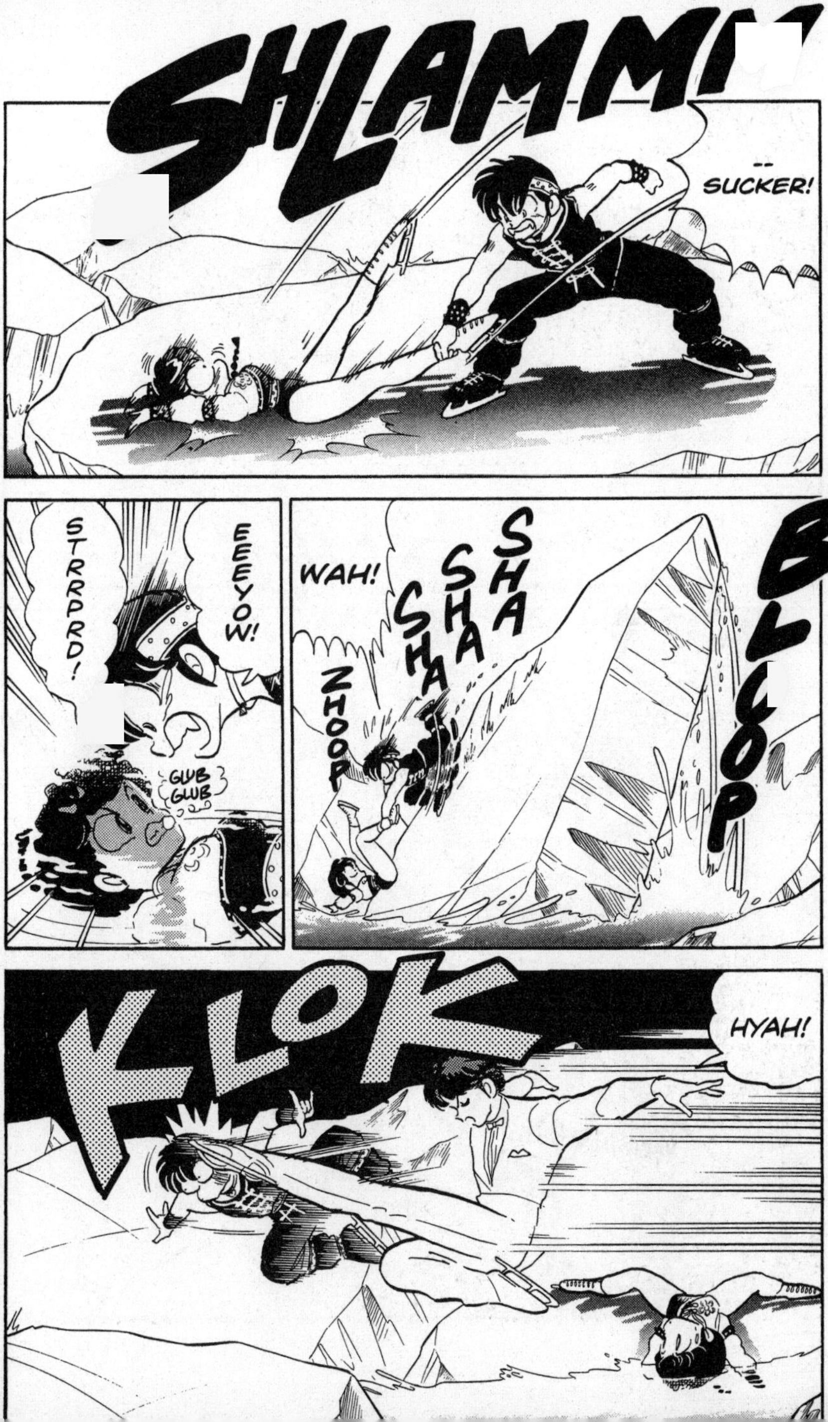
SHLAMM
-- SUCKER!
BLOOP
SHA
SHA
SHA
WAH!
ZHOOP
EEEYOW!
STRRPRD!
GLUB GLUB
HYAH!
KLOK

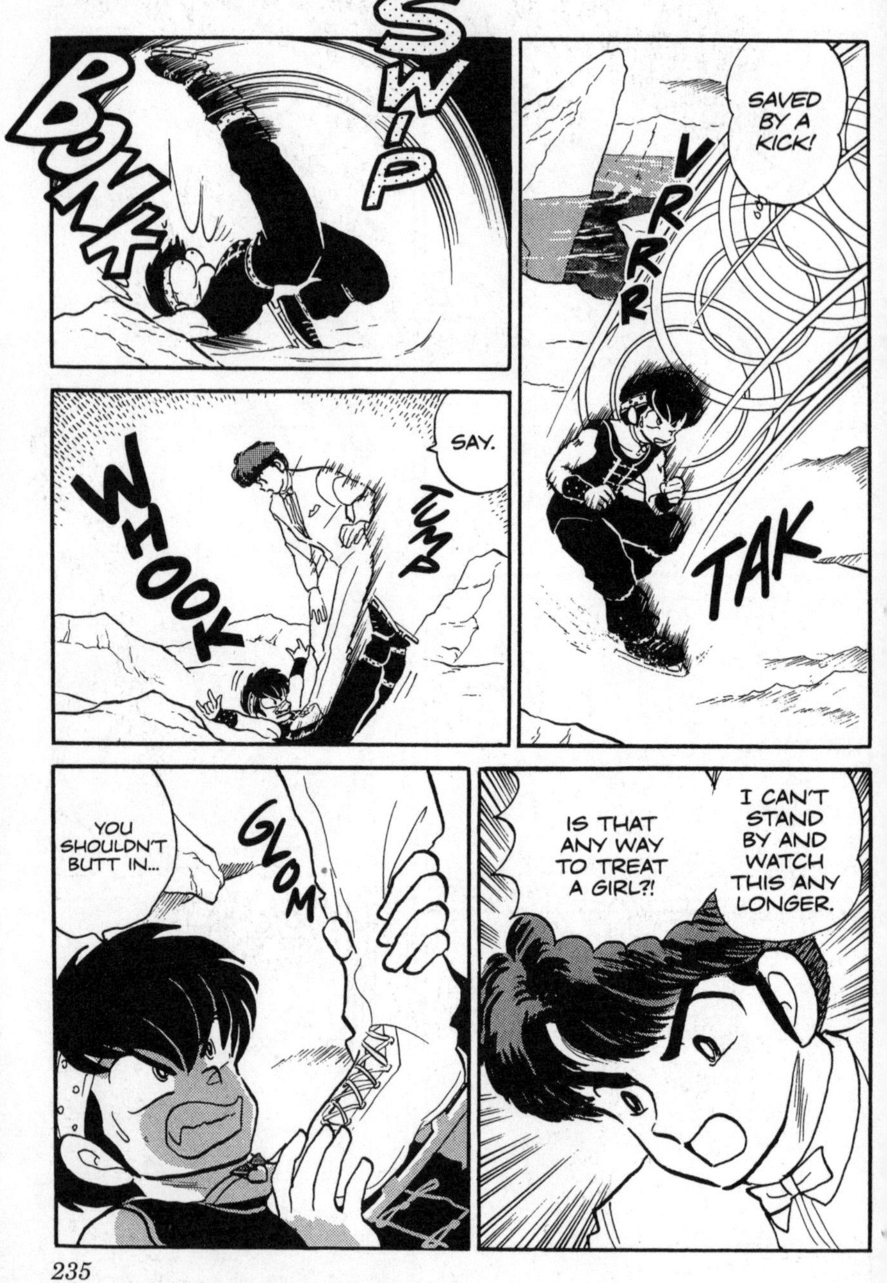
SAVED BY A KICK!
VRRRR
TAK
SWIP
BONK
SAY.
TUMP
WHOOOK
I CAN'T STAND BY AND WATCH THIS ANY LONGER.
IS THAT ANY WAY TO TREAT A GIRL?!
GLOM
YOU SHOULDN'T BUTT IN...

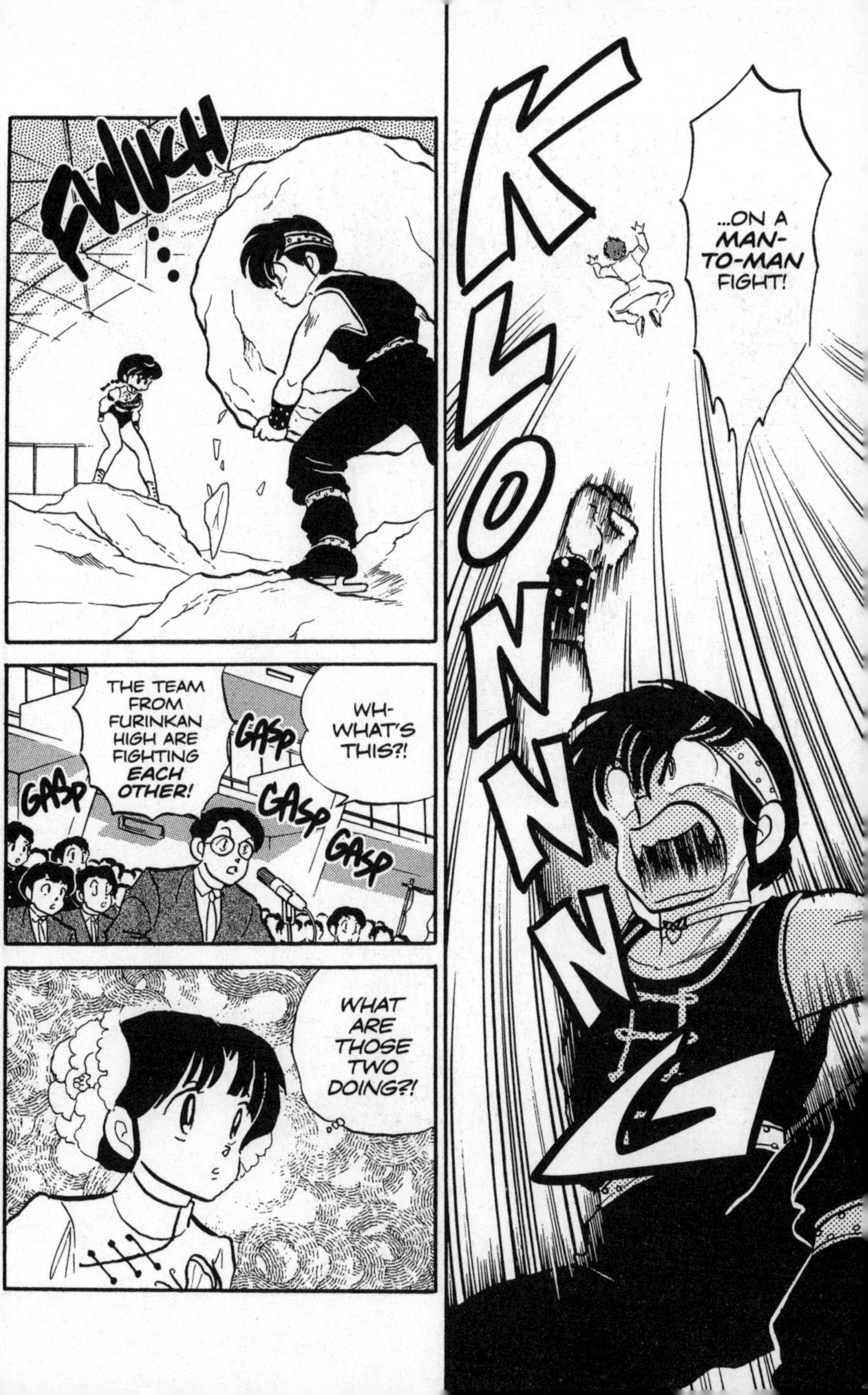
...ON A MAN-TO-MAN FIGHT!
FWUCH
WH- WHAT'S THIS?!
GASP
GASP
GASP
GASP
THE TEAM FROM FURINKAN HIGH ARE FIGHTING EACH OTHER!
WHAT ARE THOSE TWO DOING?!

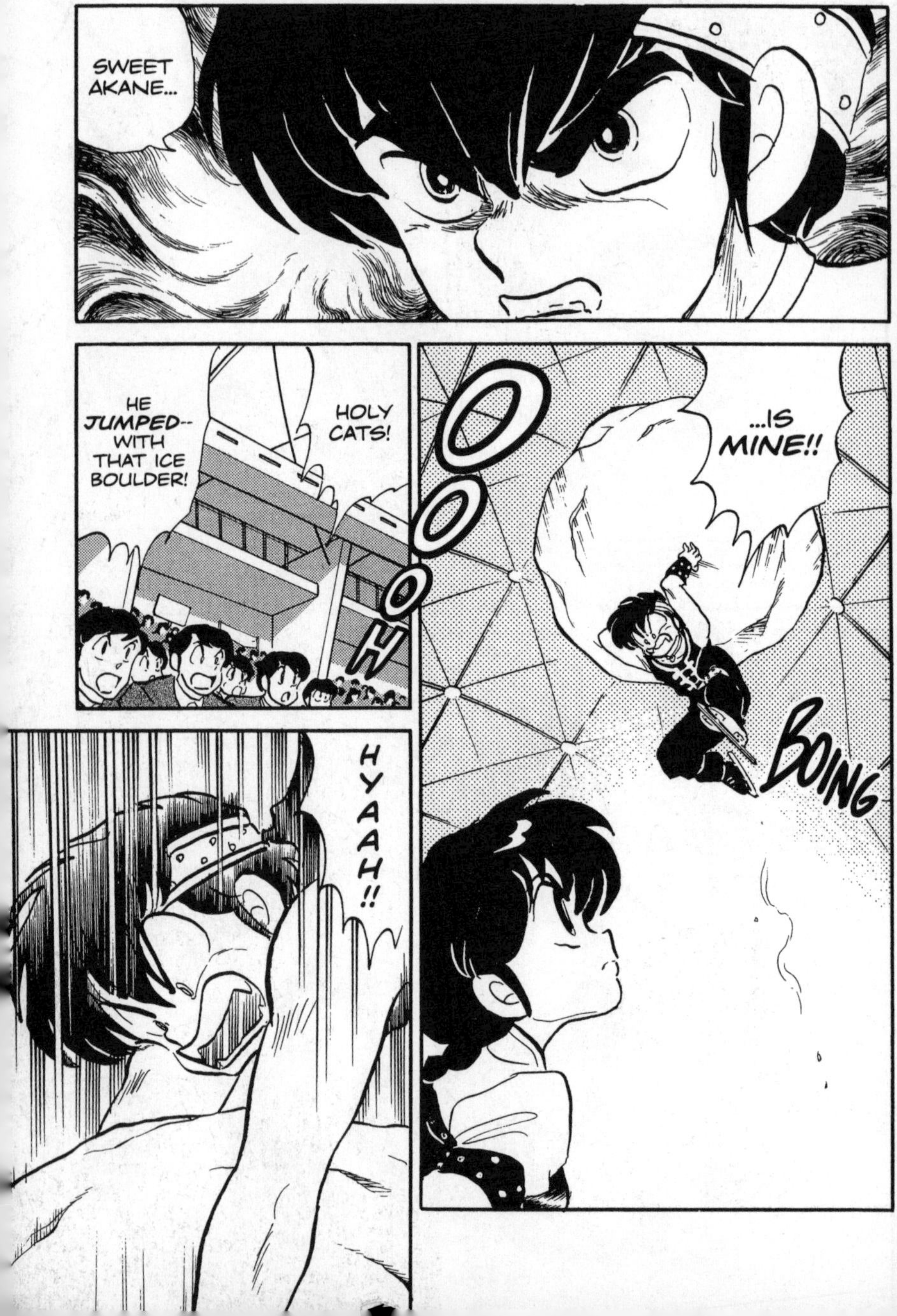
SWEET AKANE...
...IS MINE!!
OOOOOH
BOING
HOLY CATS!
HE JUMPED-- WITH THAT ICE BOULDER!
HYAAAH!!

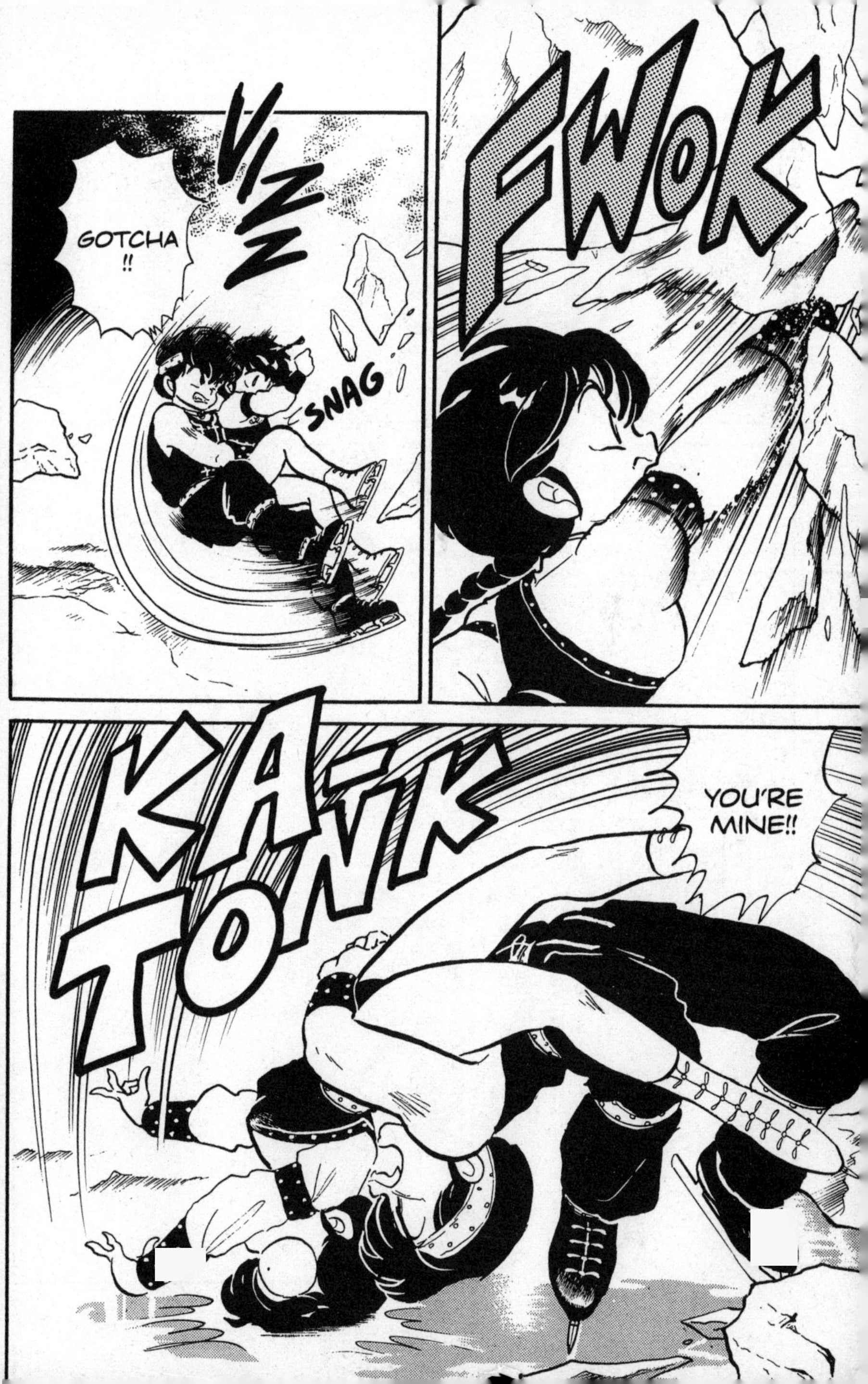
FWOK
VIZZ
GOTCHA !!
SNAG
YOU'RE MINE!!
KA-TONK

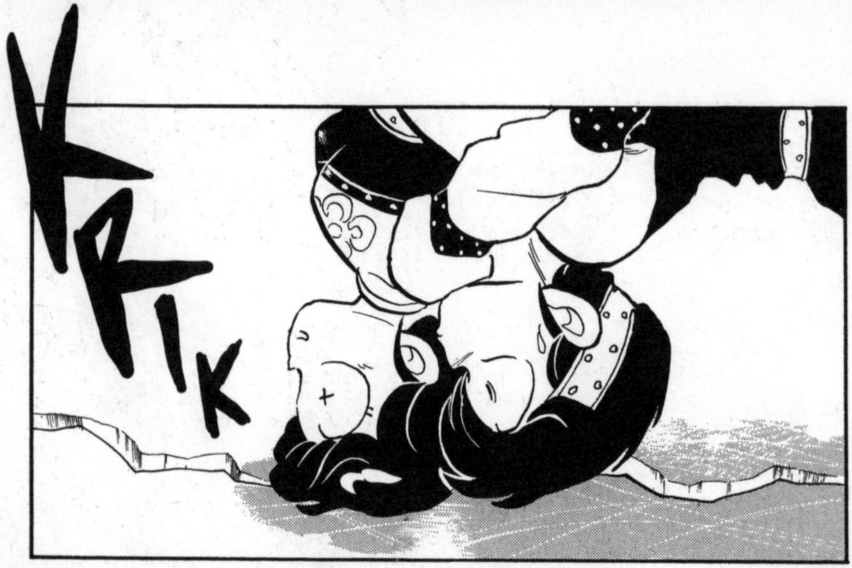
KRIK

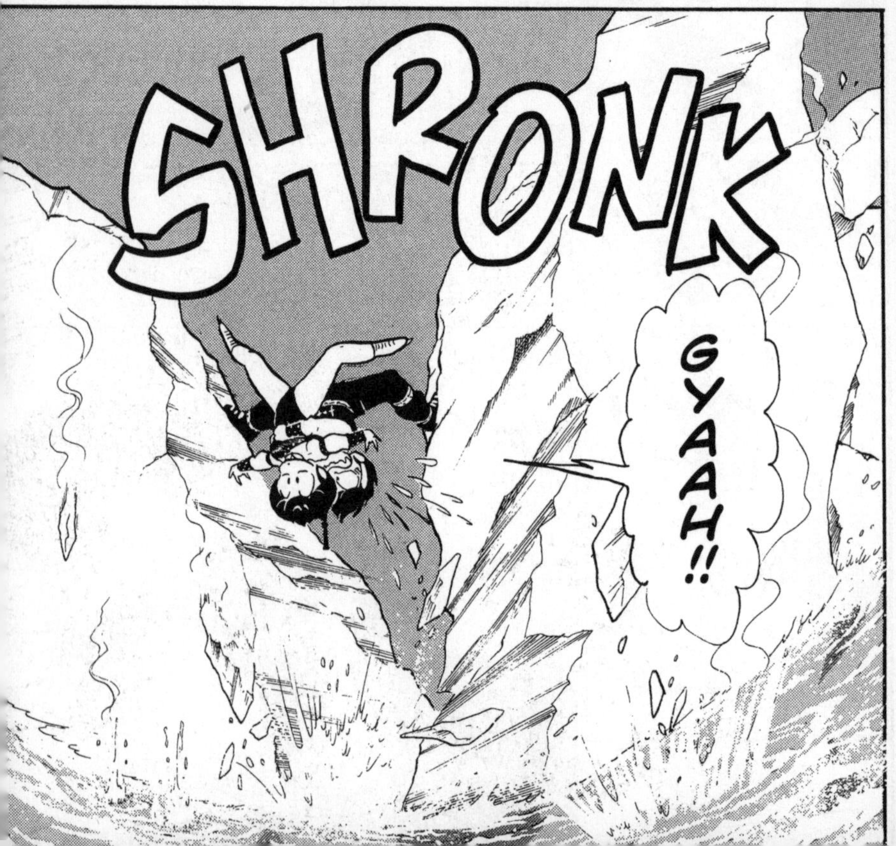
SHRONK
GYAAH!!

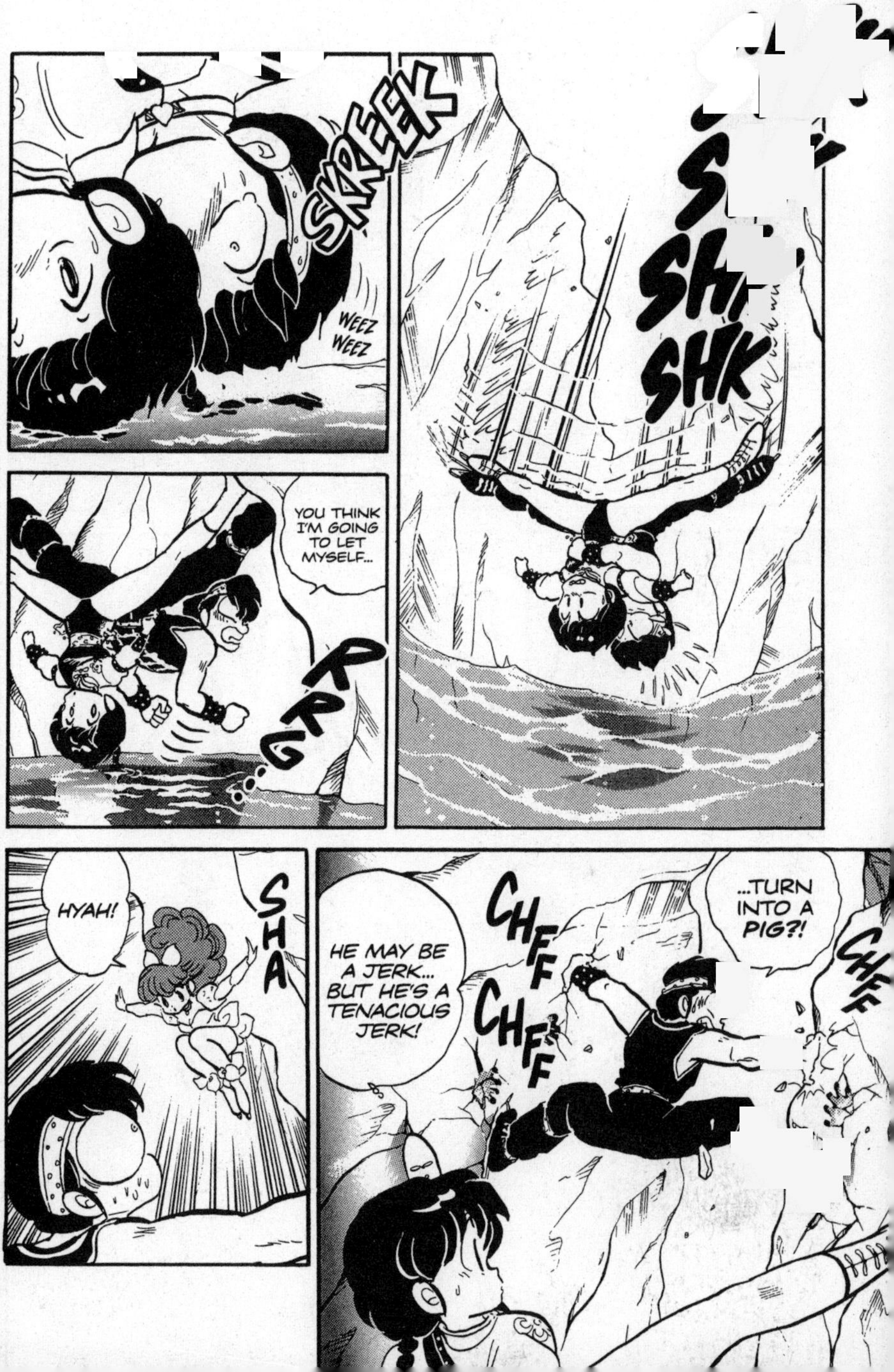
SHK
SKREEK
WEEZ WEEZ
YOU THINK I'M GOING TO LET MYSELF...
RRG...
...TURN INTO A PIG?!
CHFF
CHFF CHFF
HE MAY BE A JERK... BUT HE'S A TENACIOUS JERK!
SHA
HYAH!

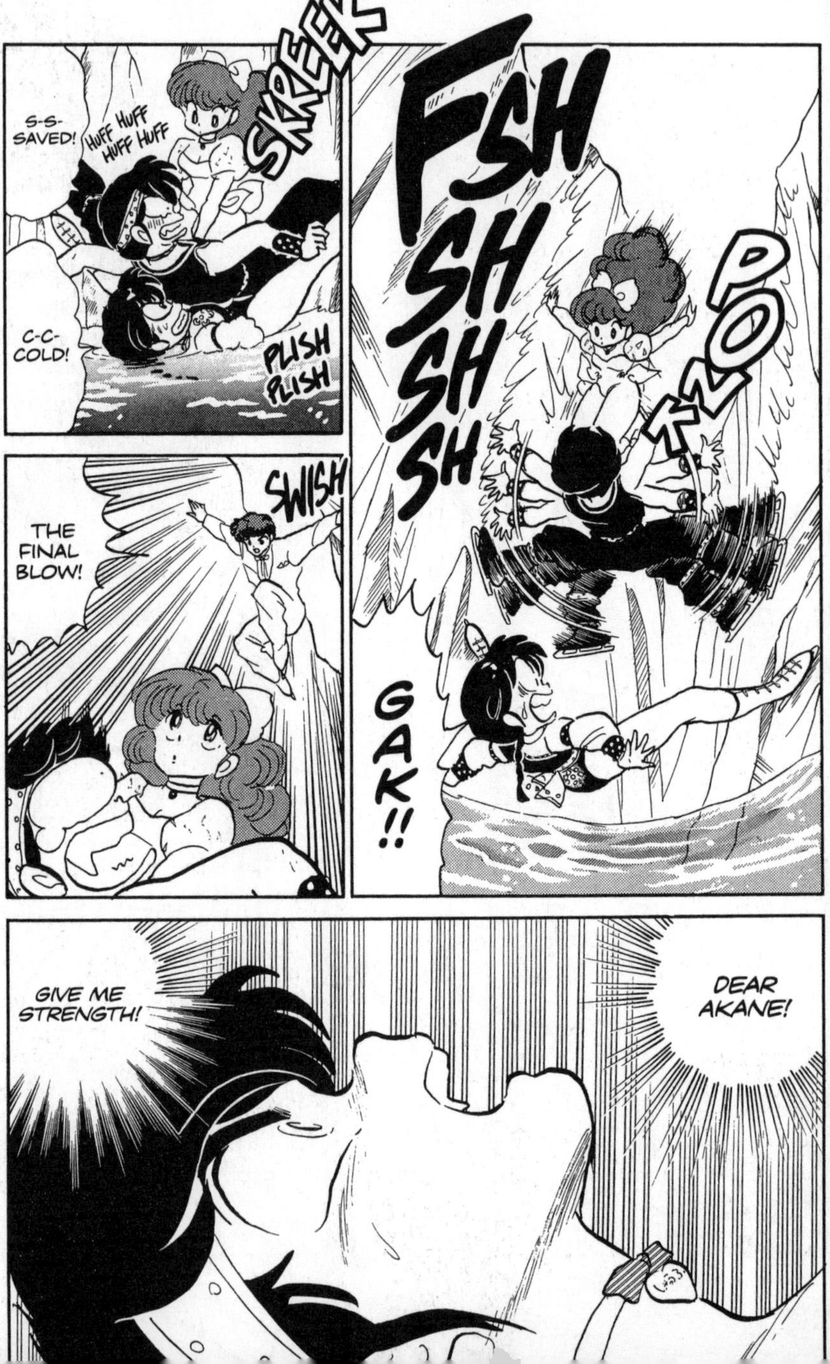
FSH SH SH SH
POK
GAK!!
SKREEK
HUFF HUFF HUFF HUFF
S-S-SAVED!
C-C-COLD!
PLISH PLISH
SWISH
THE FINAL BLOW!
DEAR AKANE!
GIVE ME STRENGTH!

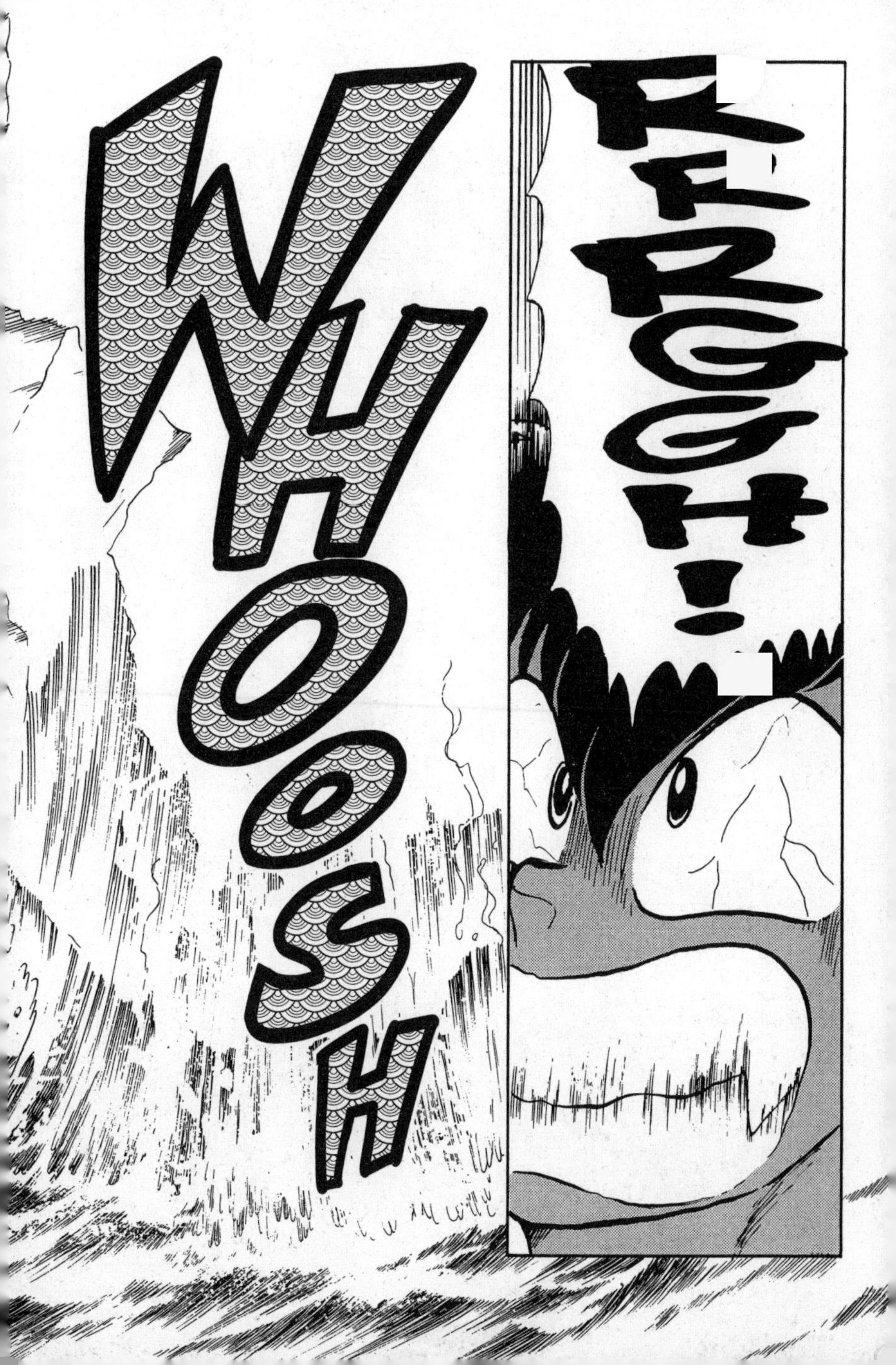
RRRGGH!!
WHOOSH

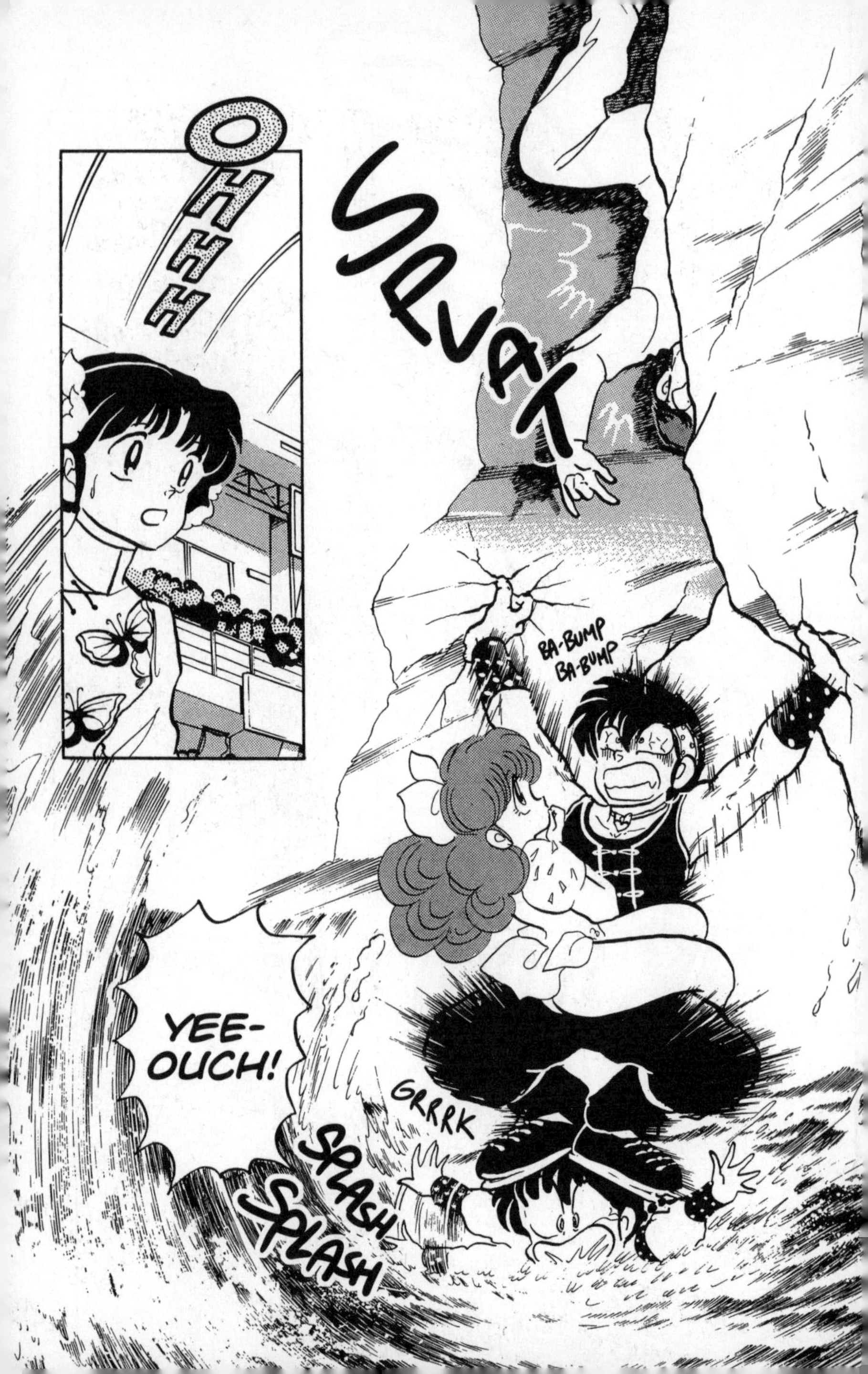
SPLAT
OHHHH
BA-BUMP BA-BUMP
YEE-OUCH!
GRRRK
SPLASH SPLASH

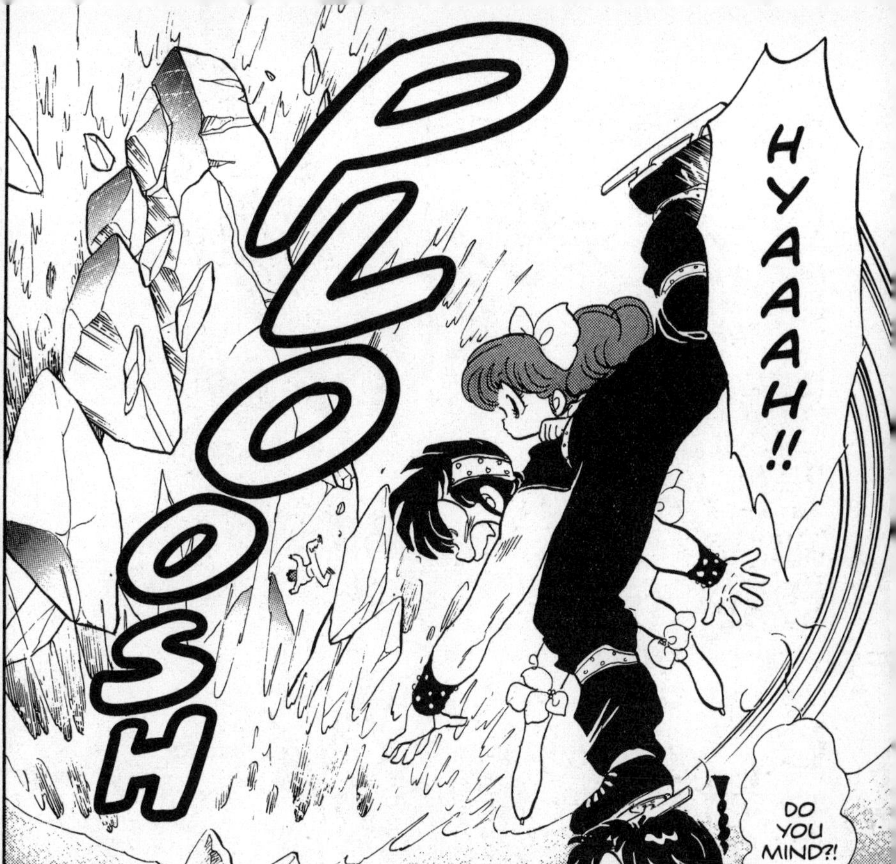
HYAAAH!!
PLOOSH
DO YOU MIND?!
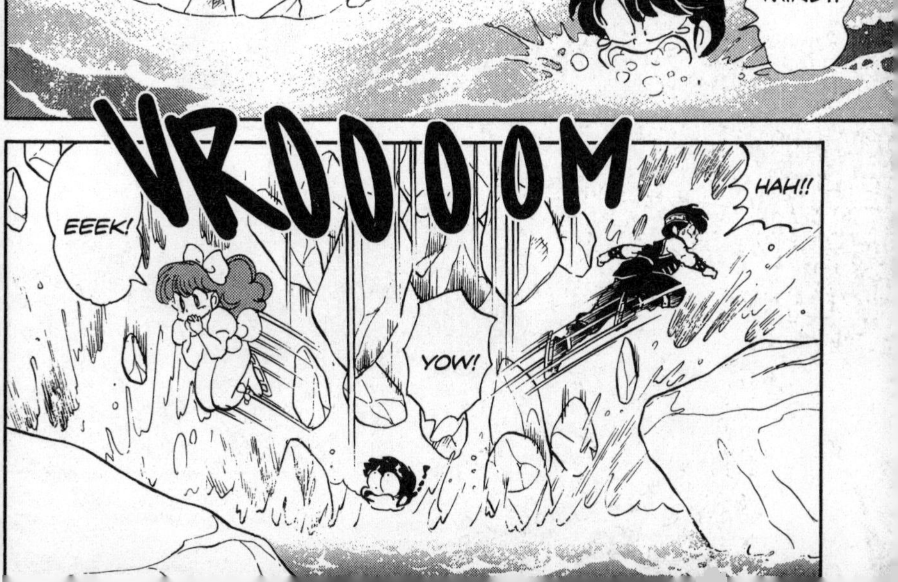
HAH!!
VROOOOM
EEEK!
YOW!

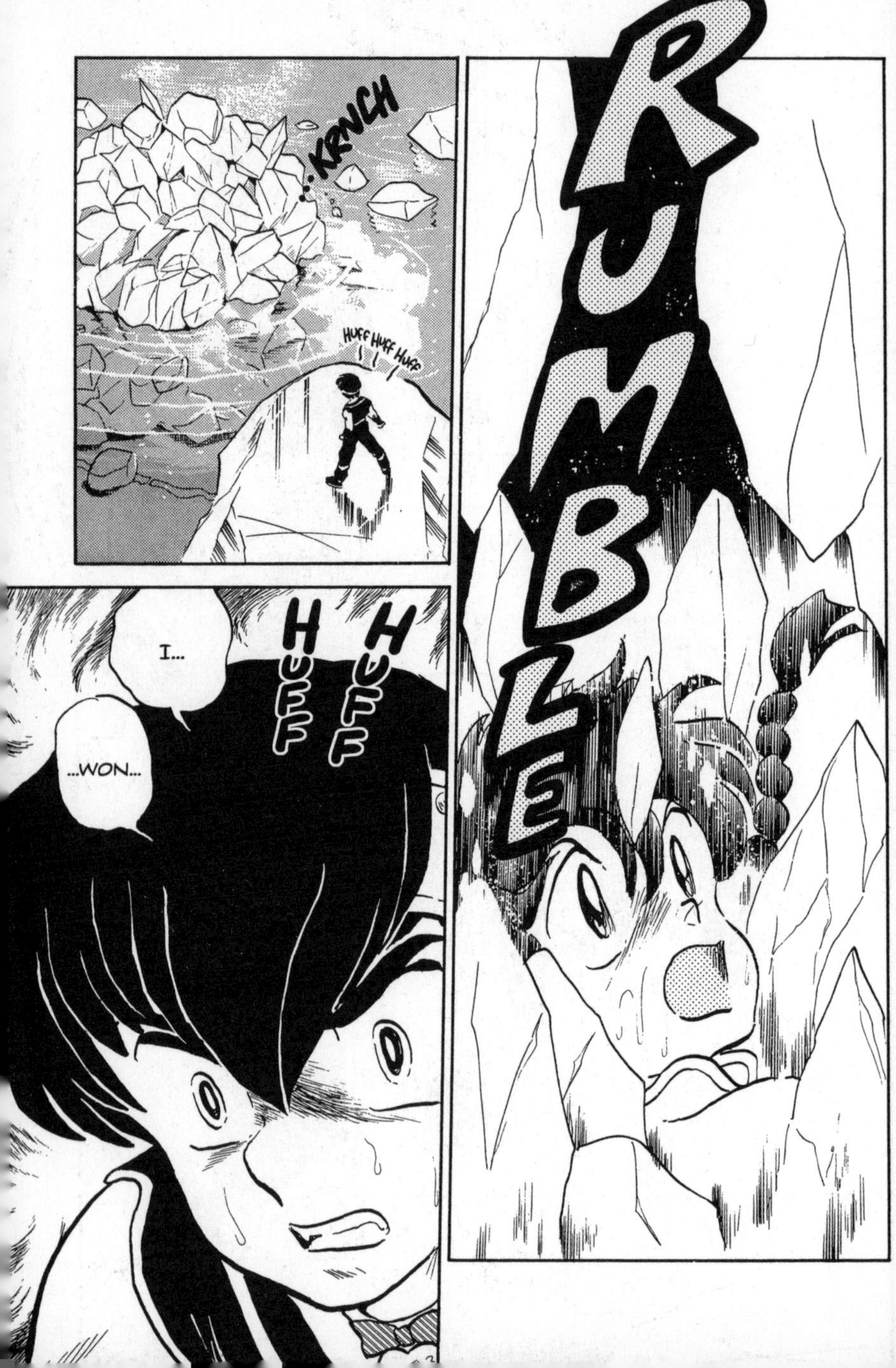
RUMBLE
KRNCH
HUFF HUFF HUFF
HUFF HUFF
I...
...WON...

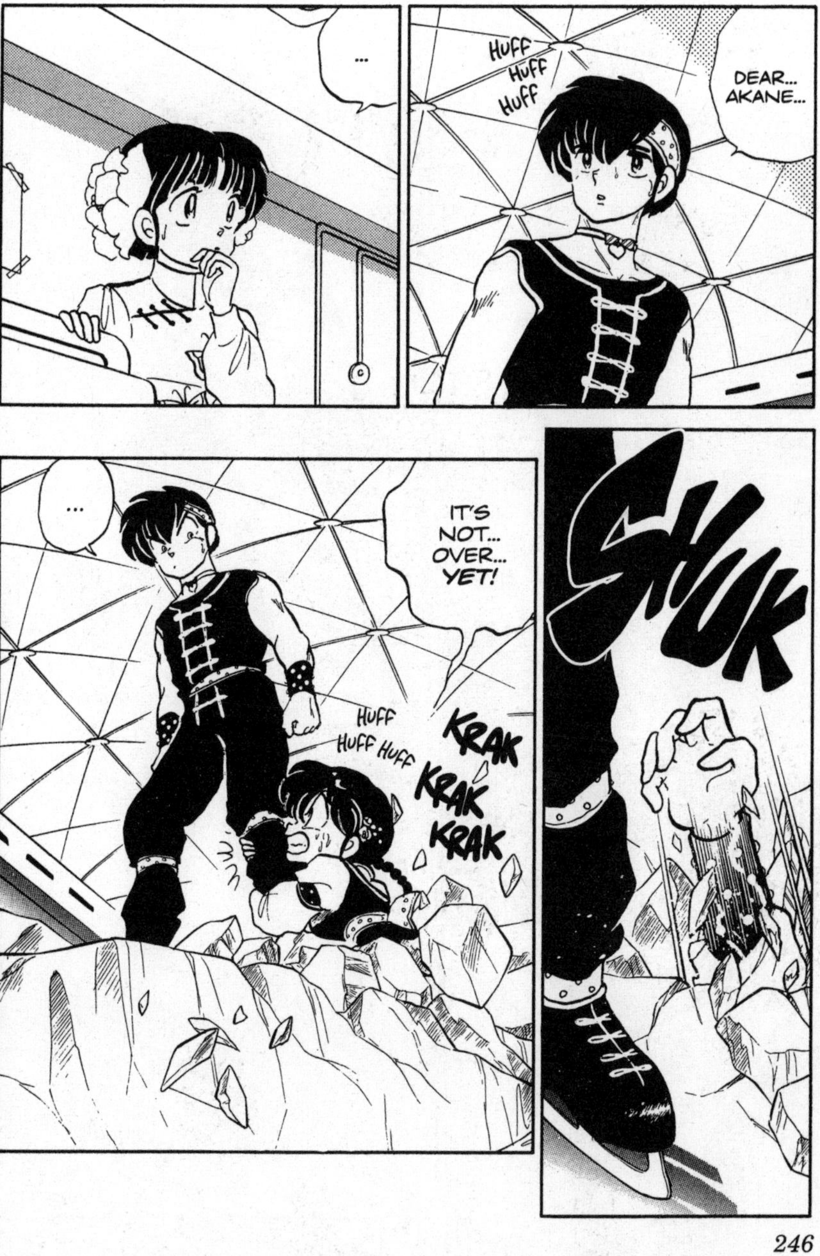
HUFF HUFF HUFF
DEAR... AKANE...
...
SHUK
IT'S NOT... OVER... YET!
...
HUFF HUFF HUFF
KRAK KRAK KRAK

PART 13
THE WATERS OF LOVE

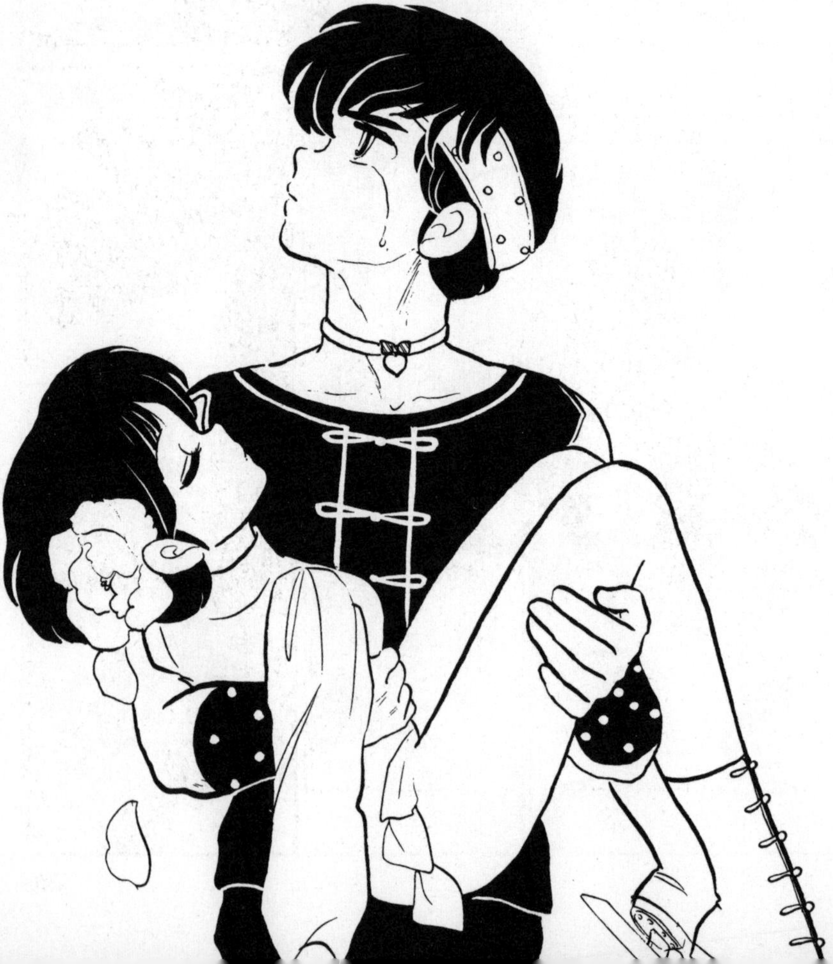

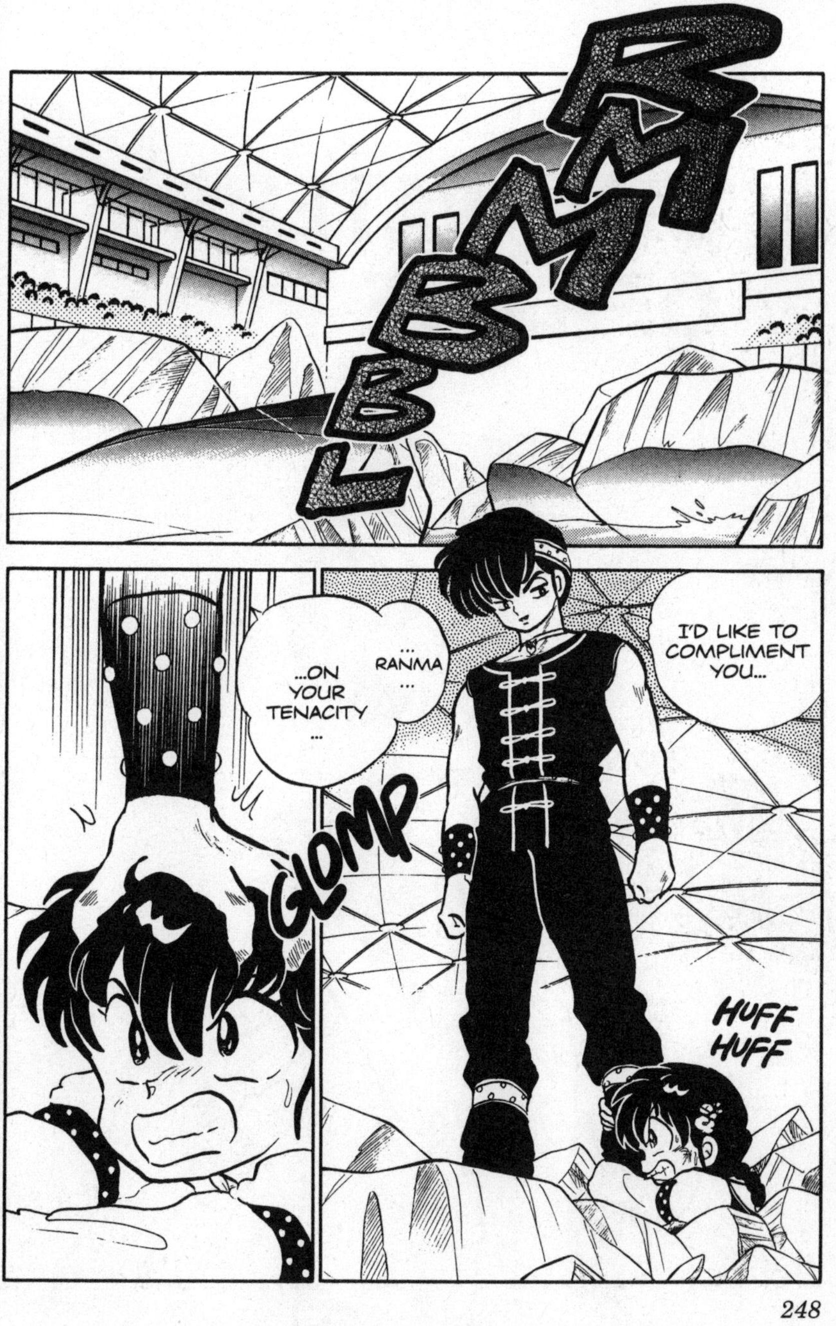
RMMBBL
I'D LIKE TO COMPLIMENT YOU...
... RANMA ...
...ON YOUR TENACITY ...
HUFF HUFF
GLOMP

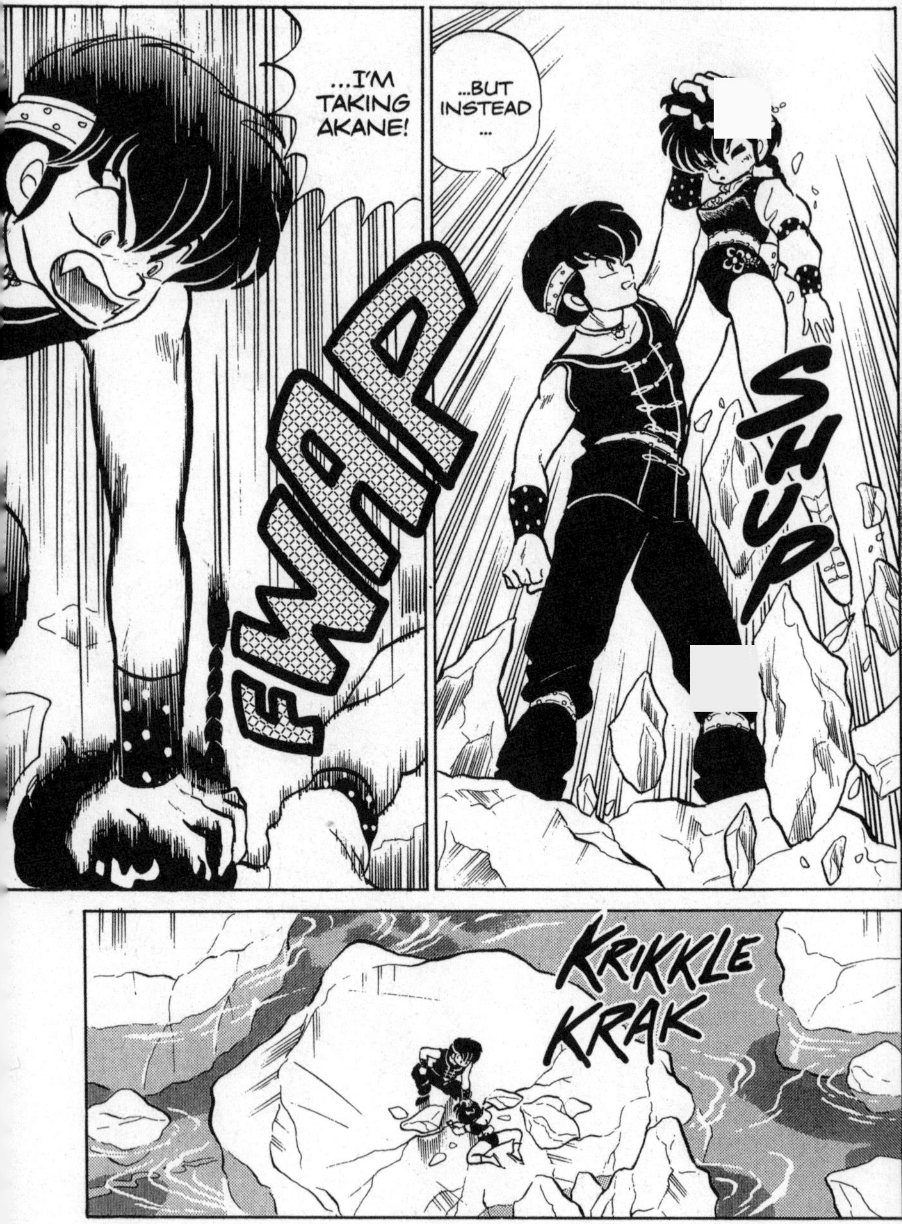
...BUT INSTEAD ...
SHUP
...I'M TAKING AKANE!
FWAP
KRIKKLE KRAK

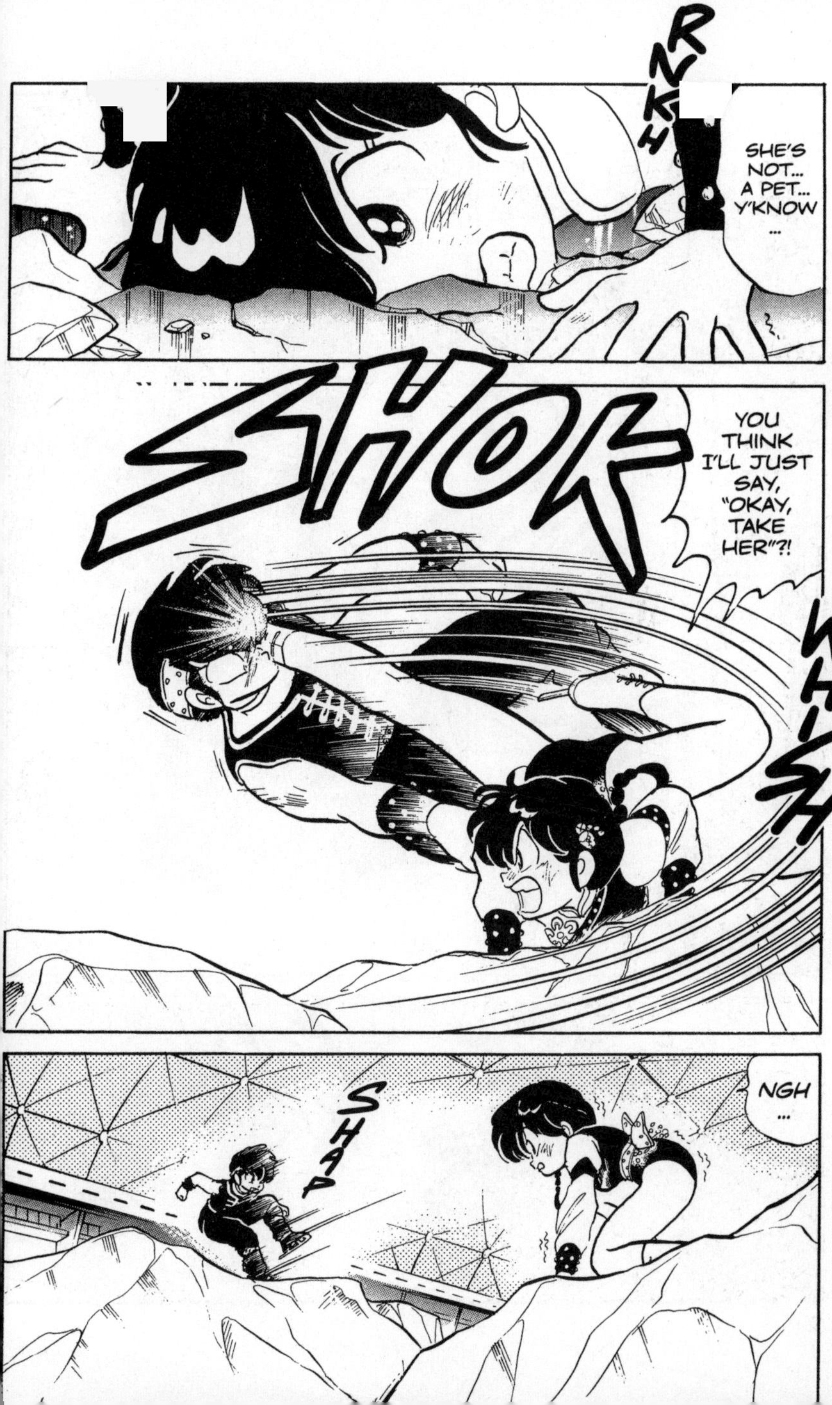
RNKH
SHE'S NOT... A PET... Y'KNOW ...
SHOK
YOU THINK I'LL JUST SAY, "OKAY, TAKE HER"?!
WHISH
NGH ...
SHAP

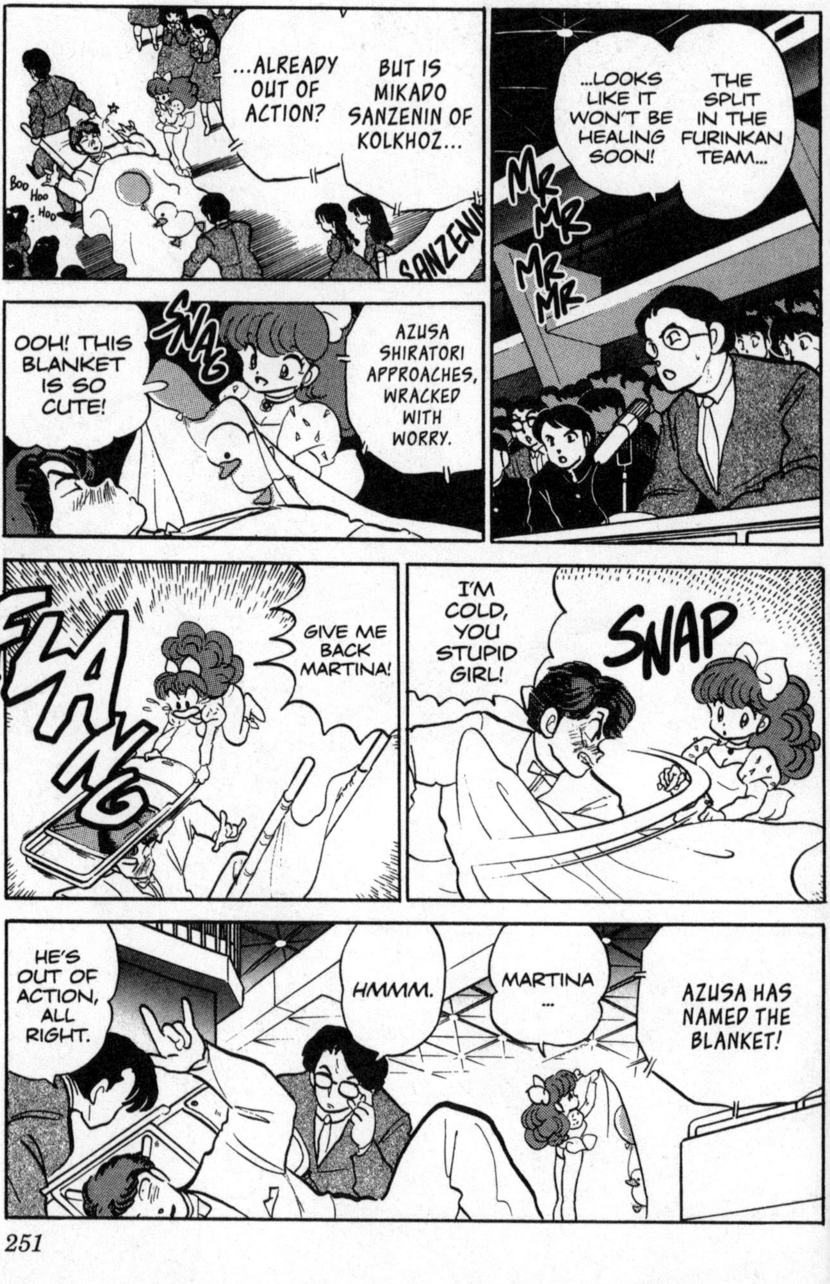
THE SPLIT IN THE FURINKAN TEAM...
...LOOKS LIKE IT WON'T BE HEALING SOON!
MR MR MR MR
BUT IS MIKADO SANZENIN OF KOLKHOZ...
...ALREADY OUT OF ACTION?
BOO HOO HOO
SANZENIN
AZUSA SHIRATORI APPROACHES, WRACKED WITH WORRY.
SNAG
OOH! THIS BLANKET IS SO CUTE!
SNAP
I'M COLD, YOU STUPID GIRL!
GIVE ME BACK MARTINA!
FLANG
AZUSA HAS NAMED THE BLANKET!
MARTINA ...
HMMM.
HE'S OUT OF ACTION, ALL RIGHT.

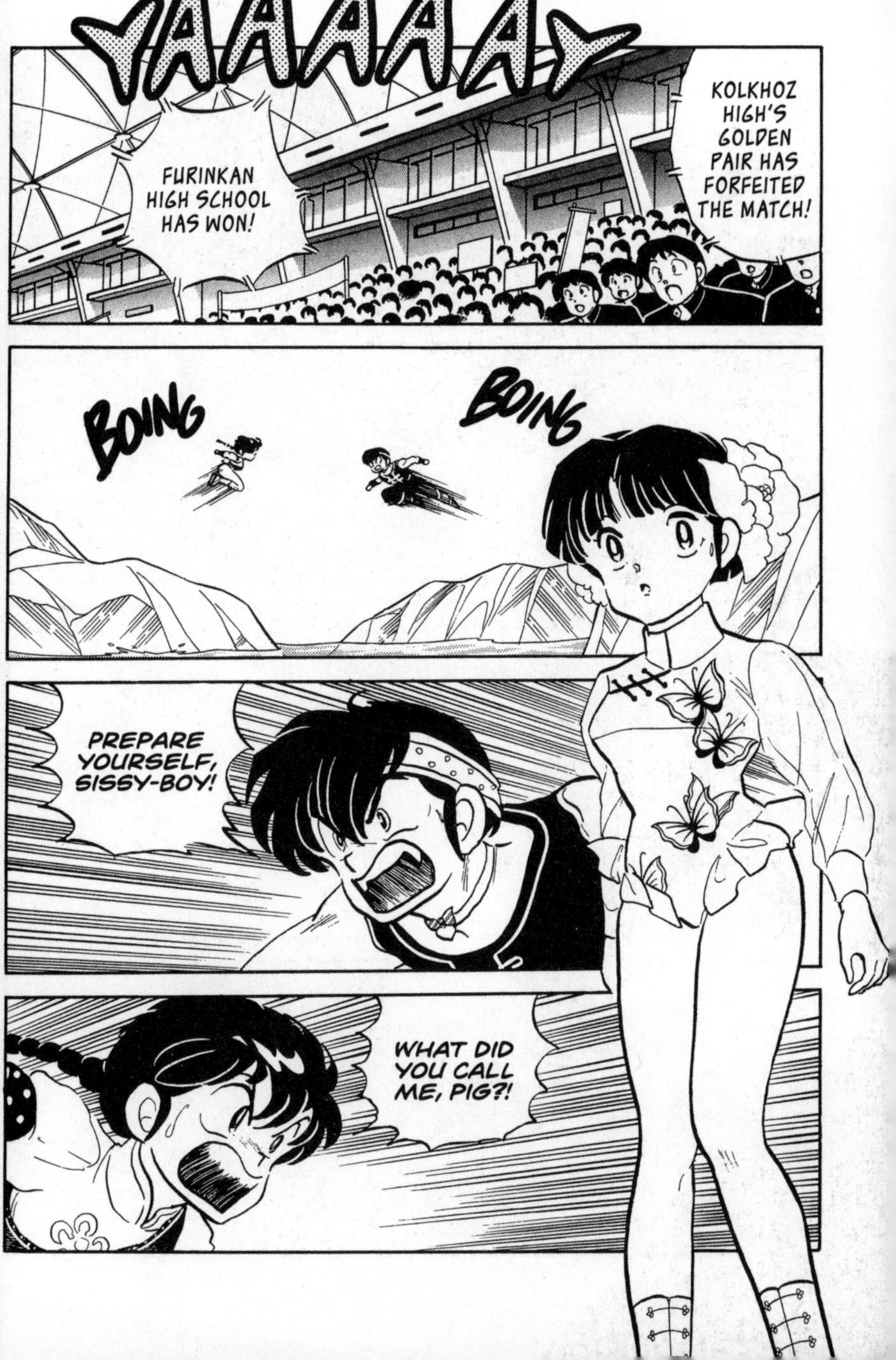
YAAAAAY
KOLKHOZ HIGH'S GOLDEN PAIR HAS FORFEITED THE MATCH!
FURINKAN HIGH SCHOOL HAS WON!
BOING
BOING
PREPARE YOURSELF, SISSY-BOY!
WHAT DID YOU CALL ME, PIG?!

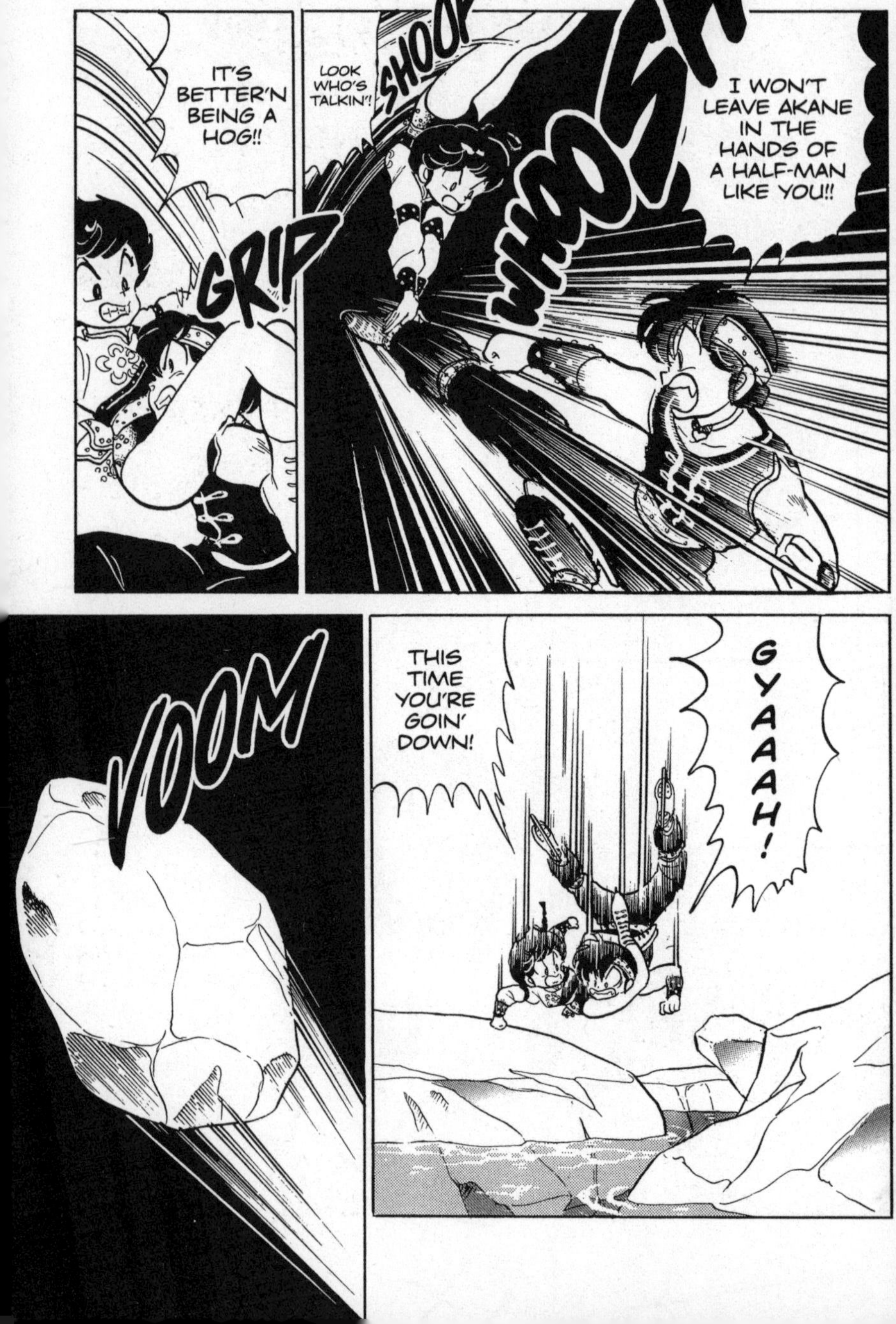
SHOOP
I WON'T LEAVE AKANE IN THE HANDS OF A HALF-MAN LIKE YOU!!
WHOOSH
LOOK WHO'S TALKIN'!
IT'S BETTER'N BEING A HOG!!
GRIP
GYAAAAH!
THIS TIME YOU'RE GOIN' DOWN!
VOOM

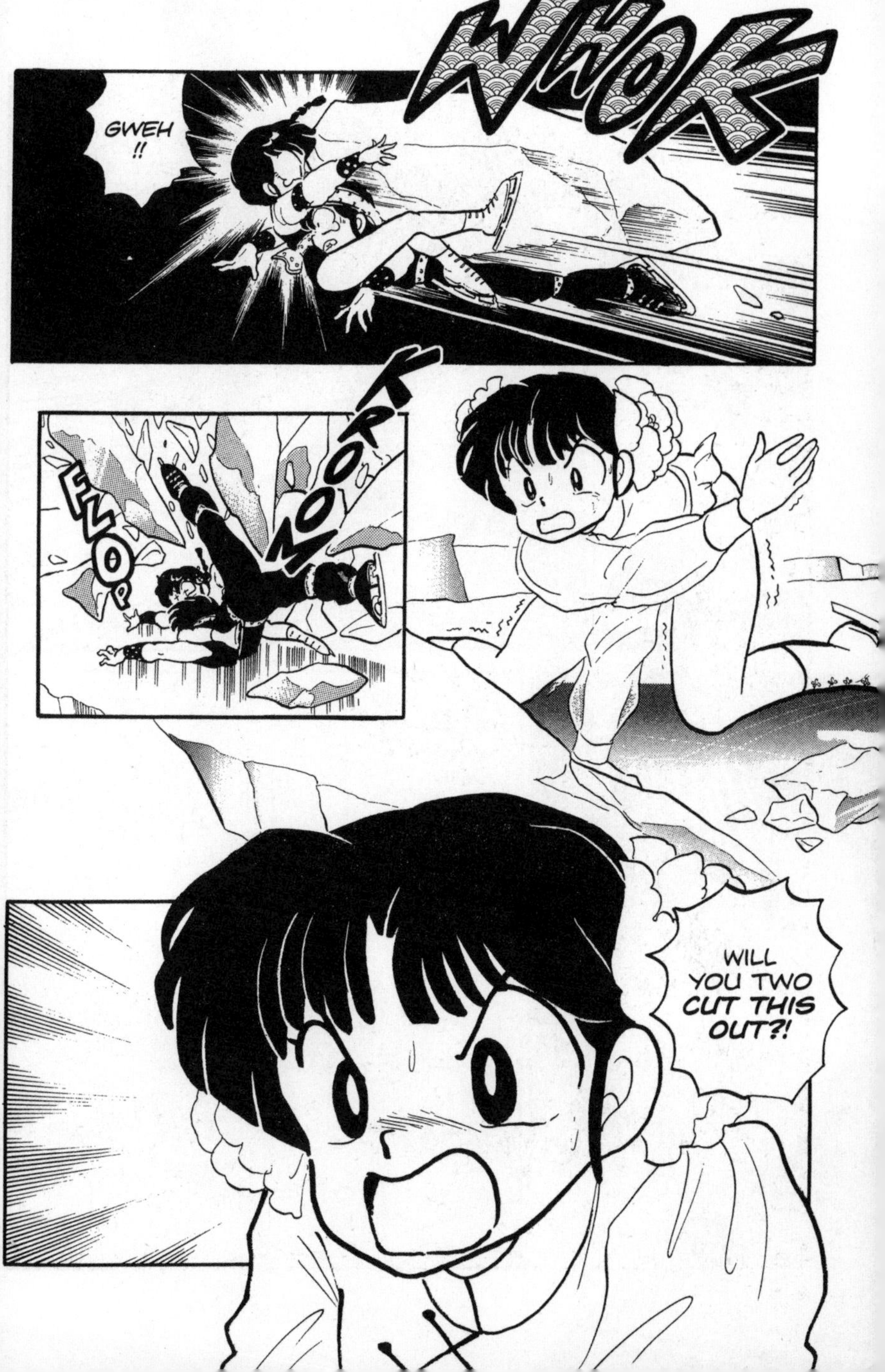
WHOK
GWEH !!
KROOM
FLOP
WILL YOU TWO CUT THIS OUT?!

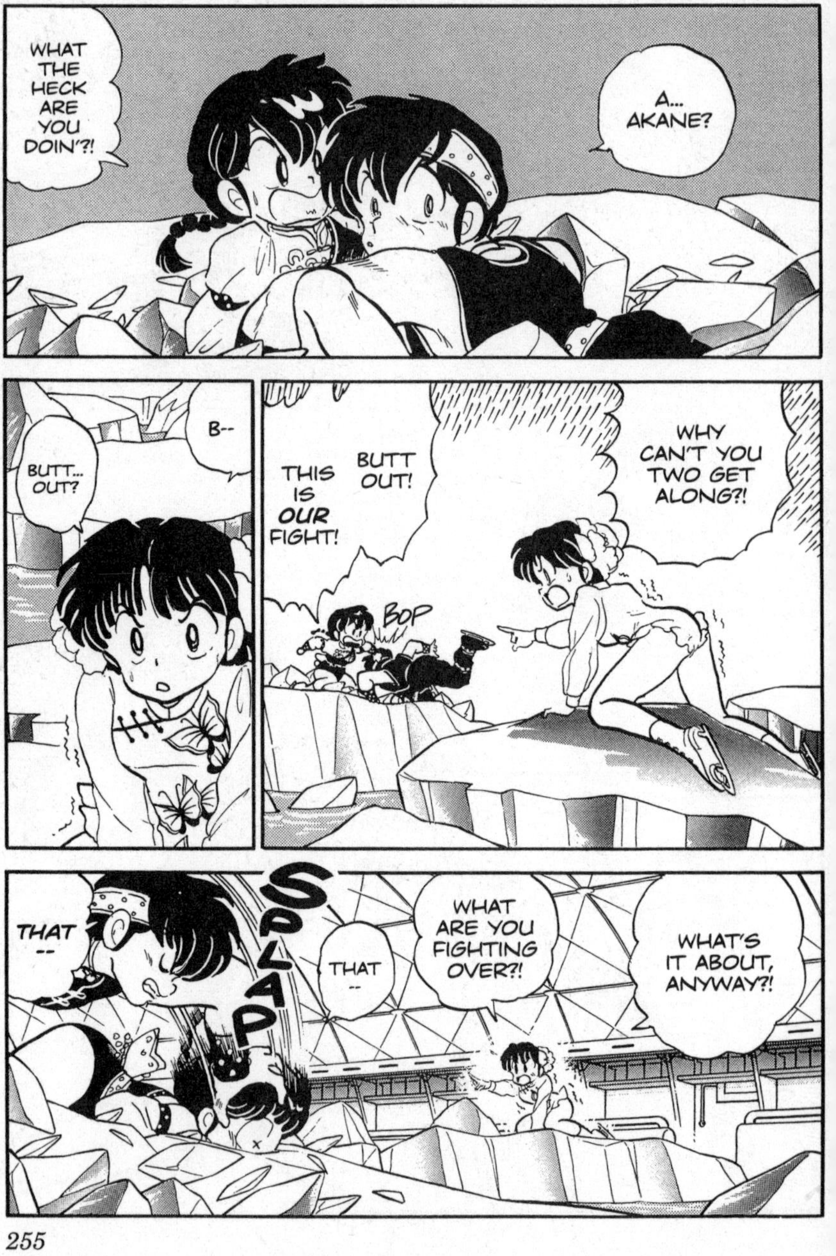
A... AKANE?
WHAT THE HECK ARE YOU DOIN'?!
WHY CAN'T YOU TWO GET ALONG?!
BUTT OUT!
THIS IS **OUR** FIGHT!
BOP
B--
BUTT... OUT?
WHAT'S IT ABOUT, ANYWAY?!
WHAT ARE YOU FIGHTING OVER?!
THAT --
SPLAP
THAT --

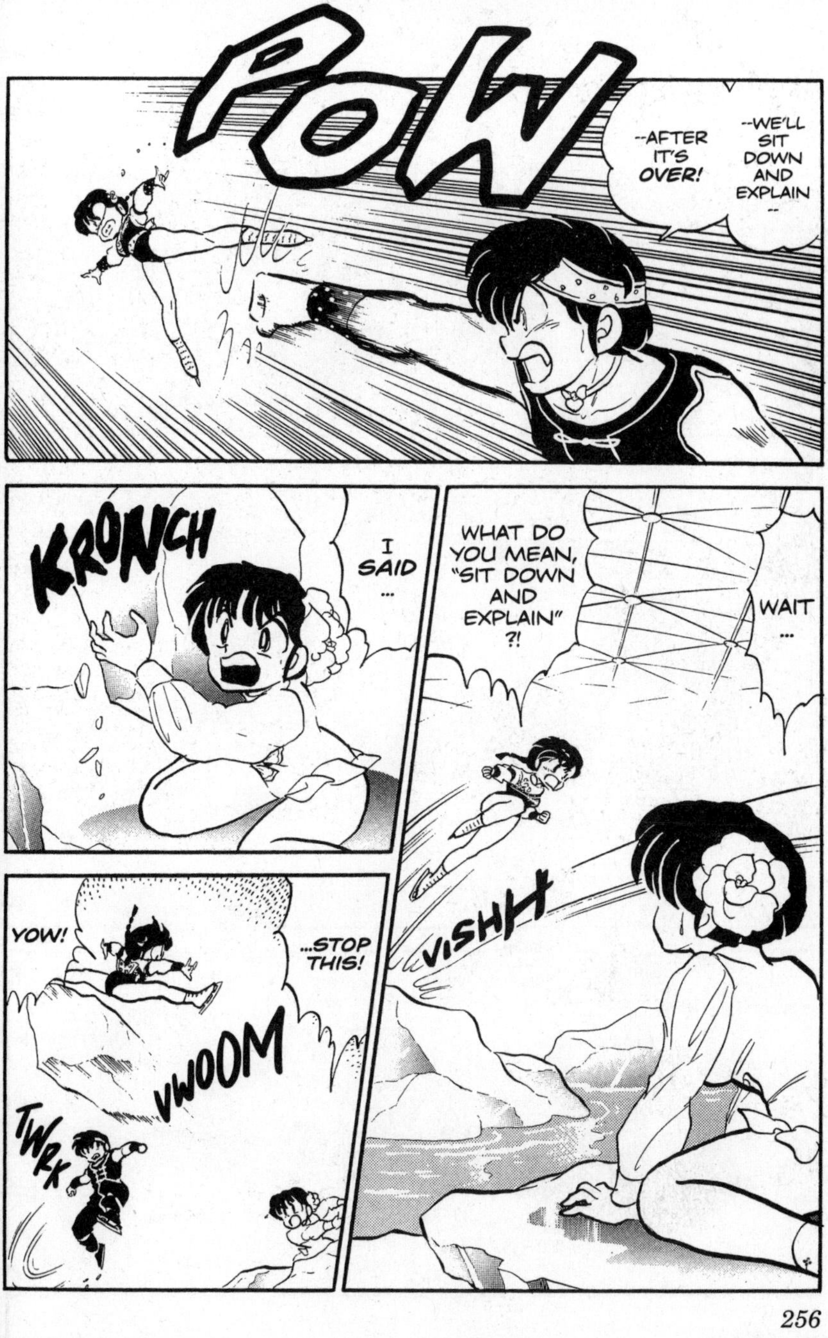
POW
--WE'LL SIT DOWN AND EXPLAIN --
--AFTER IT'S OVER!
WAIT ...
WHAT DO YOU MEAN, "SIT DOWN AND EXPLAIN" ?!
VISHHH
KRONCH
I SAID ...
...STOP THIS!
YOW!
VWOOM
TWRK

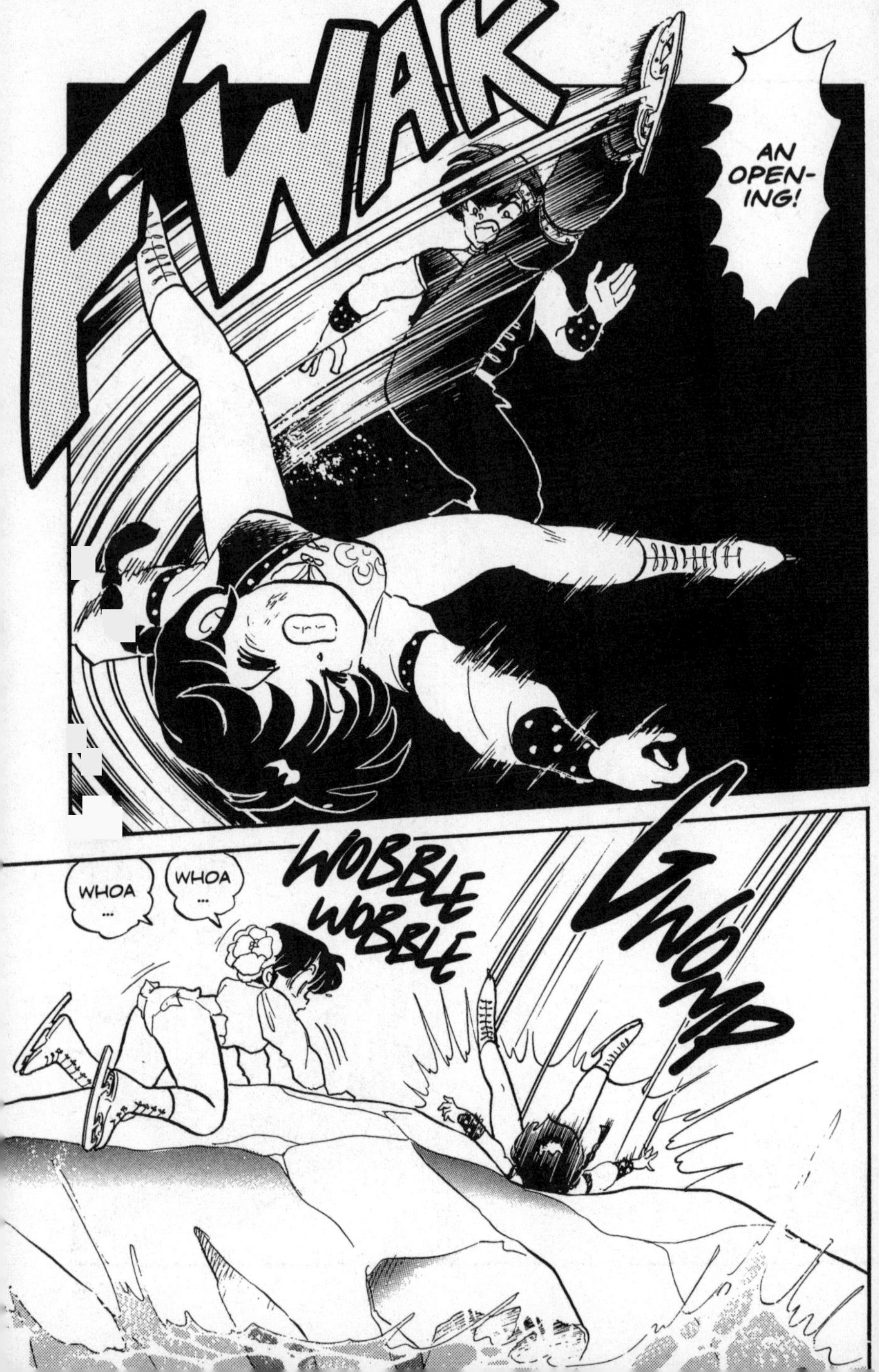
AN OPEN-
ING!
FWAK
WHOMP
WOBBLE WOBBLE
WHOA ...
WHOA ...

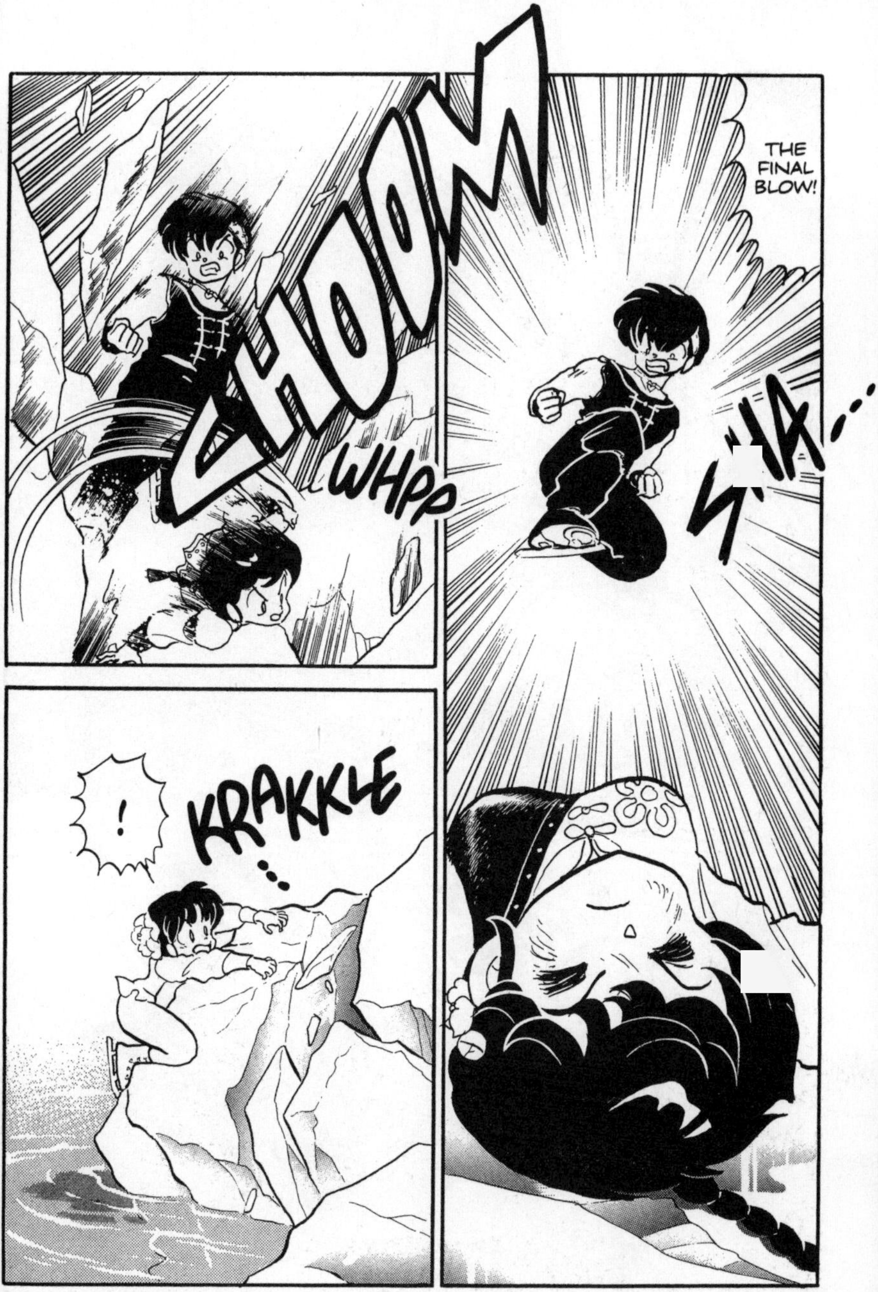
THE FINAL BLOW!
SHA...
ZHOOM
WHPP
!
KRAKKLE...

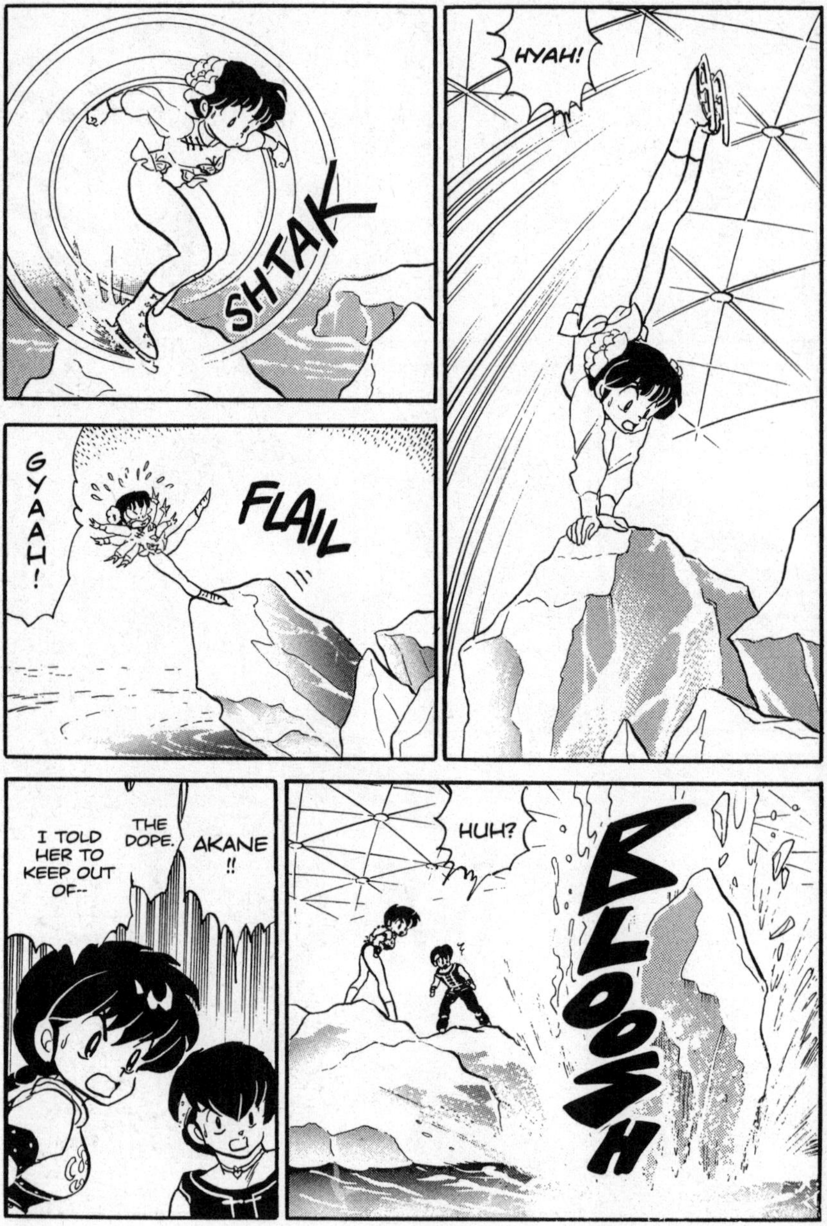
HYAH!
SHTAK
GYAAAH!
FLAIL
HUH?
BLOOSH
AKANE!!
THE DOPE.
I TOLD HER TO KEEP OUT OF--

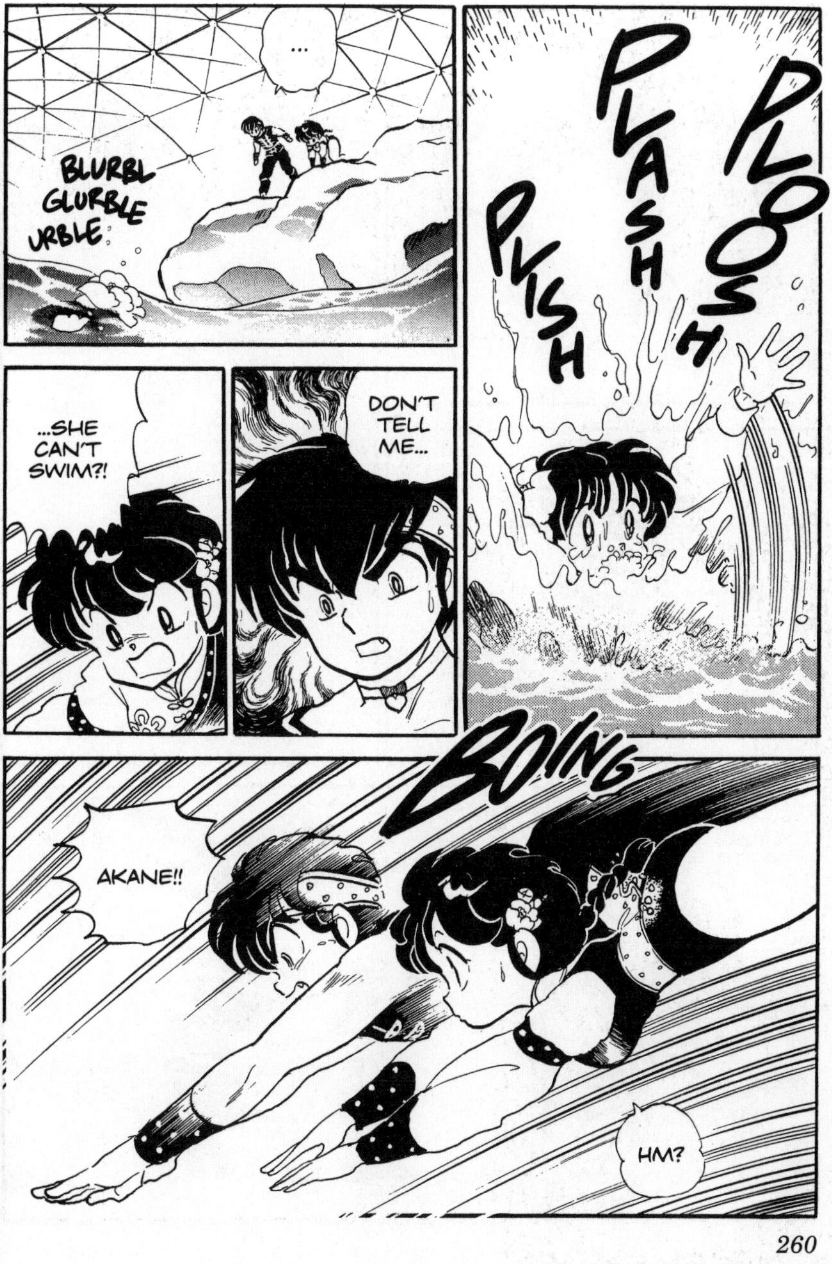
PLOOSH
PLASH
PLISH
...
BLURBL GLURBLE URBLE
DON'T TELL ME...
...SHE CAN'T SWIM?!
BOING
AKANE!!
HM?

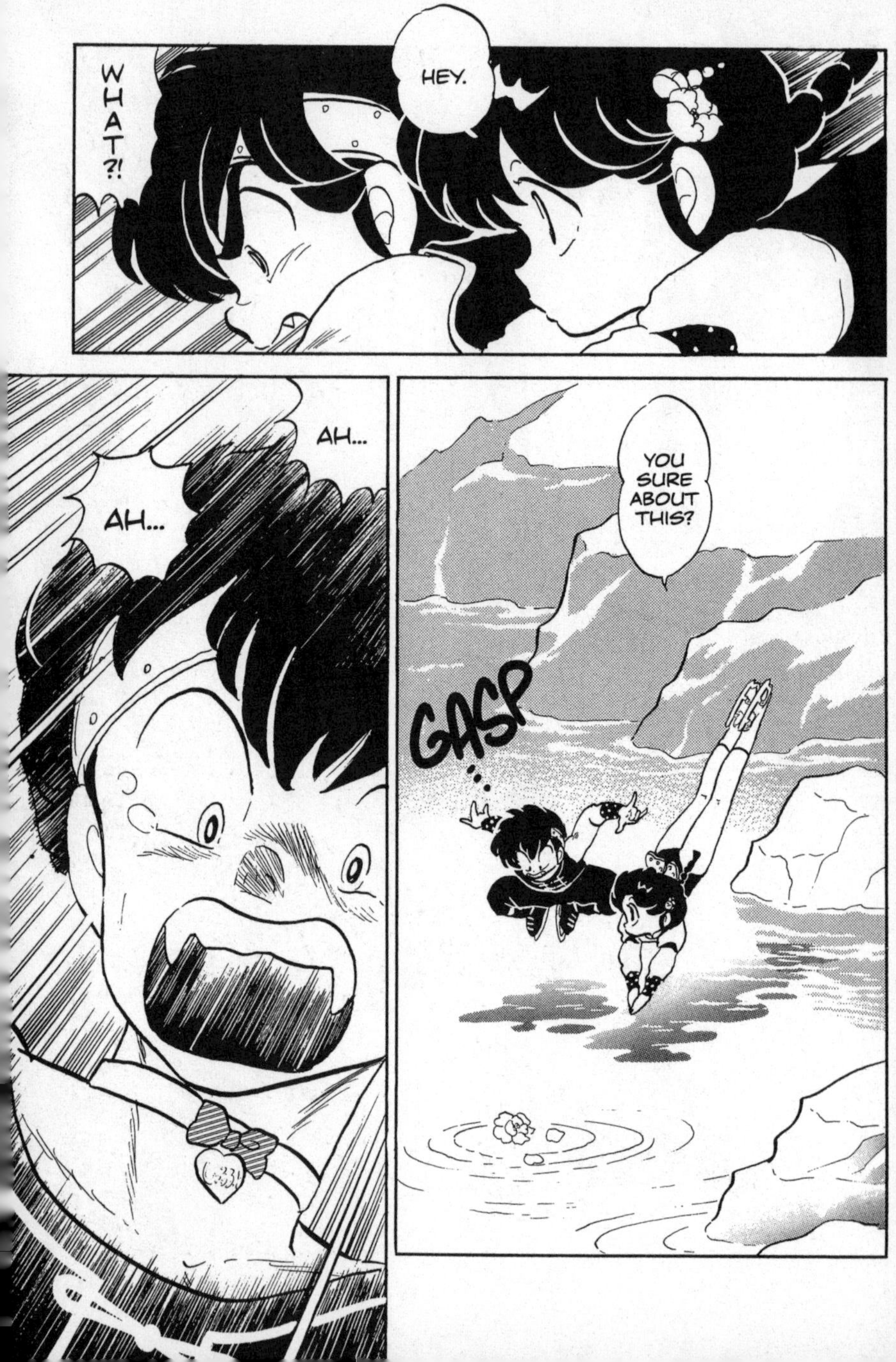
HEY.
WHAT?!
YOU SURE ABOUT THIS?
GASP
AH...
AH...

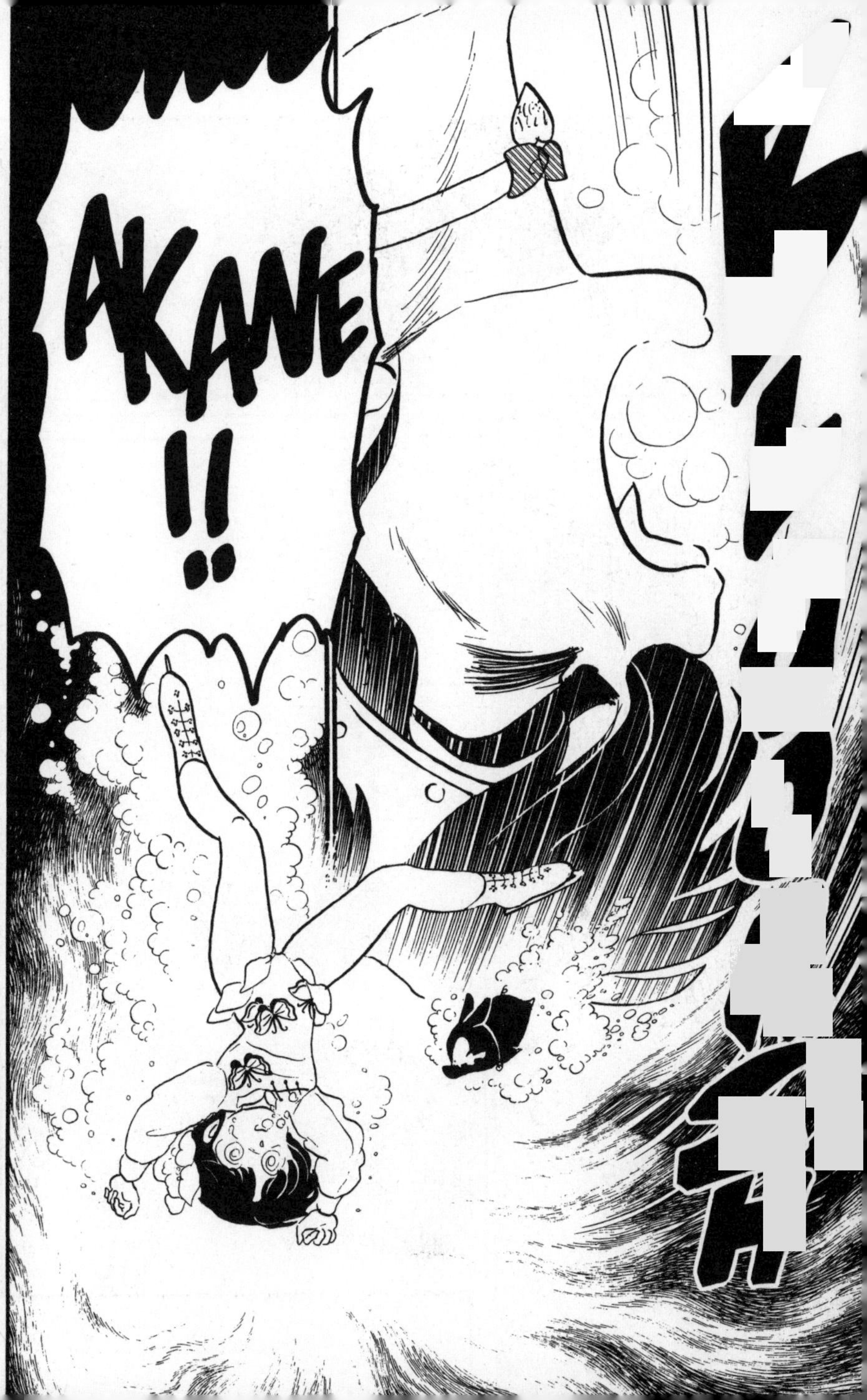
AKANE!!

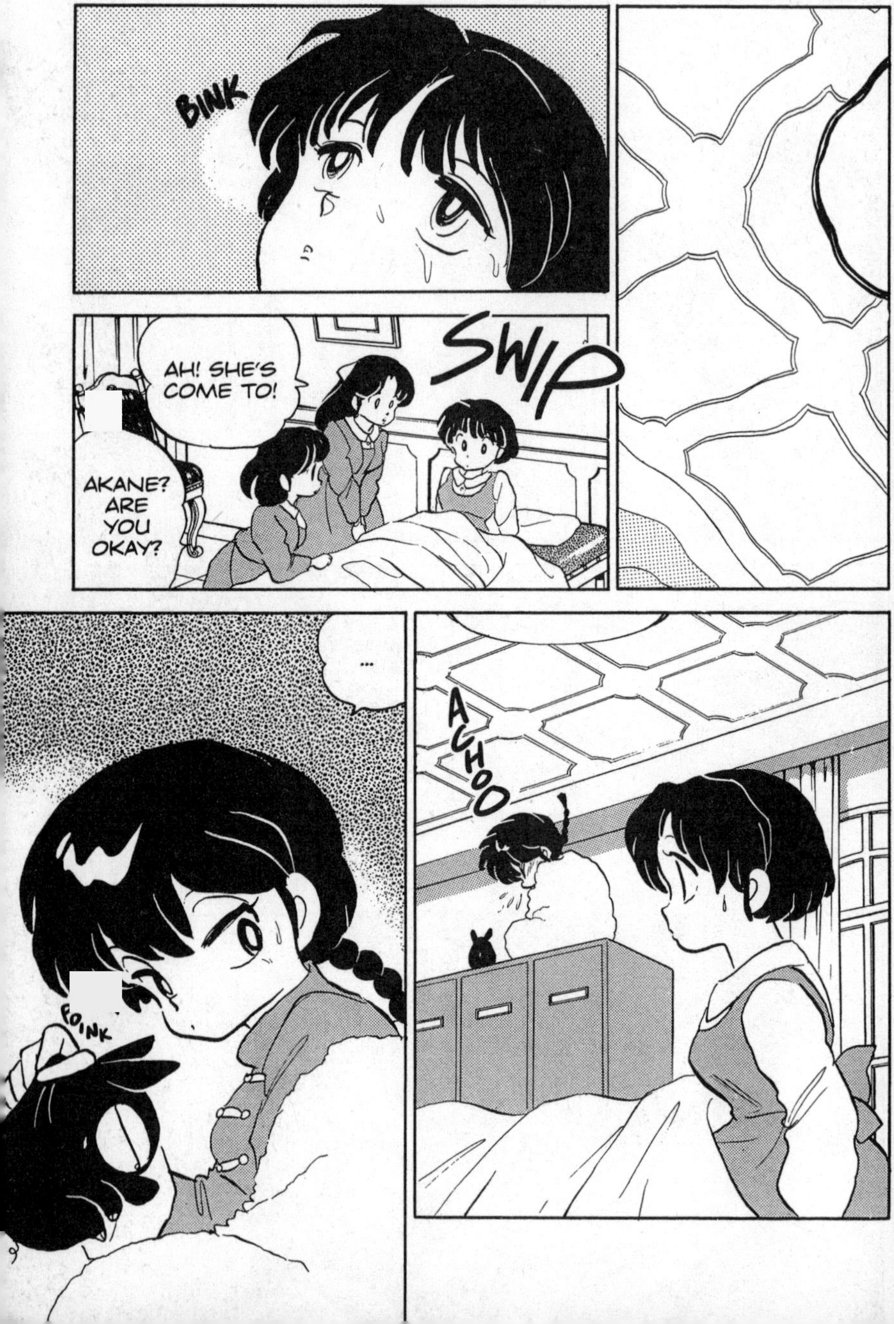
BINK
SWIP
AH! SHE'S COME TO!
AKANE? ARE YOU OKAY?
ACHOO
...
POINK

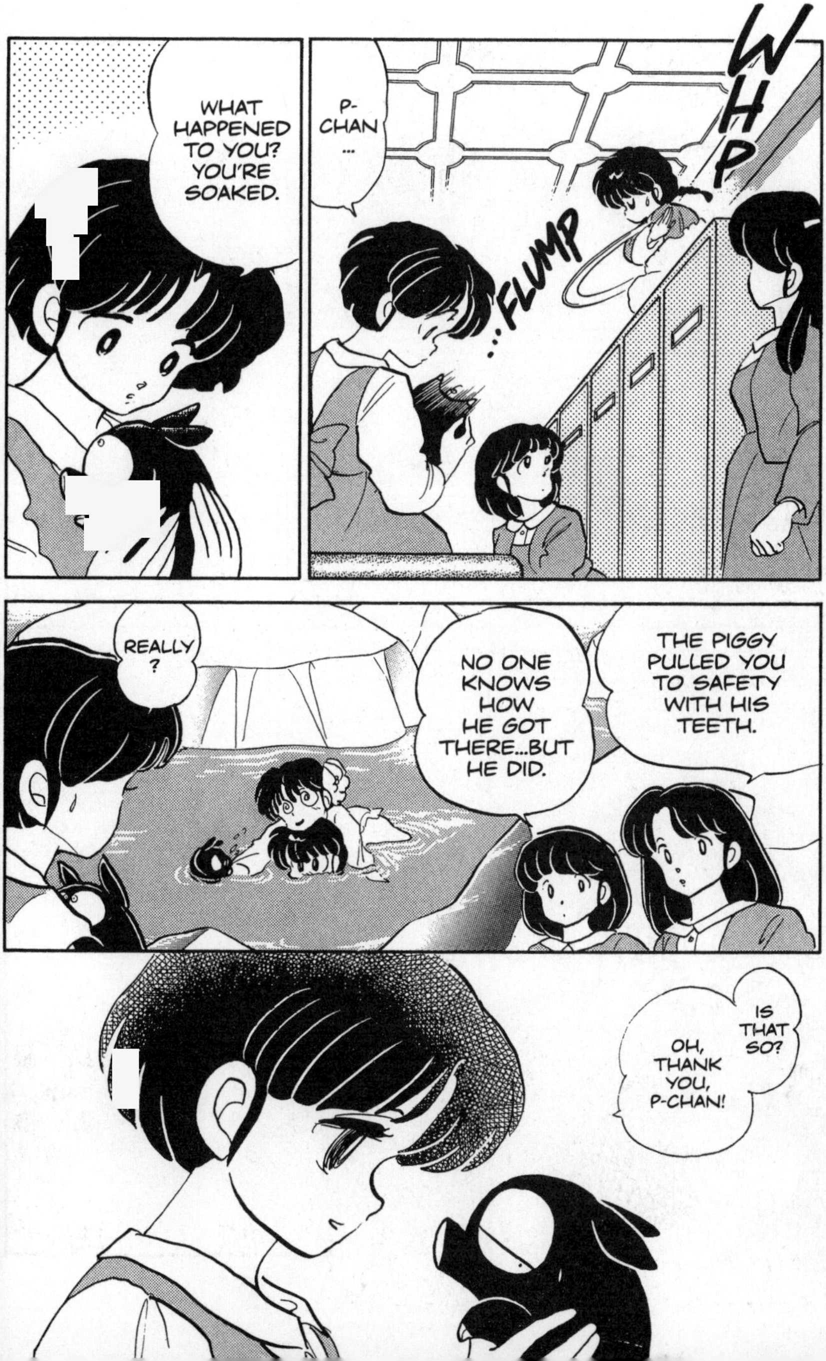
WHP
P-CHAN ...
FLUMP
WHAT HAPPENED TO YOU? YOU'RE SOAKED.
THE PIGGY PULLED YOU TO SAFETY WITH HIS TEETH.
NO ONE KNOWS HOW HE GOT THERE...BUT HE DID.
REALLY ?
IS THAT SO?
OH, THANK YOU, P-CHAN!

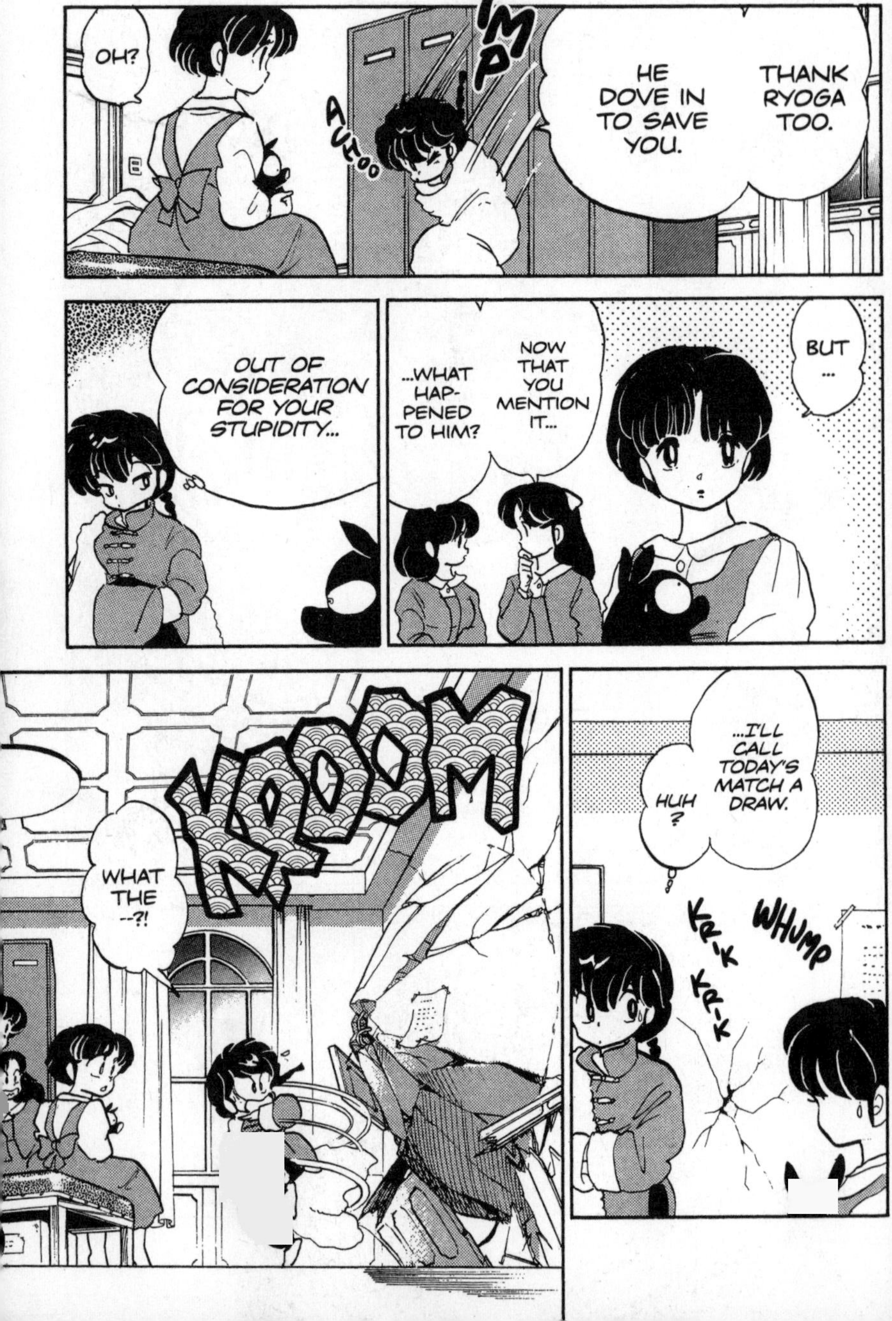
THANK RYOGA TOO.
HE DOVE IN TO SAVE YOU.
TMP
AUHOO
OH?
BUT ...
NOW THAT YOU MENTION IT...
...WHAT HAP-PENED TO HIM?
OUT OF CONSIDERATION FOR YOUR STUPIDITY...
...I'LL CALL TODAY'S MATCH A DRAW.
HUH ?
WHUMP
KR-K
KR-K
KADOOM
WHAT THE --?!

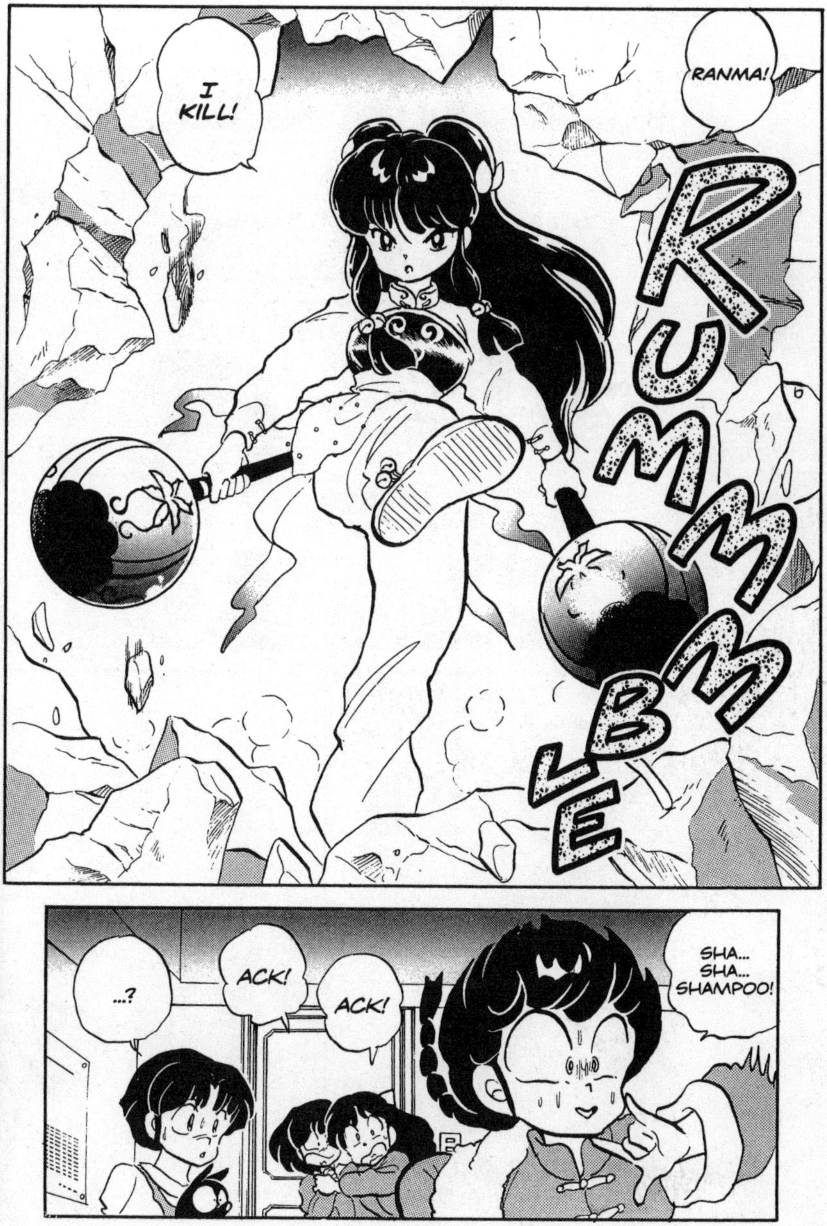
RANMA!
I KILL!
RUMMMBLE
SHA... SHA... SHAMPOO!
ACK!
ACK!
...?

PART 14
KISS OF DEATH

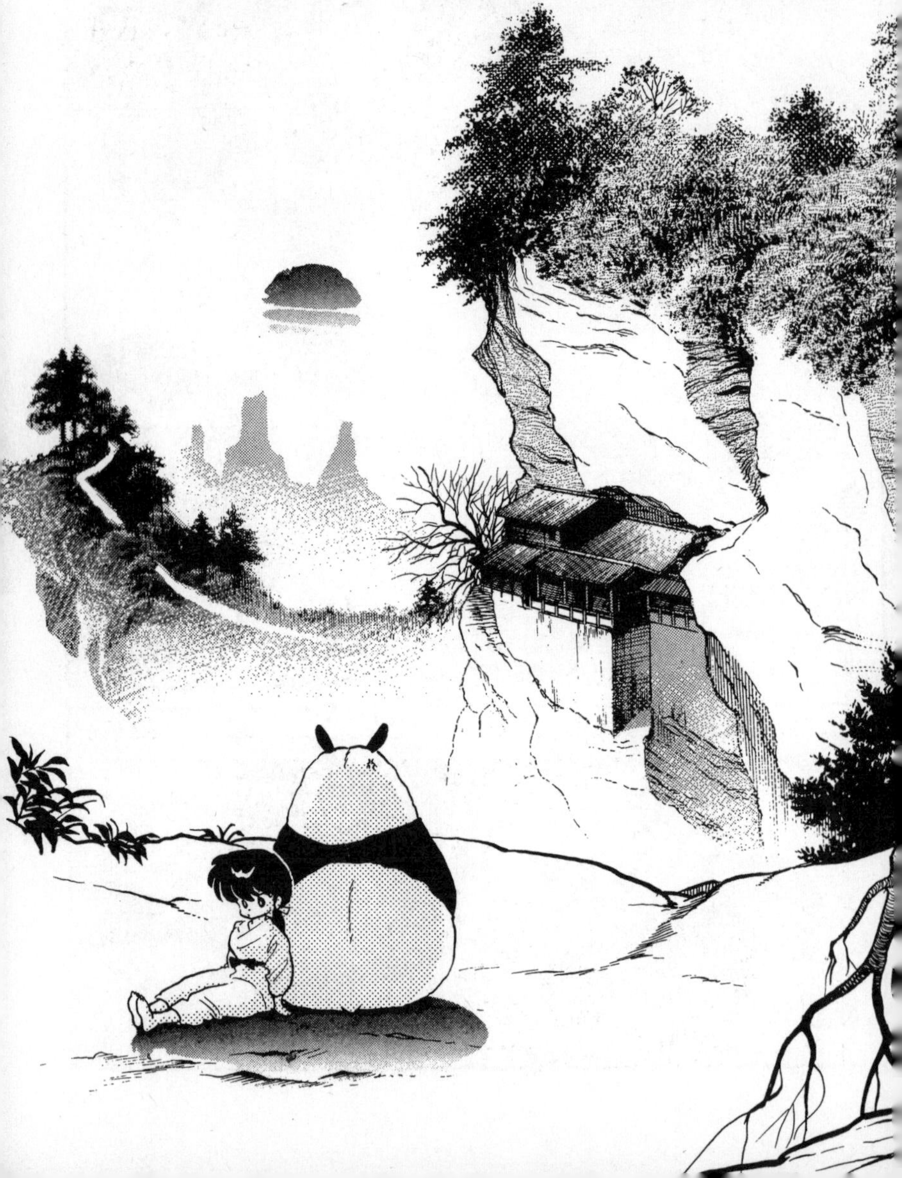

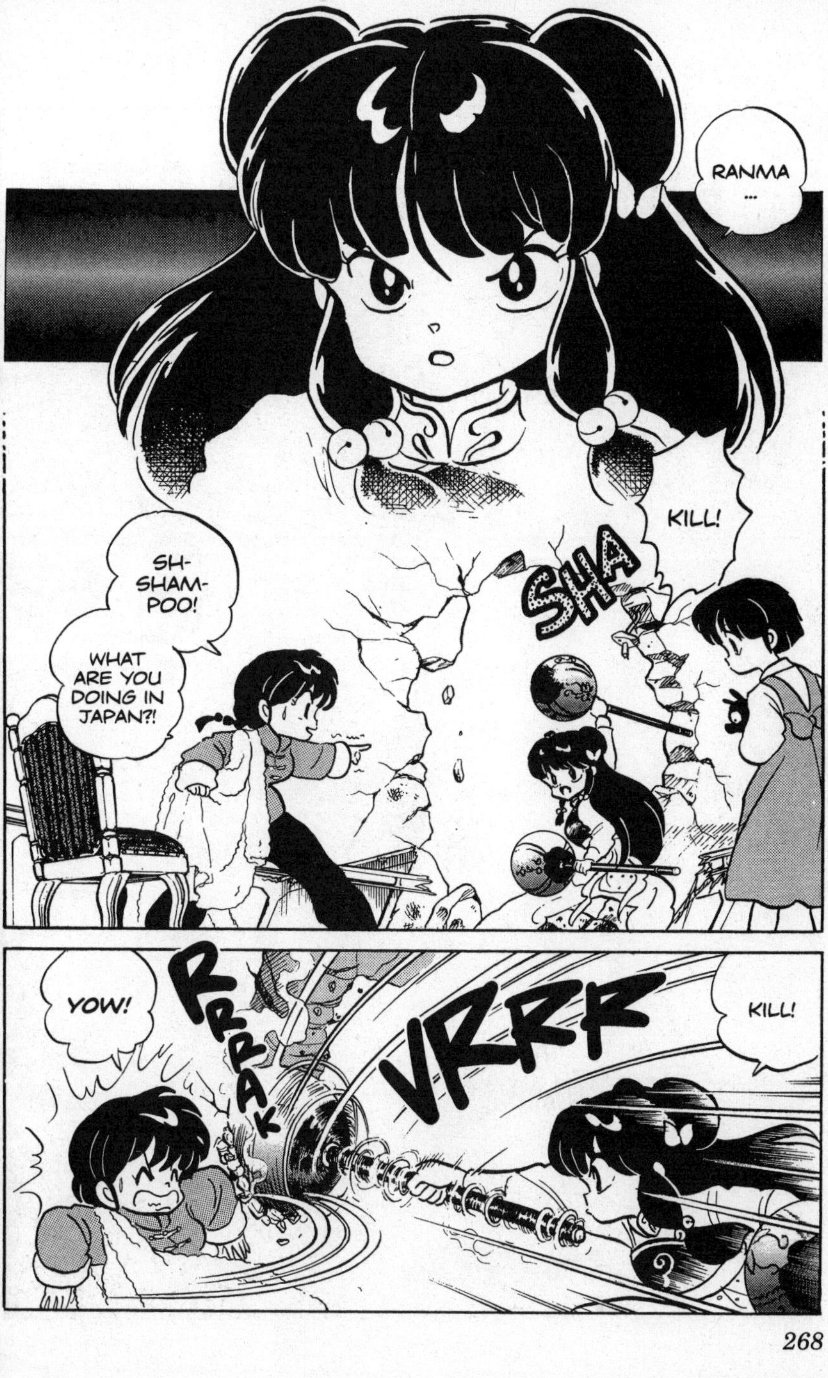
RANMA ...
KILL!
SHA
SH-SHAMPOO!
WHAT ARE YOU DOING IN JAPAN?!
KILL!
VRRR
RRRAK
YOW!

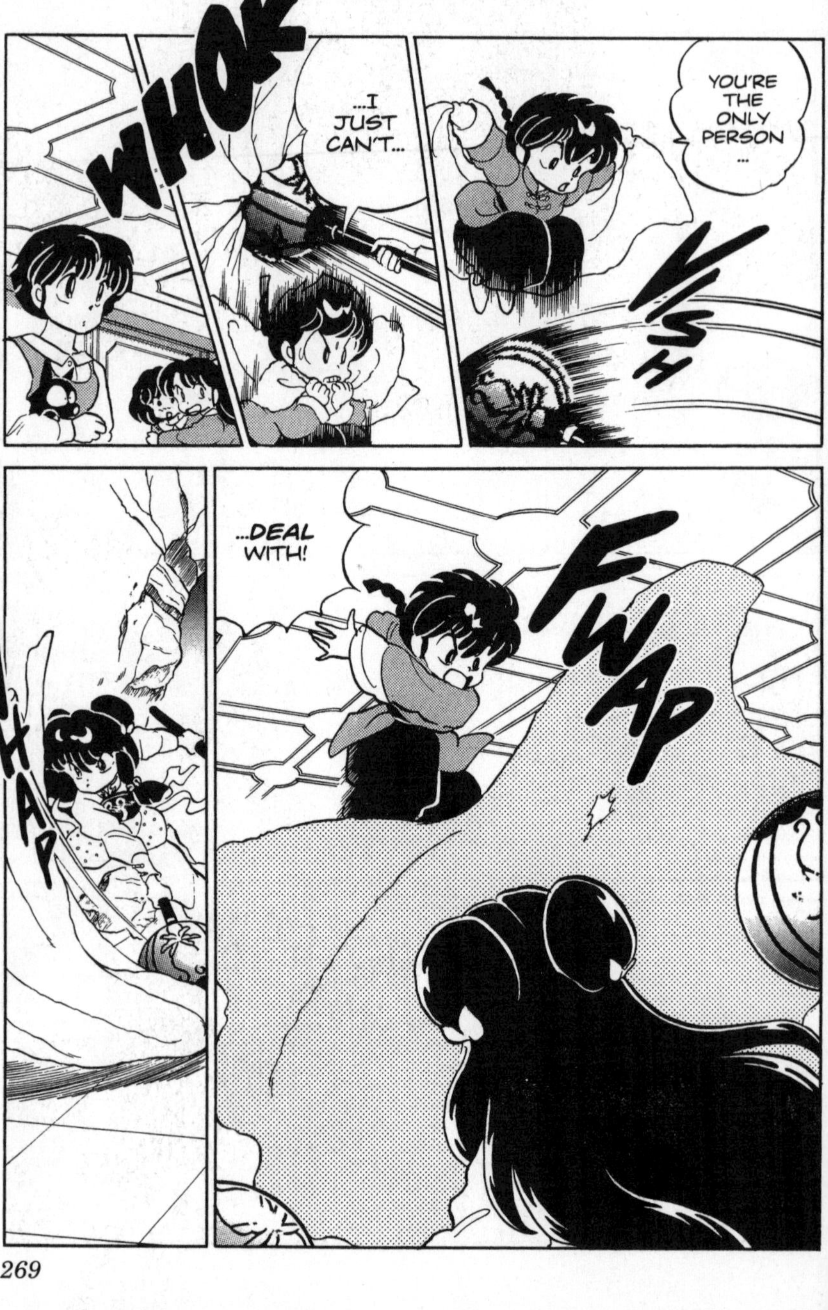
YOU'RE THE ONLY PERSON ...
VISH
...I JUST CAN'T...
WHOK
...DEAL WITH!
FWAP
WHAP

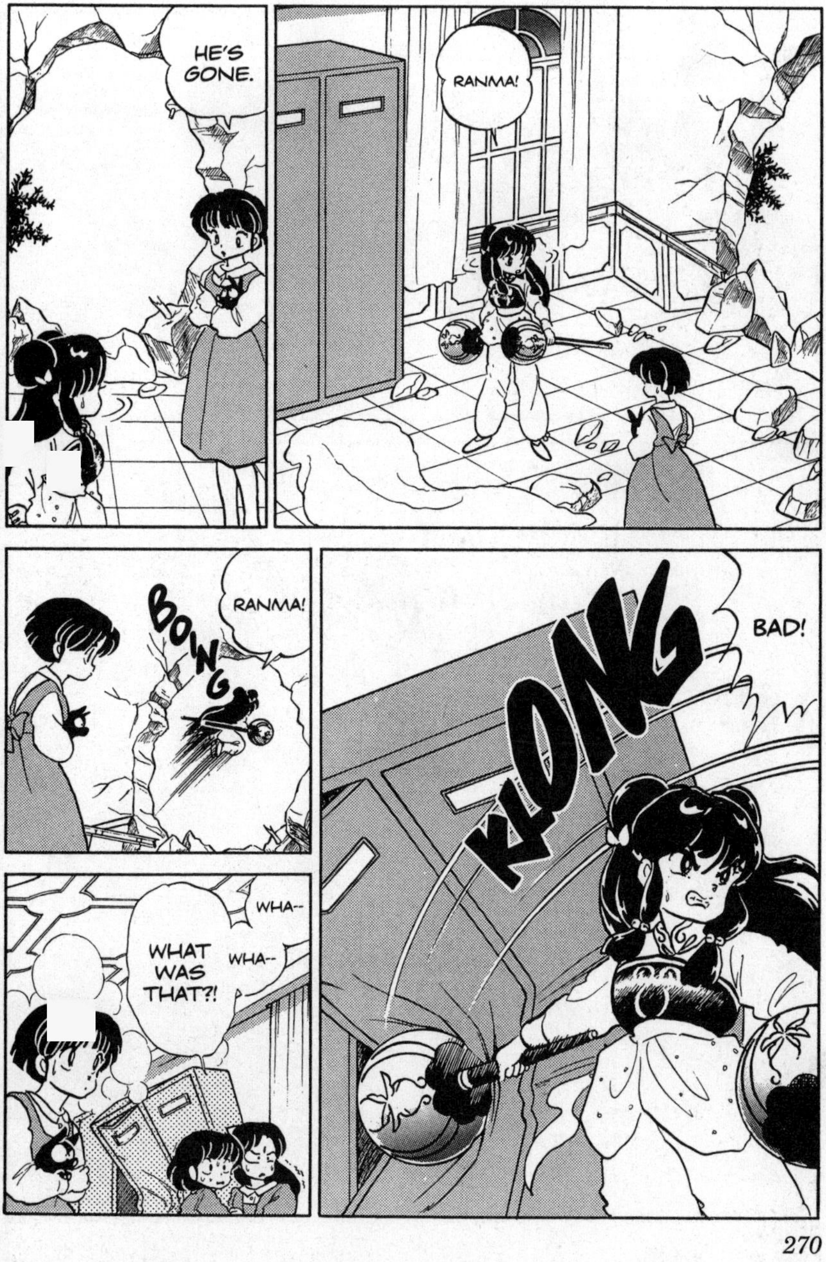
RANMA!
HE'S GONE.
KLONG
BAD!
BOING
RANMA!
WHA--
WHA--
WHAT WAS THAT?!

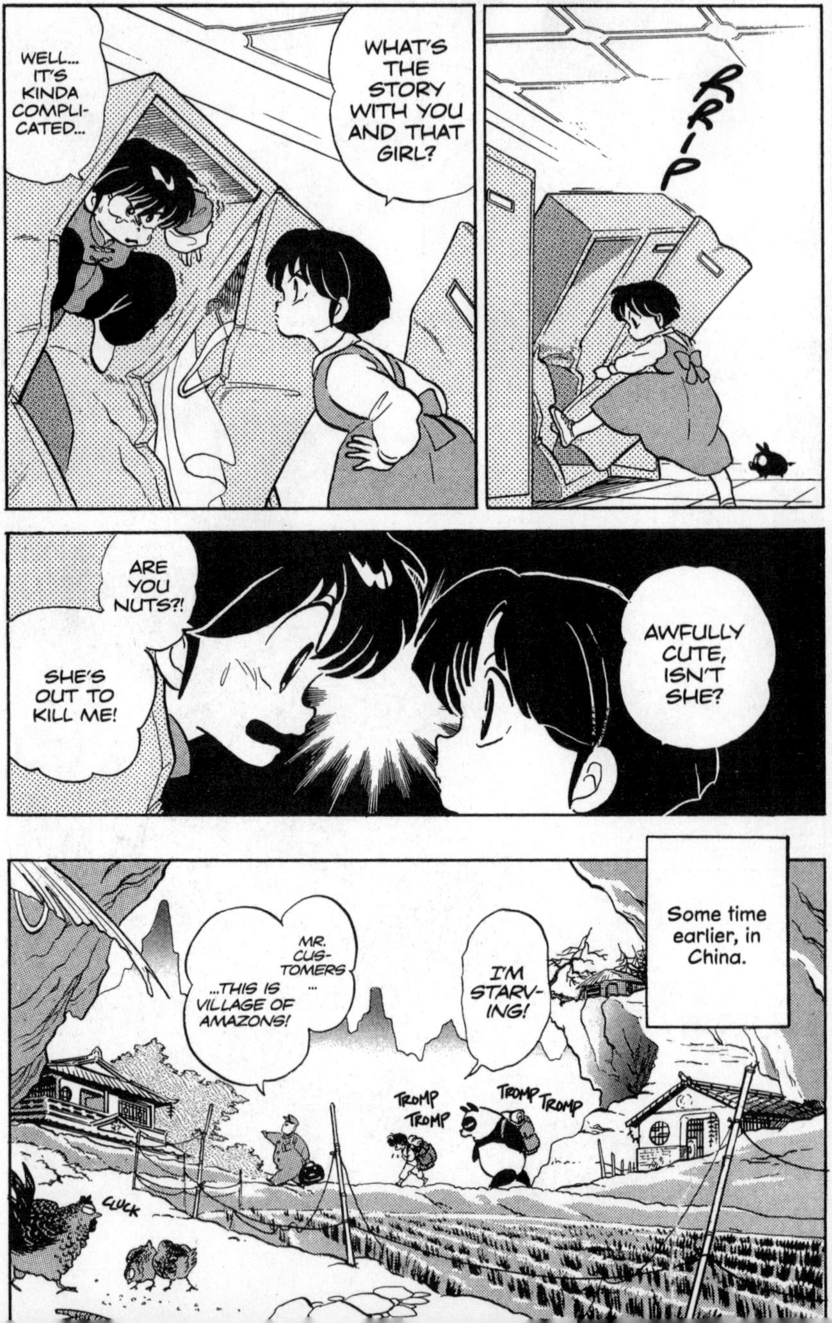
KRIP
WHAT'S THE STORY WITH YOU AND THAT GIRL?
WELL... IT'S KINDA COMPLICATED...
AWFULLY CUTE, ISN'T SHE?
ARE YOU NUTS?!
SHE'S OUT TO KILL ME!
Some time earlier, in China.
I'M STARVING!
MR. CUSTOMERS ...
...THIS IS VILLAGE OF AMAZONS!
TROMP TROMP
TROMP TROMP
CLUCK

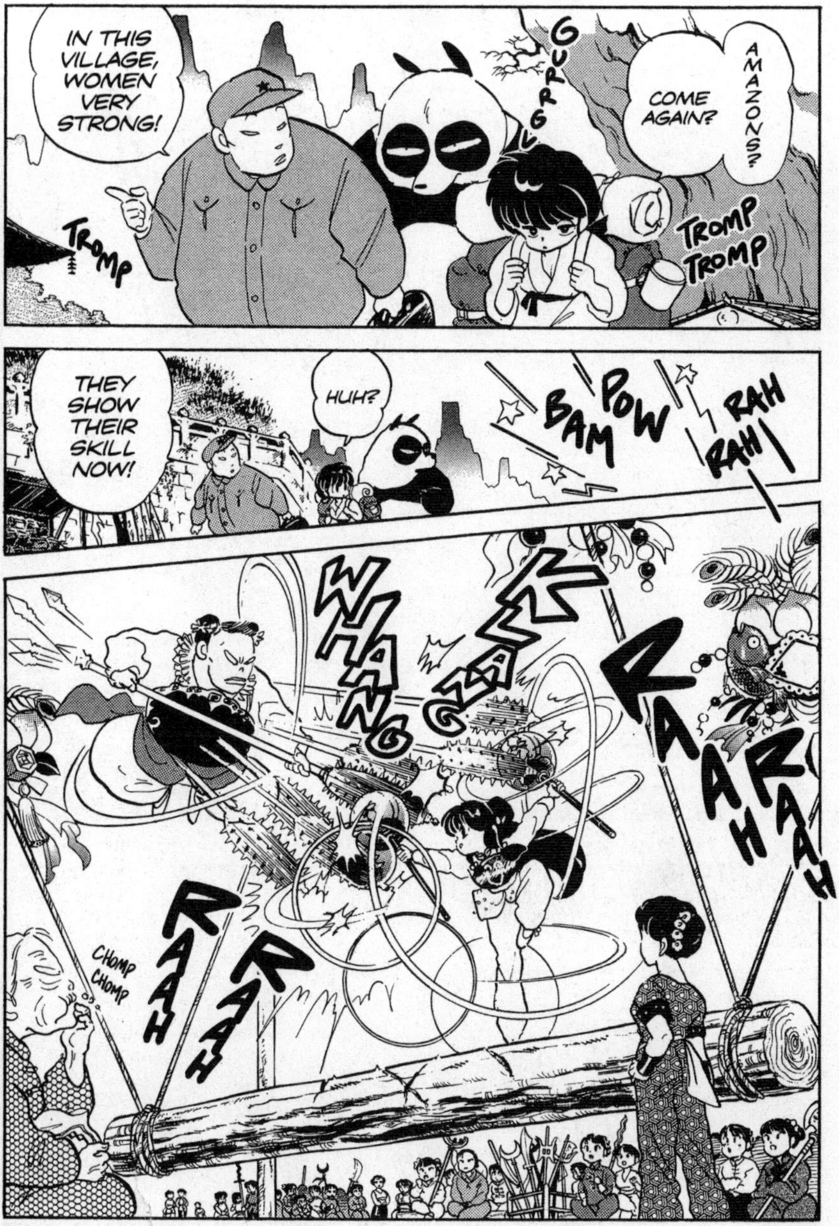
AMAZONS?
COME AGAIN?
TROMP TROMP
GURRGL
IN THIS VILLAGE, WOMEN VERY STRONG!
TROMP
RAH RAH
POW BAM
HUH?
THEY SHOW THEIR SKILL NOW!
RAAAH
RAAAH
KLAANG
WHANG
RAAAH
RAAAH
CHOMP CHOMP

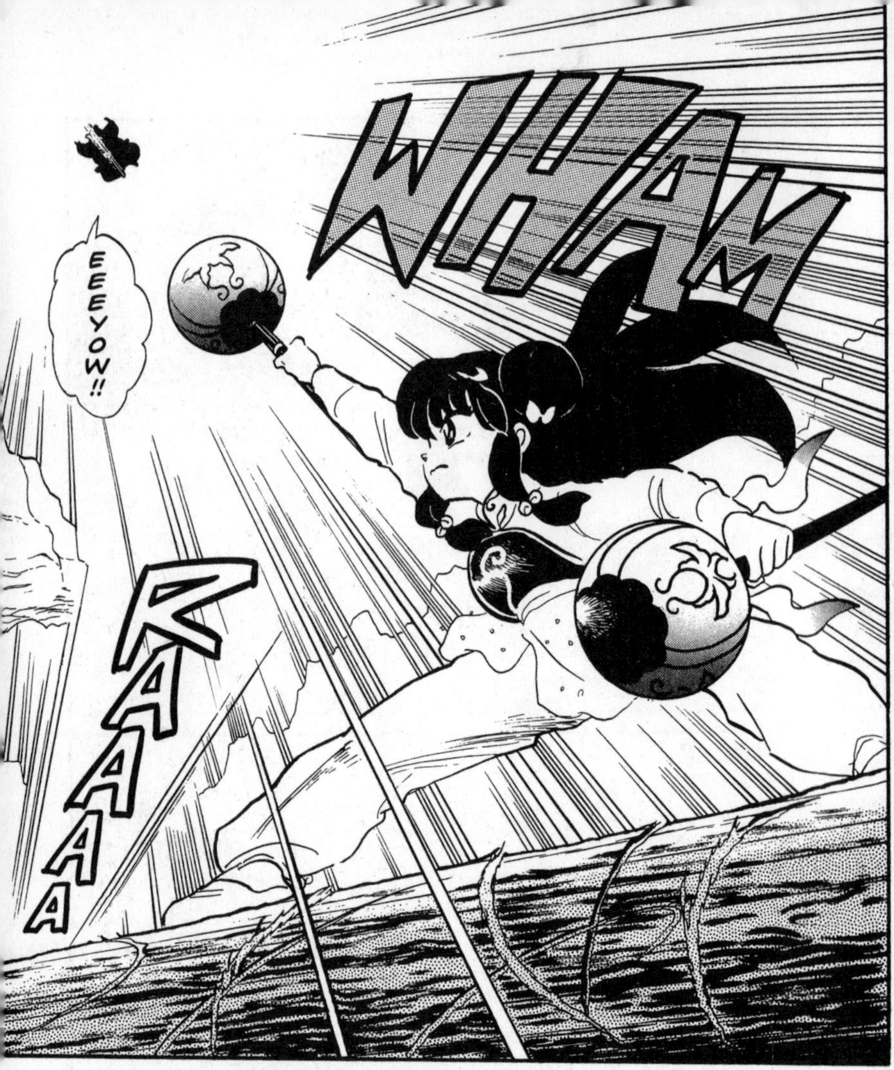
WHAM
EEEYOW!!
KRAAAAA

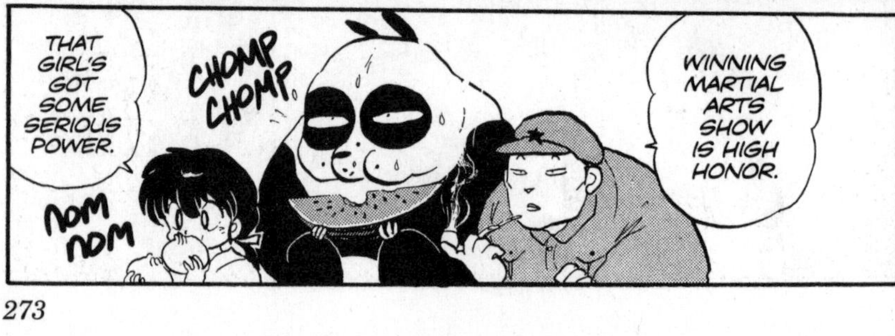
WINNING MARTIAL ARTS SHOW IS HIGH HONOR.
CHOMP CHOMP
THAT GIRL'S GOT SOME SERIOUS POWER.
NOM NOM

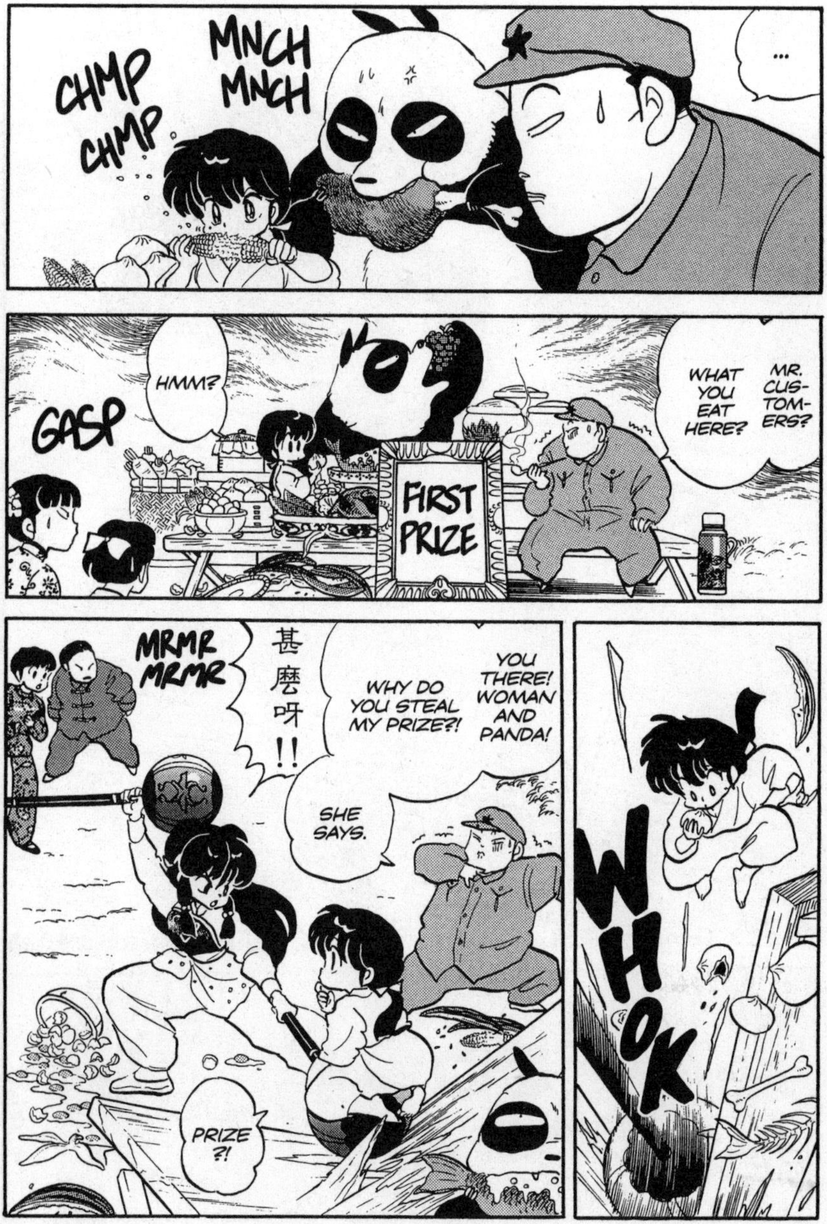
...
MNCH MNCH
CHMP CHMP
MR. CUSTOMERS? WHAT YOU EAT HERE?
HMM?
FIRST PRIZE
GASP
WHOK
YOU THERE! WOMAN AND PANDA! WHY DO YOU STEAL MY PRIZE?!
甚麼呀!!
MRMR MRMR
SHE SAYS.
PRIZE?!

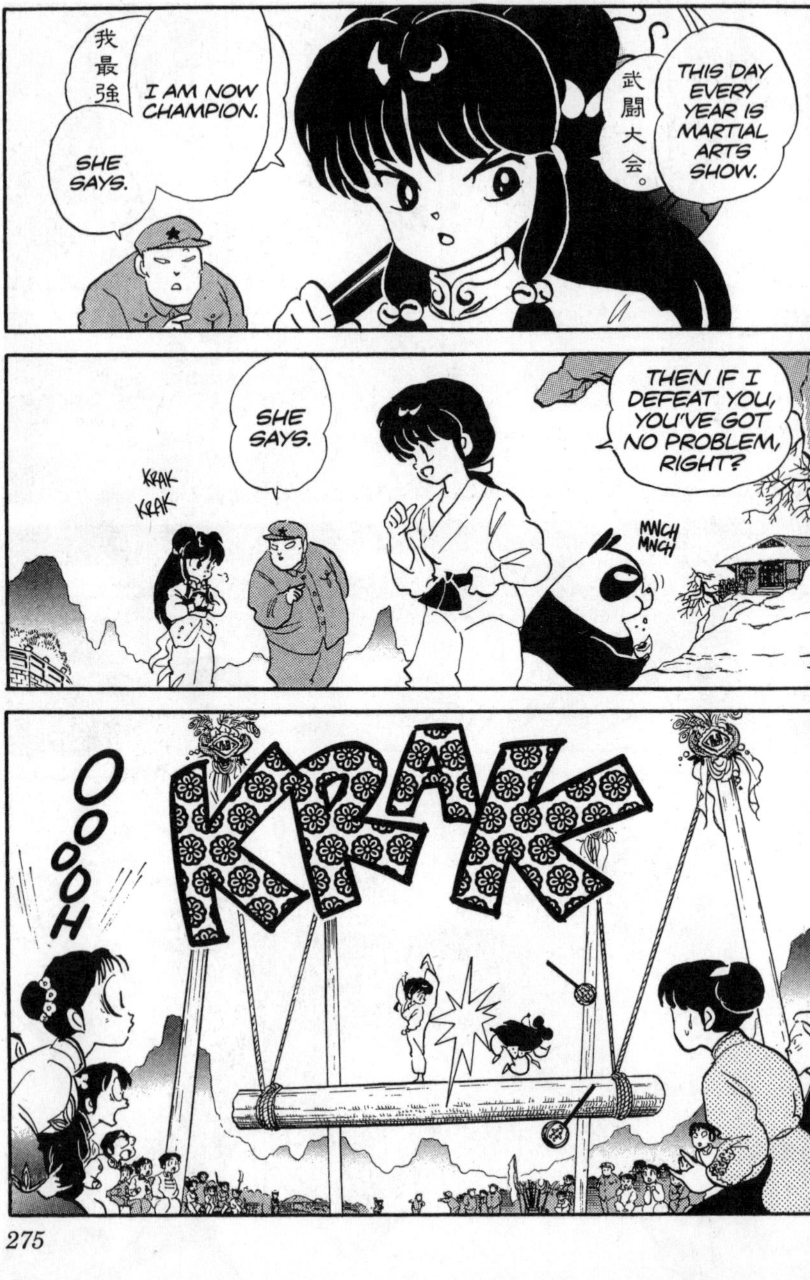
武闘大会。
THIS DAY EVERY YEAR IS MARTIAL ARTS SHOW.
我最強
I AM NOW CHAMPION.
SHE SAYS.
THEN IF I DEFEAT YOU, YOU'VE GOT NO PROBLEM, RIGHT?
MNCH MNCH
SHE SAYS.
KRAK KRAK
KRAK
OOOOOH

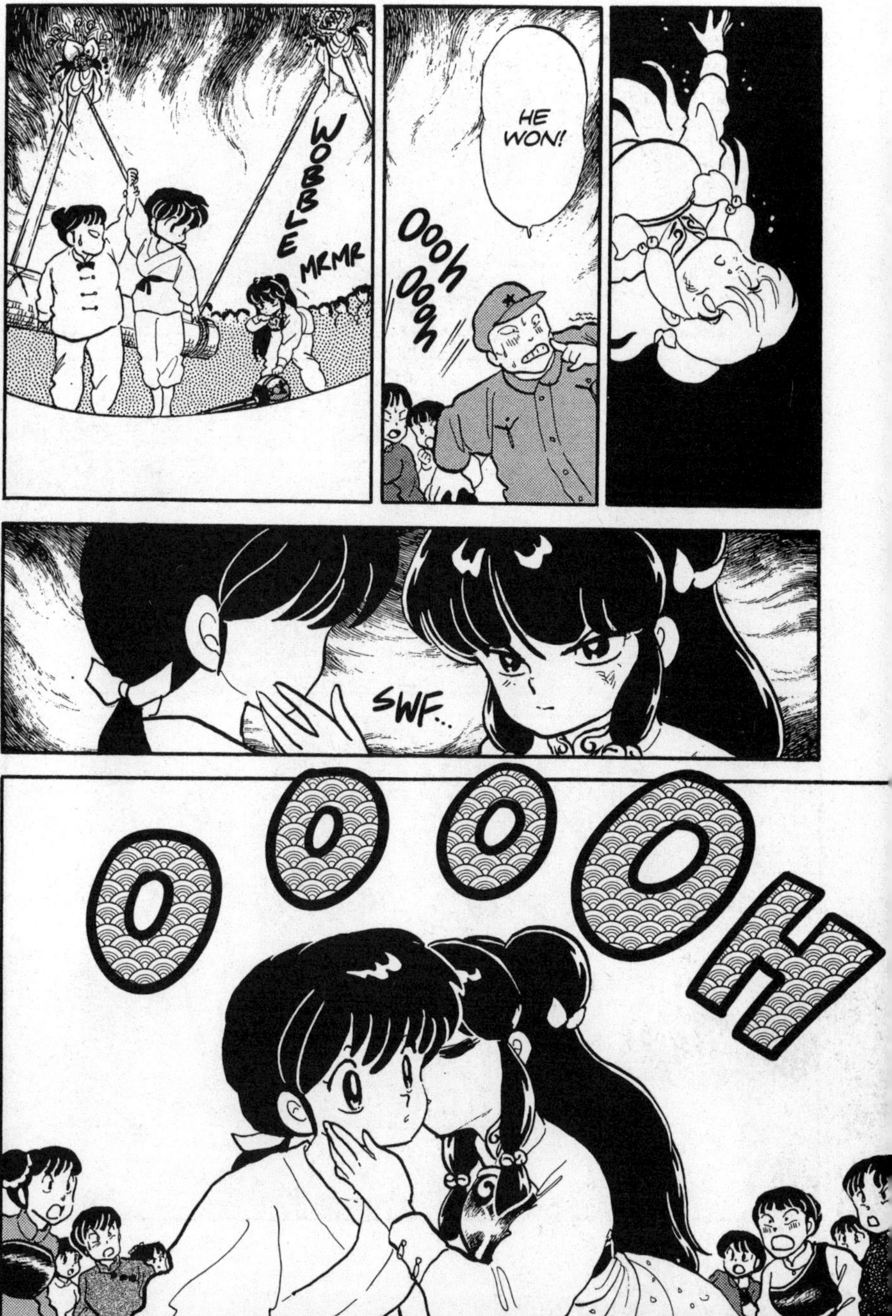
HE WON!
OOOH OOOH
WOBBLE
MRMR
SWF...
OOOOH

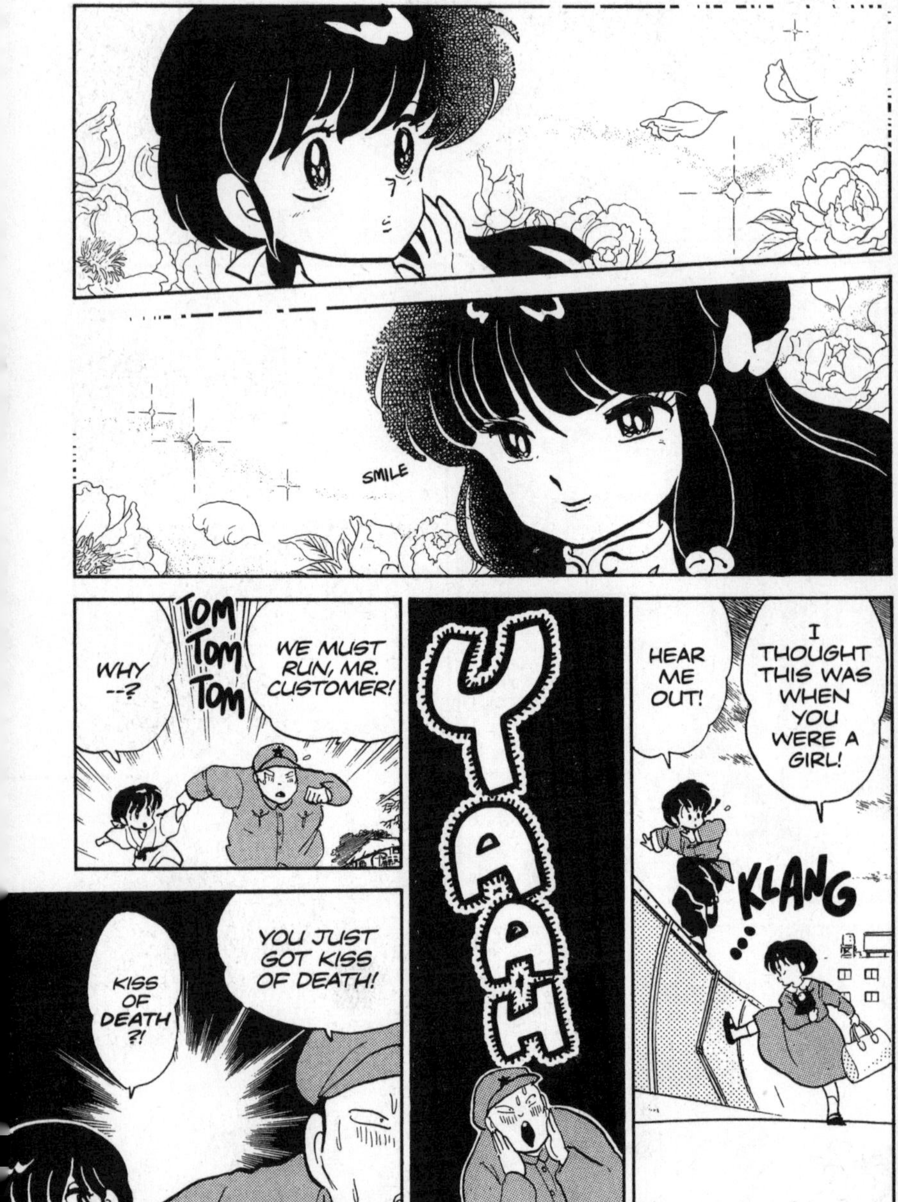
SMILE
I THOUGHT THIS WAS WHEN YOU WERE A GIRL!
HEAR ME OUT!
KLANG
...
YAAAH
WE MUST RUN, MR. CUSTOMER!
TOM TOM TOM
WHY --?
YOU JUST GOT KISS OF DEATH!
KISS OF DEATH ?!

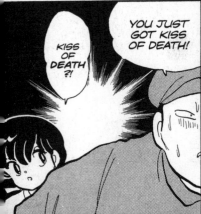

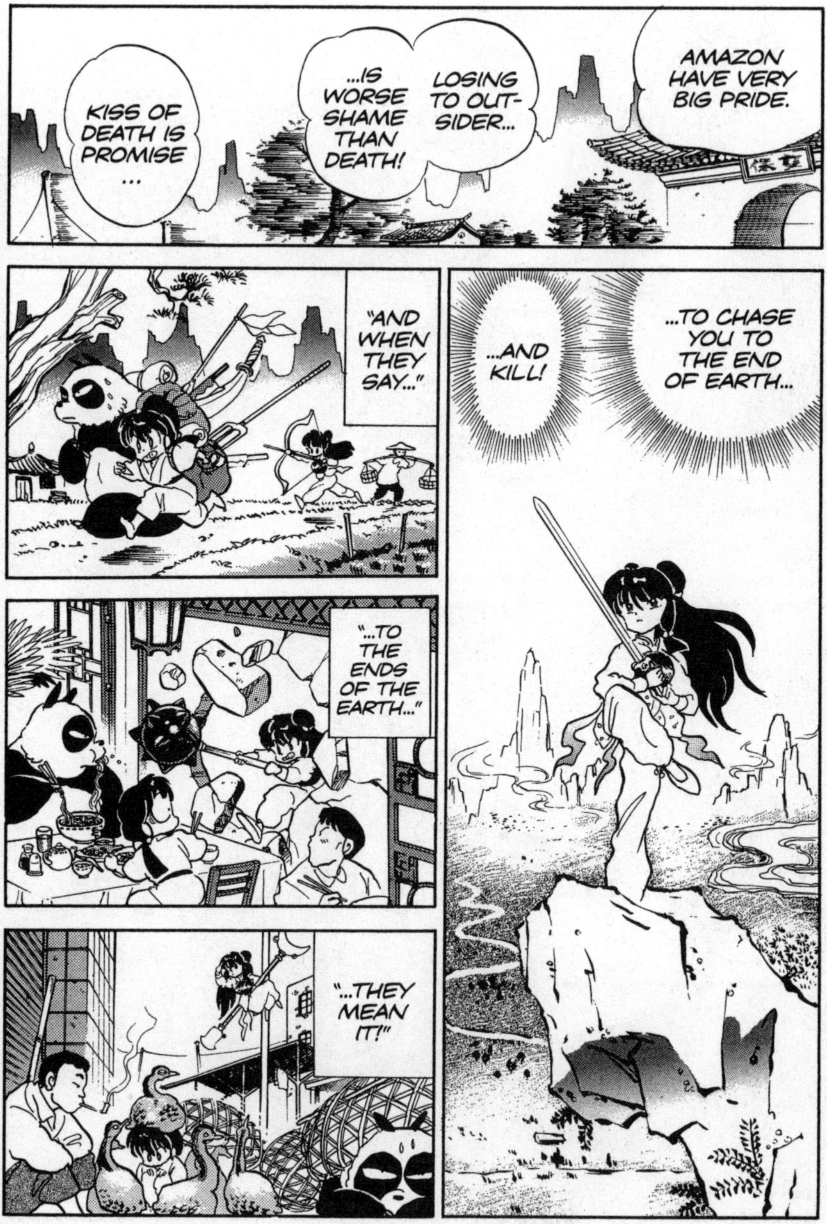
AMAZON HAVE VERY BIG PRIDE.
LOSING TO OUT-SIDER...
...IS WORSE SHAME THAN DEATH!
KISS OF DEATH IS PROMISE ...
...TO CHASE YOU TO THE END OF EARTH...
...AND KILL!
"AND WHEN THEY SAY..."
"...TO THE ENDS OF THE EARTH..."
"...THEY MEAN IT!"

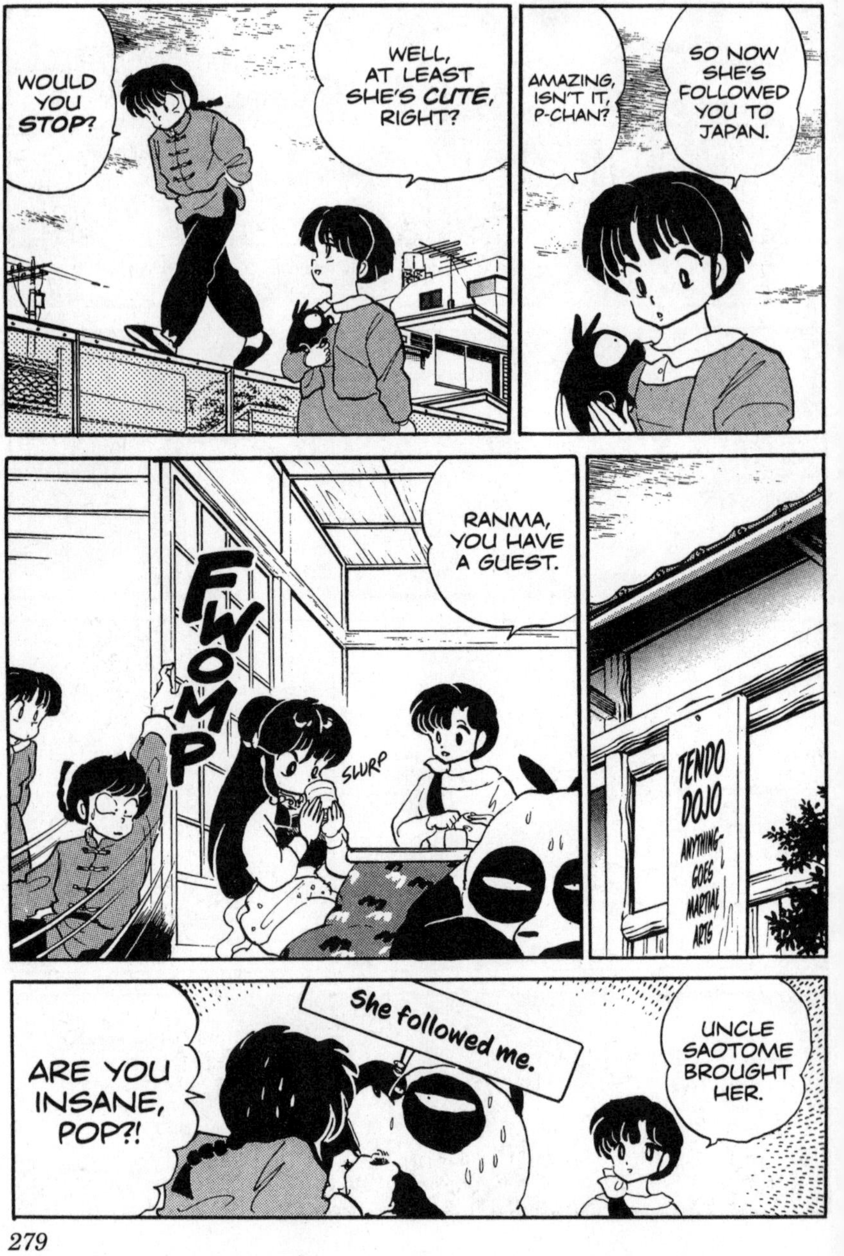
SO NOW SHE'S FOLLOWED YOU TO JAPAN.
AMAZING, ISN'T IT, P-CHAN?
WELL, AT LEAST SHE'S *CUTE*, RIGHT?
WOULD YOU *STOP?*
TENDO DOJO ANYTHING-GOES MARTIAL ARTS
RANMA, YOU HAVE A GUEST.
FWOMP
SLURP
UNCLE SAOTOME BROUGHT HER.
She followed me.
ARE YOU INSANE, POP?!

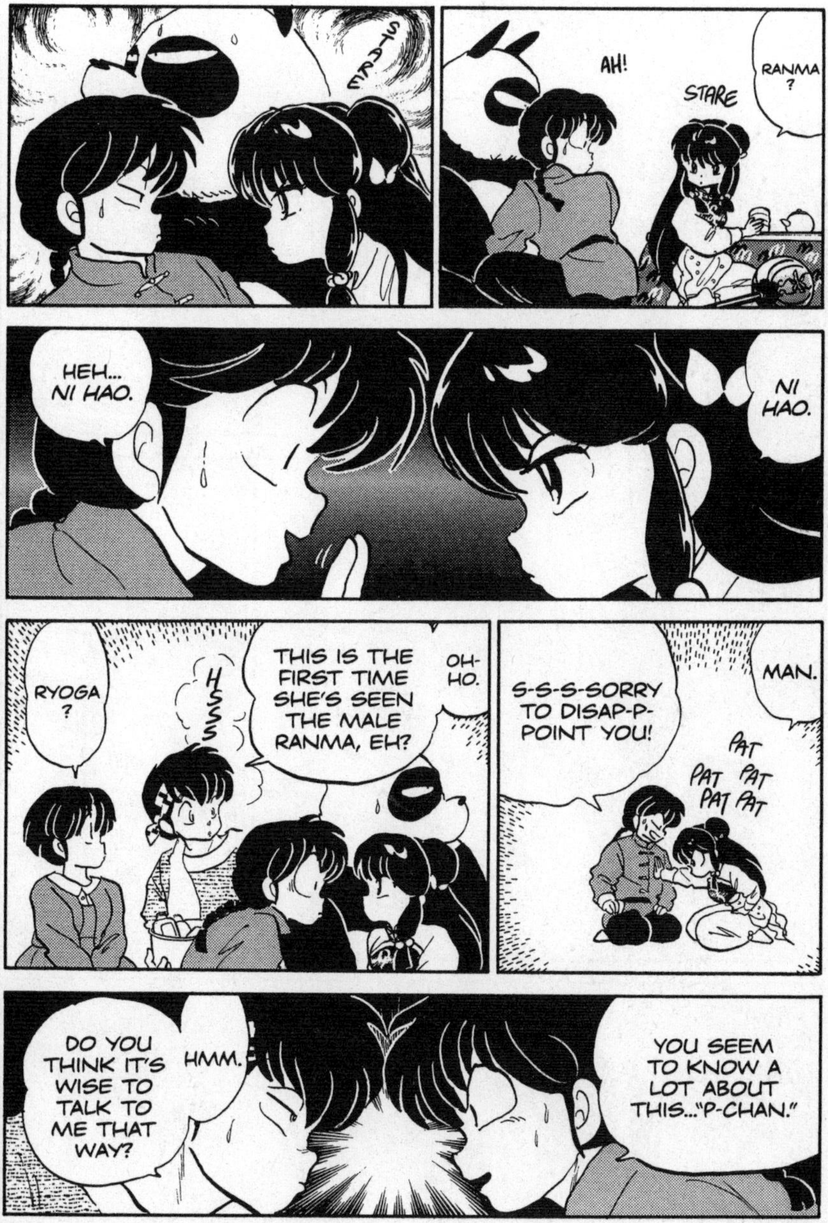
RANMA ?
STARE
AH!
STARE
NI HAO.
HEH... NI HAO.
MAN.
S-S-S-SORRY TO DISAP-P-POINT YOU!
PAT PAT PAT PAT PAT
OH-HO.
THIS IS THE FIRST TIME SHE'S SEEN THE MALE RANMA, EH?
HSSS
RYOGA ?
YOU SEEM TO KNOW A LOT ABOUT THIS..."P-CHAN."
HMM.
DO YOU THINK IT'S WISE TO TALK TO ME THAT WAY?

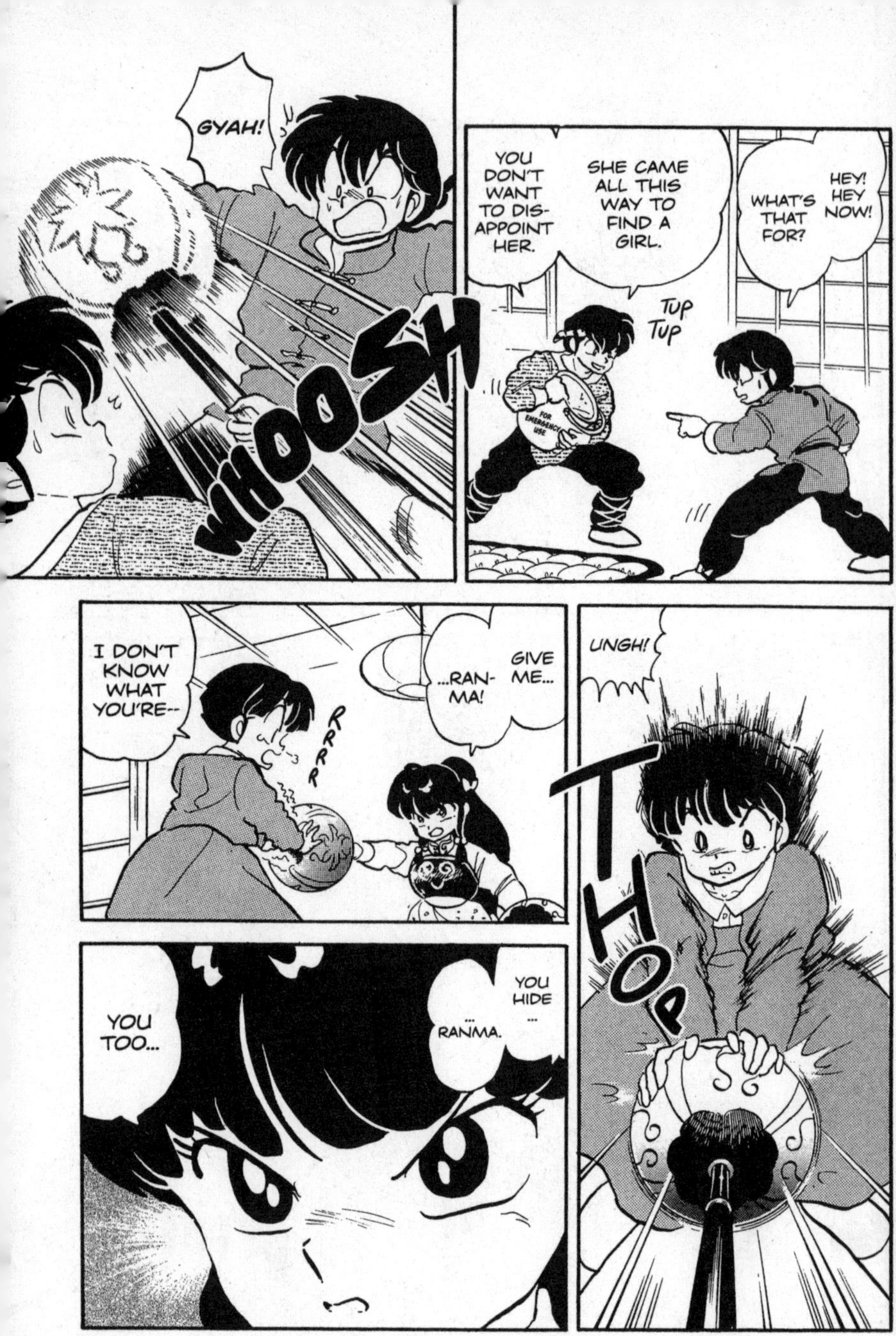
HEY! HEY NOW!
WHAT'S THAT FOR?
SHE CAME ALL THIS WAY TO FIND A GIRL.
YOU DON'T WANT TO DIS-APPOINT HER.
TUP TUP
FOR EMERGENCY USE
GYAH!
WHOOSH
UNGH!
THOP
GIVE ME...
...RAN-MA!
I DON'T KNOW WHAT YOU'RE--
RRRR
YOU HIDE ... RANMA.
YOU TOO...

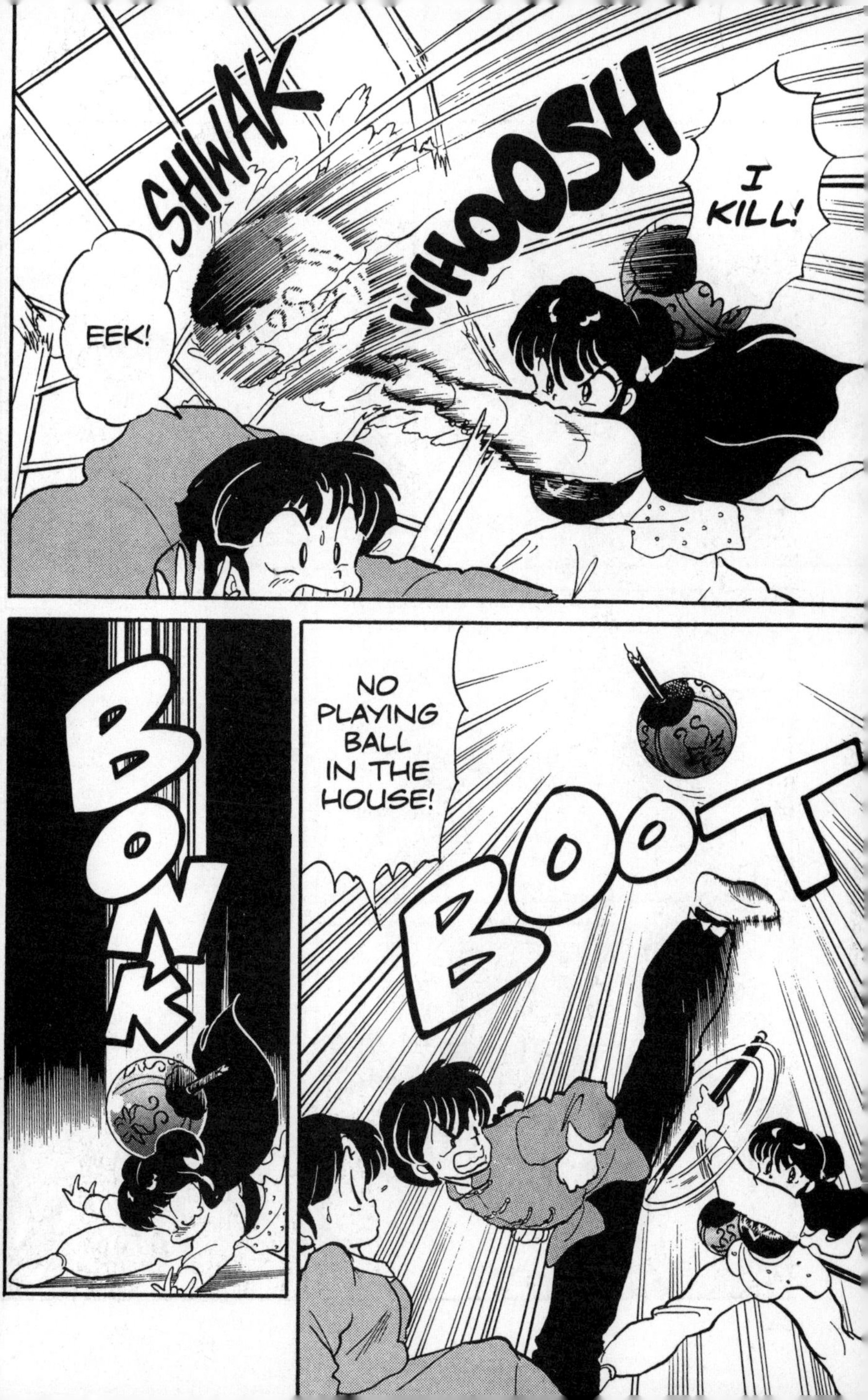
I KILL!
WHOOSH
SHWAK
EEK!
NO PLAYING BALL IN THE HOUSE!
BOOT
BONK

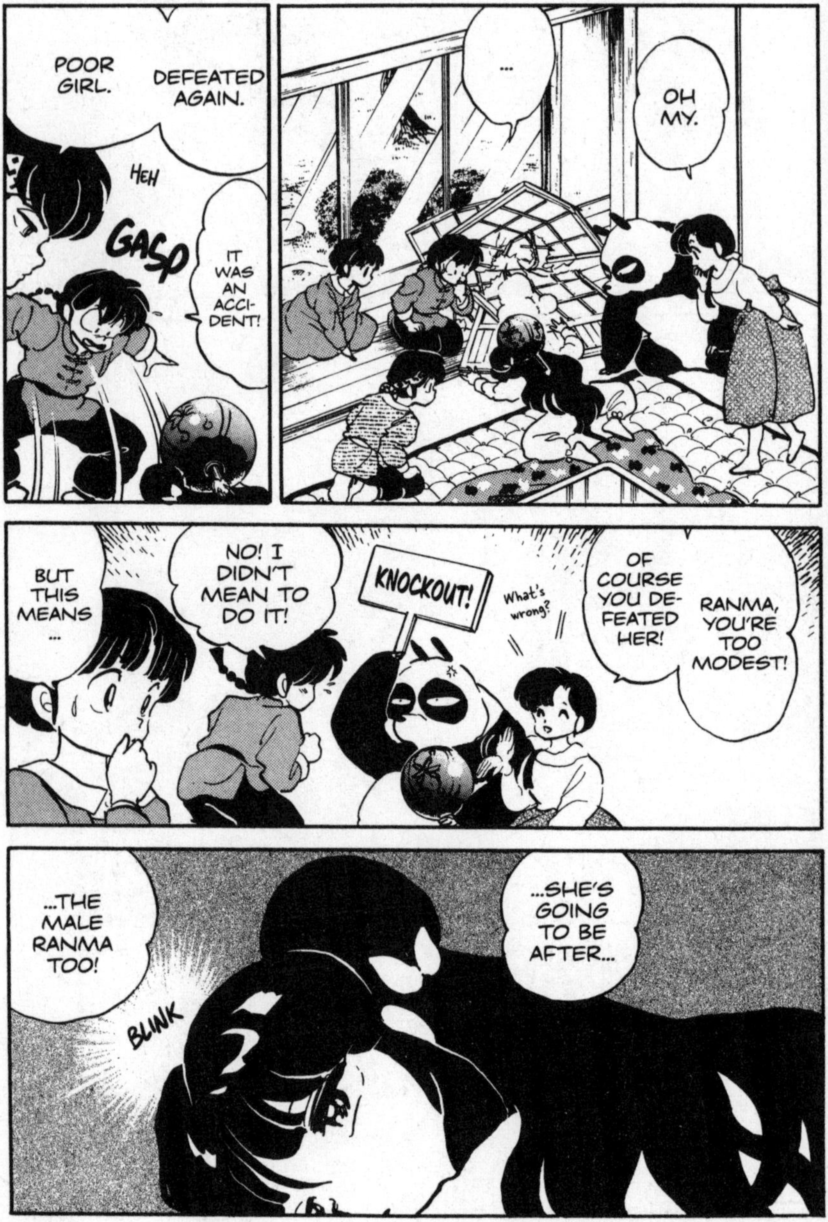
OH MY.
...
DEFEATED AGAIN.
POOR GIRL.
HEH
IT WAS AN ACCI-DENT!
GASP
RANMA, YOU'RE TOO MODEST!
OF COURSE YOU DE-FEATED HER!
What's wrong?
KNOCKOUT!
NO! I DIDN'T MEAN TO DO IT!
BUT THIS MEANS ...
...SHE'S GOING TO BE AFTER...
...THE MALE RANMA TOO!
BLINK

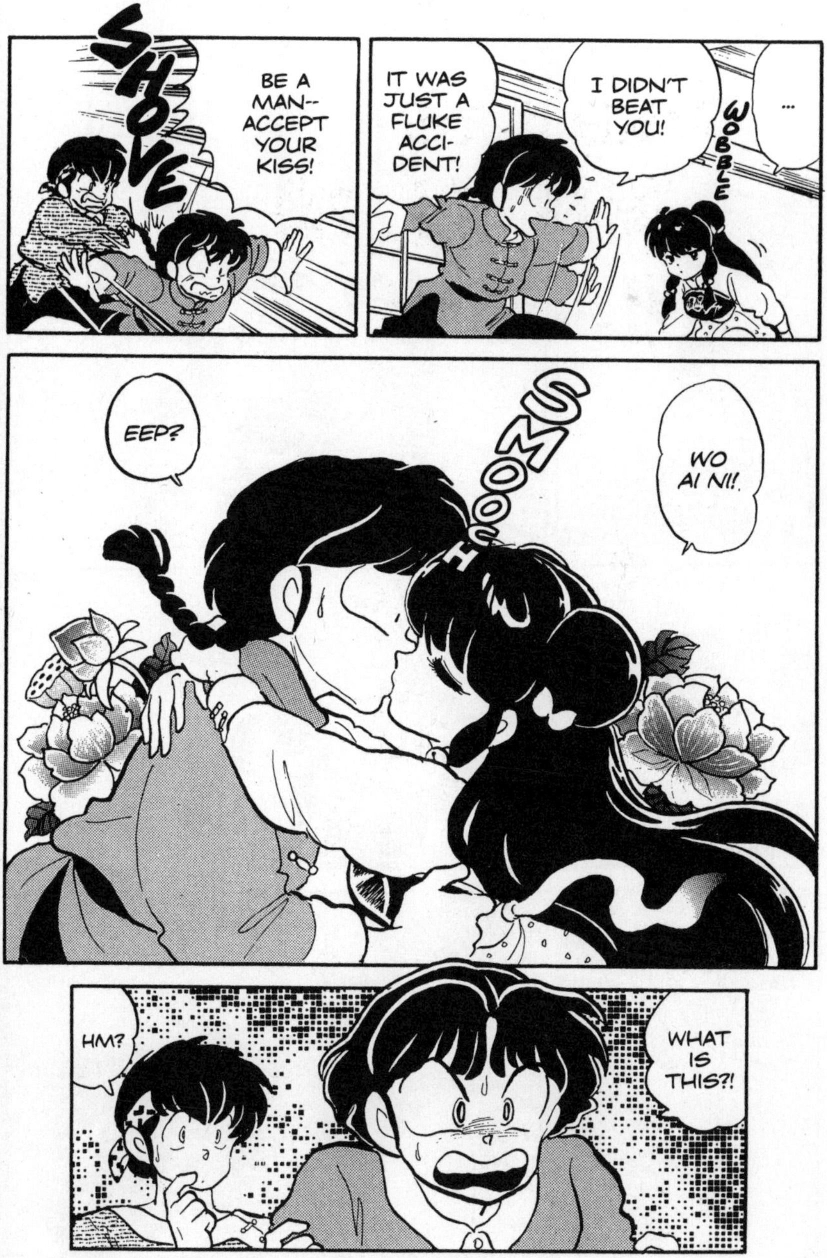
...
I DIDN'T BEAT YOU!
WOBBLE
IT WAS JUST A FLUKE ACCIDENT!
SHOVE
BE A MAN-- ACCEPT YOUR KISS!
WO AI NI!
SMOOCH
EEP?
WHAT IS THIS?!
HM?

PART 15
WO AI NI
(I LOVE YOU)

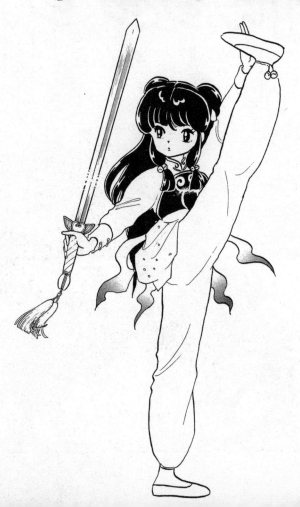

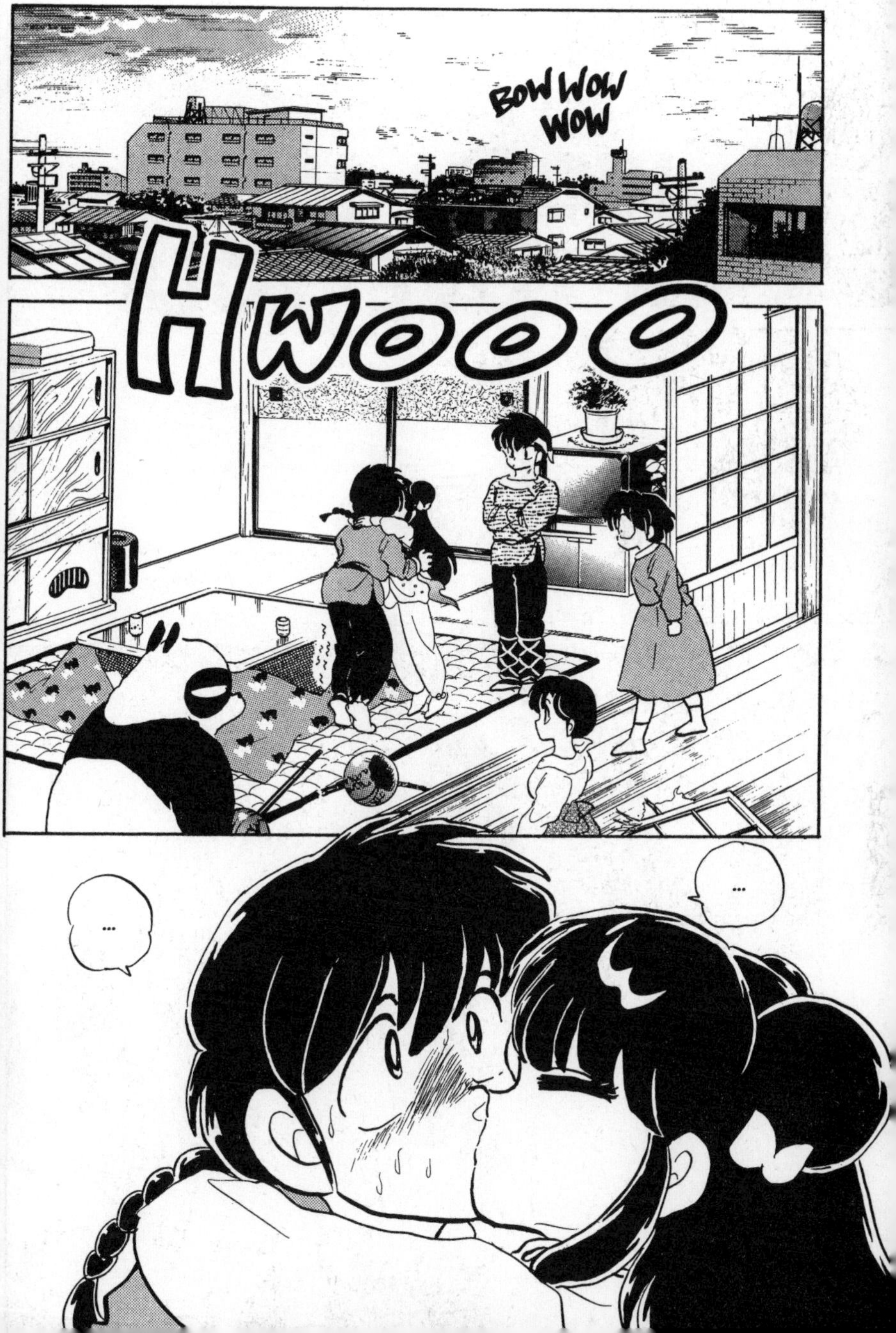
BOW WOW WOW
HWOOO
...
...

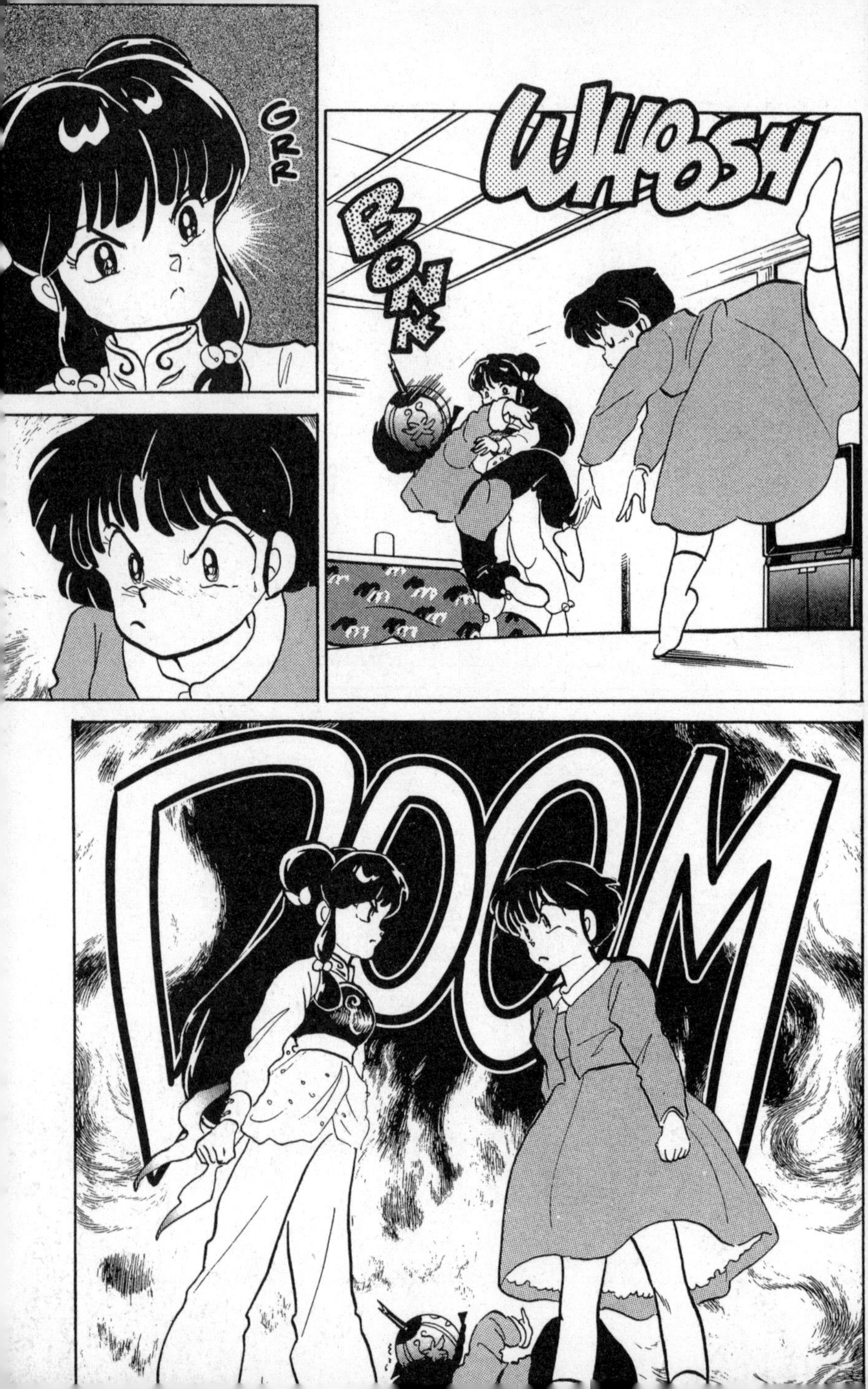
WHOOSH
BONK
GRR
DOOM

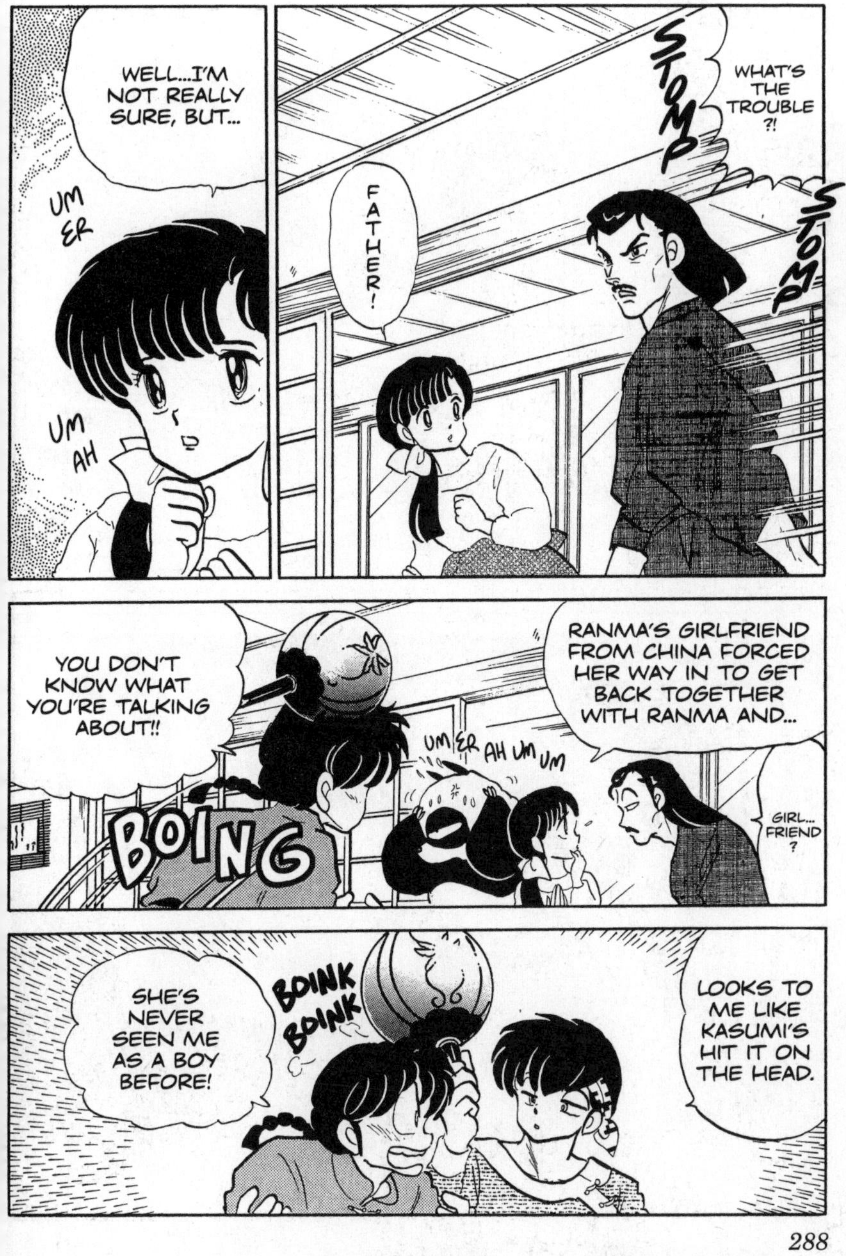
STOMP
WHAT'S THE TROUBLE ?!
STOMP
FATHER!
WELL...I'M NOT REALLY SURE, BUT...
UM ER
UM AH
RANMA'S GIRLFRIEND FROM CHINA FORCED HER WAY IN TO GET BACK TOGETHER WITH RANMA AND...
GIRL... FRIEND ?
UM ER AH UM UM
YOU DON'T KNOW WHAT YOU'RE TALKING ABOUT!!
BOING
LOOKS TO ME LIKE KASUMI'S HIT IT ON THE HEAD.
BOINK BOINK
SHE'S NEVER SEEN ME AS A BOY BEFORE!

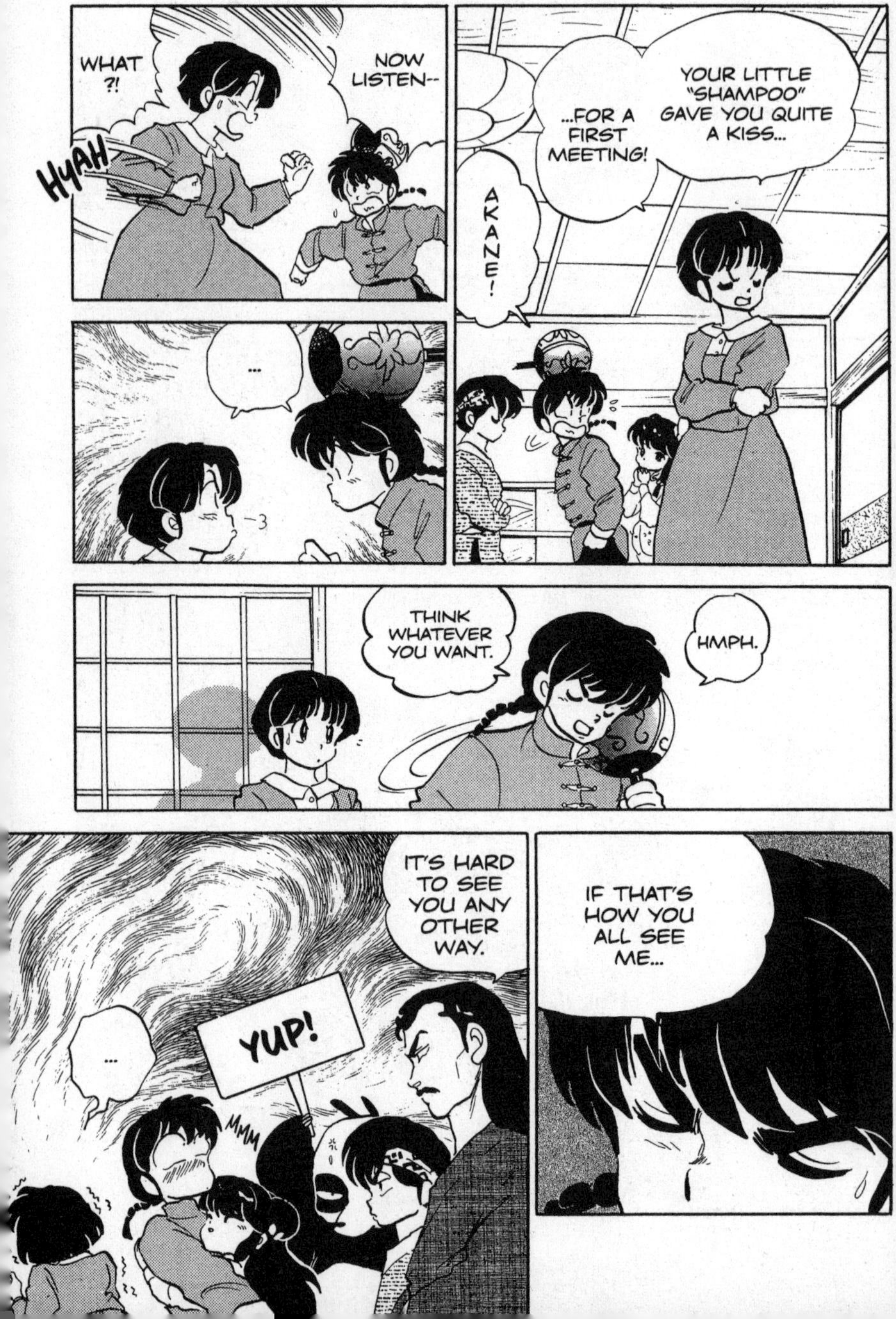
YOUR LITTLE "SHAMPOO" GAVE YOU QUITE A KISS...
...FOR A FIRST MEETING!
AKANE!
NOW LISTEN--
WHAT ?!
HYAH
...
HMPH.
THINK WHATEVER YOU WANT.
IF THAT'S HOW YOU ALL SEE ME...
IT'S HARD TO SEE YOU ANY OTHER WAY.
YUP!
...
MMM

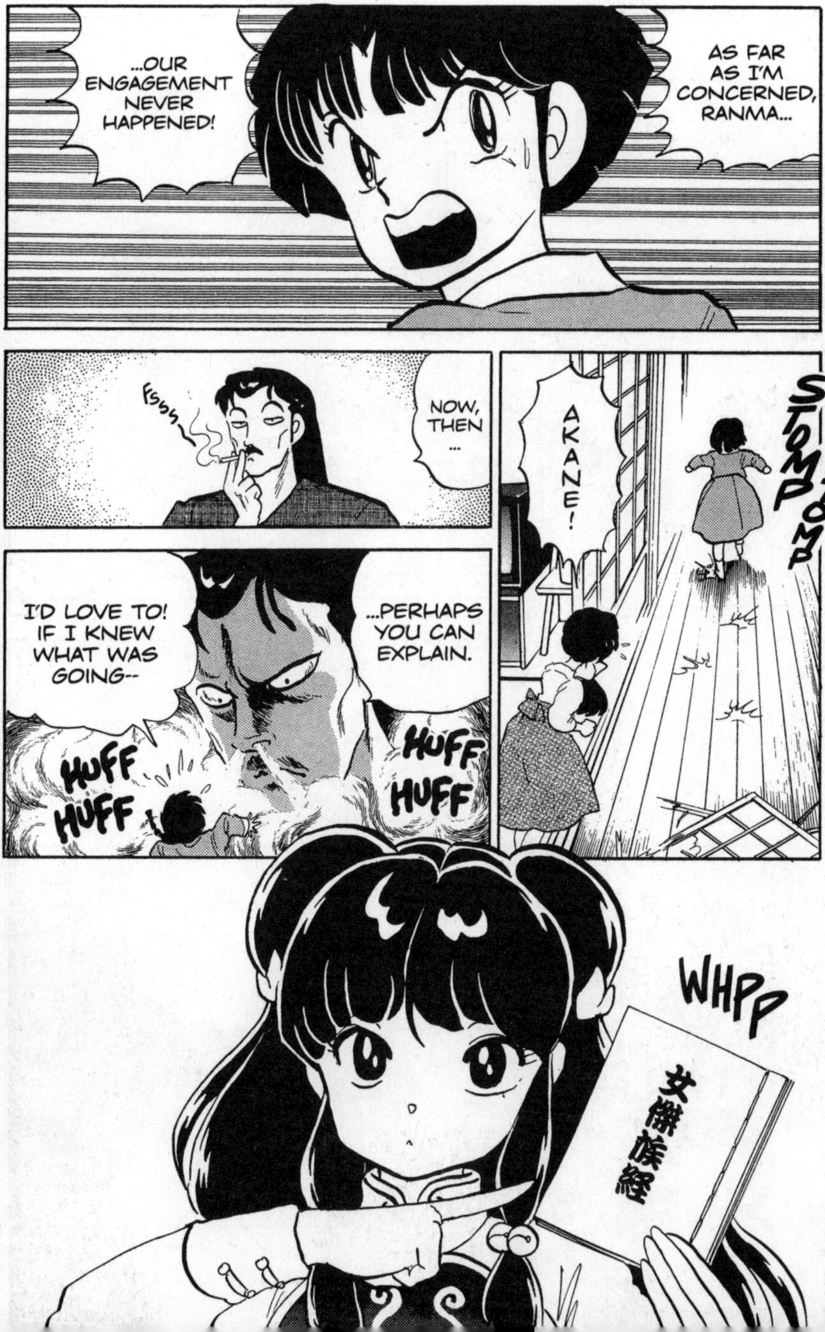
AS FAR AS I'M CONCERNED, RANMA...
...OUR ENGAGEMENT NEVER HAPPENED!
STOMP STOMP
AKANE!
NOW, THEN ...
FSSS
...PERHAPS YOU CAN EXPLAIN.
HUFF HUFF
I'D LOVE TO! IF I KNEW WHAT WAS GOING--
HUFF HUFF
WHPP
女傑族経

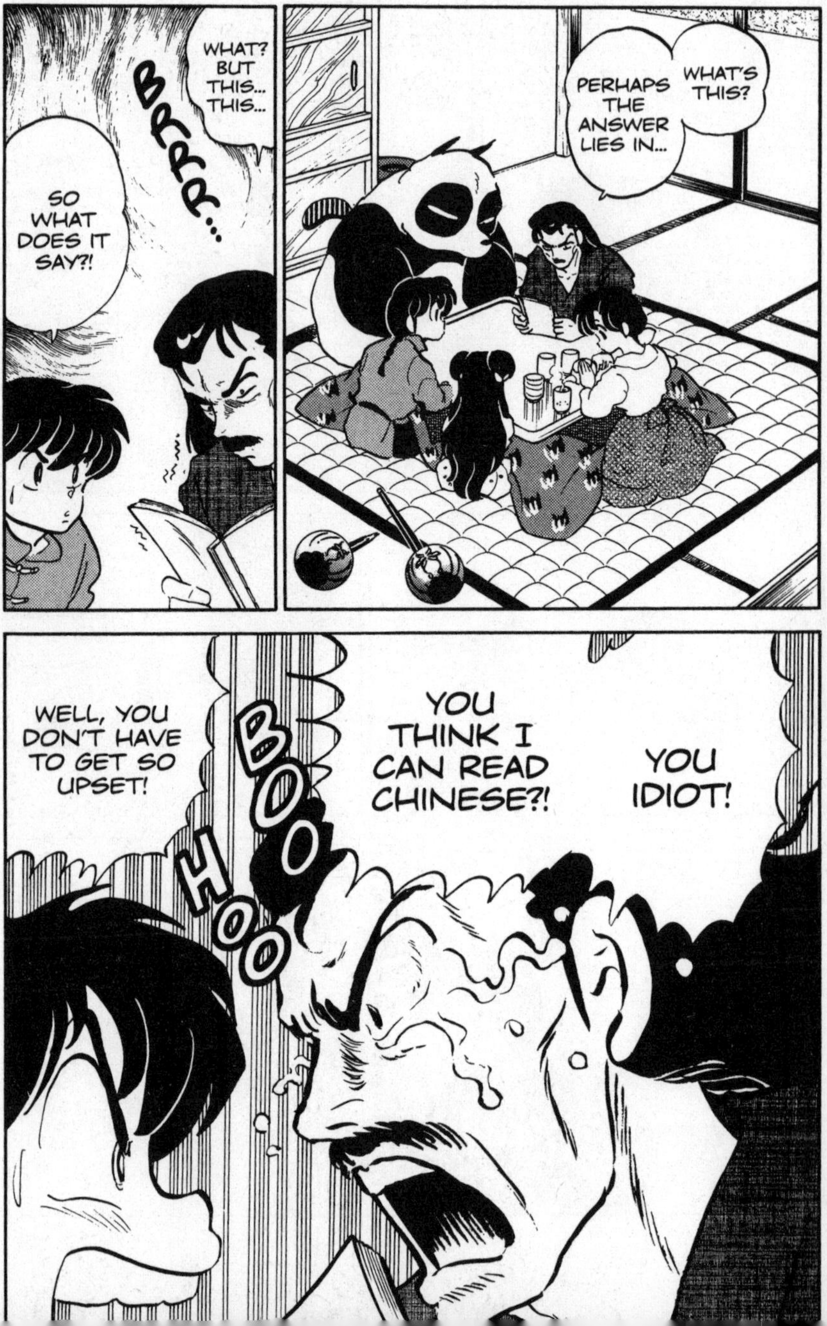
WHAT'S THIS?
PERHAPS THE ANSWER LIES IN...
WHAT? BUT THIS... THIS...
BRRR...
SO WHAT DOES IT SAY?!
YOU IDIOT!
YOU THINK I CAN READ CHINESE?!
BOOHOO
WELL, YOU DON'T HAVE TO GET SO UPSET!

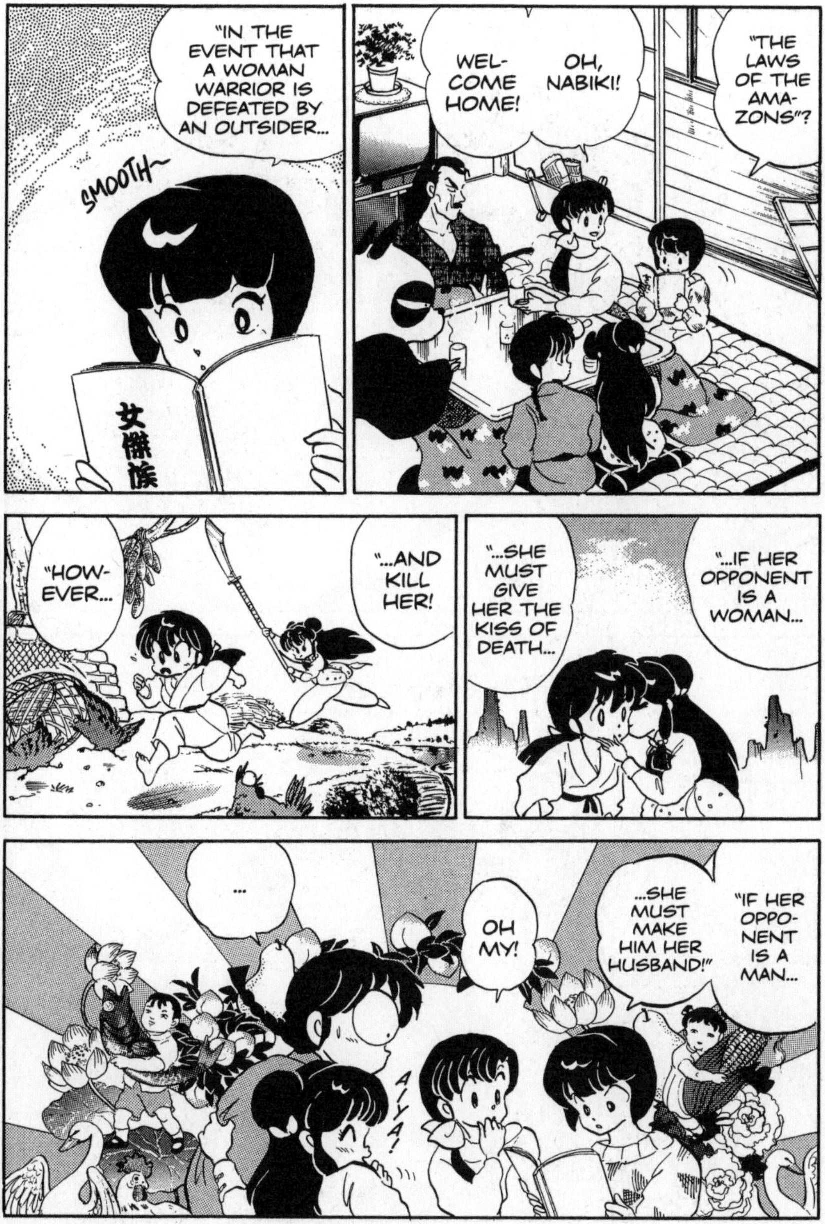
"THE LAWS OF THE AMAZONS"?
OH, NABIKI!
WEL-COME HOME!
"IN THE EVENT THAT A WOMAN WARRIOR IS DEFEATED BY AN OUTSIDER...
SMOOTH~
女傑族
"...IF HER OPPONENT IS A WOMAN...
"...SHE MUST GIVE HER THE KISS OF DEATH...
"...AND KILL HER!
"HOW-EVER...
"IF HER OPPO-NENT IS A MAN...
...SHE MUST MAKE HIM HER HUSBAND!"
OH MY!
...
AIYA!

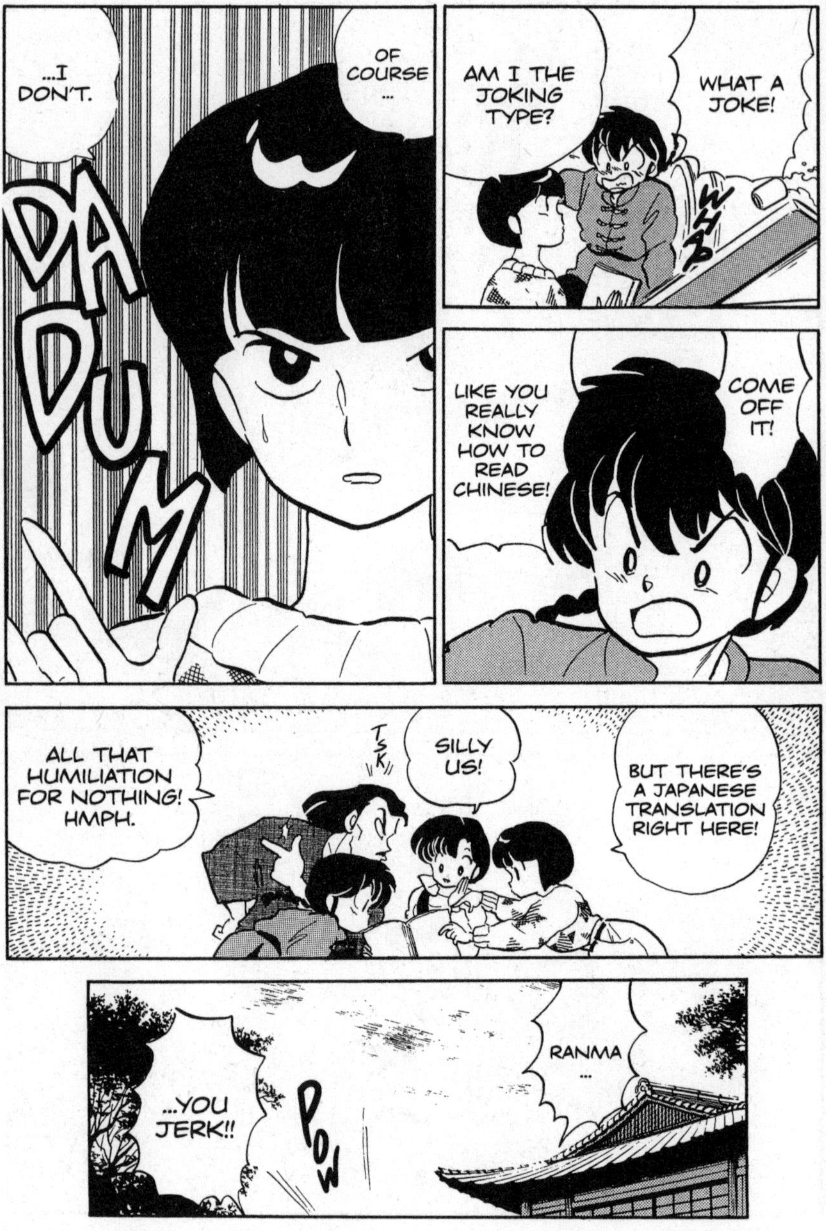
WHAT A JOKE!
AM I THE JOKING TYPE?
WHAP
COME OFF IT!
LIKE YOU REALLY KNOW HOW TO READ CHINESE!
OF COURSE ...
...I DON'T.
DA DUM
BUT THERE'S A JAPANESE TRANSLATION RIGHT HERE!
SILLY US!
TSK
ALL THAT HUMILIATION FOR NOTHING! HMPH.
RANMA ...
POW
...YOU JERK!!

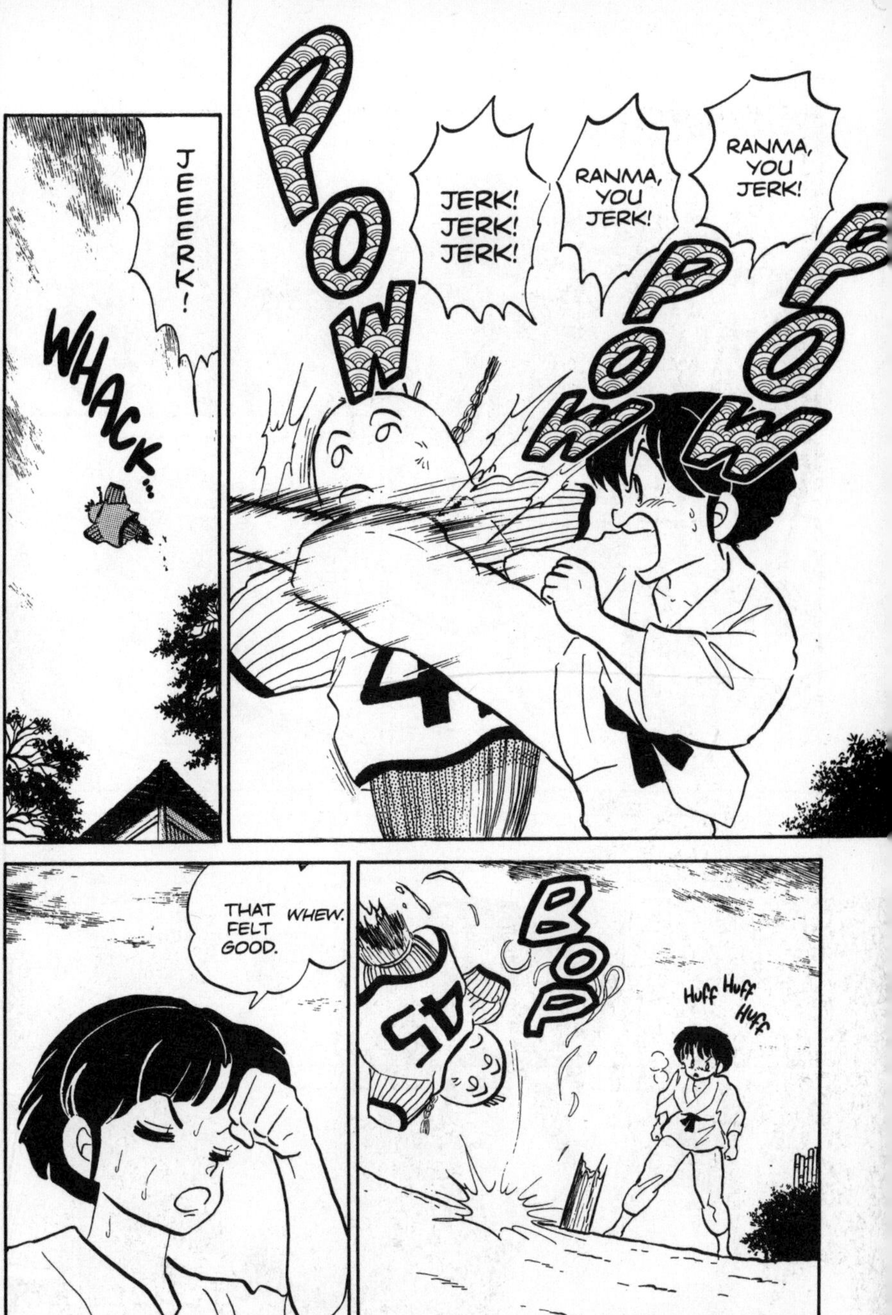
RANMA, YOU JERK!
POW
POW
RANMA, YOU JERK!
JERK! JERK! JERK!
POW
JEEEERK!
WHACK...
BOP
Huff Huff Huff
WHEW.
THAT FELT GOOD.

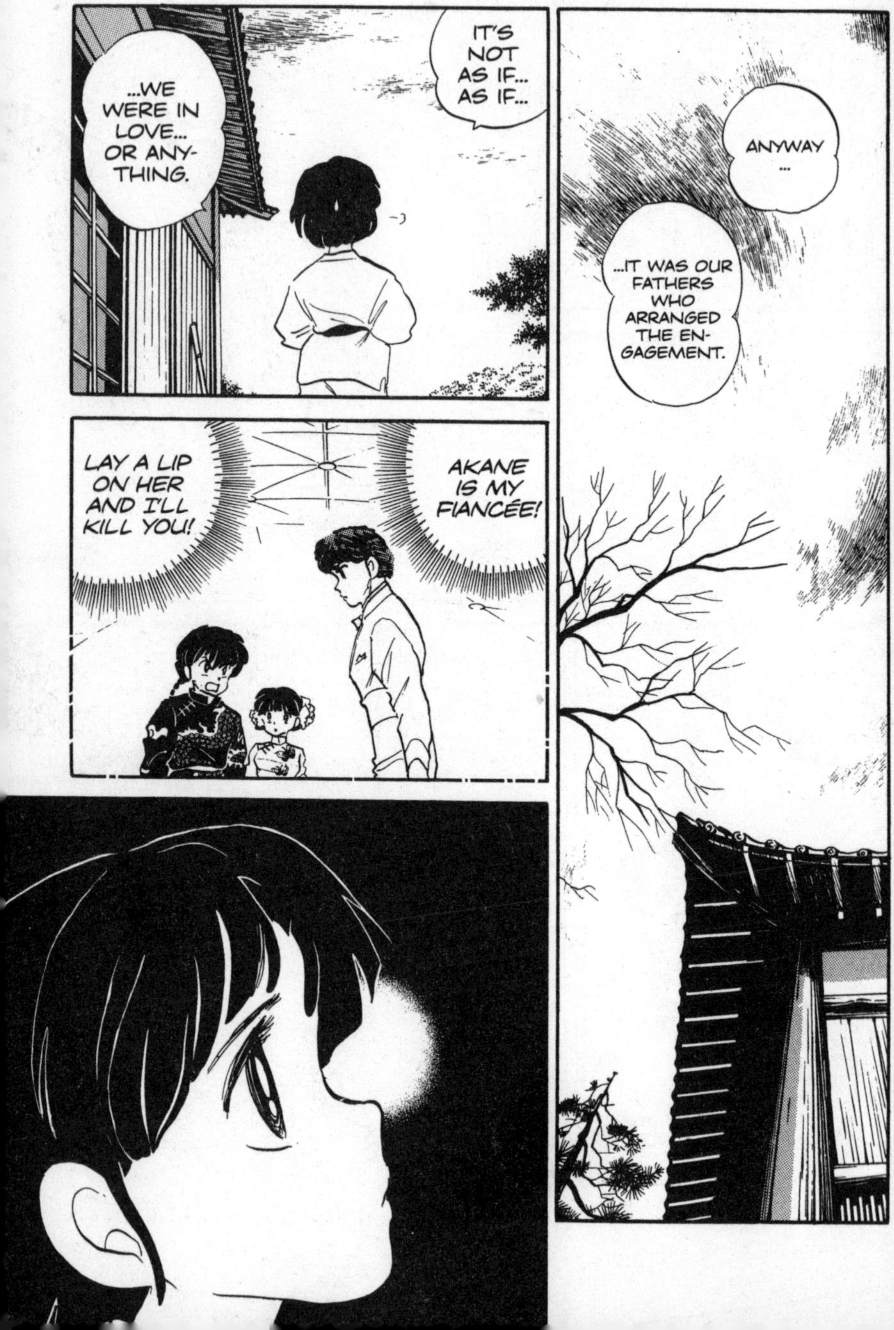
ANYWAY ...
...IT WAS OUR FATHERS WHO ARRANGED THE EN-GAGEMENT.
IT'S NOT AS IF... AS IF...
...WE WERE IN LOVE... OR ANY-THING.
AKANE IS MY FIANCÉE!
LAY A LIP ON HER AND I'LL KILL YOU!

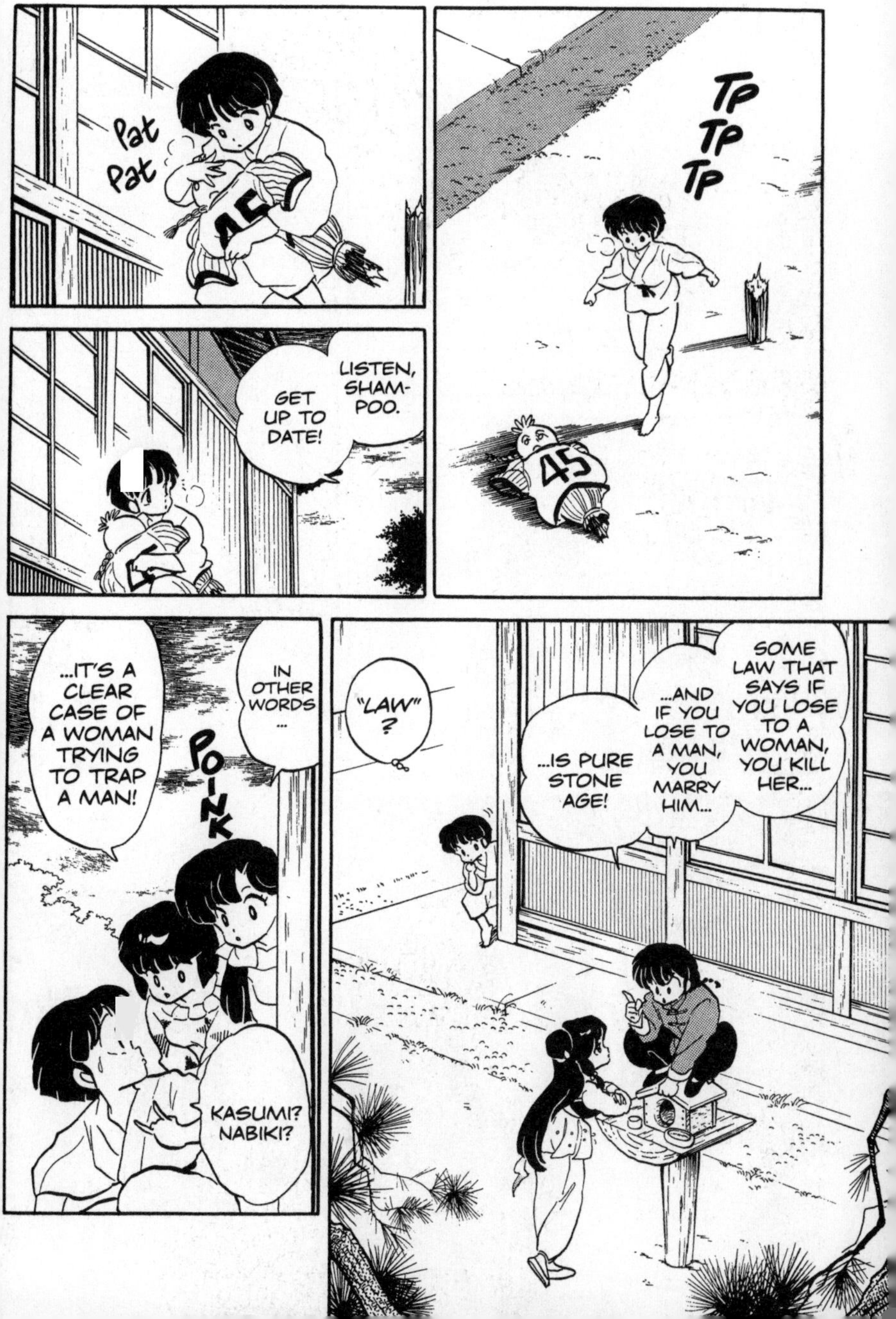
Tp Tp Tp
Pat Pat
LISTEN, SHAMPOO.
GET UP TO DATE!
SOME LAW THAT SAYS IF YOU LOSE TO A WOMAN, YOU KILL HER...
...AND IF YOU LOSE TO A MAN, YOU MARRY HIM...
...IS PURE STONE AGE!
"LAW"?
IN OTHER WORDS...
...IT'S A CLEAR CASE OF A WOMAN TRYING TO TRAP A MAN!
POINK
KASUMI? NABIKI?

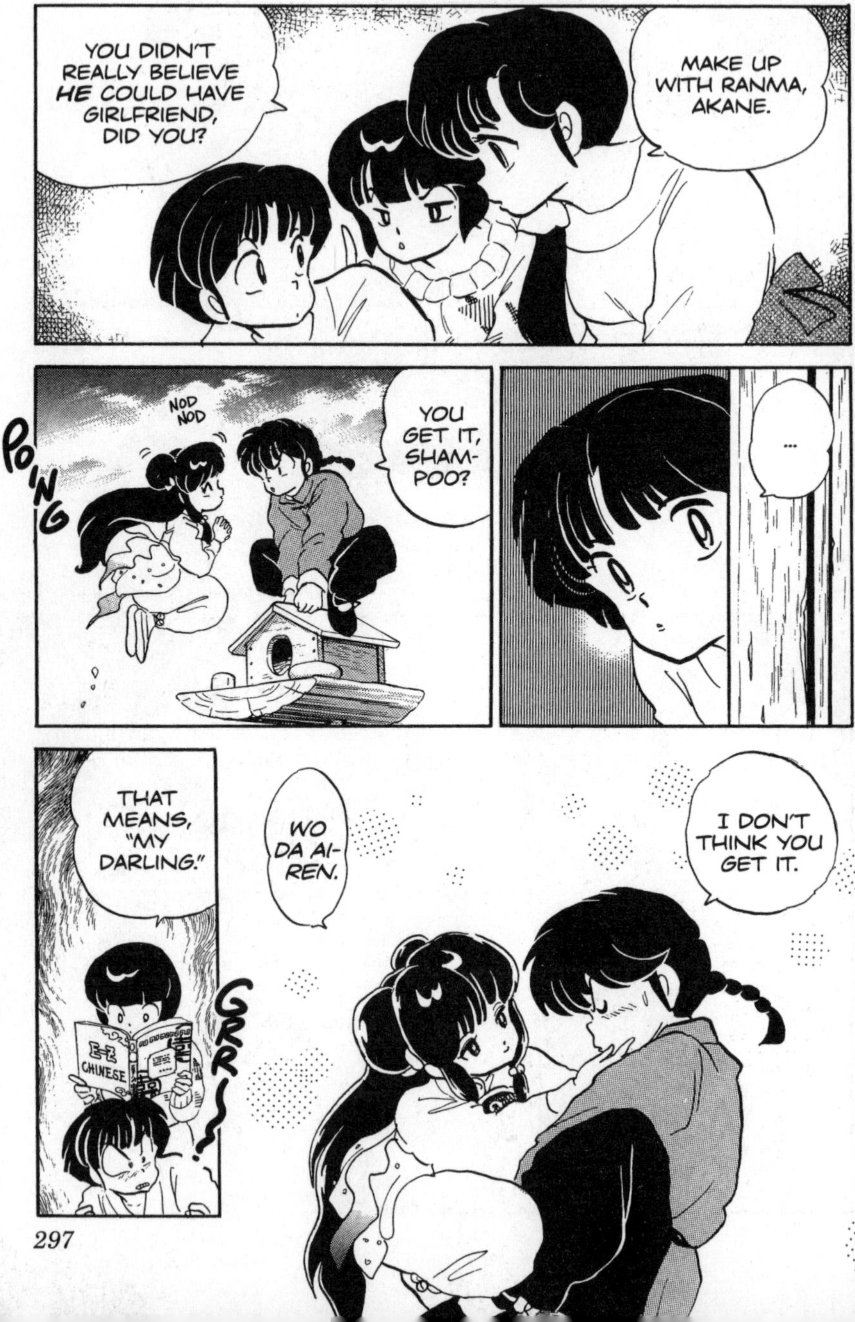
MAKE UP WITH RANMA, AKANE.
YOU DIDN'T REALLY BELIEVE HE COULD HAVE GIRLFRIEND, DID YOU?
...
YOU GET IT, SHAMPOO?
NOD NOD
POING
I DON'T THINK YOU GET IT.
WO DA AI-REN.
THAT MEANS, "MY DARLING."
E-Z CHINESE
GRRR

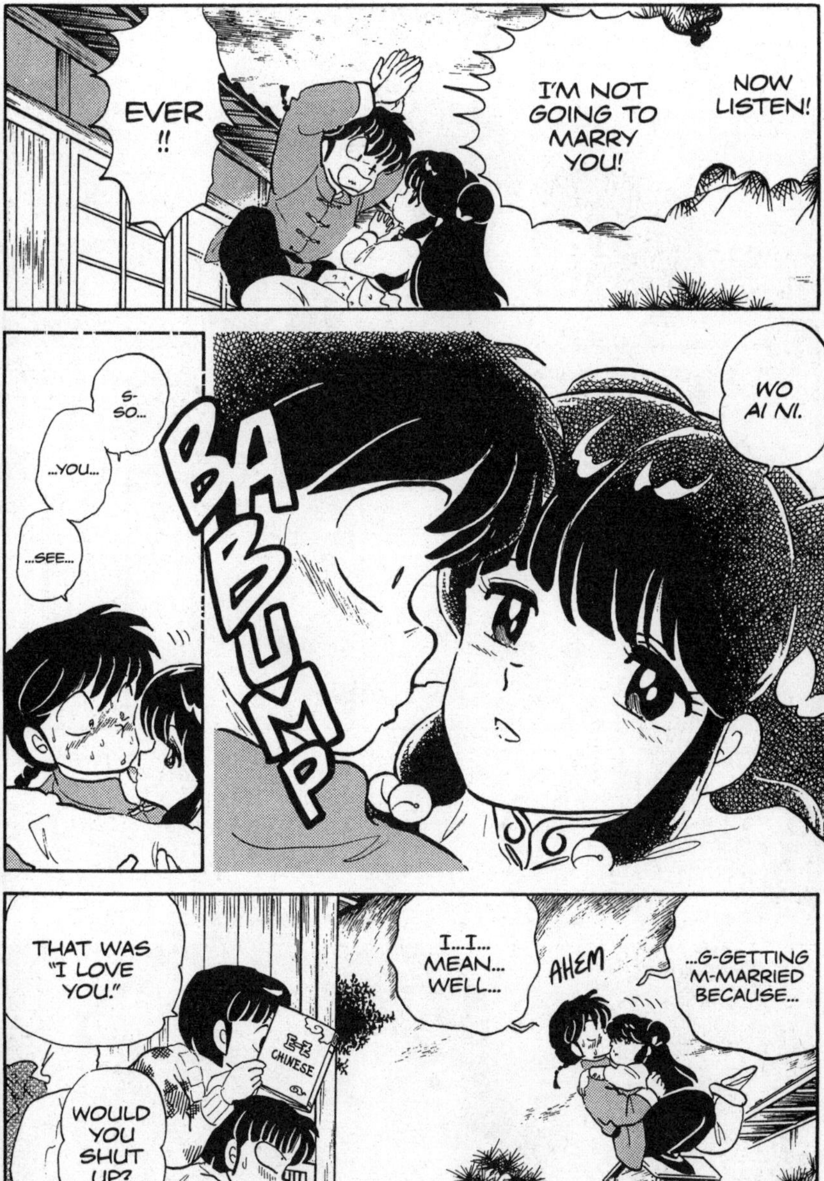
NOW LISTEN!
I'M NOT GOING TO MARRY YOU!
EVER!!
WO AI NI.
BABUMP
S-SO...
...YOU...
...SEE...
...G-GETTING M-MARRIED BECAUSE...
AHEM
I...I... MEAN... WELL...
THAT WAS "I LOVE YOU."
CHINESE
WOULD YOU SHUT UP?

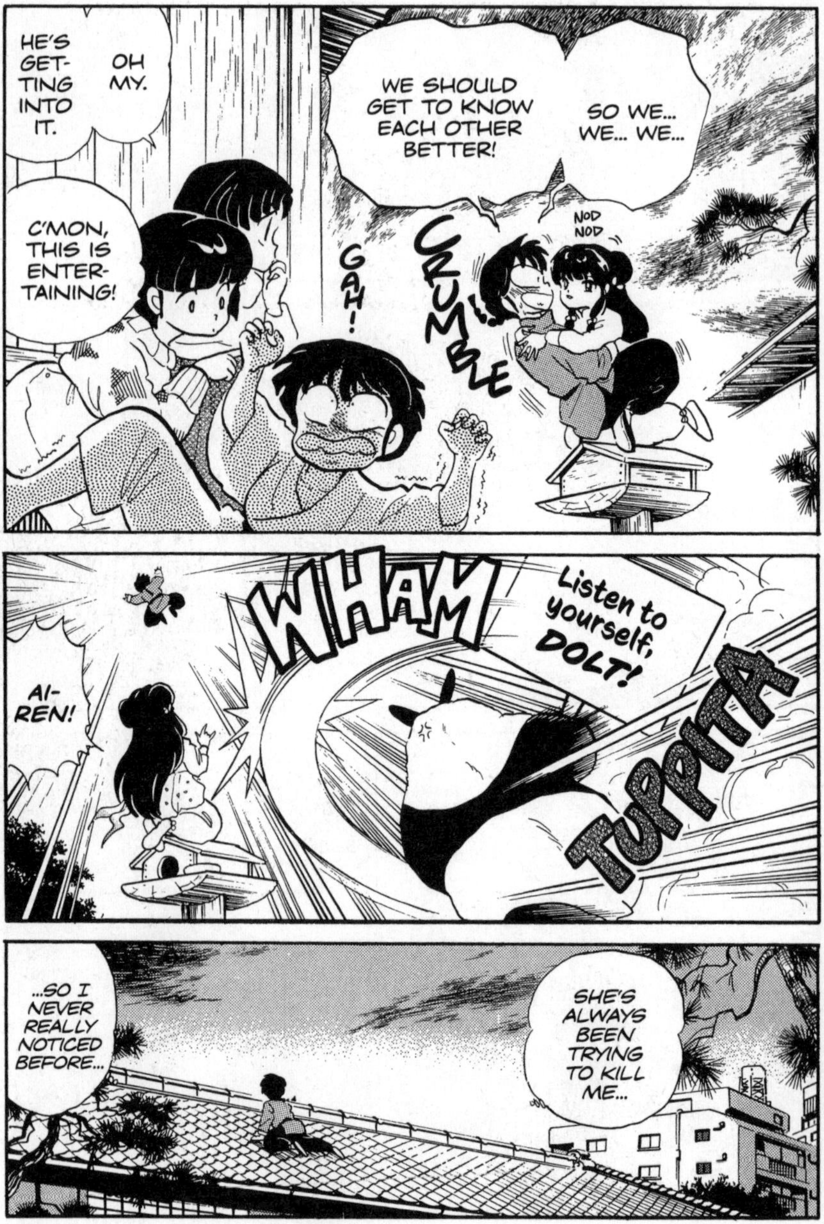
SO WE... WE... WE...
WE SHOULD GET TO KNOW EACH OTHER BETTER!
NOD NOD
CRUMBLE
GAH!
OH MY.
HE'S GETTING INTO IT.
C'MON, THIS IS ENTERTAINING!
Listen to yourself, DOLT!
TUPPITA
WHAM
AI-REN!
SHE'S ALWAYS BEEN TRYING TO KILL ME...
...SO I NEVER REALLY NOTICED BEFORE...

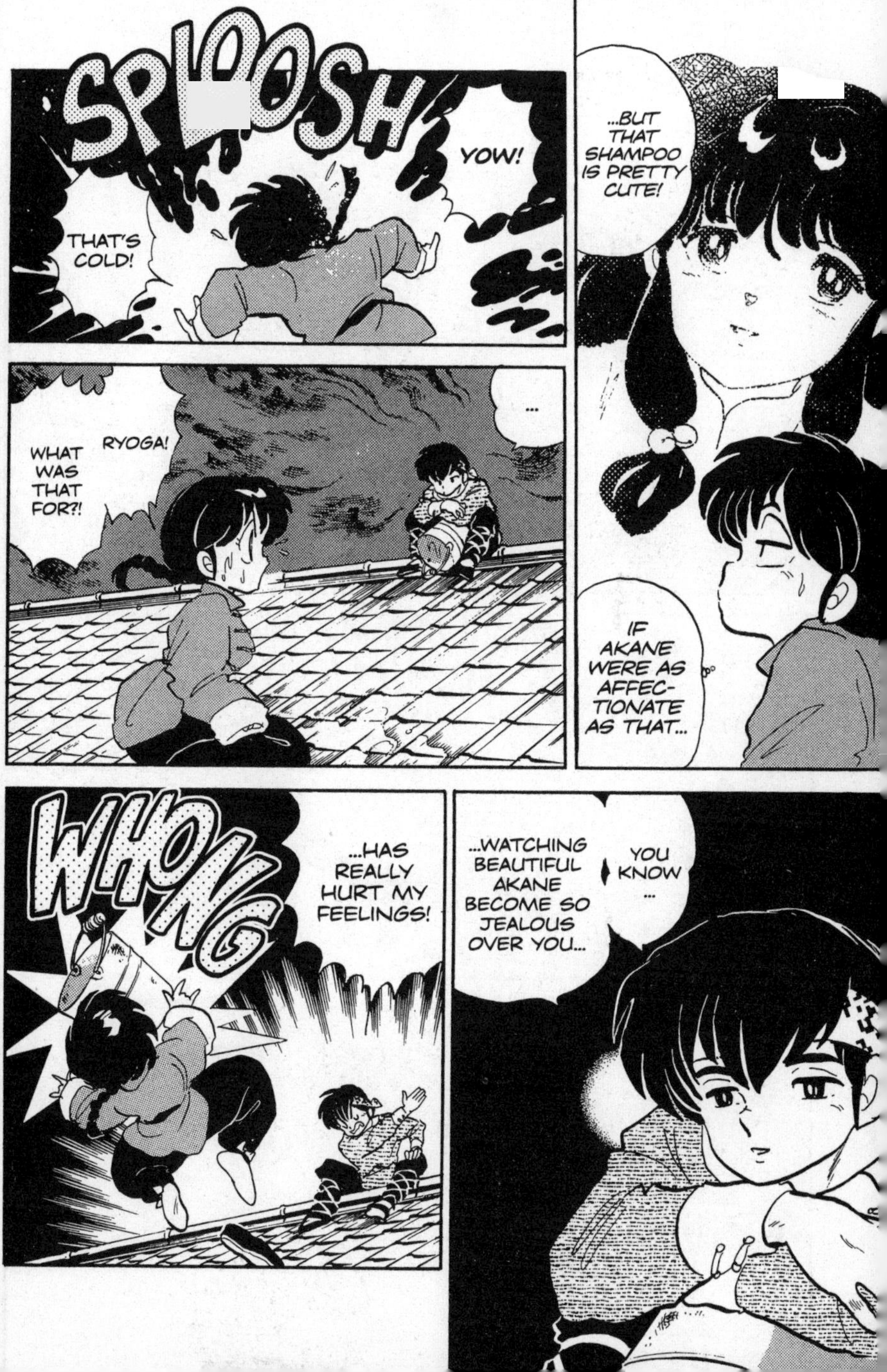
...BUT THAT SHAMPOO IS PRETTY CUTE!
IF AKANE WERE AS AFFEC- TIONATE AS THAT...
SPLOOSH
YOW!
THAT'S COLD!
...
RYOGA!
WHAT WAS THAT FOR?!
YOU KNOW ...
...WATCHING BEAUTIFUL AKANE BECOME SO JEALOUS OVER YOU...
...HAS REALLY HURT MY FEELINGS!
WHONG

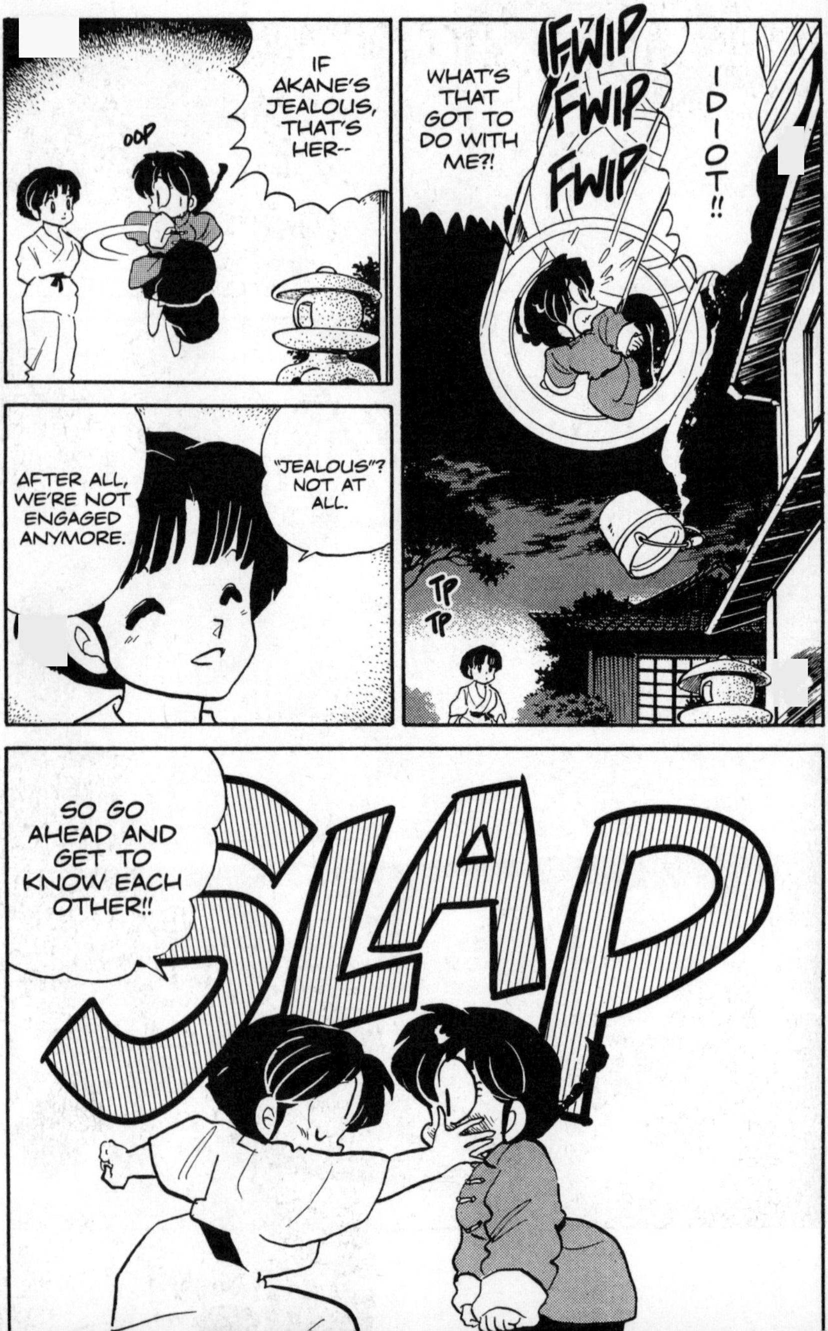
FWIP FWIP FWIP
WHAT'S THAT GOT TO DO WITH ME?!
IDIOT!!
TP TP
IF AKANE'S JEALOUS, THAT'S HER--
OOP
"JEALOUS"? NOT AT ALL.
AFTER ALL, WE'RE NOT ENGAGED ANYMORE.
SO GO AHEAD AND GET TO KNOW EACH OTHER!!
SLAP

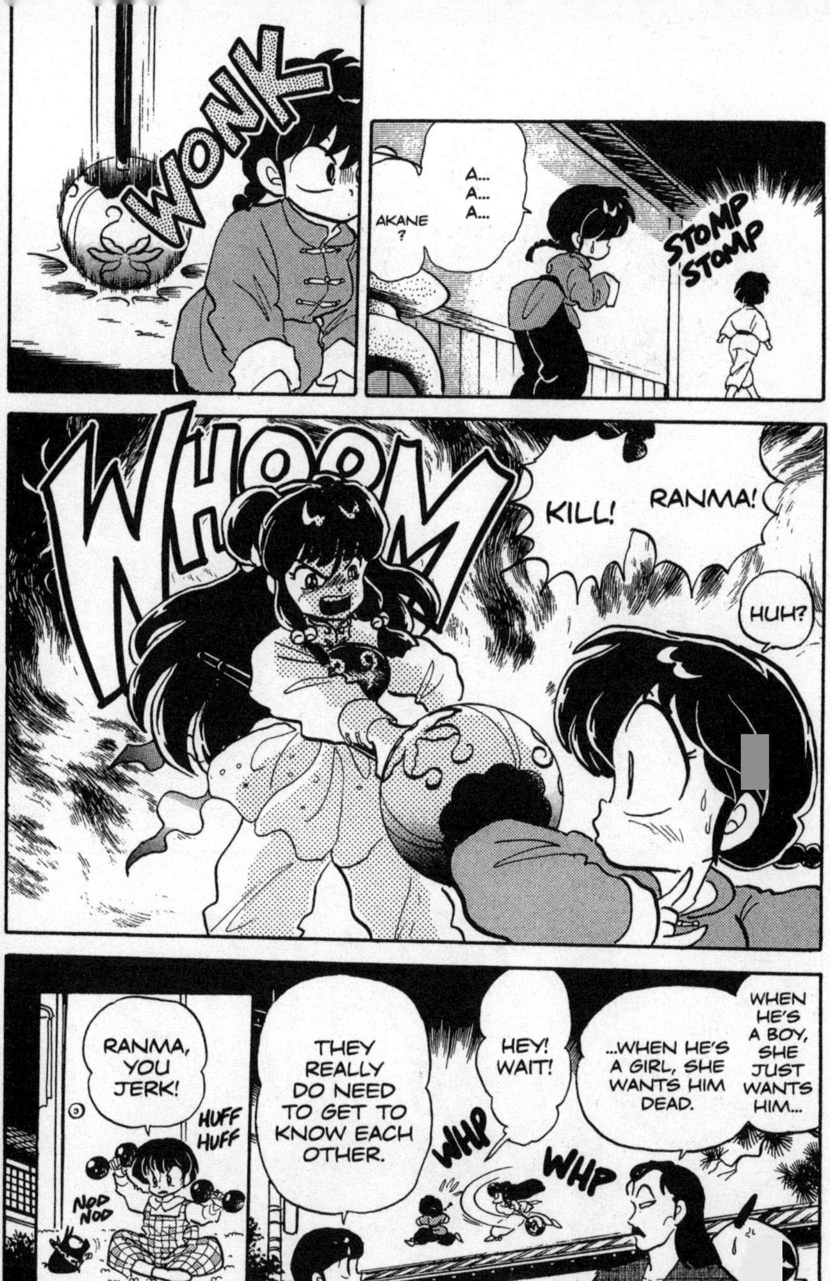
STOMP STOMP
A... A... A...
AKANE ?
WONK
RANMA!
KILL!
HUH?
WHOOM
WHEN HE'S A BOY, SHE JUST WANTS HIM...
...WHEN HE'S A GIRL, SHE WANTS HIM DEAD.
HEY! WAIT!
WHP
WHP
THEY REALLY DO NEED TO GET TO KNOW EACH OTHER.
RANMA, YOU JERK!
HUFF HUFF
NOD NOD

PART 16
AKANE GETS SHAMPOOED

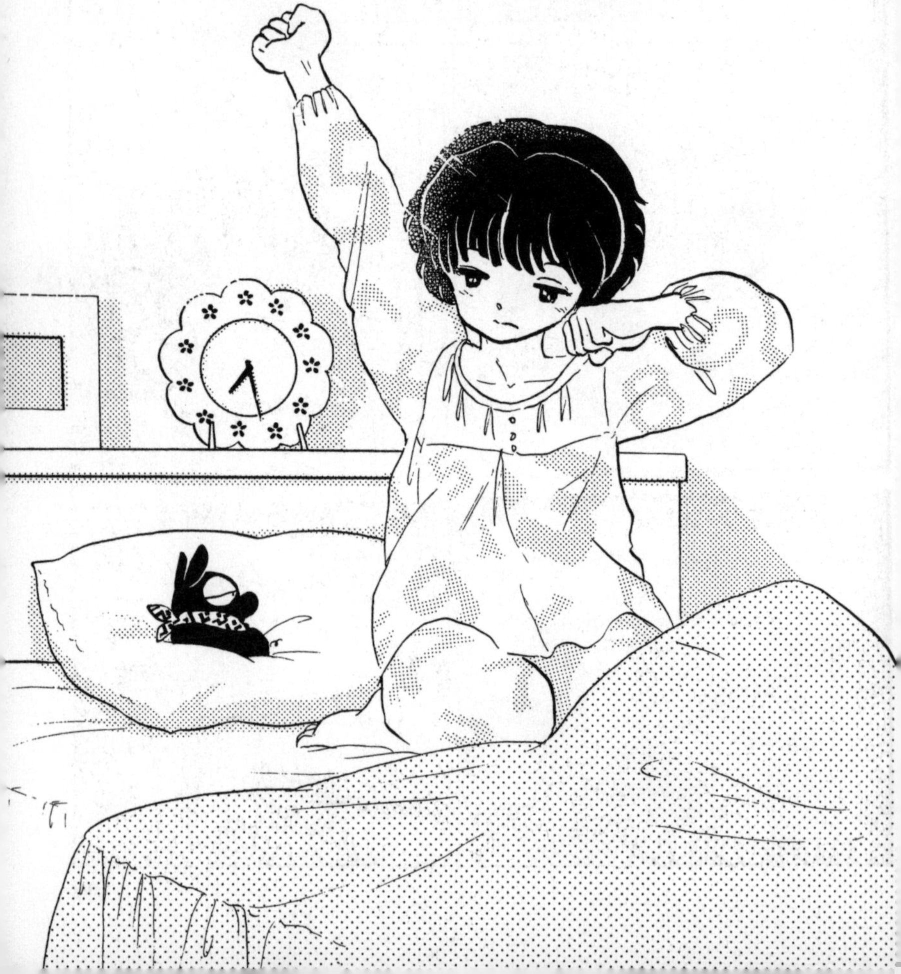

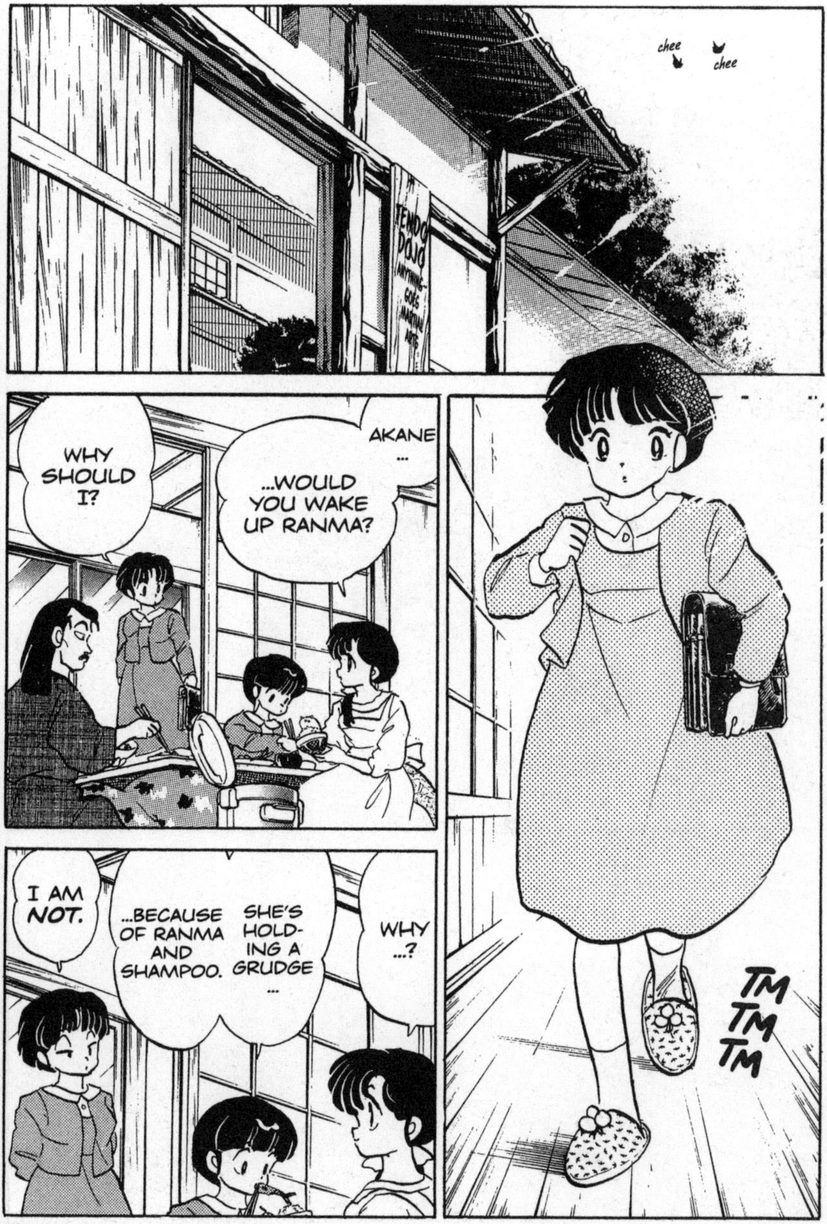
chee
chee
TENDO DOJO ANYTHING-GOES MARTIAL ARTS
TM TM TM
AKANE ...
...WOULD YOU WAKE UP RANMA?
WHY SHOULD I?
WHY ...?
SHE'S HOLDING A GRUDGE ...
...BECAUSE OF RANMA AND SHAMPOO.
I AM **NOT**.

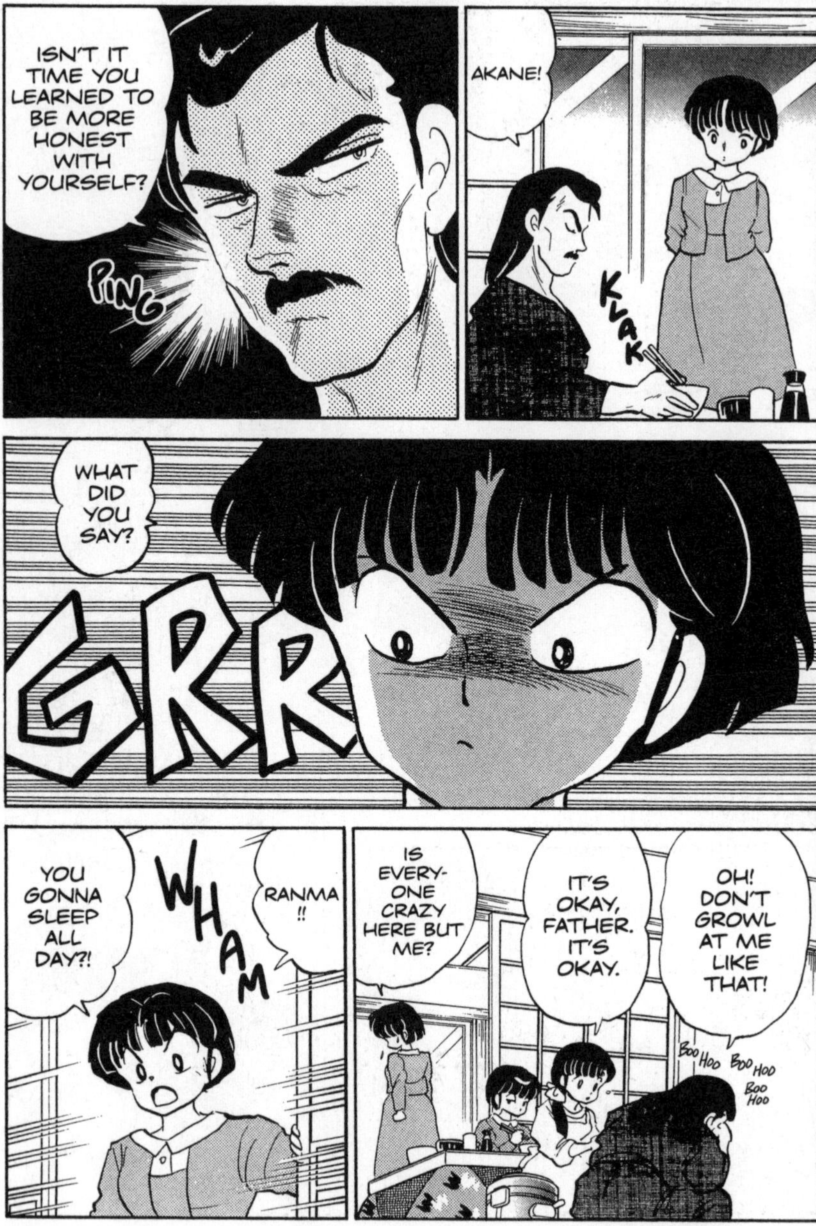
AKANE!
KVAK
ISN'T IT TIME YOU LEARNED TO BE MORE HONEST WITH YOURSELF?
PING
WHAT DID YOU SAY?
GRR
OH! DON'T GROWL AT ME LIKE THAT!
IT'S OKAY, FATHER. IT'S OKAY.
IS EVERY-ONE CRAZY HERE BUT ME?
BOO HOO BOO HOO BOO HOO
RANMA !!
WHAM
YOU GONNA SLEEP ALL DAY?!

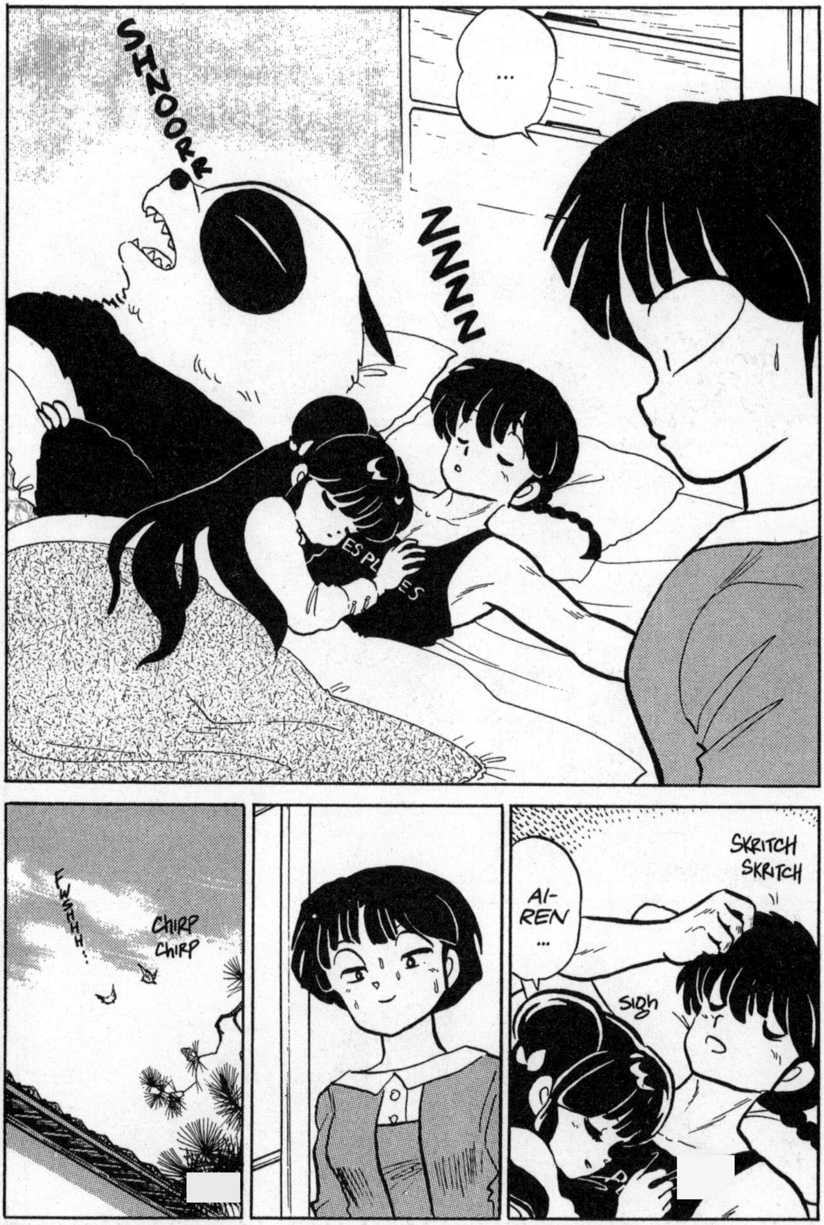
...
ZZZZ
SHNOORRR
SKRITCH SKRITCH
AI-REN ...
Sigh
CHIRP CHIRP
FWSHH...

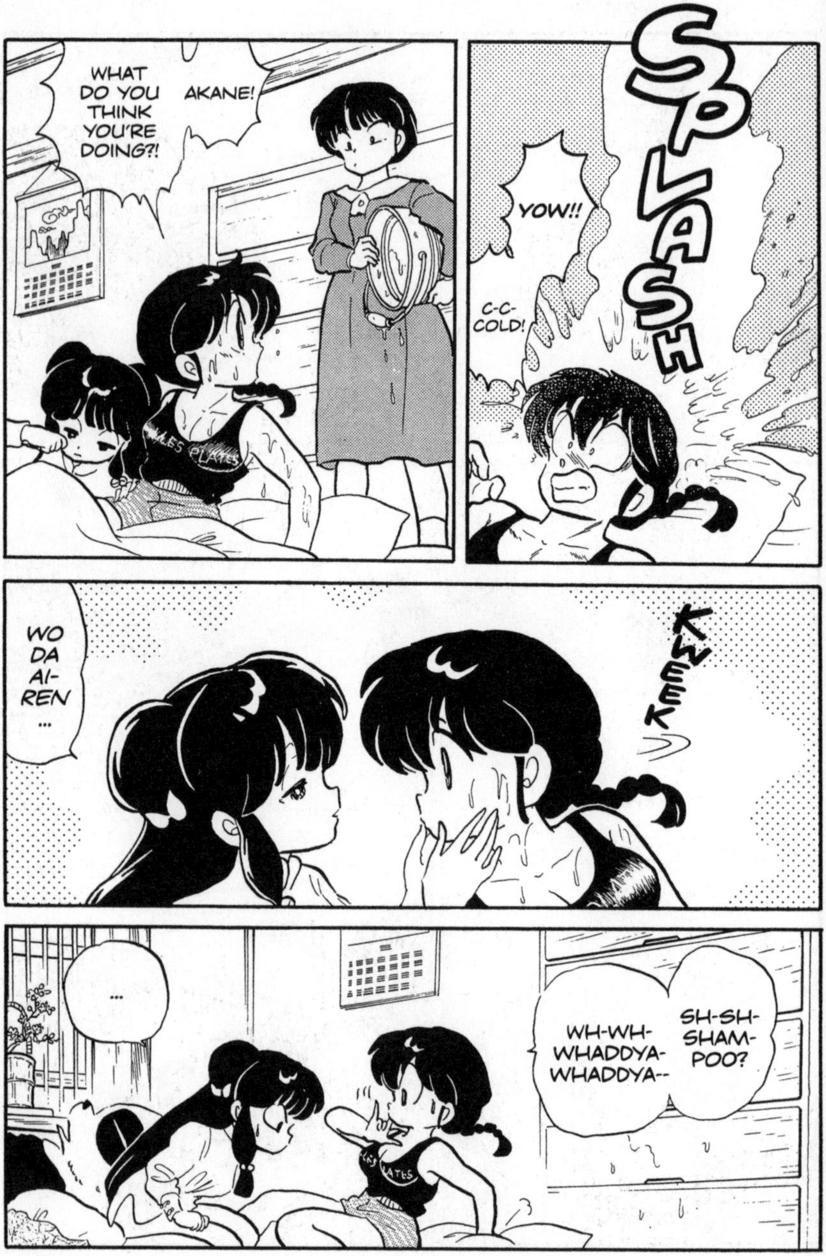
SPLASH
YOW!!
C-C-COLD!
AKANE!
WHAT DO YOU THINK YOU'RE DOING?!
KWEEK
WO DA AI-REN ...
SH-SH-SHAM-POO?
WH-WH-WHADDYA-WHADDYA--
...

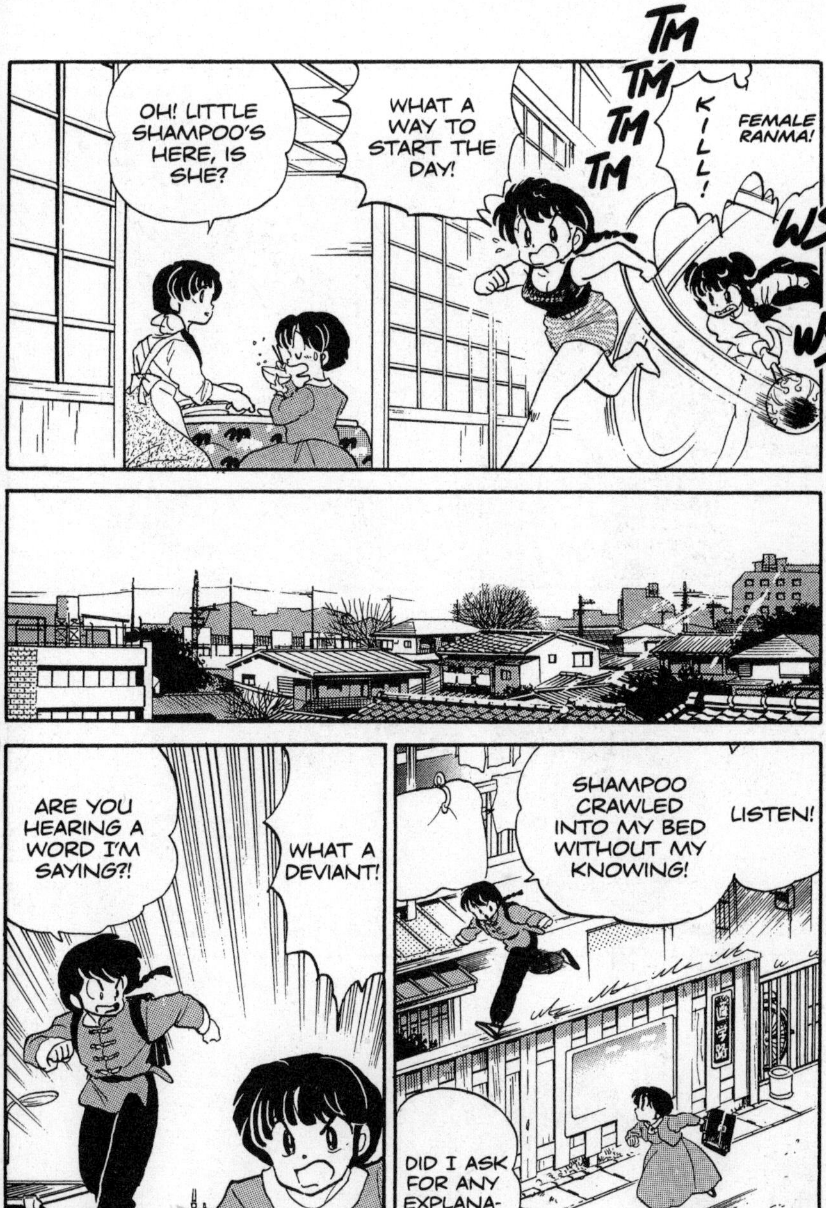
TM TM TM TM
FEMALE RANMA!
KILL!
WSH WSH
WHAT A WAY TO START THE DAY!
OH! LITTLE SHAMPOO'S HERE, IS SHE?
LISTEN!
SHAMPOO CRAWLED INTO MY BED WITHOUT MY KNOWING!
DID I ASK FOR ANY EXPLANATIONS?
WHAT A DEVIANT!
ARE YOU HEARING A WORD I'M SAYING?!

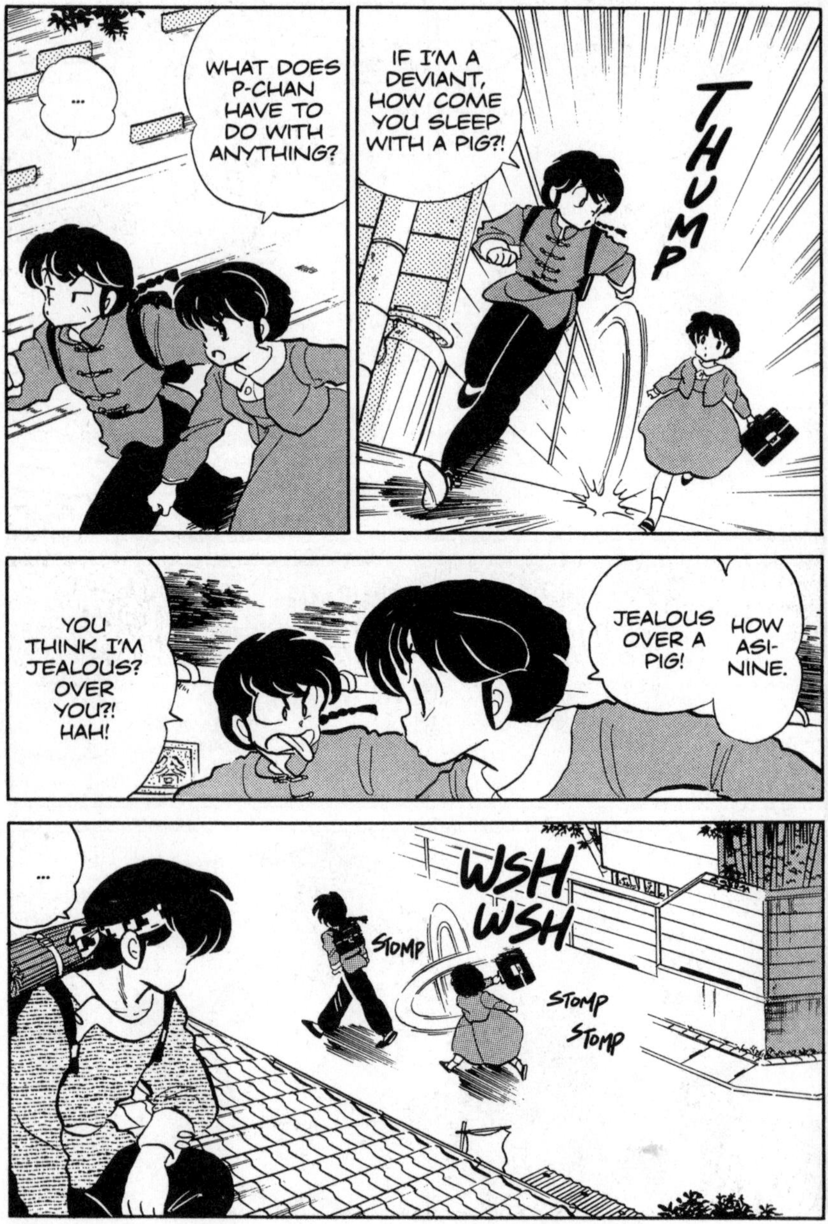
IF I'M A DEVIANT, HOW COME YOU SLEEP WITH A PIG?!
THUMP
WHAT DOES P-CHAN HAVE TO DO WITH ANYTHING?
...
JEALOUS OVER A PIG! HOW ASI-NINE.
YOU THINK I'M JEALOUS? OVER YOU?! HAH!
WSH WSH
STOMP
STOMP
STOMP
...

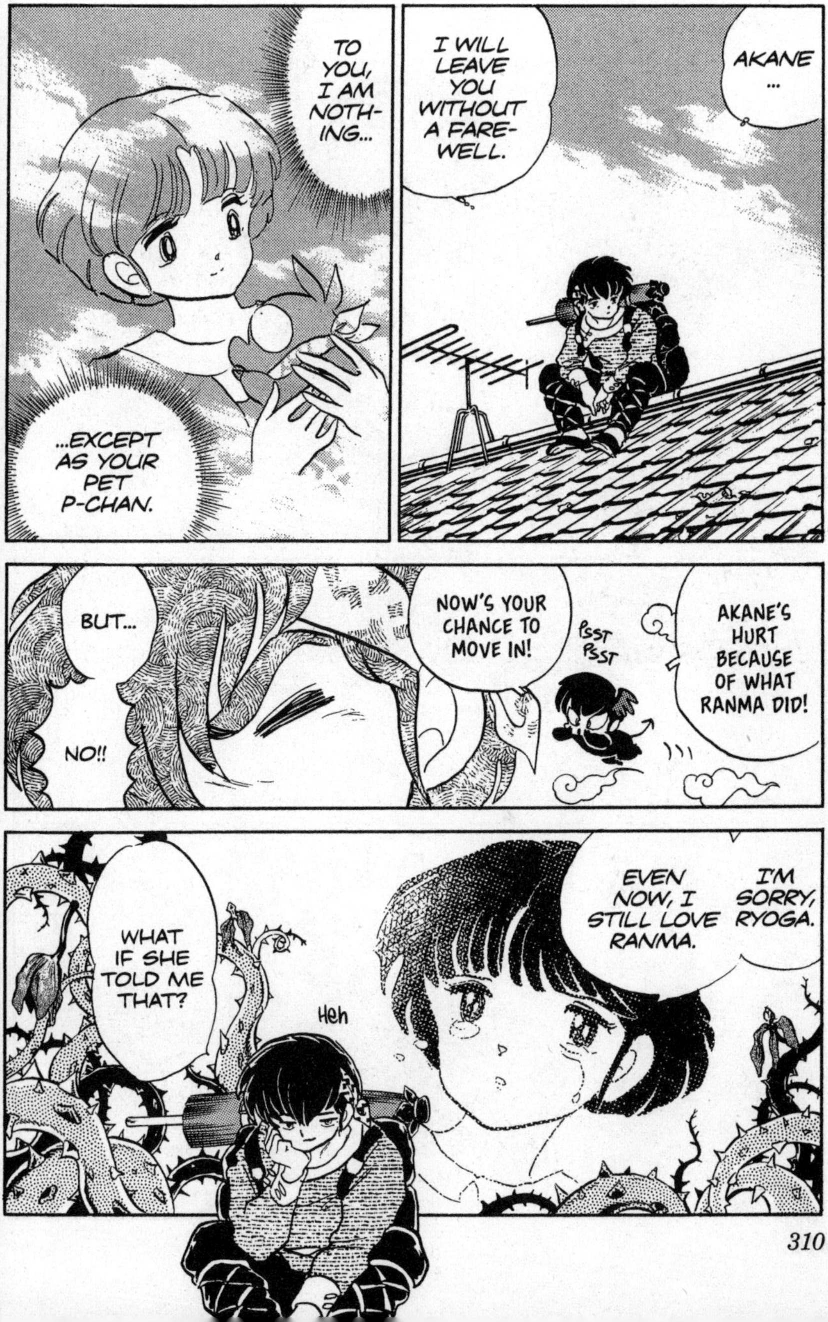
AKANE ...
I WILL LEAVE YOU WITHOUT A FARE-WELL.
TO YOU, I AM NOTH-ING...
...EXCEPT AS YOUR PET P-CHAN.
AKANE'S HURT BECAUSE OF WHAT RANMA DID!
PSST PSST
NOW'S YOUR CHANCE TO MOVE IN!
BUT...
NO!!
I'M SORRY, RYOGA.
EVEN NOW, I STILL LOVE RANMA.
WHAT IF SHE TOLD ME THAT?
Heh

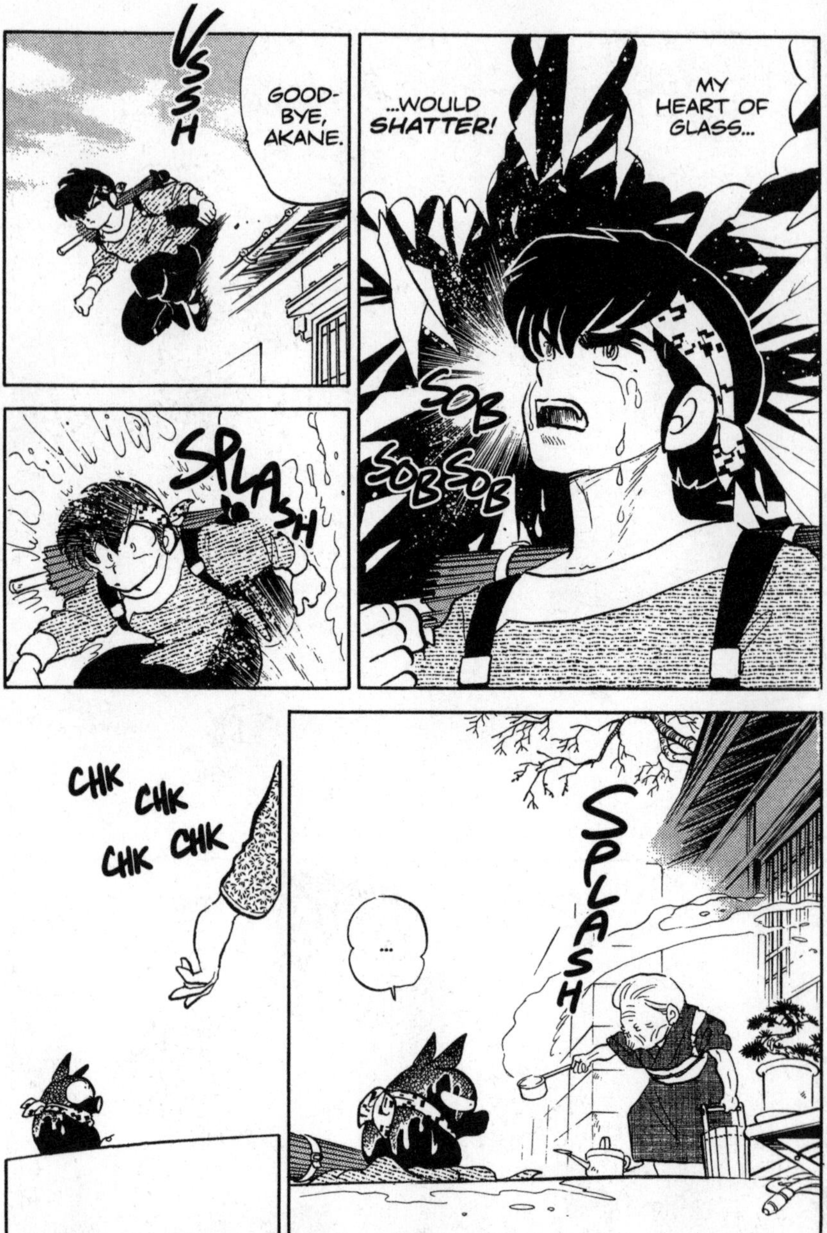
MY HEART OF GLASS...
...WOULD SHATTER!
SOB
SOB SOB
VSSH
GOOD-BYE, AKANE.
SPLASH
SPLASH
...
CHK CHK CHK CHK

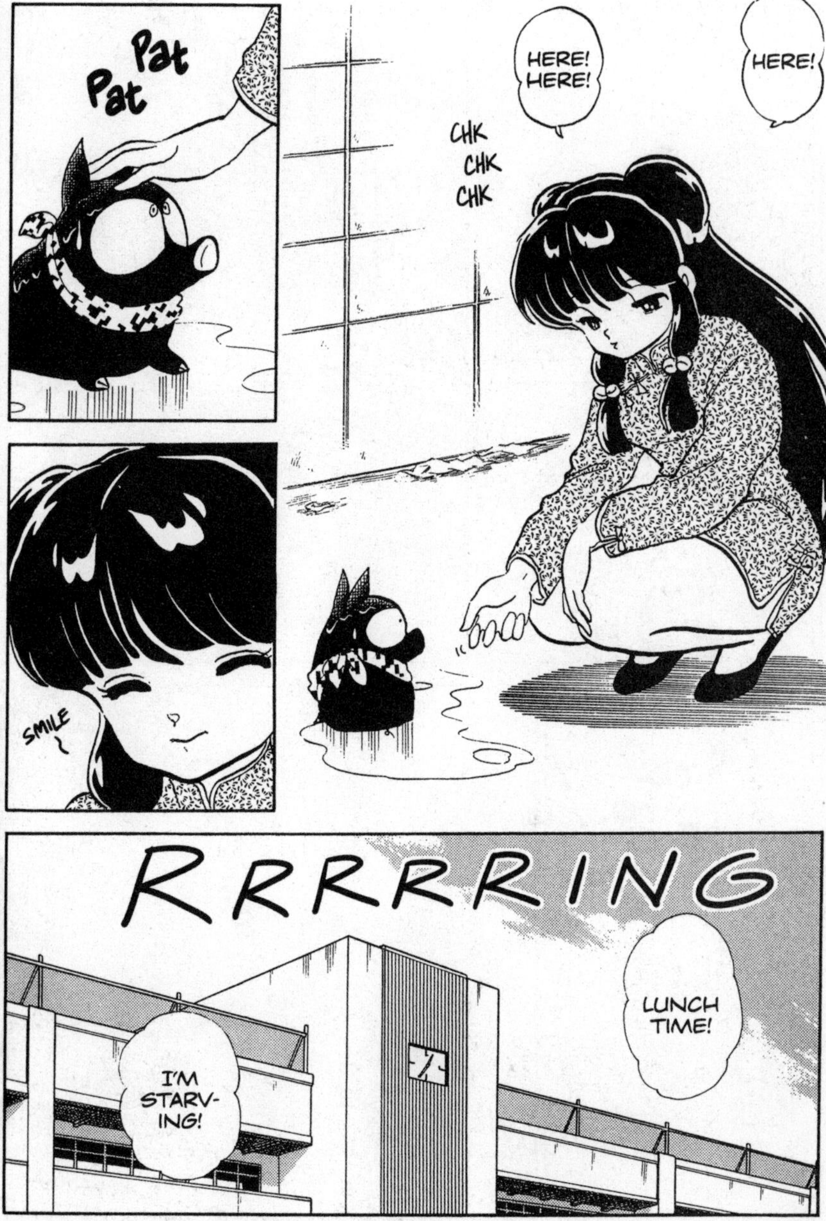
HERE!
HERE! HERE!
CHK CHK CHK
Pat Pat
SMILE
RRRRRING
LUNCH TIME!
I'M STARV-ING!

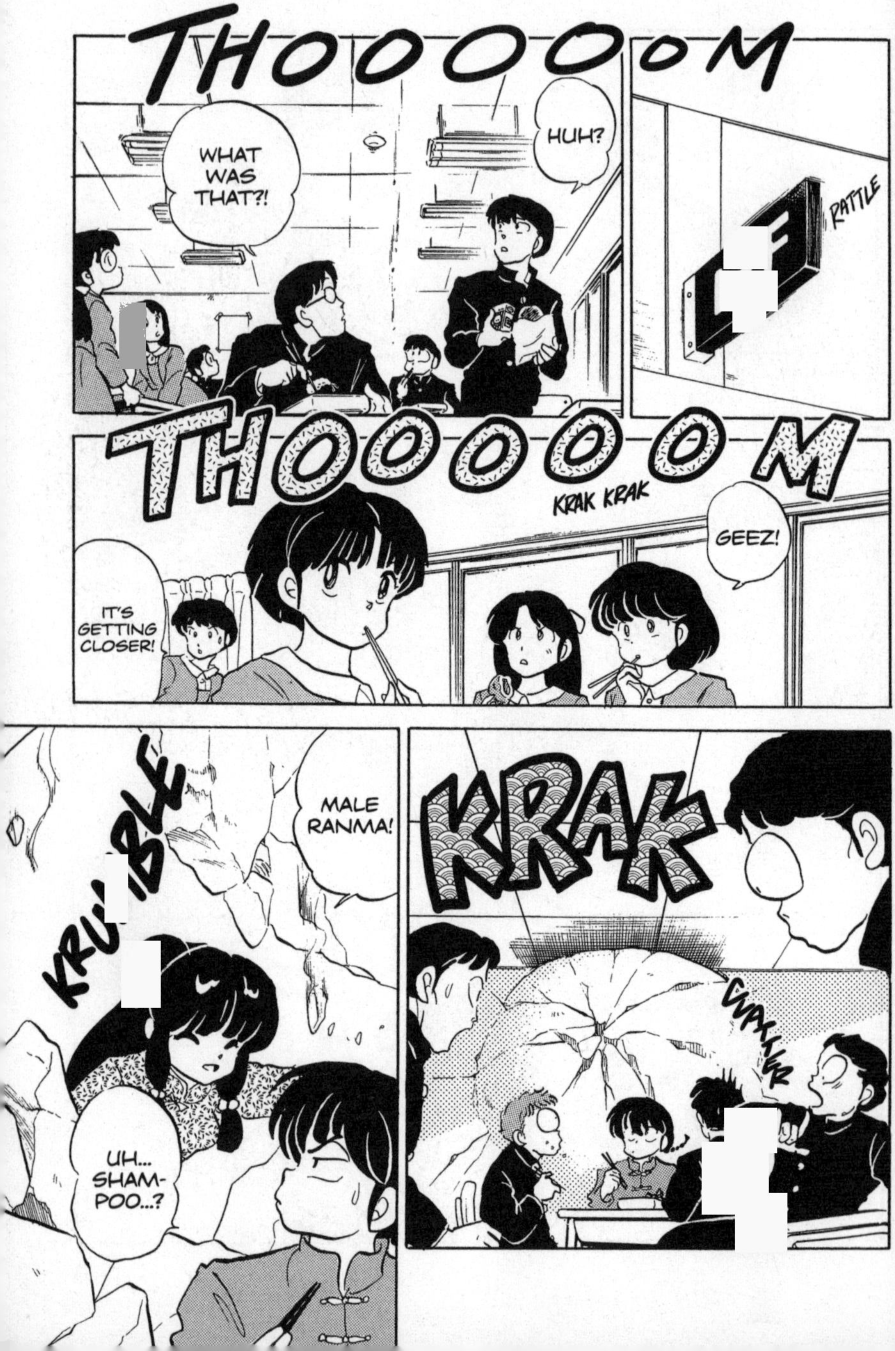
THOOOOoM
RATTLE
HUH?
WHAT WAS THAT?!
THOOOOOM
KRAK KRAK
GEEZ!
IT'S GETTING CLOSER!
KRAK
MALE RANMA!
UH... SHAM-POO...?

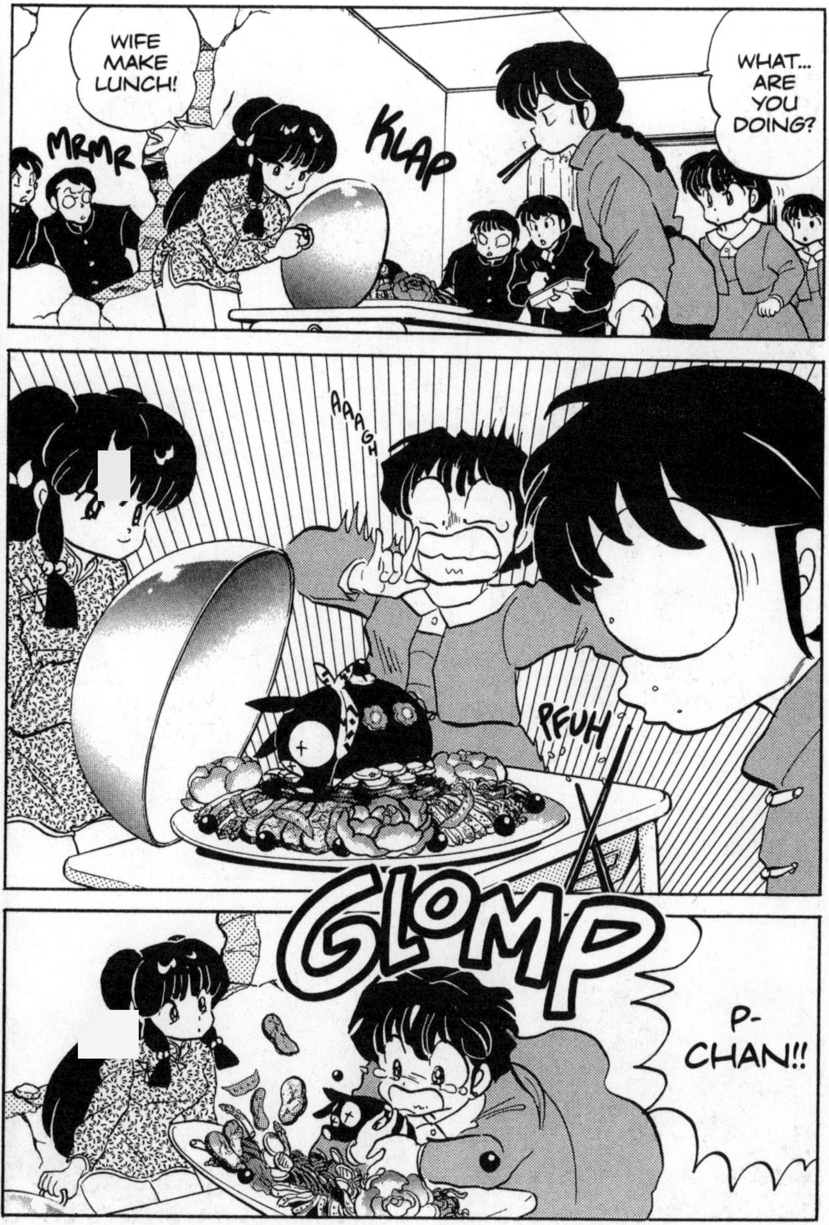
WHAT... ARE YOU DOING?
KLAP
WIFE MAKE LUNCH!
MRMR
PFUH
AAAGH
P-CHAN!!
GLOMP

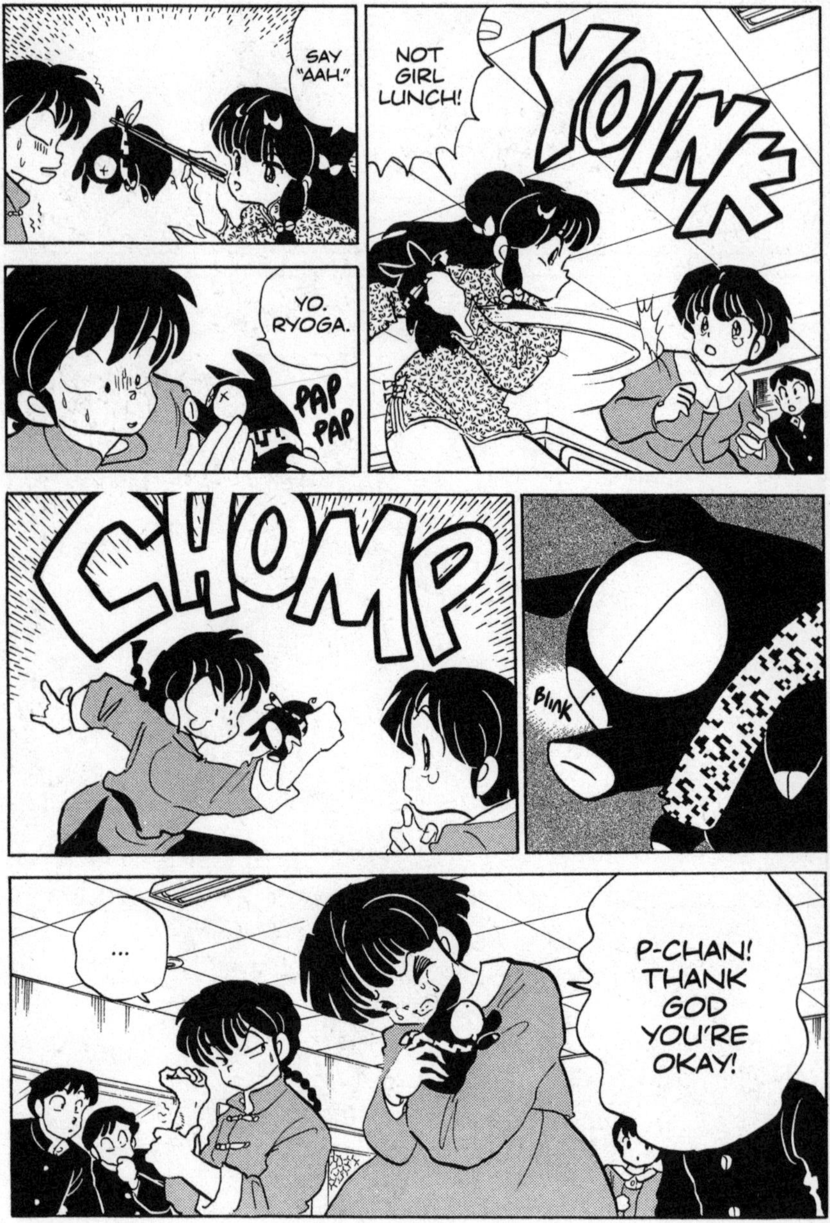
NOT GIRL LUNCH!
YOINK
SAY "AAH."
YO. RYOGA.
PAP PAP
BLINK
CHOMP
P-CHAN! THANK GOD YOU'RE OKAY!
...

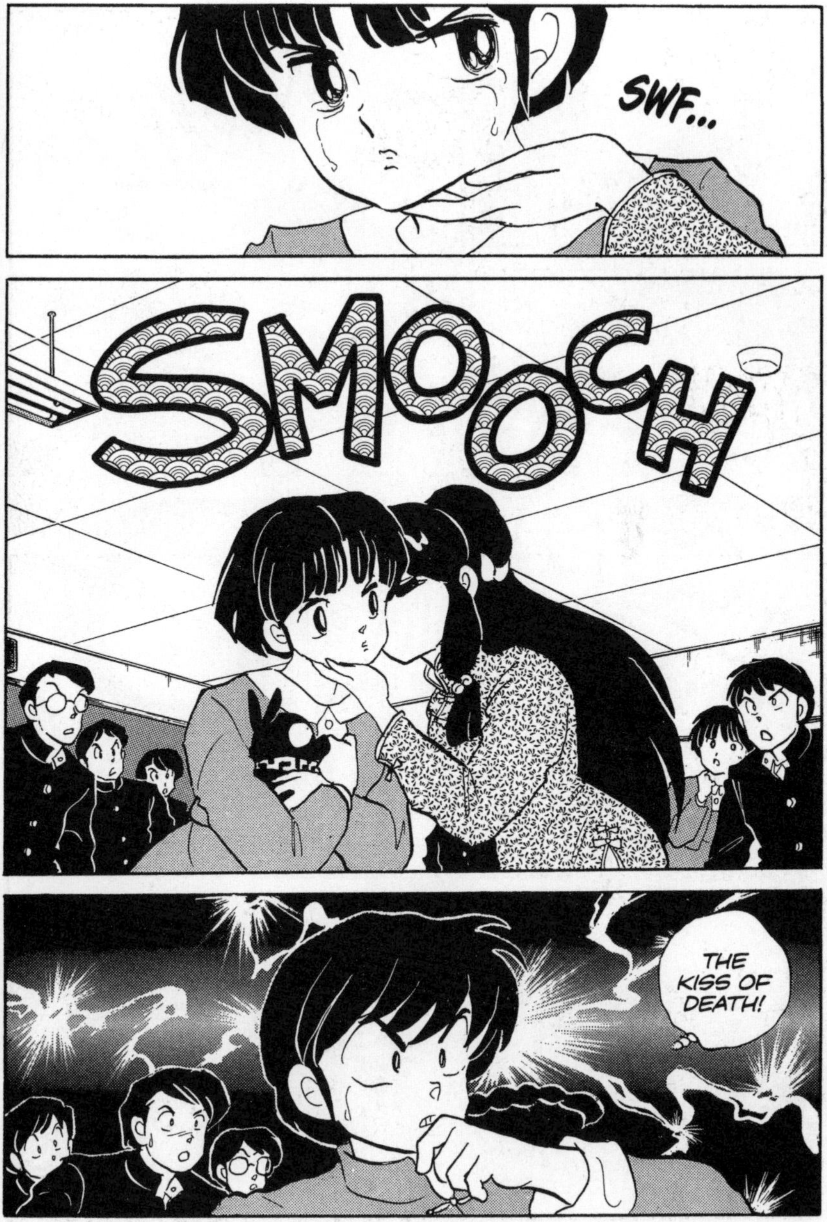
SWF...
SMOOCH
THE KISS OF DEATH!

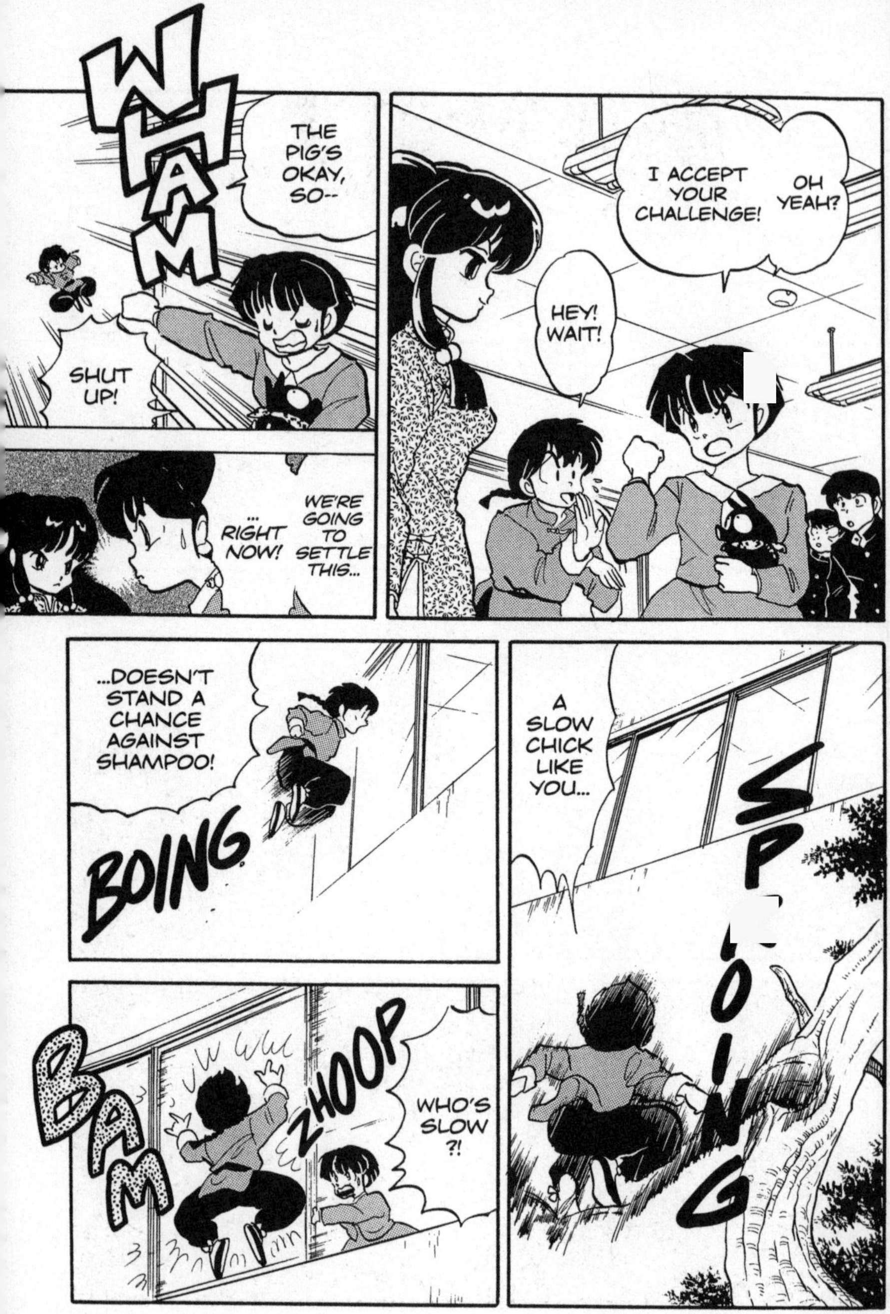
OH YEAH?
I ACCEPT YOUR CHALLENGE!
HEY! WAIT!
WHAM
THE PIG'S OKAY, SO--
SHUT UP!
WE'RE GOING TO SETTLE THIS...
... RIGHT NOW!
A SLOW CHICK LIKE YOU...
...DOESN'T STAND A CHANCE AGAINST SHAMPOO!
BOING
WHO'S SLOW ?!
ZHOOP
BAM

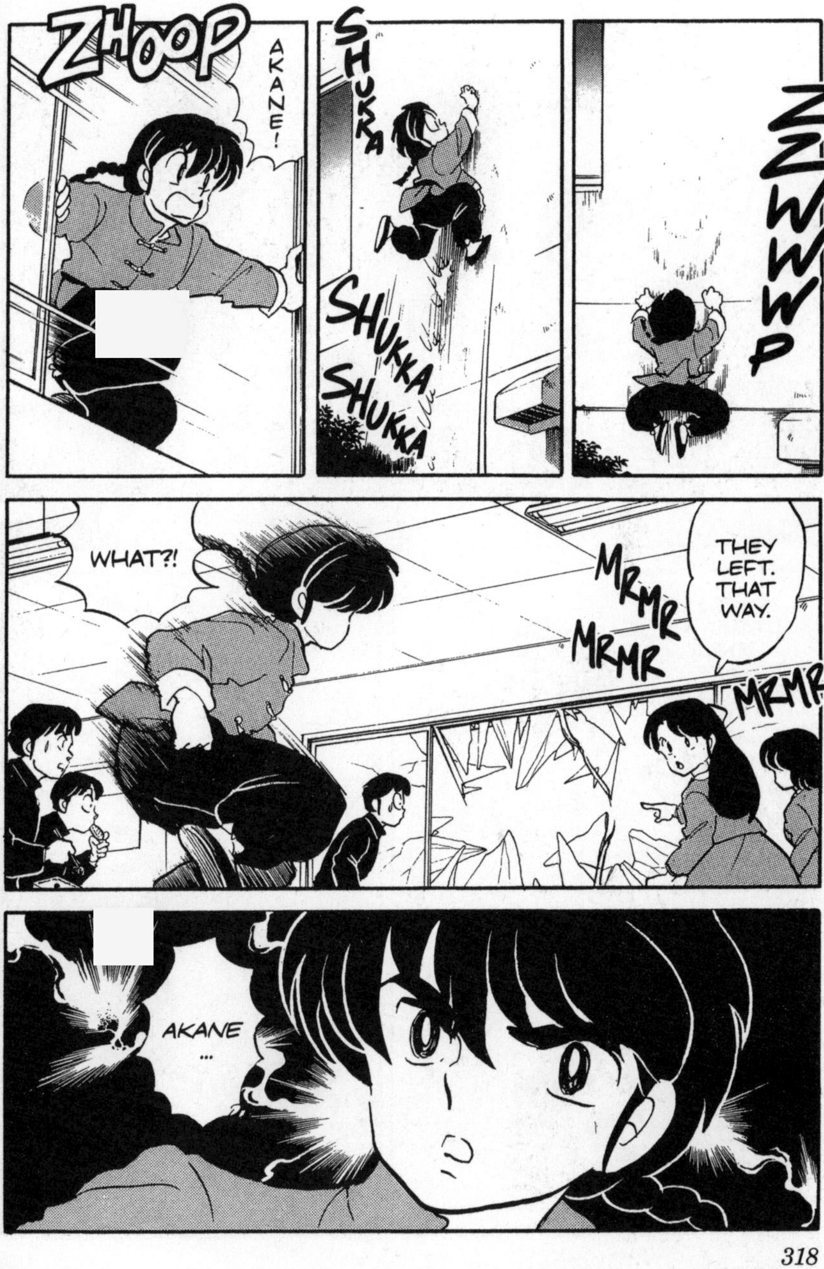
ZZWWWWP
SHUKKA
SHUKKA SHUKKA SHUKKA
ZHOOP
AKANE!
THEY LEFT. THAT WAY.
MRMR
MRMR MRMR
WHAT?!
AKANE ...

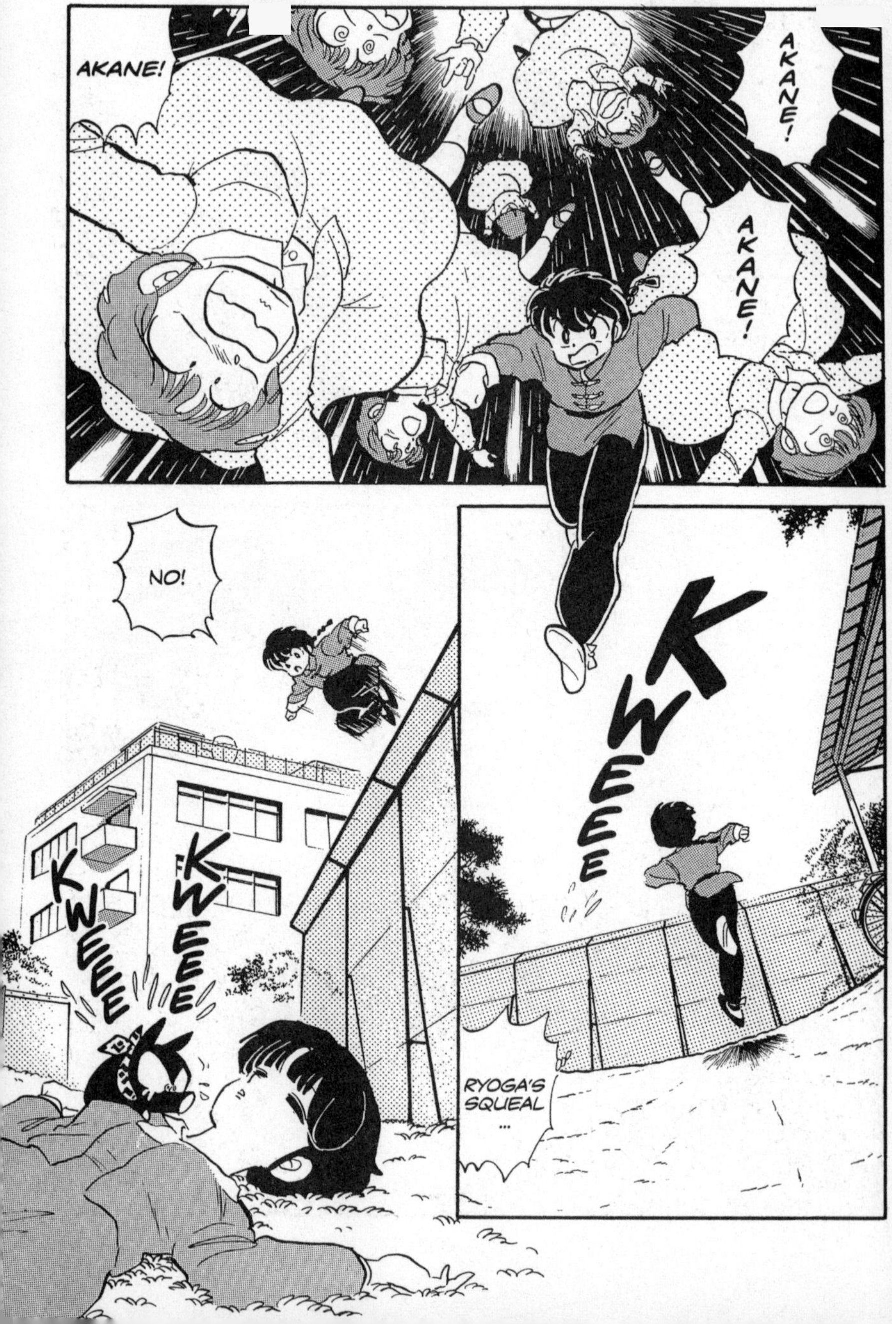
AKANE!
AKANE!
AKANE!
KWEEEE
RYOGA'S SQUEAL ...
NO!
KWEEEE
KWEEEE

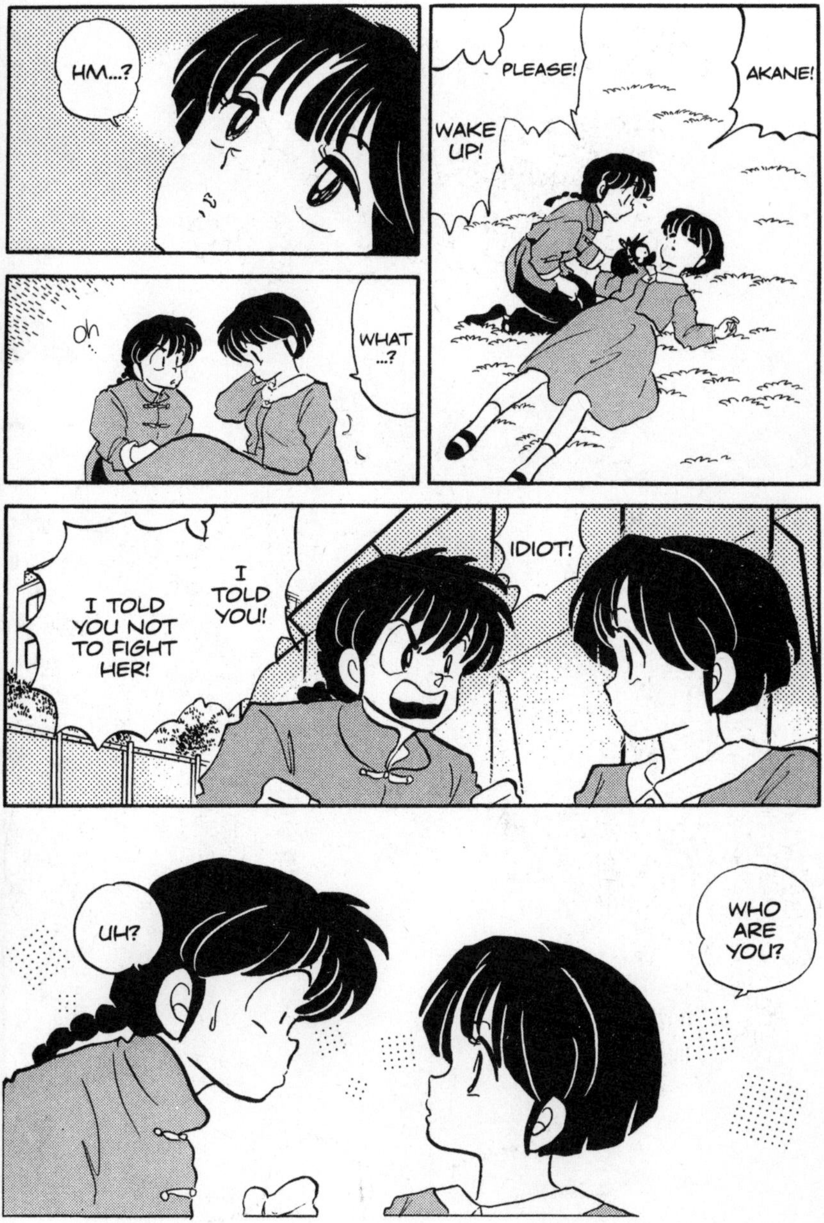
AKANE!
PLEASE!
WAKE UP!
HM...?
WHAT ...?
oh ...
IDIOT!
I TOLD YOU!
I TOLD YOU NOT TO FIGHT HER!
WHO ARE YOU?
UH?

PART 17
SHAMPOO CLEANS UP

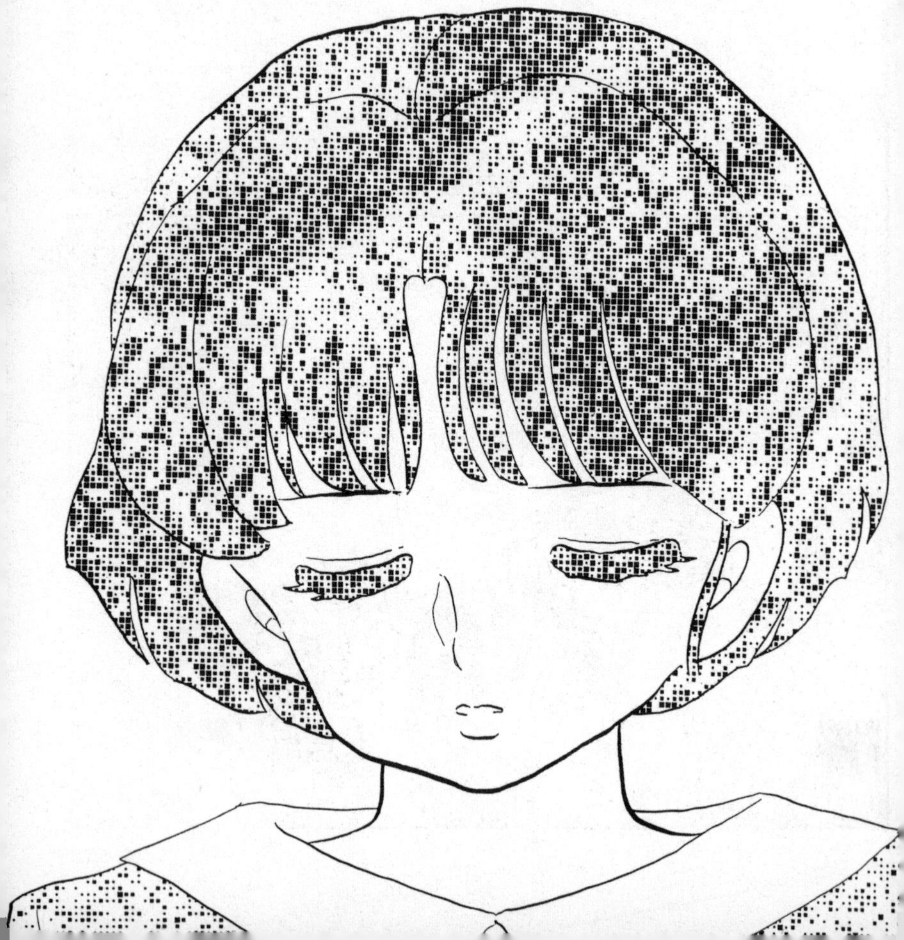

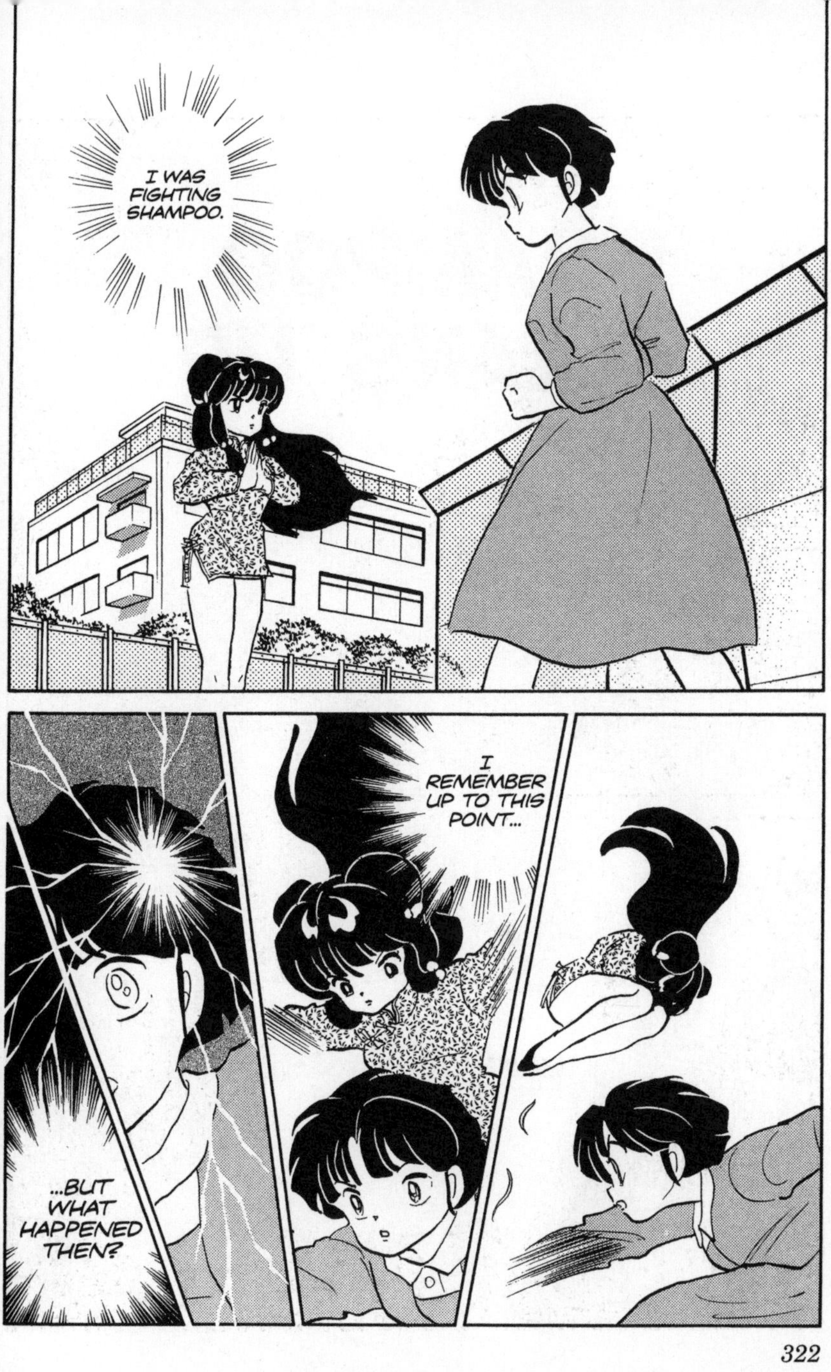
I WAS FIGHTING SHAMPOO.
I REMEMBER UP TO THIS POINT...
...BUT WHAT HAPPENED THEN?

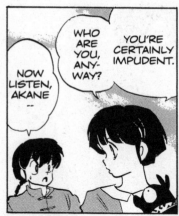

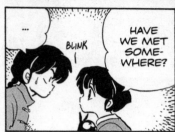

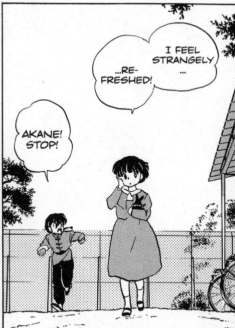

I FEEL STRANGELY ...
...RE-FRESHED!
AKANE! STOP!
YOU'RE CERTAINLY IMPUDENT.
WHO ARE YOU, ANY-WAY?
NOW LISTEN, AKANE --
HAVE WE MET SOME-WHERE?
BLINK
...
SHE MUST HAVE... AMNESIA!
HEY!
THERE THEY ARE!
AKANE!
OH!
HI, GUYS.

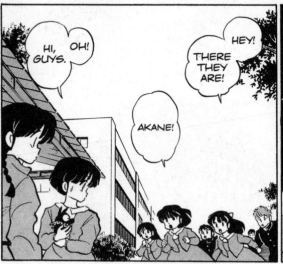

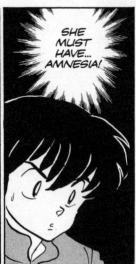

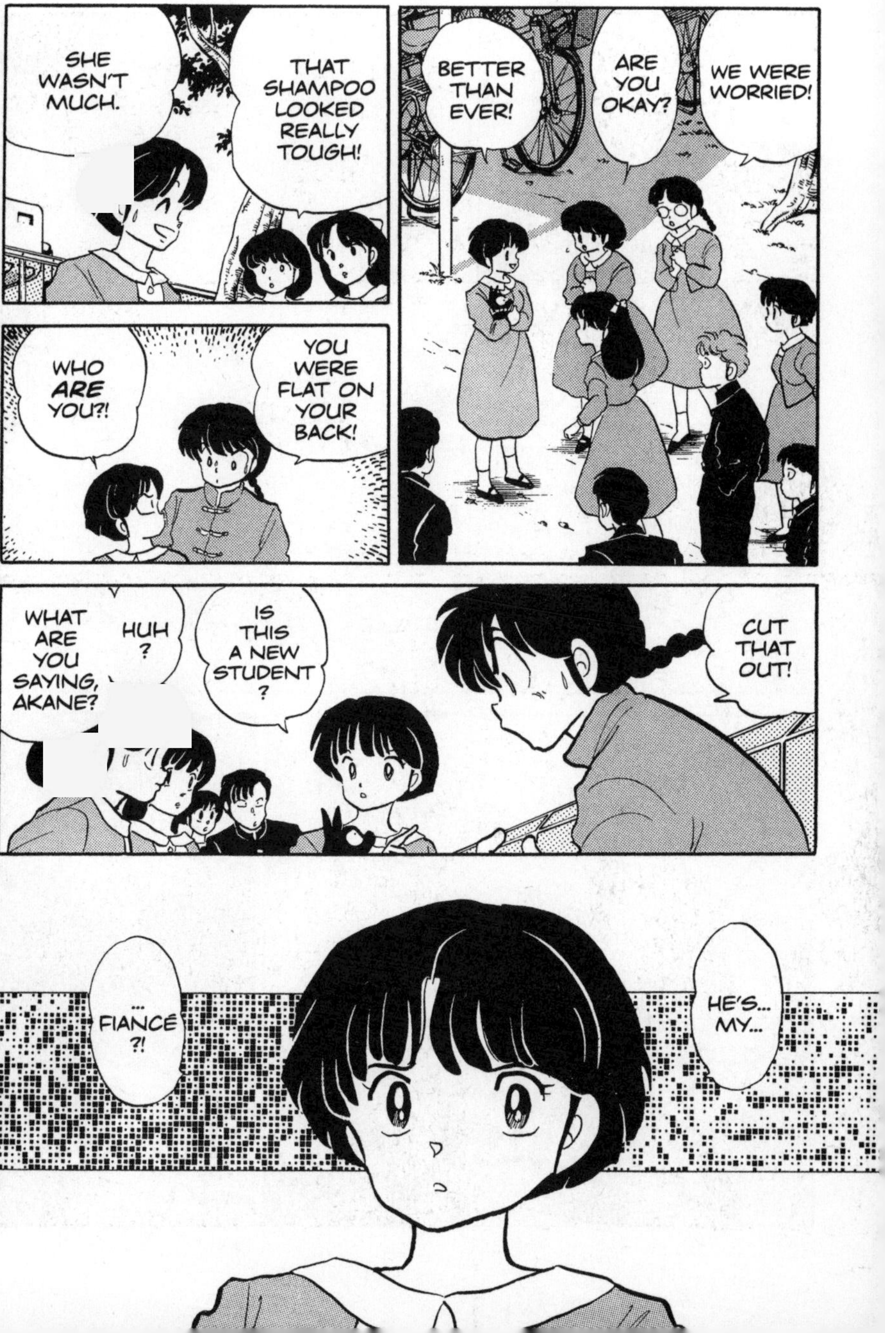
WE WERE WORRIED!
ARE YOU OKAY?
BETTER THAN EVER!
THAT SHAMPOO LOOKED REALLY TOUGH!
SHE WASN'T MUCH.
YOU WERE FLAT ON YOUR BACK!
WHO **ARE** YOU?!
CUT THAT OUT!
IS THIS A NEW STUDENT?
HUH?
WHAT ARE YOU SAYING, AKANE?
HE'S... MY...
...FIANCE?!

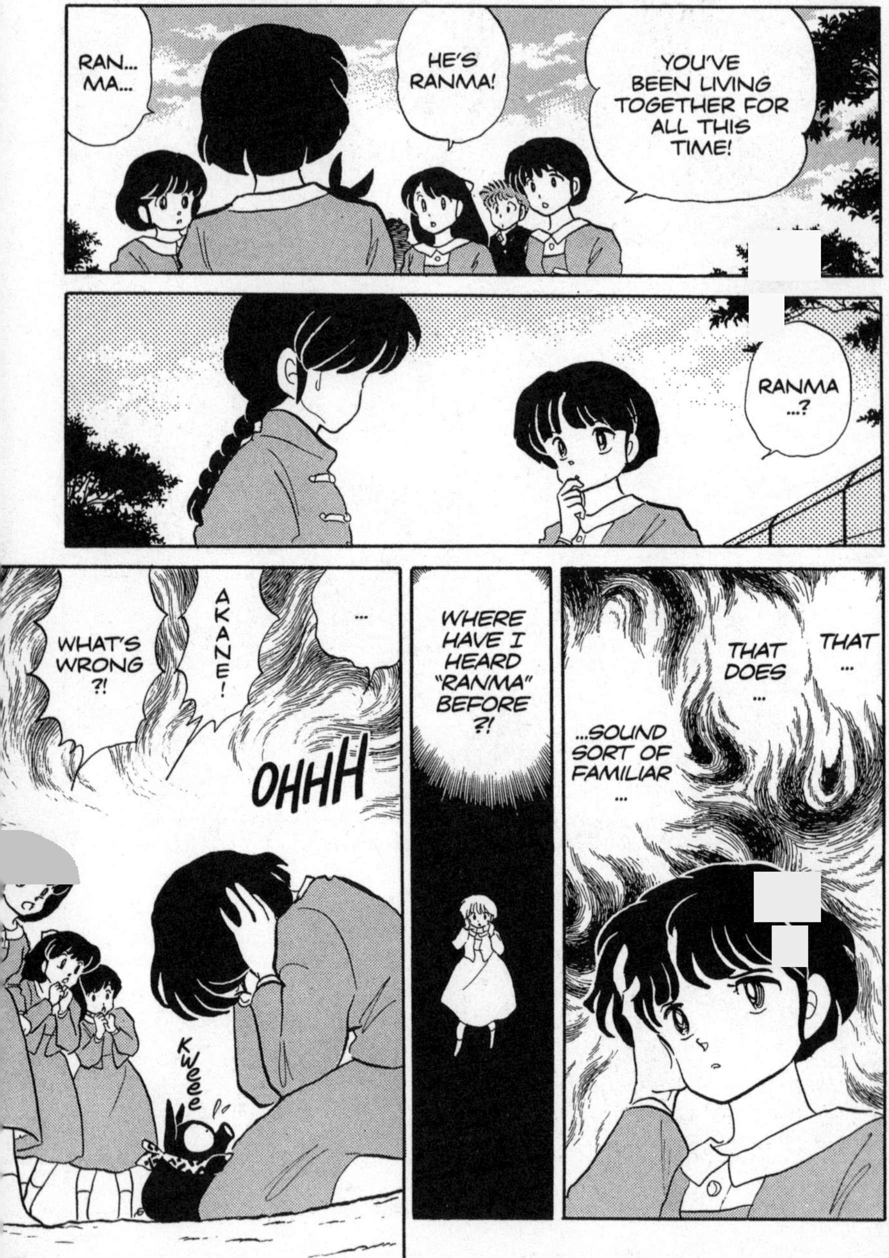
YOU'VE BEEN LIVING TOGETHER FOR ALL THIS TIME!
HE'S RANMA!
RAN... MA...
RANMA ...?
THAT ...
THAT DOES ...
...SOUND SORT OF FAMILIAR ...
WHERE HAVE I HEARD "RANMA" BEFORE ?!
...
AKANE!
WHAT'S WRONG ?!
OHHH
KWeee

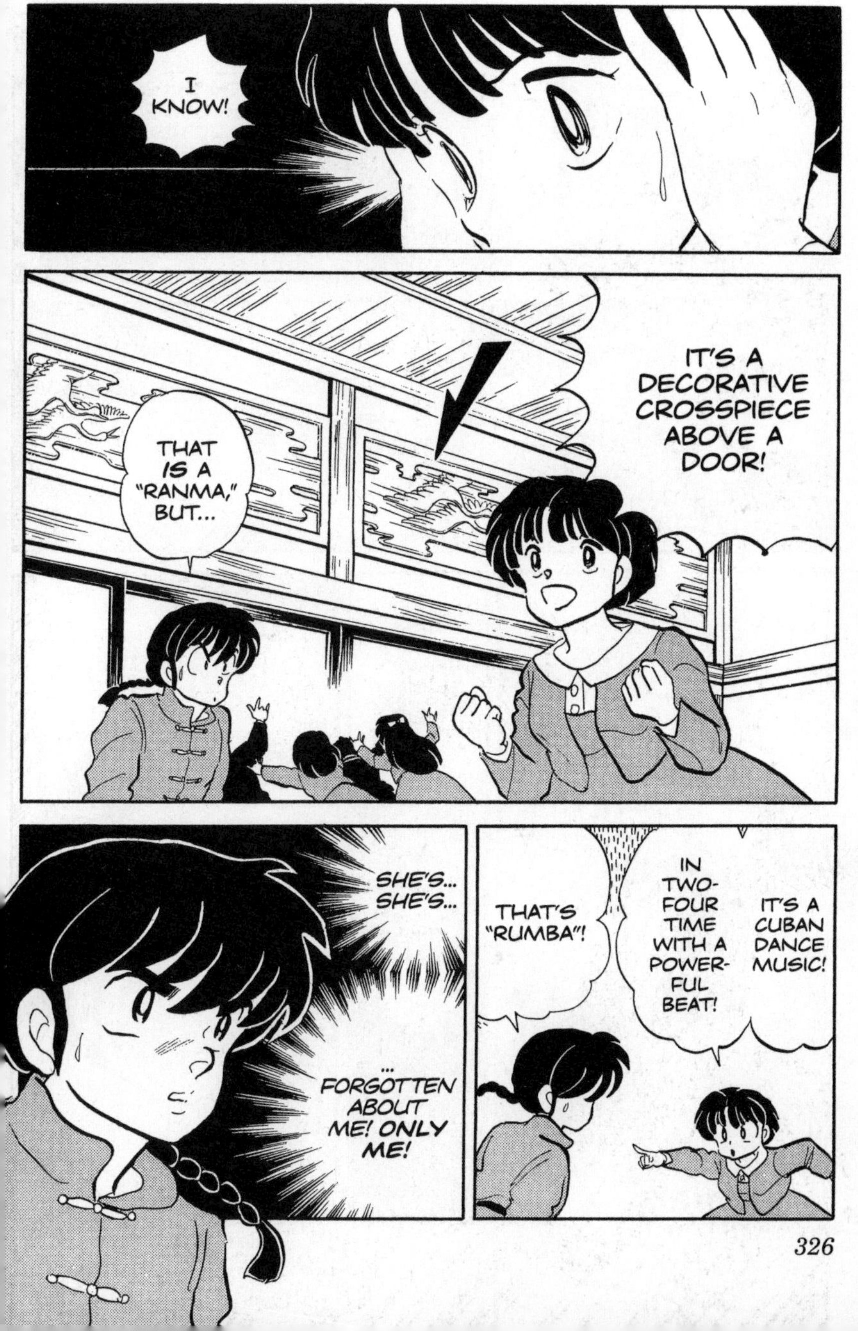
I KNOW!
IT'S A DECORATIVE CROSSPIECE ABOVE A DOOR!
THAT *IS* A "RANMA," BUT...
IT'S A CUBAN DANCE MUSIC!
IN TWO-FOUR TIME WITH A POWER-FUL BEAT!
THAT'S "RUMBA"!
SHE'S... SHE'S...
...FORGOTTEN ABOUT ME! ONLY ME!

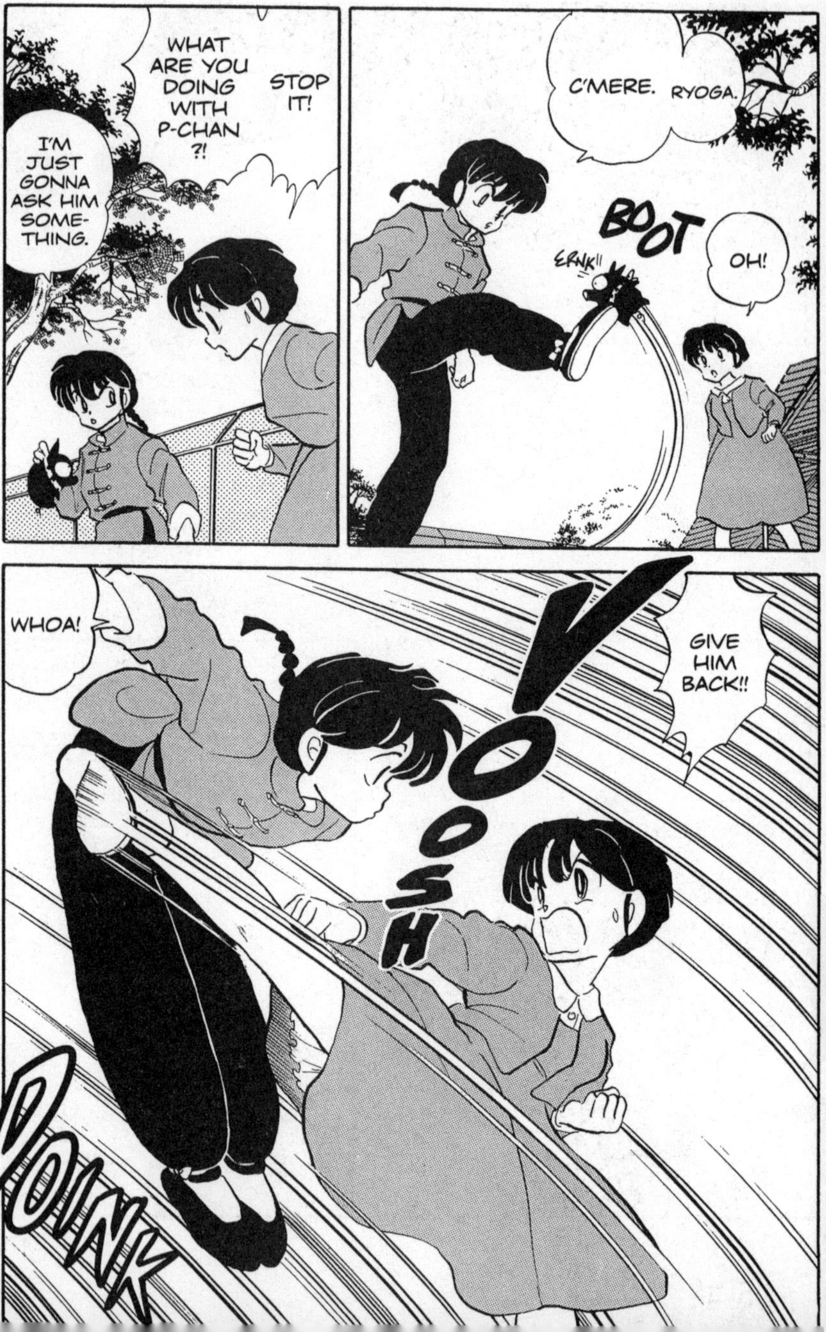
C'MERE. RYOGA.
BOOT
OH!
ERNK!!
STOP IT!
WHAT ARE YOU DOING WITH P-CHAN ?!
I'M JUST GONNA ASK HIM SOME-THING.
GIVE HIM BACK!!
VOOOSH
WHOA!
DOINK

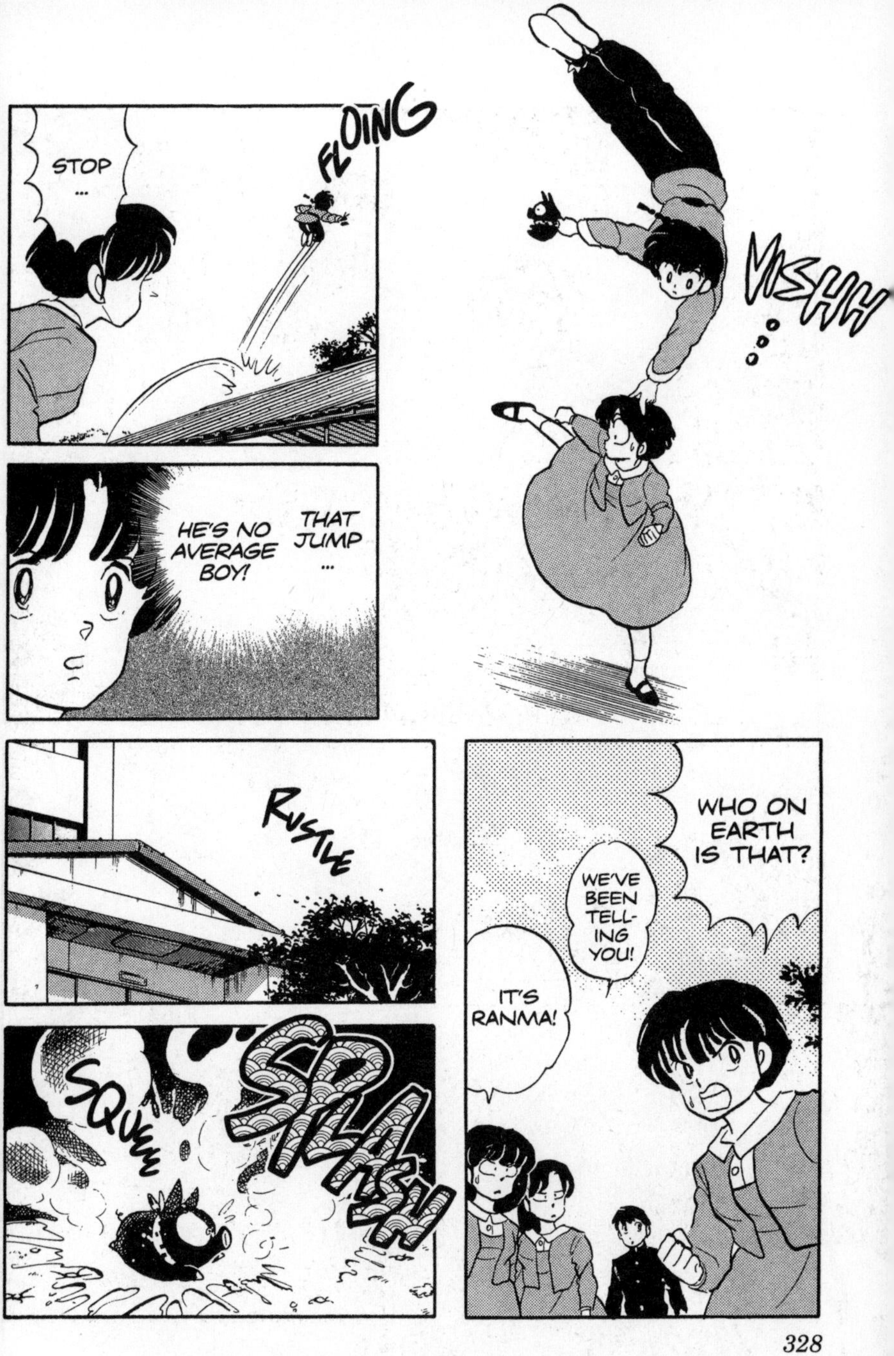
VISHH
FLOING
STOP ...
THAT JUMP ...
HE'S NO AVERAGE BOY!
WHO ON EARTH IS THAT?
WE'VE BEEN TELL-ING YOU!
IT'S RANMA!
RUSTLE
SPLASH
SQUEEE

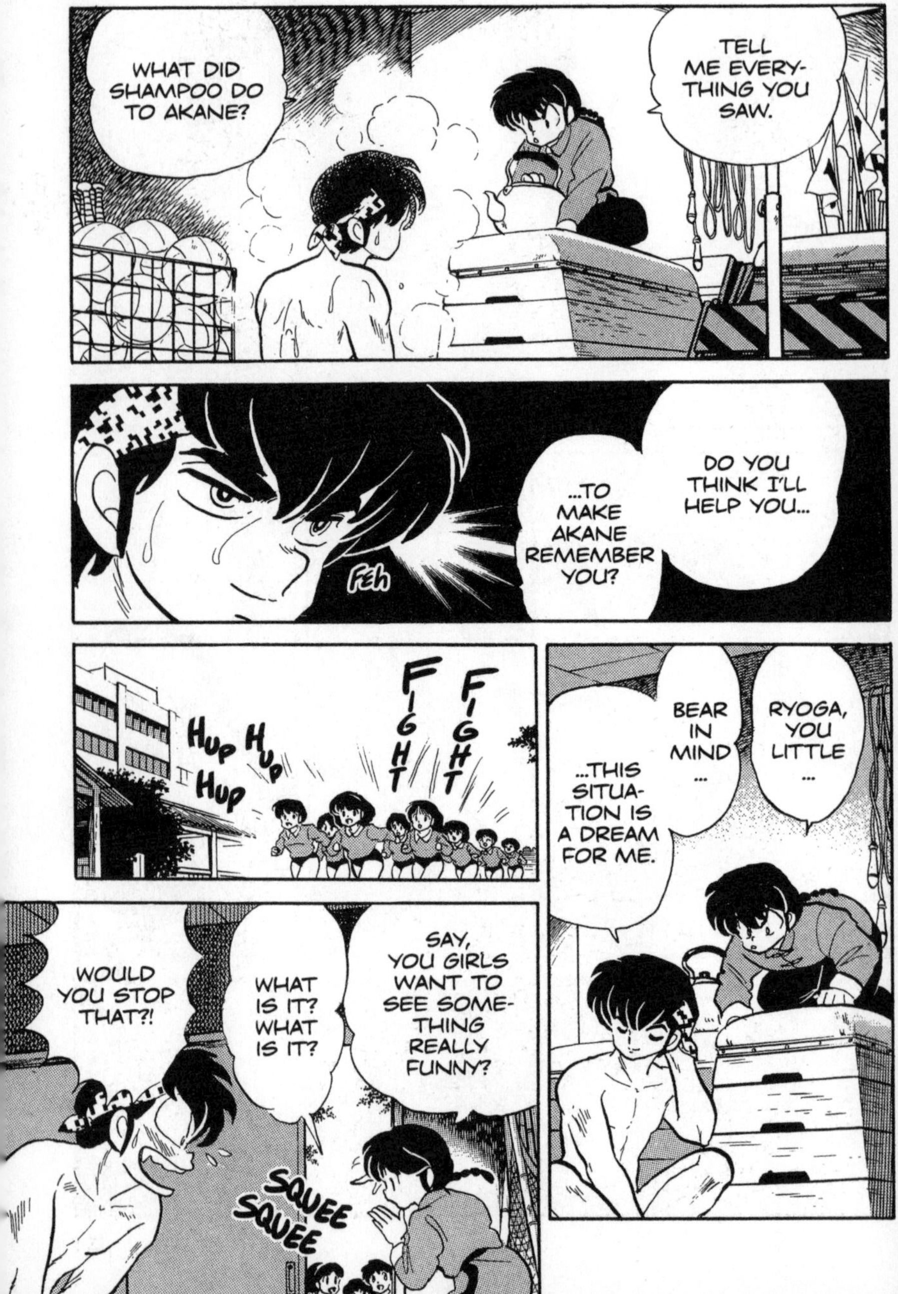
TELL ME EVERY-THING YOU SAW.
WHAT DID SHAMPOO DO TO AKANE?
DO YOU THINK I'LL HELP YOU...
...TO MAKE AKANE REMEMBER YOU?
Feh
RYOGA, YOU LITTLE ...
BEAR IN MIND ...
...THIS SITUA-TION IS A DREAM FOR ME.
FIGHT
FIGHT
HUP HUP
HUP
SAY, YOU GIRLS WANT TO SEE SOME-THING REALLY FUNNY?
WHAT IS IT? WHAT IS IT?
WOULD YOU STOP THAT?!
SQUEE SQUEE

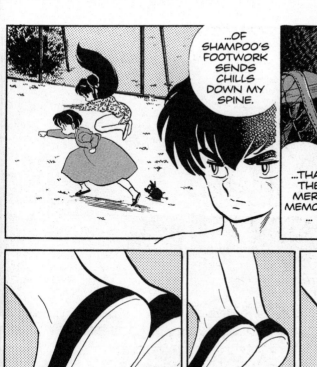

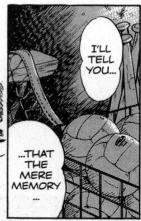

I'LL TELL YOU...
...THAT THE MERE MEMORY ...
...OF SHAMPOO'S FOOTWORK SENDS CHILLS DOWN MY SPINE.
AND THAT'S WHAT I SAW.
IN OTHER WORDS, YOU DIDN'T SEE ANYTHING!

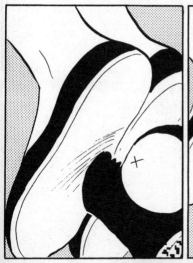

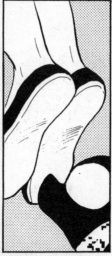

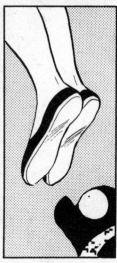

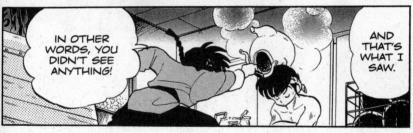

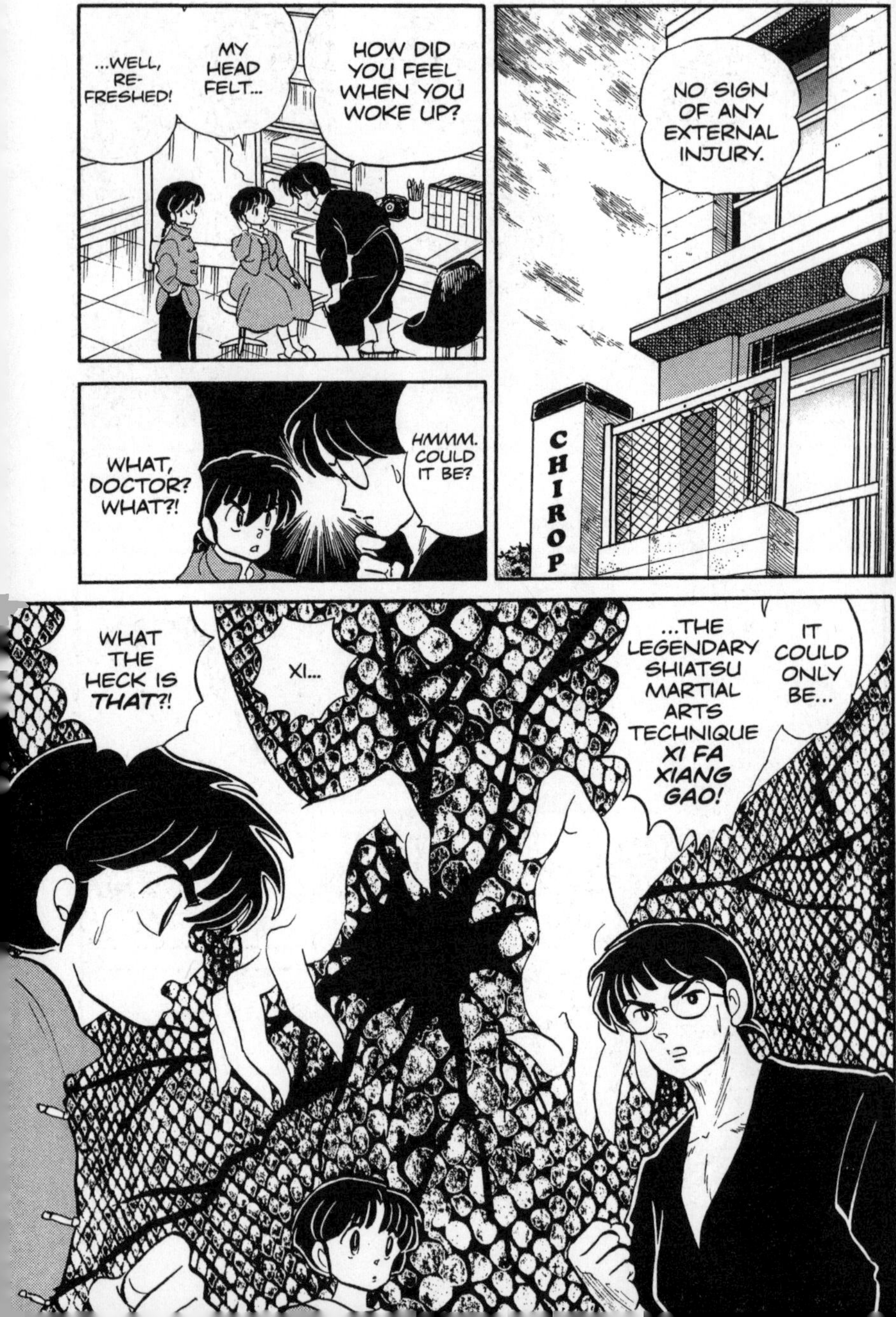
NO SIGN OF ANY EXTERNAL INJURY.
CHIROP
HOW DID YOU FEEL WHEN YOU WOKE UP?
MY HEAD FELT...
...WELL, REFRESHED!
HMMM. COULD IT BE?
WHAT, DOCTOR? WHAT?!
IT COULD ONLY BE...
...THE LEGENDARY SHIATSU MARTIAL ARTS TECHNIQUE *XI FA XIANG GAO!*
XI...
WHAT THE HECK IS *THAT?!*

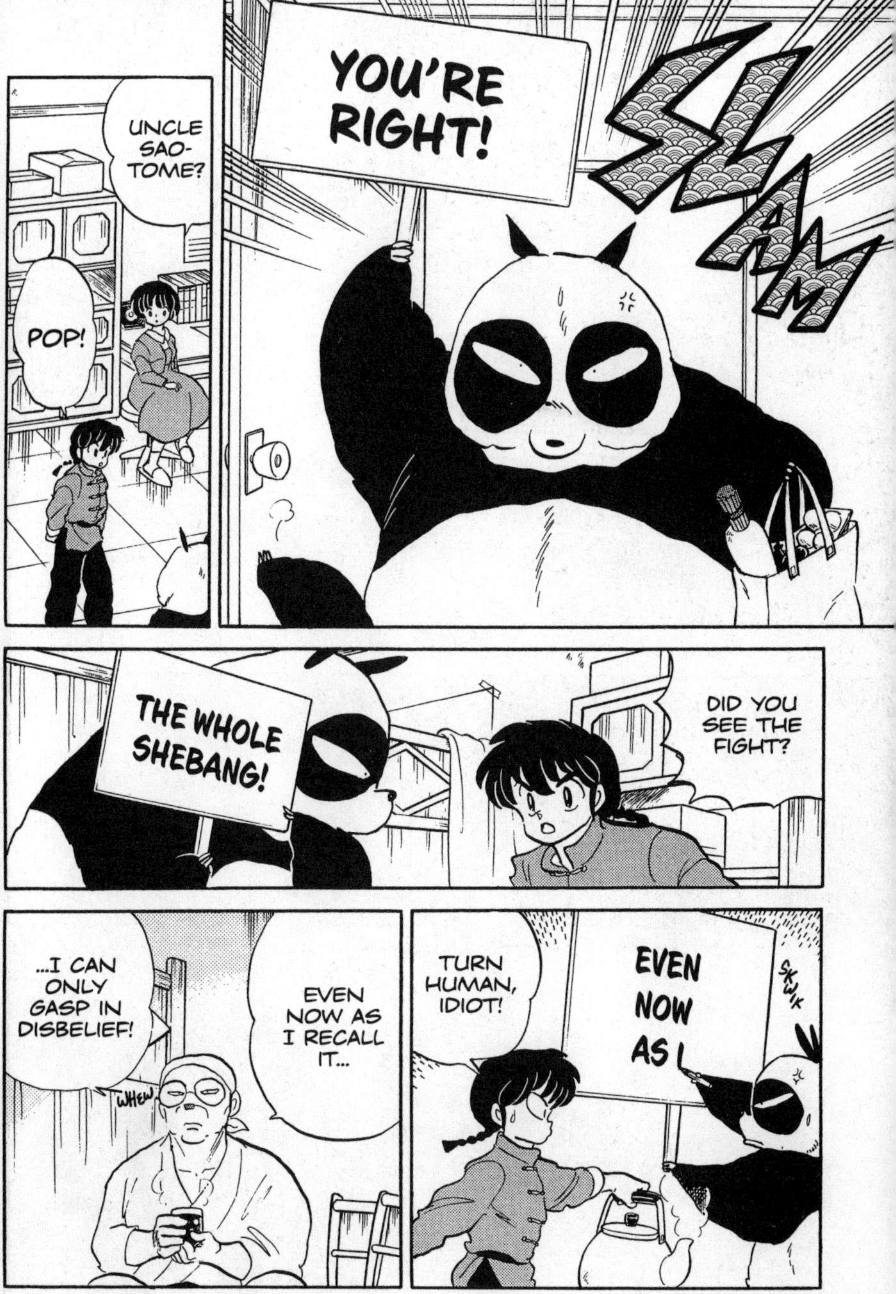
SLAM
YOU'RE RIGHT!
UNCLE SAO-TOME?
POP!
DID YOU SEE THE FIGHT?
THE WHOLE SHEBANG!
SKWIK
EVEN NOW AS I
TURN HUMAN, IDIOT!
EVEN NOW AS I RECALL IT...
...I CAN ONLY GASP IN DISBELIEF!
WHEW

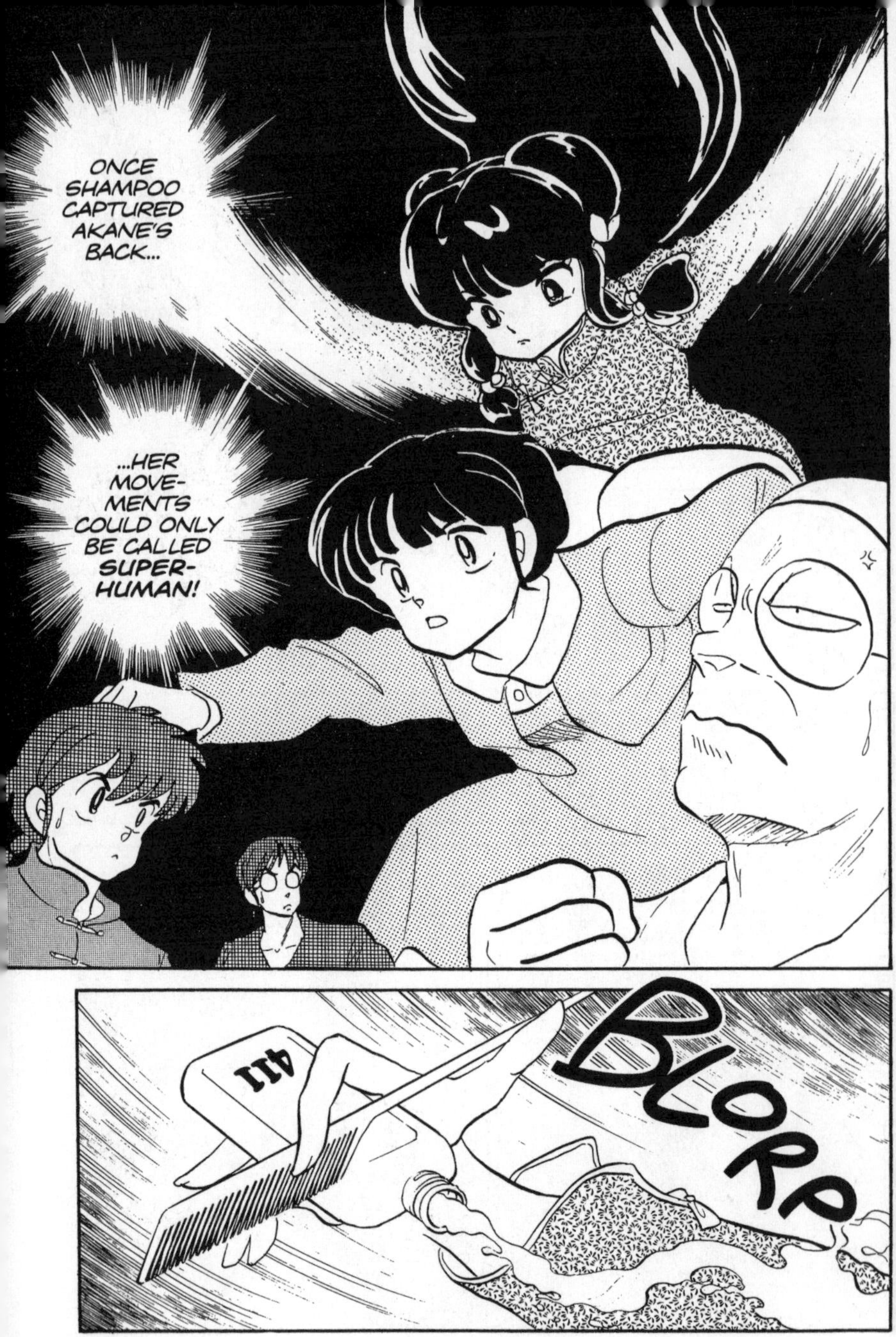
ONCE SHAMPOO CAPTURED AKANE'S BACK...
...HER MOVEMENTS COULD ONLY BE CALLED SUPER-HUMAN!
BLORP

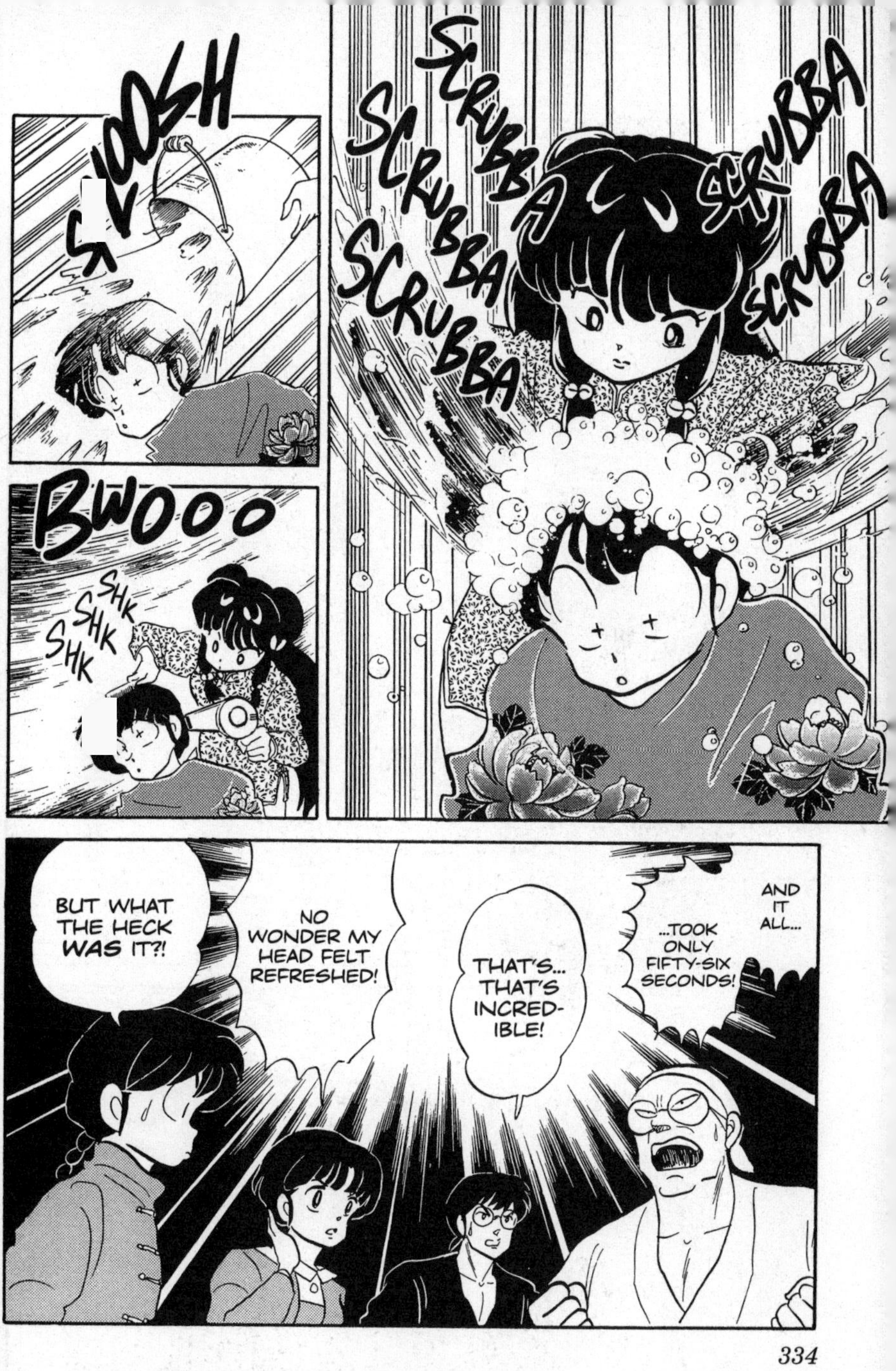
SCRUBBA
SCRUBBA
SCRUBBA
SCRUBBA
SCRUBBA
SCRUBBA
SWOOSH
BWOOO
SHK
SHK
SHK
AND IT ALL...
...TOOK ONLY FIFTY-SIX SECONDS!
THAT'S... THAT'S INCREDIBLE!
NO WONDER MY HEAD FELT REFRESHED!
BUT WHAT THE HECK WAS IT?!

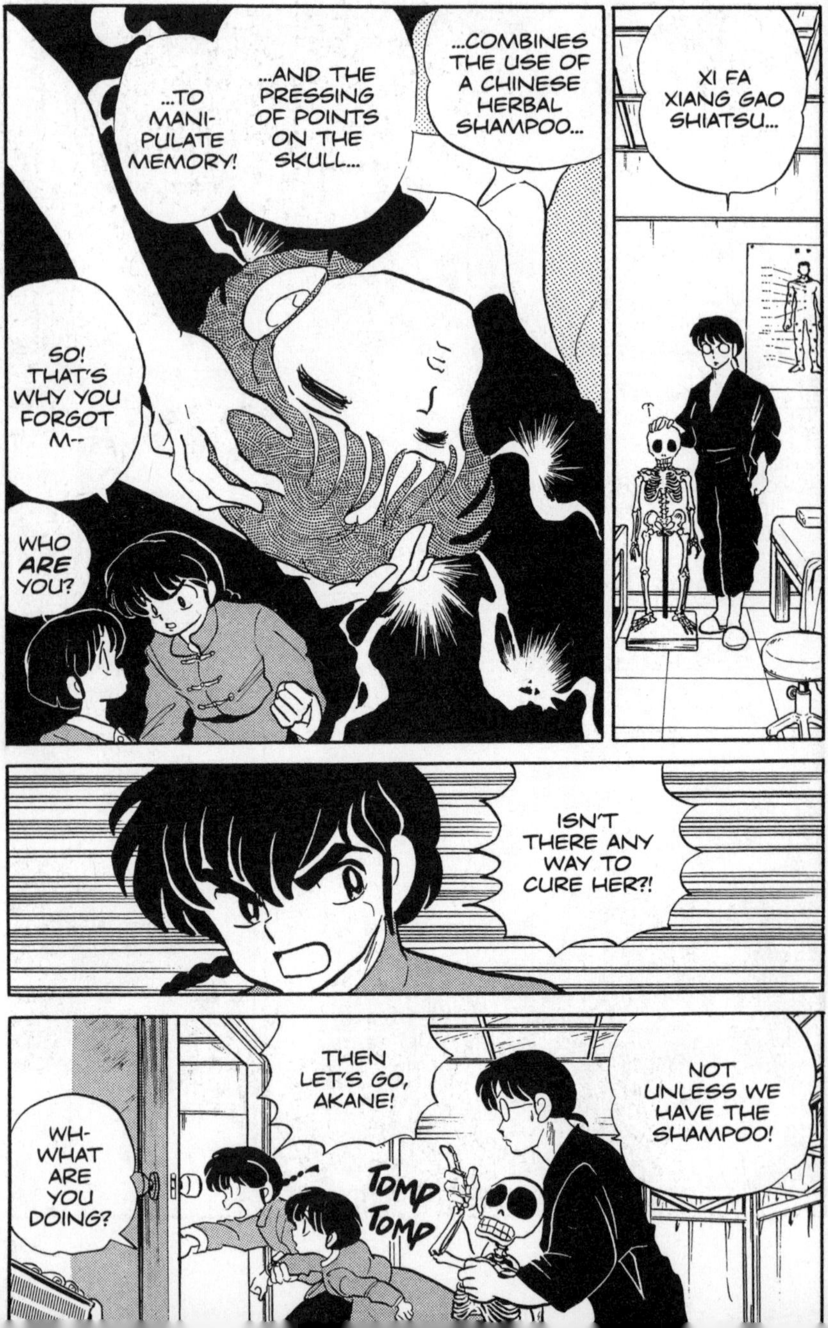
XI FA XIANG GAO SHIATSU...
...COMBINES THE USE OF A CHINESE HERBAL SHAMPOO...
...AND THE PRESSING OF POINTS ON THE SKULL...
...TO MANI-PULATE MEMORY!
SO! THAT'S WHY YOU FORGOT M--
WHO ARE YOU?
ISN'T THERE ANY WAY TO CURE HER?!
NOT UNLESS WE HAVE THE SHAMPOO!
THEN LET'S GO, AKANE!
TOMP TOMP
WH- WHAT ARE YOU DOING?

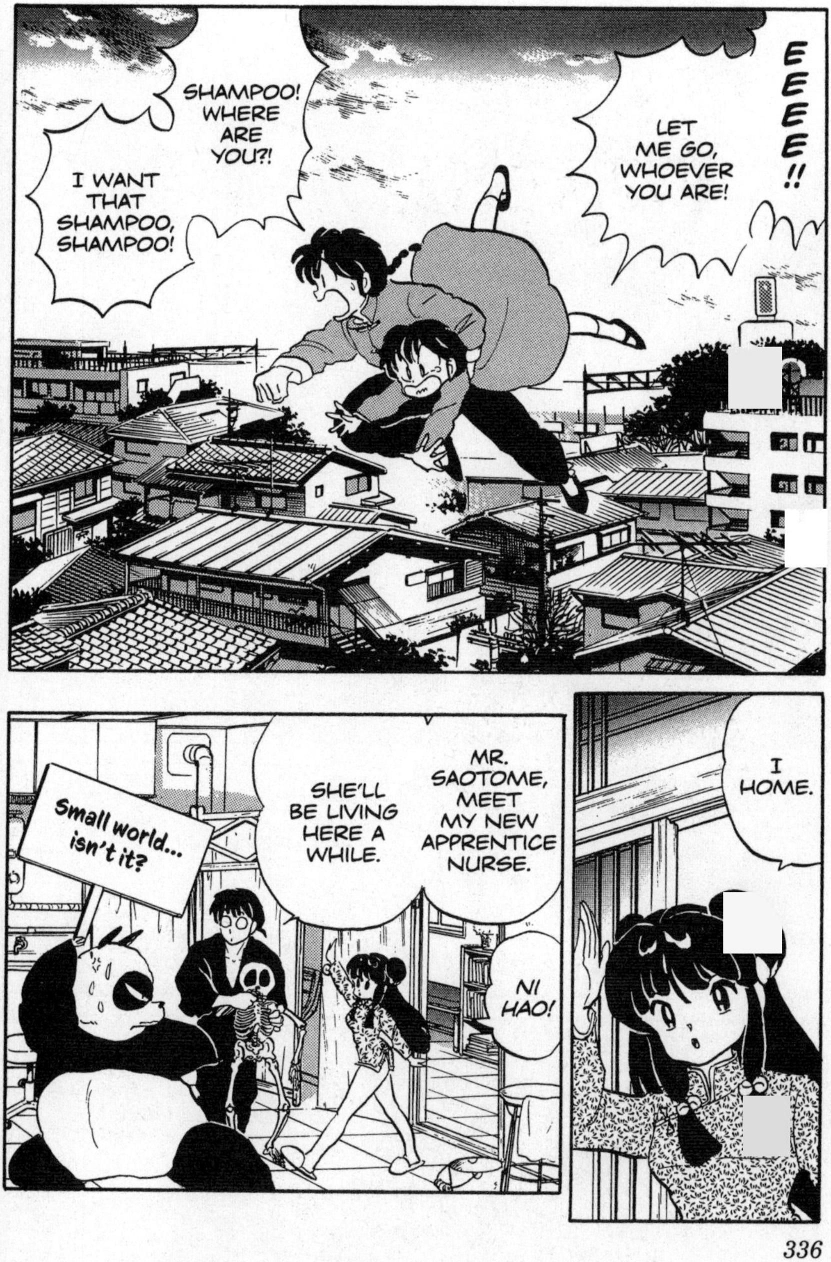
EEEE!!
LET ME GO, WHOEVER YOU ARE!
SHAMPOO! WHERE ARE YOU?!
I WANT THAT SHAMPOO, SHAMPOO!
I HOME.
NI HAO!
MR. SAOTOME, MEET MY NEW APPRENTICE NURSE.
SHE'LL BE LIVING HERE A WHILE.
Small world... isn't it?

PART 18
FORMULA #911

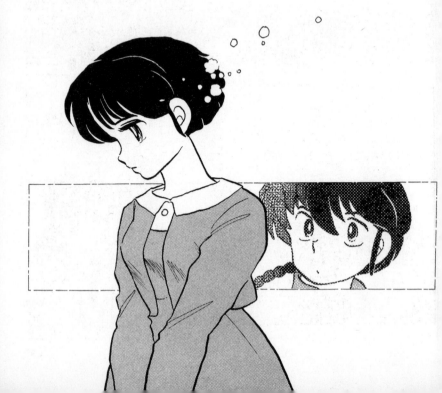

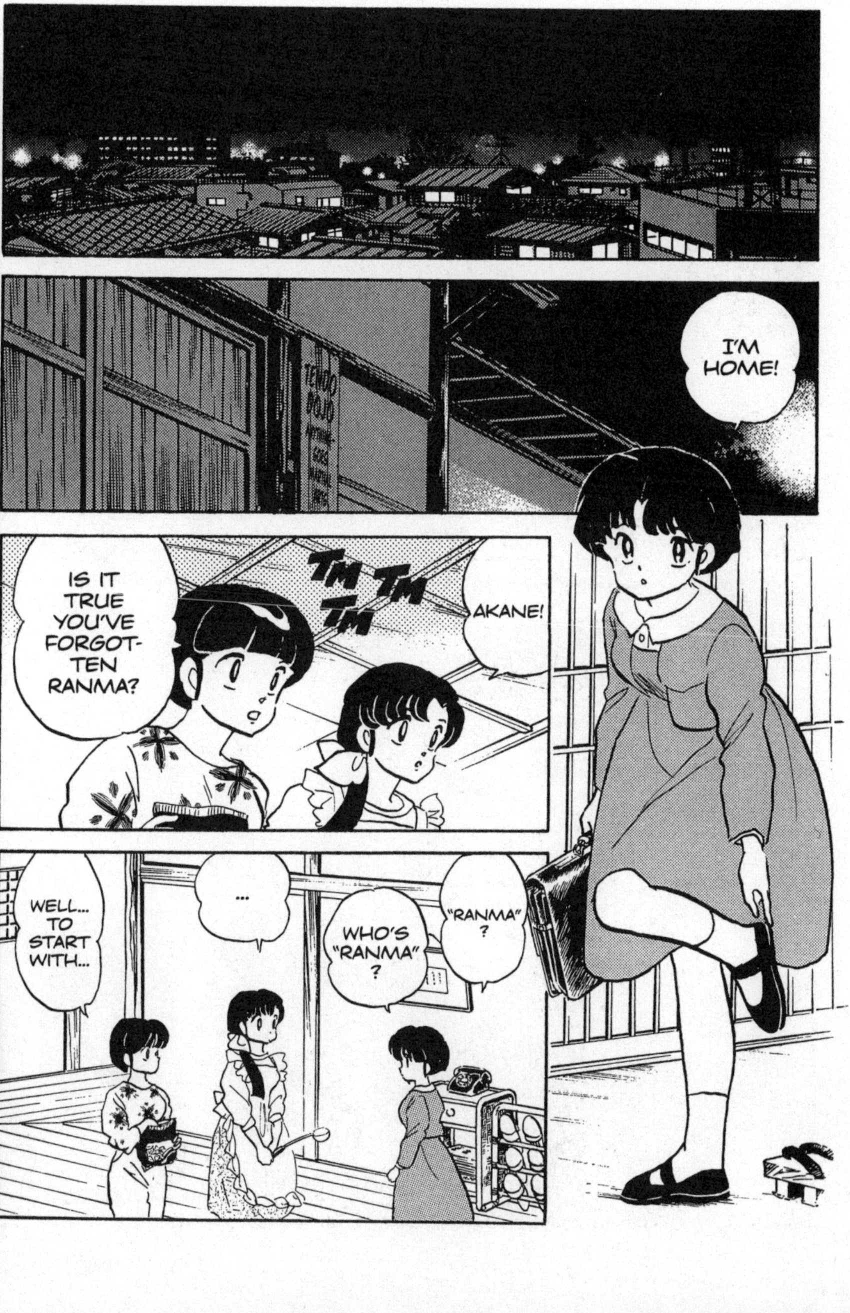
I'M HOME!
TENDO DOJO
AKANE!
TM TM TM
IS IT TRUE YOU'VE FORGOTTEN RANMA?
"RANMA"?
WHO'S "RANMA"?
...
WELL... TO START WITH...

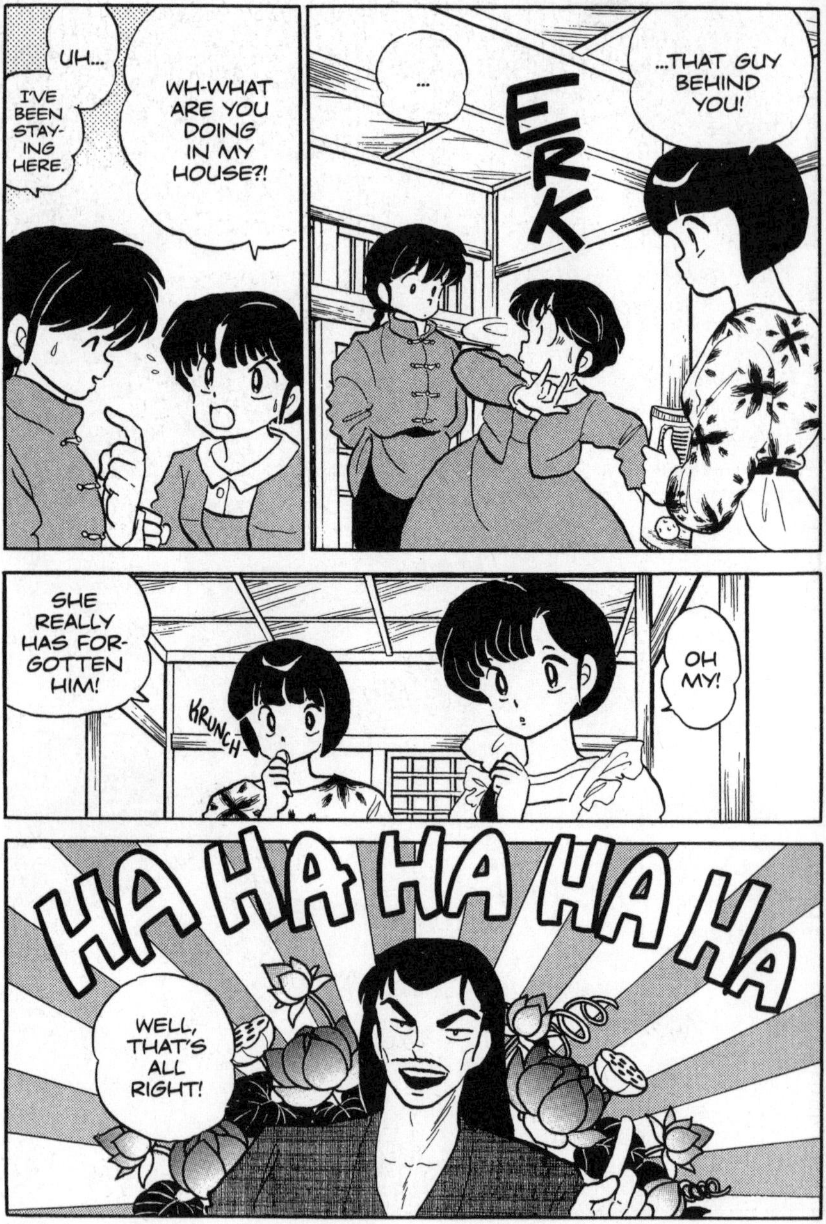
...THAT GUY BEHIND YOU!
...
ERK
WH-WHAT ARE YOU DOING IN MY HOUSE?!
UH...
I'VE BEEN STAY-ING HERE.
OH MY!
KRUNCH
SHE REALLY HAS FOR-GOTTEN HIM!
HA HA HA HA HA HA HA HA
WELL, THAT'S ALL RIGHT!

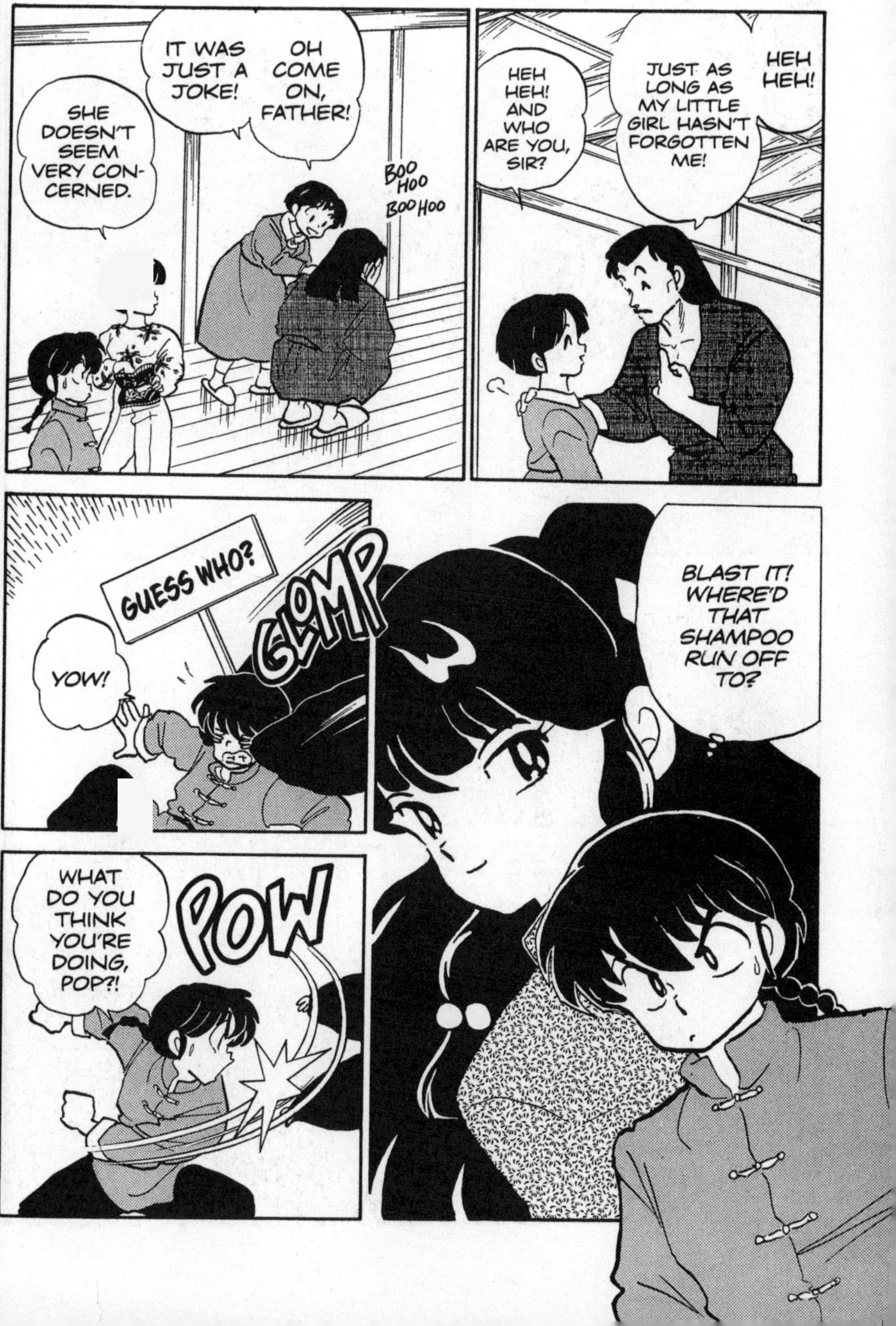
HEH HEH!
JUST AS LONG AS MY LITTLE GIRL HASN'T FORGOTTEN ME!
HEH HEH! AND WHO ARE YOU, SIR?
OH COME ON, FATHER!
IT WAS JUST A JOKE!
BOO HOO BOO HOO
SHE DOESN'T SEEM VERY CON-CERNED.
BLAST IT! WHERE'D THAT SHAMPOO RUN OFF TO?
GUESS WHO?
GLOMP
YOW!
POW
WHAT DO YOU THINK YOU'RE DOING, POP?!

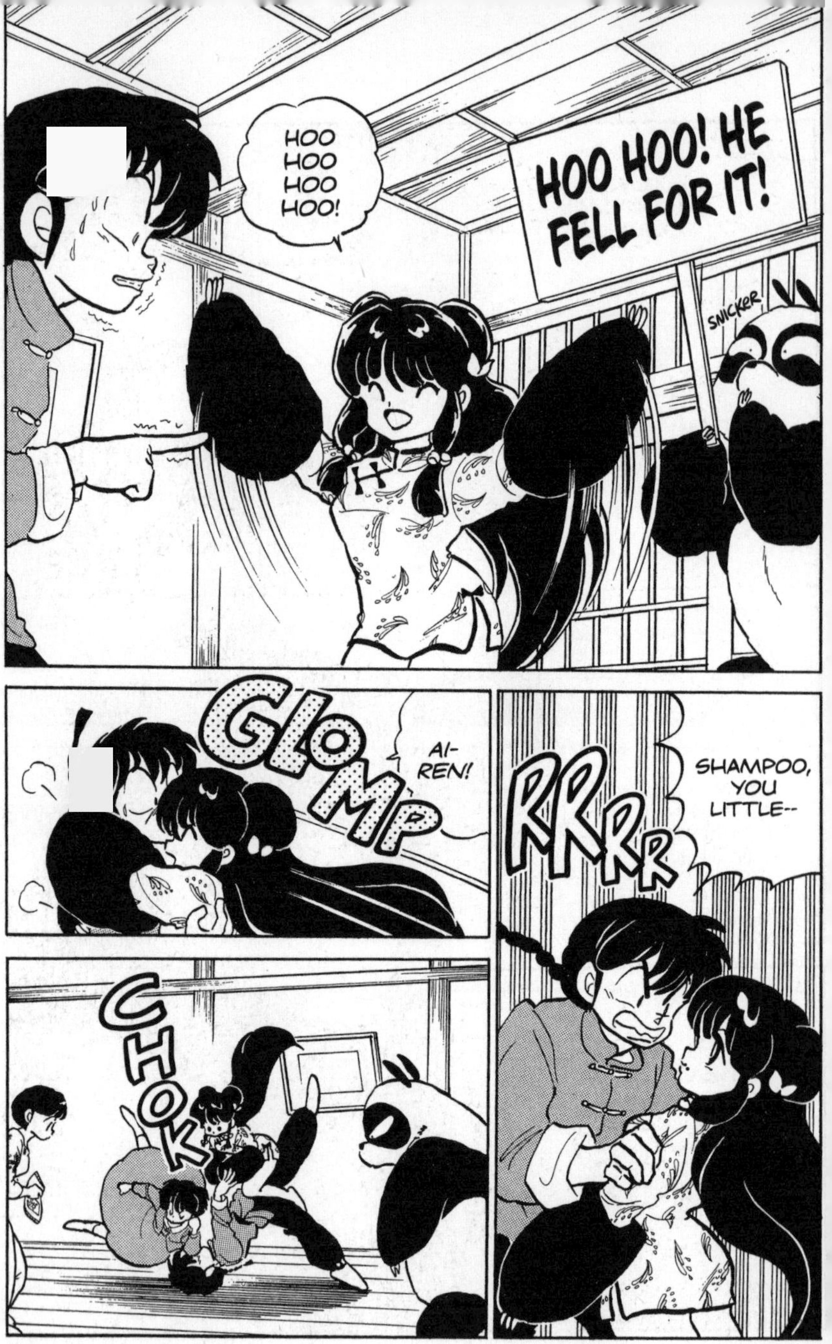
HOO HOO! HE FELL FOR IT!
HOO HOO HOO HOO!
SNICKER
SHAMPOO, YOU LITTLE--
RRRR
AI-REN!
GLOMP
CHOK

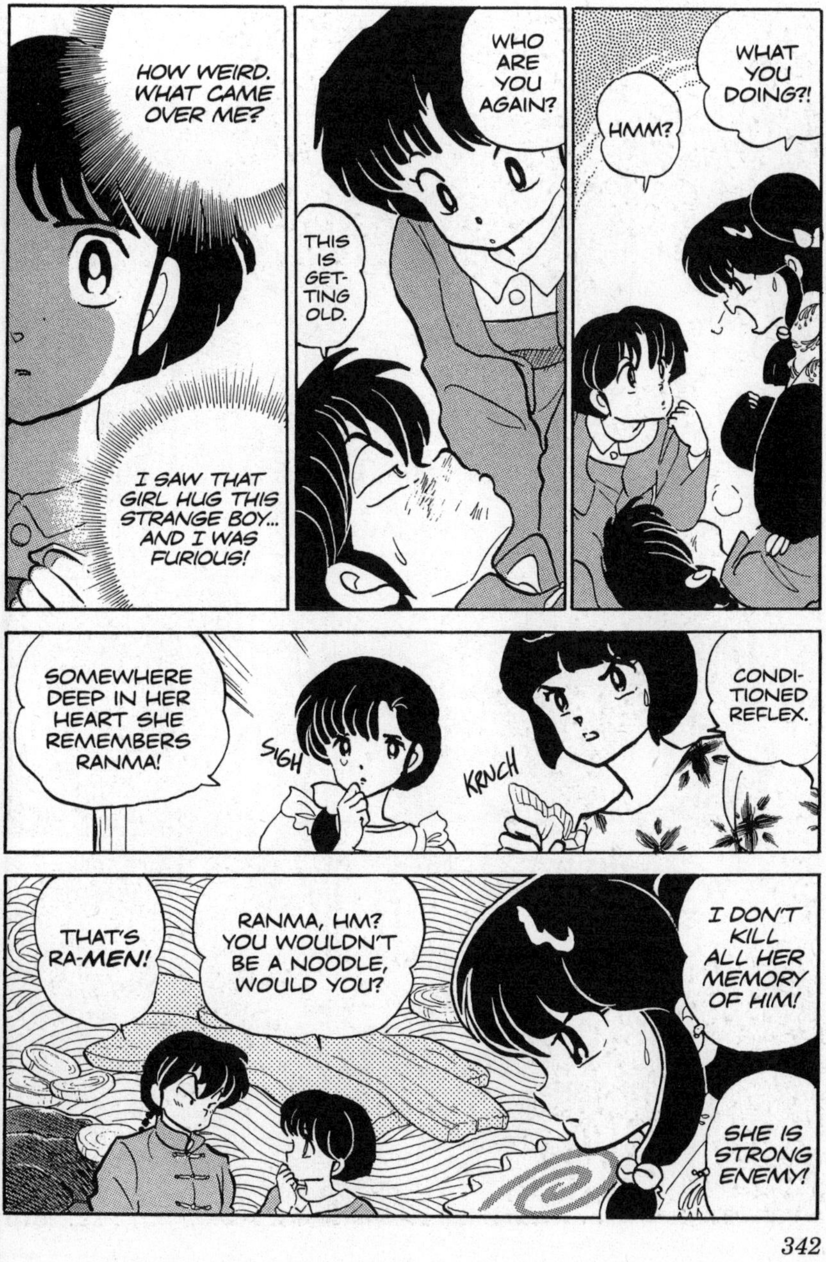
WHAT YOU DOING?!
HMM?
WHO ARE YOU AGAIN?
THIS IS GETTING OLD.
HOW WEIRD. WHAT CAME OVER ME?
I SAW THAT GIRL HUG THIS STRANGE BOY... AND I WAS FURIOUS!
CONDITIONED REFLEX.
KRNCH
SIGH
SOMEWHERE DEEP IN HER HEART SHE REMEMBERS RANMA!
I DON'T KILL ALL HER MEMORY OF HIM!
SHE IS STRONG ENEMY!
RANMA, HM? YOU WOULDN'T BE A NOODLE, WOULD YOU?
THAT'S RA-MEN!

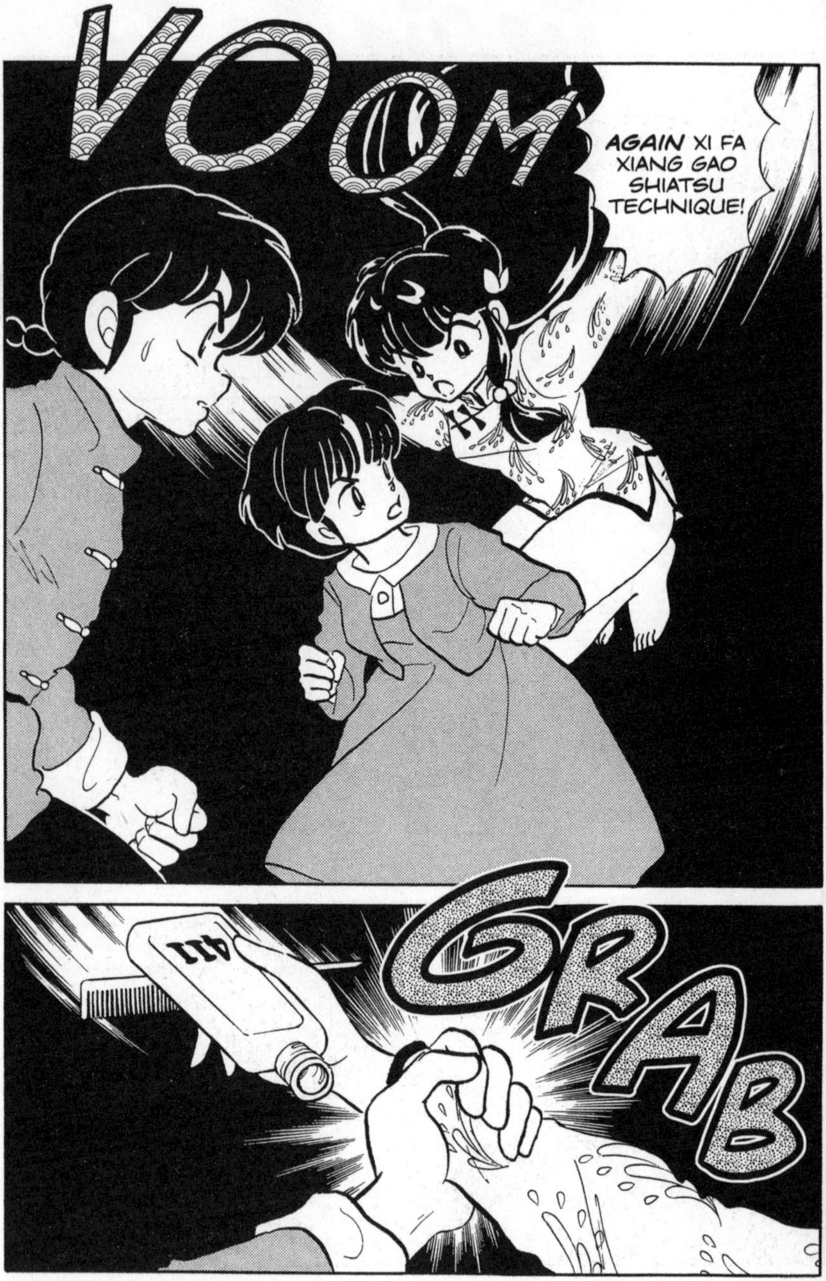
VOOM
AGAIN XI FA XIANG GAO SHIATSU TECHNIQUE!
411
GRAB

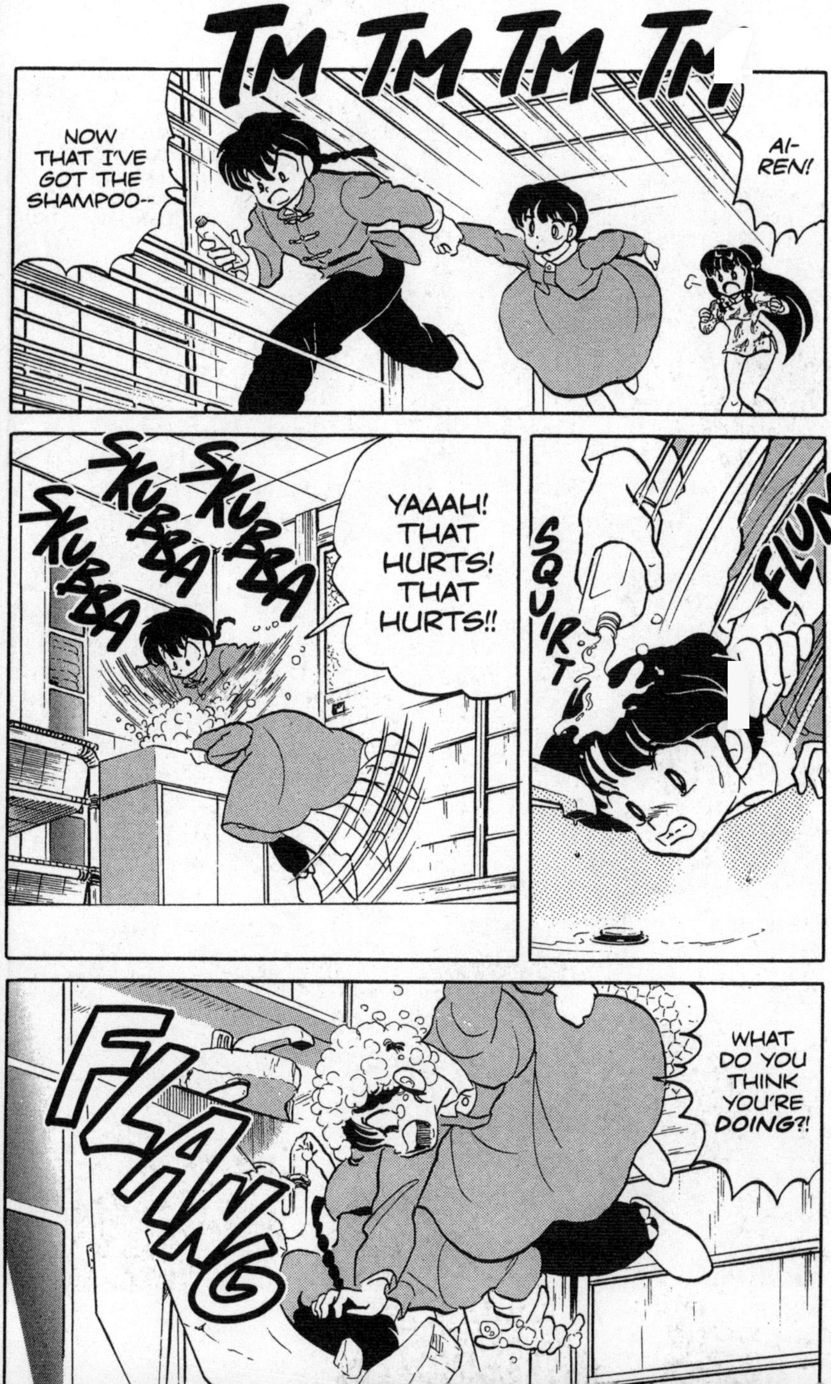
TM TM TM TM TM
AI-REN!
NOW THAT I'VE GOT THE SHAMPOO--
FLUMP
SQUIRT
YAAAH! THAT HURTS! THAT HURTS!!
SKUBBA SKUBBA
SKUBBA SKUBBA
WHAT DO YOU THINK YOU'RE DOING?!
FLANG

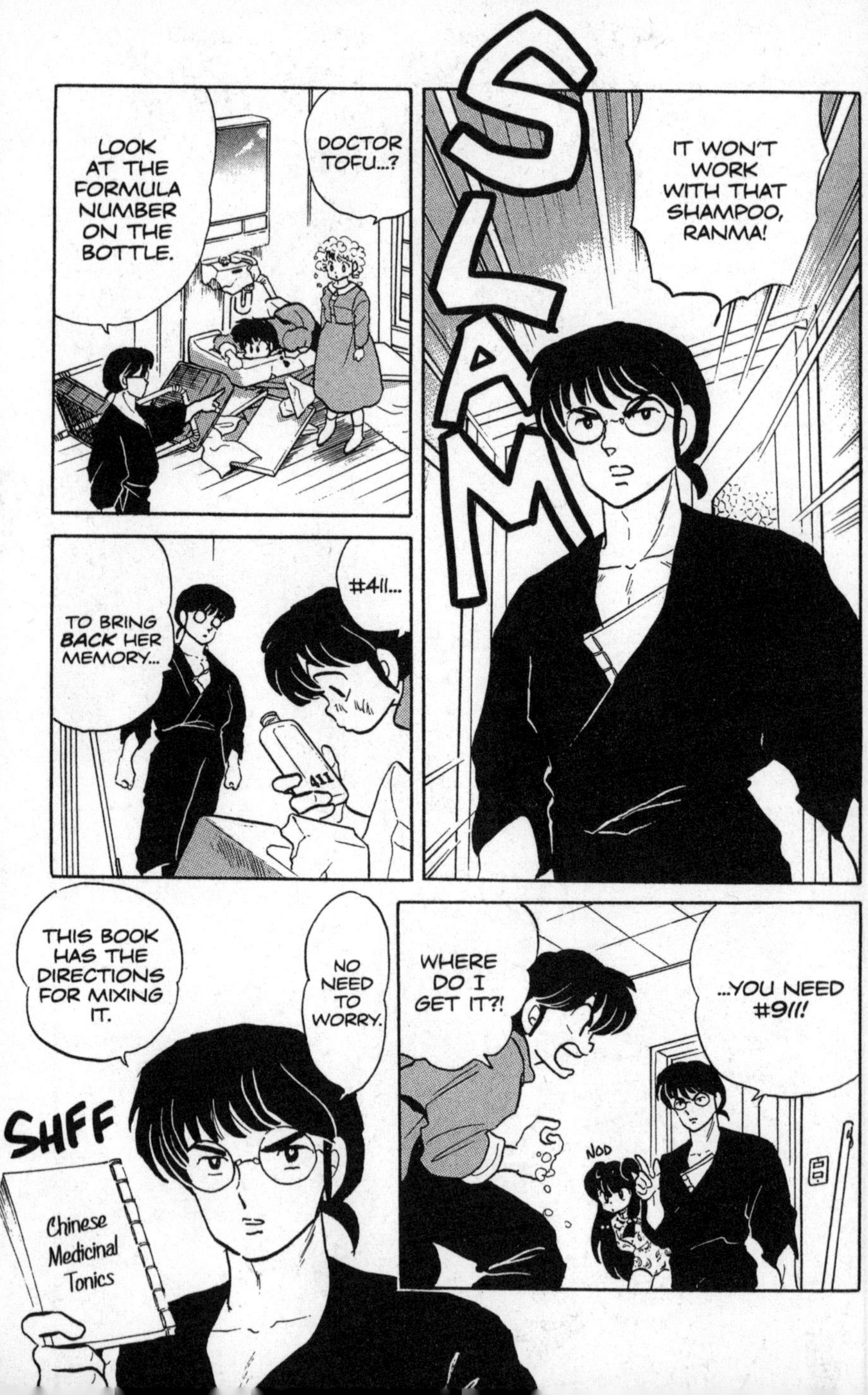
SLAM
IT WON'T WORK WITH THAT SHAMPOO, RANMA!
DOCTOR TOFU...?
LOOK AT THE FORMULA NUMBER ON THE BOTTLE.
#411...
411
TO BRING BACK HER MEMORY...
...YOU NEED #911!
WHERE DO I GET IT?!
NOD
NO NEED TO WORRY.
THIS BOOK HAS THE DIRECTIONS FOR MIXING IT.
SHFF
Chinese Medicinal Tonics

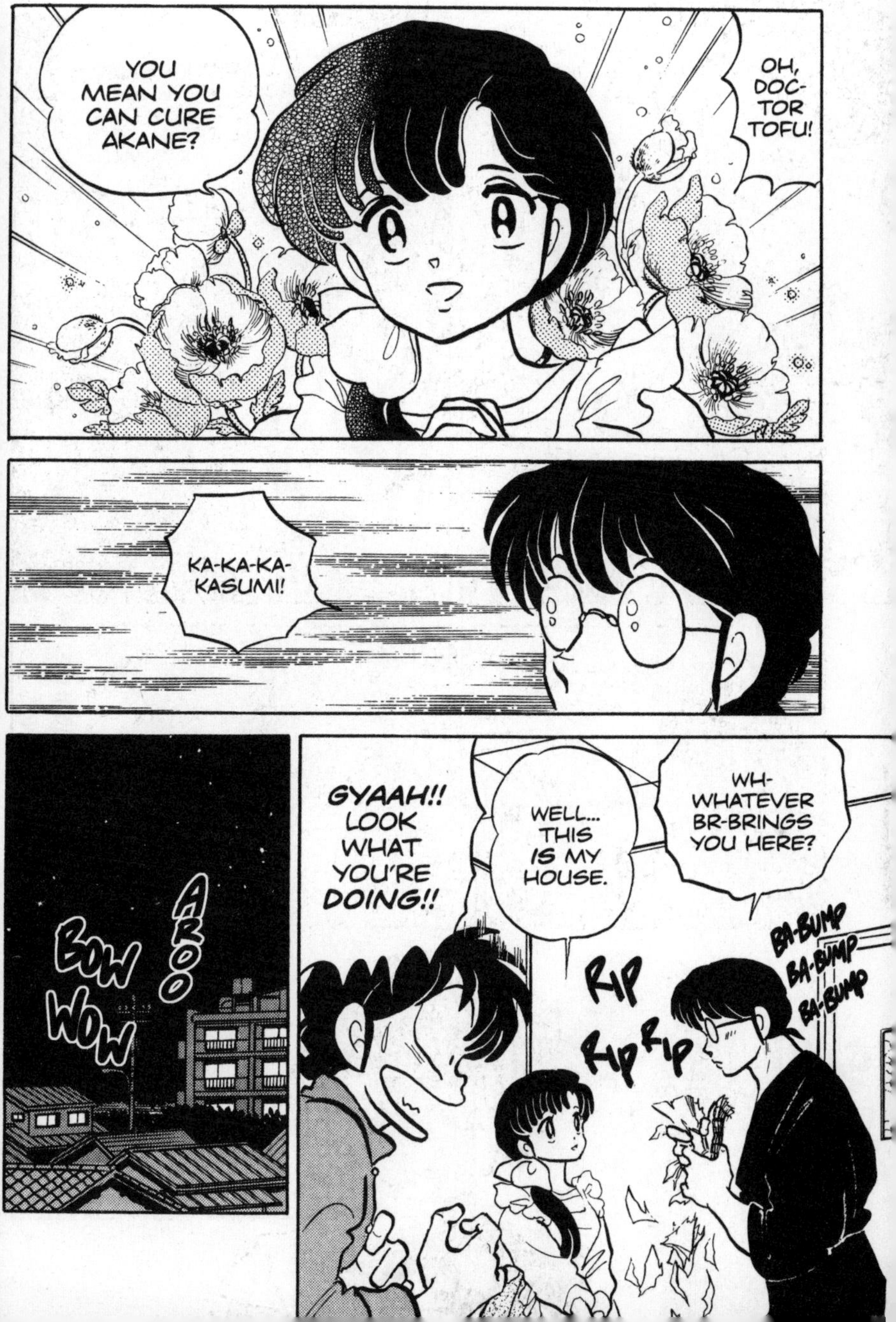
OH, DOC-TOR TOFU!
YOU MEAN YOU CAN CURE AKANE?
KA-KA-KA-KASUMI!
WH-WHATEVER BR-BRINGS YOU HERE?
BA-BUMP BA-BUMP BA-BUMP
WELL... THIS IS MY HOUSE.
RIP RIP RIP
GYAAH!! LOOK WHAT YOU'RE DOING!!
AROOO
BOW WOW

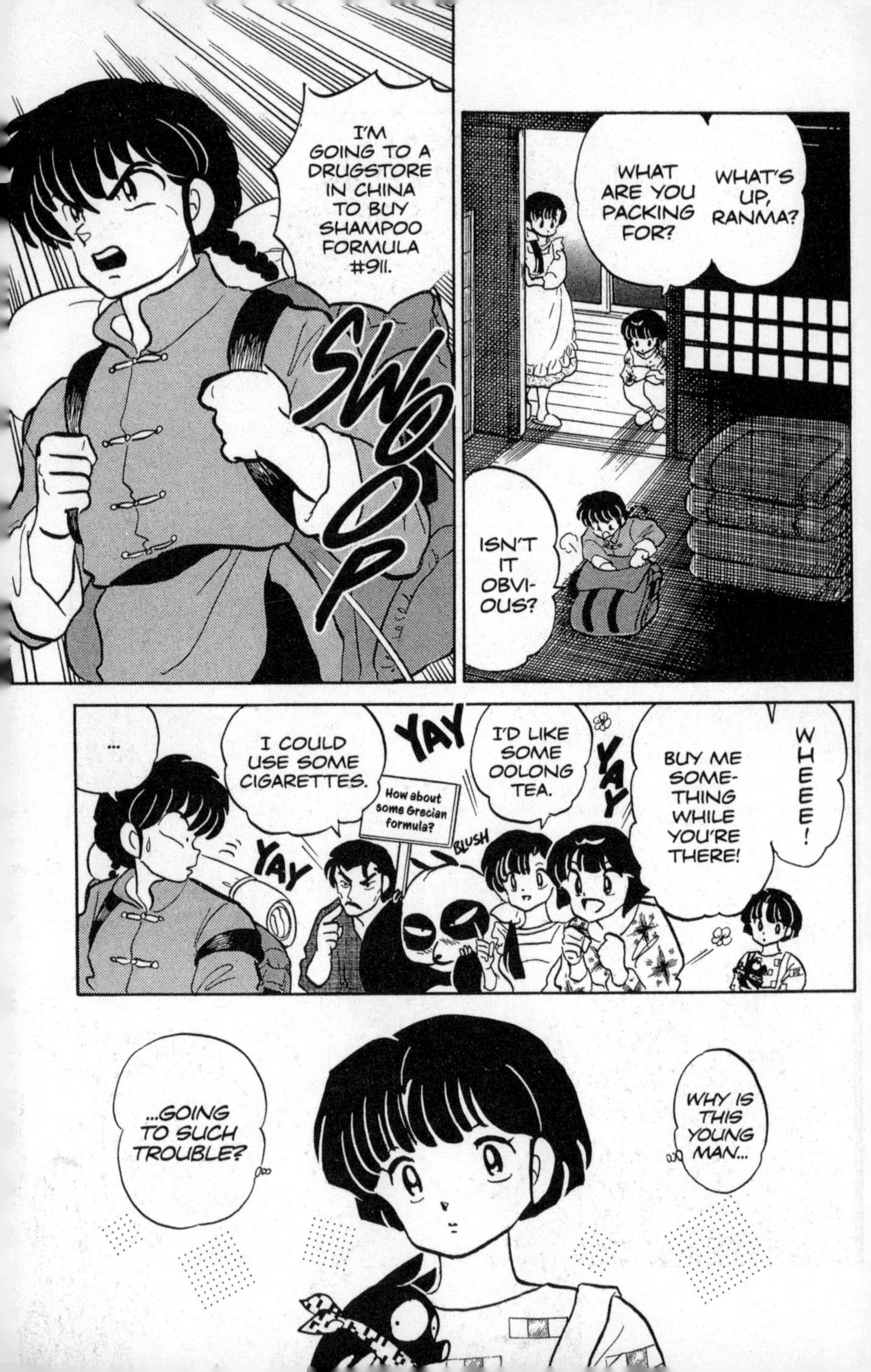
WHAT'S UP, RANMA?
WHAT ARE YOU PACKING FOR?
ISN'T IT OBVIOUS?
I'M GOING TO A DRUGSTORE IN CHINA TO BUY SHAMPOO FORMULA #911.
SWOOP
WHEEE!
BUY ME SOMETHING WHILE YOU'RE THERE!
YAY
I'D LIKE SOME OOLONG TEA.
YAY
BLUSH
How about some Grecian formula?
I COULD USE SOME CIGARETTES.
YAY
...
WHY IS THIS YOUNG MAN...
...GOING TO SUCH TROUBLE?

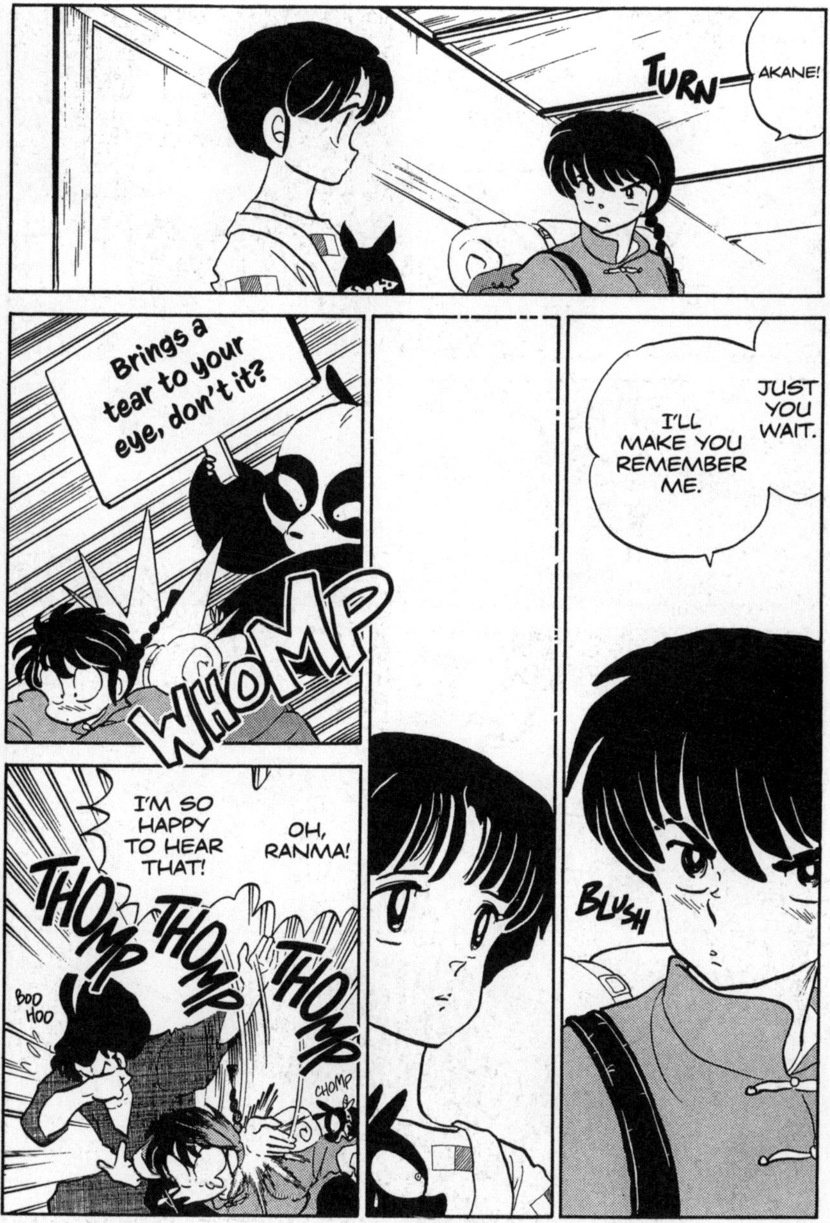
AKANE!
TURN
JUST YOU WAIT.
I'LL MAKE YOU REMEMBER ME.
BLUSH
Brings a tear to your eye, don't it?
WHOMP
OH, RANMA!
I'M SO HAPPY TO HEAR THAT!
THOMP
THOMP
THOMP
THOMP
BOO HOO
CHOMP

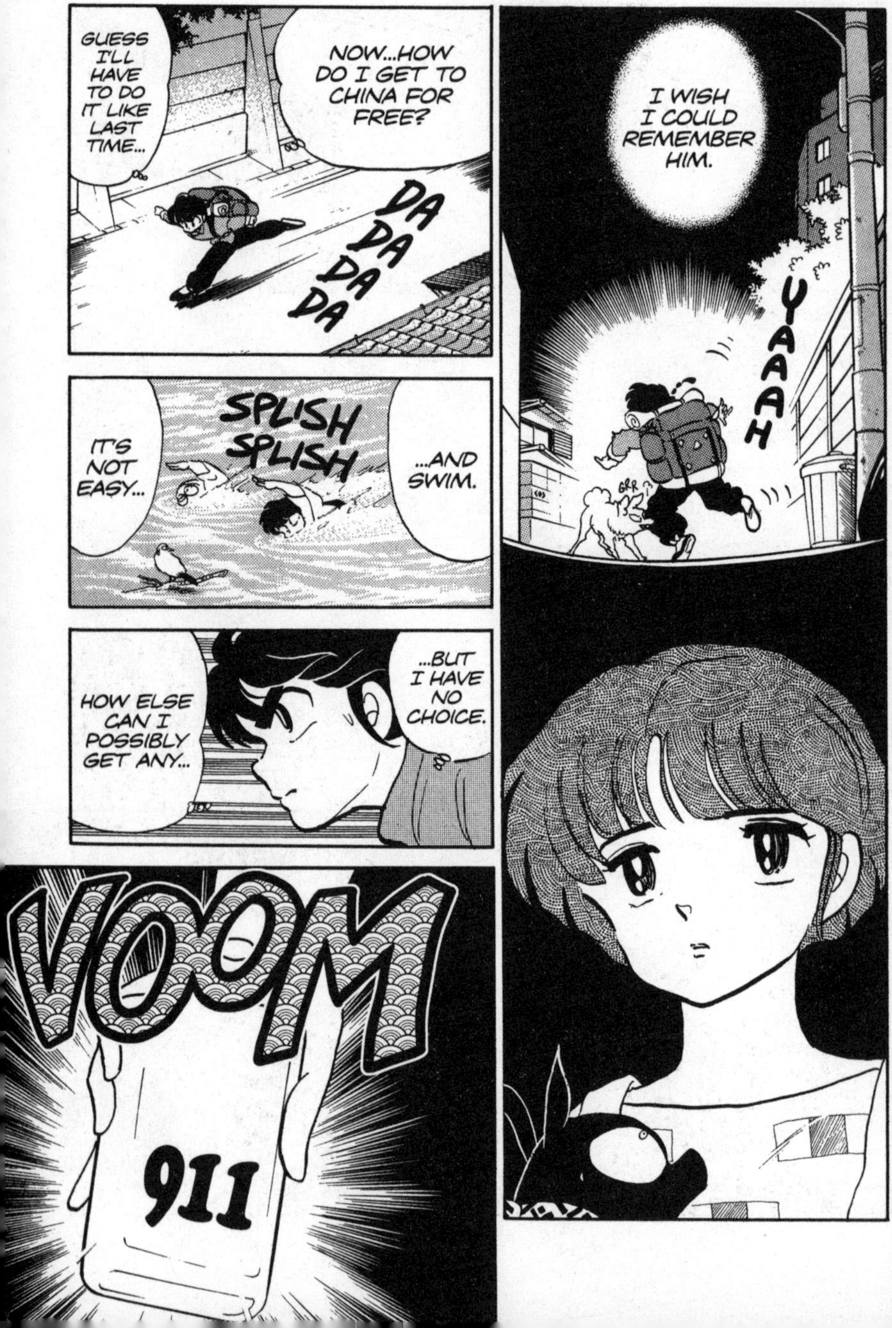
I WISH I COULD REMEMBER HIM.
YAAAAH
GRR
NOW...HOW DO I GET TO CHINA FOR FREE?
GUESS I'LL HAVE TO DO IT LIKE LAST TIME...
DA DA DA DA
...AND SWIM.
SPLISH SPLISH
IT'S NOT EASY...
...BUT I HAVE NO CHOICE.
HOW ELSE CAN I POSSIBLY GET ANY...
VOOM
911

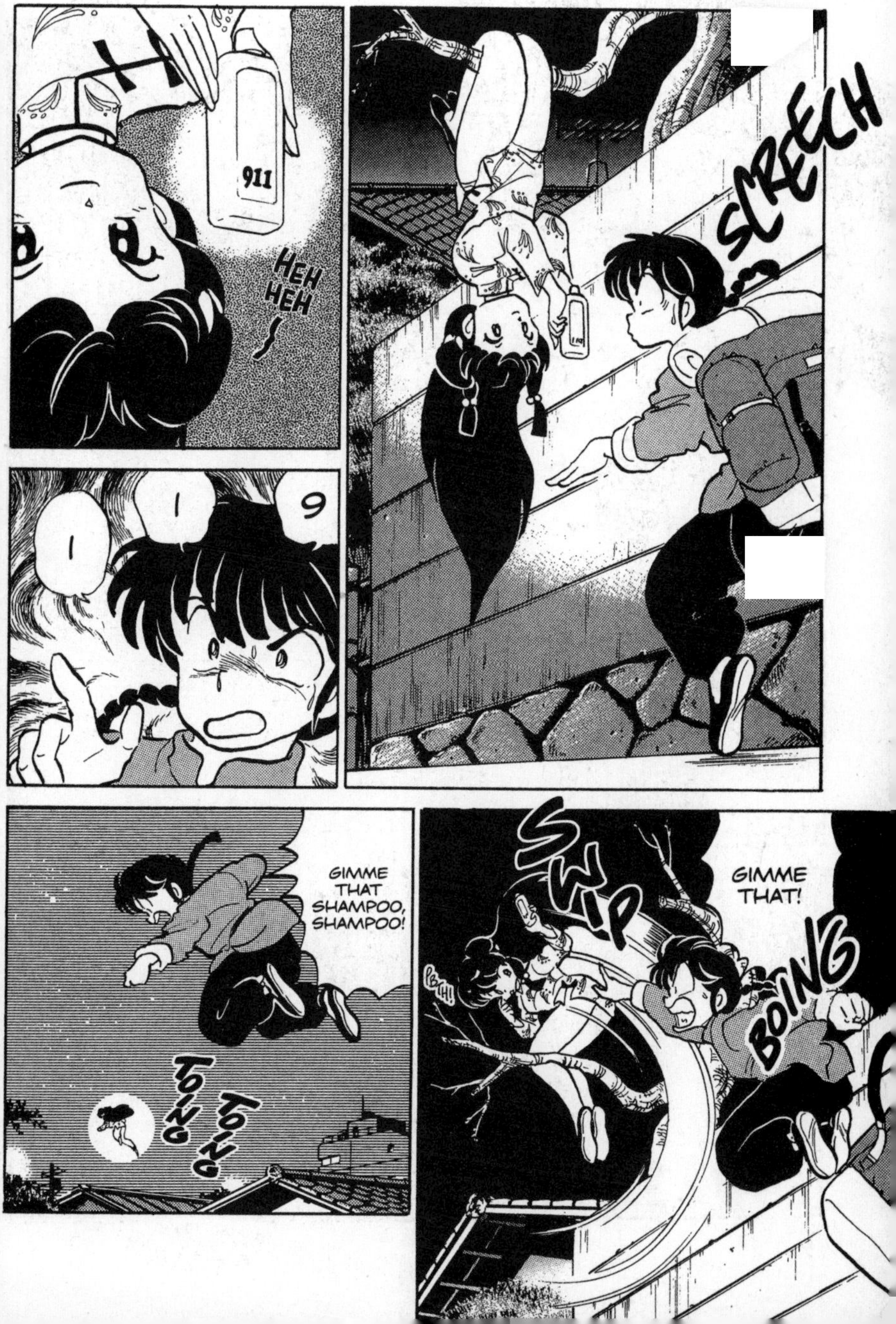
SCREECH
911
HEH HEH!
1 1 9
SWIP
GIMME THAT!
PBTH!
BOING
GIMME THAT SHAMPOO, SHAMPOO!
TOING TOING

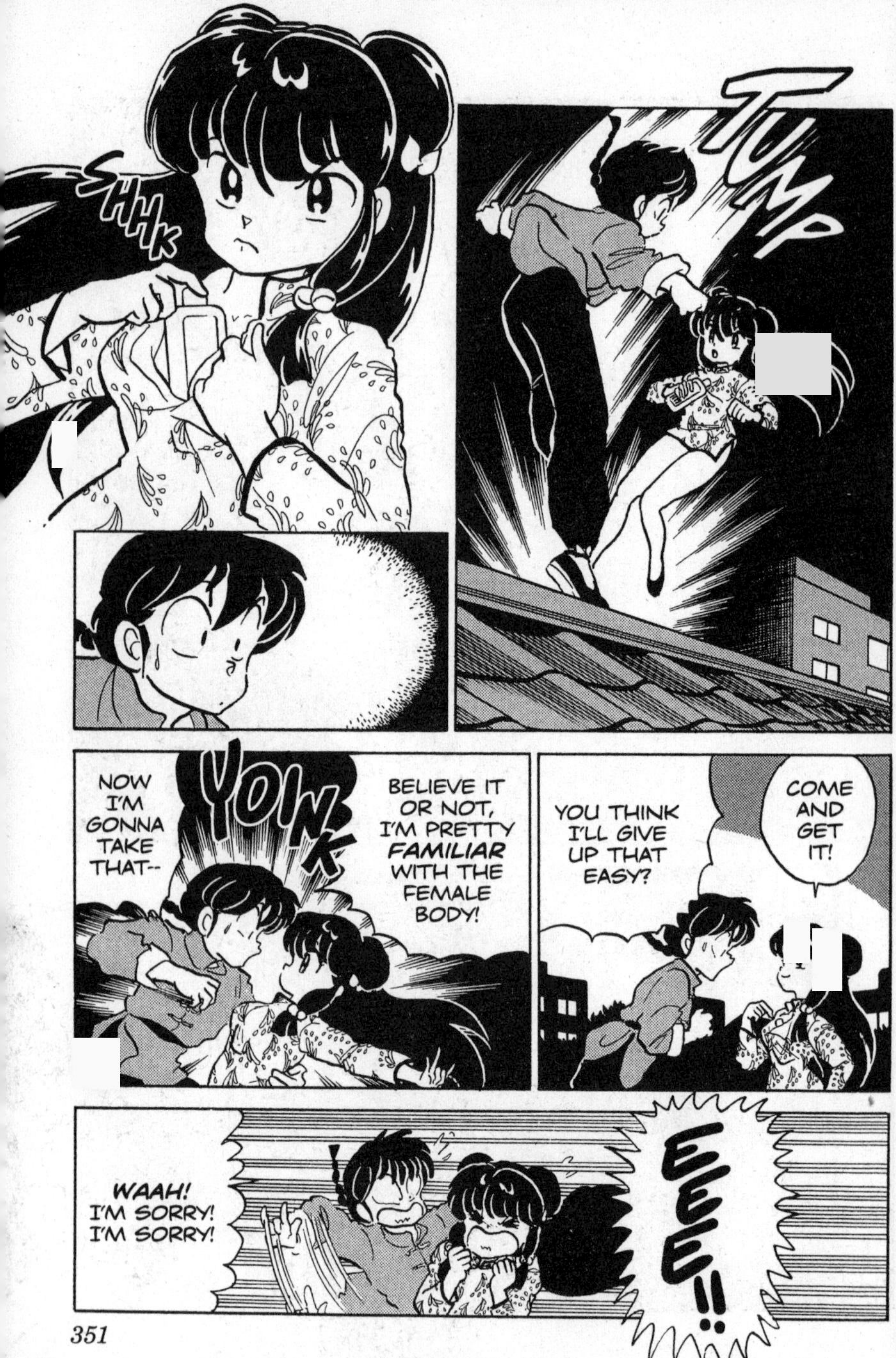
JUMP
SHHHK
COME AND GET IT!
YOU THINK I'LL GIVE UP THAT EASY?
BELIEVE IT OR NOT, I'M PRETTY **FAMILIAR** WITH THE FEMALE BODY!
YOINK
NOW I'M GONNA TAKE THAT--
EEE!!
WAAH! I'M SORRY! I'M SORRY!

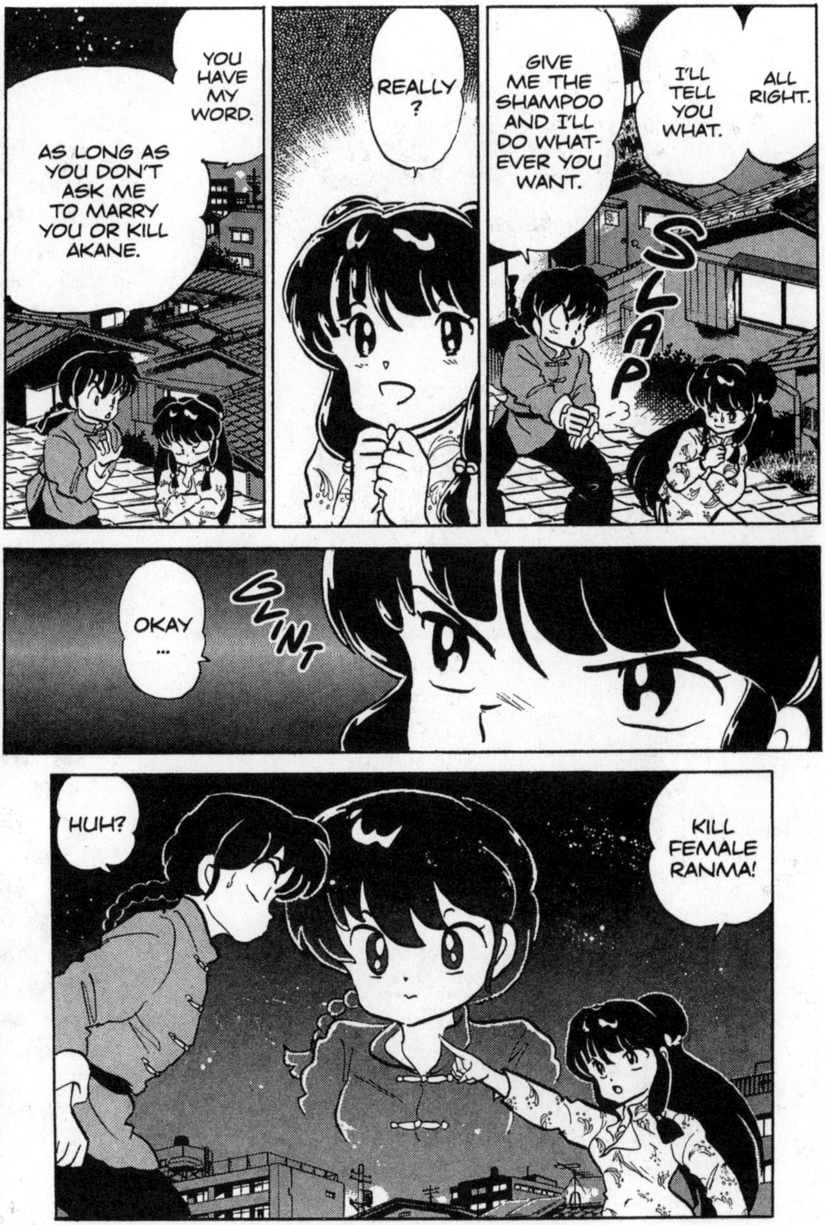
ALL RIGHT.
I'LL TELL YOU WHAT.
GIVE ME THE SHAMPOO AND I'LL DO WHATEVER YOU WANT.
SLAP
REALLY?
YOU HAVE MY WORD.
AS LONG AS YOU DON'T ASK ME TO MARRY YOU OR KILL AKANE.
GLINT
OKAY ...
KILL FEMALE RANMA!
HUH?

PART 19
BIE LIAO (GOODBYE)

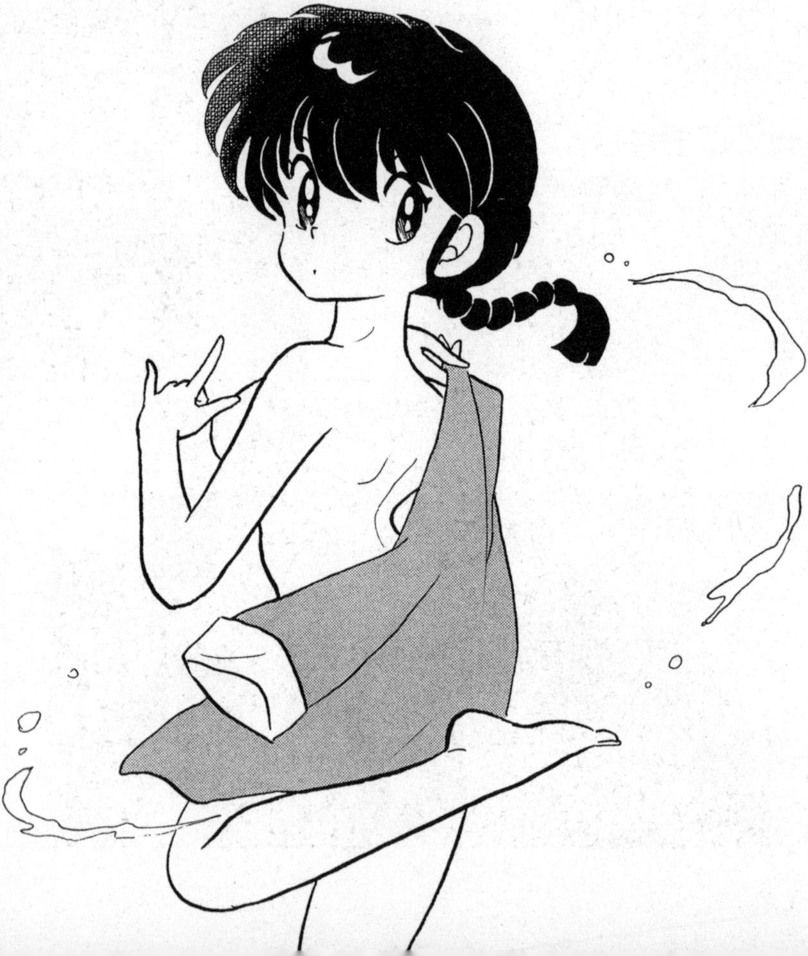

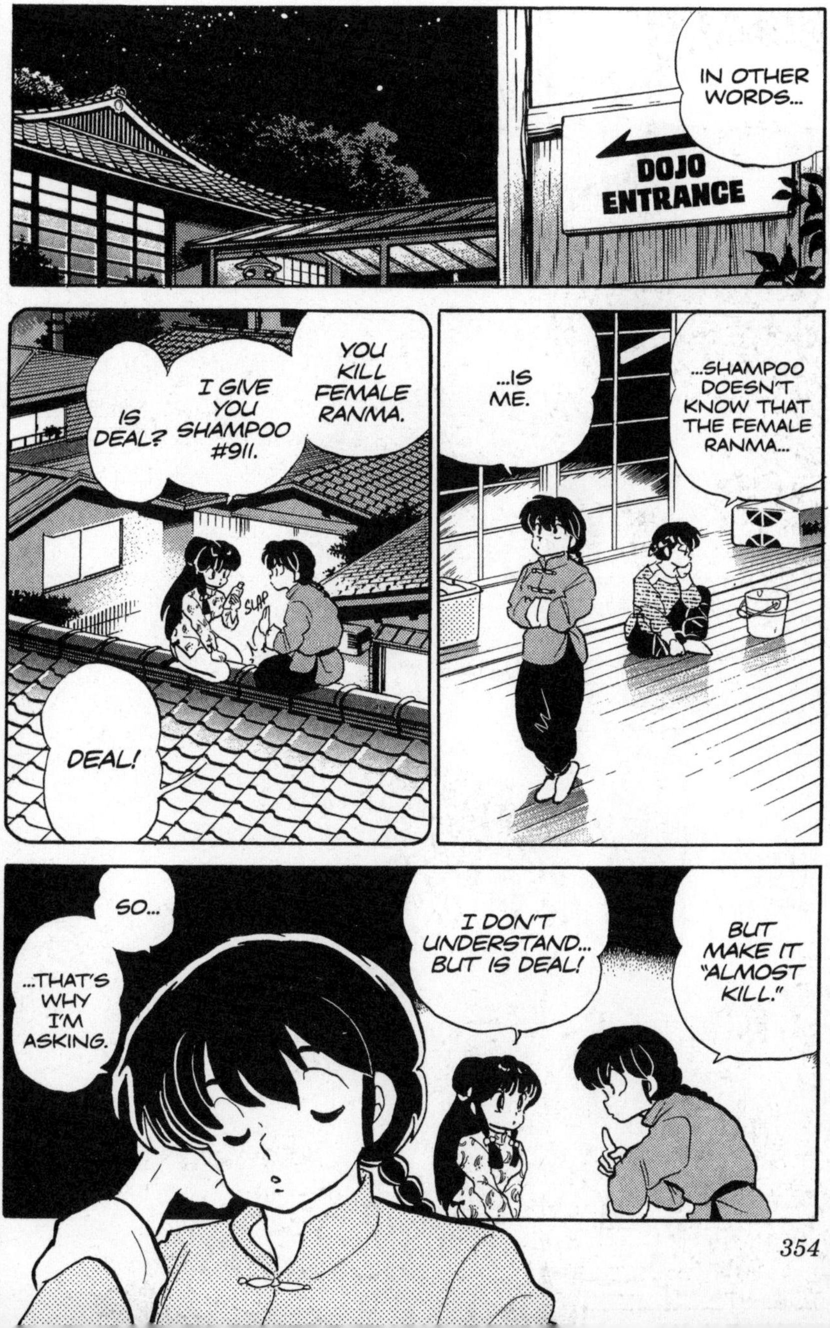
IN OTHER WORDS...
DOJO ENTRANCE
...SHAMPOO DOESN'T KNOW THAT THE FEMALE RANMA...
...IS ME.
YOU KILL FEMALE RANMA.
I GIVE YOU SHAMPOO #911.
IS DEAL?
SLAP
DEAL!
BUT MAKE IT "ALMOST KILL."
I DON'T UNDERSTAND... BUT IS DEAL!
SO...
...THAT'S WHY I'M ASKING.

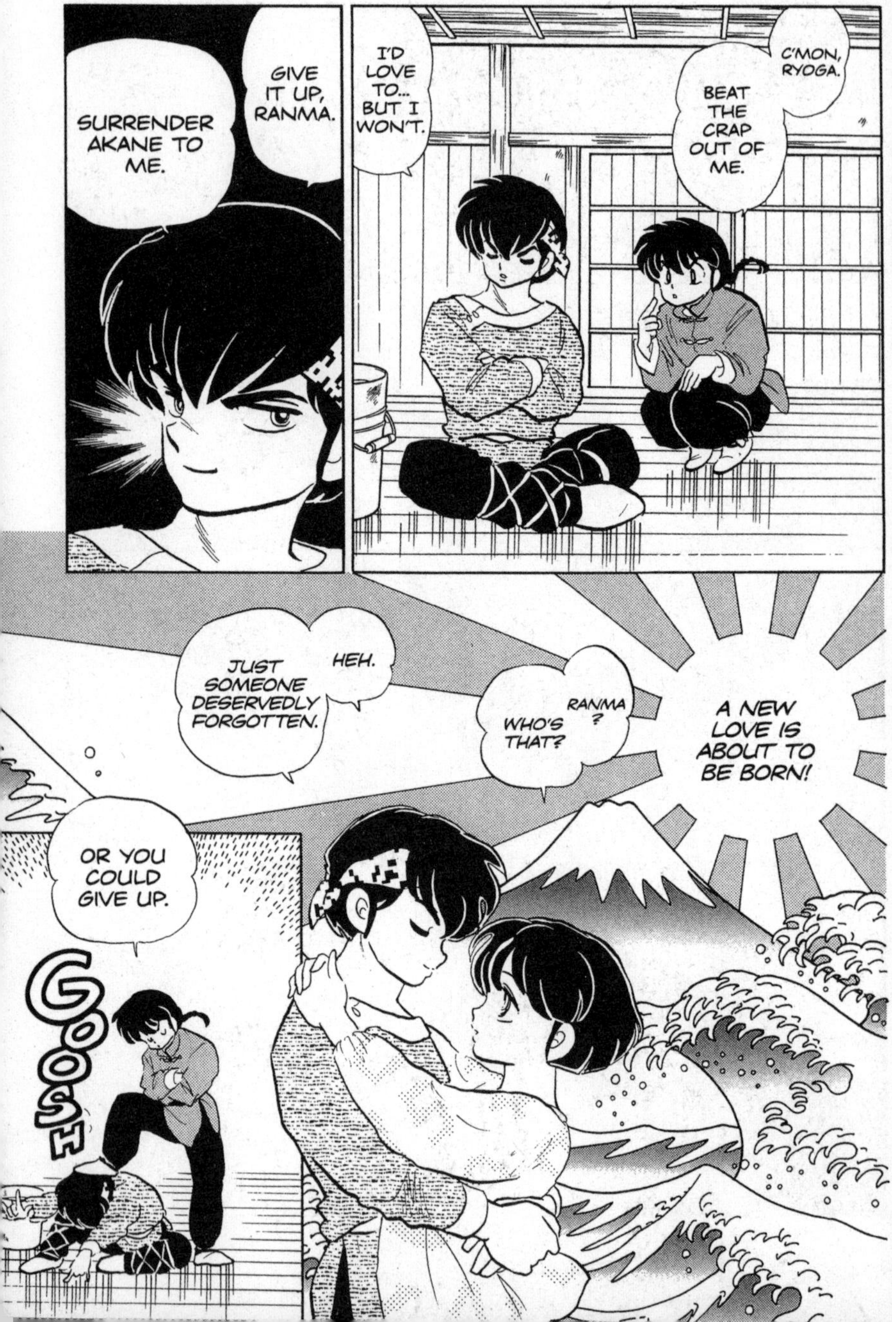
C'MON, RYOGA.
BEAT THE CRAP OUT OF ME.
I'D LOVE TO... BUT I WON'T.
GIVE IT UP, RANMA.
SURRENDER AKANE TO ME.
A NEW LOVE IS ABOUT TO BE BORN!
RANMA?
WHO'S THAT?
HEH.
JUST SOMEONE DESERVEDLY FORGOTTEN.
OR YOU COULD GIVE UP.
GOOOSH

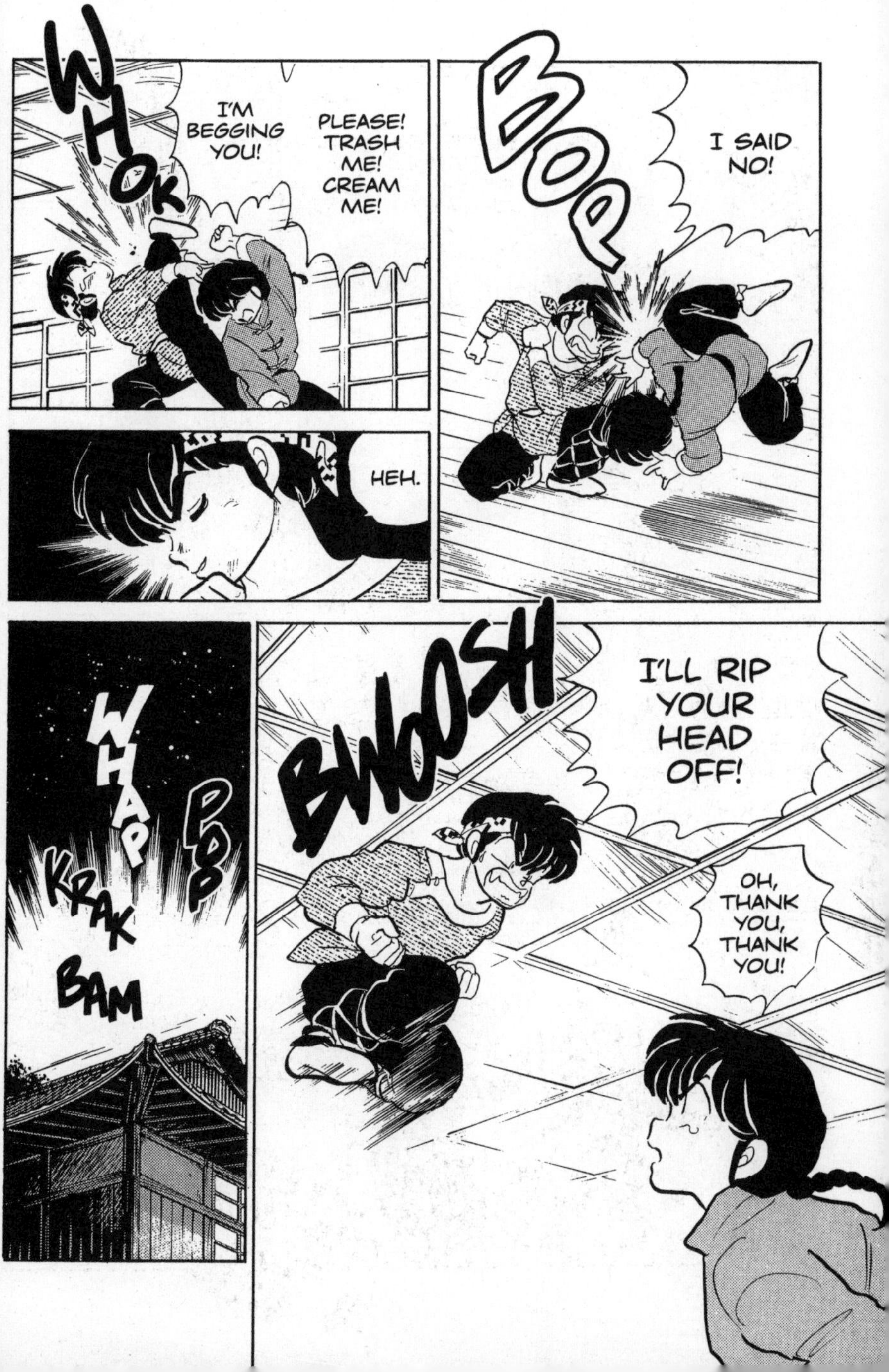
BOOP
I SAID NO!
WHOK
PLEASE! TRASH ME! CREAM ME!
I'M BEGGING YOU!
HEH.
BWOOSH
I'LL RIP YOUR HEAD OFF!
OH, THANK YOU, THANK YOU!
POP
WHAP
KRAK
BAM

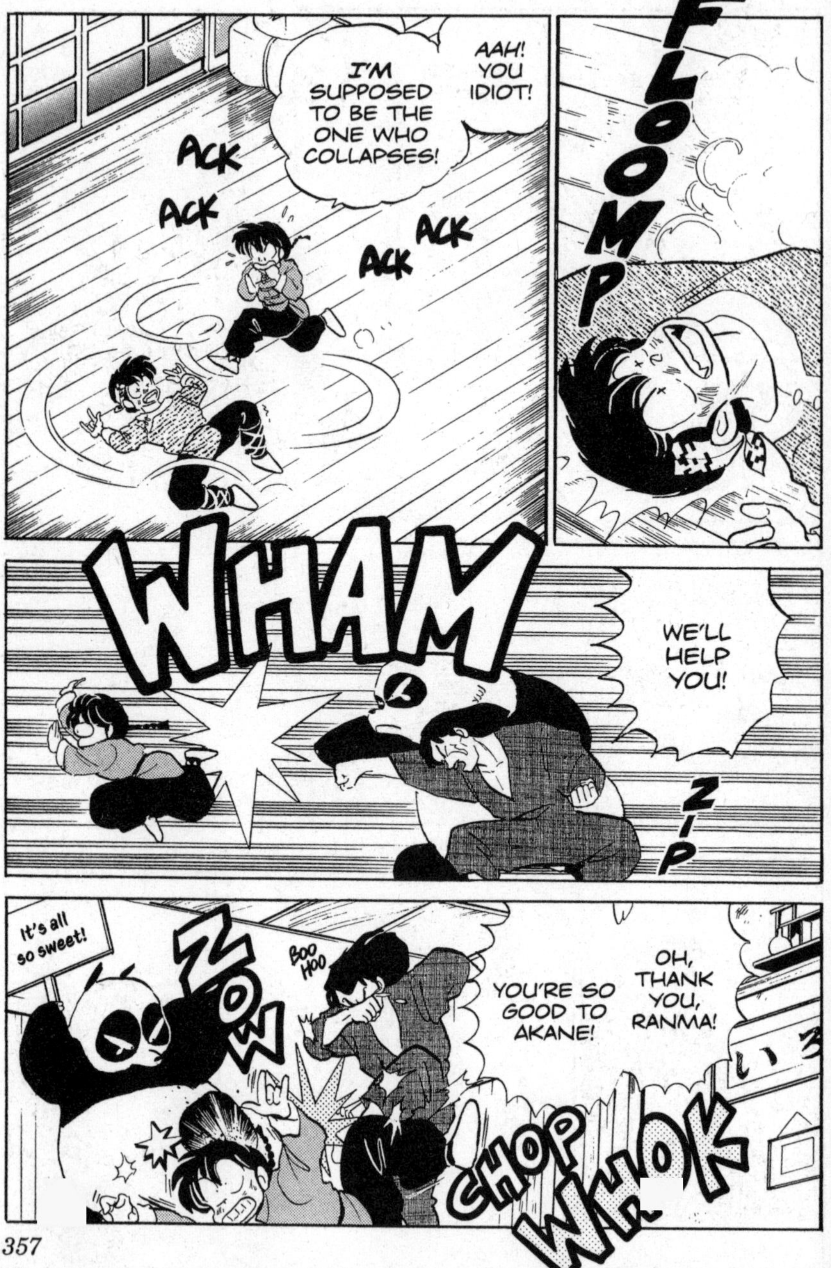
FLOOMP
AAH! YOU IDIOT!
I'M SUPPOSED TO BE THE ONE WHO COLLAPSES!
ACK
ACK
ACK
ACK
WE'LL HELP YOU!
WHAM
ZIP
OH, THANK YOU, RANMA!
YOU'RE SO GOOD TO AKANE!
BOO HOO
NOW
It's all so sweet!
CHOP
WHOK

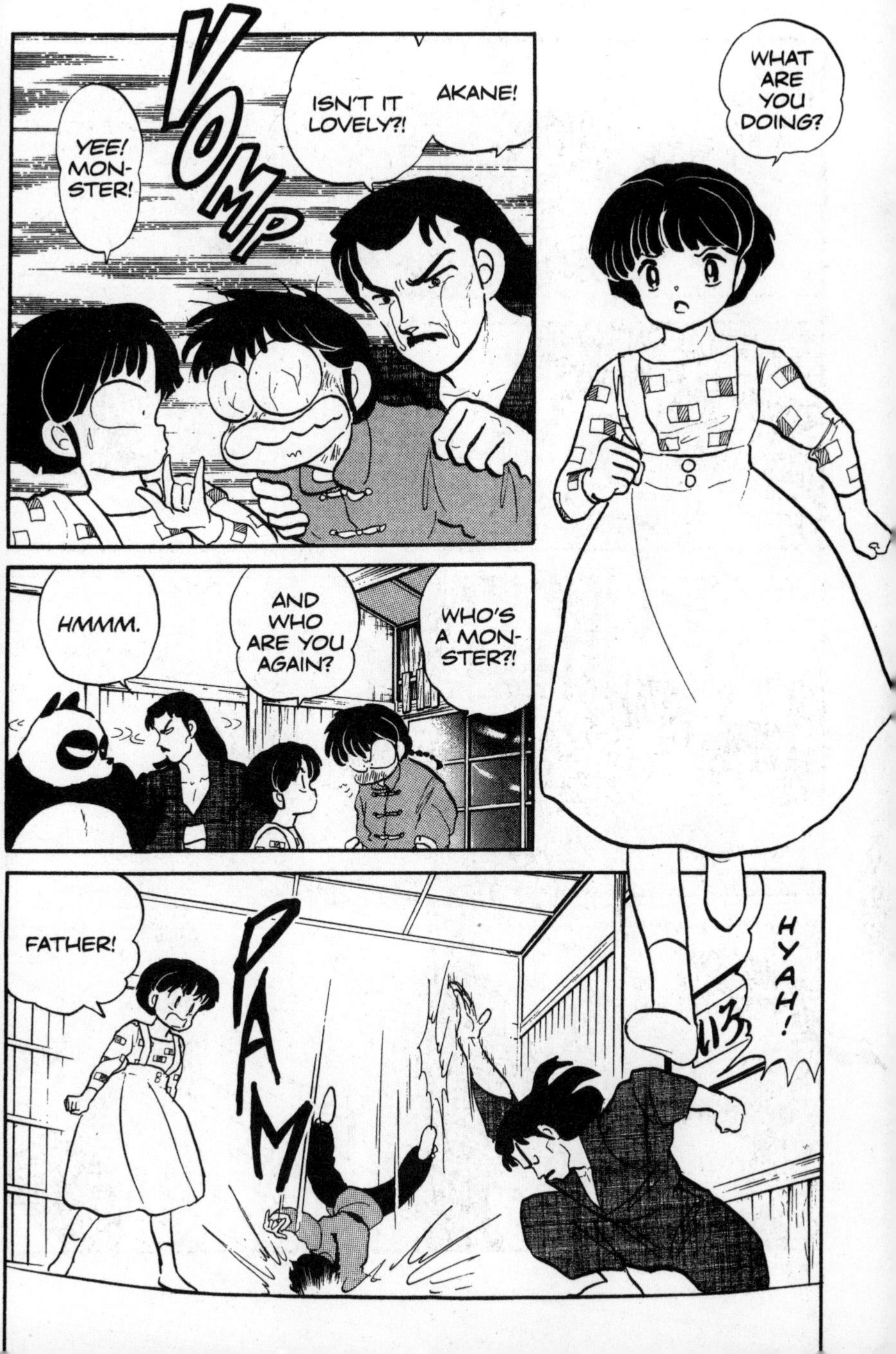
WHAT ARE YOU DOING?
AKANE!
ISN'T IT LOVELY?!
VOMP
YEE! MONSTER!
WHO'S A MONSTER?!
AND WHO ARE YOU AGAIN?
HMMM.
HYAH!
PAM
FATHER!

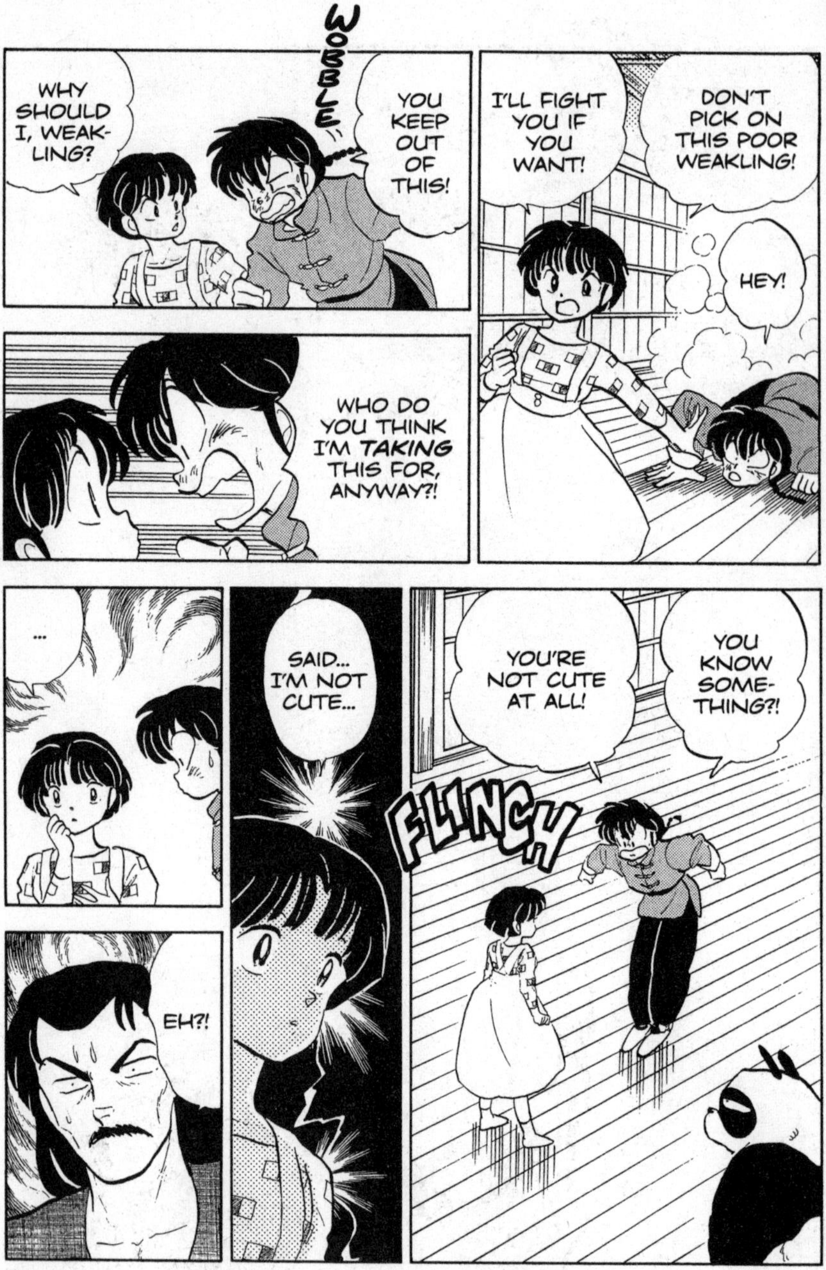
DON'T PICK ON THIS POOR WEAKLING!
I'LL FIGHT YOU IF YOU WANT!
HEY!
WOBBLE
YOU KEEP OUT OF THIS!
WHY SHOULD I, WEAK-LING?
WHO DO YOU THINK I'M *TAKING* THIS FOR, ANYWAY?!
YOU KNOW SOME-THING?!
YOU'RE NOT CUTE AT ALL!
FLINCH
SAID... I'M NOT CUTE...
...
EH?!

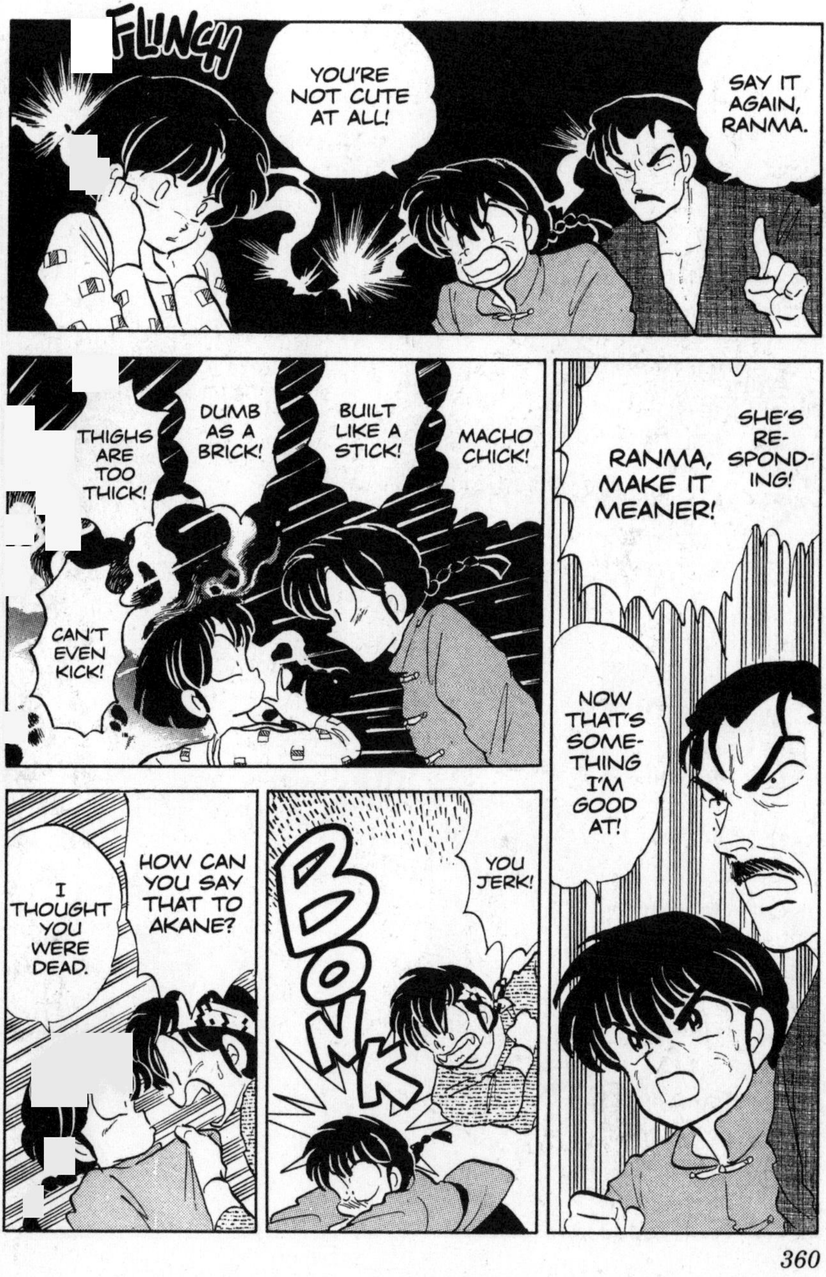
SAY IT AGAIN, RANMA.
YOU'RE NOT CUTE AT ALL!
FLINCH
SHE'S RE-SPOND-ING!
RANMA, MAKE IT MEANER!
NOW THAT'S SOME-THING I'M GOOD AT!
MACHO CHICK!
BUILT LIKE A STICK!
DUMB AS A BRICK!
THIGHS ARE TOO THICK!
CAN'T EVEN KICK!
YOU JERK!
BONK
HOW CAN YOU SAY THAT TO AKANE?
I THOUGHT YOU WERE DEAD.

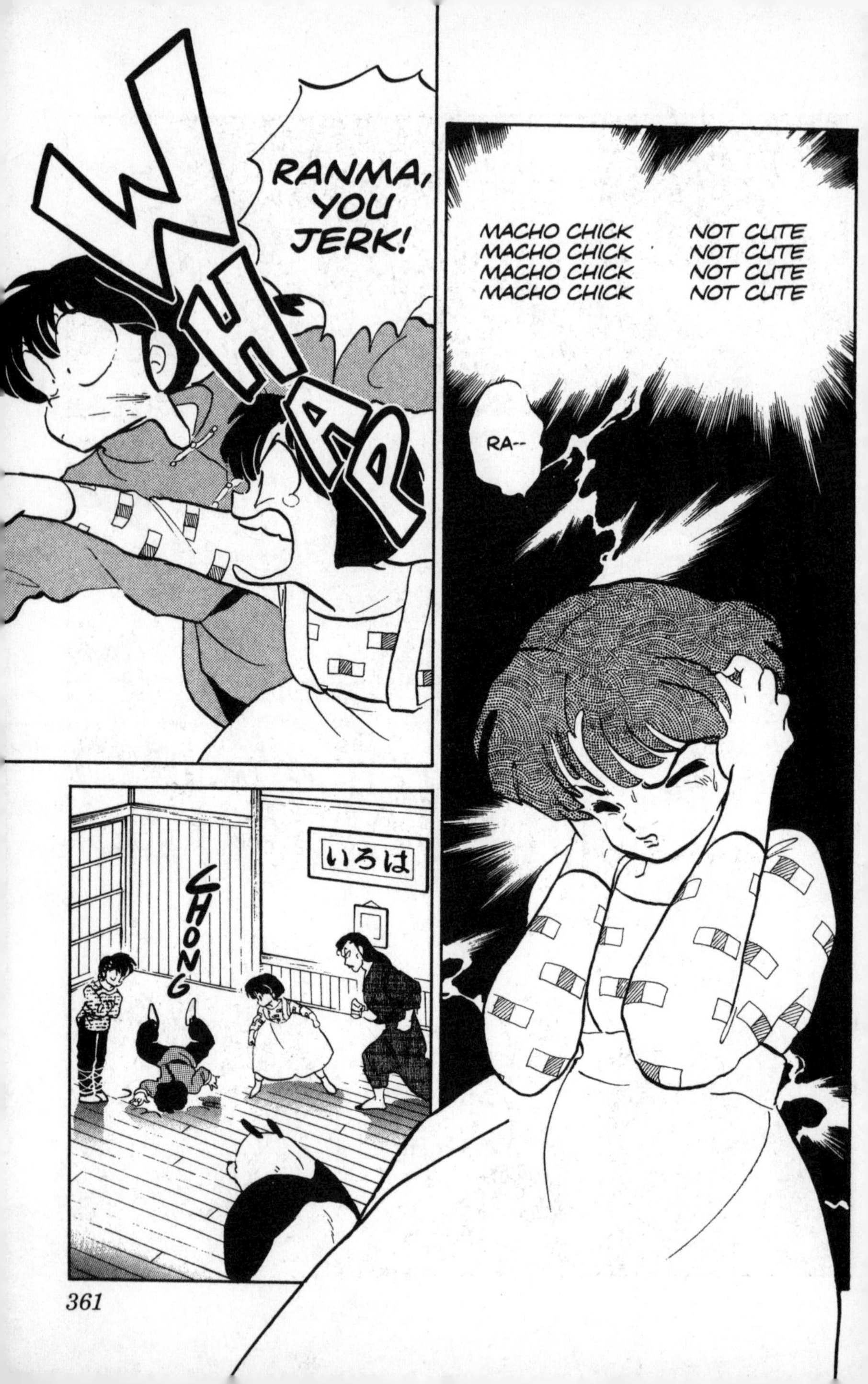
MACHO CHICK NOT CUTE
MACHO CHICK NOT CUTE
MACHO CHICK NOT CUTE
MACHO CHICK NOT CUTE
RA--
RANMA, YOU JERK!
WHAP
いろは
CHONG

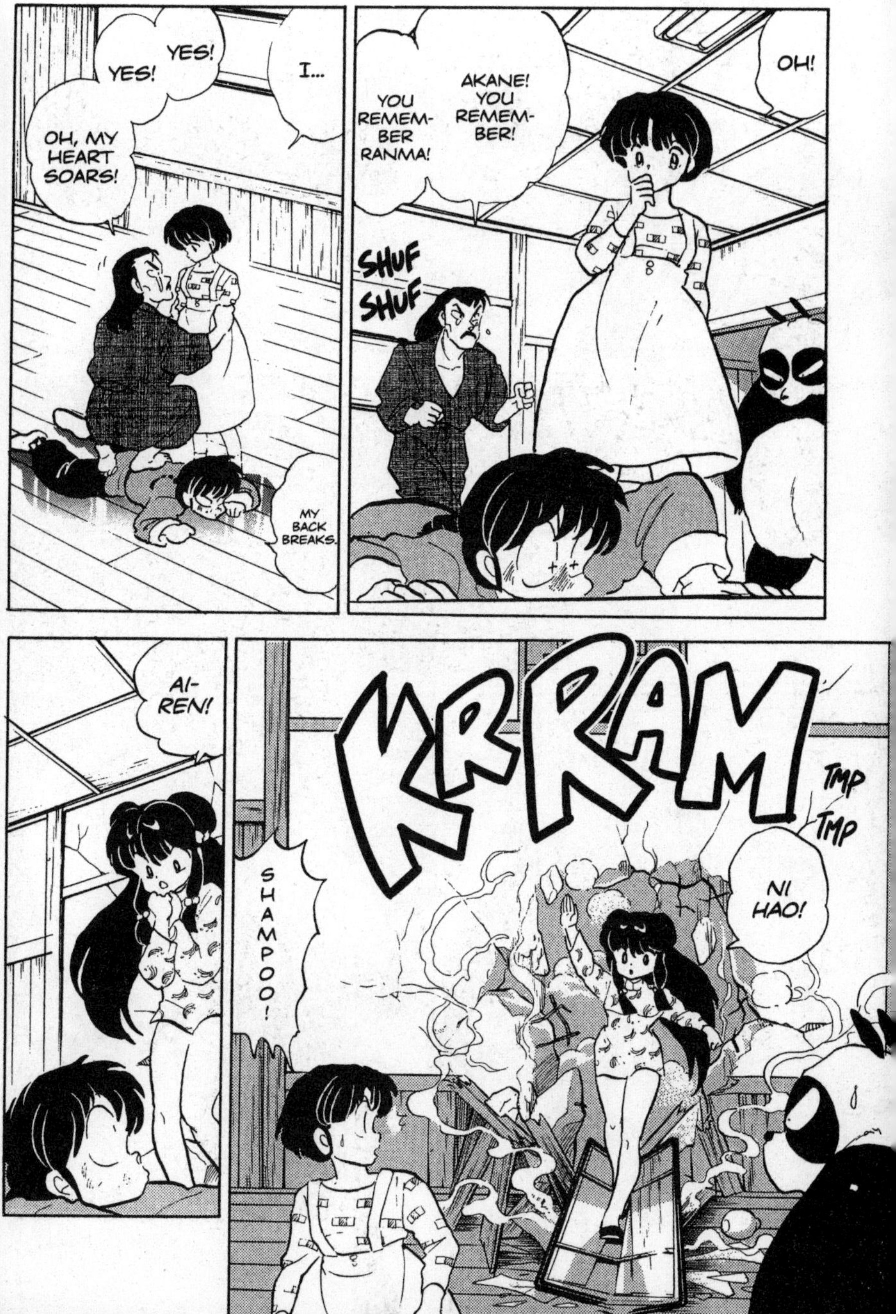
OH!
AKANE! YOU REMEM-BER!
YOU REMEM-BER RANMA!
SHUF SHUF
I...
YES! YES!
OH, MY HEART SOARS!
MY BACK BREAKS.
KRRAM
TMP TMP
NI HAO!
SHAMPOO!
AI-REN!

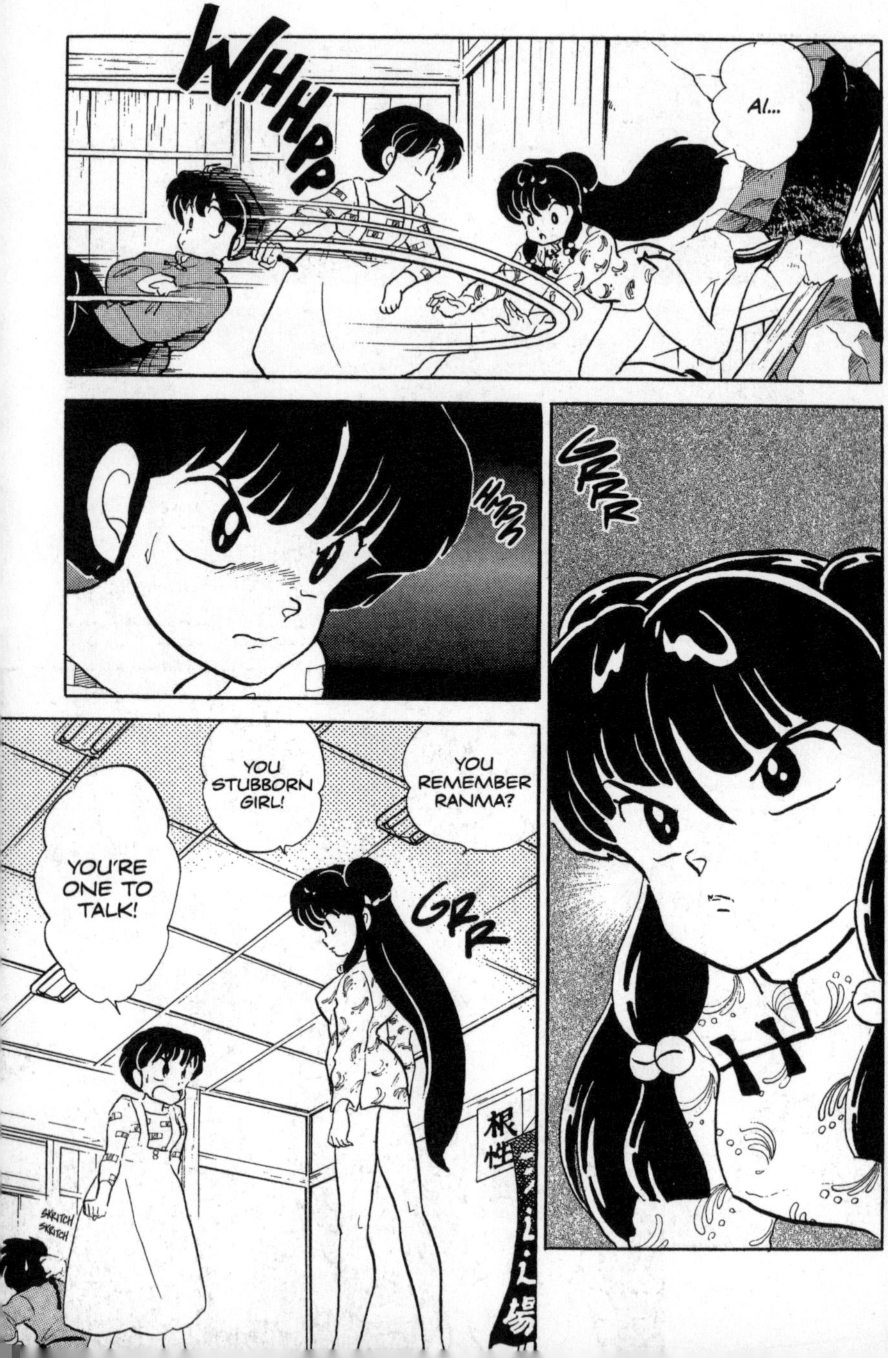
AI...
WHHPP
GRRR
HMPH
YOU REMEMBER RANMA?
YOU STUBBORN GIRL!
GRR
YOU'RE ONE TO TALK!
根性
SKRITCH SKRITCH

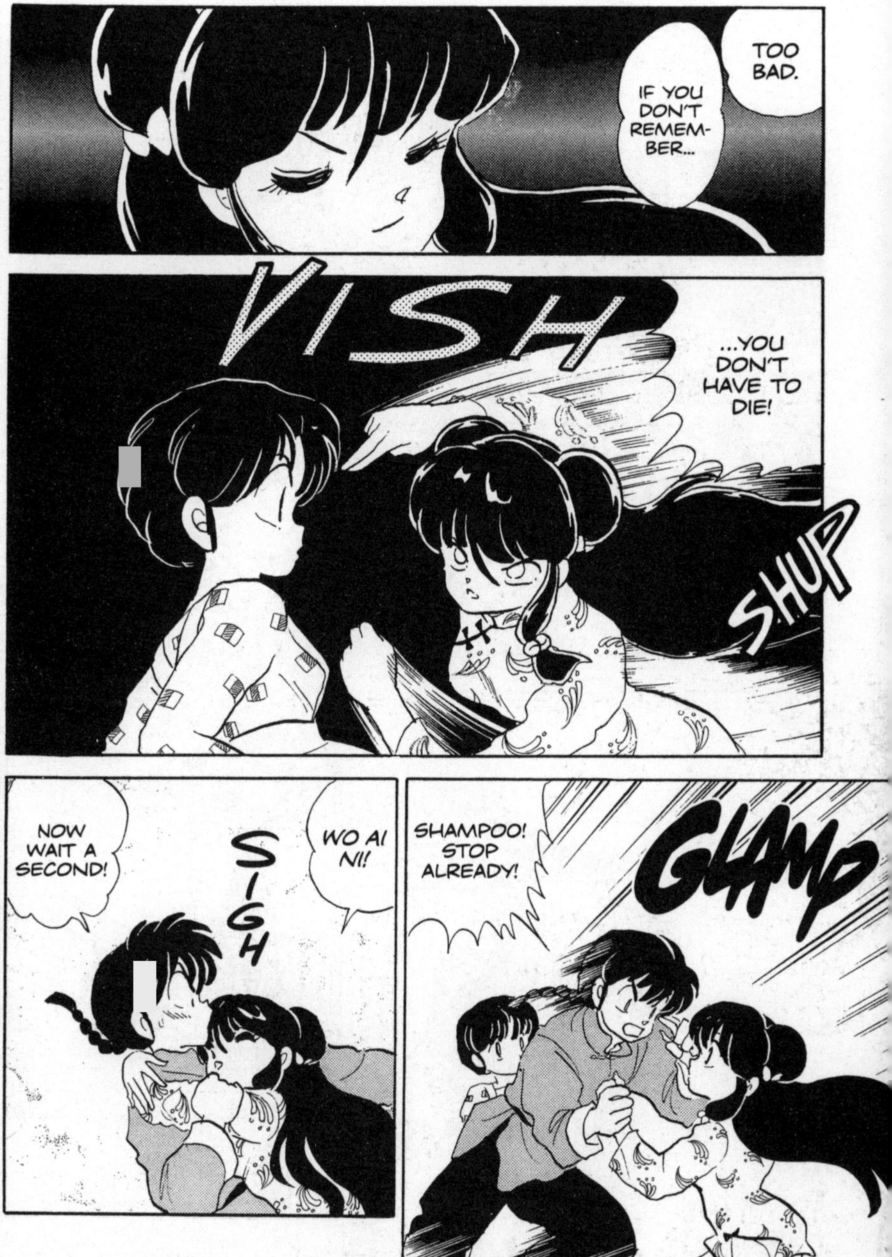
TOO BAD.
IF YOU DON'T REMEMBER...
VISH
...YOU DON'T HAVE TO DIE!
SHUP
SHAMPOO! STOP ALREADY!
GLAMP
WO AI NI!
SIGH
NOW WAIT A SECOND!

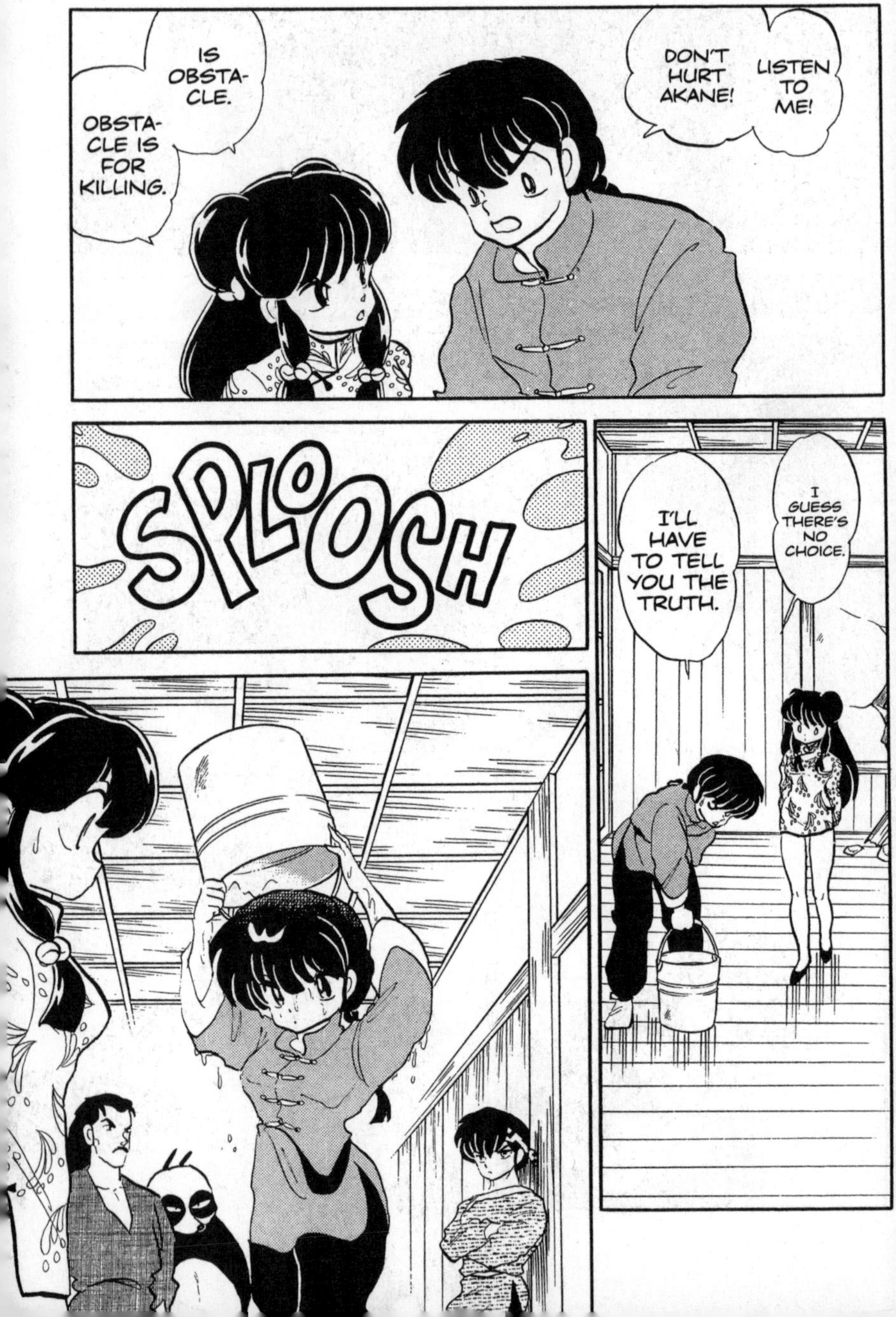
LISTEN TO ME!
DON'T HURT AKANE!
IS OBSTA-CLE.
OBSTA-CLE IS FOR KILLING.
I GUESS THERE'S NO CHOICE.
I'LL HAVE TO TELL YOU THE TRUTH.
SPLOOSH

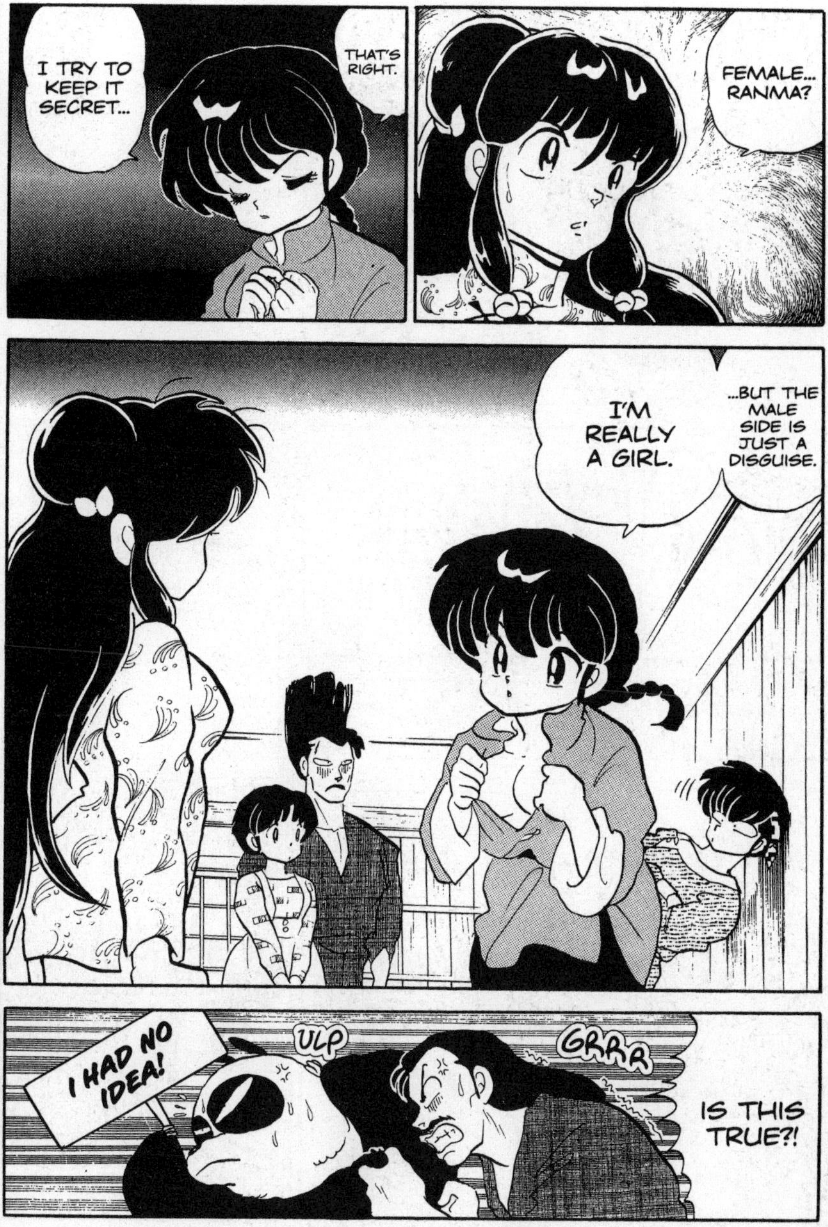
FEMALE... RANMA?
THAT'S RIGHT.
I TRY TO KEEP IT SECRET...
I'M REALLY A GIRL.
...BUT THE MALE SIDE IS JUST A DISGUISE.
IS THIS TRUE?!
GRRR
ULP
I HAD NO IDEA!

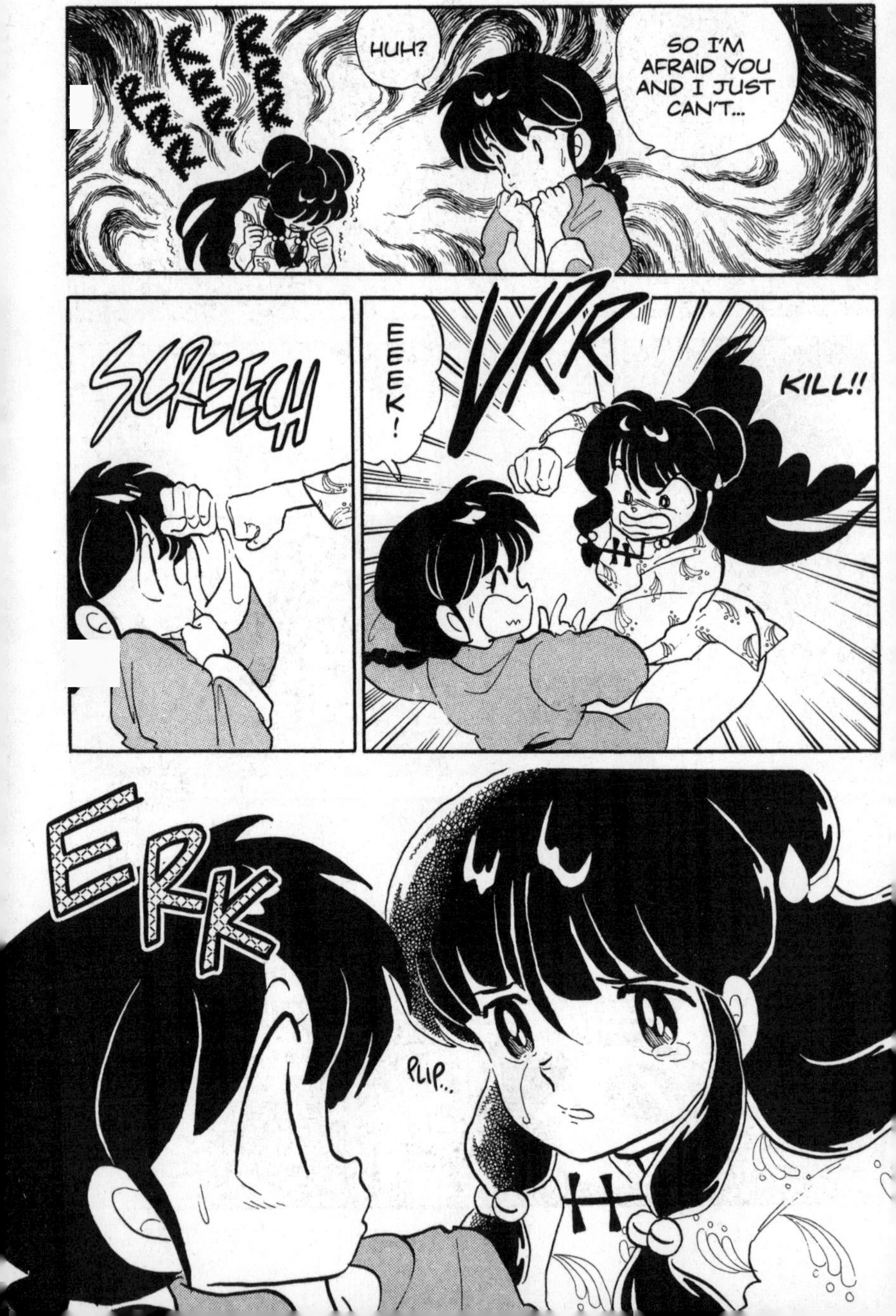
SO I'M AFRAID YOU AND I JUST CAN'T...
HUH?
KILL!!
VRR
EEEK!
SCREECH
PLIP...
ERK

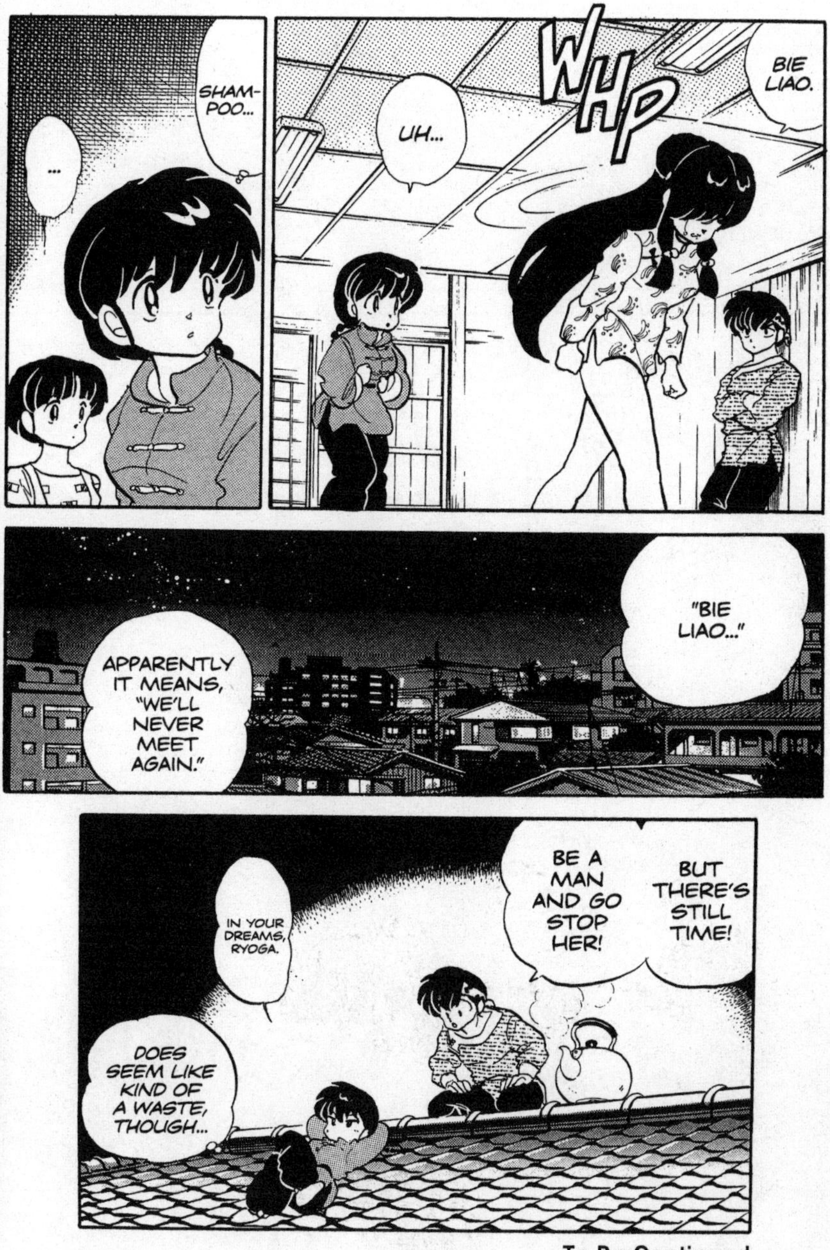
BIE LIAO.
WHP
UH...
SHAM-POO...
...
"BIE LIAO..."
APPARENTLY IT MEANS, "WE'LL NEVER MEET AGAIN."
BUT THERE'S STILL TIME!
BE A MAN AND GO STOP HER!
IN YOUR DREAMS, RYOGA.
DOES SEEM LIKE KIND OF A WASTE, THOUGH...

To Be Continued

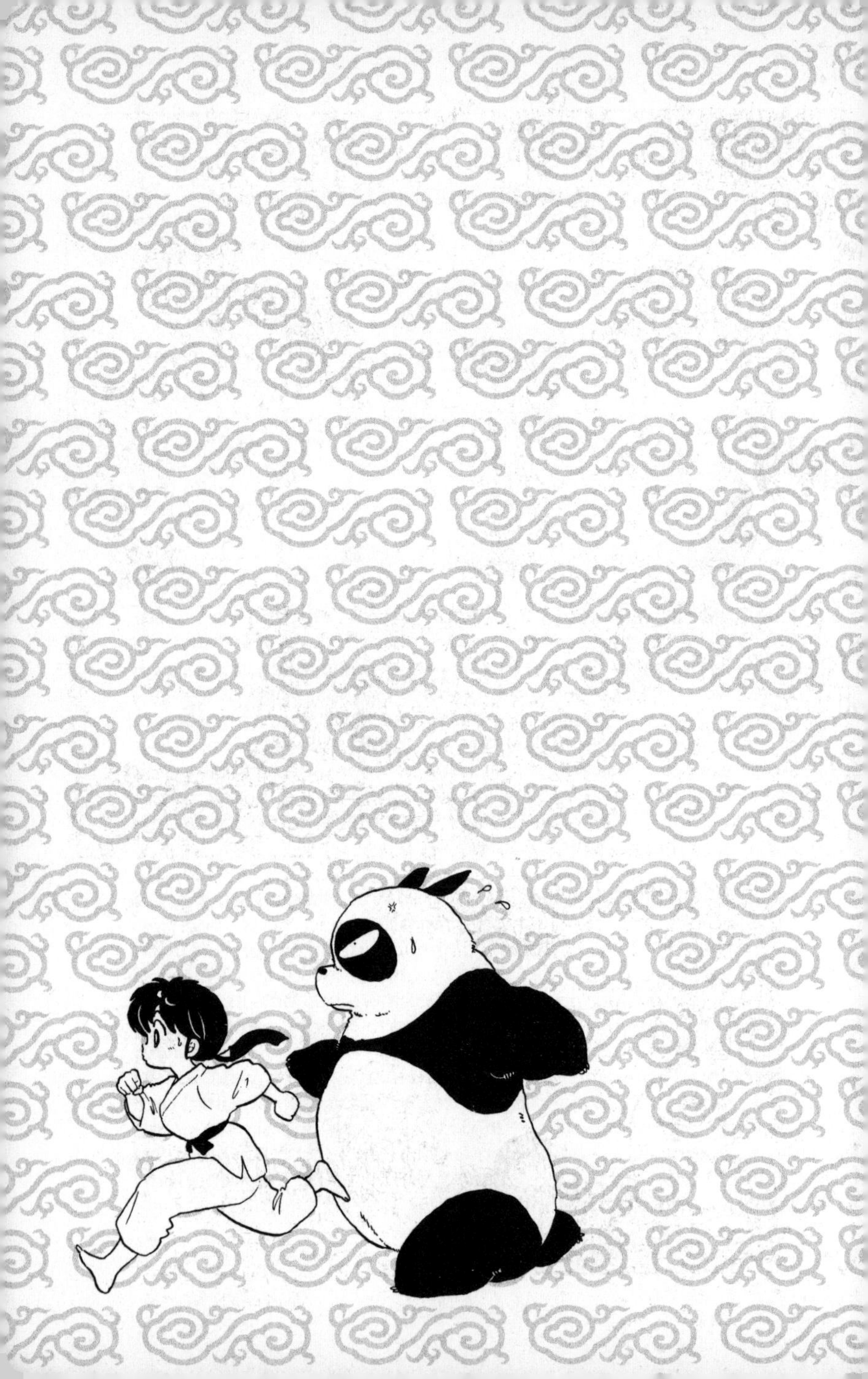

Rumiko Takahashi

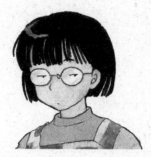

The spotlight on Rumiko Takahashi's career began in 1978 when she won an honorable mention in Shogakukan's annual New Comic Artist Contest for *Those Selfish Aliens*. Later that same year, her boy-meets-alien comedy series, *Urusei Yatsura*, was serialized in *Weekly Shonen Sunday*. This phenomenally successful manga series was adapted into anime format and spawned a TV series and half a dozen theatrical-release movies, all incredibly popular in their own right. Takahashi followed up the success of her debut series with one blockbuster hit after another—*Maison Ikkoku* ran from 1980 to 1987, *Ranma ½* from 1987 to 1996, and *Inuyasha* from 1996 to 2008. Other notable works include *Mermaid Saga*, *Rumic Theater*, and *One-Pound Gospel*.

Takahashi won the prestigious Shogakukan Manga Award twice in her career, once for *Urusei Yatsura* in 1981 and the second time for *Inuyasha* in 2002. A majority of the Takahashi canon has been adapted into other media such as anime, live-action TV series, and film. Takahashi's manga, as well as the other formats her work has been adapted into, have continued to delight generations of fans around the world. Distinguished by her wonderfully endearing characters, Takahashi's work adeptly incorporates a wide variety of elements such as comedy, romance, fantasy, and martial arts. While her series are difficult to pin down into one simple genre, the signature style she has created has come to be known as the "Rumic World." Rumiko Takahashi is an artist who truly represents the very best from the world of manga.

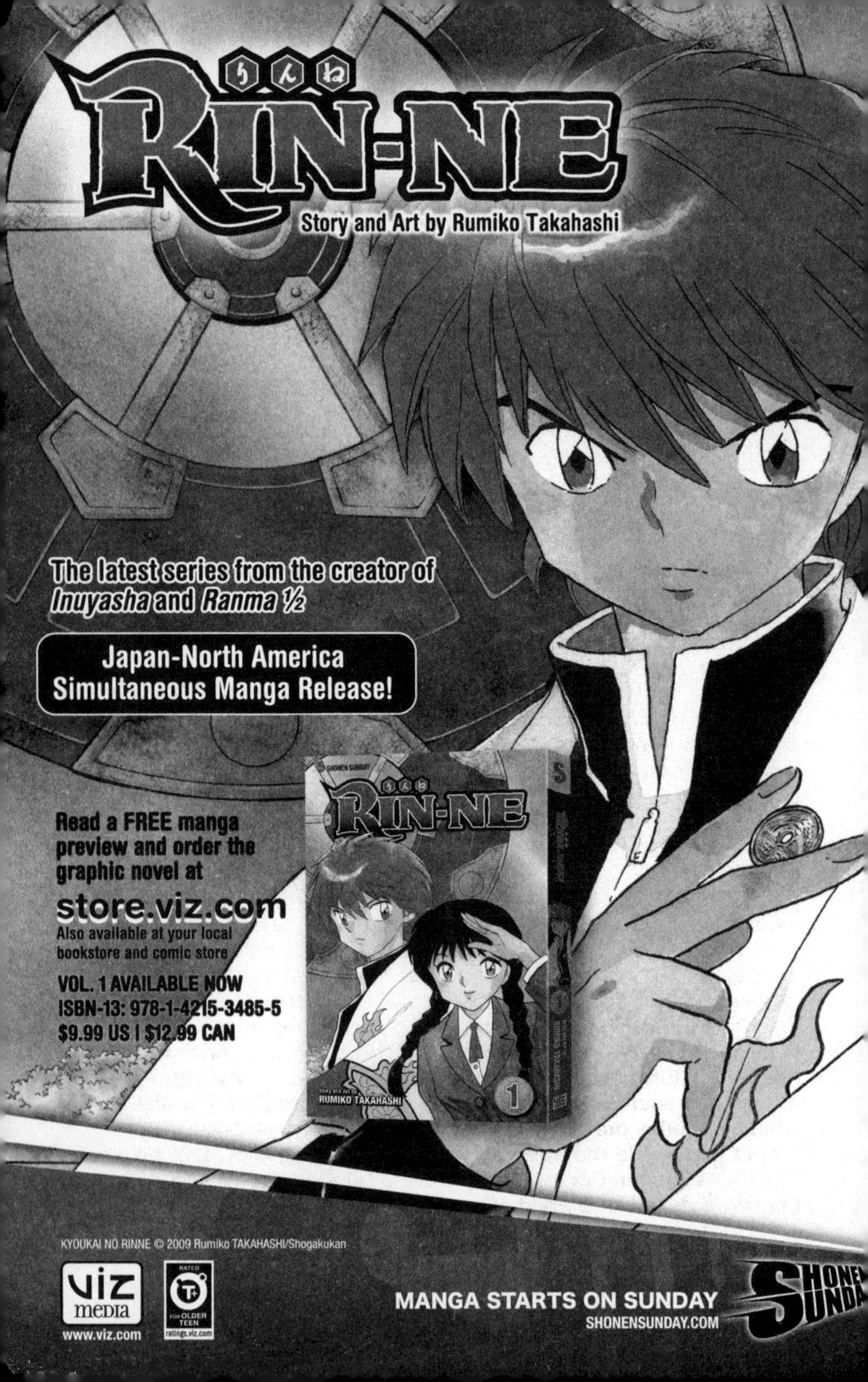

RIN-NE

Story and Art by Rumiko Takahashi

The latest series from the creator of
Inuyasha and *Ranma ½*

**Japan-North America
Simultaneous Manga Release!**

Read a FREE manga
preview and order the
graphic novel at

store.viz.com

Also available at your local
bookstore and comic store.

VOL. 1 AVAILABLE NOW
ISBN-13: 978-1-4215-3485-5
$9.99 US | $12.99 CAN

KYOUKAI NO RINNE © 2009 Rumiko TAKAHASHI/Shogakukan

www.viz.com

RATED
T+
FOR OLDER
TEEN
ratings.viz.com

MANGA STARTS ON SUNDAY
SHONENSUNDAY.COM

SHONEN SUNDAY

Ranma½ Returns!

REMASTERED AND BETTER THAN EVER!

One day, teenaged martial artist Ranma Saotome went on a training mission with his father and ended up taking a dive into some cursed springs at a legendary training ground in China. Now, every time he's splashed with cold water, he changes into a girl. His father, Genma, changes into a panda! What's a half-guy, half-girl to do?

Find out what fueled the worldwide manga boom in beloved creator Rumiko Takahashi's (*Inuyasha*, *Urusei Yatsura*, *RIN-NE*) smash-hit of martial arts mayhem!

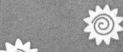

Story and Art by Rumiko Takahashi

GET IT ON DVD AND LIMITED EDITION BLU-RAY BOX SETS STARTING SPRING 2014

Watch it for FREE on vizanime.com/ranma
Get it on Blu-ray and DVD this Spring.
Packed with tons of extras!
Available at DVD and Blu-ray retailers nationwide.

AND OWN THE MANGA IN THE ORIGINAL RIGHT-TO-LEFT ORIENTATION!

- Discover the details with remastered pages!
- Now in all new 2-in-1 Editions!

©Rumiko Takahashi / Shogakukan
RANMA1/2 © 1988 Rumiko TAKAHASHI/SHOGAKUKAN

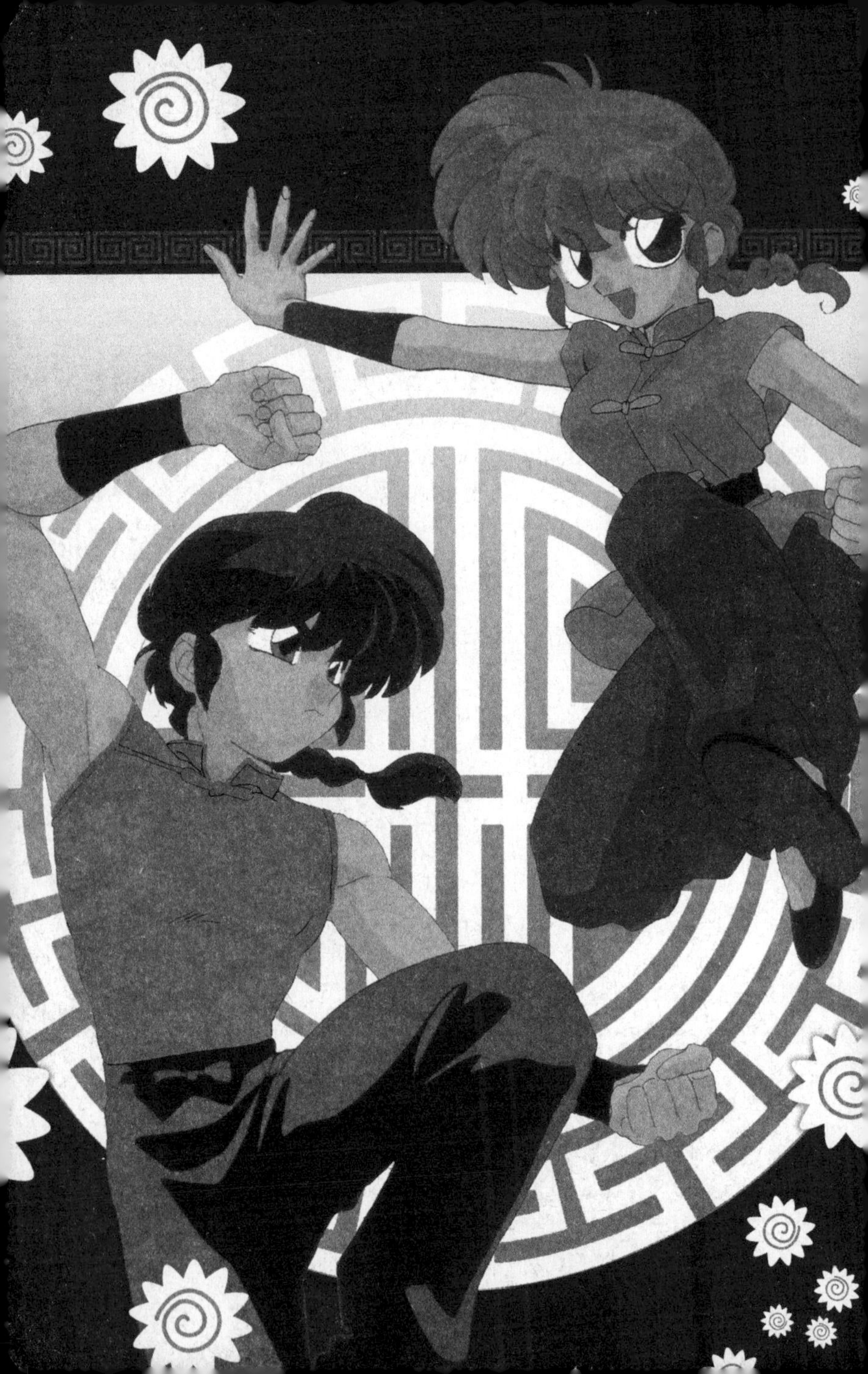

ᑌIᘔᗰᗩᑎGᗩ
Read manga anytime, anywhere!

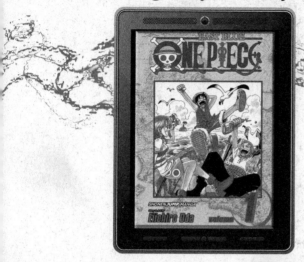

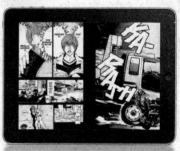

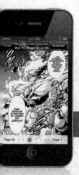

From our newest hit series to the classics you know and love, the best manga in the world is now available digitally. **Buy a volume*** of digital manga for your:

- iOS device (**iPad®, iPhone®, iPod® touch**) through the **VIZ Manga app**

- Android-powered device (**phone or tablet**) with a browser by visiting VIZManga.com

- **Mac or PC computer** by visiting VIZManga.com

VIZ Digital has loads to offer:

- 500+ ready-to-read volumes
- New volumes each week
- FREE previews
- Access on multiple devices! Create a log-in through the app so you buy a book once, and read it on your device of choice!*

To learn more, visit www.viz.com/apps

* Some series may not be available for multiple devices.
Check the app on your device to find out what's available.

DEATH NOTE © 2003 by Tsugumi Ohba, Takeshi Obata/SHUEISHA Inc.
NURARIHYON NO MAGO © 2008 by Hiroshi Shiibashi/SHUEISHA Inc.
ONE PIECE © 1997 by Eiichiro Oda/SHUEISHA Inc.

ratings.viz.com   viz.com/apps

DISCOVER ANIME
IN A WHOLE NEW WAY!

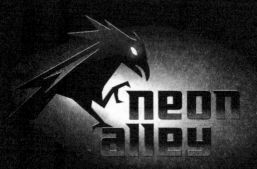

www.neonalley.com

What it is...

- Streaming anime delivered 24/7 straight to your TV via your connected video game console
- All English dubbed content
- Anime, martial arts movies, and more

Go to **neonalley.com** for news, updates and to see if Neon Alley is available in your area.

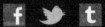

NEON ALLEY is a trademark or service mark of VIZ Media, LLC

W9-AJL-575

Hey! You're Reading in the Wrong Direction!

This is the end of this graphic novel!

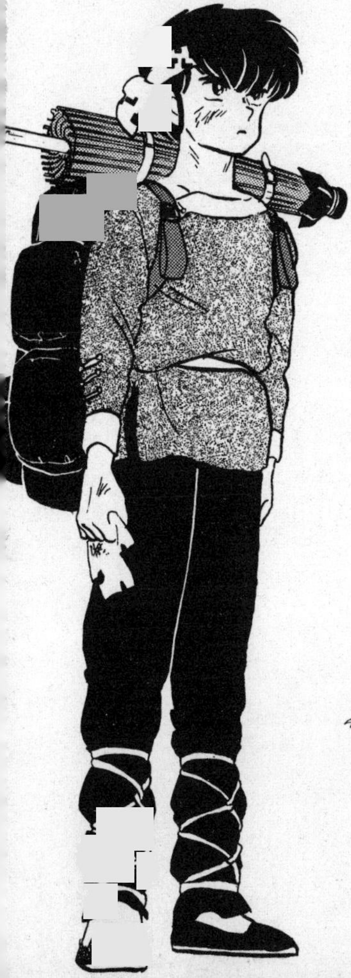

To properly enjoy this VIZ graphic novel, please turn it around and begin reading from right to left. Unlike English, Japanese is read right to left, so Japanese comics are read in reverse order from the way English comics are typically read.

This book has been printed in the original Japanese format in order to preserve the orientation of the original artwork. Have fun with it!

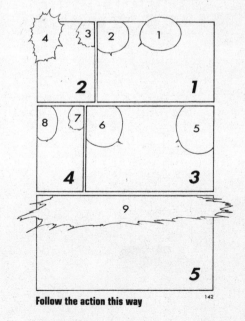

Follow the action this way

142